PSYCHOLOGY IN INDUSTRIAL ORGANIZATIONS

FIFTH EDITION

PSYCHOLOGY IN INDUSTRIAL ORGANIZATIONS

Norman R. F. Maier
University of Michigan

Gertrude Casselman Verser
University of Minnesota

Houghton Mifflin Company   Boston

Dallas   Geneva, Illinois   Hopewell, New Jersey   Palo Alto   London

To Ayesha
and to Dan

Credits The chapter opening photographs are used courtesy of the following firms and individuals: Page 2, Julie O'Neil, Stock, Boston. Pages 4 and 194, IBM. Pages 40 and 66, Ellis Herwig, Stock, Boston. Pages 92, 160, 282, and 582, Donald Dietz. Page 124, Eric A. Roth, The Picture Cube, Boston. Page 142, Ann McQueen. Page 160, Peter Menzel, Stock, Boston. Page 220, International Telephone and Telegraph Corporation. Page 256, Ford Motor Company. Page 320, T. C. Fitzgerald. Page 364, Minneapolis-Honeywell. Pages 398 and 484, Elizabeth Hamlin. Page 436, Raytheon Company. Page 464, Bohdan Hrynewych. Page 522, Daniel S. Brody, Stock, Boston. Page 546, AT & T. Page 582, Jonathan Rawle. Page 598, Christopher Morrow, Stock, Boston.

Printed in the U.S.A.

Library of Congress Catalog Card Number: 81–81702
ISBN: 0–395–31740–1

CONTENTS

PART TWO

ANALYZING WORK GROUP INTERACTIONS

PART FOUR

MOTIVATING WORKERS FOR OPTIMUM
PERFORMANCE

CHAPTER THIRTEEN

JOB MOTIVATION 321

CHAPTER FOURTEEN

EVALUATING JOB PERFORMANCE 365

CHAPTER FIFTEEN
JOB FATIGUE: PHYSICAL AND PSYCHOLOGICAL 397

CHAPTER SIXTEEN
ACCIDENTS IN THE WORKPLACE 437

CHAPTER SEVENTEEN
ANALYZING JOB TURNOVER 465

CHAPTER EIGHTEEN

COUNSELING SKILLS FOR MANAGERS 485

PART FIVE

THE ORGANIZATION
AND THE ENVIRONMENT

CHAPTER NINETEEN

PHYSICAL AND SOCIOECONOMIC ENVIRONMENTS OF
ORGANIZATIONS 523

PREFACE

Fifty years of research and original thought have gone into the writing of this text. Its objective is simple to state, though not easily achieved: to provide the most useful scientific background possible in the areas of industrial and organizational psychology for managers and students of organizations.

In order to provide this background, the text reviews and explains the work of thousands of scientists, managers, and engineers in studies ranging in time from the World War I era to the present day. But it is important to understand that this book is not an encyclopedia of applied psychology. The studies cited are a *selection* of the hundreds of thousands that might have been included. They have been chosen because (1) they are classics in their field, which have served as the bases for further research, and/or (2) they help explain an approach to interpersonal relations developed by Norman Maier that seems to be the most practical and most useful to operating managers.

The text is divided into five major parts: (1) Understanding the Behavior of Individual Employees; (2) Analyzing Work Group Interactions; (3) Matching the Worker to the Job; (4) Motivating Workers for Optimum Performance; and (5) The Organization and the Environment. Parts One and Two outline basic psychological principles, Parts Three and Four explore a number of specific areas of application, and Part Five discusses new ideas and techniques of organizational psychology.

Along with a great deal of specific information about how and why various psychological phenomena occur, the book also includes, in the form of role-playing and other exercises, the means to develop necessary skills to *use* the acquired knowledge to solve on-the-job problems. Thus, both psychological theory and managerial practice are emphasized in the text.

Many developments have occurred in the field of industrial psychology since the fourth edition was published, and the text covers these. This fifth edition contains new material on common nondirective counseling situations, the physical and socioeconomic environment of business, career planning and development, leadership, new examples of business situations stressing management and white-collar problems, more recent research findings, and new approaches to motivation. In addition, references have been extensively updated. The *Instructor's Manual* for this edition contains information and suggestions about conducting the laboratory exercises and also includes test items.

The nature of the field of psychology and

its relative youth as a science invite controversy and challenge in the matter of choosing the "best" or "most advanced" theories. Psychology has not progressed to the point where new general theories can be devised that disprove the validity of all previously contending ones.[1] The material presented here represents a distillation of the thinking of its authors, but various psychologists reading it might well disagree with this or that particular statement. When appropriate, contrasting theoretical approaches are examined. But there is also a responsibility on the part of each reader to analyze and consider all statements made, to test individually their usefulness and accuracy in his or her observations and interactions.

The current revision of this book was greatly facilitated by the willing help of many people in business as well as academia. Chief among these were: Professors Allen Solem, Richard Gaumnitz, Albert Wickesberg, and Bruce Erickson of the Department of Management, Graduate School of Business Administration, The University of Minnesota; the staff of Houghton Mifflin Company; and business leaders such as William T. Ylvisaker, of Gould, Inc., Dr. Eric Vetter of Russell Reynolds, and Richard Lane, of B. F. Goodrich. Special thanks go to professors who reviewed the manuscript at various stages: Alexis M. Anikeeff, University of Akron; Lloyd S. Baird, Boston University; Richard Barthol, University of California, Los Angeles; Robert S. Billings, The Ohio State University; Robert B. Hessert, Bloomsburg State College, Bloomsburg, Pa.; and H. Meltzer, Washington University, St. Louis, Mo.

G.C.V.

[1]See Kuhn, T. S. *The structure of scientific revolutions*. Chicago: University of Chicago Press, 1962.

PSYCHOLOGY IN INDUSTRIAL ORGANIZATIONS

P A R T

UNDERSTANDING
THE
BEHAVIOR
OF
INDIVIDUAL
EMPLOYEES

O N E

Ralph Worth has just received a surprise legacy from his great-aunt: a solid oak table. Unfortunately, the antique table is blackened with old varnish and needs a prop under one leg in order to stay upright. Ralph has several choices: (1) he can ignore the obvious blemishes and just use the table as it is; (2) he can send the table to an expert and pay that person to make the table beautiful; or (3) he can take the time and effort himself to acquire the basic knowledge and skills needed to bring out the full potential of a valuable piece of furniture. If he takes the third alternative, Ralph not only will have a handsome piece of furniture and the pride of personal achievement, but he also will have acquired knowledge and skills that can be used in the future on other more complex and more challenging projects.

Management today, faced with problems related to interpersonal relations, has a similar set of choices. A manager may be aware, for example, that group meetings are taking too long and accomplishing too little, or that a worker's productivity has dropped significantly, or that another worker is not succeeding in a new position. The choices for this manager are: (1) to ignore the problems and forgo the group's or the employee's potentially valuable contribution; (2) to refer the problem to an expert (personnel manager or consultant); or (3) to acquire the skills necessary to solve the problem.

There are, of course, occasions when the wisest decision is to ask for the advice of an expert. But in most cases, the interpersonal problems of subordinates can be handled best by the group's leader — provided that leader has the necessary skills and knowledge to do a good job. Just as Ralph Worth can get a sense of personal accomplishment from repairing the furniture himself, so the skilled manager can feel a similar satisfaction in solving an organizational problem. Most important of all, the manager learns that basic interpersonal skills, once acquired, never become obsolete.

Understanding human beings would be much simpler if each person reacted in the same way to the same situation. But, as we shall learn in Part One, the exact same situation does not exist for any two people. Although the dominant stimulus remains the same for most people (in any given situation), individual interpretations of its meaning vary. Since we cannot see the world exactly as others do, the most useful approach is to try to understand the organizing principles underlying the ways that people generally attempt to interpret the world they see.

The five chapters in Part One ("Applying Psychology to Business Organizations"; "Causation and Purpose in Behavior"; "Motivation and Behavior"; "Frustration: Behavior Without a Goal"; and "Attitudes and Behavior") describe these underlying principles, as psychologists understand them today. The material is not a simple survey of all possible opinions, but is a selection based on a consideration of the views of many scientists and the experiences of many managers. It explains the reasons for behavior that may seem unreasonable or irrational; as these chapters reveal, there is a logic of emotion as well as of the intellect. The role-playing and other exercises will help you gain experience in using basic psychological concepts. The final ingredients necessary for professional expertise, however, must be provided by you — your desire to acquire these tools, and the experience gained as you use them.

CHAPTER ONE

APPLYING PSYCHOLOGY TO BUSINESS ORGANIZATIONS

■

The Historical Role of Applied Psychology
How Principles of Applied Psychology Are Developed
The Manager as Applied Scientist
Applying Psychological Principles in Using This Text

■

BUSINESSES PRODUCE GOODS and services; they require materials, machines, capital, and people. Because people are involved, psychology — the science of mental processes and behavior — is relevant to business.

Before the advent of psychology, instinct and common sense were management's only resources for dealing with employees. Instinct and common sense provided early entrepreneurs with methods to control workers, including fear. As industries grew, this method of motivation through fear became more sophisticated. Organizational leaders administered punishment to uncooperative employees in order to serve what they saw as *the organization's needs*. Eventually, more positive methods of motivation came into use, but management still maintained power through its ability to allocate rewards.

THE HISTORICAL ROLE OF APPLIED PSYCHOLOGY

ENGINEERING TECHNIQUES AND PRINCIPLES OF MANAGEMENT

Early in the twentieth century, scientists and engineers like F. W. Taylor[1] conceived of workers as "human machines" and attempted to analyze their jobs in order to increase their efficiency and productivity. F. B. Gilbreth, for example, divided jobs into a series of separate motions, timed each part, and then attempted to devise the most efficient method for performing each job.[2]

During these years, while engineers were studying workers in an attempt to increase efficiency, administrators reviewed their experiences with employees and derived sets of principles for "proper" management. This approach is often called *classical management theory*. The use of written rules was a result of the bureaucratization of industry, which occurred as the complexity and size of corporations increased. The entrepreneurial firm became outdated — no one person could oversee all employees, so professional managers (following written policy) were hired to deal with specialized problems. The organization was still thought of in nonhuman terms. Although some people saw the corporation as a giant machine, others like R. C. Davis, viewed it as an abstract legal entity, created and administered by a rational system of rules and authority.[3]

Managers were advised by writers of the classical school (like L. Gulick and L. Urwick,[4] and H. Fayol[5]) what to do in any given circumstance. Management was normative, that is, based on the prevailing social customs, rather than on scientific evidence. These theories were often based on erroneous or limited assumptions implicit in "universal" principles.

THE FIRST APPLICATION OF PSYCHOLOGY IN INDUSTRY

In 1927, however, Elton Mayo began investigations at Western Electric's Hawthorne works in Chicago.[6] These findings revealed the importance of considering a worker as a person with feelings, and the work situation as a society in miniature. Psychology and sociology thus became as relevant as engineering and economics to the running of a business.

Supervisory training programs began to place emphasis on developing good interpersonal relations. While legalistic handling of grievances continued, the fact that knowledge of psychology was valuable to managers also gained acceptance.

THE CURRENT ROLE OF APPLIED PSYCHOLOGY

Recent developments have made many past managerial practices infeasible. Government

Many women entered industry during World War I at a time before psychology was applied to the work situation. Here Boston Edison women learn how to operate a circuit breaker. (Courtesy of Boston Edison Company)

regulations restrict monopolistic practices and hold companies accountable for environmental damage; laws prevent discriminatory practices, dishonest packaging, and inadequate wages; and unions influence wages, hours, and fringe benefits.

Changing social conditions and values influence job expectations, attitudes about personal freedom, and individual values. Under these new circumstances, individuals no longer are prey to manipulation through basic needs like hunger, security, and health; instead, such needs as self-esteem and self-actualization are determining the motiva-

tions of increasing numbers of people.[7] Thus, the methods that generated our current affluence have also changed our motivations and values and have complicated, as well as enriched, our lives.

Organizational decisions are now understood as *interactive*: individuals at all levels influence the organization and are in turn influenced by it. New management practices must also take into account advances in technology, increases in the size of organizations, economic trends, and full employment goals. Other changes through government legislation, such as equality of job opportunity, while moving society toward a more just and humane world, further restrict an organization's freedom of action.

Although these changes must be integrated into management practices, they often require reformulating company policy, re-educating employees, and sometimes coping with the sheer physical size of many organizations, which in itself creates problems in implementing change swiftly. Finally, of course, merely changing laws and policies cannot change management and employee attitudes overnight. Thus, how rapidly and thoroughly businesses can change depends in part on the innovative and effective solutions developed by organization members through the use of principles of applied psychology.

THE FUTURE ROLE OF APPLIED PSYCHOLOGY

Some of the problems that applied psychology can help management solve in the 1980s include an increasing employee demand to express individuality on the job as well as elsewhere, changing definitions of *success* that include personal fulfillment as well as economic security,[8] and a growing proportion of workers over sixty years old (because of the inroads of inflation on fixed incomes and recent changes in laws dealing with mandatory retirement).[9] Other federal regulations, like those involving the hiring and promotion of women and minority group members, will continue to provide challenges to management's ingenuity.[10] During the twenty-year period from 1955 to 1975, more than one hundred federal laws affecting management/employee relations were passed.[11] Incorporating these laws into organizational policy while optimizing efficiency requires well-trained and creative managers.

Although events in recent years have

added to the complexity of the management task, some useful new ideas derived from psychology have been applied to help solve problems. Managers are learning how to use workers' potential to improve the design and productivity of their jobs,[12] and they are adapting successful techniques developed by managers in other cultures.[13] A central figure in this adaptation process is the personnel specialist, now often given the title vice president of human resources. The title is recognition of the fact that to be competitive in the 1980s, companies will have to use their scarce resources wisely — from oil supplies to human talent.[14]

HISTORICAL AREAS OF THE APPLICATION OF SCIENCE TO BUSINESS

Over the years, the various applications of psychology to business have involved practically all branches of psychology and all phases of industry.[15] Table 1.1 shows the fields of industry in which psychology has played and is playing an active role. The first column represents earlier developments. Some of these fields use both psychology and engineering knowledge; others involve only economics, business, or physiology. Only in the development of employment tests was psychology the primary discipline.[16]

The second column in the table represents fields in which psychological research played a major role and in which psychology largely replaced common sense. This period roughly spans the years 1935–1965. The third column includes fields that depend largely on the acceptance of psychology as a mature discipline. In recent years, executives have turned to the behavioral sciences for answers when common-sense responses have proved to be inadequate. Omitted from the table are the related fields of marketing,

TABLE 1.1 APPLICATION OF SCIENCE TO BUSINESS

EARLIEST FIELDS OF APPLICATION (BEFORE 1935)	HUMAN RELATIONS ERA (1935–1965)	MOST RECENT FIELDS (1965–PRESENT)
Financial incentives	Nonfinancial incentives	Organizational environment
Job training	Supervisory leadership	Decision making
Fatigue and boredom	Interpersonal relations	Organizational change and development
Lighting and ventilation	Employee attitudes	Career planning
Employment tests	Morale surveys	Physical/psychological effects of stress
Labor turnover	Executive appraisal	Effects of automation and computer use
Motion and time study	Interviewing	
Safety	Counseling	
Discipline	Engineering psychology	

labor-management relations, industrial medicine, and psychiatry, since they are specialized topics that fall outside the primary concern of this book.

Workers' Values and Applied Psychology All the fields in Table 1.1 represent areas in which advances can be made. The third column represents new areas that have developed in response to a growing respect for the dignity of the individual. This change is reflected in our social values, as society has assumed more responsibility for the health and welfare of all people. Business assumes responsibility for workers' mental health and job satisfaction not only because they affect workers' efficiency, but because society expects it. Thus, organizational applications of psychology change both because of increasing scientific knowledge and because of changing social values.

As concern for employee welfare increases, work efficiency sometimes conflicts with social considerations. For example, in a plant that runs two or three shifts a day, workers have to adjust physiologically each time they rotate shifts. From the objective point of view of health and productivity, shifts should be permanently assigned, but

this alternative is not acceptable to workers. Another work pattern, the four-day, forty-hour week, has been tried with mixed results and little overall acceptance.[17] Other methods have been used that allow employees more freedom to set their working hours.

"Flex-time" is one alternative to the 9-to-5 workday. Although details vary from one company to another, basically, every worker must be available during a common five-hour period, and total hours to be worked during a week are set. Workers choose their starting and ending times individually, however. In one company, surveys after one year on flex-time schedules showed that both managers and employees had a more positive attitude toward the company and a lower rate of absenteeism than a control group that had followed a traditional work schedule.[18]

It is expected that business will have to continue to take into account workers' values. This shift in focus may necessitate some managers to sacrifice traditional concepts of what is best for workers and who makes such judgments. The ability of industry to satisfy values that conflict with productivity is limited, however. Efficiency creates both leisure and wealth. A society that sacrifices the value of efficient work methods in order to gain costly social values ultimately may not be able to afford them. It is important that workers understand that productivity increases are one key to future growth.

Applied Psychology Is Not Universally Used. The reader who has worked in business may find that actual management practices seem different from those discussed here. Practice lags behind theory for pragmatic reasons. Managers are reluctant to try new methods until they have been proved elsewhere; they are hesitant to give up the security of accepted ways; and their pay-offs are often only short term, which may create problems or worsen chronic ones. The value of this book is that it presents practices that have been empirically tested and have a variety of application possibilities.

HOW PRINCIPLES
OF APPLIED PSYCHOLOGY
ARE DEVELOPED

TWO KINDS OF
INTEREST IN KNOWLEDGE:
CURIOSITY AND APPLICATION

Scientific knowledge satisfies curiosity. Scientific investigators, like explorers, want to discover something. They ask why and how an event occurs in nature, and they obtain the answers by making investigations. "How do geese know when to migrate?" and "How do bees find nectar and return to their hives?" are examples of questions that people have wondered about for thousands of years.

A scientist designs tests and experiments to acquire answers. Each experiment is an attempt to narrow the field of possible answers. They lead eventually to satisfactory conclusions — which in turn might raise other questions.[19] All investigators are not concerned with the immediate practical value of information. The objective may be to find a coherent pattern in the data, which then becomes the basis of a general theory.

A second way to look at scientific knowledge is to ask how it can be used. Let us suppose an individual knows how bees find a source of honey. What *use* or application can be made of that information? First thoughts suggest that the information might provide ways to improve the production of honey. A creative person, however, might think of more ingenious ways to apply the information,[20] such as developing a new kind of guidance control for missiles that involves cues used by bees but overlooked by humans. Often, unusual bits of information find unexpected uses. For example, the solar battery was put to practical use when exploration of space became a reality. Conversely, many down-to-earth applications have derived from technology developed for space programs (for example, nonstick coatings for cooking utensils and heart pacers). Thus, scientific data in itself may not *seem* useful; it is necessary to find a way to use it. Discovering new information and finding a use for it represent different scientific operations and purposes.

Since accurate data and well-supported theories deal in some way with reality,[21] they can be useful when applied to a life situation. For this reason, pure research (the quest of knowledge for its own sake) represents a good long-term investment. For example, cancer research today is focused on questions like "How do normal cells behave?" as well as on finding cures to specific forms of cancer.[22]

The above analysis of applied science is oversimplified, however. Often, when attempting to put scientific knowledge to work, new problems arise. This forces the practical person to become curious and to raise the same kinds of questions as the scientist.

The Divergent Approach to Application One approach to the application of knowledge is to take some information or a theory and think of the ways in which it can be used. For example, take the learning principle that retention of material to be memorized is better if a rest period follows each repetition than if repetitions follow one another. This knowledge could be applied to memorization of poems, speeches, plays, skills, and jobs. Little ingenuity is needed to make this application, and no new relationships are required. If, however, this information were put to use in an unusual way and some new relationship emerged, we might more rightly call it an invention. (In using the knowledge of electricity to make an electric light, Thomas Edison went beyond the obvious application of knowledge, and so he is credited with an invention.)

Another application of this principle is evident in this next case. One company employed a large number of women who had just graduated from high school. After being hired, the women participated in a three-month training program. It was suggested that, instead, the company try employing high school students during their senior year on a part-time basis. It was found that the women who worked two hours per day for one school year were better qualified than those who had trained for three months full-time. This application of the learning principle approaches innovation because it required some rethinking of the training program and changes in company practices.

The Convergent Approach Another approach to applying knowledge is to begin with a practical problem. For example, a manager might ask whether psychology has any information that will increase job satisfaction. Immediately some areas come to mind. What about the psychology of individual differences, boredom, and intelligence? Each may impinge on the problem in a different way. This type of application is characterized by the convergence of separate areas of knowledge that might suggest a new kind of work pattern, one that not only enlarged the job to increase interest, but also permitted goal setting and individual initiative. Often the manager finds that the psychologist has knowledge that suggests the necessity for certain changes and the psychological unsoundness of things that seem to be a matter of common sense.

Exploring the Gap Between Science and Life In following the convergent approach, gaps in our knowledge soon appear. The method raises many problems in life that do not occur to the theoretical investigator. Businesses are concerned with problems associated with boredom, delegation of authority, promotion, seniority rights, and so on. Although these are psychological problems, they are not likely to be discussed in a text on pure psychology. Often limited laboratory knowledge may suggest practices that backfire. For example, laboratory studies indicate that competition often increases motivation, but attempts to promote competition in industry may cause superior workers to slow down to protect their less able peers.

Although laboratory studies may suggest leads for solutions, life problems place knowledge in a different setting. Thus the process of trying to solve life problems again raises the question why. What is boredom and why does it occur? Why is it so difficult to delegate responsibility, and why is delegation desirable? Why should there be so much disagreement over the question of whom to promote? Why do people want to change one another, and why do people resist being changed? What is the fuss over seniority, and why should people feel they deserve more rights when they have seniority? These questions can be raised out of pure curiosity, without any concern about how to deal with them. Although an understanding of the *Why* may lead to direct application, the application is not a prerequisite for raising the question.

An example of how application raises new problems comes from studies of learning, a subject that has been explored extensively. It is central to many theories of psychology and has been explored by experimenting with the mastery of a great variety of tasks, comparing the abilities of animals at different levels of the evolutionary scale, studying the changes occurring with growth, noting the effects of injuries to the brain, studying the effects of diet and drugs, and setting up varying experimental conditions. Questions designed to test theories and the effects of experimental variations largely determine laboratory research.

Training computer programmers, radar technicians, and troubleshooters to locate malfunctions in equipment is a life-situation problem. It is reasonable to suppose that application of learning principles should facilitate such training. Nevertheless, R. M. Gagné[23] found the many data from the psychology of learning to be of little value in training workers in such skills. In many instances, the data led him astray. Training was more efficient when the specific task to be learned was analyzed. Making a detailed study of the task, breaking it into meaningful component parts, and arranging a proper sequence are examples of guiding principles that were more helpful in training such workers than a knowledge of learning principles. This experience does not mean that learning principles are incorrect; rather, it demonstrates that training involves more than is apparent from a study of learning, and that we do not yet completely understand the learning process. As a consequence, these training problems must be investigated further, both in the laboratory and in business situations. The gap between pure science and life then becomes evident and can be explored.

Figure 1.1 illustrates this third type of application — modern technology. Here the connection between science and life becomes a new area rather than a bridge across a gap. The circle represents this new area of scientific exploration brought into focus by attempts to apply scientific knowledge to life's problems. This area not only includes the space between science and life, but also overlaps them, showing that applied science invades or modifies some of our life problems and also influences scientific thinking.

VARIED APPROACHES TO DEVELOPING PSYCHOLOGICAL CONCEPTS

There are several possible approaches to scientific exploration. One is for the research worker to leave the laboratory and explore problems in the organization; it is called the *field approach*. Its effectiveness depends on comparisons of differing conditions and populations already existing.[24] The field approach requires effective selection of sites, conditions of work, and populations so that differences in results can be related to the factor investigated. Studies of the relationship between productivity and morale, effects of organizational changes on communication, behavior of small and large work groups, and so on, are examples of research that can be carried out through the field approach. Survey methods (which use interviews and questionnaires to determine opinions, attitudes, and motivations), case

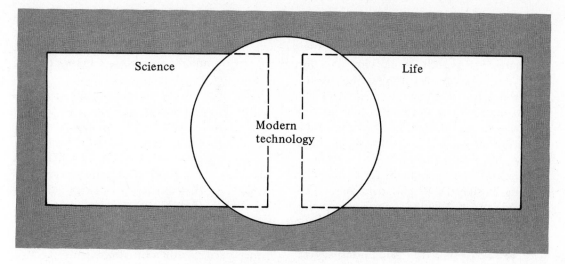

FIGURE 1.1 EXPLORING THE GAP

The new area of investigation is represented as a circle; it not only includes the gap between science and life areas but also overlaps and enlarges them.

studies, and feedback procedures are common techniques.

The main problem with the field approach is the difficulty of finding companies that match on all relevant variables. Frequently, field researchers take advantage of special circumstances — observing a company reorganize after a fire or natural disaster, for example. Such special studies cannot undertake rigorous before-and-after measurements, but do produce much data about the effects of crucial events on an organization.

A second approach is to take organizational problems to a laboratory where lifelike conditions are simulated. This method allows more rigid controls and permits repetition of a single experimental condition, so individual variations can be explored. This is the *experimental approach* to life problems. In taking the problem into the laboratory, however, some of the realities of life are lost.

There was a time when the psychological laboratory was purposely isolated from life

so that the data would not be contaminated by variables in real-life situations. Responses were measured by instruments in order to reduce the need for language; tests were run under controlled environmental conditions (specific temperature, noise, lighting); and subjects were tested in separate cubicles to prevent social effects. Only the experimental condition studied was subjected to variation. These controls were regarded as merits of scientific experimentation because the aspect of behavior studied was isolated.

Then came Gestalt psychology, which emphasized the dangers of isolating psychological processes because an organism functions as a whole in real life.[25] K. Lewin, a follower of this school of thought, was considered a pioneer when he experimented with real-life situations in order to study behavior.[26]

Many laboratories now simulate life situations. Various kinds of social situations are created in which power or prestige factors, personality conflicts, leadership styles, and prejudices are introduced into the experimental design to reproduce some of life's problems.[27] Research on solving business problems is being done by having subjects play the roles of company executives and employees.[28] It becomes clear that solving problems involves more than facts and logic when dealing with life situations. Research interest has increased in "business games," in which groups of individuals compete in running businesses.[29] The participants are required to make a series of decisions dealing with investments, budgets, and the like, and learn the consequences of each decision they act upon. Some of these "games" last several days and simulate the operation of a business over a year or more.

By creating a situation in the laboratory, a given circumstance can be repeated with many groups. Because a particular kind of conference problem, for example, can be repeated many times in a simulated situation, the effect of conference methods and conference skills can be studied and compared. The more closely the laboratory situation simulates the life situation the more accurate and dependable the results and conclusions are. The findings may still need to be verified under real-life conditions; if the findings fail to meet this test, researchers have probably overlooked some important factor. A new research problem is then created — that of discovering the discrepancy between the laboratory and the real-life test conditions.

In recent years, researchers have found other ways to integrate the laboratory and field approaches. Armchair theorizing has been supplemented by *grounded theory*,[30] derived from data collected in the field and then analyzed and organized into a logical system. People called *change agents* and *action researchers*[31] go into a company that has asked for their help in solving a specific, costly,

and painful problem; the data that they collect and the changes that they initiate to solve the problem become insights to guide future efforts by other researchers, whether the solution succeeded or failed.[32]

Use of the grounded theory approach has led to an awareness of the limits of the scientific method in resolving organizational problems that involve people. Researchers employing this method feel that there is a place in organization theory and research for subjective, clinical data, as well as quantitative information.[33] Other researchers, however, may fault such an approach because of its failure to produce data that can readily be generalized to other situations, or replicated by other experimenters.

No single ideal way of developing psychological applications for organizations is likely to be uncovered. The best approach for those who evaluate research findings would be to ask, "Was the method selected appropriate to the problem under study?" and "Can the conclusions made be justified, given the approach and analysis used?"

THE MANAGER AS APPLIED SCIENTIST

The source or the solution of problems in business, like those in science, is not clearly labeled. It is a primary responsibility of the business manager to analyze the nature and source of problems correctly and then to attempt to resolve them. The following section provides one way of breaking down problems for analysis, and it also suggests chapters in this book that give further information on each area discussed.

POSSIBLE PROBLEM AREAS

The Situation Ordinarily the manager of any group is in charge of a situation. In business,

A supervisor has charge of a work situation, which, in addition to employees, may include machines, tools, and other equipment, and can change some aspects to better the situation. (Declan Haun from Black Star)

a manager or supervisor heads a work situation that includes machinery and/or office equipment, as well as a physical work area. It is within a supervisor's control to alter some aspects of this situation and to recommend other changes. Many problems can be solved by making changes in the physical environment: the machinery, the desks, the equipment, or the spatial relationships of employees. Thus the situation in which people work and interact represents one direction in which a manager may look in order to improve performance. Working with the overall situation is a way in which he or she can attempt objective problem solving. The

potentialities of problem solving in the objective situation will be discussed in detail in Chapters 2, 19, and 21.

The Individual Managers constantly interact with individuals. Whether giving instructions, making assignments, conducting interviews, meeting others informally in the elevator or coffee shop, or facing an emotionally disturbed employee, a manager is interacting with other employees. In this area of interpersonal relations, problem-solving activity may center around feelings and attitudes. A manager's knowledge and skills in dealing with these human relationships can influence each individual's performance and job satisfaction. Essential principles in these areas will be discussed in Chapters 5, 8, 12, 18, and 22.

The Group Usually a manager has more than one employee reporting to him or her. Thus a manager must relate not only to each individual but to a combination of individuals — a group. So an additional area for problem solving is introduced, the problem of being fair.

A manager cannot grant one individual's request without influencing the expectations and judgments of others in the group. What constitutes fair treatment can be interpreted differently by each person. Since these opinions sometimes conflict, misunderstandings can result.

Group problems, viewed from the position of the supervisor, are primarily leadership problems. These will be dealt with in detail in Chapters 6, 7, 21, and 22.

DIAGNOSING THE LOCATION

A manager, therefore, may solve some problems by making changes in the work situation, in interpersonal relations, or in inner-group relations. For example, a problem involving two persons who do not get along with each other may be handled either by separating them (changing the work situation/environment), or by effectively correcting one of them (changing through interpersonal relations), or by improving communications between them (changing the inner-group relationships). Another problem might be solved more effectively by using one route rather than the other two. The person who can diagnose and pinpoint the difficulty is in the best position to select the most fruitful approach. The chapters that follow will help improve your ability to analyze problems and implement solutions.

APPLYING PSYCHOLOGICAL PRINCIPLES IN USING THIS TEXT

Management training should produce three kinds of learning. The most obvious is *acquiring information,* which includes general knowledge, job knowledge, technical know-how, and facts and principles in the behavioral sciences. This acquisition is the intellectual aspect of any learning and is gained through lectures, textbooks, and other learning aids.

Less obvious in most management-training situations is the *development of skills in leadership and group problem solving.* To become a mechanic, a person must be trained in certain skills, but those individuals who become managers are seldom given practice training. Essential skills for managers include sensitivity to feelings, ability to state problems so as not to offend, ability to teach, skill in interviewing, and conference skills. Practice in managerial skills is provided in this text by role-playing exercises at the end of some chapters to help bridge the gap between knowing and doing.

The third kind of learning is the *acquisition of constructive attitudes.* A manager who dislikes working through others will have difficulties even after thoroughly learning the basic principles and practicing them in training problems. If managerial training can develop an interest in organizing work as well as doing it, in seeing problems as challenges rather than headaches, and in reacting to employees as people to be understood rather than to judge, a manager will have positive relationships with workers and behave differently toward them. Class discussion, group problem solving, and role-playing provide this learning opportunity. Text cases and exercises are designed to help develop such constructive attitudes.

NOTES

1. Taylor, F. W. *The principles of scientific management*. New York: Harper & Row, 1911.
2. Gilbreth, F. B. *Primer of scientific management*. New York: Harper & Row, 1912.
3. Davis, R. C. *The fundamentals of top management*. New York: Harper & Row, 1951.
4. Gulick, L., and Urwick, L. (Eds.). *Papers on the science of administration*. New York: Columbia University Press, 1937.
5. Fayol, H. *Industrial and general administration (1916)*. London: Pitman, 1930.
6. Mayo, E. *The human problems of industrial civilization*. New York: Macmillan, 1933.
7. Maslow, A. H. *Motivation and personality*. New York: Harper, 1954.
8. Yankelovitch, D. Turbulence in the working world: Angry workers, happy grads. *Psychol. Today,* 1974, *8,* 80–89.
9. Ross, I. Retirement at 70: A new trauma for management. *Fortune,* 1978, *97*(4), 106–110ff.
10. Smith, L. Equal opportunity rules are getting tougher. *Fortune,* 1978, *97*(4), 152–154ff.
11. Meyer, H. E. Personnel directors are the new corporate heroes. *Fortune,* 1977, *93*(2), 84–88ff.
12. Ways, M. The American kind of worker participation. *Fortune,* 1976, *94*(4), 168–171ff.
13. Kraar, L. The Japanese are coming — with their own style of management. *Fortune,* 1975, *91*(3), 116–121ff.
14. Meyer, H. E., op. cit.
15. Munsterberg, H. *Psychology and industrial efficiency*. Boston: Houghton Mifflin, 1913.
16. Viteles, M. S. *Industrial psychology*. New York: Norton, 1932.
17. Poor, R. *4 days, 40 hours*. Cambridge, Mass.: Bursk & Poor, 1969.
18. Golembiewski, K. T., Hilles, R., and Kagno, M. S. A longitudinal study of flex-time effects: Some consequences of an organizational development structural intervention. *J. App. Behav. Sci.,* 1974, *10,* 503–532.
19. Pirsig, R. M. *Zen and the art of motorcycle maintenance: An inquiry into values*. New York: William Morrow, 1974. Part I.
20. Gordon, W. J. J. *Synectics: The development of creative capacity*. London: Collier-Macmillan, 1961.
21. See Zukav, G., *The dancing Wu Li masters: An overview of the new physics,* New York: William Morrow, 1979, for a discussion of the relationship of *theory* to *reality*.
22. Nesbitt, M., Pediatric Oncologist, The University of Minnesota. Speech Presented on Minnesota public radio, December, 1979.
23. Gagné, R. M. Military training and principles of learning. *Amer. Psychologist,* 1962, *17,* 83–91.
24. Bonchard, T. J., Jr. Field research methods: Interviewing, questionnaires, participant observation, systematic observation, unobtrusive measures. In Dunnette, M. D. (Ed.), *Handbook of Industrial and Organizational Psychology*. Chicago: Rand McNally, 1976.
25. Köhler, W. *Gestalt psychology*. New York: Liveright, 1929.
26. Lewin, K. *Resolving social conflicts*. New York: Harper, 1948.
27. Cartwright, D., and Zander, A. (Eds.). *Group dynamics* (3rd ed.). Evanston, Ill.: Row, Peterson, 1967.
28. Maier, N. R. F. *Problem solving discussions and conferences*. New York: McGraw-Hill, 1963.
29. Ricciardi, F. M., et al. *Top management decision simulation*. New York: American Management Assn., 1958; Biel, W. C. Training programs and devices. In R. M. Gagné (Ed.), *Psychological principles in systems development*. New York: Holt, 1962.
30. Glaser, B. G., and Strauss, A. L. *The discovery of grounded theory: Strategies for qualitative research*. Chicago: Aldine, 1967.
31. Beer, M. Technology of organizational development. In M. D. Dunnette (Ed.), *Handbook of industrial and organizational psychology*. Chicago: Rand McNally, 1976, 937–993.

32. Argyris, C. *Behind the front page: Organizational self-renewal in a metropolitan newspaper*. San Francisco: Jossey-Bass, 1974.
33. Buss, A. R. The emerging field of the sociology of psychological knowledge. *Amer. Psychol.*, 1975, *30*, 988–1002; Elms, A. C. The crisis of confidence in social psychology. *Amer. Psychol.*, 1975, *30*, 967–976; Gadlin, H., and Ingle, G. Through the one-way mirror. *Amer. Psychol.*, 1975, *30*, 1003–1009; Ghiselli, E. E. Some perspectives for industrial psychology. *Amer. Psychol.*, 1974, *29*, 80–87; Korman, A. K., and Tanofsky, R. Statistical problems of contingency models in organizational behavior. *Acad. Manage. J.*, 1975, *18*, 393–397; Moberg, D. J., and Koch, J. C. A critical appraisal of integrated treatments of contingency findings. *Acad. Manage. J.*, 1975, *18*, 109–124; Sarason, S. B. Psychology to the Finland station in the heavenly city of the eighteenth century philosophers. *Amer. Psychol.*, 1975, *30*, 1072–1080; Warr, P. Theories of motivation. In P. Warr (Ed.), *Personal goals and work design*. New York: Wiley, 1976.

SUGGESTED READINGS

Cummings, L. L. Toward organizational behavior. *Acad. Mgt. R.*, January, 1978, 90–98.
Dubin, R. *Handbook of work, organization and society*. Chicago: Rand-McNally, 1976.
Filley, A., House, R., and Kerr, S. *Managerial process and organizational behavior*, 2nd ed. Glenview, Ill.: Scott, Foresman, 1976.
Katz, D., and Kahn, R. *The social psychology of organizations*, 2nd ed. New York: Wiley, 1978.
Simon, H. *Administrative behavior*, 3rd ed. New York: Free Press, 1976.

LABORATORY EXERCISE
SMALL-GROUP DISCUSSIONS

A. PREPARING FOR DISCUSSION

The instructor will
1. Divide the class into groups of five or six persons.
2. Ask each group to select a discussion leader.
3. Instruct leaders to conduct a discussion on a current controversial topic, such as, "What are the most effective responses of managers to the continuing increase in government regulation of business?" or "To what individuals or groups, other than stockholders, does business have a responsibility?"

B. DISCUSSION PROCEDURE

1. Each discussion leader should develop a final list of no more than three factors from the group's discussion. The discussion may require twenty-five to thirty minutes.
2. It is suggested that leaders first develop a relatively complete list, encouraging participants to be uncritical of each other.
3. Each factor should be briefly recorded.
4. When the group ceases to produce new ideas, the discussion should turn to an evaluation of the items. The objective is to reduce the list to the best three factors.

C. REPORTS TO CLASS

1. Each group leader should report the group's contributions to the class instructor, who writes them on the board, abbreviating lengthy statements.

2. It is best to have each group make one contribution at a time, in turn, so as to keep all groups actively interested.
3. Duplicate entries should be starred.

D. METHOD USED

The discussion method experienced in this laboratory period is known as "Phillips 66,"* "discussion 66," or just "buzz session." Groups of twenty to one hundred persons can be divided so that everyone can participate in the discussion. The discussion topic should be clearly stated and should be one that the group feels competent to handle. Experience has shown that the time allowed should depend on the complexity of the topic and on the size of the group. In all cases, the time should be long enough to allow interaction and a jelling of ideas. Although the original idea ("66") was for groups of *six* to discuss for *six* minutes, it appears that only superficial problems can be handled in so short a time. Attempts to use groups of more than eight persons are unsatisfactory; groups of three to six are most successful.

The number of ideas to be reported by each group should be fewer than the number of persons in a group. This prevents the group product from being a list of the contributions made by each member. Good discussions require resolution of differences in opinion, and one way to introduce such differences is to require the group to be selective and integrative rather than merely additive.

* Phillips, J. D. Report on discussion 66. *Adult Educ. J.,* 1948, *7,* 181–182.

CHAPTER TWO

CAUSATION
AND PURPOSE
IN
BEHAVIOR

∎

The Psychological Approach
How Behavior Varies with the Nature of the Stimulus
How Human Nature Determines Behavior
Applications of the Causation Formula to the Job
Differences to Be Expected Between Managers and Workers

∎

THE ACTIVITY OF SCIENCE should lead to an understanding of nature. Psychology as a science, therefore, devotes itself to exploring behavior, with understanding as its goal. Using the information that psychologists have researched concerning behavior, managers who understand the possible causes of behavior are better equipped to deal with, and solve the problems confronting them in a work situation.

THE PSYCHOLOGICAL APPROACH

UNDERSTANDING VERSUS EVALUATING BEHAVIOR

We *understand* behavior when we know what caused it or what made the person do it. We *evaluate* behavior when we approve or disapprove of it.

Both understanding and evaluation are common human reactions. Our systems of values, whether they are religious, cultural, or philosophic, furnish frames of reference that we use to appraise ourselves and others. Our laws reflect these values, and persons who break these laws are subject to punishment.

But our understanding of why, for example, a worker steals from a company can be separated from our judgment of that person or act. When we discover that an individual embezzled company funds to pay off some gambling debts, we understand that person better, but this does not mean that we approved or support the action. Thus, the first step in a scientific approach to behavior is to attempt to separate value judgment from behavior analysis.

The psychological approach to correction is more effective than the legalistic approach. The former tends to bring into focus the objective to be achieved; hence, it has a fu-

ture reference, whereas the legalistic focuses on behavior that has already occurred and has a past reference. Since our major concern is influencing future behavior in work situations, this book emphasizes the psychological approach.

FACTORS INFLUENCING BEHAVIOR

Behavior is always the product of two factors, the nature of the organism that behaves and the nature of the situation in which the organism finds itself. The situation is a source of stimulation, and behavior is the organism's response to stimulation. Often we are not aware that we have been stimulated and assume that our behavior is spontaneous, yet spontaneous responses are more likely to be the exception than the rule. For example, a person may suddenly look at the clock to see if it is time for lunch. What was the stimulus for this behavior? It might have been a minor stomach contraction, the sound of someone eating an apple, or the chiming of the clock. One aspect of the psychologist's job is to locate the stimulus or the pattern of stimuli in order to understand the behavior under investigation.

An individual or a particular organism behaves by responding to the stimulation received from the environment. The make-up of a particular individual, therefore, contributes to the behavior. The nature of an individual depends on heredity, physical and emotional environment, culture, and learning. Individuals differ not only in their appearances but also in their sensitivities, response repertoires, intelligence, interests, motivations, and personalities. Any aspect of human beings that has been measured has revealed differences, and the psychologist must take these variations into account.

Individuals not only show differences, they also show similarities in behavior. These similarities may be biological or cultural in nature, or they may be the result of common experiences. For example, people are alike in that they can see better under good illumination, yet they differ in their visual acuity. The psychologist is concerned with the contribution of the organism to behavior and also with the determination of the similarities and differences that exist within and between species, cultures, and groups.

INTERACTION BETWEEN PERSON AND SITUATION

Researchers have found that in simple reflex behaviors, the stimulus acts on the organism and elicits the response, and that the organism plays no active part in selecting or interpreting behavior. But for the behaviors with which we are concerned, the organism — a human being — does *interact* with the environment.

We speak of the interaction between stimulus and organism, because the condition or nature of the organism affects its interpretation of the stimulus, while simultaneously the stimulus affects the organism. Therefore, a hungry person sees food differently from a person who has just eaten, because the supplementary stimulations in the body alter the properties (for each individual) of the external stimulus. We must distinguish between the *physical* properties of a stimulus and *the properties it has for the organism.* If a person sees and reacts to a stick of wood as to a snake, for instance, we can best understand that person's behavior if we consider the stimulus to be a snake, not a piece of wood. Since the organism contributes to the determination of the nature of a stimulus, behavior is the product of an interaction between the stimulus and the organism, rather than a reaction of the organism to the stimulus. The product of this interaction in psychology is called *perception.*

One example of how the same pattern can be perceived in quite different ways is illustrated by Figure 2.1. This figure may be seen as a pair of *X*s or as an upright and an inverted *V*. To argue about which view is right is futile; both interpretations are consistent with the nature of the figure. If a person expected to see *X*s, he would be more likely to see them than another who expected to see *V*s.

Let us suppose that seeing an *X* makes you angry. If someone innocently places the letter before you, is she responsible for your anger, or is your interpretation responsible?

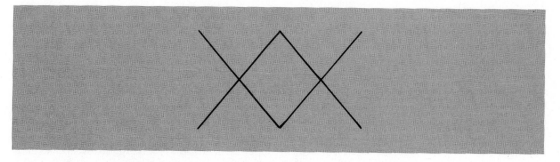

FIGURE 2.1 VARIATIONS IN THE PERCEPTION OF OBJECTS
This figure may be seen as two *X*s or as an upright *V* superimposed on an inverted *V*. Or it can be seen as a *W* resting on top of an *M,* or as a diamond. What is seen depends on a perceiver's point of view.

There are even more ways of seeing this figure. Now she suggests that the figure represents a *W* on top of an *M,* and you too can see these letters. You will even see a diamond with whiskers on its sides as soon as it is suggested. With a nonemotional stimulus like this, most people can be openminded and see other points of view when they are suggested.

The importance of interaction is evident when we consider the following example. Employees at the ACF Company react differently to a particular supervisor, Carol Adams. Some resent her presence because they see her as a slave driver; others are callous and overlook her remarks because they see her as a nervous, high-strung person; still others are glad to have her around to help them and regard her simply as a person doing her job. Carol Adams, on the other hand, perceives herself to be a goodhearted woman who works for the interest of her workers and believes that she should have a little more respect and cooperation for her efforts. Thus, the perceptions that people have of themselves and others derive from their own personalities and viewpoints, as well as from observable data.

An understanding of behavior requires not only that we determine the stimulus to which an individual reacts, but also that we discover how the stimuli are organized. It is perceptions that give stimuli their meanings, and individuals' responses are determined by these meanings. For example, quick movements are often seen as threatening; slow movements, as friendly.[1] Animals and small children exhibit reactions that show this different interpretation of these movements, regardless of the intent of the individual making the gesture. Thus, slow-moving people are generally regarded as more gentle and kind than fast-moving people, and people in a hurry are sometimes thought to be angry. The fact that angry movements *are* quick supports these simple interpretations.

BEHAVIOR AND ACCOMPLISHMENT

The behavior of an organism leads to a consequence, or *accomplishment,* which may be desired or undesired by the organism. Migration behavior in birds, for example, takes them to a more suitable climate; on the other hand, when a person drops a heavy tool on his foot, it may injure the foot. Accomplishments are always the *products* of behavior and should not be confused with the *causes* of behavior. Causes precede the results of an action.

The reason accomplishments frequently become a source of confusion is that they are the aspects of behavior that often are disturbing to others. When a traffic violation results in an accident, it is taken more seriously than one resulting in a near miss. The person who shoots and kills is guilty of murder, but the person who shoots and misses is guilty only of intent. Thus, the accomplishment of behavior causes us to evaluate it and to focus on the organism. Punishment, rather than prevention of a repetition of the behavior, becomes the focus of attention. It is difficult for us to analyze behavior dispassionately when it has harmful effects.

Often we falsely attribute motives to others on the basis of their accomplishments. For instance, a worker drops a wrench while working aloft; if it drops near me, I may accuse the person of trying to kill me. Or an employee leaves a lighted cigarette on the edge of a desk and is accused of disrespect for company property. Or a neighbor crosses a property line in mowing the lawn and is accused of trying to steal the land from the owner. Or a nation builds up its armed strength to defend its borders, and a hostile nation accuses it of planning an invasion. Misunderstandings thus arise when we falsely attribute intent to an action. Behavior and its accomplishments are only part of the story. We must seek out the stimulus conditions and relate them to the behavior.

Accomplishment enters into the causation sequence only when it plays a part in the organism's planning. In such cases, the accomplishment is something that is anticipated; it is part of the organism's make-up, hence precedes the behavior. This is the meaning of *purpose*. But birds do not plan their flights; their behavior results from a reaction to the shorter periods of daylight, a decrease in available food, and temperature gradients.

The person who drops a tool may do so because of distraction, lack of training, or many other combinations of stimulus and organismic characteristics. The individual who drives through a red light may not see the light or may be in a hurry, anticipating getting to work on time rather than receiving a traffic ticket. Whatever the accomplish-

ment, it serves as an opportunity for learning, which alters the organism and thereby may influence future behaviors by providing new anticipations.

THE CAUSAL SEQUENCE IN BEHAVIOR

The psychological approach to behavior follows the formulation shown in Figure 2.2. S represents the situation that supplies the stimulation to the individual or organism, O. The double-headed arrow indicates that O interacts with S, giving rise to the organism's perception or interpretation of the S. The response of the organism is shown by the single-headed arrow leading to B, which represents behavior. The interaction between S and O, therefore, precedes the behavior.

The behavior in turn acts on the outside world, and this leads to an accomplishment, A. The accomplishment may alter the stimulating conditions and thereby influence the subsequent behavior, or it may initiate new

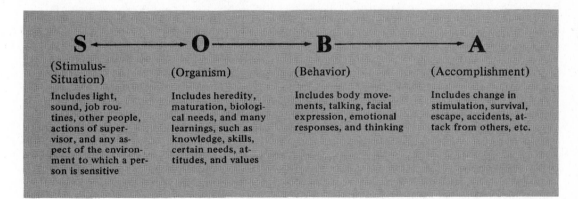

FIGURE 2.2 THE CAUSAL SEQUENCE
To explain behavior, we must include a description of the S as well as the O. The interaction between them must precede the behavior that results from the interaction. The behavior (B) causes the changes that alter the relationship between the organism (O) and its world. The change produced by behavior is an accomplishment (A), which may be desirable or undesirable. In either case it may alter the stimulus-situation for the organism, or it may serve as the stimulus for other organisms.

behaviors by creating new situations for the organism. The person who runs a red light may save time, receive a traffic ticket, or suffer an injury. In any event, a new situation has arisen that in turn initiates another unit of behavior. Although the accomplishment is a product of the behavior that precedes it, the nature of the accomplishment can play a part in subsequent behavior, providing that the organism has learned something. This learning may be profitable or detrimental. The individual who runs the red light may be rewarded by saving time, and as a consequence may run a red light on a future occasion and then be involved in an accident.

Since chance factors influence accomplishment, in the sense that the same behavior can have a number of different results, it is difficult to control accomplishment. Managers who understand causes for behavior, however, can use their knowledge to influence it.

The *S-O-B-A* sequence can be illustrated by a simple situation. A person is pricked with a pin, jumps, and escapes the pinprick. Here the pinprick is the *S,* the person is the *O,* the jump is the *B,* and escape is the *A.* In examining such a sequence, we should identify each factor. An explanation of behavior that does not identify the stimulus is incomplete, yet it is often overlooked. People are likely to say they jumped to get away from the pin or from the pain, or simply because they wanted to. The first explanation makes accomplishment the cause, the other two mention only the organism.

PURPOSE IN HUMAN BEHAVIOR

Let us take a complex situation and see how effectively we can explain behavior in terms of an interaction between stimulus and organism.

Walter Kubek is running down the street. We stop him and ask why he is running, and he replies, "I'm running to catch the 4:15 train to Chicago."

Should we accept this answer as an explanation? Catching the train would be the accomplishment of his running; how then could it be the cause? Moreover, if the train turned out to be an hour late, it would not be necessary for him to run, yet this fact would not have prevented the running. The reason he has given is not accurate.

Now let us explore the antecedent conditions. First, we must find a stimulus. A little reflection reveals that he must have looked at a watch or a clock. If a clock is the stimulus, it follows that the behavior of a given organism will change if the stimulus is altered. If his clock were to be set ahead, Walter Kubek would run when he did not need to, for the sake of accomplishment; he can also be made not to run, when for the sake of accomplishment he should, by setting his clock back. Because altering the clock will influence the running behavior of a given individual, we must accept it as a stimulus.

Now we must explore the contribution of the organism (in this instance Walter Kubek) to the behavior in question. People in general do not run when they see a clock; we have a special kind of individual. All things we say about him, however, must be reducible to antecedent events. It is reasonable to suppose Walter Kubek (1) has a need for this train (motivation); (2) knows the train schedule, the distance to the station, and that running saves time (knowledge); and (3) has the ability to run (aptitude and physical make-up). All these conditions existed before the running took place and so are antecedent events. Altering any one of them will modify his responses to the clock: a telegram stating that he is not needed in Chicago will alter his behavior; he will also respond differently if misinformed about the train time or about the distance from the station; and if he had a bad heart or paralyzed legs, he would not run even if the need for catching the train were urgent.

Walter Kubek should have answered our question by saying that the clock indicated that he might miss the train. Then why does he explain his behavior in terms of consequences or purpose? Purpose refers to anticipations or expectations. Anticipations are a product of many past learnings and are a part of his make-up, as are all his memories. He anticipates that the train will leave at 4:15 because it has left at this time on previous occasions. Relying on expectations is quite effective because many of today's events are duplicates of yesterday's. When he refers to catching "today's" train, he is actually describing his memory of past trains.

But we must not confuse an anticipation with a cause. Present events are not always duplicates of the past. Take the example of an employee who stops being tardy for a week after being reprimanded. Will the reprimand method work a second time? Will it work for all tardy employees? Are there different causes for tardiness? If so, might it be better to explore the S and the O before accepting anticipated events as dependable explanations? As a matter of fact, most common-sense explanations of behavior omit reference to the contribution of the S, which we shall see later is important in changing behavior.

BASIC CAUSES
OF BEHAVIOR OFTEN
UNKNOWN TO THE INDIVIDUAL

Although the expressed explanation of behavior may reveal a person's anticipations and desires, the accounts that people give of their responses may be incidental or even inaccurate. The important causes of behavior are often unknown to the individual, since they do not reach the level of consciousness. A person who fears snakes seldom knows why. The fear may have originated in an incident in early childhood. The incident is repressed and apparently forgotten, but the fear of the snake that the incident generated remains. Or we may take the case of a worker who attributes a decline in productive ability to fatigue, whereas the more basic cause may be worry over personal problems.

Sometimes people may think they know the *why* of an action and be entirely mistaken. For instance, a group of workers may say they are out on strike to get higher pay, but it is possible that low pay is not the true cause of their strike. Under other conditions of work, the same group might not go out on strike. Clean toilets, sanitary drinking fountains, security in their jobs, and sympathetic consideration of their problems may prevent workers from striking for higher pay, whereas unsatisfactory working conditions may make employees so dislike a job that they demand higher wages if they are to continue to work. It is not always the most poorly paid group that strikes for higher wages, a fact that sometimes puzzles the employer. The cause of such behavior cannot be found merely by analyzing demands or expressed purposes. These demands are responses to some kind of stimulation, and the effective stimuli *may not even be known to the individuals who make the demands.*

When people do not get along, they quarrel about almost anything, and what they quarrel about is not necessarily the basic cause of the trouble. The important thing is to get at the cause of the lack of congeniality;

the bickering will then take care of itself. Investigations of this sort of problem clearly show that actual causes may be unknown to the individuals and that these causes frequently go back to situations entirely unrelated to the present difficulty. Sometimes supervisors will find a few individuals among their employees who always have something to complain about. The cause for the lack of congeniality in this case is usually psychological illness on the part of the habitual complainers, rather than work-related problems.

EXCUSES ARE NOT CAUSES

Many reasons given for behavior are excuses rather than causes. People may give seemingly logical reasons for evading income taxes, opposing certain laws, voting for particular candidates, considering their employers unfair, or underpaying their employees. But none of these reasons may actually be the causes of the individuals' points of view or behavior. Sometimes people know that their expressed reasons are false, but often they themselves are so convinced by their reasons that they believe these must be basic causes. The psychologist — and the manager — cannot risk using such material as a basis for analyzing behavior. For this reason, it is preferable to analyze situation and behavior data rather than to rely on verbal reports.

HOW BEHAVIOR VARIES WITH THE NATURE OF THE STIMULUS

A person acts differently in different situations. Sometimes we may forget this obvious fact and blame the individual for the changed behavior. We know, for example, that honesty depends on the situation (a complex stimulus) in which people find themselves, yet we sometimes classify people as honest or dishonest.[2] If the situation determines whether or not the behavior is honest, then people will differ only in the number of situations in which honest behavior appears. Consequently, most people will be honest in some situations and dishonest in others, and only an extreme minority of them will be consistently honest or consistently dishonest.

The frequency of honest behavior can be increased by training and also by changing the situation. Locked cars, sophisticated auditing methods, and well-lighted and busy streets reduce the amount of dishonest behavior. J. Jacobs points out that the crime rate in modern housing areas can be reduced by arranging construction so that there are many eyes in the close vicinity, particularly the eyes of persons who live in the neighborhood.[3] Long halls and dim stairways in apartment buildings encourage crime. Even social pressure, such as that furnished by honor examinations, may serve as a stimulus for honesty. Students refrain from cheating because they have learned that their associates disapprove of such behavior.

In a work situation, the amount of labor trouble, turnover, and breakage varies with the situation. Supervisors who create a favorable work climate by showing consideration for the workers' needs have fewer grievances and less turnover.[4]

In industry, we find that in many plants there is resentment at punching a time clock. When fifteen minutes are deducted if a worker is two minutes late, we find workers waiting until the full fifteen minutes are up before they check in. Other workers begin clearing their desks ten or fifteen minutes before the end of the work period, or refuse to work a few minutes overtime to finish a job. This behavior may be called petty and be a source of irritation, yet it is directly

The use of time clocks to check in employees can produce counterproductive actions and attitudes. (Frank Siteman)

related to the stimulus-situation. In companies where a responsible individual passes judgment on tardiness and arbitrary methods are not used, such behaviors occur less frequently.

HOW HUMAN NATURE DETERMINES BEHAVIOR

Heredity is a significant factor in determining the nature of the individual. The importance is clear when we compare the physical features of parents and offspring and see the similarities. The potential abilities of chil-

dren also tend to be similar to those of their parents. If we have a particular talent, there is a greater than chance probability that our brothers and sisters will also share this talent.

As a child grows, ability to learn increases; as a consequence, behavior is further modified. We speak of such changes in behavior as being *acquired*. Knowledge, skill, and language obviously are acquired and represent important modifications of behavior. Learned modifications in behavior are not passed on to children, but must be acquired by them through their own personal experience. Such aspects of behavior are culturally determined.

Because human characteristics are both inborn and acquired, we must always distinguish between these two types of influence. We cannot expect skill from an untrained individual, nor can we automatically expect two individuals with the same training to be similar in their skills or in their ability to produce. Blaming a person for not doing a job that requires a skill that he or she has little inborn capacity to acquire is as pointless as blaming one chemical substance for not being another. It is as unjust as censuring someone for not having a skill before training the individual.

APPLICATIONS OF THE CAUSATION FORMULA TO THE JOB

Once we accept the view that all behavior is dependent to both the S and O,* many new opportunities for influencing behavior become apparent. Since all behavior is influenced by these two independent factors, a basic change in either will alter behavior. Managers must analyze conditions of work problems carefully so that the changes are made in the right direction, do not introduce worse problems, and are not uneconomical.

CHANGING THE STIMULUS-SITUATION (S)

Imagine a situation in which many errors are made on a job. What are some changes in the S that might be made? Immediately we think of such improvements as better lighting, reduced noise, a change in work procedure, or eliminating interruptions. By making further checks, we can rule out some of these and clarify others. If the lighting conditions are different in two parts of the

* Refer again to Figure 2.2 for the causation formula.

room, a comparison of errors occurring in the two sections will increase knowledge of the influence of the lighting factor. By exploring and making a variety of comparisons, we can suggest practical changes in the S. The fact that the supervisor and other employees are also stimuli should be considered as well.

If errors are greater in one unit than in another, we should locate the S factors that differ in the two units and see if any of the differences will yield a clue. Exploratory analysis of this kind should precede any contemplated changes.

Examples of accomplishments due to improved behavior that resulted from changes in the S include:

1. Reduction in highway accidents through the addition of a white line in the center of the road
2. Reduction in industrial accidents through the introduction of safety devices
3. Better inspection due to increased lighting
4. Better production due to less close supervision
5. Prompter return from coffee breaks as a result of improved elevator service
6. Improved care of trucks through having each driver use the same truck every day

CHANGING THE ORGANISM (O)

Opportunities for changing the O are less numerous, but they also require analysis. Some employees make many errors, whereas others make few. If employees working under similar conditions consistently perform differently, it is reasonable to explore ways for changing the O.

One way to change the O in a given job is to exchange one worker for another. Such a move indicates a problem of placement, which will be developed more thoroughly in subsequent chapters. Suffice it to say here that many differences among individuals should be taken for granted before this move is explored too seriously. Of course, it is better to place people properly at the outset than to make many changes in placement after employment.

A more common way to change the O is through education and development of skill. If experienced employees perform better, training should be considered. Training is also indicated if employees who do the best work use methods that the less effective employees do not.

Modifying a person's attitudes or needs also makes changes in the O. If certain employees are social misfits or unusually lacking in job interest, the problem may be one of emotional or social adjustment. Insofar as such adjustments can be improved and needs can be altered, changes in the O will occur.

Examples of accomplishments due to improved behavior that resulted from working with the O include:

1. Increased job satisfaction and work performance through the use of aptitude tests. (When managers place employees on the basis of test results, they are manipulating the O. Behavior in a given work situation is improved by placing the proper Os in it.)
2. Decreased accidents and increased production due to job training
3. Increased production due to reduced emotional conflict
4. Improved morale through use of feedback sessions

WHEN TO CHANGE THE S AND WHEN TO CHANGE THE O

Since both the S and the O influence behavior, only one may need to be changed in any given instance. It is sensible to determine, for example, what each type of change will

cost and which can be accomplished more easily.

Opportunities for changing the S are often overlooked, and attempts are sometimes made to change the O in the wrong way. Such situations occur partly because supervisors become emotionally involved when things go wrong. Under such conditions, they concentrate on assigning blame, and possibilities for preventing future trouble are overlooked because they are angry. Becoming angry with employees does not increase their judgment or skill. If insufficient judgment or skill was a factor in causing the problem initially, it is apparent that the employees should have been screened better or received better training before being placed on the job.

As in dealing with mechanical problems, there are general guides that can be of help in locating a problem. One guide is to determine how widespread a problem is. For example, if the average tardiness is excessive, we should determine whether this figure is due to a few persons or whether it involves all employees. If a problem exists because of 5 percent of the employees, it is reasonable to approach the problem by making a study of the O. If 90 percent of the employees are involved or contribute to a condition, it is wise to spend a good deal of effort exploring the S.

ANALYZING GRIEVANCES

In a certain company, for instance, the number of grievances to be processed was excessive.* Analysis of the outcomes revealed that

* A grievance is a complaint against the company that has been formalized and is handled through a systematized procedure established by collective bargaining. For example, an aggrieved employee goes to the union steward, who thereafter represents the employee to the company. The steward attempts to reach a solution in conference with the supervisor. If this fails, the case is appealed, and higher levels of management become in-

the number of cases won by the company compared favorably with other companies. This fact suggested that the company was not particularly stubborn or backward as far as general policy was concerned. The grievances were then classified in various ways in order to find a common factor. Classifying grievances on a departmental basis revealed no pattern that indicated that type of work was a factor. Analysis by topic revealed no basic factor, such as overtime, disciplinary problems, or disputes over seniority. There seemed to be no one practice or work relationship to correct.

The next breakdown was in terms of stewards. This indicated that some stewards were involved in more grievances than others, but there were inconsistencies. A breakdown of the grievances in terms of supervisors revealed that 10 percent of the supervisors were involved in 46 percent of the grievances.

From this analysis it became apparent that the best way to reduce grievances was to train or remove certain supervisors. Before this analysis, the company had felt that it was doing well in labor relations when it won a high percentage of decisions, and supervisors were often blamed when a case was lost. The analysis indicated that the supervisors with the most grievances also had the best records as far as victories were concerned. These supervisors were found to be poor because their workers were willing to make trouble even though they had weak cases.

THE SAME BEHAVIOR MAY HAVE DIFFERENT CAUSES

Any given kind of behavior may have many causes. In one company, for example, a

---

volved. Filing a grievance is similar to taking a case into court in that the procedure is formalized and the goal of winning the case often clouds the issue.

truck driver's skill was increased greatly by providing him with a truck with less leg room. Because of having rather short legs, the driver had previously had difficulty operating the brake pedal. The reduction in his collision record due to the change in trucks so impressed his department head that this incident generated a bias in favor of what was called a "safe" truck. But other drivers' accidents might be caused by inattention, poor training, or emotional upset — not short legs. Therefore, such overgeneralization of solutions should be avoided.

In another situation, a woman working at a drawing board leans back in the chair and gazes out the window. Why? Immediately, explanations that come to mind include:

1. The woman's eyes are tired.
2. She is trying to concentrate better.
3. Something is worrying her.
4. Her work has run out temporarily.
5. She is waiting for the supervisor.
6. She is bored.
7. She is loafing.

Because of a number of possible causes, in order to deal adequately with the woman's behavior, it is necessary to determine which is the cause in this particular instance. The first two items suggest no need for changing the behavior. The third suggests that the person may require help, whereas the fourth may mean that she is completing more work than is expected. The fifth explanation suggests a need to improve supervisory coverage or training. And the sixth and seventh causes indicate a need to improve her motivation or job placement.

The kind of treatment of the S or the O that will work in one case may not work with another individual — or even with the same woman on a different occasion. Perhaps in the situation described, the woman is bored. Her motivation is improved by

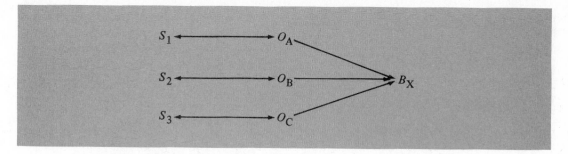

FIGURE 2.3 THE SAME BEHAVIOR MAY HAVE SEVERAL CAUSES

There is no one solution to problems like tardiness, inspection errors, and daydreaming, because various persons might engage in any of these behaviors for different reasons. S_1, S_2, and S_3 indicate three different situations in which individuals O_A, O_B, and O_C find themselves. The resulting behavior, B_X, can be the same for all three persons, but the best way to change B_X might be different in each instance.

giving her more interesting work to do. Sometime later, she is observed repeating the behavior of gazing out the window. Its cause this time is an attempt to concentrate better and requires no change. Unfortunately, many managers do not recognize Victor Hugo's insight concerning a person absorbed in thought: "There is an invisible labor as well as a visible labor."

There is no one solution to problems of tardiness, overstaying rest pauses, quitting early, making clerical errors, and giving poor service; thus, there is no escape from the necessity of analysis. Figure 2.3 describes in diagram form why the same behavior might require different remedies for different individuals.

THE SAME CAUSE MAY HAVE MANY BEHAVIORS

Any given cause may provoke one kind of behavior in one individual and a different kind of behavior in another. Let us choose a single factor, such as worry. How might a home problem affect an employee's behavior on the job? The following behaviors are possible:

1. Daydreaming
2. Neglecting to follow safe practices
3. Poorer attention to quality of work
4. Increased work pace
5. Hypersensitivity to supervisor's remarks and consequent uncooperative behavior
6. Disagreeableness to other employees
7. Failure to report for work

Persons with the same poor home conditions might behave differently, and their conduct on the job would reflect their conditions in various ways. Since an employee's behavior gives no clue to the causes, a manager cannot deduce the nature of the remedy from the behavior. Unexpected benefits may appear, however, when a manager makes certain corrections on the job, because a great number of behaviors may thereby be improved. For example, if a company offered a counseling service to help employees with difficult emotional adjustments to home problems, the benefits could be numerous though perhaps difficult to measure. Figure 2.4 shows how behavior varies for different individuals in the same situation and why a correction in the S could result in several behavior changes.

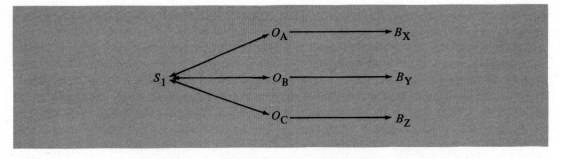

**FIGURE 2.4 THE SAME SITUATION MAY CAUSE
A VARIETY OF BEHAVIORS**

Several people, O_A, O_B, and O_C, in the same situation, S_1, may respond differently by showing behaviors B_X, B_Y, and B_Z.

DIFFERENCES TO BE EXPECTED BETWEEN MANAGERS AND WORKERS

Since actions and thoughts depend on the organism and the situation, workers and managers will not agree with each other on a good many questions. From the economic viewpoint alone, they are in different situations and have different backgrounds of experience. Workers are interested in high wages; management is interested in good profits. At times these goals may conflict. The solution to a problem involved in an issue hinges on the question of what constitutes a fair division of the return from goods produced. Any satisfactory adjustment requires an appreciation of the fact that disagreement originates in differences in points of view and is not a question of right or wrong. In order to preserve an economic system that permits development of such different interests, both parties must recognize the basis of the difference. To condemn one party for not agreeing with the other is to demand that people with different past experiences and in different situations show the same behavior. This amounts to demanding an adjustment that does not naturally occur in human nature.

Other basic differences between managers and workers may be caused by variations in social and economic security, the pleasantness or unpleasantness of the work performed, opportunities for travel and relaxation, educational backgrounds, and opportunities for satisfying the ego. An overall difference in intelligence and expectations will affect ambitions, interests, and aptitudes and will make one individual more dependent on leadership than another. These and many other factors can lead to conflict between employer and employee, but differences among groups of people (or among individuals) are sometimes assets that, if properly used, can result in more effective work efforts and a more satisfying society.

When groups with differing interests recognize that all points of view must be acknowledged and understood, they can approach their differences as problems to be solved, rather than as signs of perversity and wickedness in others. Employees and managers can accomplish much at a conference table if there is mutual respect. Failure to respect different points of view is actually a refusal to recognize the fact that experience and heredity determine the way people see things and the manner in which they react to them.

Actually, employers and employees can agree on many issues despite differences in experience. Increased production can benefit both. In plants where understanding and good relations exist, workers, as well as managers, have frequently contributed to improved methods of production. Points of agreement cannot be found, however, as long as each party is ready to gain its ends at the expense of the other.

A history of workers' insecurity in their jobs is the background for many of the differences between managers and employees. It has caused unions to demand seniority rights and to oppose methods designed to increase efficiency in production. With proper understanding among organization members, all can benefit from increased production. Workers may thereafter tend to favor improvements and may even suggest them. Many companies are learning that such cooperation makes it possible not only to survive in competitive markets but also to grow.

NOTES

1. Schneirla, T. C. An evolutionary and developmental theory of biphasic processes underlying approach and withdrawal. In M. R. Jones (Ed.), *Nebraska symposium on motivation*. Lincoln, Nebr.: University of Nebraska Press, 1959.
2. Hartshorne, H., and May, M. A. *Studies in deceit* (Vol. 1). New York: Macmillan, 1928.
3. Jacobs, J. *The death and life of great American cities*. New York: Harper, 1961.
4. Fleishman, E. A., and Harris, E. F. Patterns of leadership related to employee grievances and turnover. *Personnel Psychol.*, 1962, *15,* 43–56.

SUGGESTED READINGS

Luthans, F. *Organizational behavior,* 2nd ed. New York: McGraw-Hill, 1977.
Porter, L. W., Lawler, E. E., and Hackman, J. R. *Behavior in organizations.* New York: McGraw-Hill, 1975.
Senger, J. Seeing eye to eye: Practical problems of perception. *Pers. J.,* October, 1974, 744–751.
Tosi, H. L., and Hamner, W. C. *Organizational behavior and management: A contingency approach.* Chicago: St. Clair, 1974.

LABORATORY EXERCISE

GROUP PROBLEM SOLVING:
THE CASE OF THE SHOE ASSEMBLY OPERATORS

Preface to Group Problem Solving

Life situations do not present a problem as such, neatly tied in a package and labeled. We only see symptoms that something is wrong. It is up to problem solvers to locate the obstacles in the job situation and then find ways to remove them. Thus, life problems differ from textbook problems because the solvers must locate the problem given only the facts that are known. Much of the ability to solve life's problems depends on skill in locating the main obstacles. Some life situations permit the solvers to find ways of obtaining additional information, but in the situation presented below, no additional information is available. In this case, the problem solvers will be outsiders; they do not have to live with the solution and therefore can be more objective. Nevertheless, different groups may make quite different recommendations, even though the members within each group are agreed on their solution.

A. READING OF SCRIPT

1. Two persons will be chosen by the instructor to read the parts of Bill Wilson and Martha Johnson.
2. The instructor will read aloud the background of the case (section G.1 below).
3. Arrange an office setting for Johnson (desk or table, and chairs) in front of the class, and place at an angle so that both chairs half face the class.
4. Johnson takes the seat behind the desk; Wilson takes the other chair. They begin reading the script (G.2).

B. SOLVING WILSON'S PROBLEM

1. When the reading is completed, the participants will rejoin the class.
2. The instructor will now take over and will
   a. Divide the class into groups of four to six persons. Each group will serve as a consulting firm to solve the problem for the company.
   b. Request each firm to recommend no more than three specific corrective actions. No additional information can be obtained (for example, interviewing the workers). Vague solutions cannot be implemented (for example, "improve working conditions") and should be rejected. The thirty-day warning given Bill by Mrs. Johnson can be rescinded.
3. A copy of the materials (G.1, 2, and 3) should be available to each group for reference in discussing all aspects of the problem.
4. The groups are now to discuss Wilson's problem and to agree on the three recommendations that they feel are the most likely to produce results.
5. When about half the groups have finished, the instructor should ask the remaining groups to try to finish in the next three minutes. (About twenty-five to forty minutes should be adequate.)

C. COLLECTING CONTRIBUTIONS FROM GROUPS

1. Each group in turn will report its first suggestion to the instructor, who will briefly record these on the blackboard.
2. Continue until all groups have reported their three items.

D. CLASSIFYING SUBMITTED SOLUTIONS

1. Discuss each solution to determine whether it represents a change in the *S* or the *O*. (Training or discharging Bill is a change in the *S* because he is part of the situation for the operators.) Altering needs is a change in the *O*, but using incentives is a change in the *S*. In case of

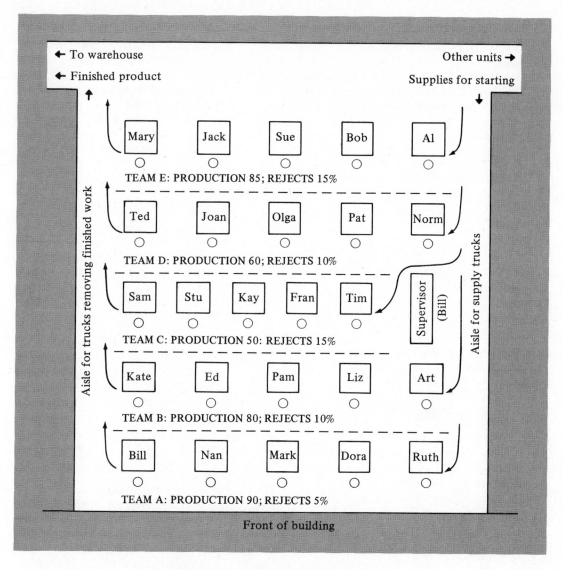

FIGURE 2.5 SEWING ROOM LAYOUT
The five teams of workers do the same kind of work, and the product moves from starters (extreme right of each team) to finishers (extreme left of each team). Each team's production and percentage of rejects are shown. The production standard is eighty items per team and the quality standard is 8 percent rejects. The problem employees are Pat, Norm, Fran, Tim, Liz, and Art.

doubt, record both *S* and *O*. When the type of change is determined, the instructor should place an *S* or *O* in front of the item.

2. When all solutions have been classified, the instructor should count the number of *S*- and *O*-type changes. Normally, there are more *S*s than *O*s, so the groups can be described as *S*-minded.

E. CLASSIFYING WILSON'S AND JOHNSON'S SOLUTIONS

1. List the solutions discussed by Wilson and Johnson in the interview. (The script may be re-examined.)
2. Place an *S* or an *O* in front of each item. Almost always there are more *O*s than *S*s, so Wilson and Johnson are described as *O*-minded.

F. OUTSIDERS' SOLUTIONS VS. INSIDERS' SOLUTIONS

1. Make a list of the causes for the differences between the group solutions and those of Wilson and Johnson.
2. In what ways do outsiders (consultants) have an advantage over insiders (Wilson and Johnson)?
3. *S*-type solutions are not necessarily better than *O*-type solutions, but a failure to consider them indicates emotional involvement.
4. If the consulting groups engaged in problem solving, what were Wilson and Johnson doing?

G. MATERIALS FOR THE CASE

1. Background

For the past six months, Bill Wilson has been the supervisor of a final assembly operation of twenty-five workers in a shoe factory. The workers are all union members. Until recently, his main problem was getting out enough production. Three months ago, however, all shoe assembly operations were changed over from an hourly to a team piece-rate system, so that pro-

duction now is fairly satisfactory. Quality is now the big problem; not only are there too many rejects, but serious complaints are coming in from sales personnel. Since the workers are not paid for rejected items, it is difficult to understand why they are not more careful.

Bill has been called in by his department head, Martha Johnson, to discuss the matter.

2. Script

Martha: Bill, I want to talk to you again about the kind of work your unit is turning out. What's the matter down there anyway?

Bill: I just don't know. On the old hourly rate, the operators weren't turning out anything, and now on this new group piece-rate, a lot of the work they do isn't any good. When I make them do it over, they say I'm picking on them.

Martha: Steve and Jane aren't having the trouble with their operators that you do with yours.

Bill: Well, I'm not having trouble with all of mine. There is just this small group or five or six who are the real troublemakers. They all want to be finishers or anything but what they are. I've got them spotted next to my desk where I can keep an eye on them, and I tell them that I won't move them until they learn to cooperate. Even so, I'd like to see Steve or Jane or anybody else get any work out of them.

Martha: You're not trying to tell me that just a few out of more than two dozen make your crew look that bad.

Bill: No, but they are the worst ones. I called all the people in the "C" and "D" teams together last week and gave them a good talking to, and now they're worse than ever. Production and quality are both down.

Martha: I'm beginning to think that you don't have *any* that are any good.

Bill: No, that's not right. I'll take the people in my "A" team and put 'em up against any we've got. As a matter of fact, all my finishers are a pretty decent bunch. The "B" team has a couple of good workers in it and there's nothing wrong with the "E" team.

Martha: Yes, but their rejects are too high.

Bill: Well, that might be true, but those people really produce. Maybe if I can get them to slow down a little, the quality will go up. It's going to make them sore, though.

Martha: That's *your* problem. You're not afraid of them, are you?

Bill: No, but they didn't even like it the other day when I got after them for talking on the job. Come to think of it, all that talking may be the reason they don't pay any attention to quality.

Martha: Well, tell them that if they don't cut it out, you'll break up their little club. You're the boss down there, aren't you?

Bill: Well, you've got me there. I hired everybody in Team "E" in one batch with the understanding that they could work together, and I hate to go back on my word.

Martha: Well, give them a good lecture and threaten to do it.

Bill: I know, but it's a headache, and those people stick together, so you can't locate the troublemaker. For example, I gave Team "C" a safety lecture the other day after Fran got her hand caught, and all they did was to gripe and pick on me about everything under the sun. I never saw such a bunch of losers in my life.

Martha: What's eating them anyway? Certainly there must have been some one thing they mentioned.

Bill: Oh, it was just the same old complaining about all of them wanting to be finishers. After they've been on the job a few weeks, they think they know everything.

Martha: Sounds like you've been giving some of those new folks a lot of half-baked ideas about the jobs around here. What's there to being a finisher anyway? The pay is the same.

Bill: I don't know. I think it's just a dumb idea they've got in their heads. I know the end job's no easier.

Martha: Was that all they griped about?

Bill: No. Quite a few of them were mad because they said they couldn't make the production standard. Most of them think it's too hard to reach anyway.

Martha: I haven't heard any other complaints about it. After all, eighty items isn't so high. Why should your teams complain when none of the rest of them do?

Bill: All I know is that they do. Except for Team "A" and a few others who really turn the stuff out, they're just about the worst bunch I ever saw. I don't know why I have to have all of them.

Martha: Bill, we've been over all this before, and I'm tired of listening to you feel sorry for yourself. Either get those operators working, or we'll have to put somebody down there who knows how to run things. I don't want to be rough about it, but that's the way it is. I'll give you thirty days to get that mess straightened out, and I'll back you up on anything that seems reasonable. If you can show me some results by the end of that time you can stay; if you don't, we'll have to find something else for you. Is that clear?

Bill: I guess so. But after racking my brains like I have for the past six months, I don't know what you or I or anybody else can do with that group. I've tried everything.

CHAPTER THREE

MOTIVATION
AND
BEHAVIOR

■

The Nature of a Motivating Situation
Studying Needs
Studying Goals
When Goals Conflict: Decision Making and Choice Behavior
Alternative Approaches to Motivation Theory

■

ALTHOUGH MOTIVATION IS a critical determinant of behavior, it is often regarded as the only one. Employees may be ineffective because they lack essential aptitudes, because they have not been adequately trained, because their motivation is low, or because they have poor job attitudes (due to personal or social maladjustment). Any one of these deficiencies could account for below-average performance on the part of the employee, so the manager's response would differ according to the kind of problem. The remedy for deficient aptitude is good selection and placement; for inadequate training, better or additional training; for low motivation, finding additional ways to motivate; and for poor attitude, a search for the factors that are at the root of the negative job and social adjustment.

THE NATURE OF A MOTIVATING SITUATION

THE RELATIONSHIP BETWEEN NEEDS AND GOALS

A motivating situation has both subjective and objective aspects. The subjective aspect is the individual's *needs, drives, motives,* or *desires.* The objective aspect is an object outside the individual, which may be called a *goal.*

When the natures of the need and of the goal are such that obtaining the goal satisfies and therefore removes the need, we speak of the situation as *motivating.* For example, hunger is a need and food is a goal. Food is of such character that, when obtained, it satisfies the hunger need. People work because they have learned that working achieves goals that satisfy their needs.

Initially, both a need and the proper goal must be present to arouse behavior. Thus, the hunger need and the food goal are both necessary to produce eating behavior. Hunger and water, or thirst and food also are combinations of need and goal, but they are ineffective because they are improperly paired. Needs by themselves may produce restless behavior, but such general behavior is in contrast to motivated behavior that is goal-oriented. However, restless behavior may lead to discoveries; when a need is associated with a satisfying discovery, future need conditions arouse memories that are called *anticipated goals.* For example, the restlessness of a hungry cat causes it to wander into a field of corn, where by chance it discovers a mouse. After this, the hunger state causes the cat to recall the goal, and so the cat now goes to the field and hunts in anticipation of a mouse. Most motivated human behavior is guided by anticipated goals. Anything associated with the goal object may serve as a cue for it.

The strengths of both needs and goals vary from time to time and from individual to individual. Hunger, for example, can be increased by lengthening the period of food deprivation. Presentation of the same goal, therefore, will produce stronger motivation in individuals in whom the need is intense than in individuals in whom the need is slight. Hungry animals will take more punishment to obtain food than will partially satisfied animals; similarly, a hungry person will take greater risks to obtain food than will a well-fed individual. The same degree of hunger will be associated with different degrees of motivation when various food goals are used. A child may do more for a piece of candy than for a slice of bread. It is clear, therefore, that the intensity of motivation can be altered either by changes in the need or by changes in the goal.

PROBLEM-SOLVING BEHAVIOR

Behavior that brings the individual to a need-satisfying goal is *adaptive*. Because such behavior makes sense, we often refer to it as purposeful. Many adaptive responses are of a purely routine nature, and we may be unaware of the fact that they are need satisfiers. We dress in the morning, go to a certain place for breakfast, arrive at our job, do our work, and so on, without really making decisions, forgetting that these habits are learned ways of reaching objectives, or goals.

We become especially conscious of the need-satisfying nature of our behavior under two conditions: (1) when two or more possible behaviors lead to different goals, sometimes even satisfying different needs; and (2) when an obstacle blocks or prevents the learned behavior from being expressed. The first is a choice situation and requires a decision; the second is a problem situation and requires a solution.

Motivated behavior contrasts with frustrated behavior (see Chapter 4) because it points to, or is directed toward, an anticipated need-satisfying goal. If the desired goal is not obtained, failure is experienced; if the goal is attained, success results. Behavior is adaptive when the anticipated goal satisfies the need.

Behavior is not necessarily unadaptive when there is a failure to reach the anticipated goal. For example, an employee might work fast to gain attention and praise from the supervisor, but instead this speed might cause an accident and he or she might be reprimanded for carelessness. However, if an employee persists in repeating behavior that leads to failure, the behavior can rightly be called unadaptive. Motivated behavior, then, is a *means* to an end and is evaluated in terms of the end it achieves. It differs from frustrated behavior, which often is an *end* in itself because the consequences of such behavior do not influence its basic character. Motivated behavior is terminated when the goal (consequence of behavior) is achieved, but frustrated behavior is terminated when it spends itself.

STUDYING NEEDS

INNATE NEEDS

Some needs are inherent in the nature of the organism and occur in all animals and human beings. These needs may be called *natural* or *innate,* since their appearance is independent of past experience. In animals, hunger, thirst, maternal drives, sex, and perhaps curiosity are generally regarded as constituting the basic needs.

ACQUIRED NEEDS

Acquired needs, on the other hand, are dependent on experience. For example, if other children in the neighborhood have tape recorders, the youngster without a tape recorder acquires a need for one and will work hard to satisfy this need. Needs for such goals as videotape recorders, a certain standard of living, or pleasant working conditions are acquired by the experiences that the environment offers. An example of an acquired need in business is the coffee break. Acquired needs are just as real and intense as natural needs; they differ only in the way that they are obtained.

From the very nature of acquired needs, it follows that people cannot revert to methods of living that are more primitive than the ones to which they are accustomed without experiencing deprivation. To argue that workers are better off today than their predecessors were a century ago and therefore should be more satisfied is fallacious. People had fewer acquired needs a hundred years ago. To speak of modern advantages as luxuries, hence unessential, is to deny the reality of acquired needs. As more people acquire new needs, a greater number recognize these possibilities and so acquire the needs in turn. The accumulation of needs serves to drive the desired standard of living upward.

Because acquired needs originate in past experiences, people differ considerably in the needs that they develop and respect. A woman who needs tea in the afternoon, for example, will respect the time and effort another takes to obtain tea, but might disapprove of that person's request for smoking facilities. People understand behaviors that satisfy needs with which they are familiar, and for this reason there is acceptance and respect for behaviors that satisfy innate needs. Time off for meals, for instance, is never questioned. Parents are understanding when their children want food, but may question the need to follow current fads in dress. Similarly, they might be unwilling to conclude that their child's need for entertainment exceeded that for food if the child used lunch money to buy a comic book. *When persons choose to satisfy their needs in a different order of importance than we ourselves do, we tend to question their judgment, even their intelligence, rather than recognize a difference in needs.*

Thus, groups that differ most in experience will have the greatest differences in needs, show the least understanding of one another, and experience the poorest communication. The following list pairs examples of such groups, which are dissimilar in their social experiences and therefore are unlike in their acquired needs:

□ Parents and Children
□ Management and Employees
□ Long-service employees and New employees
□ Rich people and Poor people
□ Early settlers and Native Americans

Members of one group — parents, for example — may be critical of the choices made by members of the other (children), and communication between them is frequently less than perfect. This failure to understand changes and differences in acquired needs causes each generation as it grows older to long for the "good old days."

SOCIAL NEEDS

Like most animals, human beings are social creatures. We feel the need to belong or to be members of a group. The family is the original social group, and every child early in life experiences the need to be wanted and loved. When this love is lacking, the child is seriously affected. Problem children are likely to be rejected children. Rejection is sensed by both a child and an adult not only through specific behaviors of parents or supervisors, but also through their attitudes.[1] It appears that one person's attitude toward another cannot be successfully hidden in any close relationship.

The need to be wanted and to belong continues throughout life. Problem employees are usually those who feel unwanted and rejected at home or on the job. Older employees often begin to feel insecure when retirement approaches, because they fear they no longer are needed. Good adjustment depends on having social needs satisfied. Companies frequently encourage clubs and social activities to increase opportunities for belonging to some group. Union membership frequently serves this function.[2]

An important activity in this area is the proper orientation of new employees, and those recently transferred or promoted. Such persons leave a situation in which they have a known position and status and enter one in which they alone are strangers. Successful attempts to bridge this gap not only will reduce turnover but will also influence the employees' long-term attitudes toward the situation. A first impression is often a lasting one.

Social needs, in addition to the need to affiliate or belong, include such intangibles as status and pride.[3] The need to feel that one is a person of consequence (the *ego* need) expresses itself in many ways. To achieve social status and gain the respect and admiration of others, people will work, compete, and deny themselves many of the more obvious incentives. Some people may choose lower-paying white-collar jobs instead of higher-paying blue-collar jobs, and for others a change in title will sometimes give more satisfaction than a raise in pay. G. K. Ingham interviewed many employees and found that those with high social needs tended to work for small companies where informal social relations were common, whereas those who were financially motivated chose large companies where the pay was higher for the same work.[4]

One aspect of social needs that has an important effect on business requires special attention: the problem of "saving face." A company may spend a good deal of money to cover a mistake made by an executive in order to protect that person's feelings and the reputation of the company. One company, for example, had an outdated machine custom built rather than purchase a more efficient modern design that could have been delivered immediately and would have cost thousands of dollars less than the custom machine. The problem arose because the junior engineers had disagreed with the head engineer over the merits of the old machine. Since he had insisted that the old machines

were superior to the new models, a new model could not be purchased without his losing face.

Many disputes between workers and management are face-saving problems. What may begin as a difference of opinion over a small matter can become a heated issue over who is right. It develops into a dispute over a matter of principle. Walk-outs listed in the records as being due to a supervisor's disciplinary action against an employee, to a company's exercising its right to put devices on trucks to record road stops, or to a dispute about overtime, may be caused by a factor like face saving, though it does not appear on the records. To understand the real reasons behind a walk-out, we must recognize the possibility that it may have been caused by the unwillingness of the disputing parties to back down from their positions.

Face-saving situations are also common in our day-to-day dealings with individuals. Some people, for example, will quit a good job rather than make an apology. Supervisors will sometimes try to fire a good worker who shows them up in front of other people or who questions their right to give an order.

Recognizing a face-saving problem for what it is not only makes it possible to prevent differences from being made personal issues, but also helps a manager deal with such occurrences. They can be prevented by keeping problems impersonal and objective. But when problems do become face-saving situations, finding a way for each party to have an out and seeing that neither party claims a victory over the other can resolve the situations successfully.

PERSONALITY AND NEEDS

Certain needs are associated with personality; among these are fear of failure, and the needs for affiliation, achievement, and power.[5] These needs are fairly stable characteristics that influence the way individuals respond to challenges, risks, and group tasks. Scores on tests used to measure such needs are treated as unrelated variables. For instance, scores on one measure of the need to achieve and on a questionnaire measuring the fear of failure show some individuals high on both motives, others low on both, while the majority have scores higher on one than on the other.[6] In short, these needs, along with those for affiliation and power, may occur together. These motives are different but not necessarily mutually exclusive.

The personality differences in needs reveal themselves when persons choose work partners. A laboratory experiment revealed that persons with high achievement-need scores and low affiliation-need scores tend to select a competent nonfriend as against a less competent friend, whereas persons with low achievement-need scores and high affiliation-need scores tend to choose a friend.[7]

Persons who have a high need for achievement are attracted to challenging tasks, the most attractive being those giving them a 50-50 chance of success. Persons high in fear of failure avoid such tasks; they find that easy tasks are not threatening and failure at difficult ones can be excused. High-need achievers tend to assume responsibility for outcomes (success or failure), whereas low-need achievers are more inclined to ascribe outcomes to external factors.[8]

Supervisors must learn to react to differences in the way competition, hazards, threats of discipline, and pressure affect different individuals. The same methods that motivate some people may frustrate others. These differences may be even more relevant with regard to executive development.

Testing the validity and usefulness of the need for achievement and related concepts has been done in a field setting. Assuming that economic achievement requires initiative that is promoted by high-achievement needs, D. C. McClelland and D. G. Winter designed a training program for businessmen in communities in India.[9] The training was geared to stimulate economic achievement. Need achievement (nAch) tests were given at the beginning and end of the course, and significant changes showed in the scores. But with regard to such personal values as cautious fatalism, respect for powerful "others," traditionalism, conforming to caste rules, and submissive conflict avoidance, no changes occurred. Thus, the effects of training seemed to have influenced specific values but did not generalize to related values and justify claims for personality changes. Nor was there evidence to justify the conclusion that the changes in need achievement scores caused any changes in entrepreneurial behavior, as business training had been part of the program.

But accelerating economic achievement by altering such needs as achievement, fear of failure, affiliation, and so on, remains an interesting but complex endeavor. For example, eight different measures of need achievement used by various experimenters have failed to correlate significantly.[10]

IS THERE A NEED HIERARCHY?

Is there a possible ordering of the variety of needs described above? A. H. Maslow[11] has proposed that needs can be ordered from the lowest level (physiological) to the highest, and that as each need level is satisfied, the needs at the next level begin to determine behavior. His sequence is as follows:

1. Physiological needs (hunger, thirst, and so on)

2. Safety needs (security, health)
3. Belonging and love needs (identification, affection)
4. Esteem needs (prestige, success, self-respect)
5. Need for self-actualization (desire for worthwhile accomplishments, self-fulfillment, personal growth)

According to this point of view the deprivation of satisfaction of lower-level needs prevents emergence of behaviors influenced by higher-level needs. It does not follow, however, that satisfactions of lower-level needs ensure the functioning of those at the next level; rather, potential higher-level needs emerge and influence behavior only after there is opportunity for satisfaction of lower-level needs.

Maslow's theory, perhaps because of its apparent simplicity and its consistency with many common sense ideas, became widely known among managers and scientists during the 1970s. However, researchers have had difficulty testing the theory, and it has been criticized on several grounds.[12] Maslow based his theory largely on psychiatric and clinical data rather than on controlled studies, and many of his original conclusions were based on logical arguments that can be questioned, rather than on quantitative data. For example, Maslow presents the need for self-esteem as being fulfilled by the approval and praise of others — a position vigorously contested by some psychologists today.[13]

The interpretation of some of Maslow's terms has also been questioned. For example, how can an individual possibly fulfill all of his or her potential? Also, the theory says little about how a person chooses the nature or extent of the areas to be developed by self-actualization.

Finally, the emergence of higher-order needs is predicated on the satisfaction of lower needs, but the nature of need satisfaction is such that it is transitory at best. Eating satisfies hunger, but only for a few hours. Thus, lower-level needs are never outgrown. Although the theory has provided an interesting framework, the question of why some people actively seek higher-order-need satisfaction *as well as* lower-order-need satisfaction has still not been clearly answered.

ARE SATISFACTION AND DISSATISFACTION OPPOSITES?

The existence of a need hierarchy does not necessarily mean that all the various need levels are latent, or innate. It is possible that as needs are satisfied, new ones are acquired. Thus, as employees gain job security and good living wages, they acquire other needs. Managers were studied who had experienced high job satisfaction; they mentioned such sources as advancement, responsibility, recognition, and achievement most frequently. However, when they talked about events associated with poor job attitudes, they did not mention a lack of satisfaction in these areas. Instead, the items brought up most frequently were criticisms of company policy, supervision, interpersonal relations, and salary.[14] F. Herzberg therefore concluded that *dissatisfactions* are not due to the absence of the sources of *satisfaction,* which raises another problem for the assumption of a hierarchical ordering of needs. His evidence indicates that (1) the satisfaction of needs, (2) the failure to satisfy needs, and (3) the sources of dissatisfaction should be carefully differentiated in studies of need satisfaction.

A person in a life situation experiences a combination of all three conditions, and the result varies from day to day. The factor of frustration must also be evaluated because deprivation of strong needs may cause frustration, whereas deprivation of less intense needs can be motivating. One study showed that employees most disappointed with promotions had the poorest motivation to learn, whereas the moderately disappointed groups had the best motivation.[15] Dissatisfaction may also arise when need satisfaction occurs but is regarded as unfair. A study of absenteeism[16] revealed that employees who felt they should be receiving more pay showed significantly more absences than those who felt their pay was fair. However, the actual pay had no relation to absences.

Herzberg's ideas about the sources of satisfaction and dissatisfaction have stimulated a good deal of interest and research. However, problems and questions regarding the methodology and conclusions of the study have arisen,[17] as they did in other pioneering studies, such as that of the Hawthorne plant (see Chapter 1). For example, the analysis of the managers' responses has been criticized as being arbitrary or misleading in some cases. Also, it has been suggested that perhaps defensiveness on the part of the managers caused them to attribute successful past experience to their own efforts and merit and to blame past failures on outside, environmental influences.[18]

DEALING WITH NEEDS

Just because people have unsatisfied needs does not mean that they must all be gratified. This gratification is not only impossible but undesirable, because without active needs people would not be motivated. However, it is important to know the needs of an individual if we wish to understand that person's behavior. Extreme deprivation, such as occurs in starvation, not only increases the food interest and does physical damage, but causes important psychological changes to occur.[19] These include loss of a sense of

humor, moodiness, unsociability, and various anxieties. Rejection and deprivation of social needs produce various kinds of poor adjustment, including delinquency, and are also reflected in physical ailments.

Cases of extreme need deprivation are not a common problem for supervisors, who are chiefly concerned with evaluating individual differences. The objective is to treat each person in accordance with his or her needs. *The person with the needs is in the best position to communicate them, but such communication requires an understanding listener.* The key to the nature of the need is to discover *why* a person wants something.

Managers often deal with groups as well as with one-on-one encounters. To discover the needs of various groups, the manager can use surveys to determine the need differences within and between work groups. Through surveys, S. W. Gellerman found that white- and blue-collar workers differ in some of their aspirations, as do young and old workers, the skilled and unskilled, and the successful and unsuccessful.[20] Modern survey designs and analyses permit some understanding of the *why* behind the expressed wants and dissatisfactions. Knowing how group needs differ is important in determining how to improve unsatisfactory conditions.

Knowing prevailing needs is also helpful to managers in order to negotiate union contracts realistically, rather than politically. A satisfactory union contract gives consideration to the needs of all employee groups. Examples of terms that may cause dissatisfaction are: shortening the wage-progression schedule, which will increase wages for short-service employees, but neglect those with long service; some retirement plans, which have value only to employees who remain with the company until they reach retirement age. To be perceived as fair by all workers, a labor contract cannot include clauses that consistently favor some groups over others.

STUDYING GOALS

REAL GOALS

Goals, when obtained, tend to satisfy needs. Eating food eliminates the state of hunger; drinking water removes sensations of thirst; sexual behavior alters the physiology of the glands; the exploration of a new area satisfies curiosity.

The acquired needs, similarly, are satisfied by the attainment of specific objects. A couple may be satisfied by the purchase of the house they have picked out, and an employee may be satisfied when the desired promotion materializes. However, in the case of acquired needs, it frequently is difficult to determine whether the goal received has satisfied a real need or only an apparent

Special recognition of employees, for long-time service, for example, provides an alternate form of satisfaction. (T. C. Fitzgerald)

need (one expressed to cover up some other need). Furthermore, a simple need may have a number of satisfying goals. For our purpose, we shall think of the real goal as the one that is the main determiner of the behavior under consideration.

SUBSTITUTE GOALS

When real goals cannot be attained, a person often will accept substitutes. Finding substitutes prevents frustration, creates extra opportunities for setting up motivating conditions, and extends need satisfactions to a greater number of people. The childless couple may shower love on a dog; the child may accept some fruit in place of candy; and the worker may accept a raise in pay rather than a promotion. In each case, the substitute must have some relation to the real goal, and its effectiveness is relative to its need-satisfying properties.

The importance of considering the relationship between needs and possible goals can be made apparent by an illustration. Suppose a job as supervisor becomes available in a plant. Immediately, several employees may feel that they want it, and all but one will have to be denied the satisfaction of this desire. However, closer examination may reveal that, although several workers want the position, their reasons for wanting it vary. Table 3.1 shows the different needs seven such persons might have. Each employee sees something different in the job, and although all may want it, each wants it for a different reason. Furthermore, the substitutes from which each would derive satisfaction differ. Thus, increases in take-home pay, various forms of recognition, more suitable work, or better supervision might each become a substitute for a promotion, depending on the nature of the need. As a matter of fact, some of the substitutes may have as much or even more

TABLE 3.1 SUBSTITUTES FOR THE POSITION OF SUPERVISOR

PERSON	CONDITION	NEED	SUBSTITUTE
A	Has five children	Food, clothing, etc.	More overtime
B	Wears overalls to work; spouse is a schoolteacher	Prestige	Cleaner work
C	Dependent on others	Recognition	Praise
D	Buying house	Job security	Assurance of steady work
E	Bored with job	Responsibility	More complex job
F	Dislikes boss or group	Escape	Lateral transfer
G	Has seniority	Face saving	Chance to suggest candidate

need-satisfying potentials than the initial so-called real goal. Certainly some substitutes are more practical from the company's viewpoint, and they might reasonably be given without even thinking of them as consolation goals.

Thus, many promotion problems can be solved by first exploring the needs of various employees by means of interviews or discussions. Some employees actually do not wish a new job, yet are disturbed when it is given to someone else. Failure to receive a particular promotion often creates a face-saving problem because some employees imagine that others wonder why they did not get promoted. A closer examination of such problems will suggest various ways in which face-saving opportunities can be created.

ATTRACTION AND AVOIDANCE RESPONSES

In the sense that goals satisfy needs, they have a positive, or *attracting,* influence and lead to pleasure. Unpleasant situations have an opposite effect, so we tend to avoid them. *Avoidance* does not satisfy needs, unless one wishes to say that the body has a need to avoid pain. Because people tend to move toward positive goals and avoid negative situations, we may think of them as being pulled toward certain activities and pushed away from others. There are, therefore, two ways of influencing behavior, one associated with reward, the other with punishment.

Both methods are logically possible. People will do a job to obtain rewards, and they will do it to avoid punishment. People will pay their utility bills before the tenth of the month to gain a discount, or they will do so to avoid a fine. However, the two methods do not have the same psychological effect, and this difference may be overlooked. In one experimental situation, for example, when children were told to stop playing with a particular toy, they obeyed, but many cried and did not resume play with other toys; however, when told to play with a different toy, the children also stopped playing with the particular toy but were not emotionally disturbed and continued to play with other toys.[21]

USING REWARD VERSUS USING PUNISHMENT

Before deciding whether to use reward or punishment as a motivator, we should analyze the situation. To what extent does the situation demand avoidance behavior and to what extent does it demand positive action? Most training problems require learning *what to do* rather than *what not to do.* If a person is taught the correct job method, learning what not to do is unnecessary. There may be hundreds of incorrect methods. Many disciplinary problems can be translated into a matter of substituting desirable behaviors for undesirable ones.

A study of productivity of railroad workers, for example, showed punishment to be counterproductive. The supervisors of low-producing groups were seen by their workers as assigning personal blame and/or exacting penalties when someone failed to do a good job. Nonpunishing behavior, on the other hand, was more characteristic of the supervisors of high-producing sections.[22]

Although punishment is effective in motivating avoidance behavior, this training objective can be lost because some uncontrolled factors may have introduced unwanted conditions.[23] Some possible undesirable effects are:

1. Punishment may frustrate the person punished and thereby produce hostile and childish behavior (see Chapter 4). *Uncooperative and emotionally unstable individuals are most likely to be frustrated by punishment and are the very persons most likely to receive it.*

2. The wrong association may be formed when one person punishes another. This produces avoidance of things other than those intended, such as the avoidance of getting caught.

3. Threat of punishment highlights what *not* to do, thus possibly suggesting an action not previously considered by the individual threatened. When you are told, "Don't think of how the roof of your mouth feels," you are unwittingly made aware of these sensations and actually do what you are requested not to do. "Don't kill a child" is an instruction given to drivers who have neither the desire nor the intent to kill a child. On the other hand, a sign saying "School — Children Crossing" is a positive instruction and suggests the desired action. A company once displayed over the time clock a list of twenty-two different violations and the punishment that went with each. It is doubtful whether any employee could have thought of so many ways to cause trouble.

4. In the use of punishment, the objective often is to inhibit or prevent behavior, rather than to train an avoidance response. Inhibiting is not constructive training, but is a surgical approach. It is more constructive to substitute an alternative response for a poor one.

5. Punishment and the thought of being punished create a hostile state of mind, thereby setting up an unfavorable attitude. All events and experiences occurring during this state of mind become associated with it. Employees who are punished for poor workmanship are prone to develop unfavorable attitudes toward the job. The reverse is true of reward.[24]

6. The threat of punishment creates fear and reduces the acceptance of ideas. Experimental evidence supports the belief that fear-arousing approaches designed to change behavior may indeed effectively arouse fear but may also accomplish less change in behavior than a moderate and reasonable approach.[25]

The fact that dangers are often inherent in employing punishment does not indicate that it should never be used. But managers should develop the habit of uncovering or inventing positive motivators whenever possible.

WHY POSITIVE MOTIVATION IS DIFFICULT

If punishment has so little justification, why has it stood the test of time so well? *One reason is that we punish not to train but to vent anger.* Our attention is attracted to situations when something goes wrong, and then we are irritated. As a consequence, we have neither the time nor the patience to make a constructive response. At such times, the use of positive methods is contrary to our natural impulses. It is a fact that persons are inclined to punish when frustrated.[26] Interpersonal skills ideally should be developed to the point where we do not become irritated when things go wrong: first, because we cannot succeed in hiding irritations, and second, because the attempt to hide them is bad for the person who tries and confusing to the person on the receiving end of the relationship, according to studies of child-parent relationships.[27]

The use of punishment is prevalent also because the negative approach is simpler than the positive. We do not have to know how to improve a job in order to find fault with the way it is done. Thus, we may find fault with secretaries, supervisors, and violinists without being able to show them how to do better. The positive approach assumes that a person knows not only what is wanted but how it can be accomplished.

ACTIVITIES AS NEED SATISFIERS

Goals are generally regarded as need satisfiers; when it is found that organisms strive for a certain object, it is customary to assume the existence of a need. This approach to behavior makes attainment of the goal the end product of the activity, and the activity itself serves merely as a means. However, some activities are enjoyed and continued for their own sake, not for what they lead to.[28] A person will continue walking because it is enjoyable, not because it takes her to a restaurant for food or to friends who satisfy social needs. Exploratory activity might be explained by assuming curiosity needs, but the desire to explore is created by the situa-

tion, and it seems unnecessary to assume that an inner craving must precede the activity of exploring something new.

To reduce the joy of all activity to curiosity, affiliation needs, or achievement needs tends to overlook the possibility that certain activities may simply be interesting. Some activities are boring, and we perform them only if they lead to need satisfiers. But some activities are attractive in themselves, and a person will perform them even if they lead to a loss in need satisfaction or to punishment.

In studying the most satisfying aspects of managers' jobs, F. Herzberg's investigators[29] found that the six most frequently mentioned sources of satisfaction were: (1) achievement, (2) recognition, (3) the work itself, (4) responsibility, (5) advancement, and (6) salary. "The work itself" is in third position. The report describes instances of satisfactions gained from the work itself, regardless of achievement and recognition. *Work that required creativity, was challenging, contained variety, and permitted an opportunity to do the job from beginning to end was deemed most satisfying.*

The postulation of needs for such sources of satisfaction would confuse the issue rather than clarify it. A person might be unable to describe a satisfying job unless he had previously held one. Joy in activity, it would seem, does not always indicate that a need is being satisfied any more than boredom implies unsatisfied needs.

Perhaps the greatest gap in our understanding of motivation results from failure to explore the interests and joys of an *activity* as a *goal* because of the tendency to define satisfaction as need fulfillment. This definition causes behavior to be treated as a means to an end, when there is reason to believe it can be an end in itself. For example, a study made of a national sample of employed men

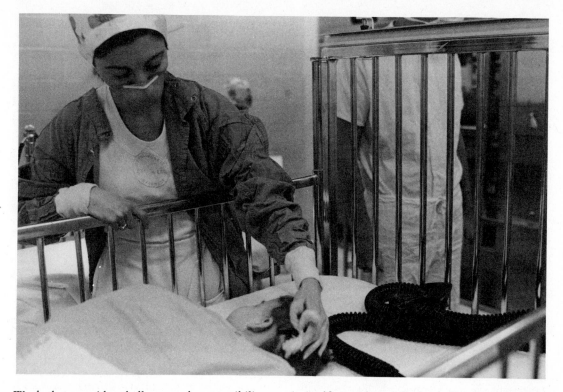

Work that provides challenge and responsibility can in itself provide satisfactions. (Ann McQueen)

found that even if there were no economic necessity for working, most of them said they would work anyway.[30]

WHEN GOALS CONFLICT: DECISION MAKING AND CHOICE BEHAVIOR

Choice behavior occurs when there is a conflict between two conditions of motivation. If persons are motivated in only one way, there is no doubt about what they will do, but when two motives are present at the same time, there is a probability of two kinds of behavior being enacted. In the end, one behavior wins out, but in the meantime,

the persons have to make a decision. If the decision is difficult, the individual may experience a sense of internal conflict.

CONFLICT IN MOTIVATION

There are three basic types of conflict in choice situations.[31] Each is represented by a separate diagram in Figure 3.1. The first type is *a conflict between two positive goals*. If some office workers are offered a choice between a certain increase in the pay rate or an increase in fringe benefits, they will have to choose between two attractive goals. Eventually, the alternative that seems to offer the greater total need satisfaction will be chosen. It must be recognized, however, that needs are an individual matter and that all individ-

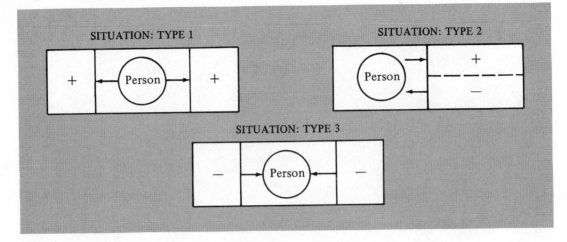

FIGURE 3.1 THREE BASIC CHOICE SITUATIONS

Type 1. The person must choose between two or more different goals, each of which satisfies a need. Type 2. The person must choose between going toward and going away from something that has attracting and repelling qualities. Type 3. The person must choose which of two unpleasant behavior routes to follow.

SOURCE: Adapted from *A Dynamic Theory of Personality* by K. Lewin. Copyright © 1935 by McGraw-Hill Book Company. Used with permission of the McGraw-Hill Book Company.

uals will not necessarily make the same choice.

The more evenly balanced the attracting forces are, the more difficult it will be for one force to win out to produce a decision. If analysis does not produce a choice, then it is futile to continue the state of indecision. Flipping a coin would be an aid to many who have difficulty in choosing in such cases when all possibilities are satisfying.

The two goals involved in a choice situation may satisfy either the same need (for example, two kinds of food) or different needs (food and water). The important element in this situation is that two or more mutually exclusive behaviors are aroused and block each other.

The second type of choice situation arises when there is *a conflict between both positive and negative aspects associated with the same action.* People avoid a course of action that leads to punishment or dissatisfaction, but if a positive goal is also present, they will be impelled both toward and away from the goal object. If these opposing forces are approximately equal, an approach-avoidance conflict in motivation occurs. For example, because work on the night shift interferes with the normal mode of living, people dislike it. Rather than force the choice in order to staff this shift, management could increase the night pay rate. At a given differential pay rate, the proper proportion of individuals would be induced to choose the night shift. The use of ticket rebates to get volunteers to leave overbooked plane flights also employs this principle. People will accept some unpleasantness if thereby they attain certain desired goals. This approach does not use coercion but allows choice, and the action is determined by the positive aspects of the goal.

UNDERSTANDING THE BEHAVIOR OF INDIVIDUAL EMPLOYEES

The reverse of the above situation may also occur. Robbing a bank offers attractions in the way of finances, but connected with this behavior is the possibility of an unpleasant prison term. In all cases the conflict is resolved in terms of the relative intensities of the repelling and attracting forces.[32]

The *third type* of choice situation involves a conflict between *two avoidance situations.* The individual in this case must choose between the lesser of two evils, such as the unpleasantness of being transferred versus that of being discharged. This type of choice situation has no positive aspect and is perceived as unpleasant.

ASSISTING OTHERS IN DECISION MAKING

Insofar as managers or parents are in a position to introduce rewards and punishments into a situation, they can influence the choices that others will make. Perception of eventual rewards will cause people, whether children or employees, to choose to do unpleasant things; punishments, if wisely used, will discourage undesired behavior. Supervisors, parents, and friends can assist in the organizational decision-making process by encouraging those faced with difficult or conflicting choices to discuss alternatives with them.[33]

When managers confront subordinates with a choice in connection with new jobs, the subordinates are not likely to feel they are free agents — rather they are inclined to feel they must accept the suggestion or offer. Employees frequently accept transfers and even promotions that they do not want because they fear they will be bypassed in the future if they turn down the "opportunity." Managers should be aware of this problem, and if it is possible, they should give a subordinate a choice between two possible job changes. Giving another person a choice between two alternatives is always desirable, even if the person *must* choose one of them. Employees will accept a transfer more readily if they can participate by choosing between two or more jobs or locations. However, giving an employee the alternatives of transferring or quitting provides only the illusion of choice.

A CHOICE ALWAYS INVOLVES THE SELF

The need in every motivating situation is located in the individual who is behaving. It follows, therefore, that behavior is oriented with reference to the self. Ordinarily, we speak of self-oriented behavior as selfish. It would be more useful to distinguish between social and antisocial behavior.

If we choose activities that raise the standard of living for everyone, we are called benefactors, yet we also have satisfied personal needs. To expect a city dweller to struggle for the interests of the farmer, a business manager to encourage unions, or any American to be glad to pay taxes is not psychologically sound. Therefore, the resolution of conflicts between individuals depends on finding common goals. However, fears and distrust must first be removed. Workers do a good day's work when they see that it is in their own interest, and managers institute reforms when such action is in line with their needs.

ALTERNATIVE APPROACHES TO MOTIVATION THEORY

The search for a better understanding of the factors that underlie behavior has always been a major concern of psychology.[34] Although various approaches have been labeled *theories,* there is currently no single overall system of theorums and postulates explaining motivation that is accepted by all psychologists. Therefore, the following material represents partial approaches, each of which is convincing to some, but not all, psychologists.

Some approaches to studying motivation can best be understood in the context of the $S \leftrightarrow O \rightarrow B \rightarrow A$ model discussed in Chapter 2. Psychologists have investigated the $S \leftrightarrow O$ interactive relationship to try to determine more specifically the aspects of the stimulus-situation (represented by S in the formula) that are most significant for a given individual or group.

Scientists, such as Maslow, Herzberg, and others, have examined motivation from the perspective of the *needs* of the organism. Which are most salient? Which are most dominant in a given individual and why? A third research approach has been to concentrate on the *goals* of the organism and attempt to ascertain why particular goals are set and how they are accomplished.

Still other studies have viewed the crux of motivation as being a matter of *choice,* or *decision making.* These studies in organizational psychology have been designed to help answer such questions as "Why does a person choose one behavior over another?" and "How does the person decide how much effort to expend on an activity and how long to continue with it?" Clearly, the latter approach is intended to concentrate on issues related to such topics as job satisfaction, pay/reward systems, and job turnover.

SITUATION/ORGANISM APPROACHES TO MOTIVATION

Some psychologists have approached the interactive process between the individual and the situation by using a "contingency" perspective. That is, instead of trying to define one behavioral model that could be stretched to explain all the differences observed in people/environment interactions, followers of this approach have assumed that there is no universal interaction mode. Instead, these studies examined the variables that moderate or influence the basic $S \leftrightarrow O$ responses. Much research of this type has concentrated on the variances in certain aspects of the individual that might help explain observed differences in behavior.[35]

Although work in this area has revealed many interesting relationships,[36] the usefulness of this approach appears to be limited.[37] One major problem has been the inability to find consistent moderator effects even when the major variables involved are virtually identical. Perhaps this is because any given factor becomes more or less important to an individual over time.[38] L. J. Cronbach,[39] among others, has suggested that this type of approach to motivational theory building has limited usefulness. Others see a more fruitful path in investigating situational (S) rather than personality (O) variables.[40]. Some, however, warn that there are problems inherent in the method of approach itself that prevent the revelation of highly significant differences.[41]

Attribution theory (another area of investigation related to the $S \leftrightarrow O \rightarrow B \rightarrow A$ model) refers to the tendency of individuals to attribute motives, intentions, and attitudes to others and themselves.[42] These attributed motives and feelings are based on the individual's observations and subjective ideas about what causes events.

A related concept, which has also sparked a good deal of research, is *locus of control.*[43] This idea, originally studied by J. B. Rotter, distinguishes individuals on the basis of their tendency to attribute the causes of behavior to external factors (such as luck, or knowing the right person) or to internal factors (such as effort or intelligence).[44] Our basic attributions about how events are caused, it is theorized, in turn affect our choices in daily behavior (see discussion of expectancy theory, opposite).[45] One danger in attribution theory, it has been pointed out, is that this approach overemphasizes attribution of causality compared to other important variables also operating simultaneously, such as needs and expectations.[46]

NEEDS AS MOTIVATORS

Although scientists in some of the studies cited above used concepts like the *need for achievement* in their work, need-based or "drive" studies have been criticized.[47] As the results of various studies have come in, scientists have recognized that all drives are not simply to reduce stimuli, but that, as suggested earlier in this chapter, activities can be need satisfiers in themselves, and that human beings seek a personally optimal, rather than a minimal, level of stimulation.

D. C. McClelland, however, who has provided much information about the need for achievement, has continued to pursue the need-based approach to motivation and has also studied the need for power in detail. We shall examine some conclusions of this and related studies in later chapters.[48]

GOAL-ORIENTED MOTIVATIONAL STUDIES

Recent goal-setting research has concerned itself extensively with two areas: the processes underlying how goals are set, and the effects of external (situational) factors on the goal-setting process.[49] A primary theorist in this areas has been E. A. Locke, who argues that knowledge of the individual's intentions to work toward a goal are basic to the understanding of work-related behavior.[50] His

studies and others have generated material that can be useful to managers who are trying to help employees develop and achieve specific task goals.[51]

MOTIVATION AND CHOICE BEHAVIOR

An approach that has interested many researchers has been termed *expectancy theory*.[52] This approach postulates that people make behavioral choices based on the expected (perceived) pay-off of various alternatives.[53] The value of the various possible alternatives is subjectively determined by assessing the likelihood of each alternative and its relative importance or reward for the individual. As indicated above, this approach is felt to have potential for generating a better understanding of why some people work harder than others for a given reward, and why some people seek higher rewards (and responsibility) than others.

However, as with the contingency theories, it has been found that the generalizability of the data (the ability to apply specific findings to the population in general) is limited. Outside factors and other moderating variables make prediction difficult.[54]

Expectancy theory has also been criticized on theoretical grounds.[55] It describes behavior under certain circumstances — that is, those when various alternatives and outcomes are known and the individual clearly prefers one to the other, therefore rationally optimizes in selecting a behavioral course. But research over the years in both psychology and microeconomics indicates that rationality is sometimes not the basis for human decision making.[56]

Equity theory is similar to expectancy theory in that it involves a subjective comparison and choice process.[57] According to this approach, people gauge their behavior and output level according to their assessment of the available rewards. If individuals believe an inequity exists between their rate of rewards and their efforts (compared to others), they will attempt to bring behavior and/or rewards to a more equitable state. As with the other approaches, both confirmation and problems have been uncovered.[58] Many criticisms of expectancy theory apply to equity theory as well: (1) little is known about how individuals select "significant others" in generating data for the decision process; (2) inputs (efforts) and outcomes are hard to define realistically; (3) the input-outcome relationship is unclear (although it obviously differs from one circumstance to another); and (4) little is known about how the various factors change over time.[59]

As indicated at the beginning of this section, there is no universally accepted, all-encompassing theory of motivation today. Consensus cannot be reached because competing theories of motivation do not really compete directly — the focus of each differs, thus the behavior explained differs — and a single fair test to compare the validity of one theory in relation to another cannot be designed.[60] Even if a single theory of motiva-

tion could somehow be established and accepted, its usefulness would be limited, since it would inevitably be extremely complex and unwieldy. For example, G. Graen attempted to synthesize just a few concepts from various approaches — such as path-goal utility, expectancy, and internal (O) versus external (S) factors — to explain why superior work effort occurs.[61] The results demonstrated many interrelationships, all of which presumably affect behavior, but it would be extremely difficult for a manager to try to consider every one of them systematically when attempting to influence employees' motivations.

Of course business people would like to find a handy rule of thumb that contains the quintessence of all human behavior. But when issues are inherently complex, the effort to compress them into a "transistorized" packet is fruitless. It will probably be more useful for a manager to consider each of the various approaches to motivation (with its unique strengths and weaknesses) for the insights it can provide rather than to try to fit all of human behavior into one theory or approach.

NOTES

1. Baldwin, A. L., Kalhorn, J., and Breese, F. H. Patterns of parent behavior. *Psychol. Monogr.*, 1945, *58*, 1–75.
2. Walker, C. R., and Guest, R. H. *The man on the assembly line.* Cambridge, Mass.: Harvard University Press, 1952.
3. Schacter, S. *The psychology of affiliation.* Stanford, Calif.: Stanford University Press, 1959.
4. Ingham, G. K. *Size of industrial organization and worker behavior.* London, England: Cambridge University Press, 1970.
5. For an overview of theory and research, see: McClelland, D. C., et al. *The achievement motive.* New York: Appleton, 1953; Atkinson, J. W. (Ed.). *Motives in fantasy, action, and society.* Princeton, N.J.: Van Nostrand, 1958; McClelland, D. C. *The achieving society.* Princeton, N.J.: Van Nostrand, 1961; Schacter S. *The psychology of affiliation.* Stanford, Calif.: Stanford University Press, 1959; Kagan, J., and Lesser, G. S. (Eds.). *Contemporary issues in thematic apperceptive methods.* Springfield, Ill.: Charles C. Thomas, 1961; McClelland, D. C., and Winter, D. G. *Motivating economic achieve-*

ment: Accelerating development through psychological training. New York: Free Press, 1969; Atkinson, J. W., and Feather, N. T. (Eds.). *A Theory of achievement motivation.* New York: Wiley, 1966.

6. Atkinson, J. W., and Litwin, G. H. Achievement motive and test anxiety conceived as motive to approach success and motive to avoid failure. *J. Abnorm. Soc. Psychol.,* 1961, *63,* 552–561.

7. French, E. G. Motivation as a variable in work-partner selection. *J. Abnorm. Soc. Psychol.,* 1956, *53,* 96–99.

8. Feather, N. T. Valence of outcomes and expectation of success in relation to task difficulty and perceived locus of control. *J. Person. Soc. Psychol.* 1967, *7,* 372–386; Rotter, J. B. Generalized expectancies for internal vs. external control of reinforcement. *Psychol. Monogr.,* 1966, *80* (No. 609).

9. McClelland, D. C., and Winter, D. G. *Motivating economic achievement.* New York: Free Press, 1969.

10. Weinstein, M. S. Achievement motivation and risk preference. *J. Person. Soc. Psychol.,* 1969, *13,* 153–172.

11. Maslow, A. H. *Motivation and personality.* New York: Harper, 1954.

12. Locke, E. A. The nature and causes of job satisfaction. In M. D. Dunnette (Ed.), *Handbook of industrial and organizational psychology.* Chicago: Rand-McNally, 1976, 1297–1350.

13. Dyer, W. W. *Your erroneous zones.* New York: Funk, Wagnalls, 1975.

14. Herzberg, F., Mausner, B., and Snyderman, B. B. *The motivation to work.* New York: Wiley, 1959.

15. Sirota, D. Some effects of promotional frustration on employees' understanding of, and attitudes toward, management. *Sociometry,* 1959, *22,* 273–278.

16. Patchen, M. Absences and employee feelings about fair treatment. *Personnel Psychol.,* 1960, *13,* 349–360.

17. Locke, E. A., op cit.

18. Vroom, V. *Work and motivation.* New York: Wiley, 1964.

19. Guetzkow, H. S., and Bowman, P. H. *Men and hunger.* Elgin, Ill.: Brethren Publishing House, 1946.

20. Gellerman, S. W. *Motivation and productivity.* New York: AMACOM, 1963, Chapter 19.

21. Meyers, C. E. The effect of conflicting authority on the child. In K. Lewis, C. E. Meyers, et al. (Eds.), *Authority and frustration.* Iowa City: University of Iowa Press, 1944, Part 2.

22. Kahn, R. L. Psychology in administration: A symposium. III. Productivity and job satisfaction. *Personnel Psychol.,* 1960, *13,* 275–287.

23. Church, R. M. The varied effects of punishment on behavior. *Psychol. Rev.,* 1963, *70,* 369–402.

24. Dinsmoor, J. A. Punishment; I. The avoidance hypothesis. *Psychol. Rev.,* 1954, *61,* 34–46.

25. Janis, I. L., and Feshbach, S. Effects of fear-arousing communications. *J. Abnorm. Soc. Psychol.,* 1953, *48,* 78–92; Howland, C. I., Janis, I. L., and Kelley, H. H. *Communications and persuasion.* New Haven, Conn.: Yale University Press, 1953.

26. Watson, G. A comparison of the effects of lax versus strict home training. *J. Soc. Psychol.,* 1934, *5,* 102–105; Maier, N. R. F. *Frustration,* op. cit.

27. Baldwin, Kalhorn, and Breese, op. cit.; Durkin, H. E., Glatzer, H. T., and Hirsch, J. S. Therapy of mothers in groups. *Amer. J. Orthopsychiat.,* 1944, *14,* 68–75.

28. Henle, M. On activity in the goal region. *Psychol. Rev.,* 1956, *63,* 229–302; Klinger, E. Development of imaginative behavior: Implications of play for a theory of fantasy. *Psychol. Bull.,* 1969, *72,* 277–298.

29. Herzberg, Mausner, and Snyderman. op. cit.

30. Morse, N. C., and Weiss, R. S. The function and meaning of work and the job. *Amer. Social Rev.,* 1955, *20,* 191–198.

31. Lewin, K. *Dynamic theory of personality.* New York: McGraw-Hill, 1935, p. 123.
32. Silberman, C. E. *Criminal violence, criminal justice.* New York: Random House, 1978.
33. March, J. G., and Simon, H. A. *Organizations.* New York: Wiley, 1958, Chapters 3 and 6.
34. Campbell, J. P., and Pritchard, R. D. Motivation theory in industrial and organizational psychology. In M. D. Dunnette (Ed.), *Handbook of industrial and organizational psychology.* Chicago: Rand-McNally, 1976, pp. 63–130.
35. Jacobs, R., and Solomon, T. Strategies for enhancing the prediction of job performance from job satisfaction. *J. Appl. Psychol.,* 1977, *62,* 417–421; Steers, R. M., and Spencer, D. G. The role of achievement motivation in job design. *J. Appl. Psychol.,* 1977, *62,* 472–479; Stone, E. F., Mowday, R. T., and Porter, L. W. Higher order need strengths as moderators of the job scope-job satisfaction relationship. *J. Appl. Psychol.,* 1977, *62,* 466–471.
36. Endler, N. W., and Magnuson, D. *Interactional psychology and personality.* Washington, D.C.: Hemisphere, 1975; Sarason, I. G., Smith, R. E., and Diener, E. Personality research: Components of variance attributable to the person and situation. *J. Pers. Soc. Psychol.,* 1975, *32,* 199–204.
37. Hackman, J. R., and Oldham, G. R. Motivation through the design of work: Test of a theory. *Organ. Behav. Hum. Perform.,* 1975, *16,* 250–279.
38. Lawrence, P. R. Personal communication, 1975.
39. Cronbach, L. J. Beyond the two disciplines of scientific psychology. *Amer. Psychol.,* 1975, *30,* 116–127.
40. Campbell and Pritchard, op. cit., p. 245.
41. Blood, M. R., and Mullet, G. M. *Where have all the moderators gone? The perils of Type II error.* Atlanta: Georgia Inst. Technol. College of Indus. Manage., Tech. Reprt. #1, 1977.
42. Kelley, H. H. The process of causal attribution. *Amer. Psychol.,* 1974, *28,* 107–128.
43. For example, see Anderson, C. R. Locus of control, coping behaviors, and performance in a stress setting: a longitudinal study. *J. Appl. Psychol.,* 1977, *62,* 446–451; Anderson, C. R., Hellriegel, D., and Slocum, J. W. Managerial response to environmentally-induced stress. *Acad. Manage. J.,* 1977, *20,* 260–272; Andrisani, P. J., and Nestel, G. Internal-external control as a contributor and outcome of work experience. *J. Appl. Psychol.,* 1976, *61,* 156–165; Mitchell, T. R., Smyser, C. M., and Weed, S. E. Locus of control: Supervision and work satisfaction. *Acad. Manage. J.,* 1975, *18,* 623–631.
44. Rotter, J. B. Some problems and misconceptions related to the construct of internal vs. external control of reinforcement. *J. Consult. Clin. Psychol.,* 1975, *43,* 56–67.
45. Weiner, B. *Theories of motivation: From mechanism to cognition.* Chicago: Markham, 1972.
46. Phares, E. J., and Larriell, J. T. Personality. *Ann. Rev. Psychol.,* 1977, *28,* 113–140.
47. Salancik, G. R., and Pfeffer, J. An examination of need satisfaction models of job attitudes. *Admin. Sci. Quar.,* September 1977, 427–456.
48. McClelland, D. C. *Power — the inner experience.* New York: Irvington, 1975. And Winter, D. G. *The power motive.* New York: Free Press, 1973.
49. Mitchell, T. R. Organizational behavior. *Ann. Rev. Psychol.,* 1979, *30,* 243–281. See also Terborg, J. The motivational components of goal setting. *J. Appl. Psychol.,* 1976, *61,* 613–621 for a view opposing the idea that external factors affect motivation only indirectly.
50. Locke, E. A. Toward a theory of task motivation and incentives. *Organ. Behav. Hum. Perform.,* 1968, *3,* 157–189.
51. DeCharms, R. *Personal causation.* New York: Academic, 1968; deCharms, R. *Enhancing motivational change in the classroom.* New York: Irvington, 1976.
52. See Connolly, T. Some conceptual and methodological issues in expectancy models of work performance motivation. *Acad. Manage. Rev.,* 1976, *1,* 37–47 for an overview of studies in this

UNDERSTANDING THE BEHAVIOR OF INDIVIDUAL EMPLOYEES

area; Kopelman, R. E. Across individual, within individual and return on effort versions of expectancy theory. *Decis. Sci.*, 1977, *8*, 651–662.

53. Parker, D., and Dyer, L. Expectancy theory as a within-person behavior choice made. *Organ. Behav. Hum. Perform.*, 1976, *17*, 97–117.

54. Kopelman, R. E., and Thompson, P. H. Boundary conditions for expectancy theory predictions of work motivation and job performance. *Acad. Manage. J.*, 1976, *19*, 237–258.

55. Behling, O., Schriesheim, C., and Tolliver, J. Alternatives to expectancy theories for work motivation. *Decis. Sci.*, 1975, *6*, 449–461.

56. Slovic, P., Fischhoff, B., and Lichtenstein, S. Rating the risks. *Chemtech*, 1979, *9*, 738–744; Simon, H. A. *Administrative behavior: A study of decision-making processes in administrative organizations*, 2nd ed. New York: Free Press, 1957.

57. Adams, J. S. Toward an understanding of inequity. *J. Abnorm. Soc. Psychol.*, 1963, *67*, 422–436.

58. Austin, W., and Walster, E. Reactions to confirmation and disconfirmation of equity and inequity. *J. Pers. Soc. Psychol.*, 1974, 208–216.

59. Dunnette, M. D. *Mishmash, mush, and milestones in organizational psychology.* Speech presented at ADA Convention, New Orleans, 1974; T. R. Mitchell, op. cit.

60. Campbell, J. P., and Pritchard, R. D., op. cit.

61. Graen, G. Instrumentality theory of work motivation: Some experimental results and suggested modifications. *J. Appl. Psychol. Monogr.*, 1969, *53*, 1–25.

SUGGESTED READINGS

Matsui, T., and Terai, T. A cross-cultural study of the validity of the expectancy theory of work motivation. *J. Appl. Psychol.*, April, 1975, 263–265.

Porter, L. W., and Lawler, E. E. *Managerial attitudes and performance.* Homewood, Ill.: Irwin, 1968.

Sheridan, J. E., Slocum, J. W., Jr., and Min, B. Motivational determinants of job performance. *J. Appl. Psychol.*, February 1975, 119–121.

Steers, R., and Porter, L. W. *Motivation and work behavior*, 2nd ed. New York: McGraw-Hill, 1979.

LABORATORY EXERCISE

ROLE-PLAYING:
THE CASE OF REPORT X–303

(Students are asked not to read the case materials before participating in the laboratory exercise.)

A. PREPARATION

1. Arrange a table at the front of the room. (This should be in addition to the instructor's desk.)
2. Place four chairs around two or three sides of the table so that all occupants face the class as well as each other.
3. The instructor will choose a person to play the role of Al Jeffries, group leader. He is to leave the room and study the "Instructions for Al Jeffries" (E.1). CAUTION: The student must not be familiar with the script that will be used (E.3) and should not return until instructed to do so.
4. The instructor will select four persons to occupy the seats at the table; see that each has a copy of the script (E.3); and assign the parts of Jack, Steve, Donna, and Bill in a clockwise direction.
5. A sixth person is chosen to take the part of Al Jeffries, who makes an entrance in the middle of the script. He is an alternate of the Mr. Jeffries who has left the room. He takes a copy of the script and stands ready to go to the table and act this part.

B. READING THE SCRIPT

1. The instructor will read aloud to the class and the actors the preliminary material labeled "Situation" (E.2).
2. The instructor then gives the signal for the reading of the script.
3. Reading proceeds to the end.
4. The instructor thanks the actors for their help, asks the four engineers to remain seated at the table, and asks the person

who has read Mr. Jeffries's part to join the class.

C. ROLE-PLAYING WITH A NEW AL JEFFRIES

1. Jack, Steve, Donna, and Bill read the last six speeches, just preceding Mr. Jeffries's entrance, to get in the mood for repeating the situation.
2. They are to dispense with the script as soon as the new Mr. Jeffries enters, but to continue the business of eating lunch. As soon as Jeffries enters, they must make up their own lines.
3. The instructor signals role-player Al Jeffries to enter the room, points out to him who is playing the role of Jack, and asks him to proceed as he sees fit.
4. Role-playing should be allowed to continue to a point where the decision reached by the role-players terminates the interview or where something else happens that requires an interruption. The instructor should feel free to discuss progress or offer suggestions during these interruptions.
5. If subsequent interviews are implied in the decision, such as having a discussion with the employees as a group, role-play such meetings.

D. DISCUSSION

1. Use class discussion to evaluate the process observed. How do the observers feel about the decision?
2. List all the things Jack did in the role-playing that indicated he had a problem that was more than a dislike of writing the report. Distinctions should be made between (a) the status of the job; (b) the

number of times Jack did the work; (c) the influence of "kidding" on Jack; and (d) Jack's answer to the others about what he would do.

3. Analyze face saving and insubordination as employee behaviors, and determine extent of agreement in the class.

4. Evaluate face-saving problems of Al Jeffries, and consider what he can do to avoid them.

5. Determine whether the class considers this situation to be a problem between the group leader and the team or between Al Jeffries and Jack. (Free exchange of views should be encouraged, and differences in opinion sought.)

6. See if the class can agree on some rule that will guide them in determining when a problem involves the group and when it does not.

E. MATERIALS FOR THE CASE

1. Instructions for Al Jeffries

You are group leader for an engineering group at LSR Systems, a small research firm whose main customer is the federal government. Most of your group's work is technical, although members share the burden of paperwork connected with government-related projects.

Generally, the government reports and forms seem to have some justification, but nevertheless, the staff dislikes this aspect of their jobs. Your boss just reminded you that Quarterly Report #X–303 is due in a few weeks. Unlike the other reports (which are written by the person in the group chiefly responsible for the project), X–303 is a sort of general overview that anybody in the group could write. The group's procedure has always been to assign it to the newest team member. This quarter, that individual would be Jack Hastings.

You stop by the cafeteria where your group members generally eat together, so you can catch Jack to remind him about writing the report. In giving Jack this assignment, it is suggested that you take Jack to your office. You

should greet the group as a whole, but take Jack to the instructor's desk, which will act as your office.

2. Background Information

LSR Systems is a small research firm whose major customer is the federal government. Projects are generally long term, confidential, and well-paying. The staff has been kept small, and the atmosphere informal, even though sales have quadrupled since the firm was founded in 1972. This policy is stressed by the company's founder and president, Andy Larson. It seems to have worked well: LSR's employees — mostly engineers and scientists — have been able to complete complex projects within budget and time constraints, partly because of high rapport within project teams and high morale.

The problems that exist are mainly generated by the nature of their big customer, the federal government. Although the LSR atmosphere emphasizes informality and creativity, the employees meet with just the opposite in their dealings with the Federal Operations Office. Slow decisions (or no decisions), red tape, and resulting frustration are common. In most cases, there is some rationale for the paperwork demanded by the FOO, but no one knows why they need Quarterly Report #X–303 (rev. 1967). Everything in it is available elsewhere, it is all trivial, and it takes a very complex path while finally accomplishing nothing. Naturally, filling out this report, although all project team members have the knowledge to do so, is a job avoided by everyone. A system was worked out finally wherein the newest team member got the job for that quarter. This procedure is used generally in the company, and no one has ever questioned it.

The time is late August. A number of projects are scheduled for "milestone meetings" with government representatives in September. Groups are working feverishly to meet deadlines, and everyone is highly charged and very busy. Jack, Steve, Donna, and Bill are sitting in the company cafeteria, eating lunch and enjoying their usual style of mealtime conversation.

These four are engineers who work together on the C–5 project team; their group leader is Al Jeffries.

3. Script*

Jack: Boy, that iced tea really tastes good.

Steve: After jogging five miles, I could drink a gallon.

Donna: You guys are crazy. I'm saving my energy for work. This end-of-the-quarter stuff is killing me.

Bill: Me, too. I've got two reports still to write this week, besides an inside memo. By the way, Jack, isn't it about time for you to start work on good old X–303? I'm sure the folks in data processing can find some computer time for you for working on those difficult tables.

Steve: Sure, Jack, and you can always get Ralphie Fogarty to help you with the hard parts.

Jack: Aren't we hilarious today — what's the matter, Steve, you got jogger's cramp?

Bill: It's really a big job, Jack, but we know we can trust you to do it.

Steve: Maybe we'd better get him started. Let's see, today is Thursday, this is the North American continent . . .

Jack: Why don't you can it, Steve?

Donna: What's the matter, Jack? Don't you like the job?

Bill: Ah, it can't be that! He's been doing them for over a year now. He must like it.

Jack: You know well enough I don't like it.

Steve: Well, you keep doing it, don't you?

Jack: I'm going to get out of it, though.

Donna: This I gotta see!

Bill: What are you going to do — complain to Dandy Andy?

Jack: I don't know, but I think it's time somebody else did it.

Steve: Not me!

Donna: You won't drag me into it, either. I had my turn.

* Adapted from a case by H. F. Shout, The Detroit Edison Company, which appeared in N. R. F. Maier, *Principles of human relations.* New York: Wiley, 1952. Used with the permission of Mrs. Ayesha Maier.

Jack: For how long? One time, that's all you ever did it.

Bill: And that was enough, too, wasn't it, Donna?

Steve: What's the matter, Jack, can't you take it?

Jack: Sure I can take it — I have for the last six reports.

Donna: Looks like you're gonna make it seven reports, too.

Jack: Not me — I'm through doing all the dirty work around here.

Steve: Who do you think is going to write it?

Bill: Maybe Al Jeffries, our fearless leader himself?

Jack: I don't care who does it, but not me any more.

Donna: Yeah, you talk big, but you can't make it stick.

Bill: Yeah, Jackie, you're just asking for trouble.

(*Al Jeffries, the group leader, enters.*)

Jeffries: Hello, everybody. Say, Jack, could I see you for a minute? I don't want to break up the lunch session.

Donna: Oh, no — it's time we were getting back on the job anyway.

Jack: Yeah, sure, Al. Anything wrong?

Jeffries: No, Jack, not at all. I just wanted to remind you about the X–303 report.

(*Laugh from the group at the table.*)

Jack: What about it?

Jeffries: Well, it's due pretty soon. I think we'd better get started — wouldn't you say so?

Donna: This is where we came in, guys, let's go.

(*All but Jack leave; Jack and Al go to Al's office.*)

Jack: Yeah, Al, I guess *somebody* ought to write up that report.

Jeffries: Will you take care of that, Jack? Any time this week you can fit it in.

Jack: I wanted to talk to you about that, Al. I'd rather not do it this quarter.

Jeffries: Do what — write up the X–303?

Jack: Yeah, Al. I'd rather not do it.

Jeffries: Listen, Jack, I know you're busy, but it won't take that much time. You can get the information from the various reports the guys are working on — they'll help you out.

Jack: It isn't that — I just don't want to do it again. I've done it the last six quarters. It's not really fair to ask me to keep on doing it.

Jeffries: Well, now — I know how you feel, Jack. It's a pain, I admit — but somebody has to do it.

Jack: If you don't mind, count me out this time.

Jeffries: But I *do* mind, Jack. Everybody has to do his job — not just the enjoyable aspects, but all of it. And you *are* the newest guy in the group. So be a good sport, and do it.

Jack: I've been the fall guy around here for eighteen months. Let somebody else do it for a change!

Jeffries: Aw, come on, Jack — the other guys did it when they were first here.

Jack: Yes, but for how long? Donna did it once and so did Bill. I don't think Steve ever had to. Why pick on me?

Jeffries: No one's picking on you. We expect people to do their jobs, that's all.

Jack: Well, it's not part of my job. I'm an engineer, not a clerk.

Jeffries: It *is* part of your job, and I think we have a right to expect you to do it.

Jack: Count me out.

Jeffries: Now, be yourself, Jack. I don't want to be unreasonable about this, but, after all . . .

Jack: Well, I think I've done my share.

Jeffries: Look, we can work on a different way of handling it for the next quarter, but we haven't got the time to argue now — suppose you take care of it this time.

Jack: No, Al, I just don't feel I should be the one to do it.

Jeffries: Jack, I guess I have to say you've got to.

Jack: I'm sorry, but I'm not going to.

Jeffries: You've got no choice here, Jack.

Jack: Yeah, I do.

Jeffries: You'll write the report, Jack, or you'll get out.

Jack: You're not firing me, Jeffries. I quit. And you can give your garbage work to some new sucker. I'm through.

CHAPTER FOUR

FRUSTRATION:
BEHAVIOR
WITHOUT
A GOAL

■

The Nature of a Problem Situation
The Symptoms of Frustration
Evaluating Frustrated Behavior
The Relationship Between Frustration and Social Movements
Reversing the Process
Dealing with Frustration

■

ACTIVITY IS FREQUENTLY a matter of following learned procedures and routines. Some jobs can be performed entirely without making complex decisions. As long as life's situations remain much the same from one day to the next, a person's learned responses continue to elicit satisfactory reactions from other people and the environment without any problems.

THE NATURE OF A PROBLEM SITUATION

Problems arise for individuals when their progress toward a goal or objective is blocked, and they have no learned responses to meet the new situation. This type of situation occurs when a person comes to a decision point and must choose one of several alternatives, or when a barrier in the goal path blocks ongoing activity.

PROBLEM-SOLVING BEHAVIOR

The healthy and mature person reacts to a problem situation with problem-solving behavior, which is characterized by *variability* in thought and action. Variability in behavior may be relatively simple, like shaking a vacuum cleaner when it does not start, or it may be creative, like reorganizing a job to remove a bottleneck.

Regardless of the problem's complexity, variability is the basic characteristic of problem-solving behavior. Even when variability in behavior is simple, a chance exists of solving a problem because the person is freed from the old ineffective way of behaving.[1] Figure 4.1 shows how variability in behavior may lead a person around an obstacle and to a goal.

Clearly an obstacle that can be overcome by one individual may continue to block another; also, some obstacles cannot be overcome. What happens when the variable behavior at a given individual's disposal is inadequate? Figure 4.2 demonstrates how an individual may abandon an objective that cannot be reached and settle for a previously unnoticed substitute goal. A high school graduate's goal, for example, was a high-paying job in the drafting department of a company. When his application for the job was turned down because he lacked the required drafting courses, he accepted an offer for a lower-paying job in another department.

FRUSTRATION AS A REACTION TO PROBLEMS

When substitute goals are not available or when pressures for solving a problem are present and escape is blocked, failure may introduce tension. The person may become frustrated and unable to employ problem-solving behavior. Figure 4.3 illustrates how persistent failure in overcoming an obstacle causes it to be avoided; pressures created by deadlines or threats drive the person into the obstacle, and the confining walls of the situation prevent escape. *Under these conditions, tensions build up inside the person, and the tensions, rather than the goal, determine behavior.* Expressions like "He blew his top" or "She went to pieces" indicate that there has been a qualitative change in behavior. Such terms are used to describe the behavior because it no longer appears goal oriented. On the other hand, sensible behavior is *adaptive,* which means that the behavior leads to a goal or solves a problem.

FRUSTRATION AS A FACTOR IN BEHAVIOR

Whether an interference will produce symptoms of frustration depends on (1) the individual's tolerance for frustration; (2) the number and severity of frustrating incidents

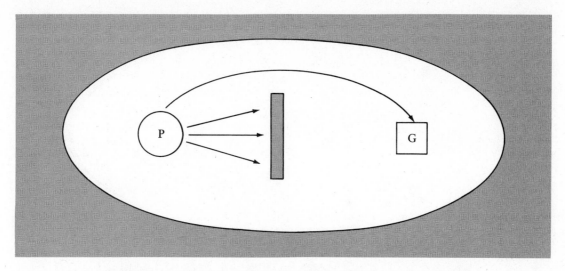

**FIGURE 4.1 VARIABLE BEHAVIOR MAY LEAD TO A SOLUTION
OF A PROBLEM**

The person (*P*) is blocked from his goal (*G*) by some obstacle. After trying several behaviors (arrows), one is found that leads to the goal.

SOURCE: Modified from N. R. F. Maier, *Frustration*. Ann Arbor, Mich.: University of Michigan Press, 1961. Copyright © 1961 by The University of Michigan.

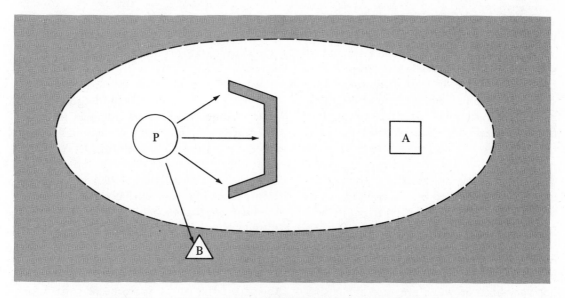

**FIGURE 4.2 INSURMOUNTABLE OBSTACLES MAY CAUSE A
CHANGE IN GOALS**

If an obstacle blocks access to Goal *A*, the person (*P*) may solve the problem by switching to Goal *B*, which may initially have been outside the situation.

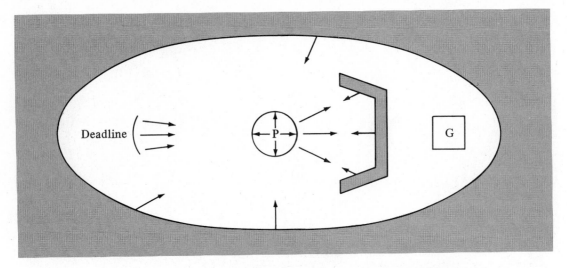

FIGURE 4.3 A PROBLEM SITUATION MAY PRODUCE FRUSTRATION

Pressures, failure, and inability to escape from a situation produce frustration. A frustrated person is under emotional tension, and this rather than the nature of the situation determines behavior.

SOURCE: Modified from N. R. F. Maier, *Frustration*. Ann Arbor, Mich.: University of Michigan Press, 1961. Copyright © 1961 by The University of Michigan.

in the recent past; (3) the pressure under which the individual is functioning; and (4) the person's interpretation (perception) of the situation. We are more apt to be frustrated by an interference caused by another person than by one caused by a physical object, because we are more likely to experience people as interferences than as problems. (Because children do not make this distinction as readily as adults, they are as likely to be frustrated by a broken toy as by their mother.) But frustration in adults does not always stem from human interference. Unemployment, a fire, or only a stalled car can cause frustration. The last situation can be frustrating when the person's tolerance is not very high or when pressure in the situation demands that the problem be solved quickly. The absolute necessity of finding a solution to a problem, or the anticipation of

punishment if the problem is not solved, tends to make problems frustrating situations.

When a situation becomes frustrating to individuals, their behavior undergoes a distinct change. What previously was healthy, unemotional activity now becomes negatively emotional and unreasonable. Variable and constructive behavior is replaced by stereotyped and destructive behavior. In extreme cases, the behavior becomes pointless, in the sense that nothing positive is gained. However, such activity sometimes obtains a constructive end in that it somehow overcomes the source of frustration. In such cases, the behavior is adaptive. We recognize, therefore, that the symptoms of frustration have a function, and that a distinction must be made between adaptive and unadaptive expressions of frustration. For example, one

The behavior of individuals when they become frustrated changes from the unemotional to the emotional. (Ellis Herwig from Stock, Boston)

computer programmer who cannot resolve the problems with "bugs" in a new program may respond by becoming obsessed with the problem and ignore all other demands until the program runs correctly. Another programmer may respond to the frustrations of the situation by drinking or by physical abuse of his family. The first response would be adaptive; the second, maladaptive.

Some writers do not make a qualitative distinction between goal-oriented behavior and behavior arising out of frustration. The following discussion is guided by the theory that frustration and motivation represent two distinct sources of action in the individual.[2] At certain times, one of these mechanisms dominates and controls the behavior;

at other times, the second takes over. Which psychological process is brought into function will depend on the individual's make-up (for example, frustration threshold), as well as on the situation.

To understand someone's behavior at any particular time, we must know which behavioral mechanism (frustration or motivation) is dominating. For instance, we can understand a person's behavior in committing a crime, provided we know the motive. Similarly, we are better able to understand the actions of a person who attacks an innocent bystander if we are aware of the attacker's state of frustration. Because such an attack does not achieve a positive goal, the behavior seems senseless from the viewpoint of motivation. Even when an attack is made on a person who is guilty of a crime, the behavior may be considered illogical in that it probably will not remedy the crime.[3]

THE SYMPTOMS OF FRUSTRATION

The major characteristics of frustrated behavior are *aggression, regression,* and *fixation.* Each of these has been experimentally produced in the laboratory. Another symptom, which may be called *resignation,* is frequently found in case-history studies. The symptoms of frustration frequently occur in mixed form; hence they are sometimes difficult to recognize unless we know what to expect. They are presented here separately for clarity, not because they represent different stages through which a frustrated individual passes.

AGGRESSION

Aggression in behavior is shown by some kind of attack. The attack may be one of physical violence against a person, such as striking the person who steps ahead in line; it may be directed toward an object, such as kicking a door when the lock doesn't work; it may be verbal abuse, directed at a spouse for buying an unnecessary item. Aggression in behavior triggered by frustration means a hostile act and is associated with the emotion of anger. A boxer who is aggressive in carrying the fight to his opponent would not be showing aggression (as the term is here used) unless the actions were determined by anger rather than strategy.

The relationship between frustration and aggression has been experimentally established and is now generally accepted.[4] This relationship is perhaps most obvious in chil-

dren because they show their aggression in less circuitous ways and are more likely to attack physically than adults are.[5]

When aggression against the frustrating agent is prevented, the aggressive energy may be directed at substitute objects. For example, a supervisor may yell at workers; the frustration evoked in the workers may then cause some of them to go home and beat their children. It has been shown statistically that parents who are unhappily married are two and a half times as likely to be abusive to their children as happily married parents are.[6] Frustrated parents take their frustrations out on their children, who in turn take theirs out on school, society, and eventually their own children.[7]

The attack on substitute objects often takes the form of *scapegoating,* in which certain individuals or groups are blamed for various evils. In such cases, propaganda writers or group leaders single out the substitute object of attack, and the aggression tends to be confined to this object, rather than to be distributed indiscriminately. The relationship between scapegoating and frustration is suggested by the fact that scapegoating becomes more prevalent during periods of widespread unrest, dissatisfaction and worry.

Slums and ghettos, where the opportunities for frustration are greatest, have the highest degree of violence and vandalism. The cost of replacement of glass in public telephone booths was found to be characteristically high in those sections of an industrial community where housing and living problems were greatest.

It should not be assumed that aggression is necessarily undesirable or unadaptive. An attack on an obstruction, be it an enemy or an object, may remove it and permit the individual to resume progress toward a goal.

Such behavior has helped lower animals to survive in the struggle for existence. In human beings, this primitive and individualistic behavior is of less value because, in this case, survival depends to a greater degree on reason and cooperation.

When aggression is directed toward obstacles that cannot be overcome, the aggression results in further frustration rather than relief. This condition also happens when the obstacle strikes back. Thus, frustration is piled on frustration, and the behavior must be regarded as unadaptive.

Substitute objects are frequently attacked under these conditions, but this behavior is also unadaptive in not being directed at the source of the frustration. The substitutes, when they are other people, also strike back. Since they are frustrated by the attacking individual, they may direct their aggression against him or her. Thus the attacking individual soon becomes regarded as an antisocial person, one who is socially undesirable. This position in society becomes a further source of frustration, and instead of having solved the original problem, the person has acquired more problems.

The attitudes of frustrated people also reflect aggressiveness because they tend to be on the defensive. They interpret compliments as insults, are overly suspicious, and want to get even with someone. These attitudes may prevail only in the frustrating situation, or like other behavior traits, they may become general and apply to innocent bystanders.

Symptoms of aggression resulting from frustration seen in on-the-job behaviors include the following: (1) excessive criticism of management, (2) constant voicing of grievances, (3) damage to equipment, (4) inability to get along with others, and (5) absenteeism. Whether the aggression expressed is justified by the frustration is a moot point, since justice for the frustrated individual is subjectively determined. People can readily prove to their own satisfaction that they are underpaid, but the real cause of dissatisfaction may be the frustration arising from unpaid hospital bills, a recent divorce, or losses in gambling. In correcting the situation, it is desirable to know whether the aggression is directed toward the true source of frustration or toward scapegoats. Sometimes management is the worker's scapegoat, and sometimes employees are management's scapegoats.

REGRESSION

Regression is a breakdown of constructive behavior and a return to childish action. In extreme cases, adults regress to the infantile stage and must be treated as babies. That regression may be produced experimentally by frustration was demonstrated at the Iowa Child Welfare Station.[8] When children were deprived of certain toys to which they previously had access, their play with the remaining toys became more primitive than when frustration was not present. This mild frustration caused the average child's play to become like that of a child one and a half years younger.

The Iowa experiments correlate with clinical studies and with many of our own personal experiences.[9] Most of us know of children who revert to wetting the bed when a new baby arrives or of children who become thumb-suckers when they first go to school or day-care programs. When children or adults are unable to act their age in situations that make demands upon them, they are exhibiting the symptoms of regression. Although one symptom does not prove the presence of frustration, it must be accepted as one of its signs.

Another regressive trait is *suggestibility*. We can easily gain acceptance of ideas for action from children because they are uncritical. A critical attitude develops with reason. If we regress to a more primitive state, we tend to lose our critical ability and become suggestible, though only to the extent that the suggested behavior is not contrary to other primitive tendencies.

Regression serves no useful purpose except temporarily to protect the ego of the threatened individual. In the development of children, the desire to grow up, to want to become more mature than they are, is recognized as a healthy sign. Adequate adjustments in childhood are a safeguard against regression in later life.

Signs of regression in employees are (1) loss of emotional control, (2) following the leader, (3) lack of responsibility, (4) primitive horseplay, (5) unreasoned fear, and (6) responsiveness to rumors. Similarly, employees who pout and who cry easily are displaying regressive behavior that may have been caused by frustration.

Supervisors, too, may show signs of regression. Managers who refuse to delegate responsibility, who have difficulty in making simple decisions, who are hypersensitive, who cannot distinguish between reasonable and unreasonable requests, who engage in broad and unreasonable generalizations on the subject of workers, and who form blind loyalties for particular persons or organizations may be showing symptoms of frustration-induced regression. When intelligent people *lose their perspective* and *fail to make obvious distinctions,* they have regressed, since inability to make fine distinctions is a sign of mental immaturity. Distinctions most often fail to be made on emotionally loaded topics. A manager may pass unfavorable judgment on a worker simply because the worker belongs to a union, and employees may pass unfair judgment on a supervisor because they generalize that all supervisors are antiworker.

ABNORMAL FIXATIONS

The term *fixation* is used here to designate a compulsion to continue a kind of activity that has no adaptive value. A fixated action is repeated, despite the fact that the person knows it will accomplish nothing. Because of the compulsive character of such behavior, its replacement by more adaptive responses is prevented. Lady Macbeth's persistent hand-washing is a classic example of the abnormal fixation.

The relationship between persistent responses and frustration has been experimentally demonstrated in a number of studies.[10] These studies also show that continually forcing an animal to attempt to solve a problem that cannot be solved is an effective method for building up a state of frustration. Punishment, when severe or when continued for a sufficiently long period, may also serve as a source of frustration and produce similar symptoms. A rat can be made to bang its head against a locked door hundreds of times without ever trying the unlocked door next to it. This behavior completely prevents the animal from ever learning a new skill, which it would readily have learned prior to the frustration. Even if the animal is taught that it can avoid punishment by choosing the other door, it still cannot make that choice. The compulsion to perform the old response makes the animal unable to practice a new alternative that it knows is better.

Analogous experiments have been performed with college students. After a period of mild frustration, their ability to learn a new problem can be reduced by as much as one-half because one of the effects of frustration is to freeze old behavior and prevent the practice of new responses.[11]

Although a fixation may have the outward appearance of a normal habit, the difference appears when attempts are made to alter the fixation. A habit is normally broken when it fails to bring satisfaction or leads to punishment, whereas a fixation actually becomes stronger under these conditions.

Punishment, therefore, may have two different effects on the organism. On the one hand, it may discourage the repetition of an act. On the other hand, it may function as a frustrating agent and produce fixations as well as other symptoms associated with frustration. Because of this dual function, punishment is a rather dangerous tool, as it may produce effects that are the opposite of those desired. (See p. 51, Chapter 3.)

Common illustrations of fixations may be seen in panic states. In a burning building, people persist in pushing at exits, even though the exits are barred. The more they push, the less opportunity for escape; nevertheless, the useless behavior continues.

Because persistent attitudes are associated with situations in which frustration has occurred, they serve as evidence to support the view that attitude fixation and frustration are related. This relationship explains why unfavorable attitudes are so difficult to change. Instead of recognizing that the person with the rigid attitude is insecure, afraid, or feels rejected, we try to use reasonable arguments without much success. If we approach rigid and persisting attitudes as problems in frustration, we may discover that such attitudes can be changed.

We often hear that older people are set in their thinking and that they block progress. It may be that it is not their age that creates the problem but the fact that older people are often made to feel less wanted than younger people. Older workers often no longer get merit-pay increases and have reached the top rate of their job classification; on some jobs they cannot keep up the pace; they cannot find employment in other companies easily, so feel they must stay on; they have been bypassed more often than younger employees; and they get less attention than new employees because they are supposed to know the job.

Examples of fixations commonly seen in industry are found in individuals who are unable to accept change. Old ways seem best, whether they concern the method of work or the nature of interpersonal relations or the economic outlook. Frustrated individuals are blindly stubborn and unreasonable, although they may consider themselves merely persistent or cautious. They defend their refusal to change by building up logical defenses for their actions.[12] Logic thus follows their decisions, rather than precedes them. Firms that are relatively free from frustrating situations and have high employee morale are made up of individuals who *seek* new ways, rather than *fear* them. To them something *new* suggests something *better*.[13]

RESIGNATION

Studies of unemployed people[14] and refugees,[15] in addition to revealing the traits already described, frequently contain evidences of a state of mind that we may describe as one of giving up. All forms of activity seem to be closed to the individual, so he or she surrenders. This is a frame of mind that oppressive leaders may desire to create. Resignation is probably a dormant condition in which all aggression has been temporarily blocked. People in this state obviously have low morale and will remain socially neutral unless their mental condition changes.

In business, the resigned individual is one who has lost hope of bettering personal conditions. "There's no use trying to do anything around here," "I've stood it this long and can wait until I retire," "I've learned to put up with conditions," and "It's always been this way and it will always be this way" are characteristic statements of hopeless and apathetic employees. Such persons depress others and make no contribution to reform.

THE COST TO BUSINESS OF FRUSTRATED BEHAVIOR

Frustrated behavior can have impact on a company's profits, as the following study shows. The study of new-product development in food-processing firms included a search for factors differentiating firms that were relatively successful in this area from those that were not.[16] The following situation was found in a firm selected for relatively poor performance in new-product development.

Scientists, members of a group that viewed itself (and was perceived by others in the company) as low in status, were largely excluded from the decision-making process in new-product development. They had become technical servants to the high-status marketing personnel with whom they worked. As a result (according to scientists interviewed), the scientists often consciously delayed technical work and took other measures to disrupt or impair the new-product-development process. Obviously, such a response by bright persons to the frustration of being treated as servants or children was not constructive for either the company or the careers of those involved. To the scientists, their responses were a way of getting back at (expressing aggression toward) the marketing personnel, whom they feared and disliked. Their behavior was not rational, but can easily be understood in terms of frustration theory.

The cost to the company — in a very competitive industry where being first to introduce a new product can be critical to success — must have been significant. Yet this cost was unknown to the organization's top managers and played no part in their policy making or interpersonal relations efforts.

This company is by no means unique in paying a price for using interpersonal and organizational policies that contribute to employee frustration. The costs to the company include not only loss of productivity and creativity, but also increased stress-induced health problems.

EVALUATING FRUSTRATED BEHAVIOR

RECOGNIZING INSTANCES OF FRUSTRATION

The symptoms of frustration should be observed primarily to determine whether an individual's behavior is a reaction to frustration or an attempt to solve a problem. Before a manager can deal with behavior properly, a diagnosis must be made. To correct behavior, it is important to attack causes rather than symptoms. Workers who violate a safety practice to save time and get better production are problem solving in that the behavior has something to do with overcoming a difficulty on the job, but persons who smoke in a restricted area in defiance of the rules may be expressing hostility. Because such behaviors are intrinsically different, the remedies also must differ.

In the first instance, if employees were

reprimanded for violating the rule, they might be more inclined to obey it in the future. Even better, the supervisor might explain why safety and production are both important. The frustrated employee, however, would not respond to a reasonable explanation for the no-smoking rule, and reprimand would only make the person feel more frustrated.

The distinction between problem-solving or goal-motivated behavior and frustration-instigated behavior is not difficult to make, for in many ways the characteristics of these behaviors are direct opposites. However, a manager should not attempt to classify specific behaviors on this basis. Safety violations, tardiness, low productivity, discontent, and filing of grievances can be caused by either frustration or motivation. In order to distinguish the cause, a large enough sample of behavior is needed so that the essential distinctions can be made.

Table 4.1 describes some of the differences that are useful in making a diagnosis of frustrated versus motivated behavior. The symptoms of aggression, regression, and fixation can be recognized in these behavior descriptions, and certain additional differentiations are possible because of the comparison with motivated, or goal-oriented, behavior.

Since frustrated behavior is unrelated to clear-cut objectives, such behavior gives no clues to a remedy. Whether a person shows aggression, regression, or fixation, all have the same cause — frustration. These symptoms might be present in a single sample of behavior. A person who gossips shows the traits of regression (tattletale behavior common in children) and aggression (injury to another's reputation) by a single act. If such an individual persists in believing a rumor when sound evidence to the contrary exists, the trait of fixation is also present.

THE PRINCIPLE OF AVAILABILITY

Since the symptoms of frustration form no logical connection with the situation in which they occur, what determines the behavior that will be expressed? Clearly, convenience or *availability* is an important condition. Objects attacked must be within

TABLE 4.1 CHARACTERISTICS OF MOTIVATED AND FRUSTRATED BEHAVIOR

MOTIVATION-INDUCED	FRUSTRATION-INSTIGATED
Goal oriented	Not directed toward a goal
Tension reduced when goal is reached	Tensions reduced when behavior is expressed, but increased if behavior leads to more frustration
Punishment deters action	Punishment aggravates state of frustration
Behavior shows variability and resourcefulness in a problem situation	Behavior is stereotyped and rigid
Behavior is constructive	Behavior is nonconstructive or destructive
Behavior reflects choices influenced by consequences	Behavior is compulsive
Learning proceeds and makes for development and maturity	Learning is blocked and behavior regresses

From N. R. F. Maier. Experimentally induced abnormal behavior. *Sci. Mon.*, September 1948, 67, 210–216.

reach. The obstacle that frustrates is often physically close at hand; hence it is sometimes attacked. Family, work companions, and others encountered in daily activities are frequently attacked just because they are so accessible.

Availability, however, does not mean mere physical nearness. Training also makes other objects accessible, even though they are not physically associated with the frustrating situation. That is, because of what we hear from others and because of the habits we have established in the past, certain objects are made available for blame and persecution in our culture, regardless of their relevance to the given situation. Thus, the military, public schools, and other social institutions have been attacked by various groups and individuals.

Availability is influenced not only by training and physical nearness but also by the simplicity of an act. Regressive behavior is immature and generally simple. Thumb-sucking may be practiced in infancy, and a five-year-old may revert to thumb-sucking because it was previously practiced and is physically handy. Strict toilet-training tends to cause children who are later frustrated to become bed wetters, because the greater attention placed on toilet habits makes this behavior more salient to strictly trained children than to others.[17]

Availability also operates in fixation. The simplest responses and those practiced at the time of frustration are likely to become fixated. If an animal is punished severely for a particular act, this very act is the one that the animal is compelled (by its fixation) to practice in the future. This suggests that a person severely punished for stealing might become a compulsive stealer, a condition known as kleptomania. Punishment does not help alcoholics, and there is good reason to believe it makes them worse.[18]

INDIVIDUAL DIFFERENCES

We have emphasized basic trends in our discussion of the symptoms of frustration. However, all people do not do the same things when they are frustrated, any more than they behave identically when they are motivated. The variations in behavior that may appear in frustrating situations have at least three basic causes. One cause of variation lies in the fact that different people may express any one of the four types of symptoms in different ways. Another is that certain people show a predisposition to display one symptom rather than the others. The final (and most important) cause is individual difference in susceptibility to frustration. Some individuals are less inclined than others to become frustrated, either because they view the situation differently or because they have a higher level of tolerance. As situations become more stressful, a greater number of people shift from goal-motivated to frustration-instigated behavior.

The causes of the differences in behavior undoubtedly depend on personality differences,* cultural differences,[19] and to some extent, differences in intelligence. Many of these differences must be attributed to heredity. Acquired differences will depend on previous experiences (1) in developing emotional adjustments, (2) in learning to cooperate, and (3) in handling feelings of insecurity and social status in a group.

The presence of individual differences complicates prediction of behavior; nevertheless, the general effect of frustration is to cause certain observable behavioral changes. A knowledge of these changes increases our understanding of individuals as well as of

---

* Socially dependent persons are more inclined to develop fixations than others; and extroverts are more inclined to show aggression than introverts, according to the work of D. I. Marquart (see note 11).

groups because it furnishes us with basic principles.

THE RELATIONSHIP BETWEEN FRUSTRATION AND SOCIAL MOVEMENTS

GOAL-ORIENTED GROUPS

Most social organizations or groups with which we are familiar are small and overlap in their membership. The various influences that they exert on customs and on manners of living tend to neutralize each other. A heterogeneous assortment of social groups within a country may influence the lives of

Workers sometimes form groups to gain a specific goal — such as child care. (David Powers from Stock, Boston)

individuals but will be unlikely to make history.

Only when a large mass of people join in a single movement do they become a social force to be reckoned with. Any important social movement can transform the social, political, and economic structure of a country. It is in the interest of the business leader, therefore, not to ignore these social trends.

Under normal conditions, social groups may be described as organizations of individuals having common interests or goals. These groups may be characterized as *goal motivated*. People who wish to attain certain ends work together for a common purpose. They have leaders who represent their interests and whose duty is to coordinate activities. Athletic clubs, bridge clubs, university organizations, political groups, and religious organizations are common examples of social groups.

SOCIAL MOVEMENTS INSTIGATED BY FRUSTRATION

It is also possible for a frustrated group of people to become organized.[20] Since aggressive behavior tendencies are present in such people, they are susceptible to being organized or united around a pattern of aggression. We have already seen that no *specific* aggression is demanded by the frustrated individual; thus, any form of aggression can have an appeal.

The study of riots and mob behavior reveals the attractiveness of destructive behavior to certain groups of people, once an avenue for such activity is opened for them or made apparent to them. It is impossible to explain mob behavior just by referring to the incident that released it. Frustrations and tensions on a wide scale or over a long period of time precede these outbursts and are the underlying causes.[21] Incidents and suggestions precipitate, coordinate, and direct the course of aggressive action, as well as furnish the security of group action.

The nonspecific nature of feelings of aggression makes it relatively easy to organize large numbers of frustrated people. Social movements of this type are potentially large, and the program of action is destructive. Such a movement can be very strong because the action of a large mass of people is channeled and synchronized.[22] Thus an organized minority can overpower the unorganized majority.

The leader of a movement organized around a pattern of aggression is in a very powerful position. He or she determines the form the aggression will take and times the action. The large supply of destructive energy generated by frustration is ready to be harnessed, and the leader may not only do the harnessing, but may also do the driving. In this capacity, the leader becomes a determiner of history if the movement comes to power. The tragedy of Reverend Jim Jones and his followers in the jungles of Guyana provides an example of the potentially disastrous effects of an organization built on individual and group frustration.[23]

The other types of behavior characteristic of frustration lend support to an organization built around aggression. Regressive tendencies make people suggestible and easily led; they become uncritical and are not likely to recognize inconsistencies. The tendency to fixate makes their behavior stereotyped, so they can be made to persist in any activity in which they get started. Taken together, the effects of frustration make possible a fanatical type of social movement in which the individuals are relatively homogeneous and are dominated by hatred and destruction. They are persistent, irrational, and ready to follow a leader. Whether they will sweep away those things that are good or evil in society depends largely on circum-

stances outside themselves. If the activity is directed at innocent bystanders, social progress is impeded. If it is directed at groups of individuals interested in reform, social regression may occur. Frustration-instigated social movements thus constitute a social risk, since they are not oriented to a future goal. Insofar as goals are mentioned in the propaganda of such movements, they are accessory factors that may influence sympathetic individuals.

Frustration-instigated movements may form the nucleus of a force from which violent revolution develops. The Nazis in Germany in the 1930s, for instance, exploited a frustration-laden situation and eventually brought about World War II. To suppose that leaders create unrest is to miss an important point. Unrest may be taken advantage of by a potential leader, but the causes of unrest lie in the frustrations already there. No leader can organize a mass of well-adjusted people into a destructive movement. This point is illustrated in the case histories of former members of cults.[24]

The manner in which frustration influences the character of a social organization is well illustrated by a comparison of the communist and socialist movements. The economic beliefs of communism and socialism are similar, but the character of the two movements is different. Communism is militant in nature, placing a great emphasis on the overthrow of capitalism. The words *down with,* so frequently used in communist slogans, are aggressive. Socialism, on the other hand, emphasizes the better life and offers a means of dealing with problems arising when private capital is not available. Its slogans tend to describe goals. This distinction explains why communism has been accepted more readily in countries that are in the throes of economic poverty or depression, whereas socialism has prospered in relatively wealthy and stable European countries.

An absolute standard of living, however, does not determine the extent of frustration; instead, the *relative* standard of living does. Frustration is always an emotional reaction on the individual's part, not a description of the situation. Therefore, in considering economic frustration it is essential to determine how people view their standard of living in comparison with that of others, rather than to determine what an individual's standard of living actually is.

One effect of frustration on behavior is to cause individuals to lose sight of a goal in favor of behavior that releases tension. That this behavior causes problems in business can be seen in union contract negotiations. Employees and management both do better when the company prospers, and both suffer when the company is in decline. And yet, many actions by management, union representatives, or both, in union negotiating can only be understood in terms of frustration, rather than in terms of mutually shared goals. Seeing negotiation as a matter of winning or "beating the enemy," or holding out even when economic and logical considerations weigh against it are telltale signs of regression and aggression that are characteristic of frustrated behavior. Of course, contract bargaining does not inevitably involve frustration. But the differing perceptions and lack of trust ofen brought to the bargaining table may lead to an interaction based on irrational, frustrated acts, rather than realistic, constructive problem solving.

REVERSING THE PROCESS

We have seen that a problem situation normally sets problem-solving behavior in motion. But if the individual becomes frustrated by the problem or enters the problem situation with a lowered tolerance (low frustration threshold), variable constructive behaviors characteristic of problem-solving activity are replaced by hostile, childish, and rigid behaviors. Actually, the lower brain centers that control the autonomic nervous system play a dominating role in determining behavior, so that rational cortical activity is to some extent shunted out.[25] To restore the problem-solving activity, this process must be reversed: the pent-up emotions must be released and the real problem located in order to restore the problem-solving state of mind.

Although the problem itself may generate the feelings, these feelings do not describe the problem and are likely to be misleading. Figure 4.4 illustrates how a problem condition may be buried in a mass of emotional reactions. Problem-solving behavior begins when the person wishes to explore what can be done about a problem. An amputee, for instance, must reach the state of mind of seeking what can be done in order to enjoy as rich a life as possible despite his handicap; a retired couple who cannot live on a pension must face the problem of finding additional income or ways to reduce expenses. Some problems are difficult, and solutions may not readily be forthcoming. Thus, a disturbed person may require help in finding a solution as well as in achieving release from pent-up feelings.

DEALING WITH FRUSTRATION

Although some methods for dealing with frustration in individuals and in groups will be discussed at length in later chapters, it is desirable at this point to indicate the variety of approaches that exists. Supervisors should never depend on a single simple remedy for

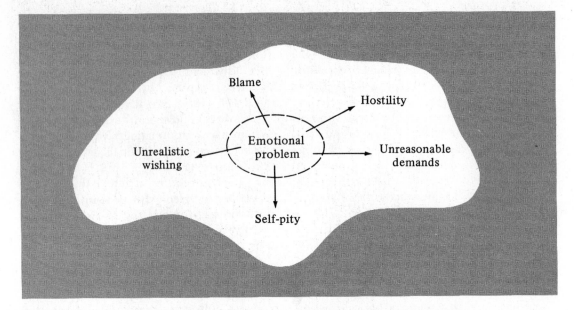

FIGURE 4.4 PROBLEMS EMBEDDED IN FRUSTRATED FEELINGS
The state of frustration is accompanied by varied and mixed feelings that hide or distort the real problem from the frustrated individual as well as from others. These feelings must be removed before the problem can be brought into focus and solved. Therapy is a process of releasing frustrated feelings under conditions that permit relief, discovering and clarifying the problem, and finding an acceptable solution.

all problems, for circumstances often exclude one solution but permit another. If a variety of approaches to a problem can be considered, it is often possible both to select a method that is best adapted to the individual's needs and to be sure that the practical aspects of the situation have been properly evaluated. Naturally, prevention of frustration is more desirable than the best cure.

THE CONSTRUCTIVE VIEWPOINT

When an employee slams a door after being reprimanded, this behavior can be seen as a sign of disrespect — a hostile act directed toward the reprimander — or as a symptom of frustration. If the reaction to the hostile behavior is striking back, a bad situation will be made worse. If the action is allowed to

pass and the act accepted as natural for a frustrated person, an unhappy situation does not deteriorate into a worse one.

Often people feel that unless they defend themselves from attack, they will appear to be weak. This interpretation assumes that the other person is doing some problem solving, which is not the case with frustrated behavior. An employee's criticism of a supervisor's action does not mean the supervisor must generate a defense. A well-adjusted person must expect to be a scapegoat at times, both at home and on the job. This acceptance of the realities of life does not mean that one individual should accept being continually pushed around. Rather it means that there may be better ways for dealing with such attacks than striking back.

UNDERSTANDING THE BEHAVIOR OF INDIVIDUAL EMPLOYEES

First, however, the individual must learn how to avoid becoming angry. An important attitude in avoiding anger is to be able to see frustrated behavior as a condition that creates problems and to see a frustrated person as one in need of help. This attitude is not an act of generosity; it can be self-oriented because it can prevent mistakes from being made and can encourage a problem-solving state of mind.

This problem-solving attitude applies to dealing with disgruntled individuals as well as finding ways to handle violence, such as that occurring during long strikes. Sometimes prolonged strikes create face-saving problems: for example, management wishes to discharge certain individuals for irresponsible behavior during a strike, and the union refuses to settle unless such individuals are protected. Past punishment and the threat of punishment do not deter destructive behavior caused by frustration; they increase it. Punishment is only a deterrent to the establishment of motivated behavior.

Regressive and fixated behaviors are less likely to elicit hostility than are acts of aggression. However, we are likely to misjudge persons showing these behaviors and treat them as incompetent and stubborn people. Instead, these behavior characteristics should be used as clues to detect instances of frustration.

CORRECTING THE SITUATION

Perhaps the most desirable procedure for dealing with frustration is to correct the situation that produced the behavior. The behavior of school bullies, for example, has been improved by giving them special instruction in reading to bring their performance up to that of other children in their class; some instances of adolescent delinquency have been stopped by correcting a physical abnormality; antisocial children have been helped by creating situations that gave them the experience of being accepted as members of a club; and vandalism has been reduced by recreation programs. Parental rejection is a common source of childhood frustration, and counseling parents is often the best way to cure their children. Similarly, supervisory training in human relations can reduce the number of frustrated employees. The importance of creating a situation in which a person feels accepted is strikingly demonstrated by the fact that even in the ultimate frustration of a prison setting, work situations can be created that will call forth cooperative behavior from inmates.[26]

Unfortunately, remedies are often not easy to put into practice, even when the situation allows. Frustrated people can be obnoxious, and it is more natural to want to punish them than to accept them.

CATHARSIS

The term *catharsis* refers to the relief created by the mere expression of frustration. In the Hawthorne study, interviewers were encouraged to make it easy for employees to express their hostility.[27] This climate creates a situation in which the person is free to release pent-up feelings. Because frustration builds up emotional tensions and creates a state that replaces rational behavior, it is necessary to reverse this process before an individual can return to rationality.[28]

We can appreciate the benefit that catharsis gives if we recall the relief experienced, for instance, after writing a hostile letter to someone who has been unfair. It is not necessary to mail the letter in order to feel the relief. The *expression* of the emotion, not what the behavior does to the other person, is important. But because the expression of frustration frequently injures or annoys another person, the benefits of expression often are lost. Thus it is useful to write hostile letters, but not to mail them. In fact, the very desire to mail them may be gone the next day.

The laboratory exercise at the end of this chapter is designed to show how expression of feeling can reduce frustration. Accepting feelings and trying to understand them rather than judging or criticizing them is most likely to clarify problems and reduce the tendency to find fault.[29] Since a manager is inclined to give advice and to pass judgment, the situation presented requires the suppression of this inclination.

The procedure of catharsis can be used with groups also, particularly when the members have a common problem. Understanding supervisors often hold feedback sessions in which employees are encouraged to say what they think, and the supervisor accepts the statements without arguing and without holding anything that is said against any member.

The following case illustrates such a session. Mr. Allen, a department head, found that someone had left a lighted cigarette on a toilet seat in the women's washroom, and it had left a large black burn. He became angry because to him this was showing disrespect for company property. Since he had the power to do so, he prohibited smoking in the washroom. The response of the women affected by this rule was hostility, reflected in their manner, job performance, attendance, and service. Supervisory personnel believed that the order was unfortunate, but they felt they could not rescind it.

One supervisor, Arnold Pond, was encouraged to hold a feedback session with the twenty-four women in his group. He opened the meeting by indicating that he would like to talk about the matter. The women responded by showing little interest since there was "really nothing to discuss." They felt that the order was silly and should

be changed. He indicated a desire to learn what it was about the rule that upset them. The discussion revealed the following four areas of feeling:

1. The ruling was unfair — all employees were punished because one woman had done some damage. Some doubted that it was done by an employee.

2. They wanted to know who had complained. It appeared that no one in the group knew, and none objected to the damaged seat. Since they had to use the washroom and the department head did not, they wanted to know why he changed the rule.

3. The ruling indicated that the company was getting awfully cheap. Prices of toilet seats were bandied about. If the company had so little money, why were not economies made in important areas? One woman suggested that they chip in and buy a toilet seat. Another suggested the purchase of two. A third woman suggested that the second be given to the department head.

4. They wanted to know what the department head was doing in the women's washroom.

Each of these areas released a good deal of hostility, and as the meeting progressed the participation increased. After the feelings had been exhausted, Mr. Pond said he understood their feelings but was not sure he understood why smoking in the washroom was so important since they could still smoke in the lounge.

He was told that they smoked while they did their hair in the washroom. He then asked why they did not fix their hair in the lounge where smoking was permitted. The response was, "Because there is no mirror in the lounge." He then asked, "If there were a mirror in the lounge, would that help?" They gave an affirmative response. He then asked, "Would you like me to buy a mirror for the lounge?" This suggestion was greeted favorably. He was able to get a mirror, and it was generally agreed that the property-damage and morale problems were both solved.

This example shows how soluble problems often lie beneath a mixture of feelings and demands. Managers often fear that requests will be so unreasonable that they cannot be discussed. They often avoid discussing such touchy topics and overlook the fact that the opportunity to express unreasonable feelings in a noncritical situation results in more reasonable people and permits the discovery of soluble problems.

CREATING OUTLETS FOR TEMPORARY FRUSTRATION

A thoughtful manager may let an employee blow off steam in an interview or discussion, but what about the frustrated employee who has no one to go to? Can a company furnish outlets for the frequent temporary frustrations on the job?

Sometimes outlets are feasible, but companies are reluctant to initiate them. For example, in exploring the switchboard panels in some telephone offices, a consultant found marks made by shoes. They were not scratches but were caused by kicks. It is not uncommon for telephone operators to be insulted, and they are not permitted to talk back. In interviews, the employees indicated that they kicked the panel as a result of their frustration. This action hurts, however, and with some shoes it could cause injury. So in order to make aggression less painful, the consultant suggested to managers that the panel be padded, but the suggestion was not taken seriously. Although the company medical department conceded that there were a number of cases of toe injuries in their records, no information was available on the causes.

In another instance, it was suggested by Maier that department stores should have a rubber dummy and mallet placed below the counter. Then sales personnel could excuse themselves from disagreeable customers and release their frustration by hitting the doll. This idea has not been adopted despite interview data from sales clerks suggesting that frustration with customers is a significant unsolved problem in retailing, and leads to a high level of expensive employee turnover.

The Matsushita Electric Industrial Company of Osaka, Japan, has set up a "human control room," designed to promote employee harmony and allow employees to give vent to their feelings.[30] With a portrait of the big boss benignly smiling on the wall, employees may smack a dummy, slug a punching bag, or select bamboo sticks from a handy rack and belabor a stuffed figure. A sign on the wall says: "To your heart's content, if you please." Executive Kuninari Azuma, who developed the plan, states that workers return to their jobs calmer and happier after working off their anger.

COUNSELING

Many instances of frustration occur in daily life. In most of these day-to-day problems, time dissipates the emotions aroused, and no serious damage is done. Although it would be desirable to avoid these difficulties, we may consider them routine; we would speak of the behaviors as frustrated acts rather than describe the persons involved as frustrated individuals.

When unresolved frustrations go far back in an individual's life, however, the feelings engendered by them continue to function and are reflected in practically all of a person's dealings with other people. Childhood experiences, such as the insecurity created by quarreling parents, a broken home, or a parent's rejection, are common sources of frustration that may mar a personality. Conditions or situations of this nature are too long-standing to correct in an employee, and it is therefore more important to develop an adjustment in the individual. We cannot expect time alone to heal the frustrations arising from childhood insecurity, shocking experiences, or physical handicaps. The causal conditions may actually snowball because the individual has difficulty in relationships with others. Such conditions may be relieved by expression, but the counseling process must be carried further to have lasting value. Managers and lay counselors can do much to help such persons reach a better adjustment. In some instances, psychiatric treatment is in order, and counselors can advise disturbed persons to seek skilled help.

For our present purposes, the difference between a temporary state of frustration and a personality disorder is important. The latter has a long history and requires professional treatment. It is also important to recognize that continued stress either off or on the job may result in behavioral change. Excessive absenteeism, alcoholism, excessive accidents, interpersonal difficulties, frequent medical visits, and sudden changes in behavior patterns are cues (symptoms) that the psychiatrist uses to indicate the existence of stress situations.[31] Work as such does not produce mental breakdowns, but working conditions may uncover and aggravate underlying tensions, conflicts, and emotional complexes already present.[32] An understanding listener can do much to help disturbed individuals overcome their resistance to seeing a psychiatrist.

FRUSTRATION AND STRESS

In recent years, the role of stress in physical illness has become a popular topic among business consultants and managers.[33] Stress has been known to be concomitant with organizational complexity and job responsibility, but data from longitudinal studies recently confirmed a relationship between responses to stressful situations and physical health.[34] Also, diseases often related to stress on the job (ulcers, heart disease, alcoholism) are found to be on the rise among women at a time when they are beginning to assume a significant proportion of jobs at higher organizational levels.[35] Whether this increase in disease among women is a temporary phenomenon associated with the difficulties of breaking new ground as executives, or whether it reflects the general stresses experienced by all executives, it is too soon to say.

One fact that has been discovered is that stress-related illnesses are more common at the middle-management level than among top executives. One possible explanation is that the frustration caused by trying and failing is the primary producer of stress-related illness, rather than such causes as competitive behavior, job complexity, and responsibility.

Although no cause-and-effect conclusions can be drawn, it is of interest that the Japanese level of heart disease (a common killer of American executives) is one-tenth that of the level in the United States, yet the Japanese are certainly competitive in world trade and industry.[36] Diet has been suggested as one important factor, but another may be related to the Japanese management style, which emphasizes participation and consensus in decision making.[37]

The long-term study by G. E. Vaillant (see note 34) found that it was not the amount of stress per se, but the individual's reaction to it that led to long-term mental and physical health or disability. Means of dealing with stress (such as the hostility and childishness seen in frustrated behavior) that repelled others were characteristic of those Harvard graduates in the forty-year study who were most likely to be dead or disabled by age fifty-five.[38] On the other hand, those men who were able to deal with conflicts or problems in ways characterized as mature (humor, suppression of impulses) were, in 80 percent of the cases, found to be in excellent health still at age fifty-five, whatever the levels of stress they had encountered in life.

Many methods sought by individuals who feel frustrated or unable to cope with their problems have proved of little use and, in fact, can be harmful. A survey of one or more participants in 130 group therapy programs offered in the United States in recent years indicated that benefits are ephemeral for most.[39] Although a high percentage (80 percent or more) reported receiving help from such methods as biofeedback, T-groups, and est, psychological follow-up tests indicated that only one-third of the participants (at most) gained long-term benefits. At the same time, in 10 percent of the cases studied, it was judged that psychological harm had been done to the participants.

Although learning to recognize and deal with frustrated persons is an important part of a manager's interpersonal skills, it is important that the approach be one that precludes the possibility of psychological damage. Such a method will be discussed in Chapter 18.

NOTES

1. Maier, N. R. F. The behavior mechanisms concerned with problem solving *Psychol. Rev.*, 1940, *47*, 43–58; Maier, N. R. F. The integrative function in group problem solving. In Aronson, L. R., Tobach, E., Lehrman, D. S., and Rosenblatt, J. S. *Development and evolution of behavior: Essays in memory of T. C. Schneirla.* San Francisco: W. H. Freeman, 1970.

2. Maier, N. R. F. *Frustration.* New York: McGraw-Hill, 1949. Reissued Ann Arbor, Mich.: University of Michigan Press, 1961; Yates, A. J. *Frustration and conflict.* New York: Wiley, 1962.

3. For technical studies that deal with the basic distinction between motivation and frustration, see: Eglash, A. Perception, association and reasoning in animal fixations. *Psychol. Rev.*, 1951, *58*, 424–434; The dilemma of fear as a motivating force. *Psychol. Rev.*, 1952, *59*, 376–379; Fixation and inhibition. *J. Abnorm. Soc. Psychol.*, 1954, *49*, 241–245; Feldman, R. S. The role of primary reduction in fixations. *Psychol. Rev.*, 1957, *64*, 85–90; Feldman, R. S. The prevention of fixations with chlordiazepoxide. *J. Neuropsychiat.*, 1962, *3*, 254–259; Jenkins, R. L. Adaptive and maladaptive delinquency. *Nerv. Child.* 1955, *11*, 9–11; Klee, J. B. The relation of frustration and motivation to the production of abnormal fixations in the rat. *Psychol. Monogr.*, 1944, *56*, 1–45; Maier, N. R. F. Frustration theory: restatement and extension. *Psychol. Rev.*, 1956, *63*, 370–388; Maier, N. R. F., and Ellen, P. Can the anxiety-reduction theory explain abnormal fixations? *Psychol. Rev.*, 1951, *58*, 435–445; Maier, N. R. F., and Ellen, P. The integrative value of concepts in frustration theory. *J. Consult. Psychol.*, 1959, *23*, 195–206; Salter, A. *Conditioned reflex therapy.* New York: Capricorn, 1961; Shimoyama, T. Studies of abnormal fixation in the rat. I. Effects of frequency of punishment in the insoluble situation. *Jap. J. Psychol.*, 1957, *28*, 203–209.

4. Dollard, J., et al. *Frustration and aggression.* New Haven, Conn.: Yale University Press, 1959, reissued in paperback, 1961; McNeil, E. B. Psychology and aggression. *J. Confl. Resol.*, 1959, *3*, 195–293; Scott, J. P. *Aggression.* Chicago: University of Chicago Press, 1958.

5. Sears, P. S. Doll play aggression in young children. *Psychol. Monogr.*, 1951, *65*; McNeil, E. B. Psychology and aggression. *J. Confl. Resol.*, 1959, *3*, 195–293; Feshbach, S. Dynamics and morality

of violence and aggression: Some psychological considerations. *Amer. Psychologist,* 1971, *26,* 281–292.

6. Watson, G. A comparison of the effects of lax versus strict home training. *J. Soc. Psychol.,* 1934, *5,* 102–105.

7. Merrill, M. A. *Problems of child delinquency.* Boston: Houghton Mifflin, 1947.

8. Barker, R., Dembo, T., and Lewin, K. *Frustration and regression.* Iowa City: University of Iowa Press, 1942; Kleemeier, R. W. Fixation and regression in the rat. *Psychol. Monogr.,* 1942, *54*(4) (whole No. 246), 34.

9. Bostock, J., and Shackleton, M. The enuresis dyad. *Med. J. Australia.* 1952, *3,* 357–360; Baruch, D. W. Therapeutic procedures as part of the educational process. *J. Consult. Psychol.,* 1940, *4,* 165–172; Axline, V. M. *Play therapy.* Boston: Houghton Mifflin, 1947.

10. Hamilton, G. V. A study of perseverance reactions in primates and rodents. *Behav. Monogr.,* 1916, *3,* 1–65; Hamilton, J. A., and Krechevsky, I. Studies in the effect of shock upon behavior plasticity in the rat. *J. Comp. Psychol.* 1933, *16,* 237–253; Patrick, J. R. Studies in rational behavior and emotional excitement: II. The effect of emotional excitement on the rational behavior in human subjects. *J. Comp. Psychol.* 1934, *18,* 153–195; Maier, N. R. F., Glaser, N. M., and Klee, J. B. Studies of abnormal behavior in the rat: III. The development of behavior fixations through frustration. *J. Exp. Psychol.,* 1940, *26,* 521–546; Kleemeier, R. W., op. cit.; Maier, N. R. F., *Frustration,* op. cit.; Maier, N. R. F., and Ellen, P. Studies of abnormal behavior in the rat: XXIV. Position habits, position stereotypes and abortive behavior. *J. Genet. Psychol.,* 1956, *89,* 35–49; Ellen, P. The compulsive nature of abnormal fixations. *J. Comp. Physiol. Psychol.,* 1956, *49,* 309–317; Solomon, R. L., and Wynne, L. C. Traumatic avoidance learning: The principles of anxiety conservation and partial irreversibility. *Psychol. Rev.* 1954, *61,* 353–385.

11. Marquart, D. I. The pattern of punishment and its relation to abnormal fixation. *J. Psychol.,* 1944, *19,* 133–163; Marquart, D. I., and Arnold, P. A study in the frustration of human adults. *J. Gen. Psychol.,* 1952, *47,* 43–63.

12. McNeil, E. B. Personal hostility and internal aggression. *J. Confl. Resol.,* 1961, *5,* 279–290; Miller, D. R., and Swanson, G. E. *Inner conflict and defense.* New York: Holt, 1960.

13. Ways, M. The American kind of worker participation. *Fortune,* 1976, *94*(4), 168–171ff.

14. Eisenberg, P., and Lazarsfeld, P. F. The psychological effects of unemployment. *Psychol. Bull.,* 1938, *35,* 358–390; Zawadski, B., and Lazarsfeld, P. The psychological consequences of unemployment. *J. Soc. Psychol.,* 1936, *6,* 224–251.

15. Allport, G. W., Bruner, J. S., and Jandorf, E. M. Personality under social catastrophe: Ninety life-histories of the Nazi revolution. *Charact. and Person.,* 1941, *10,* 1–22.

16. Verser, G. C. *The effect of an imbalance of power on new product development in marketing-oriented firms.* Doctoral thesis. Ann Arbor, Mich.: University Microfilms, 1978.

17. Bostock and Shackleton, op. cit.

18. Menninger, W. *Man against himself.* New York: Harcourt, Brace, & World, 1966; Presnall, L. P. *Recent findings regarding alcoholism in industry.* New York: National Council on Alcoholism, 1967.

19. Miller and Swanson, op. cit.

20. Maier, N. R. F. The role of frustration in social movements, *Psychol. Rev.,* 1942, *49,* 586–599; Cohen, N. (Ed.). *The Los Angeles riots: A sociopsychological study.* New York: Praeger, 1970.

21. Lee, A. M., and Humphrey, N. D. *Race riot.* New York: Dryden, 1943.

22. White, R. K. Hitler, Roosevelt and the nature of war propaganda. *J. Abnorm. Soc. Psychol.,* 1949, *44,* 157–174.

23. Greenberg, J. Jim Jones: The deadly hypnotist. *Science News,* 1979, *116,* 378ff.

24. Edwards, C. *Crazy for God: The nightmare of cult life.* Englewood Cliffs, N.J.: Prentice-Hall, 1979;

Horowitz, I. R. (Ed.), *Science, sin, and scholarship*. Cambridge, Mass.: MIT Press, 1979; Underwood, B., and Underwood, B. *Hostage to heaven*. New York: Potter, 1979.

25. Gardner, E. *Fundamentals of neurology*, 3rd ed. Philadelphia: Saunders, 1958; Jost, H., Ruilmann, C. J., Hill, T. S., and Gulo, M. J. Studies in hypertension: I. Techniques and control data; II. Central and autonomic nervous system reactions of hypersensitive individuals to simple physical and psychological stress. *Jour. Nerv. ment. Dis.*, 1952, *33*, 183–198; Cofer, G. N., and Appley, M. H. *Motivation theory and research*. New York: Wiley, 1967, Chapter 9.

26. Wilson, D. P. *My six convicts*. New York: Rinehart, 1951.

27. Roethlisberger, F. J., and Dickson, W. J. *Management and the worker*. Cambridge, Mass.: Harvard University Press, 1939.

28. Rogers, C. R. *Counseling and psychotherapy*. Boston: Houghton Mifflin, 1942.

29. Ginott, H. *Between parent and teenager*. New York: Macmillan, 1969.

30. Jampel, D. Hate your boss? Slug him. *Mechanics Illustrated*, 1962, *58*, 86–87.

31. Howe, H. F., and Wolman, W. Guide for evaluating employability after psychiatric illness. *J. Amer. Med. Assn.*, 1962, *181*, 146, 1086–1089.

32. Himler, L. E. *Dealing with difficult personality problems in an organization*. Ann Arbor, Mich.: University of Michigan Bureau of Industrial Relations, 1955; Kahn, R. L., Wolfe, D. M., Quinn, R. P., Snoek, J. P., and Rosenthal, R. A. *Organizational stress: Studies in role conflict and ambiguity*. New York: Wiley, 1964; Rogers, C. R. *On becoming a person*. Boston, Houghton Mifflin, 1968.

33. See, for example, *Executive stress: A management tool*. Seminar topic advertised by American Manage. Assoc., Dec., 1979; Levinson, H. On executive suicide. *Harv. Bus. Rev.*, 1975, *53*, 118–122; Ogilvie, B. C., and Porter, A. Business careers as treadmills to oblivion: The allure of cardiovascular death. *Human. Resour. Manage.*, 1974, *13*, 14–18.

34. Vaillant, G. E. *Adaptation to life*. Boston: Little, Brown, 1979.

35. Stress has no gender. *Bus. Week*, November 15, 1976, 73–74.

36. McQuade, W. Good news from the house on Lincoln Street. *Fortune*, 1980, *101*(1), 86–88ff.

37. Kraar, L. The Japanese are coming — with their own style of management. *Fortune*, 1975, *91*(3), 116–121ff.

38. Vaillant, op. cit.

39. James, R. D. Group therapy's help in coping with stress is minor, studies show. *Wall St. J.*, 1979, *59*(127), 1ff.

SUGGESTED READINGS

Bach, G. R., and Goldberg, H. *Creative aggression*. New York: Avon, 1974.

Ivancevich, J. M., and Matteson, M. T. *Stress and work: A managerial perspective*. Glenview, Ill.: Scott, Foresman, 1980.

Kahn, R. L., et al. *Organizational stress: Studies in role conflict and ambiguity*. New York: Wiley, 1964.

Kiev, A., and Kohn, V. *Executive stress*. New York: AMACOM, 1979.

Selye, H. *The stress of life*, rev. ed. New York: McGraw-Hill, 1976.

Shostak, A. B. *Blue-collar stress*. Reading, Mass.: Addison-Wesley, 1980.

LABORATORY EXERCISE

ROLE-PLAYING:
THE CASE OF THE FRUSTRATED SUPERVISOR

(Students are asked not to read the case before participating in the exercise.)

A. PREPARATION FOR ROLE-PLAYING

1. The class is to be divided into pairs of students seated side by side.
2. One member of each pair is to take the role of Jim Wells; the other member, the role of Bill Jackson. Read only the instructions for your own role.
3. Bill Jacksons leave seats; at a given signal they return and role-playing begins.

B. ROLE-PLAYING

1. The pairs play simultaneously. They should finish after about fifteen minutes.
2. When half of the pairs have finished, the instructor can give the others a two-minute warning.

C. DISCUSSION

1. Determine how each Bill Jackson feels toward Jim Wells.
2. Determine how each of the Bills feels toward Joe.
3. Determine what was done in each case with Joe.
4. Discuss what Jim could have done to make Bill feel better about Joe.
5. Other points should be discussed as the class wishes. No specific conclusions need be attempted by the class or contributed by the instructor. The objectives are to increase sensitivity to feeling, stimulate a permissive attitude, and develop listening skills.

D. FOLLOW-UP (USE ONLY IF TIME PERMITS)

1. Assign role of Joe Blake (E.3) to a class member.

2. After Joe has read the role, he should be seated at a desk, supposedly having returned to the job.
3. Various Bills will have been willing to take Joe back, but they will disagree on how he should be treated or talked to. Several viewpoints for the proper treatment should be posted.
4. Bills having differing opinions should then be assigned to go to Joe's desk and demonstrate how they think Joe should be handled. These demonstrations should be terminated as soon as Joe has had a chance to respond, thus indicating how he feels about the approach. After several demonstrations, this aspect of the case may be opened for general discussion.

E. MATERIALS FOR THE CASE

1. Role for Jim Wells, Division Supervisor

You are the supervisor of a division employing about seventy-five men and women and six first-line supervisors. You like your job and the supervisors and employees who work for you, and you feel that they are very cooperative.

This morning you noticed that one of your first-line supervisors, Bill Jackson, was rather late in getting to work. Since Bill is very conscientious and was working on a rush job, you wondered what had happened. Bill is thoroughly dependable, and when something delays him, he always tries to phone you. You were about to call his home when one of Bill's men, a young fellow named Joe Blake, came in. Joe is a good-natured kid, just out of high school, but this time he was obviously angry and said that he was going to quit unless you got him another job. Evidently Bill had come in, started to work, and then lost his temper completely when young Joe didn't do something quite right.

Although Bill occasionally has his bad moods,

it is unlike him to lose his temper this way. This latest rush job may have put him under too much pressure, but even so, his outburst this morning seems difficult to explain. But you are determined not to get into an argument with Bill or criticize him in any way. You will listen to what he has to say and indicate that you understand how he feels. If Bill seems more angry than Joe's mistake would reasonably justify, perhaps there is something behind all this, and Bill would probably feel a lot better if he got it off his chest.

You talked with Joe for several minutes, and after he had told his side of the story, he felt better and was ready to go back on the job. You just phoned Bill and asked him to drop around when he had a chance. Bill said he'd come right over and is walking toward your office now.

2. Role for Bill Jackson, First-Line Supervisor

You have just come to work after a series of the most humiliating and irritating experiences you have ever had. Last night your next-door neighbor, Sam Jones, had a wild, drunken party at his house that kept you awake most of the night. Jones is a blustering, disagreeable man who has no consideration whatever for others. When you called him at about 3:00 A.M. and told him to quiet down, he was abusive and insulting. But when you finally got some rest, you overslept.

Since you were in the midst of a rush job at the company, you skipped breakfast to hurry to work. As you were leaving the house, you noticed that someone had driven a car across one corner of your lawn and torn out several feet of your new hedge. You were certain that Jones or one of the drunks at his party had done it, so you went right over to Jones's house, determined to have it out with him. He denied everything, and practically threw you out.

When you came to work, more than an hour late, your nerves were so ragged that you were actually shaking. Everything conceivable had gone wrong. The last straw was when you discovered that Joe Blake, a young high school recruit, had made a mistake that delayed you several hours on your rush job, or at least it would have if you hadn't caught him in time. Naturally you gave him a good going over for his carelessness. Blake said he wouldn't take that kind of abuse from anyone and walked out on you. You noticed that he went in to see your supervisor, Jim Wells. Obviously, he is in there accusing you of being rough on him. Well, if he has gone in there complaining, you'll make him wish he'd never been born. You have had all you can stand, and the big boss had better not get tough with you because he'll have one hell of a time getting the job done without you. Jim had that complainer in there and talked to him for quite a while before he phoned you to come in. You are going to Jim's office now and have no intention of wasting time on words.

3. Role for Joe Blake
(Use only if Section D is incorporated)

This morning when you came to work, Jackson wasn't there. Since you are just out of high school and are learning the job, Mr. Jackson always outlines the program you follow each day.

You know that your unit is in the middle of a rush job, and so you became anxious about getting started. After waiting half an hour, you decided to see what you could do about setting up the operation by yourself. You had a good idea about what was wanted and after looking over the job and doing some figuring on it, you felt you had it ready to go. Just as you'd finished your preparations, Jackson showed up. Instead of praising you for your initiative, he lit into you for a small technical oversight you'd made. At first you couldn't believe your ears, but he went on abusing you and talking about the damage you would have done if he hadn't caught the mistake in time. You decided you wouldn't work for a boss like that and told him you weren't used to that kind of treatment. You went to Mr. Wells's office and told him you wanted a transfer. Mr. Wells listened to your side of the story and suggested you wait awhile until things simmered down. Mr. Wells is a reasonable guy, so you decided to go along with his suggestions.

CHAPTER FIVE

ATTITUDES
AND
BEHAVIOR

■

A Practical Demonstration of the Effect of Attitudes on Production
A Closer Examination of the Nature of Attitudes
The Effects of Attitudes
The Measurement of Attitudes   Experimental Findings
Ways to Improve Employee Opinions and Attitudes

■

PSYCHOLOGISTS ARE AWARE that an individual's attitudes are important factors that moderate how a stimulus/ situation is experienced. Therefore, knowing workers' attitudes can contribute to an understanding of how they react.

As we saw in Chapter 2, the behavior of an individual depends on the manner in which a stimulus or situation is experienced. The reactions of a plant manager, for example, may be quite different from those of a worker employed at that plant because each experiences the plant situation in a different way. As contingency theories demonstrate, we cannot even assume that the workers in that plant all will agree on the nature of this complex stimulus. But taking individual variations into account is impossible; therefore, it is of interest to determine whether there are common trends among employees, so that some guide to an understanding of work behavior may be obtained.

Before we deal with the general question of attitude, it is useful to know to what extent an employee's attitudes toward the company or plant, the manager, the immediate supervisor, or the other employees influences his or her behavior on the job. Managers who are interested only in obtaining a good day's work from each employee may feel that what the employees think about them or the company is irrelevant. Some employers are especially concerned with their employees' well being and take a personal interest in employees' attitudes toward their work situation. If the subject is to be a central concern of management, attitude must be shown to have a direct bearing on efficiency. That attitude may also bear on other problems will be seen when we consider its effect on labor relations, labor union activities, social legislation, and the quality of job applicants.

A PRACTICAL DEMONSTRATION OF THE EFFECT OF ATTITUDES ON PRODUCTION

THE HAWTHORNE STUDY

The pioneering research program undertaken by the Western Electric Company's Hawthorne Works clearly demonstrated the effect of employee attitude on production.[1] The experiments were begun to investigate the effects on production of such physical factors as temperature, humidity, lighting, rest pauses, and length of workday. An experimental room was designed in which a standard operation could be performed under varying conditions without disrupting the work of the remainder of the plant. The results of the preliminary studies revealed that the physical factors under investigation could not explain many of the results. Although the introduction of rest periods of varying lengths, rest periods with lunches, and different lengths of work periods showed trends in production that indicated their beneficial effects, a general upward trend not accounted for by these factors was evident. The general trend became very clear when removal of the favorable conditions did not result in a return of production to its previous level.

Analysis of the data revealed that more favorable work attitudes had gradually developed among employees. Because the experimental room was in the charge of an observer rather than a supervisor, the employees felt more free. They talked freely with him, and they developed confidence in the company. As a consequence, conversation between employees became more frequent, their social relationships were more friendly, social activities were carried on outside the work situation, absenteeism declined sharply (in one case, to nearly one-fourth of that outside the experimental room), and production rose.

Increased cooperation between employees was apparent from the fact that workers helped each other; when one had an off-day, another made up for it. Employees felt free to set their own pace. Although part of the cooperative effort was due to the fact that pay was based on the production of the group, this factor did not account for all the changes.

In another experiment in the same study, a fall in production was associated with a rumor that a job was to be moved from the Chicago plant to New Jersey. The feeling of insecurity caused by this rumor immediately had an effect on attitudes, and production fell, even though there was no conscious intent to reduce productivity and employees lowered their pay by doing so.

NEW INSIGHTS

The importance of attitude revealed in these experiments caused the investigation to take an entirely different turn. Emphasis was placed on improving supervision to obtain more favorable work attitudes, and an extensive program of employee interviewing was begun. Interviewers were trained to listen and to encourage free expression. They were careful not to take a stand on any issue and avoided any attempt to change an employee's point of view.

The interview material clearly showed that opinions about the company were influenced by home conditions (for example, indebtedness encouraged the opinion that pay was inadequate), by the employee's social position in the work group (the privileges and opportunities held in comparison with those of others), and by visible working conditions. The investigators began to realize that *the factory was a social as well as a work environment* and that these background conditions could not be ignored in the study of employee satisfactions and productivity.

The actual interviewing program had some immediately beneficial effects, in addition to furnishing insight and material for future investigation:

1. It allowed for correction of unfavorable work conditions. Although actual working conditions are known to managers, they do not know how employees feel about these conditions. This feeling is an important factor in efficiency.

2. It caused supervisors to realize that their methods were being studied, thus stimulating them to greater effort and interest in their work. The results of the study also aided in the selection and training of interviewers and furnished valuable case material to be used as a basis for the training of supervisors.

3. The employees benefited by the lift that they experienced. There was no question about the desirable effect of expressing their feelings and emotions freely. They saw improvements in working conditions where none had been made (for example, improved lighting); they also saw improvements in the skills of their boss.

To gain further understanding of some of the social factors, a final experiment was conducted. The experimental group of workers was again segregated in the experimental room, but the departmental supervisor was kept in charge. This time, the segregated group did not improve its proficiency. Although it developed a social structure, its informal organization resisted change. Incentive group pay in this case elicited different attitudes from those found in the previous experimental group. Such values as the following ones became apparent:

1. If you turn out too much work, you are a "rate buster."
2. If you turn out too little work, you are a "chiseler."
3. Do not tell the supervisor anything that will cause a peer to be punished, or you are a "squealer."
4. Do not act officious, or you are "for the company." According to this code, inspectors must not act like inspectors. If they do, there are many ways in which the worker can interfere with production to punish them.

THE PLANT AS A SOCIETY

Another interesting development at Hawthorne was the appearance of informal organizations and social hierarchies within the experimental room. Each kind of work acquired a social level, or status. Sometimes the mere location of the work (front or back of room) became a distinguishing feature, even if the work was the same. Other factors influencing the social status of the job were type of work, wages, vacations with or without pay, the kind of desk or work space, and any other feature that tended to go with one kind of work and not with another. Social meanings became attached to these distinguishing features, the meanings being derived from attitudes toward social status. The same words spoken by persons having different status had altogether different meanings. An office manager's mild criticism might be called a bawling-out, whereas a unit supervisor's violent criticism might be passed off almost unnoticed.

The workers also formed subgroups, and the social relationships of each individual in the room were almost entirely limited to that person's subgroup. As all members of a social group tend to have a common interest, the key integrating object in this case seemed to be the inspector. Workers having the same inspector tended to become a closed group. Since the grouping was not on the basis of social status, workers of varied social status appeared within each group. Although these groups developed different interests and different loyalties, the workers occupied social positions within the group according to their status. Those low in status accepted the role of "go-fer" and brought back hamburgers for high-status members.

Observations of this sort demonstrated the intricate informal structure that appears in any group of workers.[2] Whether members of this informal organization resist change or cooperate depends on the nature of the group, which in turn is affected by how the situation is handled. When actions taken by management respect the wishes of all persons involved, and when situations are open, responsible, and high in social status, cooperative behavior is most likely to appear. In a repressive atmosphere, workers know many ways to curtail productivity, the most common method being the limitation of each individual's production to a specified number of units per day.

SOME IMPLICATIONS

Recognizing the importance of the complex attitudes and the social factors in the work situation, the Hawthorne plant embarked on a counseling program.[3] The counselor had no jurisdiction over workers. The counselor could hear complaints, draw people out, help them understand themselves, and help supervisors understand many problem cases by drawing attention to certain factors in their lives or in the work situation.

Such counseling programs can lead a precarious existence because of their private nature. The programs at American Telephone and Telegraph, for example, have not survived. Subsidiaries within the system (which pioneered this approach) discontinued it after twelve to fifteen years. Varied factors led to dissatisfaction with the program. Many supervisors did not understand its purpose and saw the counselors as threats to their positions; top management wanted proof that the program was a paying proposition, and the counselors felt that this request infringed on their right to keep confidences; initiators and supporters of the program either retired or died.

None of the reasons for counseling programs' discontinuance at AT&T refutes the values gained from the Hawthorne study. Rather, they indicate that the applications of these research findings must become acceptable to company management. Three widespread effects of this research are: (1) training supervisors to understand employees better; (2) including trained counselors in personnel departments; and (3) expanding medical departments to include psychiatric help. The approach that seems to have gained the most acceptance by higher management is that of improving supervision. The content of management and supervisory training programs includes an increasing amount of behavioral science material.

A CLOSER EXAMINATION OF THE NATURE OF ATTITUDES

ATTITUDES AS A FRAME OF REFERENCE

Psychologically, an attitude is a mental set; it represents a predisposition to form certain opinions. If employees are asked what they think about the rate of pay, their answer is an opinion. Attitude, on the other hand, is more general and influences opinions. An unfavorable attitude toward the company will cause a worker to express a series of unfavorable opinions. Opinions on matters not covered by direct questions can be predicted, once knowledge of an attitude has been gained. If something happens to change the attitude, opinions on certain topics will show a marked modification.

In a sense, an attitude is a *frame of reference*. How a frame of reference influences our specific views can readily be illustrated by the diagrams in Figure 5.1. In these diagrams the interpretation of the inner figure depends on the outer frame. In *a* and *b,* the inner figures are the same, yet one appears as a diamond and the other as a square. The same geometrical figure can be either a square or diamond, depending on how it is framed. If we think of the inner figure as a given objective fact (the rate of pay, for example), the diamond as a favorable opinion (pay is good), and the square as an unfavorable opinion (pay is too low), then it follows that our opinion of the objective fact depends on the frame of reference. This outer frame corresponds to one's attitude, which may be *liking* or *disliking* the company. The attitude toward the company as well as the rate of pay influences the opinion expressed about pay.

When a individual's frame of reference is discovered and added to a knowledge of that person's values and personality, we can often predict the opinions that the individual will hold or the judgments that the individual will be likely to make under specific circumstances. Models based on this social judgment theory have been used to describe and analyze business and political events and behavior.[4]

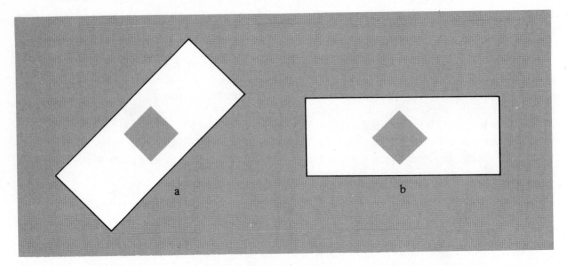

FIGURE 5.1 THE INFLUENCE OF A FRAME OF REFERENCE

Just as the frame gives specific meaning to the inner figure, so an attitude determines an opinion. A change in attitude may radically change opinions. When a person's attitude toward the company changes from an unfavorable to a favorable one, opinions about the company's pay, training methods, and promotion opportunities tend to improve.

Source: After K. Koffka, *Principles of Gestalt Psychology,* 1935, p. 185, with permission of Routledge & Kegan Paul, Ltd.

ATTITUDES, FACTS, AND OPINIONS

When attitudes are treated as a frame of reference, they become a general background of feeling against which factual events can be viewed. Thus, attitudes form frames of reference that supply the unique loading of feeling and emotion to our perceptions of things and events. Usually we classify attitudes as favorable or unfavorable. For example, there are favorable or unfavorable attitudes toward races, political parties, social groupings, religious denominations, labor unions, and work groups, which means that we view members of such groups with either friendly or unfriendly eyes. Other examples of attitudes are conservatism or liberalism in economic issues, trust or suspicion of employees in general,[5] and a feeling of superiority or inferiority to other groups of people.

Opinions, however, are specific in that they refer to an interpretation of some particular event, behavior, or object. To say that a rate of pay is unfair, that a law puts labor or management at a disadvantage, that corporation taxes are too high, that employees do not do a good day's work, or that behavior on the picket line is disorderly, is to express opinions.

Opinions represent an *evaluation,* not a *description,* of the factual evidence. They are always interpretations, and in this sense the individual adds something to the objective events in question. When these interpretations have an emotional loading, the framework is largely one of attitude, whereas when the interpretations lack emotional content, the framework is largely intellectual. *Because behavior is a response to the organism's interpretations, opinions determine behavior regardless of whether the opinion is justified.*

UNDERSTANDING THE BEHAVIOR OF INDIVIDUAL EMPLOYEES

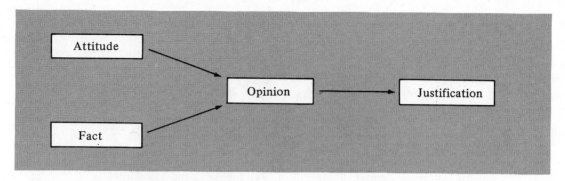

FIGURE 5.2 FACTORS CONTRIBUTING TO OPINIONS
A given opinion represents an interpretation of facts, but the nature of this interpretation depends on the attitude of the individual. However, when people are asked why they have a particular opinion, they are likely to give a justification. The opinion causes the justification; the justification does not describe the cause of the opinion.

Figure 5.2 shows the functional relationships between facts, attitudes, and opinions. It is important to note that an opinion is preceded and influenced by facts, and/or attitudes; although an attitude is like a generalization, it is not to be confused with a generalized conclusion. In other words, opinions do not lead to attitudes; opinions reflect attitudes, and attitudes can be detected from expressed opinions.

It should also be noted that justifications are the product of opinions and should not be confused with their cause. A justification is an individual's defense of an opinion, and the nature of the defense depends on the opinion to be defended. When the opinion changes, the defense changes, but a destruction of the defense does not destroy the opinion.

The relative influence of facts and attitudes in shaping opinions may vary from one extreme to another. A supervisor who has an attitude of suspicion toward employees in general interprets a worker's inactivity as *loafing*. Such an opinion could be based almost entirely on attitude, and there need be little or no factual support of this interpre-

tation. At the other extreme, an opinion such as *"increased lighting will cut down our errors,"* may represent an opinion influenced almost entirely by facts.

Opinions based largely on facts offer no problem. Such opinions change readily when conditions or facts are altered. But opinions based on attitudes constitute a particular problem because unfavorable attitudes can continue even after the facts have been corrected. The suspicious supervisor who accused a worker of loafing will not change this opinion even after finding that the worker has completed all the work, but will simply continue to watch for an instance of loafing.

THE EFFECTS OF ATTITUDES

ATTITUDES DETERMINE MEANINGS

Disagreements over the nature of a given set of facts are possible because attitudes influence the way that facts are experienced. Our various prejudices offer many illustrations of attitudes that determine the meanings that facts may assume. The actual facts that conflict with a prejudice are rationalized to fit with the general attitude; this rationalization protects the attitude from change. The following excerpt describes how some people might react to factual information about Mr. Miller, who is Jewish.

An individual's attitude toward women managers may sometimes be hidden or unrecognized by the individual. (The Wool Bureau)

> If Mr. Miller succeeds in business, that "proves" that "Jews" are "smart"; if Mr. Johansen succeeds in business, it only proves that Mr. Johansen is smart. If Mr. Miller fails in business, it is alleged that he nevertheless has "money salted away somewhere." If Mr. Miller is strange or foreign in his habits, that "proves" that "Jews don't assimilate." If he is thoroughly American — that is, indistinguishable from other natives — he is "trying to pass himself off as one of us." If Mr. Miller fails to give to charity, that is because "Jews are tight"; if he gives generously, he is "trying to buy his way into society." If Mr. Miller lives in the Jewish section of town, that is because "Jews are so clannish"; if he moves to a locality where there are no other Jews, that is because "they try to horn in everywhere." In short, Mr. Miller is automatically condemned, no matter who he is or what he does.[6]

More recently, reactions similar to those concerning Mr. Miller have been found among male managers who were evaluating the success of female managers. Success which was ascribed to skill or intelligence when male managers were involved, was ascribed to luck or the favorable prejudice of others when achieved by female managers.[7] In another instance, a male middle-manager who considered himself unbiased in his attitude toward women was asked to join an after-hours poker game. He was interested until he heard that a woman engineer with whom he worked would also be in the group. "Working with her is one thing," he said, "but if she gets lucky and wins some of my money, I couldn't take it." The idea that she might win because of greater skill never occurred to him. In these instances, the meaning of the behavior was largely determined by the attitude, as opposite behaviors (facts) were given similar (bad) meanings.

The degree to which meanings are determined by attitudes varies, but the meanings and importance of things are always influenced by attitudes. We cannot dismiss distortions of meaning by calling people prejudiced or ignorant. Prejudice is someone else's unfavorable attitude. To have attitudes is human. Criticizing people for having prejudice causes defensive behavior and increases their rationalizations.

How do attitudes influence behaviors on the job? A particular manager, Chuck Brown, believes that business gives jobs to people and that people ought to be appreciative and give a full day's work in return for a full day's pay. Another manager, Kathy James, believes that business needs employees to get its job done and that it is her job to build up a good team. Both Chuck Brown and Kathy James are presented with the following facts:

1. Labor turnover has increased 30 percent in the last two years.
2. Tardiness and absenteeism are greater for employees under 20 than for those 30 or over.
3. Employees resent being told that they cannot use company phones for personal calls.
4. Nearly 50 percent of the employees are from one to five minutes late when returning from their rest pauses.

If we imagine ourselves to be first Brown and then James, we will realize the differences in meaning that these facts will have for the two managers, as well as the differing effects on their subsequent behavior.

ATTITUDES RECONCILE CONTRADICTIONS

Many people hold what appear to be conflicting opinions. Such apparent contradictions in thinking are not always due to lack of intelligence, as is frequently supposed. They are made possible by the development of certain attitudes. With the proper attitude as a background, intelligent people can reconcile what to others are obvious contradictions. It is possible, for example, for one person to hold any of the following pairs of opinions, which another person would see as contradictory:

- ☐ a. I'm saving enough money so that I'll have a good income when I retire.
- ☐ b. I'm underpaid and can't live the way someone in my position should.
- ☐ a. A person ought to be put in his place if he does the wrong thing.
- ☐ b. My boss had no business making a fuss over the small oversight I made.
- ☐ a. I started smoking when I was sixteen.
- ☐ b. My boy is only a junior in high school, and he's too young to smoke.
- ☐ a. Responsibility helps a person grow up.
- ☐ b. The trouble with employees today is that they won't take orders.

This phenomenon of contradictory opinions was further explored in a study by B. M. Staw.[8] When the people in an experiment were confronted with data indicating that one of their past decisions had been a poor one, they reconciled the contradiction between the error and their self-respect by altering their expressed attitude so as to redefine the poor alternative in a more favorable way. When offered the chance to choose again, they were even more likely than before to choose the alternative that the evidence had shown to be inferior.

When we recognize that many of our beliefs are based on attitudes, we are likely to react more reasonably because we do not suffer from righteous indignation. We can be tolerant of another's viewpoint if we know that we are both prejudiced. If each of us insists on being right, we merely become more prejudiced.

When a supervisor characterizes a work stoppage as loafing and the worker considers it resting, the difference in meaning is based on difference in position. When a manager thinks a certain employee is the logical one to be transferred, will that employee accept the reasons? These are important everyday problems in business. We cannot prove to another logically that our interpretation is *the* right one. Rather, the cause of the difference (that is, the attitude) must be altered if a meeting of minds is to occur.

Similar to attitudes that give rise to opinions of superiority are attitudes that differentiate opinions concerning in- and out-groups. Persons who belong to one social group (union, church, or even race) are judged differently from those outside that group. The differential attitude toward the out-group is not so unfavorable as it would be toward an inferior group; nevertheless, sympathy and tolerance tend to be denied to the outsider. It takes less evidence to prove that persons outside the group are incapable of performing their duties or are unworthy of help and protection than it does to prove the same things about members of the group. Loyalties and prejudices are frequently in-group and out-group attitudes, respectively, and although they are prevalent and normal, they must be listed as sources of error in arriving at objectively sound conclusions.[9]

ATTITUDES ORGANIZE FACTS

It is difficult to see a set of facts and then refrain from grouping or organizing them in a certain way. For example, a list of words, such as *uniforms, boots, messkits,* and *jeeps,* tends to become organized conceptually: they suggest soldiers on military maneuvers. This suggestion becomes a frame of reference into which the above elements are fitted, and the individual words derive additional meaning from their relationships to the frame of reference. The word *uniforms* receives a style and a meaning that go be-

yond the given facts. This is Stage 1 of Figure 5.3. If we next add the words *tents, maps,* and *binoculars* to the list, it may be perceived as suggesting an upcoming attack on the enemy. These added items serve to elaborate the meanings of the first list of words. The addition of the word *back-packs* to the list might cause some uneasiness in the perception, but by some adjustments, the phrase can be reconciled as appropriate to a long march. Thus, in Stage 3, the frame of reference is modified to include *back-packs,* but the change is awkward — more of a patch job. But once the adjustment is made, the war scene suffers no dissonance. However, if we add just the word *Scoutmaster* to the list, a sudden reorganization of the frame of reference occurs: the military encampment changes into a Boy Scout overnight campout. The boots are for hiking, not marching; the maps show the way to secret fishing holes; and the binoculars are for sighting birds, not enemy soldiers. This shift in meaning came suddenly, and the uncertainty of meanings caused by some entries (such as *back-packs*) is eliminated by the new frame of reference.

Let us transfer this stage procedure to a business situation in which an employee who for some time had been receiving the top rate of pay for his job classification went to the supervisor of the group to complain about wages. During the interview, the worker made the following statements:

> The only pay increases that I have had in ten years are those where the top rate has been raised. Everyone gets those increases. I think that I should get an increase once in a while that isn't due to the top being raised.
>
> A person with a good attendance record should be given an increase for that reason alone.
>
> New people come into the office, and

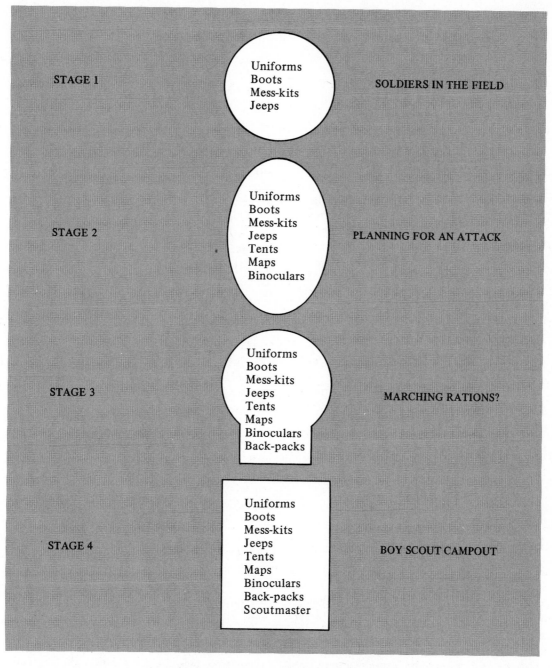

FIGURE 5.3 ATTITUDES ORGANIZE FACTS

The same words are experienced differently when the frame of reference is changed. Stages 2 and 3 represent minor changes in meanings caused by additional items, but the addition of incongruous words in Stage 4 requires a reorganization, which results in a change in meanings of the initial items. Shifts in attitude are equivalent to such reorganizations.

they get increases whether they are any good or not.

Lots of people working for the company get more money than I do, and I'm just as good as they are.

I know someone like me who works for another company and gets $170 a month more. This company is making lots of money now, and if others can pay those salaries, so can this company.

I have had to fight for every raise I ever got, and that's what I'm doing now.

You brought a new worker into our group the other day. If you had given the rest of us in the group a raise, then we would work harder and you wouldn't need to hire anyone.

If there's no more money for me here, why don't you transfer me? They have lots of good jobs in other departments, and they don't work as hard as I do.

You don't want me here. You just want young people. I'm getting old so I guess that I should get out.

(Crying) No one pays any attention to me any more.

All my troubles seem to have started since my mother died last year. Since then things haven't gone good for me.

If I could find a roommate for my apartment, maybe things would be better, but I can't find anyone I like.

I won't be working very long anyway. I'm buying a savings bond every week and that has mounted up, and with my pension I can get along all right.

At the outset, these statements appeared both unreasonable and unrelated. Toward the end of the interview, however, the supervisor may have concluded that this worker was lonely. This new frame of reference (looking at the employee as a lonely individual, rather than as an old grouch) caused all the statements to make a new kind of sense. In this frame of reference, the worker's talk about a pay raise that others don't get now communicates a need for personal attention, not a problem of giving him an individual pay raise over the top rate.

Another example of misinterpretation possible in a business situation follows. When a group of older employees has been described by a prejudiced supervisor as having an equal production rate but as being less friendly, the implication may be that they are less satisfactory. The reasons implied are that despite all their experience, they produce no more than a younger group, and that in addition, they are hard to get along with. Given a supervisor with a friendly attitude, the same description may mean highly satisfactory — the reasons implied being that the older workers do just as well as the younger ones despite age, and that in addition, they are more businesslike and less prone to socializing on the job. Thus, the frame of reference determines the meaning that the terms are given. Conflicting interpretations of the same facts are a common basis for arguments.

ATTITUDES SELECT FACTS

In addition to organizing facts, an attitude also selects them. From a mass of objective information, people tend to select the facts that favor or are more consistent with their attitudes, and to ignore or discount those opposed. Like perception, an attitude is analogous to a filter or a screen: certain materials can pass through it and others cannot. For example, persons with a positive attitude toward a race, a religion, a political party, or a company will select from the known facts only those that are congruent with their attitude and will ignore those that are not. They then use these selected facts to prove the correctness of their attitudes. In turn, persons with a negative attitude may select from the same body of information but tend to use only the facts that support their point of view.

An experiment involving simulated conflicts in attitude showed that people select the facts that support their attitude and use those facts as reasons for the attitude.[10] Even when one of the persons is cued to be a good listener and to be understanding rather than persuasive, selection still occurs. Because biased persons are often unreasonable and tend to mention only the facts that support their position, it is difficult for others to remain neutral. As a result, in a short time they interpose the previously unmentioned facts. Thus, they select the facts supporting the opposite position and behave like biased individuals. In this way, prejudiced people trap reasonable ones into behaving at their level.

Disagreements and failures to communicate in organizations are frequently not due merely to conflicting information but to conflicting meanings resulting from differing points of view or conflicting goals. In dealing with others, supervisors and managers should remember that *another person's attitude is not effectively changed by an opponent's selection of facts.*

THE MEASUREMENT OF ATTITUDES

To analyze the factors that influence attitudes scientifically, it is necessary to obtain some objective measurement of attitudes. Some discussion of techniques will further clarify the nature of attitudes, as well as exemplify methods that have been used in business.

The simplest method of measuring attitudes is merely to count the number of people who are for or against something. This approach does not measure the degree of feeling in any individual but registers only the direction of the attitude. When groups of people are studied, however, the number of people having a given attitude is some index of its strength. This measure is essentially what the political poll takers accomplish in their analyses. It is possible, though, that a large number of people might be mildly opposed to something, but would not be greatly disturbed if they had to accept it; or a smaller group might be strongly opposed to it, and its adoption might cause a violent minority reaction. In such cases, the number of people holding an opinion would not accurately indicate its actual social significance.

To make possible a study of the strength of attitudes in the individual, more refined instruments of measurement are needed. Such instruments can be exemplified by the *attitude scale* devised by L. L. Thurstone.[11] In making up such a scale, a large number of statements bearing on the topic of the attitude to be measured are collected. These statements are then experimentally analyzed, and those that are ambiguous or do not differentiate positions for or against the issue involved are discarded. Each accepted statement is then assigned a value determined experimentally. The statements that strongly favor the issue receive a value at one extreme of the scale, whereas those strongly opposed receive a value at the opposite extreme.

To measure the attitudes of a group of people, each person is asked to place a plus sign in front of all items that they agree with, and a minus sign in front of all the others. A person's score is the *average* of the scale value of all items checked with a plus sign. Low and high scores give the boundaries of the range of attitude.

In measuring attitudes, we actually explore a set of opinions; when such a set leans in a particular direction (favorable or unfavorable) it indicates the influence of an attitude. Thus, the attitude score is derived from measures of opinions in a limited feeling area.

Projective approaches to attitude measurement are sometimes used when the respondents are unable to describe their feelings accurately, when they are hesitant about expressing themselves, or when they may not cooperate if the topic under consideration is made explicit. Such approaches encourage openness since they do not require people to talk about themselves or to state their feelings and views directly.[12] Among the projective methods most frequently used are techniques in which the respondent is asked to complete sentences,[13] arguments, or descriptions of people who would behave in specified ways. Further refinement of these approaches to attitude measurement is necessary, along with caution in using such data. Some feel that such indirect measures constitute an unwarranted invasion of the individual's privacy unless the respondent has been informed about the general purpose of the items.

Businesses cannot afford to make radical changes that may backfire. Because attitude scales can indicate changes in attitude, they can be used during change processes to measure progress or the lack of it (see, for example, the flex-time study cited in Chapter 1).

EXPERIMENTAL FINDINGS

SOME TYPICAL RESULTS OF STUDIES OF ATTITUDES

Attitude measurement has revealed that a single experience, such as a movie, can sometimes alter expressed attitudes on racial,[14] social, and economic questions.[15] Other findings have shown that (1) unemployment disturbs former religious and economic values;[16] (2) radical students are more inclined to be highly intelligent than nonradical ones, although children of professional classes tend to be conservatives;[17] (3) a speech given in person is more effective in influencing attitudes than the same speech given over the radio, whereas the latter is more effective than the same speech read in a newspaper;[18] (4) judgments made by an individual in a two-person group were more strongly influenced by the other member when the person was a stranger rather than a friend or acquaintance;[19] (5) support for civil liberties is significantly associated with the increase of years of higher education;[20] (6) beliefs can be changed as a result of posthypnotic suggestion;[21] (7) shifts in attitude, when they occur, often go from negative to positive agreement without an intermediate stand in the neutral position;[22] (8) radical attitudes are more difficult to modify than conservative attitudes.

Social psychologists continue to devote considerable study to the means by which attitudes are developed and by which they can be changed.[23] One approach is Festinger's theory of cognitive dissonance. This theory holds that persons who know various items of information that do not fit together psychologically (for them) will attempt to make these dissonant items more consistent.[24] In other words, when our experiences do not agree with expectations that we have accumulated throughout a lifetime, we try to reduce the inconsistency. We may change our attitudes or opinions; in fact, we may even go so far as to distort our perceptions or the information we receive regarding the world about us.

One phenomenon, illustrated in a variety of experiments, shows how attitudes may change once an irrevocable choice has been made between two attractive alternatives. In this instance, we tend to experience an increase in the desirability of the chosen alternative, a decrease in the attractiveness of the rejected alternative, or both. In this fashion, we make our attitudes toward the alternatives more consistent or less dissonant with our choice than would be the case if the alternatives continued to be viewed as equally attractive.

ATTITUDES BASED ON INFORMATION VERSUS THOSE BASED ON EMOTIONAL INVESTMENT

Much of the research on attitude and opinion change uses topics of an unemotional nature. A topic such as "Is the Electoral College necessary?" would elicit little emotional response from most people. Thus, propaganda and logic presented for or against the topic might generate opinions having no deep-seated emotional investment. Attitudes developed by rational appeals might successfully be reversed by additional facts or logic.[25]

Generally speaking, attempts to change attitudes (measured before and after exposure to biased writings) are temporary and depend on the perceived credibility of the propaganda[26] and the speaker. Attitudes already held are more easily strengthened than changed by supplying more information.[27]

When participants are required to write their own argument on an issue rather than to read a supplied argument, opinion change is greater and more persistent, thus demonstrating the value of participation.[28] Another study showed that expressed opinions are more resistant to change than those privately held.[29] Thus, committing oneself tends to make opinions more rigid.

Fear is a more effective tool in influencing behavior than in changing attitude. A number of variables affect whether a strong fear is more effective in a situation rather than a mild fear.[30] For example, attitudes toward dental hygiene are influenced more by mild fear appeals ("If you don't brush, you'll have more cavities") than by intense fear statements ("If you don't brush, your teeth will fall out"). On the other hand, information regarding the loss of eyesight, which induced relatively high fear levels, was effective in influencing behavior.[31]

ATTITUDES WITH STRONG EMOTIONAL INVESTMENT

Attitudes against war are more resistant to change through propaganda than attitudes toward margarine as a substitute for butter. The former is likely to require an emotional investment and the latter is not.[32] Emotionally loaded attitudes resist rational and persuasive approaches, and it is not uncommon for them to be strengthened rather than weakened by such approaches.

Unfavorable attitudes often stem from unhappy experiences and frustration. A single experience, such as being beaten and robbed, can develop a strong negative attitude toward crime that will resist logic.[33] Information and social factors tend not to alter these attitudes unless they remove the source. Changes in attitudes having such origins may be effected by therapy.[34]

ATTITUDES BASED
ON GROUP AFFILIATION

We cannot determine all the factors that influence the formation of attitudes. Data collected from public opinion polls indicate that opinions vary with a number of factors. A striking difference in political and economic opinions can be obtained when respondents are grouped according to income, age, geographical location, size of community, amount of education, party affiliation, and religious denomination. The influence of family is apparent when we see that most people adhere to the religion of their parents, and that more people hold political affiliations similar to those of their parents than different from them.

If Mr. and Mrs. Jones were to describe accurately why they are Republicans, they could include among their reasons that it is because they have a good income, live in a prosperous section of the community, are beyond middle age, come from Republican homes, wish to identify themselves with the Republican status group, and so on. Such reasons are seldom given, however. The Joneses are more likely to say that they vote Republican because that party has the best candidates, the best program for developing the country, the best foreign policy, and so on. When people are asked about their opinions, they do not mention an attitude as a factor, but instead present a set of justifications (refer again to Figure 5.2).

When attitudes are not based on facts, arguing (introducing new facts and appealing to logic) has little effect on them. If our mythical Joneses were to suffer a great financial loss or to move to another section of the country, these factors could do more to alter their frame of reference than a change in the party's foreign or domestic policy.

The factors given above as causes of attitudes obviously indicate kinds of experience. Furthermore, the factors all suggest some type of group membership, from a loose one like a community to a close one like a family.[35] Attitudes are acquired from the groups with which individuals identify themselves. As this identification occurs early in life, it follows that children will have opinions on religious problems, on the relative capabilities of a party's political candidates, and on racial relations before they learn many facts. S. E. Asch points out that one reason group values and attitudes are adopted is that members feel that the group protects and promotes their interests.[36]

Various experiments have demonstrated how people are influenced by the attitudes or opinions of others. H. H. Kelley and C. Woodruff found that students were more influenced by a speech heard from outside the lecture room when told that the applause stemmed from their own faculty than when told that the applause emanated from an unknown group.[37] H. T. Moore found that 50 percent of a group of students changed their judgments about ethical matters when told (correctly or incorrectly) that the majority opinion was opposed to theirs.[38] Information about the opinion of experts had a like effect. Similar research by M. Sherif demonstrated that the prestige of authors influenced people's judgment of literary contributions.[39] Attitudes toward food purchases[40] and even confidence in the stability of business are influenced by what others think, so we have come to realize that economic laws must be modified to incorporate psychological components.[41]

Although group membership alone does not form attitudes, it is one of the more important forces. This fact suggests ways of influencing attitudes. Workers' attitudes toward the company usually change when

UNDERSTANDING THE BEHAVIOR OF INDIVIDUAL EMPLOYEES

they are promoted from worker to union steward or supervisor.[42] It also follows that if all employees *and first-line supervisors* are called "hourly" employees, whereas higher management personnel are called "salaried," first-line supervisors will develop attitudes different from those of other members of management. Classifying or grouping people is often necessary, but we should recognize that doing this affects attitudes.

An individual's attitudes developed by membership in one group might be altered most effectively by a change in group. Thus, attending college is a crucial factor in changing a student's attitudes.[43] Persons who conform most to group norms are least likely to be persuaded by appeals against them.[44]

INDIVIDUAL DIFFERENCES

Disregarding the cause and nature of attitudes and opinions, we might reasonably expect considerable individual variation. It has been found that authoritarian personalities are more influenced by remarks of authoritarian figures than by information booklets; for nonauthoritarian personalities, the reverse is true.[45] Persons who can be classified as creative or abstract thinkers are more inclined to seek information and are less vulnerable to persuasive appeals than concrete thinkers.[46] All things being equal, people are influenced more when the communicator is someone with whom listeners can identify. Thus the type of appeal and the nature of the communicator determine the effectiveness of attitude-influencing media, such as propaganda and advertising.

Although people differ in their attitudes, experiments have uncovered several facts about how they can be influenced. Since some opinions are primarily based on facts, it is not surprising that such opinions will be altered by new information. Attitudes developed by culture and group membership form emotional ties (security, affiliation, loyalty) and are influenced little by persuasion methods, regardless of whether the logic and facts used are accurate or misleading. The logic of feeling is different from the logic of intellect, and for this reason the intellectual approach has little effect. Attitudes developed through frustration have strong emotional loadings and can influence opinions that may have no basis in fact.

WAYS TO IMPROVE EMPLOYEE OPINIONS AND ATTITUDES

COMMON PRACTICES

Attitude surveys are now an accepted practice; trade magazines as well as the more technical journals frequently contain reports of significant findings. Although surveys made in different companies often yield similar results, each company must make its own survey to be clear about the types and areas of improvement needed. Survey findings can open the door to correcting unpopular practices, but they must be properly reported and interpreted. One approach involves management personnel in analysis of survey data to faciliate both communication and adequate use of findings at all levels within the organization.[47]

Attitude surveys measure symptoms, not causes. Unless properly used, attitude and opinion polls can lead to inappropriate action. A large corporation has investigated some of their experiences with attitude surveys and the meaning behind the resulting data.[48] In one work group studied, employees registered unfavorable opinions about their pay schedule. From the findings, one logical conclusion might be that they were dissatisfied with their pay rates. After some carefully planned group discussion aimed at identifying and resolving problems evidenced by the survey, however, the manager learned that employees were not dissatisfied with their pay but were critical of the way in which a related procedure was handled. In this group, merit interviews and salary changes were annual, but not for all employees at the same time. Employees not interviewed at a given period felt conspicuous by their exclusion from the interview routine, and were distressed that others in the office might make baseless inferences about their competence and merit. The group wanted the routine changed to provide for interviewing all employees during each period, despite the fact that only part of the group wbuld be scheduled for increases. This change was made, and the problem disappeared. The effectiveness of this problem solving was confirmed one year later when another attitude survey reflected no criticism of pay-related matters in this group.

In another example, workers were critical of their supervisor on a survey question about his "interest in his employees." Confronted with this kind of data, supervisors may become defensive and rationalize the criticism. Even if they accept the data, they can usually think of a host of possible explanations. In this case, the supervisor used group methods to identify and solve problems reflected in the survey. The real problem identified by the group was a unique form of insecurity. The group's work was a service provided to others, somewhat intangible and difficult to assess in terms of measurable results. The employees generally worked alone and on their own; they felt unsure about their performance and competence. They wanted the supervisor to do

more observing of their performance and to provide coaching and counseling on job techniques. The final decision also included provisions for mutual assistance among the group members, with emphasis on having senior employees help newer ones become more proficient.

In contrast to these cases, managers usually react to attitude surveys by taking the results too literally, or by acting on guesses about their meaning. Countless water coolers have been installed, parking lots assigned, procedures adopted, procedures revised, decisions made, decisions rescinded, dollars spent, facilities shuffled, and jobs reorganized on the basis of *assumptions* drawn from survey results that had little or nothing to do with the real problems. *Attitude surveys reveal only that something is wrong in the work place; they do not reveal what it is or what to do.*

Surveys reveal the importance of the immediate supervisor as well as higher levels of management in influencing employee attitudes.[49] Regardless of whether the attitudes are justified, they influence the behavior of those holding them. That attitudes about supervisors are influenced by their behavior is indicated by the similarity of attitudes among persons working for the same supervisor on different jobs, but the lack of similarity of attitudes among persons working for different supervisors on the same job.[50]

The interview method, when properly handled, is highly effective in detecting the general attitude of specific employees, even though it is not reliable for obtaining factual information. So that the interview may yield an accurate expression of attitude, the interviewer must shape the inquiry to harmonize with the interests of the person being interviewed. The sharing of attitudes in a business interview presupposes the presence of a common goal. Obviously, employees will not express honest opinions if they run the risk of putting themselves at a disadvantage by volunteering certain attitudes, or if they feel they are being cross-examined. The interview is particularly valuable in that it takes the whole individual into account rather than giving information on certain attitudes out of context.[51]

CHANGING FACTS TO IMPROVE OPINIONS

In one company, the records of thirteen employees were examined. They were regarded as qualified for supervisory positions but had been rejected because of their hostile attitudes toward the company. All had been told by their supervisors that if they improved their attitudes, they could be promoted. However, none showed an improvement. In eight cases, the attitudes seemed to stem from the experience of having been passed over for promotion; in the other instances, the source of the attitudes could not be traced. The goal of promotion would not change attitudes, but changing the facts might do so. The eight whose attitude seemed to be related to lack of promotion were promoted. All became above-average supervisors with improved attitudes.

In another company, a bell was the signal for a rest pause; it was a source of annoyance because employees, many of whom were just out of high school where class bells had been used, saw it as regimentation. Replacing the bell with musical chimes reduced the negative reaction. If employees grumble about food in the company restaurant, complain of the heat, or call their jobs boring, it is possible to effect changes that will cause such opinions to become more favorable. However, employees with unfavorable attitudes can always find something to criticize, so the opinions expressed by employees in interviews, polls, or suggestion boxes

should be studied carefully before introducing reforms. As the boss is an important factor in shaping employee attitudes, changes in supervisory behavior or management procedures represent ways of influencing attitudes because such changes alter the facts of the employees' lives.

INFLUENCING THE EXPERIENCE OF GROUP MEMBERSHIP

Because attitudes are greatly influenced by the experience of belonging to a group, anything a company does to make employees feel that they are a vital part of the organization should improve attitudes toward the company. The following are a few of many possible ways:

1. Stock-purchase or profit-sharing plans properly administered
2. Concern for the welfare of employees as evidenced by clean rest rooms, medical aid, concern for job satisfaction, and so on
3. Regulations and benefits that apply similarly to all employees
4. Creation of a climate making employees feel they are group members

USE OF ROLE-PLAYING

Role-playing is used in various kinds of training situations, one of its functions being that of developing attitudes consistent with the training objectives.[52] In these instances, individuals simulate real-life situations and trainees are placed in either supervisory or employee positions to give them the experience of approaching and viewing problems from different positions.[53]

Another use of role-playing is shown in the following case. An employee was suspended by his immediate supervisor (on the advice of the superintendent) pending the return of the manager from an executive training program. The employee had an unusually long list of demerits, ranging from excessive tardiness to frequent violations of regulations, including safety. He had received three written warnings, but the supervisor was reluctant to dismiss him because the union usually came to his rescue.

This firm's policy prior to a dismissal was to have a meeting in which union and management representatives heard the company's case, then heard the employee's version. The manager had received interpersonal-relations training, and handled this meeting somewhat differently. He asked the three supervisors involved to take the role of union members, and the three union representatives were asked to take the role of management. The case was then heard. Each group of three persons then held private discussions, and each returned with a unanimous recommendation. The union representatives, in the role of management, recommended dismissal; the supervisors, in the role of union representatives, recommended full pay for the suspension period and one more chance.

The manager then asked the six participants to return to their real-life roles and try to agree on an action. With little difficulty, the group agreed the employee should be clearly informed that he had one more chance and that he would be discharged after the next infraction. He was to receive his pay for the suspension period.

When the employee learned of the action he resigned. It appears that when he found that the union was no longer willing to get him out of trouble, he lost interest in pursuing his troublemaking activities. The manager felt the role-playing laid the groundwork for improved communication between the union representatives and the supervisors.

USE OF LISTENING SKILLS

Listening as a means of changing attitudes was referred to earlier in connection with the Hawthorne study.[54] This skill has been recognized as a first step in improving adjustment[55] and as an essential technique in interviewing.[56]

With the employee who expressed dissatisfaction with pay (pages 102 and 104), the real problem was loneliness. The supervisor discovered this state of mind by being understanding and listening to the ideas and feelings that the employee expressed. Because the supervisor did not challenge any of the worker's statements, the latter was able to move from one feeling to another until he realized his problem.

If the supervisor had argued with the employee, the real problem would not have been uncovered. Arguing has the opposite effect that listening has, because progress in the expression of different feelings is blocked if each point that an employee makes is challenged. Then the employee begins to express only points that are safe instead of those that are important. The fact that the employee felt free to express feelings led to their clarification, and this brought about a change in the feelings and in the attitudes associated with them.

The understanding attitude of the supervisor also made the employee feel accepted and less alone in the world. Evidence of an attitude change on the employee's part was revealed by the fact that the supervisor was thanked for the visit, and that the employee left in a positive frame of mind. Furthermore, the worker took steps to correct the situation by moving into an apartment building and by attending company parties. He became friendly with other workers and was soon accepted by them. All these improvements were not due solely to the interview itself, but depended also on the subsequent behavior of the supervisor, whose attitude too was changed. Now seeing the employee as a lonely person, the supervisor's behavior reflected greater concern (for example, more frequent talks, some special assignments). This altered behavior represented a change in *facts* for the employee.

The group setting may offer even better opportunities to listen, particularly when members agree and support one another. The feedback session is an example. A supervisor will find that if a group meeting is held for the purpose of discussing problems, the members will become less hostile and a soluble problem may be uncovered.

USE OF DISCUSSION SKILLS

Closely related to the use of listening to change attitudes is employment of the discussion method (see also Chapter 8). Properly conducted discussions create an opportunity for members of a group to express their feelings. In this way, attitudes toward fair distribution of overtime, favoritism, seniority privileges, introduction of changes, abuse of coffee-break privileges, and so on, emerge. In addition to clarifying attitudes and correcting some misunderstandings, discussions also introduce group-membership forces. Employees who feel that they are not getting a fair deal on overtime may find their needs for extra pay less justified than the needs of others in the group. They may also learn more about the problems faced by the supervisor, discover that there are viewpoints other than their own, and find they have responsibilities toward others.

Group discussion also uses the principle of involvement. A. J. Marrow and J. R. P. French describe how management personnel changed their strongly entrenched hostile attitude toward older women employees when the supervisors participated in planning and executing relevant research.[57] Similarly, labor unions have been found to take a constructive attitude toward improving production when they participate in solving problems in the area.[58] Another study[59] compared the lecture method (persuasion) with the group discussion method in reducing bias in the way supervisors appraised the work of employees. The lecture failed to accomplish change, whereas the discussion method reduced bias significantly.

In assessing the possibilities of discussion as a method of improving attitudes, it should be recognized that attitudes of management personnel as well as those of employees are involved. One supervisor was critical of drivers because they returned their trucks to the garage before five o'clock. Discussion revealed that the drivers were competing for parking spots in the garage, since the last drivers in had to park outside. The supervisor, on learning this, felt better about the drivers, and several solutions became obvious.

Supervisors can also profit from skillfully led meetings held to discuss common problems. Discovering that no one answer is right and that misunderstandings rather than the perversity of human nature cause most problems, airing one's feelings in a constructive situation, and experiencing security in a group — all operate to foster improved attitudes that provide a more favorable climate for the solution of problems.[60]

The fact that members of a group have similar attitudes should not mislead us into assuming that this similarity is caused by group membership. T. M. Newcomb demonstrated that persons with similar attitudes are attracted to one another.[61] Perhaps the most accurate statement of the influence of group membership is that people receive greatest satisfaction through affiliating with those who hold similar attitudes, and that such persons have the most influence on their subsequent attitudes. Thus, changes in group attitudes become an interactive process.

PERSUASION

The most common procedures used in attempts to change attitudes are argument, debates, and selling approaches. They have one thing in common: they make one point of view appear in a favorable light while the opposing viewpoints are made to appear unfavorable. The tendency is to exaggerate the two extremes and to make it appear that no middle ground exists.

Attribution theory (discussed in Chapter 3) offers an explanation for some of the cognitive processes involved in persuasion. This explanation suggests that the persuasiveness of a message is mediated by the hearer's attributions of the reason why the speaker advocates a particular position. A message seen as "what one might expect" is less likely to change the listener's mind than a stand that is seen as unexpected. If a rich person advocates the lowering of taxes, people see the message as based on self-interest and are not persuaded. When the speaker advocates a change in a tax law that may cost him or her money, listeners are more apt to find themselves persuaded. Some experiments have supported this explanation,[62] whereas others could not confirm it.[63]

Other factors that are related to the speaker/communicator have also been demonstrated to affect the reception of a persuasive message. These factors include the race,[64] the physical appearance and body position,[65] and the neatness and style of clothing of the speaker.[66] The studies show that we evaluate not only the message but the medium that carries the message in determining our opinions and attitudes.

ATTITUDE CHANGE THROUGH BEHAVIOR CHANGE

The objective of attitude change is to alter behavior. Since advertising and propaganda are largely concerned with the control of behavior, evidence of behavior change is often regarded as opinion change. Likewise, management training programs are usually designed to change attitudes in order to achieve a behavior change.

Criticism of earlier studies in the area of attitude change suggested that little research had been able to link specific attitudes clearly with appropriate corresponding behavior.[67] However, later and more sophisticated research designs and explanations have improved the understanding of the relevant links.[68]

W. Wohlking suggests the use of behavior change to produce attitude change and thereby assure persistance of the altered behavior.[69] For instance, attitudes of resistance to air travel decline rapidly once a traveler experiences a pleasant trip. Participation in interpersonal relations exercises in which people are asked to try out a procedure that they themselves would not elect to use might develop a favorable attitude or remove an unfavorable one. Thus, the question of which should come first, attitude change or behavior change, is a good one, and both approaches have their merits.

Government-imposed integration programs are an example of an approach to alter attitudes by altering behavior. The success of such programs for attitude change would partially depend on participants' experiences. The nature of attitude formation, however, would suggest that initial negative reactions may be difficult to change, even without negative experiences. Such a condition exists when companies start affirmative action hiring policies. In cases where attitudes are based on emotional factors, the facts offered by new experiences may be selectively remembered or forgotten in conformity with established attitudes. To the extent that attitudes against women and minorities are based on a lack of facts rather than on emotion, there is an intellectual basis for attitude change.

QUESTIONABLE METHODS

Brainwashing is a method of behavior change that combines interrogation, forced confession, self-criticism, repetitious propaganda, and reward and punishment in group discussion patterns. Early efforts fall short of the claims made by its proponents. Of the many thousand prisoners of war in Korea exposed to communism, only twenty-one refused repatriation when it was offered.[70] Recent attempts (for example, the Patricia Hearst case, the religious cults) have used more sophisticated techniques and achieved greater "success."

A WORD OF CAUTION

In measuring attitude changes, can we always be sure that there has been a true or basic change? H. C. Kelman distinguished between three conditions of influence: (1) compliance, where the person hopes to achieve a favorable reaction from the persuader; (2) identification, where the person wishes to establish a favorable relationship with the persuader; and (3) internalization, where the influence fits into the person's own value system.[71] In the first two conditions, the influences revealed are superficial and represent expressions of change because of external pressures. The third is a valid acceptance of influence in that it incorporates new material into the person's system of values. By the same token, conflicting material would be rejected.

In order to achieve an intrinsic attitude change, an influence would have to alter or reorganize an existing system of values and meanings. For example, let us examine some values in a job situation. The meanings of the terms *high production, no smoking, strict inspection,* and *must attend company parties* could be so organized that they would fall into a frame of reference that might be called an unpleasant and autocratic work climate. However, if we found a new boss to be understanding, friendly, and helpful, the meanings of the above terms could change to *efficiency, fire hazards, good product,* and *expected to be with the group because they want me,* respectively. An intrinsic change in attitude must introduce a new frame of reference to alter the interpretation of facts in the same way that the meaning of *high production* can change from unpleasant slave-driving to pride in efficiency. Thus, changes in basic attitudes are accompanied by a series of new insights and discoveries of new meanings and values.

NOTES

1. Roethlisberger, F. J., and Dickson, W. J. *Management and the worker.* Cambridge, Mass.: Harvard University Press, 1939.
2. Homans, G. C. *The human group.* New York: Harcourt, Brace, 1950.
3. Dickson, W. J., and Roethlisberger, F. J. *Counseling in an organization: A sequel to the Hawthorne researches.* Boston: Harv. Bus. School, 1966.
4. See, for example, Hammond, K. R., Stewart, T. R., Brehmer, B., and Steinman, D. O. Social

judgment theory. In M. J. Kaplan and S. Schwartz (Eds.), *Human judgment and decision processes.* New York: Academic, 1975, 64–83; Hammond, K. R., and Summers, D. A. Cognitive control. *Psychol. Rev.,* 1972, *79,* 58–67; Hamner, W. C., and Carter, P. L. A comparison of alternative production management coefficient decision rules. *Decis. Sci.,* 1975, *6,* 324–336; McCann, J. M., Miller, J. G., and Moskowitz, H. Modeling and testing dynamic multivariate decision processes. *Organ. Behav. Hum. Perform.,* 1975, *14,* 281–303; Moskowitz, H. Regression models of behavior for managerial decision making. *OMEGA: Intl. J. Manage. Sci.,* 1974, *2,* 677–690; Warner, H., Zill, N., and Gruvaeus, G. Senatorial decision making: II. Prediction. *Behav. Sci.,* 1973, *18,* 20–26.

5. McGregor, D. *The human side of enterprise.* New York: McGraw-Hill, 1960.

6. Hayakawa, S. I. *Language in thought and action*, 4th ed. New York: Harcourt Brace Jovanovich, Inc., 1978, pp. 142–143.

7. Terborg, J. R., and Ilgen, D. R. A theoretical approach to sex discrimination in traditionally masculine occupations. *Organ. Behav. Hum. Perform.,* 1975, *13,* 352–376.

8. Staw, B. M. Knee-deep in the Big Muddy: A study of escalating commitment to a chosen course of action. *Organ. Behav. Hum. Perform.,* 1976, *16,* 27–45.

9. Kiesler, C., Collins, B., and Miller, N. *Attitude change: A critical analysis of theoretical approaches.* New York: Wiley, 1969.

10. Maier, N. R. F., and Lansky, L. Effect of attitude on selection of facts. *Personnel Psychol.* 1957, *10,* 298–303; Mills, J., Aromon, E., and Robinson, H. Selectivity in exposure to information. *J. Abnorm. Soc. Psychol.,* 1959, *59,* 250–253.

11. Thurstone, L. L., and Chave, E. J. *The measurement of attitude.* Chicago: University of Chicago Press, 1929; Selltiz, C., Jahoda, M., Deutsch, M., and Cook, S. W. *Research methods in social relations.* New York: Holt, 1959, pp. 357–383; Clarke, A. V., and Grant, D. L. Application of a factorial method in selecting questions for an employee attitude survey. *Personnel Psychol.,* 1961, *14,* 131–139.

12. Selltiz, Jahoda, Deutsch, and Cook, op. cit.

13. Greene, J. E., Sr., and Greene, J. E., Jr. Illustration uses of the "incomplete" sentences technique in investigating certain attitudes of middle management personnel. *Personnel Psychol.,* 1961, *14,* 305–315.

14. Thurstone, L. L. The measurement of social attitudes. *J. Abnorm. Soc. Psychol.,* 1931, *26,* 249–264.

15. Rosenthal, S. P. Changes in socio-economic attitudes under radical motion picture propaganda. *Arch. Psychol.,* 1934, *25* (166), 46.

16. Ibid.

17. Hall, O. M. Attitudes and unemployment. *Arch. Psychol.,* 1934, *25* (165), 65.

18. Wilke, W. H. An experimental comparison of the speech, the radio, and the printed page as propaganda devices. *Arch. Psychol.,* 1934, *25* (1969), 1–32.

19. Ex, J. The nature of the relation between two persons and the degree of their influence on each other. *Acta Psychol.,* 1960, *17,* 39–54.

20. Selvin, H. C., and Hagstrom, W. O. Determinants of support for civil liberties. *Brit. J. Sociol.,* 1960, *11,* 51–73.

21. Rosenberg, M. J. Cognitive reorganization in response to the hypnotic reversal of attitudinal affect. *J. Pers.,* 1960, *28,* 39–63.

22. Hall, op. cit.

23. Eagly, A. H., and Himmelfarb, S. Attitudes and opinions. *Ann. Rev. Psychol.,* 1978, *29,* 517–554.

24. Festinger, L. *A theory of cognitive dissonance.* Evanston, Ill.: Row, Peterson, 1957; Cognitive dissonance. *Scientific Amer.,* 1962, *207,* 93–98, 100, 102.

25. Greenwald, A. G., Brock, T. C., and Ostrom, T. M. (Eds.) *Psychological foundations of attitudes.* New York: Academic Press, 1968; Greenwald, A. G. When does role playing produce attitude

change? Toward an answer. *J. Person. Soc. Psychol.*, 1970, *16*, 214–219; Rhine, R. J., and Severance, L. J. Ego-involvement discrepancy, source of credibility, and attitude change. *J. Person. Soc. Psychol.*, 1970, *16*, 175–190.

26. Whittaker, J., and Meade, R. Retention of opinion change as a function of the differential source credibility: A cross-cultural study. *Internatl. J. Psychol.*, 1968, *3*, 103–108; Miller, N., Maruyama, G., Beaber, R. J., and Valone, K. Speed of speech and persuasion. *J. Pers. Soc. Psychol.*, 1976, *36*, 615–624; Norman, R. When what is said is important: A comparison of expert and attractive sources. *J. Exper. Soc. Psychol.*, 1976, *12*, 294–300.

27. Haskins, J. B. Factual recall as a measure of advertising effectiveness. *J. Advertising Research*, 1966, *6*, 2–8; Klapper, J. T. *The effects of mass communication.* New York: Free Press, 1960.

28. Watts, W. Relative persistence of opinion change induced by active compared to passive participation. *J. Person. Soc. Psychol.*, 1967, *5*, 4–15.

29. Gerard, H. Conformity and commitment to the group. *J. Abnorm. Soc. Psychol.*, 1964, *68*, 209–211.

30. Karlins, M., and Abelson, H. I. *Persuasion: How opinions and attitudes are changed.* New York: Springer, 1970; Triandis, H. C. *Attitude and attitude change.* New York: Wiley, 1971.

31. Kraus, S., El-Assal, E., and De Fleur, M. Fear-threat appeals in mass communication: An apparent contradiction. *Speech Mono.* 1966, *33*, 23–29.

32. Eagly, A., and Manis, M. Evaluation of message and communication as a function of involvement. *J. Person. Soc. Psychol.*, 1966, *3*, 483–485.

33. LeJeune, R., and Alex, N. On being mugged: The event and its aftermath. *Urban Life and Cult.*, 1973, *2*(3). Reprinted in *The Aldine crime and justice manual.* Chicago: Aldine, 1974, 161–189.

34. Katz, D., McClintock, C., and Sarnoff, I. The measurement of ego-defense as related to attitude change. *J. Pers.*, 1957, *25*, 465–474.

35. Brown, J. F. *Psychology and the social order.* New York: McGraw-Hill, 1936. Contains an interesting treatment of in-group and out-group attitudes.

36. Asch, S. E. *Social psychology.* Englewood Cliffs, N.J.: Prentice-Hall, 1952, pp. 414–416.

37. Kelley, H. H., and Woodruff, C. Member's reactions to apparent group approval of a counternorm communication. *J. Abnorm. Soc. Psychol.*, 1956, *52*, 67–74.

38. Moore, H. T. The comparative influence of majority and expert opinion. *Amer. J. Psychol.*, 1921, *32*, 16–20.

39. Sherif, M. *The psychology of social norms.* New York: Harper, 1936.

40. Trier, H., Smith, H. C., and Shaffer, J. Differences in food buying attitudes of housewives, *J. Marketing*, 1960, *25*, 66–69.

41. Katona, G. *Psychological analysis of economic behavior.* New York: McGraw-Hill, 1959; and Katona, G. *The powerful consumer.* New York: McGraw-Hill, 1960.

42. Lieberman, J. The effect of changes in roles on the attitudes of role occupants. *Hum. Relat.*, 1956, *9*, 385–402.

43. Newcomb, T. M. *Personality and social change.* New York: Dryden, 1939.

44. Nahemow, L., and Bennett, R. Conformity, persuasibility, and counter-normative persuasion. *Sociometry*, 1967, *30*, 14–25.

45. Rohrer, J., and Sherif, M. (Eds.). *Social psychology at the crossroads.* New York: Harper, 1951.

46. Suedfeld, P., and Vernon, J. Attitude manipulation in restricted environments: Conceptual structure and the internalization of propaganda received as a reward for compliance. *J. Person. Soc. Psychol.*, 1966, *3*, 586–589.

47. Mann, F., and Likert, R. The need for research on the communication of research results. In R. N. Adams and J. J. Preiss (Eds.), *Human organization research.* Homewood, III.: Dorsey, 1960, pp. 57–66.

48. Private communication from John J. Hayes.

49. Likert, R. *New patterns of management.* New York: McGraw-Hill, 1961; Campbell, J. P., Dunnette, M. D., Lawler, E. E., III, and Weick, K. E., Jr. *Managerial behavior, performance, and effectiveness.* New York: McGraw-Hill, 1970.

50. Campbell, D. B. Relative influence of job and supervision on shared worker attitudes. *J. Appl. Psychol.,* 1971, *55,* 521–525.

51. Banaka, W. H. *Training in depth interviewing.* New York: Harper & Row, 1971; Black, J. M. *How to get results from interviewing.* New York: McGraw-Hill, 1970; Drake, J. D. *Interviewing for managers.* New York: American Management Association, 1972; Perkin, D. B. *Human behavior and employment interviewing.* New York: American Management Association, 1971.

52. King, B. T., and Janis, I. L. Comparison of the effectiveness of improvised versus nonimprovised role-playing in producing opinion changes. *Hum. Relat.,* 1956, *9,* 177–186.

53. Lawshe, C. H., Bolda, R. A., and Brune, R. L. Studies in management training evaluation: II. The effects of exposure in role playing. *J. Appl. Psychol.,* 1959, *43,* 287–293; Imitating models: A new management tool. *Business Week,* May 8, 1978, 119–120.

54. Dickson, W. J. The Hawthorne plan of personnel counseling. *Amer. J. Orthopsychiat.,* 1945, *15,* 343–347.

55. Rogers, C. *Counseling and psychotherapy.* Boston: Houghton Mifflin, 1942.

56. Kahn, R. L., and Cannell, C. F. *The dynamics of interviewing.* New York: Wiley, 1952; Sidney, E., and Brown, M. *The skills of interviewing.* London: Tavistock, 1961.

57. Marrow, A. J., and French, J. R. P., Jr. Changing a stereotype in industry. *J. Soc. Issues* 1945, *1,* 33–37.

58. Barkin, S. Trade-union attitudes and their effect on productivity. *Industr. Productivity,* Industrial Relations Research Assn., 1951, 110–129.

59. Levine, J., and Butler, J. Lecture versus group decision in changing behavior. In E. A. Fleishman (Ed.), *Studies in personnel and industrial psychology.* Homewood, Ill.: Dorsey, 1961, Chapter 17.

60. Dudek, D. H. The harmonious clash of ideas. *Chemtech,* November, 1979, 665–667.

61. Newcomb, T. M. *The acquaintance process.* New York: Holt, 1961.

62. Eagly, A. H., and Chaiken, S. An attribution analysis of the effect of communicator characteristics on opinion change: The case of communicator attractiveness. *J. Pers. Soc. Psychol.,* 1975, *32,* 135–144; Eagly, A. H., and Chaiken, S. Why would anyone say that? Causal attribution of statements about the Watergate scandal. *Sociometry,* 1976, *39,* 236–243.

63. McPeek, R. W., and Edwards, J. D. Expectancy disconfirmation and attitude change. *J. Soc. Psychol.,* 1975, *96,* 193–208.

64. Porter, D. T. An experimental investigation of the effects of racial prejudice and racial perception upon communication effectiveness. *Speech Monogr.,* 1974, *41,* 179–184.

65. McGinley, H., LeFevre, R., and McGinley, P. The influence of a communicator's body position on opinion change in others. *J. Pers. Soc. Psychol.,* 1975, *31,* 686–690; Horai, J., Naccari, N., and Fatoullah, E. The effects of expertise and physical attractiveness upon opinion agreement and liking. *Sociometry,* 1974, *37,* 601–606.

66. Cooper, J., Darley, J. M., and Henderson, J. E. On the effectiveness of deviant- and conventional-appearing communicators: A field experiment. *J. Pers. Soc. Psychol.,* 1974, *29,* 441–445.

67. See, for example, Wicker, A. W. Attitudes versus actions: The relationship of verbal and overt behavioral responses to attitude objects. *J. Soc. Issues,* 1969, *25,* 41–78.

68. Schuman, H., and Johnson, M. P. Attitudes and behavior. *Ann. Rev. Sociol.,* 1976, *2,* 161–207; Kelman, H. C. Attitudes are alive and well and gainfully employed in the sphere of action. *Amer. Psychol.,* 1974, *29,* 310–324.

69. Wohlking, W. Attitude change, behavior change: The role of the training department. *Calif. Mgt. Rev.,* 1970, *13,* 45–50.

UNDERSTANDING THE BEHAVIOR OF INDIVIDUAL EMPLOYEES

70. Schein, E. The Chinese indoctrination program for prisoners of war. *Psychiatry*, 1956, *19*, 149–172; Brown, J. A. *Techniques of persuasion.* Baltimore: Penguin, 1963.
71. Kelman, H. C. Compliance, identification and internalization: Three processes of attitude change. *J. Confl. Resol.*, 1958, *2*, 51–60.

SUGGESTED READINGS

Kelman, H. C. Attitudes are alive and well and gainfully employed in the sphere of action. *Amer. Psychol.*, 1974, 310–324.

Norman, R. When what is said is important: A comparison of expert and attractive sources. *J. Exper. Soc. Psychol.*, 1976, 294–300.

Pryor, M. G., and Pondy, R. W. How men and women view their jobs and what this means to the supervisor. *Supervis. Mgt.*, November, 1973, 17–25.

Salancik, G. R., and Pfeffer, J. An examination of need-satisfaction models of job attitudes. *Adm. Sci. Quart.*, September, 1977.

Smith, F. J., and Porter, L. W. What do executives really think about their organizations? *Org. Dyn.*, Autumn, 1977, 68–80.

LABORATORY EXERCISE

MULTIPLE ROLE-PLAYING:
THE CASE OF THE "OLD TIMERS"

Preface to Role-Playing

Role-playing is a procedure whereby various real-life situations are created and participants have an opportunity to practice specific interpersonal relations skills in a safe laboratory environment. Best results are obtained if the participants imagine themselves to be in the situations created for them and if they adopt the feelings and attitudes described to them as their own. Role-playing differs from acting, because the actor plays the part of someone else and must speak the lines supplied for this person, whereas the role-player remains himself or herself but is given a new name, a particular job, and certain past experiences. The interaction between the role-players should represent their own personalities *as supplemented or changed by the instructions, the situation, and the feeling engendered by the interaction.* In the interest of spontaneous interaction, students are asked not to read the case materials before participating in role-playing exercises.

A. PREPARATION FOR ROLE-PLAYING

1. In this exercise, members of the class will be asked to play the parts of persons in an actual case, the circumstances of which are given below.
2. Background material (F.1) is read aloud to all.
3. The class is divided into groups of three. (One or two groups may contain two persons in order to handle groups not divisible by three.)
4. One of the three persons in each group takes the role of Rebecca Jones; one takes the role of Dick Smith; and the third acts as observer. (In groups of two, the observer is omitted.) The sex of the role-player need not correspond to that of the role played.
5. When all have completed reading their instructions (F.2, 3, or 4), the role-players will set them aside and prepare to act out their parts as they feel them.

6. Observers should be ignored by the role-players and should make themselves as unobtrusive as possible.

B. THE ROLE-PLAYING PROCESS

1. The instructor will ask the Smiths to leave their groups. At a signal they will return, indicating their arrival in the offices of the Joneses. From this point on, participants will act in their roles.
2. Role-playing ensues for about ten minutes of interaction between the Smiths and the Joneses.
3. Each Smith and each Jones will indicate on a slip of paper whether or not the other changed his or her attitude.
4. Observers prepare to report.

C. REPORTS FROM OBSERVERS

1. A brief report from each observer concerning procedure in the group
2. The observer's opinion of good and bad practices

D. TABULATION OF FACTS MENTIONED

1. List on the blackboard the facts given in the roles of Smith and Jones.
2. With the help of the observers, indicate which of the facts were mentioned by the Smiths and which by the Joneses.

E. DISCUSSION

1. Analysis of tabulated data should permit the conclusion that the attitude selected the facts used in the discussion. (Smith would state a derogatory fact, and Jones would counter with "Yes, that may be true, but . . ." and go on to mention a favorable fact.)
2. Do the reports justify the conclusion that the Joneses who listened made more progress than those who argued?
3. The observers' opinions of attitude change should be checked against those of the role-players to evaluate observers' sensitivity.
4. Any conclusion about how the case

should be handled is premature. The important experience is developing an awareness of the numerous problems in human relationships that arise in everyday situations.

F. MATERIALS FOR THE CASE

1. Background

In a commercial office employing a large number of clerks, there was a period when business was slack and very few new employees were hired. Following the recession, business improved, and employee ranks expanded. During the past five years, many employees have been hired. Consequently, the ranks include 450 younger workers who have less than five years of service, in addition to 90 employees who have worked for the company ten or more years and 15 who have been there from five to nine years. This hiring pattern has created an unusual situation in the office: two groups with an age difference of at least five to ten years between them. With this age difference, the members of these two large groups can be differentiated, and hence discrimination can be practiced easily. Members of these two groups do not get along very well. The office force has recognized the problem and is accustomed to thinking and speaking of the groups as the "old-timers" and the "kids."

Rebecca Jones is in charge of the personnel office and for the past ten years has done all the hiring and placing of employees. All transfers, changes in pay rates, and so on, must be cleared through her. She is in a staff position, and her office was set up as a service to the line organization.

Dick Smith is the manager of one of five large offices. There are four supervisors who report to him and his position in the organization is comparable in rank to that of Rebecca Jones. Since each of them report to a different vice president, neither one has authority over the other.

Jones has asked Smith to come and see her to discuss a problem in connection with older clerks. Smith is about to enter Jones's office.

UNDERSTANDING THE BEHAVIOR OF INDIVIDUAL EMPLOYEES

2. Role for Rebecca Jones of the Personnel Office (Age Thirty-Five Years)

You have had a persistent problem with Dick Smith, the manager of a large office group in the company. He objects to older employees and refuses to accept transfers. He also gives poor ratings to the older clerks and tries to get you to find other places for them. As far as you can tell, he is prejudiced. You believe that the older workers make good, stable employees. You find them more conscientious, more dependable, more businesslike, and generally more capable. You can't understand Smith's position and therefore have decided to talk to him to see if you can't convince him to take his share of the older clerks and to give them a better deal. It's just about time for Smith to arrive. Stand up to receive him and thank him for taking time out. You've asked Smith to come to your office because you have private rooms for interviewing. If you went to Smith's office, your presence would be observed and it might start an ugly rumor about someone getting fired.

Here are things you know about the behavior of older workers compared to younger ones:

☐ Have lower absenteeism
☐ Spend more time in rest rooms
☐ Have less tardiness
☐ Are less willing to do unpleasant jobs
☐ Produce the same amount of work
☐ Are less sociable
☐ Object more to changes
☐ Can do a greater variety of jobs
☐ Know the company set-up better
☐ Adapt more slowly to new jobs

3. Role for Dick Smith, Manager of the Office Force

You have had considerable trouble with Rebecca Jones in the personnel office. She isn't cooperative regarding the kind of employees you want and doesn't help you in obtaining new jobs for those you want to transfer. Mostly, the issue centers on problems concerning the older clerks. You refuse to accept workers over thirty years of age, and you try to transfer your older clerks whenever you can. You like a young force. You have had dealings with all types of employees, and you and the four supervisors who report to you all agree that older clerks are no good. You don't like to deal with them and see no reason why the company should put up with them. However, if the company wants to keep them, let those who like them take them into their units. As far as you are concerned, they aren't worth the pay they get. They are inefficient, undependable, and slow. (Assume the attitude that you dislike them.)

You have an appointment with Rebecca Jones. She asked to see you to discuss your views concerning older employees. You are a busy man and haven't the time to help Jones solve her problems, but you will be polite enough to see what she wants. Personnel people get paid for this sort of thing but you have to make up for this time out because your work piles up when you're gone.

Here are things you know about the behavior of older clerks compared to younger ones:

☐ Have lower absenteeism
☐ Spend more time in rest rooms
☐ Have less tardiness
☐ Are less willing to do unpleasant jobs
☐ Produce the same amount of work
☐ Are less sociable
☐ Object more to change
☐ Can do a greater variety of jobs
☐ Know the company set-up better
☐ Adapt more slowly to new jobs

4. Instructions for the Observer

You are overhearing a discussion between Dick Jones and Rebecca Smith. Make special note of the following:

a. The manner in which Jones leads up to the discussion of older workers
b. The relative amount each talks
c. The arguments each uses
d. Evidences of any change in attitude

Do not enter into the discussion in any way. Learn what you can by listening in, as your opinions will be asked later.

PART

ANALYZING
WORK
GROUP
INTERACTIONS

TWO

Standard questions in interviews and on application forms for management positions concern extracurricular activities — Were you captain of the soccer team? president of the student senate? editor of the high school newspaper? Companies are interested in answers to these questions because they are looking for signs in past behavior that the individual has leadership qualities. Although what comprises leadership remains debatable, as Chapter 7 will show, most people who study or who run businesses agree that the ability to lead, to motivate, to deal with employees is key to success as a manager.

How can a potential manager learn the skills and gain the insights that provide the basis for sound leadership? One way is to study the dynamics of group behavior — the forces that influence individuals to join groups, to support or defy the group's internal code of behavior, to persuade others to join or conform. By understanding these forces, the manager can learn to work with the group instead of turning the situation into a battle of wills between manager and group. Chapter 6 ("Small-Group Behavior") covers the basic issues and dynamics occurring in group behavior — both within the group and between members and outsiders.

An analysis of leadership—probably the single most important influence on group attitudes and performance — appears in Chapter 7 ("Leadership"). Executives, employees, and organizational psychologists all acknowledge that effective leadership is a significant force in organizations, that it can sometimes make the difference between survival and bankruptcy in a company. Certainly leadership affects performance at all levels.

What constitutes a good leader is a question that has been asked for many years. No single satisfactory answer has been found, but the studies reviewed in Chapter 7 show the complexities of the concept and reveal data about the factors involved in making a leader successful or unsuccessful.

Chapter 8 ("Group Problem Solving and Group Leadership") provides one route for the operating manager to increase his or her success in dealing with employees and solving tough organizational problems. For those numerous group problems in which employees' acceptance of the solution is required if it is to be successfully implemented, a specific leadership skill (integration) is described in detail. The results of effectiveness in this leadership role will include improved employee attitudes, better performance records, and a more innovative work place.

CHAPTER SIX

SMALL-GROUP BEHAVIOR

■

Approaches to Research on Small-Group Behavior
Approaches to the Understanding of Group Processes
The Experience of Group Membership
Relationships Between Groups of Peers
The Work Group and the Company

■

THE WORK GROUP performs certain vital functions in addition to its task. As the pioneering study of the Hawthorne plant showed, the task group to which a person belongs serves an important function as intermediary between that person and the organization as a whole.[1] Also the work group can fill a person's need to belong, to have organizational roots. Lastly, the work group acts as a microcosm of society: if a member violates group norms, it can exact severe psychological penalties. At the United States military academies, for instance, cadets or midshipmen who have been isolated by their peers for transgressing group norms have found this a devastating form of punishment.

APPROACHES TO RESEARCH ON SMALL-GROUP BEHAVIOR

How people react to one another in group situations has been the object of much investigation. Psychologists have examined group behavior using various approaches: *survey questionnaires, sociometry,* and *field observation.* In this chapter, we shall weigh the merits of these approaches and then review models of *group processes.*

Group interactions are both *internal* and *external,* that is, there are interactions between/among group members (internal), and there are interactions between individual group members and persons outside the task group unit. We shall first examine internal processes, that is, the experience of being a group member and dealing with others in the group. Then we shall look at group members' external interactions with peers in other functional areas and with the company management as a whole.

SURVEY QUESTIONNAIRES

The *survey approach* to measuring group conditions uses either standardized interviews or questionnaires. From a general survey, questions relevant to group conditions are used to develop an index by assigning values to alternative answers. The individual's score is obtained by adding the values assigned to each response, while the group score is obtained by adding the individual scores and dividing the total by the number of persons in the group to get an average score for that group. S. E. Seashore,[2] for example, used such group scores for classifying 228 work groups into seven levels of cohesiveness. (High cohesiveness may be defined as group members' perception of themselves as a homogeneous unit, undivided by bickering factions.) The fact that groups with high cohesive scores were happier and better adjusted suggests that high cohesive scores do measure a group climate.

Cohesiveness scores based on individual measures reflect aspects of group behavior. Highly cohesive groups are less prone to be disrupted and divided by failure.[3] Actually, threat from the outside increases a group's cohesiveness score.[4]

But one effect of the method of computing the group measure is that the score is the *average* member's report of feelings about the group. Two groups with the same average could have quite different interpersonal relationships, but the group scores would be the same.

Survey approaches to the measurement of group phenomena have some other limitations. They are based on the expressed opinions of group members, rather than on observed group behavior. Perhaps group enthusiasm (morale) and resistance to frustration can be inferred from members' attraction to one another, but the structure of the

ANALYZING WORK GROUP INTERACTIONS

group cannot be determined by the studies of individual opinions. Also, the roles that a person plays in one group may differ from roles played in another group. Communication and cooperation, too, may change in ways not shown by questionnaire results. For example, these exchanges alter when the group process changes from arguing to problem solving. The same group may carry out a variety of group processes from one day to the next, yet members would not change their responses on the questionnaires, even though their feelings were not the same toward all the group activities.

Though surveys fail to measure group behavior as such, the investigations do not necessarily lack value. The feelings that an individual experiences in being an accepted member of the work group, in having a job the company thinks is important, and in being respected by the supervisor are important and can reveal information of value to the company. Even if various investigators have used different items to make up a morale index, the results obtained with one index can be useful in evaluating departments and companies. The error lies in combining data obtained from different instruments, assuming that each instrument is valid.

Surveys may give an overall measure of employee morale, as well as information revealing the cause of specific dissatisfactions.[5] Questionnaires also may reveal the need for training, the effects of various working conditions on attitudes, the nature of employee needs, and many other relationships. If the data are to be useful, however, the questionnaire must be properly constructed and the results skillfully analyzed by qualified personnel to realize their full value.

Even when precautions are taken, we should recognize the primary limitations of the survey technique: it measures symptoms, not causes. When attitudes are unfavorable, employees are hypercritical, and as we have seen in Chapter 4, the object or condition criticized may not indicate the underlying cause of dissatisfaction.

The survey method also does not reveal the most effective practices. We can determine which of several procedures that employees like best or which work groups yield the highest production, but are limited to an evaluation of things already known and practiced. The best of all methods of supervision may not be practiced at all, hence cannot be discovered by a survey.

To get a large proportion of a company's managers interested in improving group attitudes, they must be involved in the problem. An important requisite to involvement is using data obtained in their own company. Company representatives should also be involved in collection of the data.

The reasons given to worker participants for the survey concerning how the data will be used is crucial to a later improvement of attitude.[6] The best results are gained when the data are treated as "information that may be helpful to us in suggesting ways of improving conditions." When surveys are constructed with questions obviously aimed at uncovering groups that are not operating at an acceptable efficiency rate, the surveys are self-defeating because the workers can discern the purpose and "adjust" their answers.

SOCIOMETRY: A METHOD FOR MEASURING GROUP STRUCTURE

An alternative to collecting research data by questionnaires is obtaining data by the sociometric method. J. L. Moreno developed this ingenious method of analyzing group status.[7] Called *sociometry*, his technique is relatively simple, but diagnostic. Members of a group vote on their preferences for one another in specific situations. For example, members of a work unit or office might be asked to vote on the following questions:

1. With whom would you prefer to work?
2. With whom would you like most to lunch?
3. Who would make a good supervisor?

Each person is usually asked to give three preferences for each of the questions.

Analysis of results from such questions reveals that certain individuals receive a large number of votes. Such individuals are designated as *stars*. Others receive few or no votes and are designated as *isolates*. There are also those who invariably vote for each other. These are known as *mutual pairs*. Sometimes the voting takes the form of a *triangle*, in which three persons all vote for one another. This method readily reveals the existence of small cliques in which the votes are confined to close friends, thus producing a frequent number of mutual choices and triangles.

The existence of any subgroupings immediately becomes apparent on examination of the results. The results check with general observations and also reveal details and relationships that augment any discovered by an observer in constant contact with the group. The existence of isolates is of particular interest, as they are likely to be the unhappy and poorly adjusted individuals in a group. In school situations, they can be given special attention by the teacher who can involve them in group activity and thus help improve their status in the group. Unfortunately, in both school and business, the teacher/supervisor who is untrained to deal with isolates tends to react like the other members in the group and to ignore the isolate's situation, or even to side with the

others against the isolate.[8] For this reason, when sociometry uncovers the presence of isolates, supervisors need special training so that they can help isolates make better adjustments to the group.

Stars usually take care of themselves. A knowledge of their existence, however, could serve as one of the bases for selection for supervisor training. They are the individuals who very probably possess acceptable personality traits for leadership, since there is good assurance that they will not antagonize people.

Data obtained by the Moreno technique may be graphically represented by a *sociogram*. Each member of a group is represented by a circle, and choices are indicated by lines drawn between the circles. Arrows indicate the direction of a choice. By using solid lines to indicate mutual choices and broken lines to designate one-way choices, we can differentiate between them. The number of votes received by a particular person can be given in the center of each circle, together with his or her name or initial. In the sociogram in Figure 6.1, E is a star with eight votes, and J is an isolate with no votes. A, B, and D show definite preferences for one another and, with the exception of one another, vote only for E. These three persons constitute a subgroup. If repeated sociograms reveal the same grouping, they would be evidence of the permanence and strength of the clique. Supplementary observation would reveal whether the subgroup was a disruptive force, or was merely cohesive because of conditions/relations outside of their group, such as belonging to the same lodge. To simplify the sociogram, we can diagram the mutual choices only and indicate in each circle the total number of choices received. Omission of the dotted lines would show the presence of clusters and isolates more clearly. The standing of each person in the

ANALYZING WORK GROUP INTERACTIONS

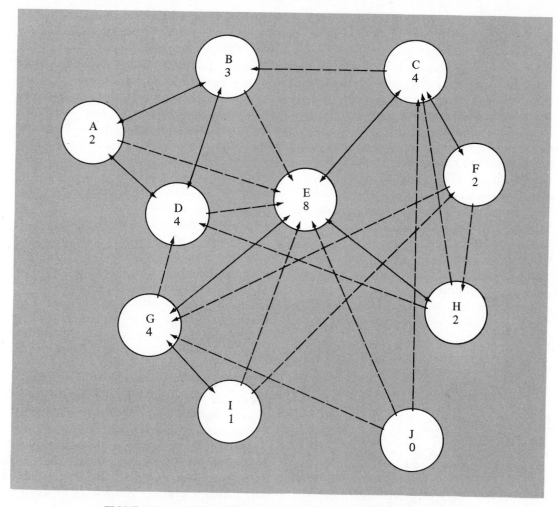

FIGURE 6.1 SOCIOGRAM OF A GROUP OF TEN EMPLOYEES

Each employee is represented as a circle, the letters of the alphabet substituted for names. Each member of the group was asked to vote for the three persons most desired as working companions. The numerals in the circles show the number of votes each received. The arrows indicate the direction of the choices; solid and broken lines designate mutual choices and one-way preferences, respectively. Individuals *A, B,* and *D* form a triangle, *E* is a star, and *J* is an isolate.

group would be revealed by the total number of votes received.

Sociometrists[9] have concluded that attractions among group members heighten cooperation and that repulsions among them cause friction. Based on this conclusion, sociometry has been applied to business situations with successful results. For example, a sociogram was made of the personnel working together in a steam laundry.[10] This revealed that certain pairs of individuals in a team of seven women rejected one another. Two members in the team were reassigned to another group and were replaced by two new members, thus removing the "rejections" and making a more harmonious group, which improved both morale and production. Similarly, when sociometric choices were used to select flying partners, morale was improved in the armed services.[11]

In another case, the benefit derived through the use of sociometry was clear. In a large housing project separated by a highway, two procedures determined the assignment of carpenters and bricklayers to crews.[12] On one side of the road the supervisor arbitrarily assigned workers to groups, and for the crew on the other side of the road, sociometric choices were followed. In the latter case, each carpenter and bricklayer indicated three preferences for teammates, and these choices were respected as far as possible in making assignments. Where the sociometric procedure was used, both labor and material costs were reduced to such an extent that every twenty-ninth building could be constructed from the savings.

Sometimes the values of work groups and management conflict. Automation is frequently rejected by employees not because they oppose efficiency, but because some of their members will be "bumped" out of their jobs.[13] On other occasions, the transfer

of a particular worker might be welcomed. The type of reaction will be influenced by the group structure.

Group structure also influences the values within a group. The appearance of cliques creates values of status that may divide an office. Secretaries may feel superior to file clerks, and office boys may develop a feeling of kinship through matching pennies in the stock room.[14]

In one study an office staff was found to have divided into friendship groups, each group having its own set of values.[15] With regard to work, the values ranged from "work hard" to "take it easy," and with regard to supervision, the attitudes ranged from friendly to hostile. In general, productivity and popularity were inversely related. This became particularly pronounced when transfers required shifts in groups and in seating. High-producing employees were rejected by low-producing groups, whereas low-producing employees were acceptable to practically all groups.

The use of sociometric methods in selection of supervisory personnel meets with a certain amount of resistance in business because of the fear that popularity and the good of the company may not coincide. This attitude makes applied research on this question difficult. Only five instances of its use have been made in companies studied by Maier. In each case the supervisor who had the responsibility of making the decision had three personal preferences. After evaluating group members, each of the five supervisors consulted with the group. Each informed the group that a promotion was to be made and that their help was needed to choose wisely. The supervisor then asked them to indicate on a questionnaire the names of the three persons they considered would make the most satisfactory supervisors. The questionnaires were not to be signed.

In all instances, the persons with the highest number of choices included at least one name that was on the supervisor's own list. The fear that the supervisor would have to ignore the group preferences was not supported in any instance. Twice the person with the greatest number of sociometric choices had limited seniority. Both cases involved individuals whom the supervisors considered to be the most capable, but whom they would not have promoted because the persons with greatest seniority were satisfactory and able to do the job. The fact that the most capable individuals had group support enabled the supervisors to promote on a basis of merit.

Isolated instances of this kind, however, are select cases and may be atypical. Only supervisors who already enjoy good relations with their groups would attempt such tests. Experimentation on a broader scale is needed to explore the matter further, but the approach is sound insofar as it makes effective use of the principles of participation. It is hoped that this limited experience will encourage others to try it.

One final example of the use of sociometry in industry is of interest. Ten women were being trained for responsible office positions involving contacts with the public. During the training period, each woman had a chat with each of the eight managers who would eventually receive the women in their sections. At the end of the training period, each manager was asked to list the names of the three trainees preferred, and each trainee was asked to list the three managers preferred. The fear that all the employees might prefer the same manager or vice versa was unwarranted. The results showed that it was possible to give every person one of his or her first three choices, and in only two instances was it necessary to resort to third choices. The person making the test considered it a success and received satisfactory reports from the managers. The motivation for trying the method was the fact that managers had previously complained about the unfairness of the assignments.

This approach is of particular interest because it holds the possibility of making an asset out of the human tendency to rely on first impressions. Since favorable impressions encourage generosity and unfavorable ones generate hypercritical judgments, biased attitudes are used to improve interpersonal relations.

FIELD OBSERVATION OF SMALL-GROUP PROCESSES

The *field-observation approach* to studying group behavior is similar to that used by a cultural anthropologist who visits some little-known tribe in an exotic location in order to systematically and thoroughly study the tribe's social relationships, accepted rules of behavior, and customs. A sociologist studying group behavior is also a participant-observer, but observes a group or groups within Western industrialized society.

A problem with the field-observation approach is that the observer's mere presence can affect the group's behavior; therefore, a sociologist sees a somewhat distorted picture of the group. To minimize this effect, a field sociologist spends long hours interacting with the group on its own terms. Studies involving such interaction have been made of many kinds of groups, including regular customers in a neighborhood tavern, professional jazz musicians, and unemployed youths.[16]

Although field observation can give a depth and breadth of knowledge about qualitative factors that are impossible to gather through survey questionnaires, this approach, too, has limitations. Field data is generally situation-specific, while questionnaires, because of standardized wording and procedure, can more easily be used to compare results in similar groups or companies. Also, collecting data in the field requires much more time than sociometric or questionnaire data collection and is generally more susceptible to interpretive bias on the part of the observer.

APPROACHES TO THE UNDERSTANDING OF GROUP PROCESSES

Because group membership is such an intrinsic part of human experience, scientists, in trying to be more objective in their study of groups, have designed *models of group behavior.* In these models, they try to capture a simplified, clarified version of what is going on between group members and in the mind of each member.[17]

THE MECHANISTIC MODEL

An early model of group dynamics likened the group to a machine.[18] Its behavior was seen as following certain patterns that could be identified and could lead to prediction of future behavior of group members. Like early physics theories that compared the universe to an eternal clock ticking off regular, identical units of time, scientists using this model emphasized group characteristics that were universal and unchanging. They sought basic principles of human social behavior and dismissed unique characteristics of particular groups as unimportant.

The usefulness of this model was demonstrated when they uncovered certain consistent behaviors and relationships (to be discussed later in this chapter). However, use of the model omitted or minimized the importance of factors that many (including business managers) must consider when

dealing with groups, for example, emotional reactions, specific group rules, and group values.

THE GROUP AS ORGANISM

A reaction to the lifelessness of the mechanistic model led to the construction of a model of groups based on the idea of the *group as an organism,* a single entity. Science fiction writers have used this concept to produce stories of individuals who share telepathically a group mind. Although the model is useful for explaining some phenomena (such as the frequent unanimity of opinion among group members), it also has shortcomings: groups as such do not decide anything, nor do organizations as such have goals. Individuals make decisions and formulate goals. Although all group members may arrive at the same conclusion, it is important to recognize that they do so ultimately as individuals, and though the group may act in concert, members' reasons for doing so may differ greatly.

THE CONFLICT MODEL

One model of group processes of particular importance in the study of organizations focuses on *conflict* and its resolution (problem solving) within and between groups. Although this approach, like the mechanistic model, is limited, it provides insights into a crucially important area of group process. The methods used in dealing with the inevitable problems encountered by all groups have a tremendous impact not only on group members' attitudes but on the very survival of the group. One type of group problem solving (with emphasis on the group leader's role) will be discussed in Chapter 8.

CYBERNETIC MODELS

More recently, sophisticated models have been developed that explicitly recognize the

ANALYZING WORK GROUP INTERACTIONS

environment (the world outside the group's boundaries) and its impact on group activities. One such model emphasizes the group's efforts to restore its equilibrium when internal or external forces threaten it.[19] Another, the structural-functional model, stresses the group's efforts to survive amid threatening conditions through adaptation, the maintenance of required behavior patterns, and the formulation and achievement of goals.[20] Possibly the most complex approach of all — the cybernetic/growth model — describes the group as an information-processing system, which aims not to restore a constant equilibrium but to adapt itself continually to the changing purposes, goals, and values of group members.[21]

THE EXPERIENCE OF GROUP MEMBERSHIP

The various approaches to understanding groups have uncovered group membership characteristics. The following sections give examples of specific research findings relating to internal group interactions and perceptions. Such findings have value to managers and supervisors as they furnish possible ways of dealing with problems within groups.

ATTRACTION TO THE GROUP AND ITS MEMBERS

Sociometric studies indicate that group members derive more satisfaction and work together more cooperatively when they are attracted to one another. The attraction may be of different kinds, depending in part on the goals and objectives of the group. A person who is preferred as a friend (social group) may not be chosen as a teammate (work group). However, individuals differ regarding whether they want friends or

competent individuals on their teams, depending on whether they have strong needs to *achieve* or to *be liked*.[22] Furthermore, individuals tend to choose as partners those with whom the relationship is reciprocal.[23] Thus, the most stable relationships occur when feelings are mutual.

SIMILARITY OF MEMBERS

Various studies have shown that members of cohesive groups (see definition on p. 126) have more influence on one another than members of less strongly unified groups. However, persons with similar attitudes are attracted, so the influence between attitudes and attraction seems to be reciprocal. T. M. Newcomb emphasizes similarity in values.[24] Undoubtedly this similarity is a factor, especially when other factors for group organization are not operating. This condition could also lead to lack of challenge and boredom, the achievement being merely a lack of strife.[25]

PROPINQUITY

Physical nearness and frequency of contact are important factors in determining social groupings.[26] Since people in work groups have little opportunity to choose their companions, it is natural that the work space and the relatedness of the work will influence friendships.

The extent to which the mere fact of having meetings develops groups and leads to group loyalties was shown in an experiment.[27] Students in four-person groups who had worked together for a semester were given a reward for their cooperation. The reward consisted of nineteen points for each group, which they could divide among the members in any way the group decided. The points allotted would then be added to each individual's examination score and would influence final grades in the course. In the

The fact of proximity may help form social groups within the organization. (Courtesy of New England Telephone)

event that the group failed to agree unanimously, each member would automatically receive four points, giving such groups only sixteen points. However, this meant that no individual would have to settle for less than four points.

Out of thirty groups, not one failed to reach a unanimous decision. Each group remained united in order to get the maximum number of points. The grade points received ranged from zero to nineteen, and in only 27 percent of the groups was the division fairly equal. The factor that most influenced the distribution of points was need. Students who were doing well in the course willingly gave up points to help keep a member from failing. This behavior represents a strong kind of unity, and the example only covers a series of fourteen two-hour laboratory sessions in a college course.

Considering the strong desire of group members to help one another, it is not surprising that groups of workers will protect a member who is threatened by manage-

ment. The mere fact of working together on a job tends to build friends. Members who "don't fit in" either learn to conform or seek work elsewhere. Studies show that the pressures to conform are very strong, and that if changes are to be introduced in a work situation, it is better to work through a group method than with individuals.[28]

POSITION IN THE GROUP

One study demonstrated a striking relationship between popularity and job satisfaction.[29] The most popular workers, when compared with the least popular ones, not only felt more satisfied with their jobs but they also (1) felt more secure, (2) considered their working conditions better, (3) felt their coworkers to be more friendly, (4) were more satisfied with their opportunities to communicate with management, (5) had more confidence in the ability of their supervisors, (6) were more inclined to believe that the company was interested in their welfare, and (7) had more confidence in the good intentions and good sense of the management. Employees' views of their jobs or their company depend not only on the nature of their work and the treatment the company gives them, but also on their status with other employees. The latter means that management should concern itself with creating conditions for employees that make for mutual feelings of being wanted and liked in a group.

THE EFFECTS OF GROUP SIZE

The dependence of group job attitudes on the group's size is also shown in survey data, which indicate that problems of job attitudes vary with large and small groups.[30] In general, maintaining positive attitudes is easier when employees are divided into small work groups. In some organizational structures where work groups are large, employees ac-

ANALYZING WORK GROUP INTERACTIONS

tually have difficulty identifying both their units and their bosses. Research with discussion groups shows that satisfaction declines if groups are increased from five to twelve; when groups exceed twelve, the skill of the leader becomes an essential feature in successful group discussions.[31] These findings suggest that large work groups should be subdivided so that the number of persons reporting to a given supervisor does not greatly exceed twelve. However, a possible source of error in survey data should be watched for: large-group members are more likely to report dissatisfactions on a questionnaire than workers in small groups because identification with the group is less strong in the larger groups.

One example of a use of this research with group size has occurred in a highly successful computer-manufacturing firm. A policy has been established that no unit of the firm in any one geographical area can have more than thirty persons (subdivided into task groups). The rationale is that the frequency and intensity of feedback needed between groups and individuals is impaired in larger units. This opinion is in agreement with a finding that research and development in a food-processing firm were apparently impaired by poor opportunities for interaction due to lack of propinquity and to large group size.[32]

GROUP COHESIVENESS AND MUTUALLY SUPPORTIVE BEHAVIOR

J. F. Muldoon elaborates the definition of cohesiveness as being a condition of a group that causes members to (1) work toward common goals, (2) think in terms of "we," (3) manifest friendliness toward one another, (4) stick together, and (5) function as a unit.[33] These qualities or dimensions are strikingly similar to those discussed later un-

der morale. Cohesiveness, however, stresses the desire to belong to a group, whereas morale stresses more the unified goal orientation.[34] Seashore, for example, found that high-cohesive groups could either show high production through cooperating with management or effectively curtail production by their united opposition.[35] Thus, production was related to high cohesiveness only when group and company goals were in harmony. The concept of high morale, as differentiated from high cohesiveness, would only incorporate groups that had goals in harmony with the leadership goals. This difference in meanings also may account for some discrepancies in the relationship between productivity and various morale measures.

A more recent study found that cohesiveness was greater in task groups when the group was successful and in socially supportive groups when members had similar values.[36] R. Likert uses the term *supportive* to describe the behavior of both leaders and group members.[37] It refers to acts that make an individual feel he or she is accepted and belongs in a group. This concept incorporates the leader as part of the group and is suggestive of a family unit.

COMPETITION VERSUS COOPERATION IN GROUPS

The group function — is it competitive or cooperative? — also influences its unity.[38] Competition tends to reduce a group's cohesiveness, and this factor becomes relevant to incentive-pay programs. Group incentives can be expected to yield group structures different from individual incentives. Intragroup competition tends to decrease cohesiveness whereas intergroup competition increases it.[39]

A study comparing intragroup and intergroup competition found that the former lessened performance and the latter increased it.[40] Another study found that cooperation increased performance in an assembly-line procedure, but made no difference when each person constructed complete units.[41]

MORALE

G. W. Allport defined *national morale* as an individual attitude in a group endeavor.[42] This statement implies that both personal and social features are involved in the mental condition we call morale. To have high morale, he believed (1) that the individual must possess firm convictions and values that make life worthwhile so that he or she has the energy and confidence to face the future; (2) that he or she must be aware of a job to be done to defend or extend those values; and (3) that those values must be in essential agreement with those of the group, and there must be a coordination of effort in attaining objectives. Another authority on this subject points out that morale involves two factors: the presence of a common goal among group members and the acceptance of socially recognized pathways toward that goal.[43]

The term *morale* thus defined refers to the relationships existing in a group of individuals.[44] We will follow the same usage and not refer to the morale of individuals.

The group conditions affecting morale include: (1) the extent to which the members of a group have a common goal; (2) the extent to which the goal is regarded as worthwhile; and (3) the extent to which members feel the goal can be achieved. Usually success raises a group's morale and failure lowers it.[45] Thus, high morale and group effectiveness interact and influence each other. One of the values of group success is that the achievement is shared, and the person who contributes the most becomes a helpful member rather than a threat.

Characteristic signs of high morale are *team spirit, staying quality, zest or enthusiasm,* and *resistance to frustration.* Groups with high morale also accomplish things with a minimum of bickering and do things because they want to rather than because they are afraid not to. In describing groups with low morale, such terms as *apathy, bickering, jealousies, disjointed effort,* and *pessimism* are relevant. Despite the fact that these two sets of characteristics are not all antagonistic, the general picture portrayed is one of opposites.

RELATIONSHIPS BETWEEN GROUPS OF PEERS

While intragroup characteristics are particularly useful to supervisors, managers are more often concerned with intergroup problems. Research has explored the problems typical to situations involving interactions between members of one group and those outside.

Although relationships in organizations are commonly thought of as vertical (between boss and employees), lateral communications are also important, particularly at intermediate levels in the organization. At one such level (lower-level managers), A. Wickesberg found that about two-thirds of their communications were to others at their level in the organization.[46]

Most research on communication between groups (that is, between members representing different groups) has focused on the potential for problems and conflict. For example, in organizations with limited total resources, groups vie for relatively greater shares in the organizational pie.

Problems multiply when groups are mutually dependent for the successful completion of an organizational task. New-product development, for instance, requires a com-

ANALYZING WORK GROUP INTERACTIONS

plex series of interactions between members of several functional groups. But differences in training, values, and goals may lead to each group's favoring a different approach and subsequently to conflict.[47]

One frequently noted effect of perceiving an outside force (an individual or group) as the enemy is that this perception tends to increase cohesiveness within the group. The pulling together of previously bickering factions during wartime or following a natural disaster is a well-known phenomenon. Within organizations, however, this characteristic reaction can have overall negative effects. If members of one functional or task group seek to achieve their group's goals, even at the expense of others within the organization, overall effectiveness will be impaired.

Some writers, notably C. Argyris and D. A. Schon, feel that the norms of modern organizational life serve to increase the potential for conflict in such situations.[48] For example, they suggest that mistrust and belief that "you can't test your assumptions about other people's motivations" lead to ineffective problem solving. To the extent that group cohesiveness and mutually supportive behavior exist within a work group, honest input and feedback may be possible.

But when the situation is perceived as *us* versus *them,* potential for conflict increases.

THE WORK GROUP AND THE COMPANY

As indicated earlier, the work group's values may encourage or diminish the achievement of goals desired by top management. Thus, group norms affect the organizational climate and organizational success.

At the same time, values and norms generated from the leadership of the organization affect group goals and values. P. Selznick[49] and others[50] have pointed out that when the individual at the top of the organization does not, or cannot, provide the organization's members with direction and a sense of mission, organizational drift sets in. With a drifting organization, the task or functional group goals are more likely to be advanced at the cost of overall organizational goals. On the other hand, when the organization is headed by an individual actively guiding the company in a well-communicated path toward specific goals, these goals become more universally accepted by its members.

NOTES

1. Mayo, E. *The human problems of industrial civilization.* New York: Macmillan, 1933.
2. Seashore, S. E. *Group cohesiveness in the industrial work group.* Ann Arbor, Mich.: Survey Research Center, 1954.
3. Lippitt, R. The morale of youth groups. In G. Watson (Ed.), *Civilian morale.* Boston: Houghton Mifflin, 1942, Chapter 7.
4. Pepitone, A., and Kleiner, R. The effects of threat and frustration on group cohesiveness. *J. Abnorm. Soc. Psychol.,* 1957, *54,* 192–199; Schachter, S. *The psychology of affiliation.* Stanford, Calif.: Stanford University Press, 1959.
5. Dunlap, J. The management of morale. *Personnel Psychol.,* 1950, *3,* 353–359.
6. Beer, M. The technology of organizational development. In M. D. Dunnette (Ed.), *The handbook of industrial and organizational psychology.* Chicago: Rand-McNally, 1976, 937–993; Mann, F. C. Changing superior-subordinate relationships. *J. Soc. Issues,* 1951, *7,* 56–63.

7. Moreno, J. L. *Who shall survive?* Beacon, N.Y.: Beacon House, 1953. See also Murphy, G., Murphy, L. B., and Newcomb, T. M. *Experimental social psychology.* New York: Harper, 1939, pp. 306–320.

8. Lippitt, R., and Gold, M. Classroom social structure as a mental health problem. *J. Soc. Issues,* 1959, *15,* 40–49.

9. Moreno, op. cit.

10. Rogers, M. Problems of human relations within industry. *Sociometry,* 1946, *9,* 350–371.

11. Zeleny, L. D. Selection of compatible flying partners. *Amer. J. Sociol.,* 1947, *5,* 424–431.

12. Van Zelst, R. H. Validation of a sociometric regrouping procedure. Supplement to *J. Abnorm. Soc. Psychol.,* April, 1952.

13. Walker, C. R. *Toward the automatic factory: A case study of men and machines.* New Haven, Conn.: Yale University Press, 1957.

14. Odiorne, G. S. The clique — a frontier in personnel management. *Personnel,* Sept.-Oct. 1957, 38–44.

15. French, J. R. P., Jr., and Zander, A. The group dynamics approach. In A. Kornhauser (Ed.), *Psychology of labor-management relations.* Champaign, Ill.: Industrial Relations Research Assn., 1949, pp. 71–78.

16. See, for example, the study by William F. Whyte, *Street corner society,* 2nd ed. Chicago: U. of Chicago Press, 1955.

17. See Mills, T. M. *The sociology of small groups.* Englewood Cliffs, N.J.: Prentice-Hall, 1967, for a more complete analysis of these models.

18. Simon, H. A. *Models of man: Social and rational.* New York: Wiley, 1957.

19. Bales, R. F. The equilibrium problem in small groups. In T. Parsons, R. F. Bales, and E. A. Shils (Eds.), *Working papers in the theory of action.* New York: Free Press of Glencoe, 1953, 111–161.

20. Parsons, Bales, and Shils, op. cit.

21. Deutsch, K. W. *The nerves of government.* New York: Free Press of Glencoe, 1963.

22. French, E. G. Motivation as a variable in work-partner selection. *J. Abnorm. Soc. Psychol.,* 1956, *53,* 96–99.

23. Shaw, M. E., and Gilchrist, J. C. Repetitive task failure and sociometric choice. *J. Abnorm. Soc. Psychol.* 1955, *50,* 29–32.

24. Newcomb, T. M. The prediction of interpersonal attraction. *Amer. Psychologist,* 1956, *11,* 575–586.

25. Hoffman, L. R. Homogeneity and member personality and its effect on group problem solving. *J. Abnorm. Soc. Psychol.,* 1959, *58,* 27–32; Hoffman, L. R. Similarity of personality: A basis for interpersonal attraction? *Sociometry,* 1958, *21,* 300–308.

26. Festinger, L., Schachter, S., and Back, K. *Social pressures in informal groups.* New York: Harper, 1950.

27. Hoffman, L. R., and Maier, N. R. F. The use of group decision to resolve a problem of fairness. *Personnel J.,* 1959, *12,* 545–559.

28. Festinger, L., et al. The influence process in the presence of extreme deviates. *Hum. Relat.,* 1952, *5,* 327–346; Jackson, J. M., and Salzstein, H. D. The effect of person-group relationships on conformity processes. *J. Abnorm. Soc. Psychol.,* 1958, *57,* 17–24.

29. Van Zelst, R. H. Worker popularity and job satisfaction. *Personnel Psychol.,* 1951, *4,* 405–412.

30. Pelz, D. C. Leadership within a hierarchical organization. *J. Soc. Issues,* 1951, *7,* 49–55; Pelz, D. C. Influence: A key to effective leadership in the first-line supervisor. *Personnel,* 1952, *29,* 209–217.

31. Hare, A. P. Interaction and consensus in different sized groups. *Amer. Soc. Rev.,* 1952, *17,* 261–267.

32. Verser, G. C. *The effects of an imbalance of power on new product development in marketing-oriented firms*. Ann Arbor, Mich.: University Microfilms, 1978.
33. Muldoon, J. F. The concentration of liked and disliked members in groups and the relationship of the concentration to group cohesiveness. *Sociometry*, 1955, *18*, 73–81.
34. Albert, R. S. Comments on the scientific function of the concepts of cohesiveness. *Amer. J. Sociol.*, 1953, *59*, 231–234.
35. Seashore, op. cit.
36. Anderson, A. B. Combined effects of interpersonal attraction and goal-path clarity on the cohesiveness of task-oriented groups. *J. Per. Soc. Psychol.*, 1975, *31*, 68–75.
37. Likert, R. *New patterns of management*. New York: McGraw-Hill, 1961.
38. Deutsch, M. A theory of cooperation and competition. *Hum. Relat.*, 1949, *2*, 129–152; Deutsch, M. Some factors affecting membership motivation and achievement motivation in a group. *Hum. Relat.*, 1959, *12*, 81–95.
39. Blake, R. R., and Mouton, J. S. Competition, communication, and conformity. In I. A. Berg and B. M. Bass (Eds.), *Conformity and deviation*. New York: Harper, 1961, Chapter 16.
40. Goldman, M., Stockbauer, J. W., and McAuliffe, T. G. Intergroup and intragroup competition and cooperation. *J. Exp. Soc. Psychol.*, 1977, *13*, 81–88.
41. Okun, M., and DiVesta, F. Cooperation and competition in coacting groups. *J. Pers. Soc. Psychol.*, 1975, *31*, 615–620.
42. Allport, G. W. The nature of democratic morale. In G. Watson (Ed.), *Civilian morale*. Boston: Houghton Mifflin, 1942, Chapter 1.
43. Katz, D. Group morale and individual motivation. In J. E. Hulett, Jr., and R. Stagner (Eds.), *Problems in social psychology*. Urbana, Ill.: Allerton Conference on Social Psychology, University of Illinois, 1952, Chapter 14.
44. Stouffer, S. A., et al. *The American soldier: adjustment during Army life* (Vol. 1). Princeton, N.J.: Princeton University Press, 1949.
45. Zander, A. *Motives and goals in groups*. New York: Academic Press, 1971.
46. Wickesberg, A. Communications network in the business organization structure. *Acad. Manage. J.*, 1968, *11*, 253–262.
47. Lorsch, J. W., and Morse, J. J. *Organizations and their members*. New York: Harper & Row, 1967.
48. Argyris, C., and Schon, D. A. *Theory in practice: Increasing professional effectiveness*. San Francisco: Jossey-Bass, 1974.
49. Selznick, P. *Leadership in administration*. New York: Harper & Row, 1957.
50. See, for example, Barnard, C. I. *The functions of the executive*. Cambridge, Mass.: Harvard University Press, 1938.

SUGGESTED READINGS

Fisher, B. A. *Small group decision making,* 2nd ed. New York: McGraw-Hill, 1980.
Jewell, L. N., and Reitz, H. J. *Group effectiveness in organizations*. Glenview, Ill.: Scott, Foresman, 1981.
Malcolm, A. *The tyranny of the group*. Totona, N.J.: Littlefield, Adams, 1975.
Senger, J. *Individuals, groups, and the organization*. Cambridge, Mass.: Winthrop, 1980.
Shaw, M. E. *Group dynamics: The psychology of small group behavior,* 2nd ed. New York: McGraw-Hill, 1976.
Shifflett, S. Toward a general model of small group productivity. *Psychol. Bull.*, 1979, 67–79.
Zander, A. *Motives and goals in groups*. New York: Academic Press, 1971.

LABORATORY EXERCISE

**GROUP DISCUSSION:
WELCOME TO THE DARVOL GROUP**

A. BACKGROUND INFORMATION AND SCRIPT READING

1. The instructor will read the background material (E.1) and will have six class members read the script as provided (F).

B. GROUP DISCUSSION

1. The class will divide into groups of four or five.
2. The groups will be asked to serve as outside advisers or consultants to Danny and Eunice; they are to make three actionable, specific recommendations about what the two newcomers can and should do in response to group members' feelings (as expressed in the script).

C. TABULATION OF INFORMATION

1. *Content analysis.* The following information should be collected from a representative from each discussion group:
   a. What aspects or problem issues were felt by the group to be most important? (List two or three.)
   b. What specific recommendations were made? (If there are repetitions of recommendations, refer back to the originals rather than rewriting each time.)
   c. How did these recommendations address the issues identified earlier?
   d. How many (ask for a show of hands) found the recommendations (overall) to be satisfactory, or unsatisfactory, or were neutral in their attitude toward the recommendations?
2. *Process analysis.* Again collect this information from group representatives:
   a. Did the group formally choose a discussion leader?
   b. If not, did an informal leader emerge?
   c. How was disagreement handled?

D. GENERAL DISCUSSION QUESTIONS

1. Why might the pressures for conformity (for example, unanimity of opinion and behavior) be greater for the DARVOL group than for the class groups?
2. What are some ways that peers can put pressure on others in their group to ensure conformity?
3. What is the management's responsibility in a situation like the one represented by the DARVOL group?
4. Under what conditions might members of class discussion groups or problem-solving groups feel greater pressure to conform to the group's agreed-upon plan or standards?
5. In what ways might uniformity of opinion and purpose affect the group's morale?

E. MATERIALS FOR THE CASE

1. Background Information

The Sheffield Lake Technical Center (SLTC) provides research and development support for the Chemical Division of AMACORP, a multinational American firm with over two billion dollars in annual sales. The 450 employees who work in the laboratory are divided into small independent groups, each dealing with a specific product or raw material. The DARVOL group (consisting of eight scientists, two laboratory managers, and six technicians) constitutes one of the largest and most successful groups.

In the scene that follows, the six DARVOL laboratory technicians are taking a coffee break in one corner of the laboratory.

- ☐ Mary: fifty-two years old, twenty years at the SLTC, the leader of group
- ☐ Bert: forty-five, twenty years at the SLTC
- ☐ Chester, forty-one, fifteen years at the SLTC
- ☐ Billy, thirty-seven, ten years with the SLTC
- ☐ Eunice, twenty-two, newly hired, with an as-

sociate degree in chemistry from the local junior college
☐ Danny, twenty-one, newly hired, also with an associate degree in chemistry

It is the first day of work in the group for Danny and Eunice.

F. SCRIPT

Billy: Hey, listen, no trouble at all. I just took this Bunsen burner the company didn't need and converted it for use as a coffeemaker. The sugar and creamer are courtesy of the company cafeteria.

Mary: Yeah, right, except they don't know it. I laugh when I see you slipping those sugars into your pocket. Like you were a spy.

Eunice: Well, it's very convenient to have everything right here. And these nice chairs, too, after sitting on that lab stool all morning.

Mary: Yeah, that was a good deal. You just have to know the system around here, that's all. You know, I was thinking maybe we ought to explain the system here to you and Danny, since you're new to the group.

Danny (jokingly): Hey, are you saying we're messing up our jobs already?

Mary: No, it's not that. I just want you to understand our way of thinking here.

Danny: Which is?

Chester: Which is not to let the bosses get the better of us. "The servant is worthy of his hire," as the Good Book says. And that's what we hold to. A fair day's work for a fair day's pay — no more, no less.

Mary: The thing is, you let them get their way here, they'll run you ragged. Believe me, I know. Been here twenty years — long as anybody. I was standing in the door when they first opened. Right, Bert?

Bert: That's right.

Mary: Bert's been here from the start, too. He knows, we all know, that you have to keep your eye on them. They got memories that go back years; you make a slip-up, it goes right into your file.

Eunice: I hope I don't make many slip-ups.

Billy: Oh, take it easy. It's not as bad as she makes out. The thing is, you gotta watch out for number one. Why kill yourself? is what I say. This can be a very nice place if you know how to work it.

Mary: That's right. I believe in being real careful with your work. And how can you be careful if you're just zipping along?

Danny: Yeah, but maybe if you work a little extra, stay over, watch for anything special, maybe the bosses will notice that; seems like that's the way to get ahead.

Chester: Ha! That's a laugh. Not in this vale of tears. No, sir. I tried that when I was young — got me nowhere.

Danny: Look — I didn't spend two years in community college to be just a bottle-washer forever. I've got little kids; I can't just relax and pick my teeth, like some people.

Mary: "Two years in community college" — I guess we should be impressed, huh, guys? You'll see how much good it does you. Remember that time when you told them about the funny way the H–202 samples turned rigid when they got cold, Bert? They told him to leave the thinking to them. Six months later, a great big project the company wanted fell through because they couldn't get the parts made of Darvol–202 to work when the weather turned cold.

Eunice: But surely, they're not all like that. I talked to Mr. Wheelock, and he was very nice to me. He's the kind of boss that makes you want to do something really great.

Mary: Yeah — so he can take the credit for it. The thing of it is, you see the bosses maybe fifteen minutes, half an hour out of a whole day. You work with us all day. You'll find things'll go along a lot smoother if we all work at the same pace.

Danny: Smoother for you, maybe, but not for me. I came here to get a good job in a good company . . .

Eunice: Me, too . . .

Mary: Listen, knocking your head against a wall is crazy. You stick with us, you'll get your cost of living, your benefits, your vacations. . . . You stick your neck out — who knows what you'll get.

CHAPTER SEVEN

LEADERSHIP

■

Theories of Leadership
Leading the Organization versus Leading a Task Group
New Issues in Leadership

■

HIGH PRODUCTIVITY is essential if the United States is to maintain its present standard of living.[1] Many factors determine whether production in a given plant or office is relatively high. Some of these factors are beyond the ability of employees to control — the relative efficiency of tools and procedures, for example, or the company's ability to stay up-to-date when technological breakthroughs are common (as in the electronics industry).

Factors within the provenance of employees, such as shared cultural values, also affect productivity. One head of a large mutual funds firm stated that if he were to leave a large portion of his investment portfolio in one country for twenty years, he would invest it in Japanese firms because "the Japanese believe in the value of hard work."[2] Although this sentiment is an overgeneralization, it suggests a shared Japanese cultural value that supports hard work. In this instance, an individual whose livelihood depends on his accurate perceptions of the profit potential of companies considers cultural values to be an important influence on productivity.

Within a given cultural environment, the values, lifestyles, and attitudes that are considered acceptable vary from company to company. The organization, particularly if the chief executive takes an active and skillful approach, generates messages to individual company members on issues that affect productivity. This organizational climate and its effects on employees will be examined further in Chapter 20.

Other processes necessary to generate high productivity take place within the minds of individual workers — that is, in the form of personal motivations to produce as much as possible. Such individual factors have been introduced in Chapter 3 and will be related specifically to work in Chapter 13.

Ample evidence shows the key role of the leader in affecting employee attitudes and productivity. Recognizing this fact, scientists have spent many years attempting to define and analyze the concept of leadership. One way of categorizing their approaches would be to divide them into these groups: (1) scientists who approach leadership as something one *has* (a personality trait); (2) those who approach leadership as something one *does*[3] (a category of behavior); and (3) those who emphasize leadership as a relationship between the leader and group members.

All research designs and leadership theories do not fit neatly into these three categories. However, the division will help provide a framework for reviewing the efforts of researchers, past and present, in order to elucidate the concept and practice of leadership.

THEORIES OF LEADERSHIP

LEADERSHIP AS A CHARACTER TRAIT

Over a period of many years, numerous business executives and scientists have tried in vain to agree on a list of character traits that describe a successful leader. The problem is that any positive trait can be taken too far: *objectivity* can become *aloofness, enthusiasm* declines into *nagging,* and so on. To get around this difficulty, H. Fayol, one of the early writers on general principles of management, suggested that the proper manager should be flexible and moderate in the application of management rules, neither too strict nor too lenient.[4] However, this approach does not provide methods for gauging "proper" levels of leniency or strictness.

Later writers attempted to be more spe-

ANALYZING WORK GROUP INTERACTIONS

cific (and scientific) by providing observable and measurable ways of determining the personality characteristics of leaders. For example, R. F. Bales analyzed small group interactions and described two types of leader personalities: one oriented to task accomplishment and the other oriented toward group process and members' emotions.[5] Efforts were also made to distinguish personality characteristics, such as dominance/submission, aggressiveness, and so on, which would systematically differentiate between these two types of leaders.

After reviewing a number of approaches linking leadership traits and productivity of group members, C. Perrow wrote that research of this type had resulted in increasing disillusionment on the part of researchers.[6] As knowledge advanced in this area, so did awareness of the complexities of human motivation and of leader/follower situations. Generally, research efforts resulted in the eventual disqualification of any and all traits from being automatically linked to leadership. It also produced a lengthening list of moderating variables that specified the conditions under which this or that personality trait seemed to be related to leadership as perceived by group members.

A review of the popular journals in the business area would suggest that many practicing managers are still using modernized versions of trait theory. In R. Rowan's article, for instance, top executives' styles are presented in terms of personal characteristics.[7] When various executives' styles are incongruent, he says, the organization suffers. One explanation for these troubles (given by an executive interviewed) involved the astrological signs of the organization's leaders! This kind of "theorizing" based on false or subjective information is frequently the basis on which executive recruiters seek out and select candidates for middle- and upper-

level management jobs. Some more psychologically oriented approaches may be used, but much of this important gate-keeping function is handled by individuals with little or no training in the behavioral sciences.

Although trait theory as an overall explanation has been mainly abandoned by organizational theorists, some fruitful research is still being done. Specifically, researchers are analyzing the trait of power motivation, that is, the desire to influence the behavior of others.[8] One important distinction made in this research is that power as a motive is not in itself a destructive force; the nature of its impact depends on the focus of efforts to use it and the intent and maturity of the individual. Power motivation can be helpful (and may be necessary) in effectively guiding others to pursue organizational tasks. According to these theorists, the trait of power becomes counterproductive when the goal of such guidance becomes the manipulation of individuals, rather than the accomplishment of the job.

LEADERSHIP AS A TYPE OF BEHAVIOR

M. P. Follett was one of the first management writers to conceive of leadership as a skill or category of behavior (see Chapter 8) in which the leader relates the efforts of individuals in such a way as to maximize the group's power rather than the leader's.[9] But her writings did not explain how to develop or select the most capable leaders who exhibit these desirable behaviors.

Later researchers used survey methods to try to uncover basic differences in behavior on the job between relatively successful and unsuccessful leaders. The Survey Research Center at the University of Michigan classified supervisors as relatively *employee-centered* or *job-centered* in their behavior toward employees.[10] This classification was based

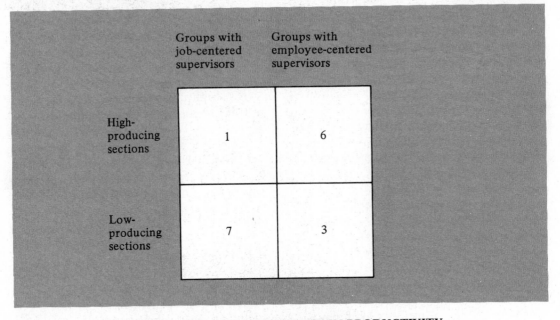

	Groups with job-centered supervisors	Groups with employee-centered supervisors
High-producing sections	1	6
Low-producing sections	7	3

FIGURE 7.1 RELATIONSHIP BETWEEN PRODUCTIVITY AND LEADERSHIP

When supervisors are classified as either job-centered or employee-centered and their work sections are classified as either high- or low-producing, job-centered supervisors are most likely to have low-producing sections and employee-centered supervisors are most likely to have high-producing units.

SOURCE: *New Patterns of Management* by R. Likert. Copyright © 1961 by McGraw-Hill Book Company. Used with permission of McGraw-Hill Book Company.

on questionnaire responses relating to supervisory behaviors. A number of studies indicate that groups with employee-centered supervisors are more likely to be among the high-producing groups, whereas groups with job-centered supervisors are more likely to be among the low-producing groups. Figure 7.1 illustrates the type of evidence used to support this conclusion.

The employee-centered supervisor takes employees' needs into account, offers employees more freedom, and gives them a sense of personal worth (that is, is supportive). *Supportive* supervisors achieve both morale and productivity, providing they have high standards of performance and communicate enthusiasm to their groups.[11]

Another classification of supervisory behavior widely used in research is based on measures of *initiating structure* and *consideration*.[12] Each is treated as a separate dimension. The dimension of consideration reflects the extent to which the leader's behavior establishes two-way communication, mutual respect, and a consideration of feelings for followers. It represents the interpersonal relations aspect of leadership. *Initiating structure* reflects the extent to which the leader facilitates group interaction toward goal attainment. These activities include planning, scheduling, criticizing, initiating ideas, and so on. Analysis of data based on these measures shows these two dimensions to be independent of each other. Both are measured

ANALYZING WORK GROUP INTERACTIONS

by questionnaire responses given by employees to describe their supervisors.

These two dimensions of leadership have been found to be related to absenteeism, accidents, grievances, and turnover. In general, these undesirable behaviors are associated with high initiating-structure scores and low consideration scores.[13] High consideration thus seems to be more related to morale and job-satisfaction factors and is similar to employee-centered supervision. High consideration was associated with production measures only when the work had no deadline. In situations where deadlines and production measures were important, high initiating structure was related to production.[14]

Some researchers and consultants felt that encounter groups (also called T-groups), which involve emotional sessions wherein participants tried to learn more about themselves and others, might be a breakthrough in managerial development by providing a way to *teach* effective leadership behaviors. It became apparent, however, that although leaders often saw themselves as being more effective with their groups after such training sessions, the groups did not necessarily agree, and the effect on productivity and effectiveness was not measurable.[15]

Many laboratory and field experiments have attempted to discover the key to a behavioral analysis that would differentiate leadership as a category of behavior. These studies include a review of the literature by D. G. Bowers and S. E. Seashore, which describes four leadership behaviors found in many studies.[16] Another study by F. A. Shull and L. L. Cummings analyzed leadership behavior in terms of differential enforcement of organizational rules.[17]

An employee-centered supervisor shows consideration to members of the group and allows them more freedom. (Peter Menzel from Stock, Boston)

Other researchers have categorized leadership behavior in terms of the conditions or situations in which certain types of behavior would be effective or ineffective. In general, this theoretical approach is called *contingency theory*. Like contingency theories of motivation, this approach hypothesizes that a given type of leadership behavior will vary in effectiveness depending on the specific circumstances in which it takes place.

F. E. Fiedler was one of the earliest theorists to describe leadership effectiveness in contingency terms.[18] Although follow-up research continues, replication of his findings (that group performance is a product of the fit between the task, the leader's motivation, and the amount of control or influence in the situation) has been partial and inconclusive. A more recent contingency approach, path-goal theory outlined by R. J. House, may prove more fruitful.[19] According to this theory, the role of the leader is to provide followers with guidance and rewards in return for effective performance (which is also satisfying to followers). The leadership style that best carries out this role depends on the personalities of individual followers, the nature of the group's tasks, and the kinds of outside threats or conflicts with which the group leader must deal.

Other researchers have used attribution theory (see Chapter 3) to explain leadership effectiveness under different conditions. It has been shown, for example, that an employee's level in the organization affects his or her conceptualization of a good leader; also the employee's sex,[20] personality,[21] and similarity to a given leader[22] have an effect on this perception.

One reason why contingency theories have not appealed to the imagination of practicing managers is that they do not include the "magic" of the more traditional, intuitive concept of leadership. It would be easier if a John Wayne type of leader could solve all of an organization's problems. But contingency-theory data suggests that this is not likely to happen.[23] As sources of problem-producing demands like government regulations or employee expectations increase, the need for a variety of kinds of leaders to solve problems will also increase. The knowledge and experience necessary to deal effectively with complex problems is too much for one "star" to deal with, however clever and motivated. In the past, changes occurred less frequently and fewer variables had to be considered, so some organizations could be led by a few great leaders. We look back at those times today and wish perhaps that they could return. But the probability is that the greater number of good leaders present in an organization will reduce the prominence of any particular one. Nevertheless, their overall importance to the successful functioning of the organization will be just as significant.

LEADERSHIP AS A RELATIONSHIP BETWEEN THE LEADER AND GROUP MEMBERS

In earlier chapters we have seen that behavior is a function of both *individual* and *situational* factors. Because of differences in individual experience and perception, people vary widely in what they perceive to be the proper leader/follower relationship and differ, therefore, on what makes a good leader. Thus, the same behavior or personality trait may connote different meanings to different group members. One person's "fascist dictator" is another's "capable, aggressive leader." For example, it was found that leaders who are more willing to permit participation in management decisions are preferred by some identifiable kinds of people, but not by everyone.[24] In one instance,

ANALYZING WORK GROUP INTERACTIONS

individuals whose upbringing and personality had led them to admire strong leaders were less favorably inclined toward participative management than those whose style of upbringing had been less strict and rigid. Similarly, individuals who scored high on a test measuring dogmatism preferred a leader who provided more detailed, structured orders; those scoring low on this characteristic preferred considerate leaders who shared power. And finally, group members' reactions to considerate versus structuring leaders were affected by the types of conflicts the group encountered. When the conflicts were within the group, a more top-down style was favored than when the perceived threat came from outside the group.

Whether we feel that another individual's actions should influence our own behavior depends partly on our perception of the structure of the organization (that is, what we see as the leader's official rights and privileges) and also on the relationship between the leader and ourselves. E. Goffman describes the way in which an individual can control the group's opinion of a situation by influencing the group's definition of the meaning of the activity.[25] He uses the word *director* to describe that member of the group who brings back into line any member of the team whose performance becomes unacceptable and gives the group members their roles.

To understand the relationship between group leader and followers better, a researcher could ask group members how the leader influenced them. But they may not know how, they may know how and not want to tell the researcher, or they may not want the group leader to know. This situation illustrates the effects, described earlier, of attitudes and expectations on a person's perception of others.

R. D. Laing illustrates the complexity that emerges when we try to unravel all the meanings and effects of leader/follower interactions.[26] Let us put ourselves in the follower position. If our expectations are not met by the leader's behavior, we may draw conclusions about his or her motivations, which in turn affect our future behavior. These changes in our behavior may then lead our leader to make assumptions (valid or not) about our intentions and to change his or her expectations about us. Some of this interaction may be conscious and rational, some may be known but be affected by emotion (or frustration), and some may be unconscious (we are not aware that our behavior or attitude has been affected). One result of these complex knots of assumption, reaction, and counterreaction is to make it difficult, if not impossible, to determine completely (1) why a given person thinks the leader is a good one, (2) how the leader has affected the followers' behavior, and (3) what behaviors on the leader's part have determined group members' opinions.

One way of thinking about the importance of expectations about leaders' and followers' behavior has been derived from the study of psychological contracts.[27] A psychological contract is an unwritten set of expectations based on past experiences, attitudes, and personality variables that people bring to bear when they are hired or are hiring someone. D. McGregor's studies indicated that leaders have expectations (justifiable or not) about the proper relationship of the worker to the company and to themselves.[28] Although the study of expectations and attributions concerning others may be helpful, it will inevitably suffer from the limitations and compexities described by Laing.

In the past, leadership studies have generally asked the queston, "What is the effect of the *leader's* behavior on the *group*?" However, some researchers have also asked, "What is the effect of the *group's* behavior on the *leader?*" This approach also interprets the leader/group member relationship as being *interactive*; that is, each has an effect on the other. Such research has suggested that the development of the leader's role is a collaborative process and is modified over time as demands change. Expectancy theory (see Chapter 3) can be related to these findings because behavior by both leader and group members is regulated by the expectations of each and by the ways in which the expectations are met, disappointed, ignored, or modified by others.

In a simulated study, some supervisors were told their employees were a superior performing group, and others were told that their employees were one of the worst groups.[29] All supervisors had the task of conducting a discussion with three employees in which the objective was to get the workers to adopt a change in work procedure. After the meeting, the employees were asked to fill out questionnaires revealing their attitudes toward their supervisors. The supervisors of the low-producing groups were found to be significantly different from those of the high-producing groups. The low-producing-group supervisors differed in these characteristics:

☐ Had more punitive attitudes
☐ Exerted unreasonable pressure more often
☐ Had less trust in employees
☐ Were less sensitive to needs and feelings of workers
☐ Were less inclined to give recognition for a job well done
☐ Had lower performance standards
☐ Had less pride in the group
☐ Gave less freedom
☐ Were poorer listeners

☐ Were poorer communicators
☐ Placed less emphasis on teamwork

Thus, this simulation produced the very leadership characteristics that are related to low-producing groups, but in this instance, the leader's perception that the group had a history of poor productivity made the leader less considerate. On the other hand, the simulation showed that a leader is more inclined to supervise less closely, be more permissive, and be more supportive with a superior group of employees. The fact that leader and follower attitudes are the product of an interaction (not one the cause and the other the effect) must be kept in mind when examining relationships between leader behavior and worker productivity.

Some findings on how groups evaluate their leaders have been surprising. For example, results of a study measuring the relative effects of quantity versus quality of speeches found that the *amount* an experimental leader (hired by the researchers) talked was more important than content *quality* in determining the groups' evaluation of leadership potential.[30] However, when individuals (again, collaborators in the experiment) were perceived by group members to be experts, they were frequently chosen as leaders, no matter how much or how little they spoke.[31]

Most contingency research relates leadership effectiveness to organizational level, type of task, and personalities of leader and followers. One recent study partially reversed the usual relationships of these variables. R. M. Kanter suggested that many characteristics of poor leaders — previously viewed as inherent in the leader's personality and as causes of poor task performance (such traits as officiousness, bossiness, overconcern with details, reluctance to delegate re-

ANALYZING WORK GROUP INTERACTIONS

sponsibility), are in fact results of inadequate access to the organization's sources of power.[32] When individual or organizational factors (for example, a female leader, a staff position, or a first-level supervisory position) increase the probability of limited access to organizational resources and power, the observed poor leadership traits are likely to be more frequently encountered.

Our earlier discussions of the effects of frustration (hostility, childishness) also seem congruent with these findings. If, for whatever reason, a supervisor cannot get resources or rewards for the followers, both leader and followers become less satisfied and more apt to become frustrated.[33] This attitude in turn, leads to less effective behavior relative to other group leaders in the organization who have the "right connections" and plenty of resources. In the organization, as elsewhere, success breeds success and failure breeds further failure.

LEADING THE ORGANIZATION VERSUS LEADING A TASK GROUP

Up to now, we have used a framework for studying leadership that differentiates approaches according to definitions of the concept. Some theorists have distinguished the necessary behavioral and personality traits on the basis of the organizational level of the leader instead. The following sections contrast leadership of an organization as a whole and leadership of a work group within an organization.

THE CHIEF EXECUTIVE OFFICER

Many people see policy making as a leadership function of the chief executive officer and upper management, as opposed to a function of middle management. Middle managers are generally held responsible for the creation, change, and elimination of *structure,* which can include levels of hierarchy, systems of rules, hiring specifications, and so on.

For P. Selznick, the most important function of the chief executive officer is to make critical, as opposed to routine, decisions.[34] These decisions may be necessary only two or three times per year, yet they have long-term effects and are crucial to the firm's long-term survival and maintenance of its image, its value set as an organization. Without this critical function being properly carried out, the organization will lose focus, and members will concentrate on personal and task group goals.

For T. Burns and G. M. Stalker, the overriding top management tasks are first, interpreting correctly the marketing and technical situation's stability; second, designing the management system appropriate to conditions; and third, making it work.[35] They call these functions *direction* and feel that they constitute the distinctive tasks of managers-in-chief. Some individuals who have written about top managers as leaders have been influenced by the theories of Sigmund Freud. A. Zaleznik emphasizes the lonely responsibility of chief executives and the importance of these leaders' development of a sense of self and of the courage to assert their individuality.[36]

Another psychoanalyst views leadership as a quality derived from a younger person's identification with an older good leader.[37] He cites the responsibility of the chief executive for engendering the ideal of the organization as part of providing a learning environment for developing managers.

Middle-level managers transmit upper management decisions to lower levels of the organization. (Ann McQueen)

LEADERSHIP FOR
MIDDLE-LEVEL MANAGERS

The linking-pin function and its importance in the organization have been described both by C. I. Barnard[38] and R. Likert.[39] According to these writers, it is the job of middle managers to transmit the values evolved by upper management to the lower organizational levels and so knit the organization together. Although the top leaders must be aware of future positive and negative impacts on the company from outside, middle managers need an internal perspective. They need to concentrate on seeing that members of their own and other task groups work smoothly without serious obstacles.

To enable a smooth-running operation, middle managers must learn to deal with various kinds of conflict. On some occasions, group members are placed in a situation that sets them in conflict with one another, but the leader is not a part of the conflict. This type of relationship is shown in Figure 7.2. Situation A would arise if, for instance, the supervisor had to assign office space in a new building and if one office were more desirable than the others.

Situation B in the figure shows the group in conflict with the leader. Such a conflict occurs when the leader wishes to introduce a change in work methods or standards, or to remove some privilege. The conflict tends

ANALYZING WORK GROUP INTERACTIONS

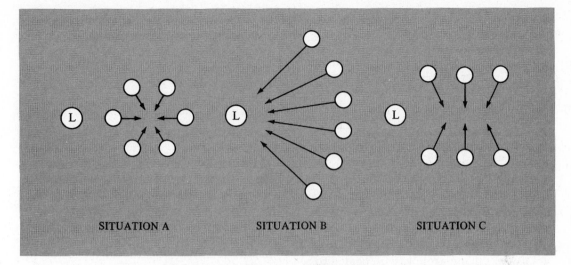

FIGURE 7.2 THREE TYPES OF CONFLICT
Situation *A* occurs when the leader must choose one person for favored treatment. All the others want the same treatment, so they are in conflict with one another. Situation *B* conflict occurs when the group members unite against the leader. This type tends to occur when the leader wishes to introduce a change. Situation *C* occurs when the group is divided into two or more subgroups, so cooperation is at a minimum.

to unify the members and strengthen their opposition.

Situation C represents a split in the group. The more the subgroups are in conflict with one another, the more they are unified within themselves. Divided job interests, differences in status, and differences in privileges can produce these subgroupings.

Techniques for resolving conflict and using the differences for constructive ends primarily depend on the leadership. *Leadership* takes on new meanings when it is seen as one of solving problems through group interaction. New conceptions and new skills are required if management is to be seen as working with groups, not as controlling the work of a certain number of individuals.

One special problem of middle managers is their two-way function (the linking-pin function) — they must communicate upward in the organization hierarchy to their own supervisor and also downward to those whom they themselves supervise. Thus, part of their task is to digest, simplify, and reorganize the data that they receive so that the information will be appropriate for the next level, up or down. This position — being sandwiched between two layers of the hierarchy, which may have conflicting perspectives, goals, and training — presents a chronic problem for managers.[40]

THE SUPERVISOR AS LEADER

Between the level of the chief executive and the level of the individual is the task group level. In the last chapter, many factors involved in determining the productivity of a work group (morale, group size, and so on) were described. But one specially important factor has been reserved for separate treatment here: the group's official leader, its supervisor.

The immediate supervisor has more influence on the attitudes of employees than the job itself does.[41] The supervisor is generally regarded as an important determiner of morale,[42] and surveys repeatedly show the dependence of productivity on supervisory behavior. A survey of office workers[43] revealed that most of the differences between the high- and low-producing work groups were related to some aspect of supervision. Some of the more important conclusions were as follows:

1. Supervisors in high-producing groups were given more freedom and more general supervision from their superiors than those in low-producing groups, who tended to receive close supervision.
2. Supervisors of high-producing groups tended to be satisfied with the amount of authority and responsibility they had in running their jobs, whereas supervisors of low-producing groups tended to be dissatisfied on these points.
3. Supervisors of high-producing groups were more aware of their leadership function and spent more time in planning and organizing the work than did supervisors of low-producing groups, who were more inclined to help out by doing some of the actual work themselves.
4. Supervisors of high-producing groups tended to give general supervision and leave details to employees, whereas supervisors of low-producing groups tended to give close supervision.

One of the most striking relationships that has been reported is that between attitude toward a superior (score on questionnaire) and productivity (based on ratings).[44] A statistical study showed these two measures to be closely related (good attitude was associated with high productivity; poor attitude, with low productivity).

NEW ISSUES IN LEADERSHIP

WOMEN AS LEADERS

In her study of a modern business organization, Kanter found that higher percentages of female managers have been in relatively low-power positions.[45] This situation seems to be a result both of the sort of jobs that women have traditionally held (advisory or staff positions) and of the underlying negative attitudes of managers toward those who are "different." Access to fellow managers is important especially for middle managers, and an inability to take part in peer networks lowers a manager's chances of performing well.

Women managers today are attempting to overcome these difficulties in various ways. As the number and acceptability of women in management grows (for example, there were five hundred women who received M.B.A. degrees in 1966 as compared to about ten thousand in 1976),[46] some alleviation of past negative attitudes and their effects can be expected. Greater acceptability may then lead to greater access to "inside information" and provide the beginnings of a path to organizational power and achievement.

CROSS-CULTURAL LEADERSHIP ISSUES

The increasing presence of women and minority-group members in managerial, professional, and supervisory positions in organizations has been one of the most important developments in management during the 1970s, but there is another small but growing group of "different" managers in the United States. The increasing interdependence of cultures and markets throughout the world is well known, as are the huge multinational firms that dominate world trade. Americans are used to the idea of other Americans opening fast-food franchises from Christchurch, New Zealand, to Abu Dhaby. Having foreign companies open plants or offices in the United States, however, is a relatively new phenomenon.

In many ways, the effects of this phenomenon have been similar to those encountered by other groups new to management: conflicting expectations, negative a priori attitudes, and shocked resentment when behavior and expectations do not match. For many years, these problems have been experienced by Americans working in managerial jobs in foreign countries as they have to some degree been prepared for cultural differences. Now, such interactions are occurring between non-American managers and relatively large numbers of American workers, who have *not* been exposed to the differing cultural values and expectations of their new bosses. As a result, some problems are occurring, but in other instances, these foreign managers have been able to get higher productivity from American workers than that in comparable plants run by American managers.[47]

If American business is to survive and prosper in a highly competitive world, it must be able and willing to learn from managers who bring different backgrounds, talents, and perspectives to their jobs. Many factors suggest that the day of the industrial giant — white, male, and Anglo-Saxon, who leads his firm to the top singlehandedly — is over, probably forever. Instead, business must learn to apply *rational* approaches to the selection and promotion of *all* kinds of employees. Such methods are discussed in the chapters in Part III of this book.

NOTES

1. Bowen, W. Better prospects for our ailing productivity. *Fortune, 100*(11), 68–70ff.
2. Templeton, J. Speech presented on *Wall Street Week*. Owings Mills, Md.: Maryland Center for Public Broadcasting, January 11, 1980.
3. Katz, D., and Kahn, R. L. *The social psychology of organizations.* New York: Wiley, 1966.
4. Fayol, H. General principles of management. In D. S. Pugh (Ed.), *Organization theory.* Hammondsworth, Eng.: Penguin Books, 1971, 101–123.
5. Bales, R. F. Task roles and social roles in problem solving groups. In E. E. Maccoby, T. M. Newcomb, and E. L. Hartley (Eds.), *Readings in social psychology.* New York: Holt, 1958.
6. Perrow, C. *Complex organizations: A critical essay.* Glenview, Ill.: Scott, Foresman, 1972.
7. Rowan, R. Watch out for chemical reactions at the top. *Fortune,* 1978, *98*(6), 92–95.
8. Kipnis, D. The power holder. In J. T. Tedeschi (Ed.), *Perspectives on social power.* Chicago: Aldine, 1974, 82–123; McClelland, D. C. *Power: The inner experience.* New York: Irvington, 1975; Miner, J. B., Rizzo, J. R. Harlow, D. N., and Hill, J. W. Role motivation theory of managerial effectiveness in simulated organizations of varying degrees of structure. *J. Appl. Psychol.,* 1974, *59,* 31–37; Winter, D. G. *The power motive.* New York: Free Press, 1973.
9. Follett, M. P. Leader and expert. In L. Gulick and L. Urwick (Eds.), *Papers on the science of administration.* New York: Institute of Public Admin., 1937.
10. Likert, R. *Developing patterns of management.* New York: AMACOM, 1955.
11. Likert, R., and Seashore, S. E. Motivation and morale in public service. *Publ. Personnel Rev.,* 1956, *17,* 268–274.
12. Stogdill, R. M., and Coons, A. E. *Leader behavior: Its description and measurement.* Research Monograph, No. 88, Bureau of Business Research, Ohio State University, 1957.

13. Fleishman, E. A., and Harris, E. F. Patterns of leadership related to employee grievances and turnover. *Personnel Psychol.*, 1962, *15*, 43–46.
14. Fleishman, F. A., Harris, E. F., and Burtt, H. E. *Leadership and supervision in industry.* Research Monograph, No. 33. Columbus, Ohio: Bureau of Education, 1955.
15. Perrow, op. cit.
16. Bowers, D. G., and Seashore, S. E. Predicting organizational effectiveness with a four-factor theory of leadership. *Admin. Sci. Quart.*, 1966, *11*, 238–263.
17. Shull, F. A., and Cummings, L. L. Enforcing the rules: How do managers differ? *Personnel*, 1966, *43*, 33–39.
18. Fiedler, F. E. *A theory of leadership effectiveness.* New York: McGraw-Hill, 1967.
19. House, R. J. A path-goal theory of leadership effectiveness. *Admin. Sci. Quart.*, 1971, *16*, 321–338.
20. Butterfield, D. A., and Barton, K. M. Evaluation of leader behavior. In J. G. Hunt and L. L. Larson (Eds.), *The cutting edge.* Carbondale, Ill.: Southern Illinois Univ. Press, 167–188.
21. Durand, D. E., and Nord, W. R. Perceived leader behavior as a function of personality characteristics of supervisors and subordinates. *Acad. Manage. J.*, 1976, *19*, 427–437.
22. Weiss, H. M. Subordinate imitation of supervisor behavior: The role modeling in organizational socialization. *Organ. Behav. Human Perform.*, 1977, *19*, 89–105.
23. Lawrence, P. R., and Lorsch, J. W. *Organization and environment.* Homewood, Ill.: Irwin, 1967.
24. Schuler, R. S. Participation with supervisor and subordinate authoritarianism: A path-goal reconciliation. *Admin. Sci. Quart.*, 1976, *21*, 320–325; Weed, S. E., Mitchell, T. R., and Moffitt, W. Leadership style, subordinate personality and task type as predictors of performance and satisfaction with supervisor. *J. Appl. Psychol.*, 1976, *61*, 58–66; Katz, R. The influence of group conflict on leadership effectiveness. *Organ. Behav. Human Perform.*, 1977, *20*, 265–286.
25. Goffman, E. *The presentation of self in everyday life.* Garden City, N.Y.: Doubleday, 1959.
26. Laing, R. D. *Self and others,* 2nd ed. London: Tavistock, 1969.
27. See, for example, Thomas, R. Managing the psychological contract — teaching notes. HBS #4-474-159. Boston: Harvard Bus. School; Kotter, J. P. The psychological contract: Managing the joining-up process. In M. A. Morgan (Ed.), *Managing career development.* New York: Van Nostrand, 1980, 63–72.
28. McGregor, D. *The human side of enterprise.* New York: McGraw-Hill, 1961.
29. Farris, G. F., and Lim, F. G. Effects of performance on leadership, cohesiveness, influence, satisfaction, and subsequent performance. *J. Appl. Psychol.*, 1969, *53*, 490–497.
30. Sorrentino, R. M., and Boutellier, R. G. The effect of quantity and quality of verbal interaction on ratings of leadership ability. *J. Exp. Soc. Psychol.*, 1975, *11*, 403–411.
31. Gintner, G., and Lindskold, S. Rate of participation and expertise as factors influencing leader choice. *J. Pers. Soc. Psychol.*, 1975, *32*, 1085–1089.
32. Kanter, R. M. Power failure in management circuits. *Harvard Bus. Rev.*, July–August, 1979; and *Men and women of the corporation.* New York: Basic Books, 1979.
33. Pelz, D. C. Influence: A key to effective leadership in the first-line supervisor. *Personnel*, 1952, *29*, 209–217.
34. Selznick, P. *Leadership in administration.* New York: Harper & Row, 1957.
35. Burns, T., and Stalker, G. M. *The management of innovation.* London: Tavistock, 1961.
36. Zaleznik, A. *Human dilemmas of leadership.* New York: Harper & Row, 1966.
37. Levinson, H. *The exceptional executive.* New York: New American Library, 1968.
38. Barnard, C. I., *The functions of the executive.* Cambridge, Mass.: Harvard University Press, 1938.
39. Likert, op. cit.
40. Roethlisberger, F. J. *Man-in-Organization.* Cambridge, Mass.: Harvard University Press, 1968.

41. Campbell, D. B. Relative influence of job and supervision on shared work attitudes. *J. Appl. Psychol.*, 1971, *35*, 521–525.

42. Baruch, D. W. Why they terminate. *J. Consult. Psychol.*, 1944, *8*, 35–46.

43. Katz, D. Maccoby, N., and Morse, N. C. *Productivity, supervision and morale in an office situation.* Ann Arbor, Mich.: Institute for Social Research, University of Michigan, 1950; Katz, D., Maccoby, N., Gurin, G., and Floor, L. G. *Productivity, supervision and morale among railroad workers.* Ann Arbor, Mich.: Institute for Social Research. University of Michigan 1951. Kahn, R. L., and Katz, D. Leadership practices in relation to productivity and morale. In D. Cartwright and A. Zander (Eds.), *Group dynamics.* Evanston, Ill.: Row, Peterson, 1953, Ch. 41.

44. Lawshe, C. H., and Nagle, B. F. Productivity and attitude toward supervisor. *J. Appl. Psychol.*, 1953, *37*, 159–162.

45. Kanter, op. cit.

46. Werner, L. MBA: The fantasy and the reality. *Working Woman,* 1979, December, 37–41.

47. Kraar, L. The Japanese are coming — with their own style of management. *Fortune,* 1975, *91*(3), 116–121ff.

SUGGESTED READINGS

Hollander, E. P. *Leadership dynamics.* New York: Free Press, 1978.

Kotter, J. P. *Power in management.* New York: AMACOM, 1979.

Sayles, L. R. *Leadership.* New York: McGraw-Hill, 1979.

Stogdill, R. M. *Handbook of leadership.* New York: Free Press, 1974.

Stoner, J. *Management.* Englewood Cliffs, N.J.: Prentice-Hall, 1978.

Vroom, V. H., and Yetton, P. W. *Leadership and decision-making.* Pittsburgh: University of Pittsburgh Press, 1973.

LABORATORY EXERCISE
PRACTICE IN DISCUSSION LEADERSHIP

A. PREPARING FOR DISCUSSION

The instructor will
1. Divide the class into groups of five or six persons.
2. Appoint one member of each group as a discussion leader.
3. Take leaders aside and instruct them to rejoin their groups and conduct a discussion on the topic, "What is the single best way to improve employee productivity?"

B. DISCUSSION TIME: ABOUT 20 MINUTES

C. REPORTS TO CLASS

1. One at a time the leaders will report the conclusion reached by their groups. The instructor will summarize the items on the blackboard under each group's number.
2. How many of the group's members accepted their group's report? Indicate number under summarized report.
3. Allow members the opportunity to criticize their group's report; summarize criticism.
4. Determine the number of members who were bored, satisfied, or interested by the discussion.

D. ANALYSIS OF REPORTS

1. Determine number of common factors in group reports.
2. Discuss the relative merits of group reports.
3. Discuss the values of specific items, such as reduced training costs due to less labor turnover, and general or vague items, such as production increases because of higher morale.

E. EVALUATION OF DISCUSSION LEADERSHIP FUNCTIONS

1. Hold a general discussion of what the various leaders did — both good and bad.
2. What could a leader do to increase the interest and satisfaction of members in the discussion?
3. What could a leader do to improve the quality of contributions?
4. What could a leader do to move discussion along?
5. What could a leader do to make participation more nearly equal for all members of a group?

ANALYZING WORK GROUP INTERACTIONS

CHAPTER EIGHT

GROUP
PROBLEM SOLVING
AND
GROUP LEADERSHIP

■

A Study of Leadership Styles
What the Group-Decision Concept Involves
Determinants of Effective Decisions
Classification of Problems
Adapting Group Decision to Operating Conditions
Training Needs   Industrial Examples of Group Decision
Why Group Decision Works

■

THOSE TRAITS AND BEHAVIORS that make for effective leaders were analyzed in Chapter 7. But how do leaders interact with their groups to achieve desired goals? What style of leadership is most effective — autocratic, democratic, or laissez faire?

A STUDY OF LEADERSHIP STYLES

BASIC TERMS DEFINED

The terms *autocracy, democracy,* and *anarchy* (*laissez faire*) describe various forms of government. In general, we think of an autocracy as strict and inconsiderate, as an arbitrary rule imposed by one person. *Democracy* carries a favorable connotation, and we think of one as being fair to people and considerate of them. Anarchy is often considered to be the absence of leadership, representing a hands-off (laissez faire) policy likely to end in chaos.

The specific definition of these terms, however, is a complex matter involving many differences of opinion over the meanings inherent in them. People may argue that democracy means majority rule, or protection of minorities through a bill of rights, or equality before the law, or a method for choosing leaders, or a method for making reforms, or some combination of these conditions.

Definitions involving complex concepts do not lend themselves to simple experimental designs. To investigate in the laboratory the way a form of government or of leadership influences behavior and to allow the testing of single variables, clear-cut, single distinctions must be made. For example, a scientist may distinguish forms of leadership in terms of the amount of freedom permitted, the degree of efficiency attained, the manner in which leaders obtain their positions, or any other measurable difference.

After somewhat arbitrarily making certain limiting and specific definitions, the laboratory investigator of leadership must simplify still further and study leadership with only one *level* of difference present: that between the leader and group members. In government and in business, hierarchies involving as many as five or six levels may exist, and because these various levels exert upward and downward influences, they must be excluded for the time being so they do not complicate the study.

EXPERIMENTAL RESEARCH ON AUTHORITY

K. Lewin selected the location of authority as a critical experimental variable.[1] Theoretically, authority could be located in (1) the leader (autocracy), (2) the group (democracy), or (3) the individual (laissez faire). Figure 8.1 shows how these three pure locations might be illustrated as the points of a triangle. (In practical situations, these three locations of authority are not likely to occur in pure states.) The sides of the triangle represent mixtures that might occur in real-life situations. (See page 164.)

In the initial research, experimenters served as leaders, and boys (about ten years old), who were invited to join a club, served as group members.[2] Experimental tests of the three pure locations of decision making yielded results clearly favoring group decision in terms of both satisfaction and productivity, whereas individual decision making generally resulted in chaos and little satisfaction. These laboratory findings became the stimulus for much research and for many practical applications and misapplications. For example, since autocracy was inferior to democracy in these experimental

ANALYZING WORK GROUP INTERACTIONS

Autocratic leaders impose their decisions on the group. In group decision, leaders do not impose preconceived solutions on the group; the group solves the problem presented by the leader. (Top, courtesy of Boston Edison Company; bottom, Chris Morrow from Stock, Boston)

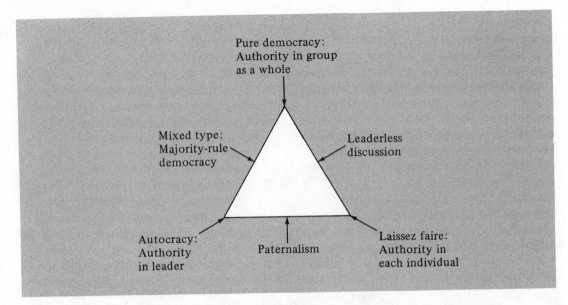

FIGURE 8.1 DIFFERENCES BETWEEN VARIOUS TYPES OF LEADERSHIP

The location of authority, or the place where decisions are made, differs in pure democracy, autocracy, and laissez-faire situations. These extreme locations are shown as the vertices of a triangle. Intermediate locations are also possible, and these can be described as falling on the sides of the triangle. Majority-rule democracy would seem to fall between pure group decision and autocracy because it implies both participation and imposition of a majority decision upon a minority. A paternalistic leader is both autocratic (makes decisions) and laissez faire (considers the wishes of individuals), and so may be described as being a point on the base of the triangle. Since a leaderless discussion involves discussion but does not make for organized action, it may be described as a condition between pure democracy and laissez faire. Any leader may be described by location on this triangle.

Source: After K. Lewin. The dynamics of group action. *Educ. Leadership,* 1944, *1,* 195–200. Reprinted with permission of the Association for Supervision and Curriculum Development. © 1944 by the Association for Supervision and Curriculum Development. All rights reserved.

results, decisions imposed by business leaders were regarded as poor leadership methods by organizational theorists generalizing to the business situation. However, if autocratic leaders cease controlling, they do not necessarily become democratic, but merely nonautocratic. Many become permissive and follow the laissez-faire style. If one type of control is to be surrendered, the group must be reorganized to coordinate effort. Group decision represents such a new style of control, but it is not likely to arise without management training. In this sense it is an in-

vention and could not have been found by studying existing organizational behavior. The elimination of autocracy in supervisors, teachers, or parents does not necessarily replace it with something better. As illustrated in Figure 8.2, pressures to move away from autocracy can lead to laissez faire or permissiveness. But managerial training can replace autocratic leadership with group problem-solving methods.

Experiments with the group of boys demonstrated that activities could effectively be controlled by having members make the de-

ANALYZING WORK GROUP INTERACTIONS

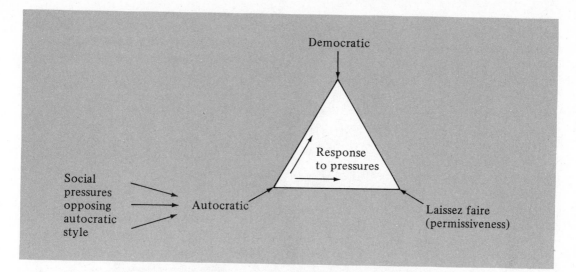

**FIGURE 8.2 AVOIDING AUTOCRACY BECAUSE OF SOCIAL
PRESSURE IS NOT THE SOLUTION**

The avoidance of autocracy does not produce democracy since democratic leadership is not the opposite of autocratic. There are two directions away from autocratic styles. Both autocracy and democracy (as defined in the text) limit freedom, but in one case the limitation is imposed by the leader, and in the other, it is agreed upon by the group.

cisions for the club activities (naming the club, determining activities, task assignments, and so on). In other experiments, food habits were changed more effectively by group decision than by persuasion of the leader.[3]

Figure 8.3 shows the results of an industrial study that illustrates how production was greatly increased by inviting workers to set their own production goals. Figure 8.4 shows how a change in work methods in another firm was successfully introduced, without the usual distrust, when workers were given the opportunity to participate in the planning. (See pages 166–167.)

GROUP DECISION VERSUS
PARTICIPATIVE MANAGEMENT

In early experiments on group decision, trained psychologists conducted the meetings, so there was a tendency to overlook the need for skills since all discussion leaders possessed them. Untrained supervisors who try to practice goal setting in their groups may be incorrectly perceived as being dissatisfied with the group or as trying to sell them on setting higher goals. The untrained group leader is also likely to fear losing control, so permits participation on an important matter only if veto power is retained.

As a result, group participation may become heavily loaded with manipulative or deceptive approaches in which employees are allowed to discuss matters, but not really to make decisions. What is called *participative management* today includes practices ranging from having a chance to express views to having a vote. In our modern society, most people favor democracy, but at the same time, they are afraid to practice it without some safeguards. People are inclined to favor having a say-so when they are doing the

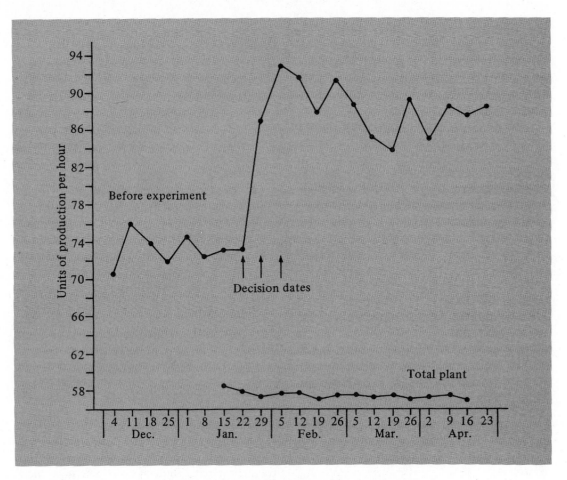

FIGURE 8.3 AN EFFECT OF TEAM DECISION
When a team of workers decided to attain a specific goal, their production showed a sharp increase, which was maintained despite the fact that the team's performance was already above the plant average. (Courtesy of A. Bavelas)

"saying," but are hesitant to accept this practice when they have to abide with someone else's "say."

An illustration of what happens under the influence of ambivalent feelings occurred in a large corporation. Coffee drinking was getting out of hand because employees were taking coffee breaks when policy did not permit them. When the violations became intolerable, top management personnel held a meeting in which they reached the decision to permit all employees a twenty-minute coffee break. The next step was to determine whether this break should be given in the morning or the afternoon. The managers felt that the sensible time was afternoon. One member remarked that employees would also choose the afternoon to have their cof-

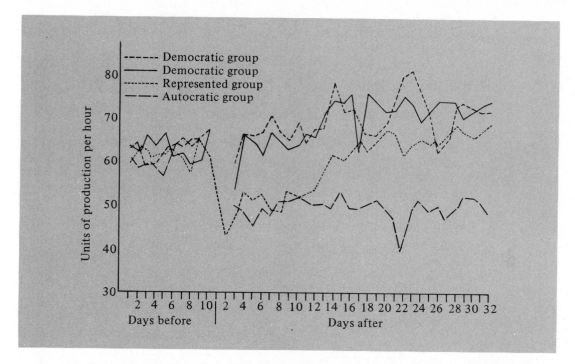

FIGURE 8.4 OVERCOMING RESISTANCE TO CHANGE
The production records for each of the four groups studied are shown before and after job change. The curve of the autocratically handled group shows a sharp drop in production when the change is made, and recovery does not occur during the period studied. The two democratically handled groups show rapid recovery and reach a production level on the new job that exceeds the old one. Production of the group that participated through its representatives shows a sharp drop and recovery gradually occurs. The gaps in the curves of the democratically and autocratically led groups indicate the period during which they were paid on a time-work basis.

SOURCE: After L. Coch and J. R. P. French, Jr., Overcoming resistance to change. *Hum. Relat.*, 1948. *1*, 512–532. Permission granted by the Plenum Publishing Corporation.

fee, so why not let them feel that they were participating in the decision? This plan was agreed on, ballots were printed, and employees voted whether they wanted a morning or afternoon coffee break. The vote showed 80 percent voting in favor of a morning coffee break. However, management decided to have the coffee break in the afternoon "where God intended it to be." Participative management of this kind does more harm than good.

WHAT THE GROUP-DECISION CONCEPT INVOLVES

LEADER-GROUP RELATIONSHIP

In order to use group decision effectively in business, it must not be confused with popular definitions of democratic or participative approaches. As initially tested, *the group-decision concept assumes a face-to-face meeting of the leader with members in which the leader (1) poses a problem and (2) leads the discussion, but the group makes the decision.* The problem concerns a matter that participants understand and in which they have an interest. The size of the group is assumed to be twelve or fewer. If the concept is to be adapted to larger groups or participants who cannot meet, certain modifications in procedure are needed.

In the Lewin experiments, the leader was not only an adult, but a psychologist as well. Thus, authority was not restricted by higher management, unions, or other work groups. Furthermore, the leader had no emotional investment in favoring certain solutions over others. This means that practical life situations introduce variables not present in these laboratory experiments.

UNANIMOUS AGREEMENT

The purpose of discussion is to reach unanimous agreement. If cooperative effort in the implementation of a decision is to result, differences must be resolved. A majority decision, on the other hand, imposes its will on the minority, the group is divided. *The voting type of democracy must not be confused with group decision.* Failure of groups to reach agreement is less likely to occur than might be imagined because discussion tends to resolve differences once the disagreement is clarified. However, one study indicates that in some groups where positions are taken before discussion, the effect of discussion is to polarize members and teach them new justifications for their positions.[4] This finding emphasizes the need for a skilled group leader.

LOCATION OF DECISION VERSUS STRICTNESS

Autocracy is often associated with strictness, and laissez faire with leniency. The location of authority, however, does not necessarily determine whether standards for work will be high or low. An autocrat can be strict or lenient, and individuals may set lenient or strict standards for themselves. Figure 8.5 illustrates how the high and low standards might be included in the concept by changing the triangle to a prism. Thus some autocratic leaders might expect higher standards of performance than others; some individuals may work harder doing what they want to do than others; and some groups might set higher goals than others. If group decision makes a group more productive than autocracy does, it demonstrates *high standards are more easily achieved through group decision than through autocracy,* not that one is *necessarily* associated with the other.

DETERMINANTS OF EFFECTIVE DECISIONS

Experiments have demonstrated that when groups rather than leaders have made a decision, behavior was more cooperative and initiative was higher. Members worked on the task regardless of the leader's presence with greater pride in their work, better group cohesiveness, greater satisfaction with the task, and more positive feeling for the leader. Whether the decision to engage in the activity selected was the best one cannot be determined, and for the purpose of the experiment, this aspect of the decision was irrelevant. However, in many practical situations, decision *quality* must be considered. It is essential therefore that a distinction be made between the objective fitness of a decision (its quality) and the degree to which the participants like it (its acceptance).[5]

QUALITY AND ACCEPTANCE

Tests in life situations indicate that participation in making decisions is more likely to

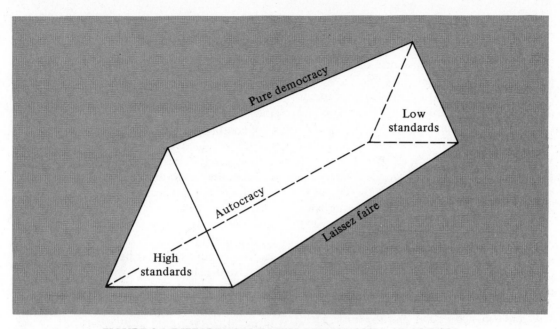

**FIGURE 8.5 DIFFERENCES IN THE EFFICIENCIES OF GROUPS
FORM A THIRD DIMENSION**

A prism is used to picture this aspect of group functioning and at the same time to describe the various locations of a decision-making function. It follows that efficiency or standards can be high or low in any type of leadership. An important problem is to determine which type of leadership can achieve high standards most easily.

motivate the group to implement *its* decisions than is the case with those supplied by the leader. We might speak of this dimension of the decision-making function as *acceptance*. People are more likely to accept the decisions when they feel responsible for them as a result of having helped to make them.

The risk involved in the use of group decision is that the decisions may lack objective quality and be influenced too much by feelings. High-quality decisions require an effective use of objective facts. Decisions made by experts or by experienced and capable leaders can generally be trusted to respect facts and protect quality.

A decision lacks effectiveness if it does not have the emotional support of those who

must execute it or if it ignores or fails to respect relevant objective facts. The formula

$$ED = Q \times A$$

describes this relationship. Effective decisions (*ED*) are a product of the degree to which the decision has quality (*Q*) (which concerns the objective facts) and acceptance (*A*) (which concerns the feelings of the persons who must execute the decisions).

In the light of this analysis, we are confronted with an interesting practical problem. To be effective, decisions should have both high quality and high acceptance, but the procedures for gaining quality and acceptance conflict. The method for achieving quality gives the decision-making responsibility to the leader where there is access to information, advice, and expert opinion; whereas the method for gaining high acceptance puts the decision-making function in the membership. Must one of these objectives be sacrificed for the other?

This conflict in methods is a management dilemma that has plagued organizations for centuries. Traditionally, achieving quality was regarded as the first step. Leaders protected quality by making the decision themselves. Once this was done, they were left with the problem of executing the decision. The oldest method for gaining acceptance was through the use of fear. Later on, paternalists gained acceptance through loyalty.

Perhaps the most common method in present practice is persuasion. A successful leader, it is argued, must be a good persuader. Participative approaches often are invoked to gain acceptance, but the leaders still retain the right to make the final evaluation and decision. Consultative managers, at best, are open to suggestions and, at worst, attempt to manipulate the group members to come around to their ways of thinking. All these changes in management styles stop short of giving up the decision-making function from fear of either endangering quality or losing control.

Despite the fear of risking quality by permitting group decision, it is not uncommon for managers to admit that they frequently make second-best decisions because the highest-quality decision is not acceptable to employees. Compromises are common results of conflicts in interest between managers and employees.

HOW Q AND A INTERACT

Let us suppose that we had to decide on the best way to do a particular job and that four solutions were possible, each differing from the standpoint of engineering excellence. On the basis of this much information, perhaps everyone would be inclined to choose the technically most efficient method. But what if the persons who had to perform the job liked this method the least? In the light of these feelings, it might be wise to choose another method in order to gain the willing cooperation of employees, as was done in the following case.

In a large power plant, the job of cleaning furnaces was a trouble spot for management because of grievances and turnover. A four-member crew had to work inside the furnace and use specific cleaning tools. The job procedure had been worked out by time-and-motion engineers, who had to consider the facts listed below.

1. Two people should not need the same tools at the same time.
2. Employees should not get in the way of each other.
3. Duplicate tools should be minimized because of space limitations.
4. The number of times a tool is picked up and put down should be minimized (because these motions are not productive).

A method based on these considerations was developed, and the workers were trained to follow the method.

Over the years workers complained about the job. Since they were not work-methods engineers, no one listened. After being trained in group decision the supervisor called a meeting and asked the workers what was wrong with their team. They agreed that one person had more of the dirty work than the others, and that this was a source of dissension. After they voiced criticisms about the job, the discussion became more constructive. Various changes were suggested and evaluated. The ideas finally developed into a modified job procedure.

This new procedure was analyzed by the time-and-motion experts. Their report indicated that the modified work procedure would cut efficiency to 67 percent of its original value. Nevertheless, the new method was put into effect with the result that it took four workers *two,* rather than *four,* days to clean a furnace.

Analysis in terms of quality and acceptance would indicate that the first method had high quality and low acceptance, whereas the modified method had lower quality (67 percent versus 100 percent), but the effect of greater acceptance more than offset the reduced quality.

The increased production made the new method more effective, despite the fact that we might agree that the engineers had the best answer from the quality point of view and the workers had the best answer from the acceptance point of view. A decision's effectiveness, quality, and acceptance should be differentiated to facilitate communication.

The importance of quality and acceptance will undoubtedly vary with the nature of the problem. Perhaps a consideration of differences in problems will suggest an approach that will avoid the management dilemma and propose a method for avoiding the conflict in methods for gaining quality and acceptance.

CLASSIFICATION OF PROBLEMS

QUALITY-CRUCIAL/ACCEPTANCE-AUTOMATIC PROBLEMS

Some problems are of such a nature that persons who have to execute decisions regarding them have no emotional interest in any particular decision. Decisions about where the company buys its raw materials, how much it charges for services or products, what is the best rate of expansion, and decisions on many technical engineering matters are readily accepted by employees. If they were involved in such decisions, they might perhaps complain about wasting their time.

The nature of solutions to such problems, however, may be highly important with respect to the quality dimension. Decisions pertaining to pricing a product or a service, or adapting growth rate to markets and economic conditions can mean success or failure for a company. Problems for which quality is important and acceptance creates little or no problem belong to this type and can continue to be solved at the leadership level.

ACCEPTANCE-CRUCIAL/QUALITY-NOT-AN-ISSUE PROBLEMS

Many problems have a great variety of possible solutions, and the differences in their objective quality are negligible. Who should work overtime, who should get the corner office vacated by a retiring vice president, who is to be sent to a training program, what constitutes tardiness, and what are proper methods for discipline are questions that management decides largely because decisions must be made, not because a particular decision is regarded as important. However, such decisions can involve a good deal of emotion. Generally, they involve the issue of *fairness.* Feelings, rather than objective facts, determine what is fair. Thus, acceptance becomes the important dimension.

It is over problems of this type that management decisions are frequently challenged. The most common word in picket lines is *unfair.* When these problems are solved by group decision, the possibilities for gains in acceptance are great, and the risks to quality are minimal. In such instances, the interests of managers and employees are least likely to conflict. Both sides favor fairness; the question is how to accomplish it. The actual conflict is often within the group. If a new truck is obtained, which driver should get it if several want it? This conflict in interest can be more effectively resolved through group discussion than through the marshaling of factual information. As a matter of fact, groups will not agree on the solution, so the most satisfactory solution will vary from one group to another even when the facts are the same. Such decisions are tailored to fit the values of the group members.

NEITHER-QUALITY-NOR-ACCEPTANCE-CRUCIAL PROBLEMS

Some decisions have to be made among alternatives that are equally good from a quality point of view; furthermore, these decisions often make little difference to those who execute them. For example, if telephone lines have to be built from point A to point B, a decision has to be made regarding which end to begin with. If the supervisor decides to begin at A, the crew might ask, "Why not begin at B?" The supervisor then feels obligated to point out why it is better to begin at A, which is hard to do when the alternatives have equal objective merit. If a group-decision meeting is held, half the crew may vote for A and half for B. Since it really makes no difference, they do not discuss the problem to resolve a difference, but find the problem interesting from the point of view of winning the debate. Such problems can best be handled by flipping a coin.

BOTH-QUALITY-AND-ACCEPTANCE-CRUCIAL PROBLEMS

With these three classes of problems eliminated, a class of problems remains in which *both* quality and acceptance are important, although their relative importance may vary. Such problems include standards for tardiness, production goals, improving service, increasing safety, improving work methods, and introducing labor-saving methods. These problems frequently involve (1) conflicts in interests (real or apparent) between managers and workers; (2) use of expert opinion; and (3) complex patterns of variables that create issues of fairness.

Two procedures are available. On the one hand, the leader can make the decision to protect quality, but in following this plan the leader needs persuasive skills in order to obtain as much acceptance as possible. On the other hand, the group-decision method insures acceptance, but the leader must have certain conference skills to optimize the quality of the decision. These discussion leadership skills are not in the form of manipulation and subtle controls, but methods for upgrading the discussion procedure, processing the information and selecting a solution. A group of persons has certain resources that, if effectively used, can make group thinking more effective than that of the leader. However, the group product also may be inferior because of interpersonal rivalry and self-interests.

How and when to use the group for improving decision quality will be discussed later in connection with problem solving. Improving decision quality becomes especially important at higher levels in the organization where much talent lies latent. As organizations increase in size and technical complexity, it becomes more essential to use group resources effectively. Individuals working alone cannot process information and generate the ideas needed. For the present, our concern is with the potential uses of group decision to gain acceptance, cooperation, and improved communication.

THE PROBLEM CHART

Since the needs for quality and acceptance of decision vary, the leader may visualize problems as occupying a position on a chart, such as that in Figure 8.6. To determine the method to follow in reaching a decision, the leader may rate the importance of quality and acceptance separately. A rating of zero to nine can designate the importance of both quality and acceptance for an effective solution. These two ratings will locate the problem on the chart. The location of the problem will suggest the most appropriate method to follow. A*q type problems fall in the upper left quarter of the chart, Q*a type problems in the lower right quarter, the a*q problems in the lower left quadrant, and the Q*A problems in the upper right.

Supervisory personnel will not usually agree regarding the way the same problems are classified. Some estimate the quality dimension more highly than others. With training, the awareness of the acceptance dimension increases, as does agreement. After

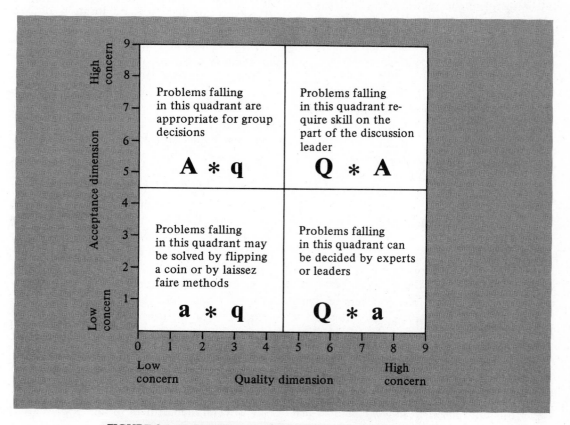

FIGURE 8.6 CLASSIFYING PROBLEMS ACCORDING TO THE ACCEPTANCE AND QUALITY DIMENSIONS

Problems may be rated in terms of the two dimensions essential for effective decisions. Each problem then becomes a point on the chart and falls in one of the four quarters. The method to be followed in solving the problem depends on the quarter in which it falls. This simple method may aid the beginner in deciding on the appropriate decision-making procedure.

training, managers classified 43.8 percent of their problems as the A*q type and only 22.6 percent as the Q*a type.[6]

ADAPTING GROUP DECISION TO OPERATING CONDITIONS

Some adaptations are required to bring the group-decision method closer to the day-to-day operating needs of a company. These adaptations can assist the practicing supervisor to relate the method to problems on the job as well as to clarify the problem areas that lend themselves to the approach.

GROUP DECISION AS A SUPERVISORY METHOD

A leadership style should be considered a method and not a description of a person. For instance, Supervisor Musante may handle a problem on vacation scheduling democratically by conducting a group-decision conference; he may behave autocratically in setting up an improved housekeeping plan by making the decision without inviting discussion; and he may behave in a laissez-faire manner by allowing employees to select work companions. The reason for pointing out the difference between types of leaders and methods is that many supervisors feel that they must accept the concepts of democratic leadership completely in order to use it at all. They resist using the method because they feel they do not have the time; they fear the method would backfire in some cases; or they feel that the method would sometimes become too involved for their level of skill. *Objections to group decision that are based on special cases where the method seems inappropriate need not prevent its use in other instances, providing we separate the method from the person.* The most democratic supervisor is the one who uses the group-decision method on the greatest number of problems. Supervisors would become more democratic if they sought new instances in which group decision could be used, instead of looking for conditions under which it could not be used.

ACCOUNTABILITY

In describing the Lewin experiments on leadership styles, the location of *authority* was the distinguishing feature. For practical purposes it seems better to distinguish the styles on the basis of the location of the *decision-making function.* The supervisor does not relinquish responsibility by sharing a problem with the group and asking them to help solve it. The leader is still accountable to top management for results. When group decision is chosen, the leader should be willing to accept responsibility because of a belief that the decision will be more effective.

THE AREA OF FREEDOM

In most firms, there is a hierarchy of management personnel. A somewhat simplified example of this hierarchy is illustrated in Figure 8.7. The figure shows only the relationship between the units and divisions in a particular department. Each square describes a position held by a particular individual, who in turn reports to the person above in the chart. For example, the first-line supervisor who is in charge of unit B reports to division supervisor K, who in turn reports to the head of department H. In a similar manner, a figure might show how the several department heads report to a plant manager, who then may report to a vice president. The person in charge of each management position shown has certain tasks to perform and certain decisions to

ANALYZING WORK GROUP INTERACTIONS

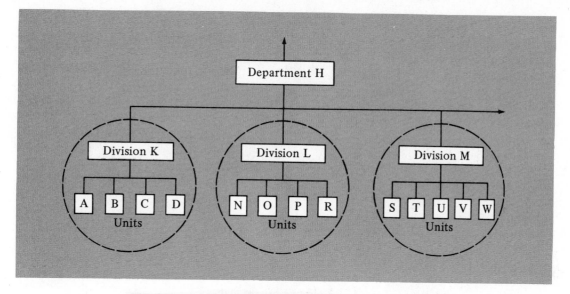

FIGURE 8.7 ORGANIZATION CHART OF A TYPICAL DEPARTMENT

The relationship between departments, divisions, and units is shown by the connecting solid lines. This chart shows only a small department within a company. The broken lines, each enclosing a division and several units, represent potential discussion groups in which the division supervisor acts as the leader. Each unit supervisor is the leader of groups of employees not shown in the chart. All management personnel are potential participants in one grouping and leaders in another.

make. The unit supervisors are in charge of a group of workers, and although each unit may perform different functions — ranging from clerical to drill press work — they are alike in that they supervise the work of non-management personnel.

Unit supervisors have to deal with disciplinary problems, scheduling work loads and vacations, maintaining quality and productivity, and so on. Division supervisors are in charge of a group of unit supervisors. Each division supervisor must plan and integrate the work of the units, see that standards between them are comparable, coordinate the work of the division with that of the others, and so forth. In higher levels in the organization, the problems encompass a wider segment of the company. The depart-

ment head must deal with problems on a department-wide basis, hence must think more in terms of principles and less of specific details.

In holding group-discussion meetings, supervisors ordinarily would meet only with their immediate subordinates, and the problem shared would be one that they had the authority to solve. It is important to keep in mind that supervisors cannot have a group decision on matters over which they have no authority. If they have the authority to make a decision, they can accept the group's decision as *the* decision, but they cannot let their group decide the problems of another level in the organization.

Figure 8.8 has been constructed to clarify the area open for group decision. The circle

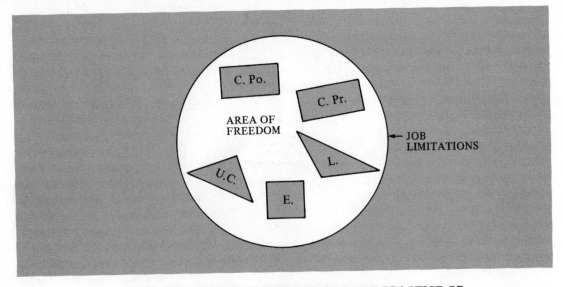

FIGURE 8.8 THE AREA OF FREEDOM FOR THE PRACTICE OF DEMOCRATIC LEADERSHIP

The circle represents the limitations that the job situation imposes on activity. *C. Po.* and *C. Pr.* represent the limitations imposed by company policies and company practices, respectively; *U.C.* and *L.* represent activity areas removed by union contracts and legislation, respectively; and *E.* represents problem areas solved by experts. The remaining area falls within the authority of a given level of supervision, and problems in this area may be solved by group techniques.

SOURCE: From N. R. F. Maier, A human relations program for supervision. *Indust. and Labor Relat. Rev.*, 1948, *1*, 443–464. Used with permission.

represents the limitations imposed by the job. A supervisor is a group leader only insofar as the job supervised is concerned. Problems about religion or politics, for example, would not be matters for group decision because they would fall outside the circle. Activities unrelated to the specific supervisor's responsibility also are outside the circle. Thus, drill press operators cannot decide to become material handlers or to change the shift on which they work.

Even when considering problems falling inside the circle defining job activity, there still are certain restrictions on the area open for group decisions. Within a supervisor's job territory, some activities have been taken away or greatly limited. Higher management has established company policies and practices felt at all job levels, which supervisory as well as group decisions cannot contradict.

Company policies (*C. Po.*) and company practices (*C. Pr.*) reduce the area of a supervisor's decision-making functions and are thus shown as rectangles in Figure 8.8. Similarly, union contracts (*U.C.*) cannot be violated or altered by group decisions. Laws (*L*), such as those governing the length of the work week, child labor, minimum wages, or establishing the rights of employees to hold union membership, also restrict the freedom of action at all levels of management. The square label *E* refers to experts. Most companies have taken away

ANALYZING WORK GROUP INTERACTIONS

some of the technical aspects of the supervisor's job and have turned them over to specialists. Lighting engineers, time-study specialists, personnel assistants, and safety engineers are a few of the organization members whose job is to supplement the activities of management throughout the plant.

The area within the circle and between the limiting geometrical figures is designated as the *area of freedom.* Problems falling within this area are the ones to consider for group decision. Since all problems of a company fall within the area of freedom of one group or another, all decisions can be group decisions, though all groups do not participate in all decisions.

THE SUPERVISOR AS AN EXPERT

In using the group-decision approach, a supervisor has two parts to play.[7] One role is that of the *discussion leader,* who has the job of conducting a good discussion. The other role is that of an *expert,* who has information that may be of value. In making good decisions, effective use must be made of available facts. Often a supervisor has access to sources of information or has had training and experience that will aid in reaching good decisions. In order not to impose their views on a group, skilled discussion leaders give their groups the benefit of their knowledge by the way in which they state the problem and supply the facts.

Let us suppose a group-decision meeting is held to determine what color the walls should be in an employees' lounge. Relevant to the decision would be knowledge of such things as the amount of light reflected by various colors, interior decorators' opinions on color combinations, and the cost of different-colored drapes. The discussion leader can supply the group with this information, using charts and samples, as the various points come up and the group asks about

them. A leader who is open-minded and sincerely wishes the group members to make the decision will find them interested in facts.

Before supplying information, a leader may explore the group's knowledge, because various members may be able to supply essential facts. When the leader does supply information, it should be done in a way that does not indicate the leader's preference for a decision. A city council, for example, can make an effective decision about the design of a new bridge, providing they have the benefit of an engineer as consultant. It would be this expert's role (1) to point out problems, such as the relationship between cost and load, style and cost, style and type of rock formation, and (2) to ask good questions about the needs and objectives of the citizens. The expert need never and *should not* express a personal choice, because this reflects a bias and may encourage controversy. Similarly, the supervisor in the role of expert should act as an unbiased resource person.

If we think of experts as individuals with knowledge greater than that of the persons with whom they deal, the supervisors become experts on several counts. They know more about company plans, company policies, what other units are doing, past records, methods, and what areas are open to choice. In dealing with new employees, the supervisors know more than employees about specific jobs, and they function as experts when training employees.

Often supervisors can phrase problems to make them fall within the area of freedom. For example, if Jean Collins knows that her unit has been allotted five hundred dollars to redecorate the lounge, she can put the problem to her group as follows: "We have been given up to five hundred dollars to redecorate the lounge. Let's discuss the matter and decide how we want to spend it." Many decisions must consider limitations and these can be clarified by the supervisor in the statement of the problem. An instance of such a problem would be: "During this overtime period, we have to have one skilled and two semiskilled operators in attendance — what is the fair way to distribute overtime so as to accomplish this?"

THE SUPERVISOR
AS DISCUSSION LEADER

Both the degree of acceptance of a decision by group members and its objective quality depend on the skill of the discussion leader. Experimental tests show that an individual performs a valuable function merely by serving as group leader[8] and becomes even more valuable by asking good questions, by setting an example of listening and trying to understand, and by not trying to sell ideas.[9] The principles and methods discussed in the chapters on attitudes and frustration can serve as aids to a leader in dealing with feelings; ability to do so becomes a primary skill area. A group's respect for, and interest in facts is elicited when true feelings can be communicated and understood. A group's problem-solving activity, which requires a consideration for factual matters and goals, places no great demands on the leader's capacity. The major difficulties are to refrain from dominating and to inhibit the tendency to make suggestions, supply alternatives, and manipulate the group by indicating the ideas favored. Relaxing and *letting the group pick up the problem is an important leadership skill* and is easiest to do when the leader has no fear that the group will reach the wrong solution. Because of emotional involvement in outcomes, it is often difficult for the leader to distinguish between solutions and problems. As a matter of fact, many supervisor

problems turn out to be "How can I get my ideas accepted by my group?"

A problem is properly isolated when it is formulated in terms of the desired goal and the obstacles that lie in its path. Group decision is the process of finding and agreeing on solutions. Presenting a solution and trying to sell it is the authoritarian approach, and it needs to be inhibited when conducting group discussions.

The use of group decision therefore represents a change in the role of the discussion leader. The use of the group method with a few basic skills will be adequate for solving problems of the A * q type. With the acquisition of additional skills in discussion leadership, a supervisor can make further gains. To achieve the maximum potential, the supervisor should receive special training in group-decision methods. These further gains are not in the form of getting the group to cooperate but in that of raising the problem-solving level of the group process, which often means that the leader's thinking also will be upgraded.

SELECTION OF PROBLEMS

Group decision makes its greatest contribution when the acceptance of decisions becomes important for their effective execution. The conservative use of group decision therefore should be in the solution of problems that primarily involve acceptance. *Whenever emotions are present and attitudes within a group conflict, the use of group decision should be seriously considered.* Problems involving work changes, fair treatment, fair standards, and job security are loaded more with feelings than with facts and readily lend themselves to group decision. It is important for the leader to evaluate problems in terms of their importance to employees. Availability of iced tea may become an important issue to a group of employees, whereas a supervisor may consider it a big fuss over nothing.

When selecting problems for group decision, a supervisor should also consider their possible ramifications. Wash-up time in a unit may create a problem for the whole department. If the area of freedom is properly clarified, such difficulties can be avoided; nevertheless, problems differ in the degree to which they involve other issues.

TIME REQUIREMENTS

Many managers initially react to the use of group decision as being too time-consuming. But most would not find spending one or two hours per week for such meetings excessive. If the meetings effectively solve one or two problems each month, considerable progress can be made over a year.

TRAINING NEEDS

BASIC LEADERSHIP SKILLS

The skills essential to the group-decision type of discussion must be consistent with the concept. Some people think that if leaders cannot dominate a discussion, as in autocratic leadership, they will be left without a function. However, a different set of skills is needed for group-decision leadership, and possibly they exceed in complexity those essential to autocratic leadership. The following are some skills that seem to be essential:

1. *The ability to state a problem in such a way that the group does not become defensive, but instead approaches the issue in a constructive way.*
Statements of problems in terms of situation, in terms of fairness, or in terms of

common objectives are successful approaches. It is important for leaders to share problems with their groups (for example, how to make the job more safe), rather than to pass judgment on them (how to get the employees to be more careful). Leaders should not suggest alternatives to choose from, indicate a preference for a solution, or criticize suggestions made by employees. In many instances, leaders show more skill when they have no preconceived idea of what should be done.

2. *The ability to supply essential facts and to clarify the area of freedom without suggesting a solution.*
Ordinarily this aspect of leadership requires little time, and it is important that the problem be turned over to the group as quickly as possible. Any facts overlooked can easily be supplied later. The most frequent fault encountered in training discussion leaders is their tendency to make long preliminary speeches.

3. *The ability to draw persons out so that all members will participate.*
This technique requires leaders who are able to (a) accept contributions (using an easel helps); (b) make reluctant individuals feel their ideas are wanted and needed; (c) prevent talkative individuals from dominating without rejecting them; (d) keep the discussion moving forward; (e) accept feelings and attitudes of all participants as valid considerations; (f) protect individuals that other group members might attack verbally; and (g) accept conflict in the group as good and essential to the resolution of the problem. Complete acceptance of decisions can occur only when there has been full participation, and this can take place only when the leader encourages expression of, and respect for all points of view.

4. *The ability to wait out pauses.*

This ability is one of the most difficult skills to perfect. Pauses trap the leader into continuing to talk, calling on persons, asking leading questions, and suggesting ideas. The same pause that can make the leader participate *too much* should instead be used to cause the group members to enter the discussion. If leaders can outwait the first few pauses (which may seem painfully long), they will have made a great advance in stimulating discussion. Calling on individuals puts them on the spot, and they may not be ready to contribute. Participation should not be forced, but should occur naturally.

5. *The ability to restate accurately the ideas and feelings expressed in a more abbreviated, more pointed, and clearer form than when initially expressed by a member.*
In performing this function, leaders demonstrate that they are paying attention, understand what is said, and accept the views and the person who expresses them. Acceptance of ideas means that the leader neither agrees nor disagrees, but respects the right of the group members to contribute.

6. *The ability to ask questions that stimulate problem-solving behavior.*
This skill is highly important in conducting discussions for solving complex problems. Questions from the leader cause all group members to think about the same thing at the same time. If the questions are good ones, they direct exploration along fruitful lines and prevent the thinking from persisting in areas where failure is repeatedly experienced.[10] Questions become bad when the group sees them as threatening (cross-examination) rather than helpful.

7. *The ability to summarize as the need arises.*
This skill is important since it can be used to (a) move the discussion along, (b) indicate progress, (c) restate the problem in a new form (in the light of discussion), and (d) point up the facts that differences exist in the group and that these differences are part of the problem. Summarizing at the end of a discussion also serves to check on understanding, commitment made, and responsibilities entailed.

8. *The ability to deal with deadlock.*
Failure to reach unanimous agreement is much less common than is usually anticipated. Conflict situations have been described in which as many as thirty groups reached unanimous agreement. Nevertheless, anticipated failure to resolve differences tends to create anxiety in leaders, and they then use persuasion. Searching for added alternatives or making failure to reach agreement into a problem for the group to solve are effective ways to deal with competing alternatives or individual hold-outs.

Practicing these skills in various situations helps leaders to hone their abilities and students to develop them. Discussion procedures and role-playing cases (like the one described in the laboratory exercise) are designed to furnish opportunities to practice and apply the principles of leadership. A person can also improve these skills by practicing discussion leadership on the job. If leaders critically evaluate their performances in relation to discussion outlines and are sensitive to the satisfaction of those participating, they can continue to improve over a long period of time. Most problems can be handled successfully with a minimum amount of skill. Ample opportunities to improve through real-life practice will present themselves.[11]

ESSENTIAL ATTITUDES
Skills must be supplemented by appropriate attitudes. Discussion leadership seems to require a respect for the feelings of others. A leader must be concerned more with understanding than with judging.

Some research shows that a leader's behavior and effect on the outcome of discussions are influenced by variations in the leader's attitude.[12] In one part of an experiment, the attitude of the leaders was manipulated in a role-playing situation by telling them that they were supervisors conducting a discussion either (1) with other supervisors or (2) with their employees. The problem was the same in each instance, but the difference in the mental set of the leaders caused them to be more permissive and open to suggestion when dealing with peers than when dealing with employees. As a result, satisfaction and free participation were greater when a leader felt the group to be peers rather than employees.

In another study, a leader who took a helpful attitude toward the group caused participants to be more satisfied with the discussion than a leader who assumed a negative, nonconstructive attitude.[13] Failure to obtain a difference in the quality of decisions in the study seemed to be due to the fact that when the leader's behavior was unsatisfactory, certain group members took over some of the leadership functions. Members summarized ideas, clarified issues, and corrected misstatements when the leader purposely was inadequate.

The research thus suggests that a leader with a given amount of knowledge and training will do the best job of conducting a discussion when the ideas and feelings of the group members are respected, and when the leader has no favored solution in mind but considers that performing the functions of leadership is part of the job.

SOCIAL PERCEPTION

People communicate not only through language, but through actions, voice intonations, and facial expressions. Frequently, a person's spoken words actually misrepresent his or her thought or feeling. In any group discussion much potential communication is lost because members fail to respond to nonverbal expressions. It is the leader's responsibility to become sensitive to the feelings of persons and go along with the group's condition at the moment.

Sensitivity to the feelings of others can be developed, but a leader must learn what to observe, and there is no simple formula to follow. This leader-sensitivity is analogous to what a car driver must learn in properly applying the brakes. In an emergency we do not use a formula and apply a particular force for a particular speed; rather, we apply the force as the car can take it. From the response of the car we can sense a slippery pavement or a soft shoulder, and in order to become a good driver we must respond to this *feedback* from the car.

A discussion leader cannot concentrate on the agenda and expect to conduct a satisfying meeting. The group will feed back reactions in many ways, and no single behavior will have a consistent meaning. A leader must get the meaning of these signs from their context, just as we get the right meaning for a word from the way it is used.

Practice in sensing when persons like or dislike each other, when they are satisfied or dissatisfied with decisions, when participants are bored, hurt, or hostile during a discussion, and so on, are important aspects of leadership training. Role-playing and evaluative analysis of past discussions are effective ways for increasing sensitivity.

INDUSTRIAL EXAMPLES OF GROUP DECISION

When supervisors change their approach from supplying decisions (and often having to spend considerable time persuading employees) to sharing a problem, the social climate shows a radical change. In some instances, employees become suspicious, but if the supervisor is sincere in inviting their help or in finding a fair solution, discussion begins. In simulated life situations, differences both in the quality and in the acceptance of decisions among leadership styles clearly favor leaders who invite the group to make the decision.[14]

Evidence from life situations is less easily obtained because the given problem cannot be duplicated to allow a comparison of solutions obtained under difference methods. However, instances of practices do serve as case studies in which crucial behaviors can be identified.[15]

The modifications (for example, area of freedom, problem classification) imposed by adapting the group-decision concept to practical situations clearly have not destroyed the way group behavior is influenced by it. The case studies reported here are included to show how the dynamics of behavior are changed when decision making is transferred to the group.

EFFICIENCY IN A REPAIR CREW

The *production index* of a telephone repair crew is expressed in terms of the average number of visits per worker per day. The company average at one time was 10.8. The best crews had a score of 12.5; the poorest, 8.5. After training in group decision, the supervisor of a crew with a production score that had ranged between 8 and 9 for the past six months called the twelve employees in his crew to a meeting and asked whether they had any ideas on how their work could be coordinated better. The supervisor asked whether there were obstacles that could be overcome if the group sat down and discussed various phases of the job. In the presentation of the problem, the leader avoided any criticism of the relative standing of the crew. The group agreed that such a discussion would be worthwhile, and their attitude was one of a sincere desire to help.

The group readily came up with criticism about the organization of the job. The group agreed that there were too many repeats. (A *repeat* is defined as a further report of trouble from a customer within thirty days after a telephone has been repaired.) Repeats measure the quality of service in that they show either that the repair job was not properly done or that the instrument went out of commission a second time for some new cause. A new cause cannot easily be prevented, but the need for the same repair indicates inadequate work. Thus, the frequency of repeats is used as the *quality index*. The company practice is to send a more highly skilled worker on a repeat, assuming that if the first worker failed to correct the difficulty, a more skilled worker might succeed. The group felt that this procedure was wrong because it did not permit a person to learn new things or to know the outcome of past efforts.

To solve this problem, the group recommended that on all repeats the person who previously visited the customer should be sent back and that the supervisor should also go to help locate the difficulty. This suggestion was particularly interesting because the workers were actually asking for training. Furthermore, by having the supervisor visit the job, they were protected from unfair evaluation.

Another item was then brought up for consideration — time wasted in travel. The company practice was to send workers on new assignments whenever someone became available. Thus, jobs were assigned according to the order in which they were received and the worker's availability. The purpose of this procedure was to keep the number of subsequents as low as possible. (A *subsequent* is second or third call from a customer before a telephone company employee arrives.) The percentage of subsequents was used as the *service index*.

The crew recommended that the district in which they worked be divided into ten territories. A map was used to make up these divisions so that about an equal amount of work would be required in each. There were twelve people in the crew, and ten were to be given territories. The remaining two workers were to be *floaters,* who would cover the district. The plan was that floaters would make up for irregular fluctuations in the repair load.

In addition, provision was made for such marked changes in load as occur after storms, fires, and so on. It was agreed that although ten employees were to work primarily in their own territories, they could be moved into adjacent territories. By this procedure, more than half the crew could be pulled into a trouble area, leaving the rest to cover their own and an adjacent territory.

The group spent the remainder of the meeting discussing assignment of territories and floaters. Two group members liked driving and wanted to be floaters. At the end of the meeting, the employees expressed pride in the territories assigned them and acted as if they owned them. During the next two years, the effectiveness of the plan was reflected in the objective records as follows:

1. Repeats, which previously averaged over 17 percent of all service calls, now were held down to an average of 4 percent.
2. Subsequents, which previously occurred about 20 percent of the time, fell to 4 percent.
3. The number of visits per worker per day

rose from an average of 8.5 to an average of 12.5, while the company average remained below 11.

The interesting aspect of this case is the way the quality of the work procedure was upgraded. Job experience introduced facts that cut travel time and motivated learning. How much improved productivity was due to greater acceptance versus higher decision quality cannot be determined.

EMPLOYEE GRIEVANCE

Mrs. G was given a voluntary transfer from her job at the university laundry to a job at the university hospital; in making the change she went from a salaried to an hourly wage. Mrs. G was told that she would lose nothing in the transfer. However, she soon learned that her vacation accrual was only one and a half days per month on her new job for her length of service, whereas it was two days per month on the old one. When she learned this she complained, and after some deliberation the personnel office ruled that she could keep her two days accrual because she had been promised equivalent benefits.

This decision created a problem. Miss L found that she had as much seniority as Mrs. G but received less vacation and so filed a grievance. It was clear that if Miss L won her case, there would be others. How could personnel go back on its word with Mrs. G or how could they persuade Miss L to withdraw her case?

A meeting was held that included Mrs. G, Miss L, two other employees who were concerned with the outcome, the department head, his assistant, the union president, the personnel manager, and her assistant. The personnel manager put the problem to the group as follows: "We have a problem in that Mrs. G is getting more vacation time than other hourly employees with the same seniority. A grievance has been filed by Miss

L, stating that she feels Mrs. G is receiving preferential treatment, and we will probably get many more grievances on the same question. The hospital policy is to accrue one and a half days per month when you have as much seniority as Mrs. G, but through what we now feel was a misunderstanding and a mistake on our part, Mrs. G is getting two days per month. Now, could you think of any way to solve our problem?"

After twenty five minutes of discussion with all taking part, Mrs. G suggested that she give up the extra half-day she was getting per month. The group-decision approach accomplished in a single meeting what would have taken upward of six months to accomplish via the channels usually followed, and the solution did not result in loss of face for anyone. The personnel staff, initially reluctant to try the method, was both surprised and pleased. Mrs. G felt more accepted in her new job because of her willingness to give up a special privilege.

Another case involved employees in a General Motors plant. Some of them were brought together to solve a problem of excess glass breakage after traditional management methods had failed.[16] The group not only identified specific causes of the problem and generated solutions, but voluntarily talked with workers in other departments whose practices had contributed to past breakage rates of up to 46 percent. A representative from plant management indicated that workers were being tapped to problem-solve more often, particularly when they had access to knowledge of the circumstances leading to the problem.

HIGHER MANAGEMENT DECISIONS

The foregoing examples illustrate participation at lower levels of management. There are three reasons for citing this type of case.

First, group decisions made with employees in management positions are not as crucial a test of the effectiveness of the group-decision procedure as are decisions made with rank-and-file employees, because the former are expected to respect management goals and consequently evidence of good-quality decisions is not especially surprising. Second, problems and decisions at higher levels of management require consideration of many details and therefore are difficult to describe. Third, the benefits of such decisions are more difficult to appraise in terms of production standards and services rendered. However, these reasons do not mean that the group-decision method is not needed, or is inappropriate, at higher levels. As a matter of fact, it is at these levels that a good deal of talent could be marshaled for creative decision making.

Examples of group decision making by higher management illustrate its possibilities and some difficulties in reporting the value of using such a method. One case involved the briefing of an airline company officer, Mr. A, who was assigned to represent his company in working out a new or supplemental contract with a municipal airport to determine charges for the various services and facilities. All airlines serving the city are represented in such cases, and a favorable contract for a particular airline depends on the number of flights, the amount of freight carried, the amount of space used, and so on. A contract that was favorable to an airline handling a good deal of freight might be unfavorable to one having many short passenger trips. Airline representatives are inclined to strive for a contract that favors their company, but the type of contract favorable in one city might be unfavorable in another. Thus, each airport represents a unique situation, which changes from time to time, necessitating the negotiation of new contracts. Furthermore, the contracts agreed to for one airport are of concern to those who must represent the company at another airport.

Individuals involved in these negotiations have their own territories, and all report to the same person. In this instance, Mr. X was Mr. A's supervisor. In the past, Mr. X's involvement in negotiations was that of supervising the work of the employee involved by being available for consultation and giving approval to certain concessions or changes in procedure.

On the occasion in question, Mr. X decided to use the group-decision approach. Mr. A had a pending contract situation, so instead of having him in for a briefing, Mr. X called a conference. The meeting included eight employees (A through H), but a ninth, I, was on vacation.

The group discussed the specific problem situation Mr. A faced, and it soon became evident that any contract he concluded would be of concern to them. Thus Mr. A learned that any contract he negotiated would raise problems for his fellow representatives. They, in turn, sympathized with his problem, exchanged ideas, and discussed various alternatives. Mr. X was surprised and impressed with the degree of involvement in alternative possibilities and with the plans of action that emerged.

When Mr. A went to the city concerned for contract negotiations, he felt better briefed than on previous occasions. He also found himself better qualified than his competitors to discuss the issues and had no occasion to call his supervisor and check on his next move. The preliminary discussion had briefed him on all eventualities.

The resulting contract was regarded by Mr. X as highly favorable to the company; he felt Mr. A had done an excellent job; and all his fellow representatives, except Ms. I, praised the contract. She felt certain factors had not been given adequate consideration. Whether this criticism stemmed from the decision's quality, which her presence might have upgraded, or whether it was due to lack of acceptance because she had not influenced the outcome could not be determined.

Another case concerns the McCormick Company, a Baltimore-based flavoring and spice manufacturing firm, where group problem solving has been a part of management policy making for nearly fifty years.[17] When C. P. McCormick took over management of the firm, he replaced an autocratic style of management with one in which managers at all levels in the organization met regularly to formulate goals, examine problems, and recommend policy to the company's board of directors. In their first five years of existence, these policy-making boards submitted 2,104 problem solutions to top management; 99.8 percent were implemented. During the same period, another management group with responsibility for increasing production raised productivity levels one-third, without added personnel or purchase of a significant amount of new equipment.

There are now ten multiple management boards active in the company. Membership on each board changes every six months, and selection of members for the next period is based on a ranking of their past performance as evaluated by themselves and their fellow board members. Board members indicate that not only is the work rewarding in itself but the experience of working with other managers at different levels and functional areas counteracts forces tending to increase conflicts between representatives of various work groups. Also, working on boards fosters the managers' identification with overall company goals, rather than with specialized or particular group goals.

The examples show that workers and supervisors approach a problem constructively if it is relevant to their jobs and does not threaten them. The contrast between what occurs and what was anticipated is often striking. This observation is frequently voiced by persons who have given the group-decision method a trial. They started with certain fears and expectations that contrasted sharply with what actually happened; with experience, they become more relaxed and look forward to surprises. They learn that it is best not to have a solution in mind, for it has been shown experimentally that the obvious preference by a power figure for a particular alternative tends to strengthen another alternative.[18]

Because people confuse the group-decision method with many current supervisory practices, it is important to make the distinction clear. Table 8.1 lists what the group-decision method is and what it is not.

WHY GROUP DECISION WORKS

All the morale-improving factors mentioned in Chapter 6 are used in group decision. The principle of participation is carried to its logical conclusion, since it is applied to the points of decision making and enforcement. The principle of mutual sacrifice is fully used, because fairness is determined by the way members of a group see it. Freedom and tolerance are present to a high degree, and when restricted, they are restricted by the group, not by the power invested in the leader. Progress is experienced when an individual perceives movement toward a goal. A group's goal is more real to its members than a supervisor's goal, so the experience of progress is more real in group decision. Furthermore, when a group specifies goals and participates in ways to measure them, the rate of progress toward its goals becomes

TABLE 8.1 CLARIFICATION OF THE GROUP-DECISION METHOD

GROUP DECISION IS	GROUP DECISION IS NOT
1. A way of controlling through leadership rather than through force	Abandoning control of the situation
2. A way of group discipline through social pressure	A disregard of discipline
3. A way of being fair to the job and all members of a group	A way of giving each individual what he or she wants
4. A way of reconciling conflicting attitudes	A way of manipulating people
5. Permitting the group to jell on the idea that it thinks will best solve a problem	A way of selling the supervisor's ideas to a group
6. A way of letting facts and feelings operate	Sugar-coated autocracy
7. Pooled thinking	A matter of collecting votes
8. Cooperative problem solving	Consultative supervision in which mere advice is sought
9. A way of giving each person a chance to participate in things that concern him or her in the work situation	A way of turning the company over to employees
10. A method that requires skill and a respect for other people	Something anyone can do if he or she wishes

apparent to group members, who monitor it themselves and are therefore free from anxiety that external monitoring would cause.

Psychologically, the group decision method fosters sound motivation, clarification of attitude differences, security of group membership, constructive social pressure, prevention or removal of misunderstanding, good two-way communication, and respect for human dignity. Simple procedures, like this method, that use many principles are efficient procedures.

When group decision is used as a problem-solving procedure, its effectiveness depends on a very thorough exploration of the problem, discovery of many varied obstacles, utilization of a large amount of information, and generation of a great variety of points of view. Problem solving as a management skill will be discussed in Chapter 22.

NOTES

1. Lewin, K. The dynamics of group action. *Educ. Leadership,* 1944, *1,* 195–200.
2. Lewin, K., Lippitt, R., and White, R. K. Patterns of aggressive behavior in experimentally created social climates. *J. Soc. Psychol.,* 1939, *10,* 271–301; Lippitt, R. An experimental study of the effect of democratic and authoritarian group atmospheres. *University of Iowa Studies in Child Welfare,* 1940, *16,* 43–195; White, R., and Lippitt, R. Leader behavior and member reaction in three "social climates." In D. Cartwright and A. Zander (Eds.), *Group dynamics,* Evanston, Ill.: Row, Peterson, 1953.
3. Lewin, K. Group decision and social change. In T. M. Newcomb and E. L. Hartley (Eds.), *Readings in social psychology.* New York: Holt, 1947, pp. 330–344.
4. Myers, D. G., and Lamm, H. The group polarization phenomenon. *Psychol. Bull.,* 1976, *83,* 602–627.
5. Maier, N. R. F. *Problem-solving discussions and conferences.* New York: McGraw-Hill, 1963.
6. Maier, N. R. F., and Hoffman, L. R. Types of problems confronting managers. *Personnel Psychol.,* 1964, *17,* 261–269.
7. Maier, N. R. F. *Principles of human relations.* New York: Wiley, 1952.
8. Maier, N. R. F., and Solem, A. R. The contribution of the discussion leader to the quality of group thinking: The effective use of minority opinions. *Hum. Relat.,* 1952, *5,* 277–288.
9. Maier, N. R. F. The quality of group decisions as influenced by the discussion leader. *Hum. Relat.,* 1950, *3,* 155–174; Maier, N. R. F., and Hayes, J. J. *Creative management.* New York: Wiley, 1962.
10. Maier, N. R. F. An aspect of human reasoning. *Brit. J. Psychol.,* 1933, *24,* 144–155; The behavior mechanisms concerned with problem solving. *Psychol. Rev.,* 1940, *47,* 43–58.
11. A more complete treatment of leadership skills will be found in N. R. F. Maier, *Problem-solving discussions and conferences.* New York: McGraw-Hill, 1963.
12. Solem, A. R. The influence of the discussion leader's attitude on the outcome of group decision conferences. Doctoral dissertation, University of Michigan, 1953; Solem, A. R. An evaluation of two attitudinal approaches to delegation. *J. Appl. Psychol.,* 1958, *22,* 36–39.
13. Heynes, R. W. Effects of variation in leadership on participant behavior in discussion groups. Doctoral dissertation, University of Michigan, 1948.
14. Maier, N. R. F. *Problem solving and creativity: In individuals and groups.* Studies 23, 26, 29, 30, 31, 33, 34, and 35. Belmont, Calif.: Brooks/Cole, 1970; Maier, N. R. F., and Sashkin, M. Specific leadership behaviors that promote problem solving. *Personnel Psychol.,* 1971, *24,* 35–44.
15. Maier, *Principles of human relations.*

16. Ways, M. The American kind of worker participation. *Fortune,* 1976, *94*(4), 168–171ff.
17. Dudek, D. H. The harmonious clash of ideas. *Chemtech*, 1979 (November), 665–667.
18. Worchel, S., and Brehm, J. W. Direct and implied social restoration of freedom. *J. Person. Soc. Psychol.,* 1971, *18,* 294–304.

SUGGESTED READINGS

Alutto, J., and Vredenburgh, D. Characteristics of decisional participation by nurses. *Acad. Mgt. J.,* 1977, 341–347.

Greene, C. N., and Schriesheim, C. A. Leader-group interactions: A longitudinal field investigation. *J. Appl. Psychol.,* February, 1980, 50–59.

Miles, R. E. *Theories of management: Implications for organizational behavior and development.* New York: McGraw-Hill, 1975.

Pennings, J. M. Dimensions of organizational influence and their effectiveness correlates. *Adm. Sci. Quart.,* December, 1976, 688–699.

Steiner, I. D. *Group process and productivity.* New York: Academic Press, 1972.

LABORATORY EXERCISE

ROLE-PLAYING:
THE CASE OF THE NEW TRUCK

(Students are asked not to read the case materials before participating in the laboratory exercise.)

A. PREPARATION FOR ROLE-PLAYING

The instructor will
1. Read general instructions (E.1) to the whole class.
2. Place data regarding name, length of service, and make and age of truck on chalkboard for ready reference.
3. Divide the class into groups of six. Any remaining members should be asked to join one of the groups and serve as observers.
4. Assign roles to each group by handing out slips with the names Walt Marshall, George, Bill, John, Charlie, Hank. Ask each person to read his or her own role only (E.2). Instructions should not be consulted once role-playing is begun.
5. Ask the Walt Marshalls to stand up when they have completed reading their instructions.
6. When all Walt Marshalls are standing, ask that each group member display the slip of paper with the role name conspicuously so that Walt can identify each worker by name.

B. THE ROLE-PLAYING PROCESS

1. The instructor will start the role-playing with a statement, such as the following: "Walt Marshall has asked his crew to wait in his office. He is out now. Apparently he wants to discuss something with the men. When Walt sits down, that will mean he has returned. What you say to each other is entirely up to you. Are you ready? All Walt Marshalls please sit down."

2. Role-playing proceeds for twenty-five to thirty minutes. Most groups reach agreement during this interval.

C. COLLECTION OF RESULTS

1. Each supervisor in turn reports the group solution. The instructor summarizes on the chalkboard by listing the initials of each worker and indicating with arrows which truck goes to whom.
2. A tabulation should be made of the number of persons getting a different truck, the crew members considering the solution unfair, and the Walt Marshalls' evaluations of the solution.

D. DISCUSSION OF RESULTS

1. A comparison of the solutions will reveal differences in the number of persons getting a different truck, who gets the new one, the number dissatisfied, and so on. Discuss why the same facts yield different outcomes.
2. The quality of the solution can be measured by the trucks retained. Highest quality would require the poorest truck (Hank's) to be discarded. Evaluate the quality of the solutions achieved.
3. Acceptance is indicated by a low number of dissatisfied participants. Evaluate solutions achieved on this dimension.
4. Locate the new truck problem on the problem chart (Fig. 8.6 p. 173).
5. List problems that are psychologically the same as the new truck problem. See how widely the group will generalize.

E. MATERIALS

1. General Instructions

Each group of six persons will be working on the same problem at the same time; members of each group will be asked to participate in solving a job problem. (This procedure is called multiple role-playing and combines role-playing and "Phillips 66" (see Chapter 1, Laboratory Exercise) to give a new kind of participation experience.)

Assume that you are telephone repair workers for a large utility. Each day you drive to various locations in the city to do repair work. Each of you drives a truck, and you take pride in keeping it looking good. You have a possessive feeling about your trucks and like to keep them in good running order. Naturally, you like to have new trucks too, because a new truck gives you a feeling of pride.

Here are some facts about the trucks and members of the crew that reports to Walt Marshall, the supervisor of repairs:

Crew	Years with company	Age of truck	Make of truck
George	17	2	Ford
Bill	11	5	Dodge
John	10	4	Ford
Charlie	5	3	Ford
Hank	3	5	Chevrolet

Most of you do all of your driving in the city, but John and Charlie cover the jobs in the suburbs. (The instructor should write the above facts on the board so that they are visible to all during the role-play.)

You will be one of the persons mentioned above and will be given some further individual instructions. In acting your part in role-playing, accept the facts and assume the attitude supplied in your specific role. From this point on, let your feelings develop in accordance with the events that transpire in the role-playing process. When facts or events arise that are not covered by the roles, make up things consistent with the way it might be in a real-life situation.

2. Role-Playing Instructions

Walt Marshall — Supervisor of Repair Crew
You are the head of a crew of telephone maintenance workers, each of whom drives a small service truck to and from the various jobs. Every so often you get a new truck to exchange for an old one, and you have the problem of deciding to which of your crew members you should give the new truck. Often there are hard feelings, since each seems to feel entitled to the new truck, so you have a tough time being fair. As a matter of fact, it usually turns out that whatever you decide is considered wrong by most of the crew. You now have to face the issue again because a new truck, a Chevrolet, has just been allocated to you for assignment.

In order to handle this problem you have decided to put the decision up to the crew. You will tell them about the new truck and will put the problem in terms of what would be the fairest way to assign the truck. Do not take a position yourself, because you want to do what they think is most fair.

George
When a new Chevrolet truck becomes available, you think you should get it because you have most seniority and don't like your present truck. Your own car is a Chevrolet, and you prefer a Chevrolet truck such as you drove before you got the Ford.

Bill
You feel you deserve a new truck. Your present truck is old, and since the more senior man (George) has a fairly new truck, you should get the next one. You have taken excellent care of your present Dodge and have kept it looking like new. A man deserves to be rewarded if he treats a company truck like his own.

John
You have to do more driving than most of the other men because you work in the suburbs. You have a fairly old truck and feel you should have a new one because you do so much driving.

Charlie

The heater in your present truck is inadequate. Since Hank backed into the door of your truck, it has never been repaired to fit right. The door lets in too much cold air, and you attribute your frequent colds to this. You want a warm truck since you have a good deal of driving to do. As long as it has good tires, brakes, and is comfortable, you don't care about the make of the truck.

Hank

You have the poorest truck in the crew. It is five years old, and before you got it, it had been in a bad wreck. It has never been good, and you've put up with it for three years. It's about time you got a good truck to drive, and you feel the next one should be yours. You have a good accident record. The only accident you had was when you sprung the door of Charlie's truck when he opened it as you backed out of the garage. You hope the new truck is a Ford because that is what you prefer to drive.

PART

MATCHING
THE
WORKER
TO THE
JOB

THREE

One of the chief goals of management is to maximize the productivity (return on investment) of organizational resources — both capital goods and labor. It is not always clear, however, how to do this or even how to determine what constitutes the maximum potential of resources. The question of capital goods is the easier maximum productivity to determine. Machines can be worked harder and harder until they break down; then calculations as to their optimal capacity and speed can be derived from fairly objective data. However, as the system becomes more complex (a huge manufacturing plant or a plant-warehouse-retail network), the calculations necessarily involve some estimates, becoming less precise, more subject to debate.

In the case of human resources, maximum, optimal, or even normal or satisfactory output is not easily determined. For one thing, motivation is a factor in human performance, whereas it is not involved in machine output, and for another, human beings can innovate, can imagine improved ways of doing a job, whereas machines operate according to a specific job method.

Over the years, psychologists and others have tried in a number of ways to find methods for improving the fit between job and worker — both by selection and training (changing the O) and by altering the job's design (changing the S) — thereby increasing efficiency and improving motivation.

Part Three describes several of the most important of these methods. Chapter 9 ("Evaluating Individual Abilities") explains why effective selection methods are the chief components in achieving a good worker/job fit. Careful selection minimizes the duration and expense of training, which, no matter how skillful, cannot undo the effects of selecting a poor job candidate. Chapter 10 ("Selection, Placement, and Career Planning") makes clear why effective selection methods are never easy. The description of the role of bias in testing and interviewing demonstrates the application of principles outlined in Chapter 5 on attitudes to this selection process. Chapters 11 and 12 ("Designing the Job for Greater Efficiency" and "Training in Organizations") describe ways that scientists have developed for improving worker/job fit by altering the design of the job and by increasing the skills of the person performing the job.

Thus, Part Three presents a comprehensive picture of methods developed to aid managers to select the best candidates for jobs, to design the job most effectively for these persons, and to provide training for maximum productivity. In doing this, managers apply the principles of motivation, frustration, attitude formation, and so on discussed in Parts One and Two.

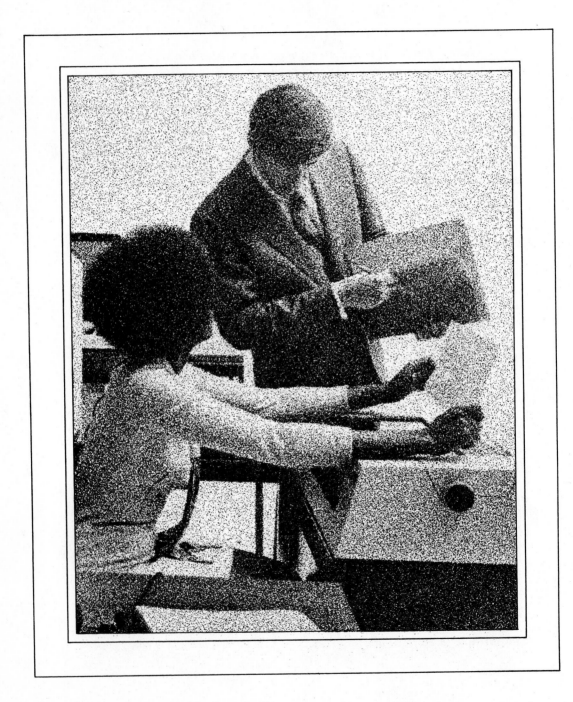

CHAPTER NINE

EVALUATING INDIVIDUAL ABILITIES

∎

The Nature of Individual Differences
Variations in Normal Distributions of Human Abilities
Deviations from Normal Distributions
Measuring the Relationship Between Human Abilities
Ability and Performance

∎

THAT PEOPLE DIFFER from one another is a truism. They not only look different, but their abilities also vary. However, the full importance and nature of variation in abilities among people are not generally appreciated. Many people believe that "practice makes perfect," yet whatever the amount of practice, some persons will never become as proficient in a certain skill as others. Sometimes people are classified as bright or dull, good or poor workers, easy-going or hot-tempered. The implication in each instance is that a person falls permanently into one of only two categories, an assumption that is fallacious.

In business, a common practice is to pay by the hour. This payment implies that a person's time is what counts rather than what is accomplished. Paying for hours spent on the job encourages workers to "put in their time," rather than to produce to the limits of their abilities. If someone falls below a certain level of performance, that person may be discharged. But frequently the actual cause of termination is related to factors other than productivity, such as attitude or attendance. On the other hand, the fact that one person may be capable of producing as much as two others and require no more equipment than one of them is not sufficiently appreciated by the average employer.

Since marked differences in ability do occur, optimal selection alone would greatly increase production. Once the most capable available workers are selected, pains can be taken to keep them and use their superior ability. Because superior individuals can do satisfactory work without much effort, they ordinarily need not exert themselves to keep their jobs. Inducements must be offered to encourage them to produce up to the level of their ability. This is not a simple problem, since other group members may object to having their own lesser abilities exposed.

The objections of less capable workers to superior performance are based largely on the fact or the impression that they will suffer thereby. It has been the experience of labor that when workers are paid for the amount they produce, some have made a lot of money. When this has occurred, they have often found that mangement is likely to lower the piece rate.[1] If managers wish to benefit from individual differences, they must do it in a way that will avoid opposition from employees. Although the improper use of a person's ability may provoke opposition, it does not follow that differences in ability should not be recognized and used.

It should be borne in mind that ability or potential skill *does not* equal performance. Ability is only one factor of several (including motivation, training, and so on) that combine effects to result in actual performance.

THE NATURE OF INDIVIDUAL DIFFERENCES

THE NORMAL DISTRIBUTION CURVE

If we subject many aspects of human beings to measurement, we find that the measured traits are distributed in the population in a particular fashion. Further, these traits are distributed in a very similar manner whenever they are measured in individuals selected randomly — that is, so as to be representative of the general population. The measured trait may be height, strength of hand grip, intelligence, ability to memorize, speed of reacting to a signal, or emotional stability. Regardless of whether we measure physical characteristics, mental traits, personality traits, sensory capacities, or muscular coordination, the manner in which they are generally distributed in the population forms a bell-shaped pattern as illustrated in Figure 9.1. The height of the curve represents the frequency with which the various scores plotted on the base line occur in a population. This curve is the theoretical normal distribution curve for individual differences. It is characterized by symmetry about a center, which is called the *average,* or *mean.*

The shaded portion in the figure includes 50 percent of the total population. Mathematical procedures are available for marking off such parts of a curve. The population represented in the curve thus can be divided into four equal parts. We can refer to individuals as being in the first, second, third, or fourth quarter of the population in regard to the particular trait measured. *The greatest variation in individual ability occurs within the first and fourth quarters.* In the two middle quarters, the individuals are more closely bunched and are more homogeneous. People tend to generalize from this fact and assume that *all* individuals perform at about this level. We are likely to overlook the fact that a wide range in ability occurs in both the upper and lower quarters. *It is these exceptional performers that are most frequently misunderstood, and it is through a proper appreciation of the upper quarter that potential gains can most easily be achieved.*

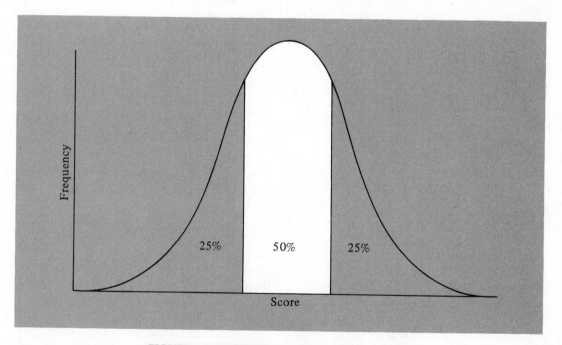

FIGURE 9.1 NORMAL DISTRIBUTION CURVE
The height of the curve indicates the frequency with which the various scores shown on the base line appear in a population. Half of the people make scores that fall in the narrow band in the middle. The other two quarters make scores that are spread over a wide range, both above and below the middle band. If the middle half is divided into two quarters, the population is divided into two groups of equal size.

EVALUATING INDIVIDUAL ABILITIES

When sufficiently large numbers of people are tested, when these are selected at random, and when the test is not too easy nor too difficult, the plot of the actual measurements obtained corresponds to the theoretical curve. In other words, the distribution curve describes the manner in which ability is distributed in a group when selective and chance factors are excluded and a good measuring instrument is used. When results do not reflect this distribution, there is good reason to investigate further to discover the cause.

The importance of any individual's score must always be judged by its position in the distribution curve. This position gives an idea of how rarely or how commonly this degree of ability occurs. The fact that a person can inspect 200 parts in an hour has little meaning, but the fact that only three workers in one hundred can do better than that shows clear superiority. To find another who would do as well would not be easy. Human ability, for the psychologist, is always a relative matter. To appreciate any one individual, we must know how that person compares with the population as a whole.

PRACTICAL IMPLICATIONS

Because about half of the people are near average in ability, such individuals are likely to be represented in any small group of employees. It is these employees whom a supervisor is most likely to understand, and it is their performance that provides a basis for what performance levels can reasonably be expected. The lower as well as the upper 25 percent of the population often will be misunderstood because they are unusual and some are very much above or below average in ability. Often both superior and inferior

producers are classified as "loafers": the superior ones because they do not keep busy and the less gifted because they accomplish less than is considered normal.

A supervisor may transfer or discharge the superior "loafer" and then find too late that two or more workers are needed to handle the job. A job that keeps an average worker busy will allow considerable leisure for one of superior ability. When extra work runs out, the supervisor who must keep the superior worker busy may become frustrated. When there is no limit to the amount of work to be done, workers of superior ability may become problem employees if they refuse to do as much as they can.

Persons below average in ability are problems because they may respond to the supervisor's demands for more work by using methods that reduce quality, by ignoring safety procedures, or by becoming hostile. Furthermore, other employees may slow down so that the poor producer's work no longer is out of line with the general level of production.

The first step in meeting the problem of individual differences in ability is to recognize them and to accept the differences as facts. To demand the same from all workers can lead to the slowest one setting the pace for all.

The concept of a normal distribution can serve a valuable positive purpose when it is used to give a supervisor some idea of unfavorable conditions in the group. Although the production figures of small groups cannot be expected to form a smooth distribution curve, certain trends can be expected. Let us examine an actual situation and see how this knowledge may be helpful.

A supervisor in the telephone industry, when asked about the productivity of employees, stated that six were above average in productivity, each doing four installations per day; six were below average, each doing three per day; and none was average since no one did three and a half installations. It is obvious that half of the workers cannot be equally superior even if only twelve people are involved. At least one or two should be able to do more than four installations if six can do four per day. It also follows that some of them should do less than three if six can do three per day. However, this condition might be explained by assuming that those who are unable to do three per day had been discharged or transferred. But most interesting is the fact that no installer completed between three and four jobs, since the ability to do approximately three and a half installations must be present in some who are doing three.

The discrepancies indicate the need for determining motivation, that is, (1) why installers turn in only complete jobs; (2) why some either hold back on production or are not interested in doing more; and (3) how workers who have difficulty in doing three installations are treated. If superior workers hold back on production to protect low producers, it would be more efficient to stop criticizing the low producers and hope superior workers would feel free to do more. How poor must a worker's production be before he or she is considered unfit for the job? The answer to this question involves supervisory attitudes, the notions of fairness in a group of employees, and some further consideration of individual differences.

In a toll-ticket–sorting unit the production figures for a group of 13 workers on a particular day were as follows: 610, 790, 910, *1005, 1060, 1090, 1150, 1195, 1255,* 1405, 1595, 1780, and 2098. Note that the production of six workers (italic scores) falls between 1005 and 1255, a range of less than

300 units. This is the middle part of the distribution curve where we find people to be very much alike in ability. The production of four superior performers has a spread of more than 600 units, and that of the three low performers ranges from 610 to 910.

The question first is whether or not the employee with production at 610 should be removed. Perhaps the previous lowest scorer already has been removed; eliminating the poorest producer always leaves another. How bad is a production of 610 when it is seen in relation to a distribution curve of the other scores?

Since scores near the average are always the ones most alike, it is reasonable to suppose that the concentration of scores between 1000 and 1300 centers on the average for this kind of activity. Roughly 1150 would be about the center of distribution. A person producing 610 units will be 540 units below average, and one worker producing 2098 units will be 948 units above. As a matter of fact, the person producing 1595 units is just as superior as the one producing 610 units is inferior.

In this instance, the poorest performers already have been removed by one method or another. To continue removing the poorest performer will cause anxiety on the part of others and lead to morale problems. Large differences in productivity are a tolerable condition when they stem from the fact of abilities spread over a wide range. As long as the superior producers are definitely farther above the central grouping than the less gifted producers are below, a good selection of employees is indicated. This favorable condition is more readily apparent when the production figures are graphically presented as in Figure 9.2 (see page 200). The superior performers more than offset the low production of the less capable workers.

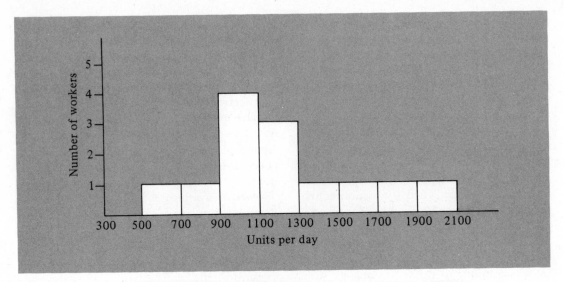

FIGURE 9.2 PRODUCTION SCORES OF A SMALL GROUP OF WORKERS

The slowest worker is less of a problem when it becomes apparent that superior workers more than make up the deficiency. Since every group must have a slowest worker, study of the distribution of production scores reveals when this condition is acceptable and when it needs correction. In this example, the slowest worker does not deviate enough to be classified as unsatisfactory.

When tests are not used to select employees, the distribution of abilities approaches what may be expected from the general population. For example, finger dexterity is an important ability for radio assemblers. Figure 9.3 shows the manner in which this ability is distributed in the population as a whole (solid line) and among forty-two radio assemblers (broken line). (See page 202.) Ability was measured by the time required to place a hundred pegs in the O'Connor Finger Dexterity Test Board. A low score therefore means superior ability. This group of radio assemblers differs from the population as a whole only by a small shift in the curve as a whole toward the right or upper range. The average time for people in general is 7.99 minutes as compared to 7.35 minutes for the assemblers. Supervisors are often mistaken in supposing that the degree

of superiority in their group is greater than it really is.

SEX AND RACE DIFFERENCES

Whether the distributions of ability between sexes and races actually differ and whether differences reported are due to biological, cultural, or educational factors are questions that cannot be answered at this time. For practical purposes the answers would have little value. The differences within a race and within a sex would show normal distributions, and if any differences in shape between these distributions did occur, it would have to be slight. (Visualize another distribution curve superimposed on the one in Figure 9.1 but placed slightly to either side.) It follows that even if the average female were slightly superior in some ability to the average male, it would still allow, for example, 48 percent

MATCHING THE WORKER TO THE JOB

The entry of more women into heretofore male-dominated jobs affirms that any differences in ability between the sexes is slight. (Courtesy of Raytheon Company)

VARIATIONS IN NORMAL DISTRIBUTIONS OF HUMAN ABILITIES

THE RANGE OF ABILITY IN DIFFERENT OCCUPATIONS

Although the abilities of an unselected group of people tend to be distributed as in the normal distribution curve, variations in the spread of the scores do occur. For some abilities, the highest score may be only one and a half times as great as the lowest score; for others, the highest score may be as great as twenty-six times the lowest. A large variation may occur even when individuals with similar training are compared.

Figure 9.4 illustrates how ability to produce may be distributed in three occupations (see page 203). Usually, the productivity levels in business do not have as wide a range as occurs in the general population. Markedly inferior workers are eliminated, and superior workers often lack motivation. Nevertheless, the productive performances of different workers are not as much alike as is usually supposed. For example, it has been found that for polishing spoons, the ratio is 1 to 5, and that for loom operation, it is 1 to 2.[4] In looping hosiery, the production of 199 employees ranged from three pairs to eighty-four pairs per hour.[5] These production figures, however, included those of inexperienced individuals. When the output of fully experienced persons only was studied, the range was from thirty to eighty-four pairs per hour.

In general, the spread of a distribution curve is greater for complex abilities than for simple ones. When the range is great, it is particularly important to encourage the superior individuals to remain with the company, as their ability is an important factor in total production. The low-producing

of the males to be superior to 50 percent of the females.[2]

The function of employee selection should be to screen for job ability. General characteristics like race and sex offer no meaningful clues for selection because *individual* differences are the important variables.

The value of certain psychological tests for measuring differences in ability has come under severe criticism because their use puts certain groups at an unwarranted disadvantage.[3] A test that systematically places a particular group at a disadvantage is obviously not a valid instrument.

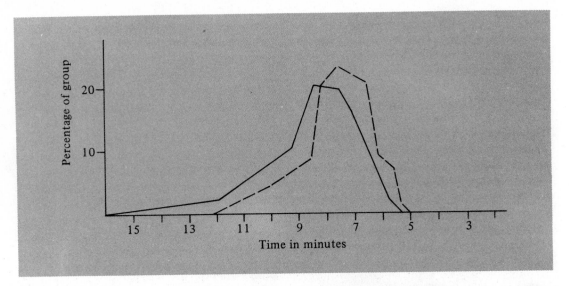

FIGURE 9.3 DISTRIBUTION OF SCORES ON O'CONNOR FINGER DEXTERITY TEST

The solid line shows the distribution for people selected at random and the broken-line curve shows the distribution for radio assemblers. Although finger dexterity is an important aptitude for this work, it will be noted that the ability of the assemblers (average time 7.35 minutes) is only slightly better than that of the population as a whole (average time 7.99 minutes).

SOURCE: From Joseph Tiffin, *Industrial psychology,* 3rd ed., p. 20. © 1952, adapted by permission of Prentice-Hall, Inc., Englewood Cliffs, N.J.

workers either should be transferred to a simpler type of operation where the distribution is less widely spread and where varying degrees of ability show minor differences in production, or should be placed in jobs different from those in which they are at a disadvantage.

DIFFERENCES IN EXPERIENCE CONFUSE THE PICTURE OF INDIVIDUAL DIFFERENCES

Practice does not equalize productive ability. Differences in ability to learn a task may actually increase the spread. Great emphasis on the number of years of experience as a qualification for a job is often a mistake. That length of experience is not a satisfac-

tory basis for choosing employees is shown in Figure 9.5 on page 204.[6] Stenographic candidates were divided into three groups: those with five or more years' experience; those with one to five years' experience; and those with less than one year's experience. The figure shows that when the experience was matched, a wide range in ability still occurred. The average ability for each group is indicated. Although the more experienced typists had a slightly higher average, the difference in no way made up for the wide variation in ability between individuals.

Since each person has an inborn capacity for learning to do certain kinds of work better than others, attempts should be made to train workers on jobs that best suit their

MATCHING THE WORKER TO THE JOB

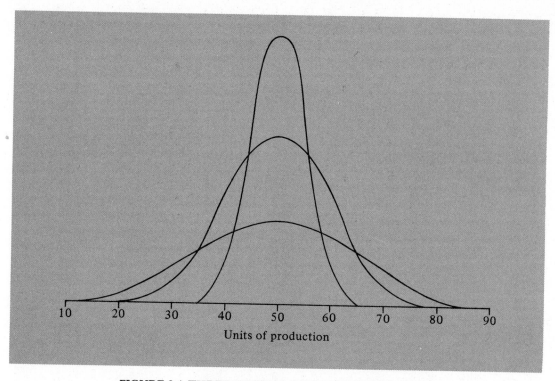

Units of production

FIGURE 9.4 THREE NORMAL DISTRIBUTION CURVES
Normal distribution curves may differ in the extent to which the ability measured is spread. The tallest curve shows that the range from lowest to highest score is less than the ratio of 1 to 2; the flat curve indicates a range in scores of more than 1 to 4. In simple occupations, there is less of a spread in ability than in complex occupations.

natural talents. Experience can develop the potentialities, but how much it will develop them depends on the original endowment. In comparing human performances, it is well to note experience in order to bring out differences in ability. For instance, one individual can do exactly as much as another, but has had less experience. In such a case, we can expect the former to surpass the latter with added experience and equal motivation. It is therefore better to employ the person with less experience. For many industrial purposes, individual differences in ability are far more important than varying degrees of experience.

Figure 9.6 on page 205 shows how three workers might profit from experience. All will eventually reach a ceiling when experience will not help. However, sharp differences among individuals will occur in the height of the ceiling, the steepness of the curve of improvement, and the degree of proficiency revealed before training. Ordinarily, persons who have the most proficiency at the outset will improve the fastest, will improve over a longer period, and will reach the highest final level. These trends are shown in Figure 9.6 for Jones, Brown, and Smith. Jones will never be a satisfactory worker since performance levels off before

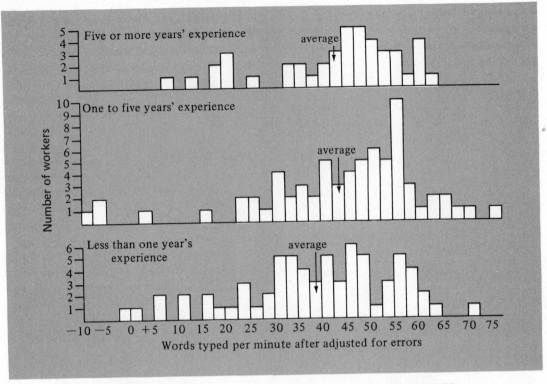

FIGURE 9.5 RANGE IN SKILL OF THREE GROUPS OF TYPISTS
The typists are classified according to length of experience. It will be seen that the variation of ability within each group far exceeds the difference in skill that accompanies experience.

SOURCE: After D. G. Paterson and J. G. Darley, *Men, women, and jobs.* Minneapolis: University of Minnesota Press, 1936, p. 94.

it reaches standard. Brown reaches the standard after about seventy days' experience, and Smith after about twenty-five days. Early performance is somewhat of an indication of how much skill employees will be able to develop.

Not only will the steepness of improvement and the overall period of improvement vary from one person to another, but variations will also occur because of the nature of the job. Jobs involving complex skills will permit improvement over longer periods of time than will simple jobs.

DEVIATIONS FROM NORMAL DISTRIBUTIONS

Although the measurement of a given ability may be adequate for testing both extremes, a normal distribution curve is not always obtained. When this occurs, we know either that we are dealing with a special group of people or that some factor is operating to influence our measurement of ability.

BIMODAL DISTRIBUTION CURVES

If we measured the strength of hand grip in a mixed group of ten- and fifteen-year-old

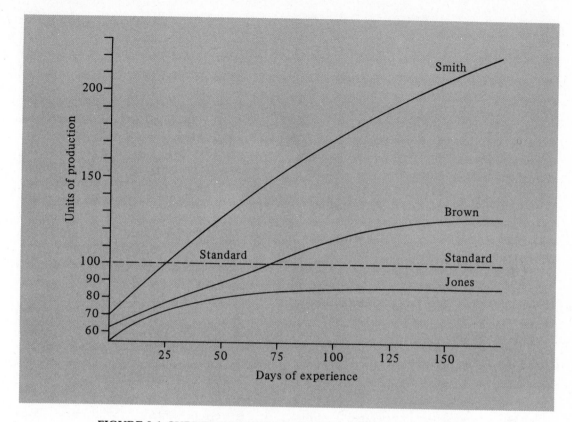

FIGURE 9.6 CURVES SHOWING RATES OF IMPROVEMENT WITH EXPERIENCE

Although all people profit from job experience or training, some profit more than others. The hypothetical curves of Jones, Brown, and Smith differ in (a) the points at which they begin; (b) the steepness of the progress; (c) the height at which the curves level off to indicate the ceiling of their progress; and (d) the length of time over which improvement will occur.

boys, the distribution curve would have two high points. Normal distribution curves are obtained from either group, but the curve for ten-year-olds would be shifted somewhat to the lower end. The two humps obtained from the measurements of the combined group represent the averages for the two ages. A theoretical bimodal curve is shown in Figure 9.7 (see page 206).

Bimodal distribution curves reveal that we have actually measured a combination of two different populations. Similar curves would be obtained if we measured the intelligence of a group of college students combined with a group of children. If two extremely different groups are combined in this manner, the distribution results in two entirely separated curves. The bimodal effect is due to incomplete separation.

In some work groups, a bimodal distribution curve for intelligence reflects the fact that persons of average ability have been discouraged and have found jobs elsewhere. This can occur when workers of superior

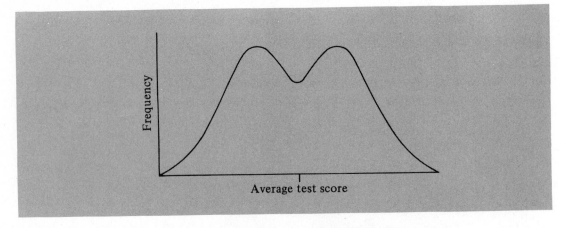

FIGURE 9.7 BIMODAL DISTRIBUTION CURVE
Curves of this type are obtained when two different populations are combined or when a selective factor, which eliminates persons of average ability, operates in a single population.

intelligence are given more desirable work within the department. The less gifted are content to remain, but the average employees in the department are not satisfied with their prospects and so seek other work. The remaining workers cease to be representative of the industrial population as a whole, because a selective factor has operated to eliminate persons with a specific degree of intelligence. If it is found that the individuals of below-average intelligence are doing satisfactory work, this selective factor is desirable. The intelligence test can then be used for selecting individuals having the desired degree of mental ability.

Bimodal distributions occur only under special conditions. People cannot be divided into two categories or types. If people were either honest or dishonest, wise or foolish, good or poor workers, bimodal curves would be the rule rather than the exception.

SKEWED DISTRIBUTION CURVES

Bimodal distribution curves differ from normal curves in that the middle group of scores is not the most frequent one. Deviations also

can occur because of increases or decreases in the number of individuals falling at either end of the curve. Such curves are described as *skewed*; they are nonsymmetrical and the high point does not lie in the center of the curve.

Three examples of skewed distribution curves are represented by solid lines in Figure 9.8. Curves A and B are both skewed, but curve A represents a selective condition in which low scores are abundant, while curve B represents a condition in which low scores have been eliminated. To determine whether a skewed condition is favorable or not, we must know what the total population looks like.

In order to produce curve A, we would have to select from a large population, shown by the broken-line curve X, retaining primarily, the lower-scoring individuals and rejecting those with progressively higher scores. To produce curve B, one could take a given population, such as represented by curve Y, and weed out the low-scoring persons, being progressively more strict as scores fell below average. Curve B would

MATCHING THE WORKER TO THE JOB

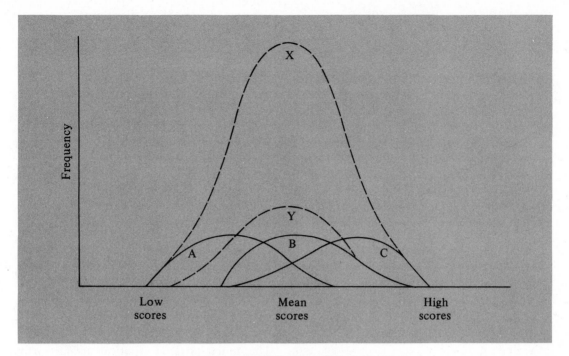

FIGURE 9.8 SKEWED DISTRIBUTIONS

Curves *A, B,* and *C* represent skewed distributions and indicate operation of a selective factor, serving either to exclude or include scores as they approach extremes. Curves *A* and *C* are skewed in opposite directions, and represent select populations taken from a large population, shown as Curve *X*. Curve *B* is skewed toward the upper end as is Curve *A*. This type of curve can be derived from a smaller population, such as that represented by Curve *Y*, and is produced by weeding out persons with progressively lower scores.

represent a favorable employment condition in that it showed that the poorest workers were most inclined to leave; curve *A* would represent an unfavorable condition in that average and poor producers are relatively more frequent than in the total population and high-producing individuals are entirely lacking.

Select populations are highly desirable in industry, since they tend to be more homogeneous in skill level and specifically adapted to do a particular kind of work. The best vocational guidance would be that which placed each individual in the kind of work that produced his or her most favor-

able position in the distribution curve. This kind of guidance would actually fit the person to the job. Since people are most contented when they are doing work that they can perform fairly proficiently, this procedure would not only increase the productive capacity of a company but would increase work satisfaction as well.

MEASURING THE RELATIONSHIP BETWEEN HUMAN ABILITIES

In business, one of the main concerns is the ability to produce. For this reason, it is desirable to learn whether specific abilities are related to competence in a given job. If marked relationships are found and the required abilities can be measured, individuals with superior abilities can be selected on the basis of such tests. The degree to which the tests are selective will in part be indicated by the strength of the relationships existing between the test scores and job performance.

Different jobs may call for the same basic abilities. For example, manual dexterity is an ability needed in many assembly-line jobs. Therefore, a person who performs the task of assembling automobile parts with marked success can be transferred to another job assembling appliances, with the expectancy of continued success. Even a worker's interests may be related to success. Generally speaking, people tend to have more ability to perform tasks for which they have special interest than to do tasks in which they lack interest.[7]

CORRELATION COEFFICIENTS

To demonstrate the relationship between two sets of measurements, we may plot one against the other on a graph. A hypothetical graph or scattergram of this nature is shown in Figure 9.9a. Each dot represents an individual. The production score for each individual can be read by noting the position along the horizontal axis; the test score can be found by reading its value from the vertical axis. This type of *scatter diagram* can be made whenever we have two sets of measurements on the same group of individuals.

If a perfect relationship exists between two sets of scores, the dots arrange themselves in the straight line shown in Figure 9.9b. When a linear relationship of this type exists, a scientific law can be formulated, and prediction is perfect. Such a relationship exists

between the length of a column of mercury and the temperature.

Another straight-line relationship occurs when the dots arrange themselves at right angles to the line of dots shown in Figure 9.9b. In this case, the highest score on one test would go with the lowest score on the other test, the second highest with the second lowest, and so on. This arrangement of dots would express an inverse relationship, such as is found between the volume of a gas and its pressure.

When the relationships are less than perfect, the dots merely tend to fall about a straight line within an elliptical area, as in Figure 9.9a. If the long axis of the ellipse is in the direction of increasing scores on both axes (that is, lower left to upper right), the relationship is positive. If the axis is at right angles to this, it indicates an inverse relationship, and the relationship is negative. The more extreme elliptical arrangements indicate high relationships. The most extreme relationship occurs when the short diameter of the ellipse is zero, and such an ellipse becomes a straight line. If no relationship exists between two tests, the dots do not tend to group about an axis. The scatter of dots thus appears circular rather than elliptical.

From inspection of scatter diagrams, we can see whether or not relationships exist, whether they are small or large, and in what direction the measures are related. By means of statistical formulae, we can express the degree of relationship by a value known as the *correlation coefficient*.

The procedure for obtaining a correlation coefficient can be found in any textbook on elementary statistics. Our present concern is with the meaning of various correlation coefficients. When a perfect relationship is found, the value of the coefficient is 1; when

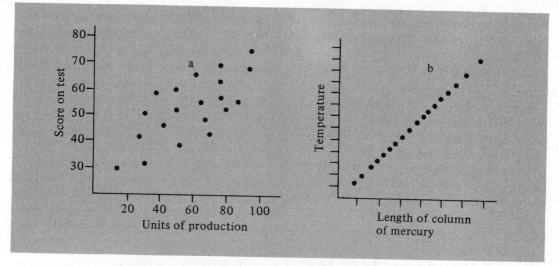

FIGURE 9.9 SCATTERGRAMS SHOWING RELATIONSHIP BETWEEN TWO MEASURES

(a) Relationship between test score and production. Each dot represents an individual, and the position of the dot indicates that person's production and test score. (b) Relationship between temperature and length of column of mercury. When the dots fall into a straight line, the relationship between the two variables is perfect.

no relationship exists, the value is 0. Values between 0 and 1, such as .2, .5, .8, indicate varying degrees of relationship. Since relationships may be positive (direct) or negative (inverse), the correlation coefficients are given a plus or minus sign, so the correlation values range from −1 to +1.

When dealing with the relationships between human traits or abilities, perfect relationships (+1) are never found. For example, relationships exist between height and body weight, intelligence and school grades, performance on certain tests and ability on a job, but none of these relationships correlates perfectly. Relationships between +.5 and +.7, however, are frequent, and this is the extent to which body weight and height are related. Individual exceptions do occur, but we could make a reasonably

accurate guess at a person's weight if we know his or her height because this consistent relationship between the two traits exists. The number of exceptions increases as the correlation coefficient decreases.

BUSINESS APPLICATIONS OF CORRELATED PERFORMANCES

A useful application of the scatter diagram arises if workers have to be shifted from one job to another. Suppose we know the correlation of performance on various pairs of jobs in an industry. If more workers are needed on some jobs and can be spared from others, workers should be shifted between correlated jobs and be expected to occupy similar positions in the distribution curves. Thus, if job *A* correlated with job *B*, it would be safe to transfer workers from the

A to the B job with a good probability that the transferred workers would be about as successful on the new job as on the old.

When workers do poorly on one job because of a lack of ability, it may be advisable to shift them to jobs that are uncorrelated or negatively correlated. In two jobs that are uncorrelated, a person's performance in one will probably be different from that in the other, if previous poor performance was not due to inadequate motivation. When a negative correlation exists, we may expect the person to place in a superior part of the distribution curve after the change.

Psychologists have constructed lists of jobs they speak of as *job families,* occupations that demand similar patterns of activity.[8] Through job analysis, the relative importance of each activity is determined, and consideration is given to the time that would be saved in training if transfers were made from one job to another. Jobs that require (1) similar activities, (2) the same worker characteristics, (3) corresponding machines, tools, or instruments, and (4) work on the same kinds of material (for example, wood) are placed in the same family. With the advent of the computer, systematic comparisons between large numbers of jobs have become feasible. Thus, simple clustering and factor-analysis techniques are now being employed in a statistical approach to the development of job families.[9] When shifts in workers become necessary, human resources are efficiently used if the transfers are made within a job family. Correlation of performance on jobs within a job family serves as a check on the degree of relatedness in each family. Job families permit lateral transfers when the jobs' grades are the same, that is, the pay scale is identical. When jobs at different levels show correlations, they supply valuable information for promotion. This vertical linking of jobs has been described as the development of career ladders.[10]

This treatment of individual differences is aimed at reducing the tendency of supervisors/managers to judge the abilities of others in the light of their own abilities, at encouraging them to look for special talents in employees, at stimulating them to make comparisons in terms of relative abilities, and at making them analyze jobs and duties in terms of human abilities. Recent theories of leadership behavior indicate that employees respond better to leaders who recognize their differences and deal with them according to individual needs and abilities.[11]

ABILITY AND PERFORMANCE

What a person is capable of doing and what is actually performed are not necessarily the same. The term *ability* refers to a person's potential performance, whereas the term *performance* refers to what a person actually does under given conditions. How a person performs on a job depends on ability as well as on willingness or motivation. We may express the relationship between these factors by the following formula:

$$\text{Performance} = \text{Ability} \times \text{Motivation}$$

According to this formula, performance has a value of zero if either ability or motivation is absent. Performance increases as either ability or motivation rises in value.

In order to measure a person's ability directly, it is necessary to observe performance.[12] To the extent that motivation is the same for all individuals in a group, variations in performance of simple tasks reflect differences in ability. In the past, psychologists have assumed that test situations are con-

MATCHING THE WORKER TO THE JOB

ducive to uniformly good motivation and that test performance scores are reliable measures of ability. When there is reason to believe, however, that the motivating conditions have been disturbed or that the ability being tested is complex and involves previous knowledge and training, test scores under these conditions cannot measure natural abilities accurately and fairly.

MOTIVATION AND PRODUCTION

Motivation also affects performance. Let us examine the effects of motivation on the shape of curves based on distributions of production in a work situation. If all persons were motivated maximally, we would expect the distribution of production to follow the normal curve, except that some low producers might be eliminated. The effect of lowering motivation would then be one of merely displacing the curve to the left without altering its shape. Figure 9.10 shows three curves, *A, B,* and *C,* representing the conditions of low, medium, and optimum motivation, respectively (see page 212).

Now let us consider the possibility that persons with differing ability may have varying degrees of motivation. One possibility is to postulate that persons of low ability tend to have low motivation, those with average ability tend to have average motivation, and those with superior ability tend to have optimum motivation. If these conditions were in fact the case, then the distribution curve of production would be more widespread than the ability to produce. The production curve would range from about fifteen units (the low-ability end of the low motivation curve) to about eighty-five (the high-ability end of the optimum motivation curve). Thus we would expect the distribution curve to approach the shape of

Curve *X* in Figure 9.11. However, this widespread curve does not describe actual findings, so the abovementioned relationships between ability and motivation must be rejected. (See page 213.)

Let us therefore change two of the assumptions and postulate that persons with low ability tend to have optimum motivation, those with average ability tend to have average motivation, and those with superior ability tend to have low motivation. If these conditions did exist, we would expect the production curve to range roughly between thirty-five (the low-ability end of the high-motivation curve) and sixty-five units (the high-ability end of the low-motivation curve). This narrow range (Curve *Y* of Figure 9.11) corresponds more closely to actual findings. The range in production measures invariably is narrower than that of ability scores. That the lower end is curtailed by selection is understandable, but the absence of high producers poses a problem even if we presumed that some of them had been promoted.

The evidence indicates that persons of low ability are highly motivated unless they become discouraged. Pressures to keep up with others are sufficient to motivate most persons. However, persons with superior ability can keep up easily, so there are no social pressures to motivate them. Thus, the potential for increasing productivity by motivation procedures lies in tapping the efforts of superior workers, and persons with low aptitudes can be helped most by special training or lateral transfers. Unfortunately supervisors are inclined to seek production improvements by trying to motivate the low producers and, as a consequence, quality decreases and errors or accidents increase. Persons who already are doing their best can produce more only by taking shortcuts. If

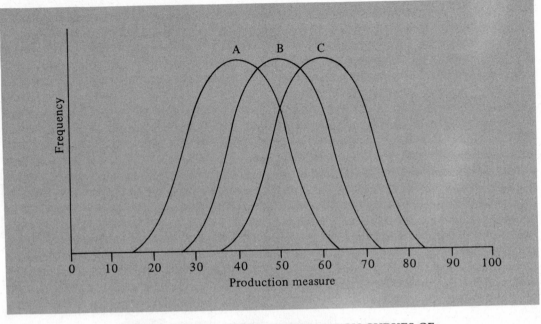

FIGURE 9.10 EFFECTS OF MOTIVATION ON CURVES OF PRODUCTION

Curves *A, B,* and *C* represent the effects of low, average, and optimum motivation on the production of a given unselected population. Increasing everyone's motivation to the same degree merely moves the production curve from left to right.

pressures are too great, they lead to frustration and a further deterioration in performance. Thus, the greatest possibilities for increasing production seem to lie in the direction of finding ways of motivating persons with superior talents.

CURVES OF RESTRICTED PRODUCTION

Another type of curve is frequently found when actual production, rather than ability to produce under carefully controlled conditions, is measured. A theoretical distribution curve of this type is shown in Figure 9.12 on page 214. It shows that expected superior producers are conspicuous by their absence. The curve is sharply cut off because

the superior individuals are producing a lesser amount than their ability warrants. Instead of being at the extreme right, these cases form a cluster, which is indicated by the sharp rise at the right end of the curve. Apparently, in this type of work situation the workers have agreed among themselves not to produce more than a certain number of units. It is at this amount of production that the curve is sharply cut off. One study has revealed that 40 percent of the workers were performing at a production level of 120 percent, when 100 percent was supposed to represent average.[13] This condition, known as *restricted production,* tends to arise when there is hostility toward the company, fear or distrust of company objectives, job inse-

MATCHING THE WORKER TO THE JOB

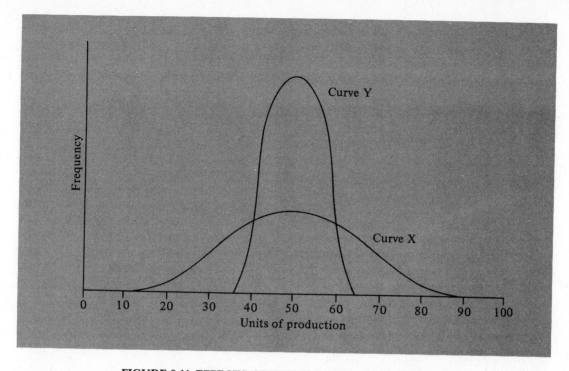

FIGURE 9.11 EFFECTS OF DIFFERENTIAL MOTIVATION
Curve X would describe the distribution of production if persons of lesser ability tended to be least motivated and persons of great ability tended to be optimally motivated. However, if persons of lesser ability were most highly motivated and persons with great ability were least motivated, a curve approaching that of Y would result. This curve most accurately describes prevailing conditions.

curity, or group pressures to protect low standards.

In *Harper's Magazine,* one worker described the means used in his plant to eliminate the "eager beaver" tendency to produce more than fellow workers considered to be adequate. At first, gentle hints were given to the eager worker; if these were not successful in curtailing production, the worker might find his street clothes in knots or encounter glue on the handle of his locker door. The writer also indicated that some workers had been known to suffer injuries from "accidental" falls while en route to lunch. Eventually the eager worker got the

point that he should not produce at a higher rate than the standard.[14] More recent discussions of blue-collar work practices indicate that such methods are still being used.[15]

Restricted production therefore implies more than lack of motivation to produce on the part of superior individuals; it indicates motivation to hold down production. Piecerate work, ordinarily designed to motivate workers to produce, is most subject to this condition of restricted production because piece-rate work shows up differences in ability. Sales personnel working on commission bases also have a wide range in earnings due to varying sales abilities and conditions. To

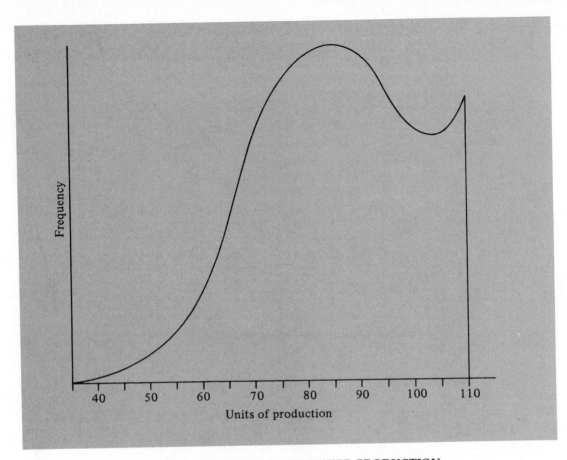

FIGURE 9.12 CURVE OF RESTRICTED PRODUCTION
This curve is cut off sharply because individuals who have the ability to produce the greatest amounts limit their production to 110 units or less. The result of this restriction in production is that a large number of individuals produce a maximum amount.

SOURCE: Adapted from *A Scientific Approach to Labor Problems* by A. Ford. Copyright © 1931 by McGraw-Hill Book Company. Used with the permission of McGraw-Hill Book Company.

reduce this discrepancy, it is not uncommon for companies to have a decreasing scale of commission percentage as earnings rise. This practice reduces both the earnings of the superior salespeople and their motivation.

The actual extent of restricted production is unknown. There is reason to believe that it is considerable. For example, the standard for bricklayers varies, but seldom exceeds 350 bricks per mason per day. It is also well known that a superior bricklayer can lay well over 2,000 bricks without lowering quality. This might require more effort than would be considered comfortable, but a mason of

MATCHING THE WORKER TO THE JOB

this caliber would probably feel little job satisfaction if required to limit production to 350.

The solution to the problem of unused ability created by various forms of restricted production requires cooperative problem solving. To blame either labor or management evades the basic issue. Workers often do not restrict production because they are unwilling to do a good day's work, but because they are afraid. Where workers are frustrated, restriction is a form of retaliation. Distrust and conflicting interests are involved, and these are states of mind that will not be altered by legislation. Instead, all interested parties must share responsibility for the resolution of their differences.

NOTES

1. Shrank, R. *Ten thousand working days.* Cambridge, Mass.: MIT Press, 1978.
2. Bardwick, J. M. *Psychology of women: A study of biocultural conflicts.* New York: Harper & Row, 1971.
3. Kirkpatrick, J. J., Ewen, R. B., Barrett, R. S., and Katzell, R. A. *Testing and fair employment: Fairness and validity of personnel tests for different ethnic groups.* New York: New York University Press, 1968; Miner, J. B. *Personnel Psychol.* London: Collier-Macmillan, 1969; Anastasi, A. Some implications of cultural factors for test construction. In A. Anastasi, (Ed.), *Testing problems in perspective.* Washington, D.C.: American Council on Education, 1966.
4. Hull, C. L. *Aptitude testing.* New York: World Book, 1928, p. 33.
5. Tiffin, J., and McCormick, E. J. *Industrial psychology,* 4th ed. Englewood Cliffs, N.J.: Prentice-Hall, 1958, pp. 25–27.
6. Paterson, D. G., and Darley, J. G. *Men, women, and jobs.* Minneapolis, Minn.: University of Minnesota Press, 1936, p. 94.
7. Pervin, L. A. Performance and satisfaction as a function of individual-environment fit. *Psychol. Bull.,* 1968, *69,* 56–68.
8. Shartle, C. L., et al. Occupational analysis activities in the war manpower commission. *Psychol. Bull.* 1943, *40,* 701–713; Shartle, C. L. *Occupational information, its development and application,* 3rd ed. Englewood Cliffs, N.J.: Prentice-Hall, 1959; *Estimates of worker trait requirements for 4000 jobs as defined in the dictionary of occupational titles.* Washington, D.C.: U.S. Dept. of Labor, Bureau of Employment Security, 1958; Mosel, J. W., Fine, S. A., and Boling, J. The scalability of estimated worker requirements. *J. Appl. Psychol.,* 1960, *44,* 156–160.
9. Dunnette, M. D., and Kirchner, W. K. A checklist for differentiating different kinds of sales jobs. *Personnel Psychol.,* 1959, *72,* 421–430; Hemphill, J. K. *Dimensions of executive positions: A study of the basic characteristics of the positions of ninety-three business executives.* Columbus, Ohio: Bureau of Business Research, Ohio State University, 1960; Orr, D. B. A new method of clustering jobs. *J. Appl. Psychol.,* 1960, *44,* 44–59.
10. Fine, S. A. *Guidelines for the design of new careers.* Kalamazoo, Mich.: Upjohn Institute, 1967; Miner, J. B. *Personnel psychology.* New York: Macmillan, 1969.
11. House, R. J. A path-goal theory of leadership effectiveness. *Admin. Sci. Quart.,* 1971, *16,* 321–338.
12. Vroom, V. *Work and motivation.* New York: Wiley, 1964.
13. Georgopoulos, B. S., Mahoney, G. M., and Jones, N. W. A path-goal approach to productivity. *J. Appl. Psychol.,* 1957, *41,* 345–353.
14. Bradshaw, C. Sure, I could produce more. *Harper's Mag.,* 1947, *194,* 396–401.
15. Shrank, R., op. cit.

SUGGESTED READINGS

Bardwick, J. M. *Psychology of women: A study of bio-cultural conflicts.* New York: Harper & Row, 1971.

Downey, H., and Slocum, J. Uncertainty: measures, research and sources of variation. *Acad. Mgt. J.,* 1975, 562–578.

Ghiselli, E. E. *The validity of occupational aptitude tests.* New York: Wiley, 1966.

Tiffin, J., and McCormick, E. J. *Industrial psychology.* Englewood Cliffs, N.J.: Prentice-Hall, 1965.

MATCHING THE WORKER TO THE JOB

LABORATORY EXERCISE
DISCUSSION: THE CASE OF VIOLA BURNS

(Students are asked not to read the case materials before participating in the laboratory exercise.)

A. BACKGROUND INFORMATION

1. The instructor will read the background material supplied and will have three members of the class act out the parts of Bill Randall, Raymond Birdsall, and Viola Burns from the script (section D).
2. The class is to divide into groups of three or four.
3. Discussions
   a. Free discussion. Half the groups should serve as consultants and try to reach agreement on one of three alternative decisions:
      1. *Encourage* Viola to take on the new job.
      2. Agree that *insufficient information* has been given for making a decision.
      3. *Discourage* Viola from taking the job by indicating that she is needed in the old job.
   b. Developmental discussion. Half the groups should serve as consultants and follow these discussion steps.
      1. Develop a list of Viola's duties on her present job.
      2. Determine which duties she does well.
      3. Develop a list of duties on her new job.
      4. Determine which of these duties that we know Viola can do well and which ones about which we have doubts or insufficient information.
      5. Determine which three duties that the new boss will consider to be most important.

6. Try to reach agreement on one of the three decisions.

B. REPORTS TO CLASS AS A WHOLE

1. Reports from the groups following the unstructured (*free*) discussion pattern and those from groups following the structured (*developmental*) pattern should be tabulated separately.
2. The instructor should tabulate the number of votes for the three alternatives, using headlines (*Encourage, Insufficient information, and Discourage*) for each group.
3. The totals for the free groups and those for the developmental groups should be compared.
4. The proportion of unanimous decisions reached for the two discussion procedures should be indicated.

C. GENERAL DISCUSSION

1. The two discussion methods have been found to yield different results, and this will probably be duplicated in class results. Why should the same facts discussed with two procedures yield different outcomes?
2. Why were such a large proportion of decisions unanimous?
3. There are two sources of error in decisions regarding promotion: (1) the tendency to favor promotions when the person makes a favorable impression; and (2) an inclination to use promotion as a reward for past performance. Which discussion procedure tends to reduce these sources of error? Discuss.
4. To what extent (if any) was the group's decision influenced by the fact that the potential job candidate was a woman?

D. CASE MATERIALS*

1. Background

Viola Burns was hired directly upon her graduation from high school and placed in the payroll office as a typist. She was intelligent, quick, cheerful, energetic, and had a pleasing manner but looked delicate and somewhat unprepossessing at first sight and was somewhat lacking in self-confidence. The paymaster had asked for a woman who was good at figures, could type with reasonable speed and accuracy, and do shorthand. Viola more than met these qualifications.

There were twenty women in the paymaster's office, and Viola readily made friends with all of them. She not only adapted herself quickly to the job but evidently enjoyed the work. She was usually the first to arrive in the morning and was frequently spoken to for her failure to quit work at noon or at night. She became an asset to the department head and within a year had demonstrated to the employment manager that she was in line for promotion. Consequently, when Bill Randall received a requisition for a secretary to one of the sales executives, Viola Burns immediately came to his mind. He went to the paymaster, Raymond Birdsall, and suggested Viola's release for transfer.

2. Script

Randall: Ray, I have a requisition from Jim Wagner's office for a bright woman to replace Agnes Brown who is leaving to be married. I think Viola Burns is just the person for the job.
Birdsall: Hey, Randall, that woman is practically indispensable to me. She's one of the best employees I ever had. You don't think I'm going to let her go, do you?
Randall: How much are you paying, Ray?
Birdsall: She's at the top of the K–6 rate.
Randall: But you're not going to stand in her

---

* Case taken from *Social Problems in Labor Relations*, by P. J. W. Pigors, L. C. McKenney, and T. O. Armstrong. Copyright, 1939. McGraw-Hill Book Company, Inc. Used by permission.

way if she has a chance for a better job and more money, are you?
Birdsall: Well, maybe I could pay her more money myself.
Randall: Maybe you could, Ray. But you're limited to the top rate for her present job classification. You can't pay her what she may eventually receive as a private stenographer.
Birdsall: No, of course not. Damn it all, the good people always go. I sometimes wonder if I'd be better off to take women that aren't quite so good, so I could keep 'em around here after I've spent time and money training them.
Randall: Well, here's your chance to decide. If I take Viola, you'll need someone to replace her. Tell me what you want, and I'll find just the right candidate for you.
Birdsall: Well, I suppose there's only one answer. You'll have to take Viola. After all, I've got to give her the break. But you find another woman as good as she is, if you can. I guess I'm better off to hire bright women even if there is a chance that I may lose them.

(Later in the day, Viola Burns is called to see Randall in his office.)

Randall: Good morning, Ms. Burns. Have a chair. I have a suggestion to make which I believe will please you. Do you know Ms. Brown in Mr. Wagner's office?
Burns: Not very well, but I know who she is.
Randall: Well, she's leaving us very soon — getting married — perhaps you have heard? I have suggested that you be considered to take her place. But whether or not you get the job depends on three conditions. The first is Mr. Birdsall's consent to release you; the second, your own willingness to give it a try; and the third, Mr. Wagner's acceptance. Now I want to tell you something about this job before you make up your mind. If you do well, you would become Mr. Wagner's private stenographer, and be the only person in his office. This is quite a change from your present job, and you might feel rather lonesome. Mr. Wagner's work requires a considerable amount of detail. You would handle his correspondence, keep his files,

MATCHING THE WORKER TO THE JOB

and run the office when he is out of town. This would involve contact with customers in person as well as over the telephone. If you should be transferred to this job, you would receive a slight increase in salary at once, and more later if you do well. Do you think you would like to try this job?

Burns: Really, I don't know, Mr. Randall. It sounds like a lot to learn, and so different from what I've been doing. I'd hate to fail. You know more about it than I. Do you think I could do it?

Randall: I'm very sure you can do it if you want to.

Burns: Is there much dictation?

Randall: Yes, there's a good deal. But I'm sure you can handle that part of it. And, of course, Ms. Brown would be with you for a couple of weeks to show you the ropes. How about it, would you like to give this a try?

Burns: Well . . . it's awfully hard to say, Mr. Randall. Could I think it over and let you know later?

Randall: Certainly, Viola, just let me know in a day or so when you've made up your mind.

(At the end of two days, Randall has heard nothing further from Viola Burns. He speaks to Birdsall during the lunch hour.)

Randall: Oh, by the way, Ray, has Viola said anything to you about taking the job at Wagner's office?

Birdsall: No, she hasn't, but I certainly hope she'll make up her mind about it pretty soon. She's not much good to anybody since you spoke to her. She goes around looking like she's lost her last friend. She even cries about it. I believe she feels she ought to take a chance but hates to leave the department and her friends.

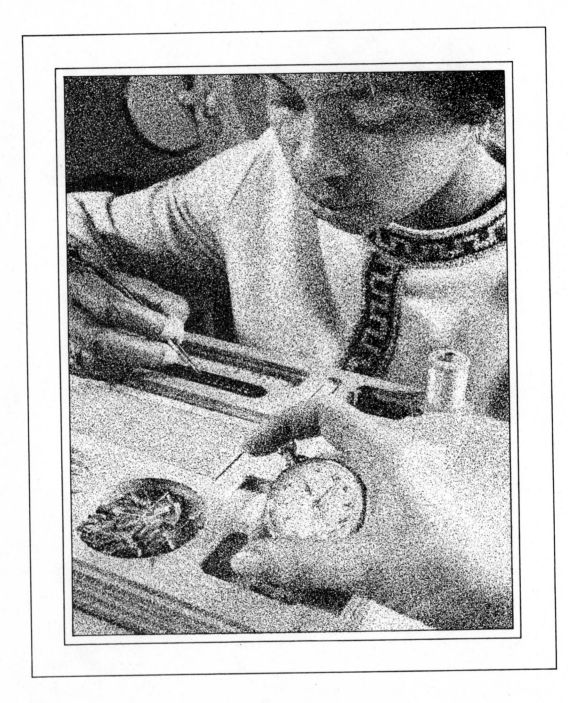

CHAPTER TEN

SELECTION, PLACEMENT, AND CAREER PLANNING

∎

Effects of Past Selection Practices
Testing: What It Can and Cannot Do
Alternatives to Testing
Recruiting and Interviewing
Careers: The Planning and Management of Human Resources

∎

TODAY, BUSINESS is going through a massive upheaval in its hiring and placement practices. Many assumptions are being examined and found unjustifiable. For example, making the possession of a high school diploma an a priori requirement for hiring was a nearly universal practice in business for many years. Even if specific skills were not needed or were taught on the job, it was felt that graduation was a sign of diligence and good character. This was an assumption, based not on matching successful job performers with this criterion, but on "common sense." Since then, court decisions (for example, *United States, et al.* v. *Georgia Power Company*) have declared such arbitrary requirements to be unfairly discriminatory and therefore illegal.

EFFECTS OF PAST SELECTION PRACTICES

DISCRIMINATION

People are frequently unaware of bias in their attitudes and behavior. For many years, commonplace selection practices had the effect of systematically and unfairly reducing the chances of being hired for thousands of Americans. "Attitudes reconcile contradictions": managers, who complained that their extensively (and expensively) educated daughters could not find positions worthy of their abilities, had no difficulty explaining why a female could not be hired for a sales position in their department. "She just wouldn't be accepted by our customers."

Tests and testing procedures used in the past, according to many researchers, also have systematically reduced the opportunity for fair representation of abilities for significant numbers of individuals.[1]

Discrimination practiced by organizational recruiters and interviewers in the past (whether conscious or not) has led to efforts to regulate these aspects of the organizational task via government statutes. Whether companies would have voluntarily changed their hiring practices to conform with new views of fairness cannot be known, but they now *must* conform to government regulations in this area or risk expensive consequences. As of mid-1978, the government agency responsible for equal opportunity in employment had 130,000 unresolved charges in its files. Since then, the agency has developed computerized methods for evaluating hiring and promotional practices in thousands of companies and for selecting for further study all of those whose hiring patterns seem discriminatory.[2]

The policy of federal agencies in this area has been to encourage and, if necessary, to force companies not only to avoid such practices in the future but, in many instances, to make reparation (for example, to provide back pay where unfair pay differentials can be shown). In the case of one firm found guilty of discrimination in the hiring and promotion of women in management, the decision required in part that the company seek out and promote into managerial positions several hundred women among those already employed as well as those to be hired in the future. In other words, companies are being told not just to mend their ways but to undo the effects of past unfair practices.

The reactions to these policies on the part of members of groups that have been discriminated against (as well as previously favored groups) have been ambivalent and emotional. Whenever people are forced to admit errors (especially those they were unaware of making) or to change long-held (if irrational) attitudes, resistance can be expected. Many women who spent fifty years as obedient daughters and supportive wives

MATCHING THE WORKER TO THE JOB

with no thought of careers outside the home were shocked at what they perceived to be a downgrading of their life's work. Employers who had hired minority group members resented their efforts' being labeled tokenism. The turmoil that these charges and their remedies produced in business reflected the turmoil occurring throughout society, as individuals in large numbers began questioning values and assumptions central to the American culture and to them personally.

Nor are we finished yet with examining our assumptions. Assertions of discrimination in hiring and promotion have come more recently from older employees.[3] Again, remedies have been sought through federal legislation, and the age for mandatory retirement for most jobs has been set at a higher level or eliminated entirely. Again, responses have been both critical and congratulatory. Young workers with ambitions to move up in the organization may view such laws as reducing their chances unfairly.

TESTING PRACTICES

Although managers have been the main target for criticism in the area of selection methods, psychologists have received their share as well. As mentioned earlier, tests designed and promoted as unbiased were found, in fact, to be *culture-bound,* that is, biased in favor of individuals with certain ethnic and educational backgrounds. Psychologists, however, have begun to reassess other aspects of testing conditions as well.

One frequent assumption has been that testing conditions provided job applicants with uniformly high positive motivation. On analysis, such assumptions seem to be naive today. For example, mathematics has been shown to be perceived by many young women as a masculine realm.[4] One young woman who from her class participation seemed to have above-average mathematical ability was counseled after receiving a failing grade in a college mathematics course examination. It was determined that, for this individual, success in mathematics was perceived as literally masculinizing. Her alternatives, subjectively seen, were to do well in mathematics or to be "normal" and "feminine." Given those perceived choices, it is not surprising that she opted to fail. A so-called unbiased test of her mathematical ability would then falsely indicate that she was below average in this area.

Perception is also a factor in another criticism of testing situations.[5] Standard practice in testing is to encourage persons being tested to be open and honest. At the same time, in many tests, those individuals in charge of the tests are vague or actually misleading about their purposes. Expecting trust and openness to be a one-way interaction is unrealistic. The result is an effort on the part of those being tested to find ways to beat the system.[6]

In the past, many psychologists have overlooked or ignored the fear, stress, and resentment that the testing situation engenders in many people. Even when such emotional reactions are explicitly recognized, instructions for dealing with them have generally been vague or patronizing.

Unfairness and insensitivity are easier to see in others than in ourselves. The same rigorous, impersonal testing methods seen by psychologists as the height of impartiality and fairness may be perceived by some job applicants as attempts to dominate, manipulate, and control their behavior.

But changes in recruiting and selection processes have occurred, and new methods have been developed. Those managers responsible for creating selection systems today must consider the cost of possible legal suits when designing their hiring systems.[7] The ideal selection process today includes vigorous affirmative action in recruiting and nondiscrimination in hiring and promotion. Moreover, it aims at overcoming as much as possible the incompatibility between the organization's ideal choice and the individual's point of view. According to one study, the optimal selection system now and in the future provides a balance among the needs of the individual, the company, and society.[8]

Business practice today falls short of these ideals. Although individuals cannot be forced to take certain tests (for example, personality tests) as a prerequisite to consideration for hiring, the nature of the applicant/employer relationship is such that it is a rare job candidate who feels free to say, "I don't want to take the test." Even in areas of technical expertise among personnel managers, such as calculating the cost/benefits of alternative selection methods, managers are found to be using older, less accurate methods when improved ones are available.[9]

Obviously, companies need to devise further methods for choosing employees that are both accurate and fair. Yet there is reason for optimism. The most difficult step in changing attitudes or behavior is to convince the persons involved that change is needed. For most Americans, that difficult first step has been taken.

TESTING: WHAT IT CAN AND CANNOT DO

The fact that some tests have been found to discriminate unfairly among job applicants does not mean that companies should abandon all testing. Current regulations in testing require that tests not be systematically biased and that performance on a test must be highly correlated with performance on the job. Attempting to follow these rules requires greater knowledge and sophistication on the part of management about the merits and limitations of various kinds of tests.

HOW TESTS MEASURE ABILITY

The use of psychological tests in business presupposes that a satisfactory *criterion* for success on a job is available. Since both test results and measurements of job performance are expressed quantitatively, the degree of correlation between the two measures can be determined. After correlations are obtained, it is possible to define the desired abilities in terms of a test score. This is an important advantage, since it replaces ambiguous and subjective descriptions of human abilities with objective and quantitative scores.

Well-constructed tests measure some aspect of human ability. If we know what workers should accomplish with their abilities, tests can be constructed to measure the desired abilities. By this procedure, tests become objective instruments for measuring human traits.[10]

Norms have been developed for standard tests; these permit interpretation of the score of an individual in terms of the frequency with which it occurs in the general population. In addition, many tests have norms for various types of work groups (select populations). Standard tests also have had their *reliability* measured, which means that if the proper procedures for administering and scoring them are followed, the test scores of a group of people will tend to be consistent when given on different occasions or by different testers. Thus, scores of a test administered to the same group on two occasions should correlate highly if chance factors have been largely eliminated. The reliability coefficient of tests thus becomes an index to indicate the degree to which the test score is an accurate one (of whatever it measures).

TEST VALIDITY

The chief requisite of any test is its *validity* — the extent to which the test measures what it purports to measure.[11] Although an instrument may be called a test of intelligence or supervisory competence, such titles mean little or nothing unless the instrument predicts the employee's subsequent performance with reference to definite criteria of job success within the organization. No test is valid for every purpose.

In developing or choosing tests, the concept of *face validity* can conceal pitfalls for the unwary. Essentially, face validity refers to the apparent validity of tests or test items that appear to be logically related to, or bear superficial resemblance to, job activities. In actuality, such items frequently do not sample relevant abilities and thus have low validity.

The use of psychological tests in business presupposes that a satisfactory criterion, or knowledge of the various criteria currently used for job performance within the organization, is available. Let us suppose that in a particular work situation 50 percent of the job candidates are satisfactory when no tests are used. Suppose further that the number of applicants is such that 50 percent of them must be hired. What effect will selection tests of varying correlations to job performance have on the number of satisfactory employees? If the only variable is the degree of correlation, a test that correlates + .3 with job performance (that is, has a low, but consistently positive relationship with job success) would raise the number of satisfactory employees to 60 percent, while a test that correlates + .8 with job performance (that is, has a very close, positive relationship with job success) would raise the number to 80 percent.

Other things being equal, the effectiveness of employee selection can be increased by increasing the number of applicants considered for a job. The more applicants to choose from, the more tests increase in value. If 50 percent of the job candidates are satisfactory when no tests are used and all persons have to be hired, even a good test can produce no improvement in the percentage of satisfactory employees. If, however, we hire 20 percent versus 80 percent of those seen, the percentage of satisfactory employees rises from 50 to 78. The *selection ratio* is that proportion hired compared to the total number of available candidates.

The selection ratio adopted will naturally vary with the available labor supply. Irrational factors (like prejudice) that artificially limit the size of the pool of candidates can reduce the company's chance to find the best candidate and can unfairly disqualify individuals.

APTITUDE TESTS

Aptitude tests are designed to measure a person's potential for succeeding in certain tasks. Aptitude, therefore, refers to a person's abilities before being trained in a specific task. Aptitude thus depends on the abilities developed through heredity and growth and the extent to which these have been improved through use and experience.

The purpose of aptitude testing is to obtain, before training, an indication of how well a person will perform a job after training. People with the same training will show great differences in their performances on a job; the cause of these differences lies in the dissimilarities in aptitude. Aptitude tests are therefore so designed that certain kinds of experience do not influence the score attained. Figure 10.1 shows four different aptitude tests, each designed to measure a different specific ability. In some instances,

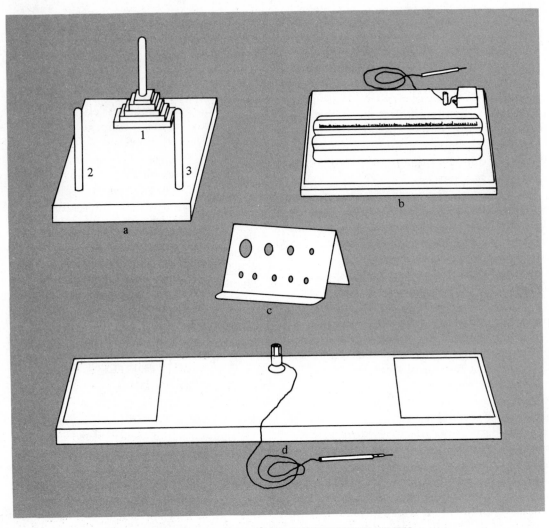

FIGURE 10.1 EXAMPLES OF APTITUDE TESTS

(a) *Pyramid Puzzle*. The pyramid problem involves moving the blocks to a designated post without placing a larger block on a smaller one. Demonstrates problem solving. (b) *Steadiness Tester — groove type*. Calibrated. Sides are electrified to activate buzzer or electric counter if user's hands are unsteady and sides are touched. (c) *Steadiness Tester — hole type*. Conventional hole type with terminals for completing electric circuit to activate buzzer or counter if sides are touched. (d) *Tapping Board*. Stainless steel metal plates at each end complete circuit when stylus contacts each successive plate. Number of taps within designated period are counted, to measure rapidity of hand movements. (All equipment made by Lafayette Instrument Co.)

items of information are included in the test, but in such cases, exposure to the information is so common that individuals with the necessary aptitudes would have acquired it.

For example, the MacQuarrie Test of Mechanical Ability has the following seven parts: (1) tracing with a pencil through gaps in straight lines; (2) tapping three times in each of a number of circles with a pencil; (3) putting a penciled dot in small circles that are irregularly spaced; (4) copying straight-line drawings; (5) locating the positions of objects in figures that are the same shape but a different size from a given pattern; (6) counting blocks that are pictured in piles where some blocks are hidden by others in the piles; and (7) pursuing with the eyes wavy lines that cross several other lines. Applicants would have no previous training in these activities, and practically all people in a given culture would have had the necessary preliminary general training to understand instructions, to hold a pencil, and to write. Despite these background similarities, large differences in test scores would be obtained from a group of people, and these are the differences that aptitude tests are designed to reveal.

Aptitude tests also include measures of bodily structure and the various aspects of sensory functions, such as vision, hearing, and balance.[12] Such factors clearly depend on developmental factors and are largely unchanged by practice or experience.

Many companies give specific training but wish to have some knowledge of the applicant's potential before making an investment in training. Such firms as telephone companies depend on public schools to give a general background training in such skills as reading, speaking, and arithmetic, and then select graduates on the basis of school grades, interview data, and test performance. Today, some firms like Control Data

are taking a more active role in training, seeking out for in-company training persons who have not succeeded in public school. Special approaches used in hiring the hard-to-employ will be discussed in Chapter 12.

MECHANICAL-RELATIONS TESTS

Among the tests of mechanical ability, we find some that measure primarily the mental aspect of mechanical relations, whereas others measure primarily certain muscular or motor abilities. It is necessary to distinguish between the two. Here we are concerned with tests that measure the understanding or comprehension of mechanical relationships. For convenience, we have called them *mechanical-relations tests*.

Various kinds of mechanical-relations tests are available, both individual and group.[13] Most of them show a high correlation with each other, so it may be supposed that mechanical comprehension is rather general in nature. The common form of the test is designed to determine whether a person has insight into mechanical functions. Some tests present pictures of pulleys or gears, and the person tested must describe which way one wheel turns when another turns clockwise. Care is taken not to require mathematical computations, as the inclusion of such items would make the test a measure of achievement rather than one of aptitude. Other tests require that parts of unfamiliar mechanisms be assembled. This task requires insight into the relationship of the various pieces and thus resembles a puzzle. Often the parts are blocks to be fitted together to produce an end product of specified shape. In the latter case, past familiarity with machinery is entirely excluded as a helpful factor.

Inventive mechanical ability is tested by showing an applicant how a particular gadget functions and requiring the person to draw diagrams to show how the inside of the mechanism must be arranged in order to work the way it does.

The selection of persons to repair equipment — from typewriters to computers — and many kinds of machine operators can be greatly improved by the use of well-selected mechanical ability tests.[14] The proper test battery to use for a given job is the one that proves itself the most selective.

CREATIVE ABILITY

For many years it was generally believed that high intelligence test scores indicating superior learning ability were indicative of the highly creative person, since differences in mental ability were assumed to be quantitative. Other studies, however, support the theory that mental processes of a different kind than learning exist.

Creative persons appear to differ more in kind than in degree from good learners. Creative ability seems to require a minimum level of intelligence but beyond this minimum, individuals vary greatly in creative ability.[15] Research with gifted children show them to vary greatly in originality, particularly in their perception of problem situations.[16]

E. P. Torrance[17] has developed a number of tests and training exercises that support the notion that productive (creative) thinking and reproductive (recall of past learning) thinking are qualitatively different.[18] In the second case, an old solution is used to solve a new problem; in the first, the solution to the new problem is a reorganization or an integration of parts of old solutions (learnings). In experimental studies in which subjects were given information to learn, they used this information differently when required to recall it than when required to use it in a problem situation.[19] If some individuals react to a problem by trying to recall the solution from their past learnings (as students do when taking an exam) and others react to the problem as something new and try to make up a solution, different kinds of mental processes are to be expected.

Recall depends on associative bonds formed during learning. However, another process, that of the *fragmentation* of associative bonds, also occurs. Once learned sequences are fragmented, spontaneous reorganizations of old learnings can occur so that *new* combinations are created. Individuals differ widely in which of these processes (reproducing or reorganizing) dominates in problem situations, but the evidence reveals marked individual differences in the way stored information is treated.[20]

Research has shown that the search for uniqueness can be influenced by training,[21] and creativity is even improved when a person is told he or she has the reputation of being creative and because of it has been approached by associates to solve a problem.[22] Guilford has developed a variety of specific tests of creativity and distinguishes between *convergent* and *divergent* processes in creativity.[23] The convergent process is one in which different things must be brought into an organized pattern (dividing a list of words into a certain number of classes), and the divergent process is one in which one starts with specific things and with them makes as many further things as possible (make many structures out of a given set of lines). There is evidence that high scores on measures of divergent process are associated with superiority in science.[24]

The abilities associated with so-called creative functions seem to be rather specific, so it is difficult to develop a test that will satisfy various criteria of creativity. In a study of the way that different individuals used learned information in a problem situation, none of the types of processes investigated were found to correlate with tests of creativity.[25] People generally agree about which persons are creative, but the characteristics of creative thinking are difficult to pinpoint. One author reports rating by peers to be a valid measure of an individual's creativity.[26] If people use stored information differently, creativity is not developed by supplying more information.[27] Rather, the development of creative solutions requires that nonhabitual kinds of thinking be used. Reorganizing old experiences is not necessarily a difficult task, merely a different approach.

At present there is confusion about the meaning of creativity. Certainly studies of creativity in different fields should not be generalized until common elements in the processes involved are securely established. Further, problem solving and creativity should be differentiated. Three basic types of problem-solving behavior can be distinguished: (1) trial and error, (2) adapting old solutions to new situations, and (3) forming original solutions by reorganizing past learning. Only the last process should be regarded as creative or productive problem solving.

Perhaps the best measure of the creative person in an organization is the individual's record for innovation and originality. Managers can make fairly accurate judgments of this ability, and for the present these should be considered in relation to tests of creativity. Creative people, unfortunately, may also be regarded as problem employees because they are likely to think differently from the rest of the group and tend not to conform.

MOTOR COORDINATION TESTS

The motor functions, such as dexterity, manipulative activity, and muscular control in general, are unrelated to the mental functions. Thus, it is not surprising to find that a very intelligent person may be awkward when it comes to assembling a simple piece of machinery or operating a lathe.

Various *motor tests* show little or no relationship with one another.[28] In one study, the average correlation between a large number of motor tests was found to be only + .15.[29] A summary of many studies indicated that the motor abilities could be divided into eleven fairly independent groups.[30] Since motor abilities are highly specific, individual tests are relatively simple, and administration does not require a great deal of time. A good sample of the pattern of motor abilities can be obtained fairly quickly. Most of the tests involve equipment, however, and must be given individually.

Typical *dexterity tests* require the applicant to place pegs in small holes arranged in various patterns. The arrangement of the holes determines the relative importance of finger and arm movements. *Precision tests* may require the testee to plunge a stylus accurately into a hole each time it is mechanically uncovered. Some tests merely record the speed with which one can tap a stylus on a metal disk and activate an electrically controlled counting device. *Tests of rhythm* require the applicant to duplicate, by tapping a telegraph key, a pattern presented on a phonograph (see Figure 10.1).

The use of a device that measures the speed with which a person can react to a signal is one of the oldest tests in use. This *reaction time* varies with the type of stimulus used and the conditions under which the test is given, as well as with the person tested. Short reaction times are helpful in most activities that require alertness.

Tests of motor coordination are usually more elaborate. They require a person to synchronize different movements of the two hands or of the hands and feet. A person may be asked to cause a beam of light to follow a given course when the horizontal movement is controlled by one lever and the vertical by another lever. The arrangement of the task is unusual in that it does not duplicate learned activity. In more simple arrangements, a person may be required to turn, as rapidly as possible, a small crank with the right hand and a large one with the left hand.

When the purpose is to test aptitude, the task required is usually one that does not duplicate some form of work. In some instances, motor tests are purposely designed to duplicate some of the activities required on a given job. When such tests distinguish between good and poor operators who possess the same degree of experience, they are highly satisfactory tests for aptitude.

Since the motor abilities are highly specific, it is possible for one test to be closely related to one manual job and poorly related to another. For operators of garment machines, the correlations between job success and a paper-folding test, a card-sorting test, and a dexterity test were .52, .35, and .21, respectively.[31] However, the test for finger dexterity, which was the poorest test for the machine operators, showed a correlation of .37 with output records for simple electrical assembly jobs.[32] Since many jobs require a number of specific abilities, best results can be obtained by combining a number of specific tests and forming a *test battery*.[33] Each test should be related to a measure of job performance, but the tests should not be related to one another because, to the extent that they were related, one test would merely duplicate the function of one of the others. For example, two tests with validity coefficients of .60 and .50 would have a combined coefficient of correlation of .78, providing the two tests were entirely unrelated to each other. If, however, the tests showed an intercorrelation of .80, their combined

value would be no greater than that of the better of the two tests used by itself.[34]

TESTS OF SENSORY ABILITIES

Vision is the important sense in most jobs. It is necessary, therefore, to determine not only a worker's visual capacity in general, but how well the vision is adapted to the particular job. Thus, for close work, persons who tend to focus their eyes relatively close produce significantly more than those who tend to focus farther away. In one case, using glasses to adapt eyes to special work resulted in increased production among hosiery loopers.

Many operations also require accurate judgments of distance. Distance perception (under 30 feet) is largely a matter of binocular vision and can be accurately measured. Many accidents in industry caused by faulty vision can thus be prevented. Hiring people who do not wear glasses does not protect the employer against workers with defective vision. Because people who wear glasses have at least had their vision tested, they may actually be a safer risk.

Since night and day vision depend on different types of receptors in the eyes, people who are alike in day vision may be highly unlike in night vision. Work that requires vision under dim illumination must therefore take this fact into account. Bus and truck drivers who have accidents primarily at night may be defective in night vision.

Color vision varies greatly, particularly among males, and color-vision tests are necessary to detect deficiencies when jobs require color differentiation. Some partially color-blind people are unaware of their defect.[35]

Visual acuity also varies with age, and many people fail to recognize the gradual reduction in ability to see at close range.

In a highly automated plant, such as this slabbing mill in Ford's Dearborn installation, the worker's visual acuity plays an important role in monitoring closed circuit television screens, gauges, and dials indicating computerized activity. Here, the worker also uses his hands to manipulate 14- to 18-ton steel ingots. (Courtesy of Ford Motor Company)

Glasses can correct these changes, but the only way to be certain that employees are obtaining these corrections is to require periodic examinations.

Other senses play vital roles in certain specialized jobs. *Hearing* perhaps is next to vision in importance, but deficiencies are more readily apparent.[36] In conversation, we can make adjustments for hearing difficulties, but this can lead to inefficiency in an office situation. Even differences that occur within the normal range of hearing will determine whether a telephone operator, for example, must have a message repeated. Exceptional auditory sensitivity has been shown to be an asset to inspectors of electrical equipment. Some persons were able to hear defects in motors and compressors when the equipment was running, whereas most could not make the necessary distinctions.

The sense of *smell* is essential to food and

wine tasters and to perfume testers, and success in these occupations undoubtedly depends on exceptional acuity. The sense of *touch* is important for lens grinders, and sense of *balance* is important to people who work aloft.

Supervisors should observe and analyze the jobs they supervise to determine whether special sensory capacities may be an asset. Most jobs make no special demands, and a person who falls within the normal range or has the minimum requirement may be as effective as a person with a high degree of sensitivity. However, in certain jobs a person gifted in a specific capacity can easily perform a task that is difficult for the average person. An electrical worker who had an unusual sense of touch, for example, was able to adjust electrical contacts without going through the usual trial-and-error adjustments made by other workers.[37]

Visual perception is dependent on the way the brain organizes the nervous impulses coming from the eyes. Whether a person will see a particular part of a complex object is therefore a matter of *perception* as well as of visual acuity. Even more common differences in perception arise when a picture contains many objects. Which details will be seen depends on the way the elements are grouped, what the subject is looking for, and the like. Asking people to tell what they see in an inkblot brings out a great variety of reactions. Experiments on perception have shown that the eye may report a detail as perfectly as does a film, but the detail may fail to be experienced by the observer. Two observers of the same picture will describe widely different versions of its details. A person's ability to observe defects in inspection work, see the conditions leading up to an accident in time to prevent it, or detect the snapping of a thread in weaving depends on perception as well as on vision.

People differ greatly also in the rapidity with which they perceive. A brief exposure (flash) will permit some people to identify a complex object, whereas others do not have time even to recognize any part of it. Fast readers are usually rapid perceivers because they can recognize words by rapidly scanning. Slow perceivers are handicapped in situations in which only a momentary glance at an object is available. This is invariably the case when objects are in motion, and motion often is a factor in industrial work.

Another aspect of perception especially important in many industrial operations is the size of the visual field. For example, some automobile drivers see only the street; others see the houses along the street as well. In tests in which the exposure to the visual object is too brief to permit eye movement, some people recognize detail far off to the side of their point of fixation, whereas others can see detail only at the point at which they are looking. Obviously, work that involves a large field of vision will be ill adapted to a person with a small perceptual field, even though visual acuity may be highly adequate.

Perception is largely a matter of training, but many differences are inherent in people and cannot be eliminated by experience. To the extent that the differences are biological, business must solve the problems by employee selection. Training will influence the kind of detail that will be recognized, but it cannot correct basic differences in perceptual speed and in the size of the visual field. Persons trained in the Chinese language will see details in a Chinese character that others will miss because their familiarity with the characters makes them react to details necessary for reading. For the same reason, a person trained in a given job can be made responsive to the kind of defect he or she is set to perceive. Speed of perception can be improved by training only insofar as it teaches people to see groupings of objects rather than individual objects. Thus, a person can improve reading skills by learning to react to groups of words rather than to single words. Even after training, however, people differ widely in their manner of perceiving.

PERSONALITY TESTS

A description of *personality tests* used in business is included here because such tests are still used, particularly in selecting among candidates for managerial jobs. There are serious questions, however, about their validity as measures of job performance.

Contrary to popular usage, *personality* should not be regarded as meaning something that characterizes the inner self, such as the spirit of an individual or the force molding behavior. The term as used by psychologists refers to a group of abilities or traits. Personality traits include such characteristics as cheerfulness, persistence, dominance, sociability, and cooperativeness. Mental and physical traits influence many personality traits, but modifications of personality arise because this group of traits is subject to change through experience, and mental and physical factors influence this experience.

In all aspects of life, the unusual or exceptional individual has the most difficult adjustments to make. Very often the inability to make human adjustments drives people to apply themselves exclusively to their work. Work is their escape, and their immersion in it frequently results in great success in fields in which human relations are relatively unimportant.

Personality also depends on heredity and on the functional condition of the body. Heredity determines the potentialities of personality development, but experience can influence their course. That some people, through heredity, are more likely to become mentally ill than others is a generally agreed-upon fact, but that some will remain relatively normal no matter what their life problems turn out to be, is a matter of debate.

The functions of the endocrine glands play an important part in general make-up and determine physical and mental growth. For instance, inadequate functioning of the thyroid gland makes people easily tired, sluggish, and unable to concentrate, whereas overfunctioning results in restlessness, irritability, and worry.

The *rating method* of personality testing uses other people's estimates of a given individual's personality traits. By using a list of pertinent traits, a group of people can rate any given individual who is known to them. Since prospective employees usually cannot be rated in this way, the method is largely limited to more effective placing of those already employed. An application of this method was found to be a good predictor of managerial success and job performance in other areas.[38]

The great virtue of the rating procedure lies in the fact that a wide range of traits can be explored with very little time and effort. The method presupposes, of course, that the employer already has determined the traits that best suit specific jobs. The limitations of the rating method will be discussed in Chapter 14.

The questionnaire method of testing personality has been widely used, largely because it is simple to administer. The applicant is required to answer a series of questions, usually with *yes, ?,* or *no*. From the responses, some understanding of the person is achieved. Widely used questionnaires are concerned with measures of emotional adjustment and tendencies toward introversion or extroversion. As emotional adjustment is essential to cooperative behavior and morale, these questionnaires or scales may be useful in detecting problem employees.

Poorly adjusted people tend to exaggerate their troubles, so that their behavior is not in keeping with the situation. They that feel they are unlucky, excessively criticized, lonely, and misunderstood. They have little confidence in other people, do not enjoy the company of others, and have family conflicts. In general, their health is poor; they have no appetite and sleep poorly. Selected questions would have some value in detecting poor adjustment.

Despite attempts to improve the questionnaire method, it has a number of drawbacks.[39] In one experiment,[40] students were asked to fill out a questionnaire designed primarily for detecting poorly adjusted individuals in industry.[41] The students were first asked to answer the questions honestly and then to answer them again under the assumption that they were applying for a job. It was found that there were more answers of the good-adjustment type under the second condition. In another study, retail sales applicants distorted their scores, whereas industrial sales applicants did not.[42] In this case, the Edwards Personal Preference Schedule was used in an actual employment situation.[43] It is apparent, therefore, that persons applying for a job can give favorable slants to their responses. If the instrument being used has been carefully validated so that a certain *pattern* of responses is significantly related to successful job performance in a given situation, the truth or falsity of the subject's answers is of little importance with reference to prediction.[44]

The Minnesota Multiphasic Personality Inventory, originally designed for clinical diagnosis, is among the questionnaires most frequently employed in personnel selection.[45] Data from this instrument must be treated in a configural, rather than in a cookbook fashion, since the shape of the profile obtained is more important than the level of single scores.[46] Thus, interpretation by highly competent examiners is imperative. Many other instruments of the self-report variety are currently available.[47] The purposes for which the questionnaire is to be used as well as the requirements of the specific situation will, of course, determine eventual choice.

Scales designed to measure specific personality traits also are available.[48] The scales are based on research that led to the isolation of primary traits, as distinct from compound traits. Such traits as persistence and honesty have been found to be compound rather than unitary. For example, persistence in enduring pain is different from plodding or keeping at a task. Similarly, honesty may vary greatly from one situation to another, so that we may speak of different kinds of honesty. For these reasons, caution must be used in generalizing from personality-test data.

Personality inventories are of greatest value when the person involved sees them as a way of gaining genuinely needed information or help. In such instances, these instruments are not seen as invading privacy, and thus faking and other types of resistance are lessened.

Projective tests require that the subject respond to ambiguous stimuli by giving them meaning or structure. The vague or incomplete nature of the material permits the individual to project his or her feelings into the situation. In the Rorschach Test, for instance, the subject is asked to locate and describe images in inkblots — much as children see figures in clouds. In the Thematic Apperception Test a person responds to rather indistinct drawings by making up a story

MATCHING THE WORKER TO THE JOB

— telling what has led to the present scene, what is now happening, and what the outcome will be. These two tests are among the most frequently used projective instruments.

The chief characteristic of a projective test is that the individual imparts meaning to the presented stimuli. These instruments are especially useful in identifying personal reactions, personality patterns, or behavioral styles that may determine the way in which a person frequently responds in real-life situations. These tests were originally developed for use in clinical diagnosis and require skill in administration and interpretation. In the hands of an inexperienced tester, they may become more a test of the projections of the tester than of the subject. In the hands of psychologists skilled in their use, however, insights can be generated that can then serve effectively as a framework against which other sources of information about the individual can be compared.

One value of projective tests is that they can obtain a global view of personality, because the respondent can react freely without being forced to use special categories or degrees of response ordinarily imposed by the nature of the test. This breadth of response can be helpful but it makes the statistical handling of test results very difficult. Projective tests have neither the mystic power to locate all the inner workings of the personality attributed to them by psychiatrically oriented movies or television programs, nor the complete lack of power attributed to them by those who insist that a test must be statistically perfect.

Comparisons of successful and unsuccessful supervisors sometimes yield certain personality differences. In one study, care was taken to choose successful and unsuccessful supervisors who were equal in skill and job knowledge.[50] When this was done, the un-successful group were persons who tended (1) to withdraw from others, (2) to be indifferent to the actions of people, and (3) to show antagonisms in their dealings with people. H. H. Meyer compared successful and unsuccessful work-group leaders in a utility and obtained similar differences.[51] He found social attitude to be the most distinguishing feature. Successful leaders were more likely to perceive others as individuals who had feelings and goals of their own, whereas the unsuccessful leaders saw things in terms of their own goals and situations. He also found that unsuccessful leaders were more inclined to engage in combative sports, although the successful leaders participated more in sports in general.

At present, the ratings of supervisors depend on how they please their superiors and carry out their orders, as well as on the productivity of their groups. Some superintendents like to see their supervisors keep busy, so evaluate them more on how many disturbances they settle or suppress than on how many they prevent. The influence of the criterion used and the relationship obtained with a personality measure is illustrated in a study by R. H. Van Zelst.[52] He used as his personality measure the Empathy Test, which measures the ability to put oneself in another's position. The test scores of sixty-four union leaders (business agents of five AF of L building trades unions) correlated .38 with percentage of votes received; .55 with scores on a supervisory test; .64 with ability to settle disputes; and .44 with enforcement of rules and regulations. The combined measures yielded a correlation of .76, which suggests that this Empathy Test may have value in selecting union leaders. Which of the four measures shown above is the best criterion of union leadership? At the present time, opinion plays a dominant role in the selection of a criterion of leadership (see Chapter 7).

T. W. Harrell approached the problem of personal qualifications associated with success in executive positions by following up three classes receiving MBA degrees from Stanford University.[53] While on campus, the students had been given a large variety of tests, including various personality scales. Earnings after five years were used as the criterion of success. When the upper with the lower third in earnings were compared, differences in thirteen out of fifty-five comparisons were significant. When data only from those employed in large companies was used, the high earners showed significant differences in personality and social interest from the low earners. The differences for the high earners were in the desirable (well-adjusted) direction. Specific measures showed them to be higher in energy levels, to have greater self-confidence, to be more socially bold, and to be more ready to make decisions.

TRENDS IN PERSONALITY TESTING

Much attention has been given to the problem of selecting managerial personnel.[54] The use of projective techniques, such as the Rorschach and Thematic Apperception Test, has become more widespread despite the fact that these techniques do not lend themselves to quantitative analysis. This trend has resulted in development of semiobjective approaches to scoring[55] and in recognition of the need for additional validation studies.[56]

In general, personality tests may be helpful in selection and placement, but they frequently do not survive rigorous validation procedures. Despite the usefulness of current tests for clinical purposes, authorities seriously question their automatic inclusion in batteries for personnel purposes and suggest that well-developed biographic inventories may prove more useful for organizations at present.

SOME LIMITATIONS

Obtaining tests that correlate highly with job performance for complex jobs is more difficult than finding ones for simple jobs. For one thing, the criterion of success on complex jobs is often more difficult to establish, and it is not uncommon for supervisors to differ considerably in what they expect from a person. Actually, the failure to agree on the criterion of job success may be our good fortune. Perhaps our hopes and faith in the future will be better served if success is not conceived of as an absolute and establishable fact.

RECENT DEVELOPMENTS IN TESTING

In the past, psychologists have used manual dexterity and other kinds of motor and sensory tests that required individual testing for accurate measurement of results. More recently, tests have been developed that allow the efforts of a number of applicants to be measured simultaneously. A study comparing results of dexterity test scores in individual versus group conditions appeared to indicate, however, that these test conditions affected results. Mean scores increased almost linearly in randomly selected groups as the group size rose from two to nine.[57] The cause of such increases cannot be stated unequivocally, but the lesson is clear — many more aspects of testing than had previously been taken into account probably can, and do affect scores. If our goal is to be fair in using tests, these factors must be understood and equalized for all job applicants.

MATCHING THE WORKER TO THE JOB

In recent years, models and procedures have been developed to ensure fairness in testing, that is, to avoid bias for or against any specific subgroup. Unfortunately, the development of such models and methods involves at some point defining the term *fairness*. Here again, an understanding of attitude formation and perception is important. Each definition is *operationalized*, that is, turned from an abstraction into a measurable phenomenon through the logic and creativity of the scientist. But such a process also involves subjective attitudes and perceptions. It can be no other way — scientists are not computers, and computers cannot generate theory. Each scientist or personnel manager uses his or her unique value orientation when defining what *fairness* is — which may or may not agree with the definitions of minority applicants, older versus younger workers, male versus female candidates, the Equal Employment Opportunity Commission versus companies, and so on. Fairness in testing is a desirable goal, but it is also important to realize that the goal is an ideal.

In Chapter 11, we shall examine ways that have been developed to analyze task components of jobs, so measures that accurately predict job success can be prepared. In addition to testing, these ways include the use of biographical data and job samples to evaluate a candidate's probability of success. Expert opinion in this field suggests that tests, especially of motor skills, can be very useful and should be included as one part of a sophisticated selection procedure, which also includes other information sources.[58] Thus, while the widespread use of some kinds of tests has (justifiably) lessened in recent years, other tests that differentiate applicants accurately and fairly will probably continue to be used.

ALTERNATIVES TO TESTING

Although court decisions concerning culture-bound tests have caused some companies simply to abandon testing, for others, it has stimulated the search for viable alternatives. Some of these, such as *biodata* (biographical data), have been known for many years, but were not relied on as extensively when tests were inexpensive, readily available, and considered acceptable.[59]

Much useful biodata can be acquired from a well-designed application form — that is, a form whose questions accurately differentiate those candidates who will do well from those who will perform poorly on the job in question.

Designing such forms is not as simple and arbitrary as it once was. Some questions asked in the past have been used to discriminate unfairly (for example, questions relating to age, marital status, and so on), and today there are restrictions on their use.

In the past, many interviewers appraised responses to application forms in terms of their own experience rather than trying systematically to match responses to later job performance. Experience can often be useful, but it can sometimes be the worst teacher rather than the best. Memories are filtered through our perception and interpreted in light of favorable or unfavorable attitudes. Therefore, greater fairness can usually be achieved by the objective comparing and weighting of biographical items.

The purpose of weighting is to yield a single score to which the most relevant items contribute the greater number of points. By properly weighting the items on the application blank, the correlation between the single score and the performance criterion can be maximized. Unfortunately, the weighting pattern and the relevant items that should be considered vary for different jobs, so that each job must be separately analyzed.[60] One study showed that secretaries who were still on the job two years after hiring showed the following biographical information: they tended to be over thirty-four years old, had children in high school, and lived within the city. Secretaries not having these characteristics were more likely to have left the company.[61] The same study showed that the previous salary of the secretaries yielded no information of predictive value.

The use of biographical data has been particularly valuable in the selection of sales personnel, and it is often difficult to prejudge the items that will be critical.[62] For example, in selecting teen-agers for door-to-door sales jobs, it had been assumed by the company that the needy would be the best candidates.[63] Actually, it was found that those who seemed to be the least in need of money were most likely to succeed.

A second use for application forms also was experimentally tested; 483 sales applicants were divided randomly into two samples. One (control) group was sent the merchandise as usual; the other (screened) group was sent a questionnaire to be returned before the merchandise was sent. Failure to return the questionnaire screened out 45 percent without reducing the number of successful applicants. The single act of returning the questionnaire was an extremely effective factor for reducing failures from 91 percent to 45 percent on a job in which failure had been the predominant outcome.

The scientific use of biodata requires adherence to certain procedures. If the data is collected by means of oral responses to an interviewer, every interviewee must be asked the same questions in the same way. If the interviewer analyzes or interprets the data, such judgments must be made in ways that ensure they are standardized, relevant, and of known validity.[64] Some people may question whether deliberately or unconsciously falsified information may not weaken or invalidate this approach. However, attempts to verify reported data have shown it to be accurate to a level of 90 percent or higher.[65] Weighted application blanks have been used successfully in predicting performance in many types of jobs — from soldiers to clerks to European sales personnel.[66]

Biodata can also be used to derive information that will lead to the use of other accurate measures of future performance. For example, analysis of the *type* of questions that differentiate successful from poor performers may lead to the conclusion that measurement of a specific aptitude could be used to increase successful selection.

Biodata as a measurement tool is superior to testing in several ways. The choice of items is empirically based, that is, drawn from real-life situations, and weighting methods are also based on observation of actual job performance. Thus, the relationship between the measure and the job is clear to all — to government regulatory agencies, to personnel department employees, and to job applicants. The interviewer does not have to weigh the ethical implications of engaging in the "covert operations" required in some kinds of tests, and the applicant can understand the relevance of the information requested and feel more confident that abilities, not group membership, are being evaluated.[67]

Motor-coordination tests have been developed to measure basic abilities applying to some degree to many kinds of jobs. But because the tests are basic, they do not accurately and completely measure the job skills needed for any specific job. *Job sampling* is a method of reproducing accurately a sample of the specific job skills needed to perform well on a certain job. This method, when carefully and expertly used, has often yielded better predictions of performance than tests.[68]

Employers have long looked at college grades to evaluate prospective employees, but little research has been done to establish scholastic success as a valid selection criterion. F. J. Williams and T. W. Harrell studied graduates of MBA programs to determine predictors of success in business.[69] They found that grade-point averages for undergraduate courses and for required courses in business school did not have significant correlation with the success criterion (salary adjusted for length of time out of school). However, grades in elective courses in business school were significantly correlated with success. Distinction in chosen areas of academic or administrative interest in college were an indication of probable success in business.

References and letters of recommendation are frequently required of job applicants despite their many apparent deficiencies. In one study, only two sources of recommendation had any correlation with performance, even when a standardized recommendation questionnaire was used, and these correlations were low. A nonstandardized letter would perhaps lead to even less correlation as it allows a respondent to select only those aspects of a former employee's performance and personality that the supervisor wishes to communicate.

RECRUITING AND INTERVIEWING

Finding the best person available for a job has become a more difficult and complex

Recruiting employees through newspaper advertisements that state the company is "An Equal Opportunity Employer" broadens the field from which potential employees may be drawn. (Bohdan Hrynewych, Stock, Boston)

process in recent years. Companies required by the Equal Employment Opportunity Commission (EEOC) to use affirmative action programs in hiring must follow prescribed practices in their search for job candidates.[70] The overall purpose of such practices is twofold: to ensure that individuals with the potential to perform well in a position are not missed in recruiting efforts, and over the long run, to bring the representation of minorities and women at various levels in the organization into line with the percentage of such groups living in the area and seeking employment.

The government has taken a part because recruiters in the past had frequently omitted or rejected good workers who did not meet arbitrary traditional ideas about "proper" employee characteristics. But few would argue that the present system is flawless. As with the civil service system, an approach intended to improve the recruiting process has brought about some progress and some new problems as well. To the extent that recruiters' and managers' attitudes are not in line with affirmative action principles, efforts to carry out the regulations are sometimes less than wholehearted. In some cases, employers already have a candidate in mind for the job, and the EEOC-prescribed process is done for show.

There is no way to *legislate* attitude change, but the fact is that business attitudes have changed to some extent with respect to the perceived ability of women and minority group members to hold responsible jobs. Eventually, it is to be hoped, such regulatory efforts as affirmative action will no longer be necessary.

That eventuality will not solve all recruiting problems, however. A survey of nearly two hundred companies indicated that although there were methods for measuring recruiter effectiveness, there were few incentives for surveyed recruiters to hire the (objectively) best candidate, since low effectiveness ratings had minimal effects on recruiters' careers.[71] Another problem is that selection criteria used by recruiters tend to be vague and subjective, and little effort is made by training departments to improve recruiters' interviewing skills. The importance and complexity of such skills will be explored in this section.

INTERVIEWING PRACTICES

In practice, most firms employ selection interviews — one survey indicated that 99 percent of the companies contacted routinely do so — despite the fact that the use of the interviewing technique as a selection tool is open to serious question. It is important to recognize that eliminating testing does not eliminate bias in selection. Conflicting opinions are rife with regard to the usefulness of interviewing, and an extensive review of the literature shows highly variable findings.[72]

"Nearly everyone uses this costly, inefficient, and usually invalid selection procedure . . . (although) nothing in the recent literature may be cited to give strong support to the use of the personal interview as a prediction tool."[73] Since interviewing is time consuming, expensive, and thus far lacking in widely accepted standards, companies could profit considerably from any improvement in its effectiveness.

The standardized or patterned interview represents an attempt to raise the validity of the interviewing procedure.[74] The interviews are structured to lead to a more systematic collection of data and to follow a similar pattern for all applicants so that comparisons can be made. The interviewer is trained to follow a specific plan for the time spent with the applicant. Often the interviewer works from a job description and may fill out a printed form, which contains rating scales for the traits to be observed. The ratings provide permanent records that are more useful in the subsequent comparison of applicants than the rather haphazard notes obtained from nonpatterned interviews are. The validity of the items included in the standardized interview should be determined in the same way as those included in tests or weighted application blanks.[75]

Another attempt to improve the value of the interview is to make a rating (five-point scale) after each question (called Q *by* Q) and thus make a series of small decisions before the total one.[76] The Q by Q interview has been shown to increase the reliability of the interview (the degree of agreement between raters), but whether the validity (accuracy) of decisions reached by this means is improved remains to be determined.

J. M. Fraser stresses the need for refining the interview and for developing skills.[77] Two prerequisites are (1) that the interviewer knows what is sought, and (2) that it will be recognized when seen. Since even experienced interviewers do not agree in their appraisals of candidates, research must determine sources of error and determine the type of training needed.[78] Even persons observing the same interview use the same behaviors to prove opposite conclusions.[79] The judgments are more accurate when the interview is heard on a tape recorder than when observed, indicating that the presence of the interviewee serves as a distraction.[80] However, exactly the opposite results were obtained in predicting grades in a statistics course.[81] The Q by Q interview was used to predict success in the statistics course study, and deception was not an issue, but the equally significant (though opposite) relationships shown indicate that behavior cues can influence judgments either negatively or positively.

BIAS IN INTERVIEWS

The prevalence of an ineffective procedure, such as the unstructured interview, indicates that some need other than good selection is satisfied by the interview. People like to see what they are buying, not because they can judge its merits better but because they want to see if they like it. This attitude also seems to be true in hiring employees. In an organization, interviewers serve as gatekeepers and must pass an opinion on whoever is admitted. They must not only select good applicants but must also please supervisors. Whether or not interviewers are aware of this dual role, they cannot escape the criticisms directed toward them when they pass on unacceptable candidates.

People have positive and negative first impressions, which are known to be unreliable, yet often are unavoidable. It is only natural for a supervisor to feel that if a new employee is needed, why not hire a likable one — someone who is his or her kind of person? The more psychologists try to objectify the interview procedure, the more they interfere with this emotional bias and destroy interest in the improved method. This bias toward people who "think like me" has been shown in a number of studies.[82]

An investigation by E. E. Ghiselli and R. Barthol offers some support for this view.[83] They found that higher management "approves of supervisors whose attitudes seem to be similar to those traditionally held by higher management." This means that people who are most like their managers are most apt to be advanced. This same bias operates in employment interviews. The effect of these biases is to create in the organization an image of a desirable personality: the individual members might change, but the personality of the image would be stable.

Bias cannot be eliminated entirely, but we need to find ways to maximize its beneficial effects and minimize its undesirable ones. As we mentioned earlier, another area of bias that still must be recognized and dealt with is that which discriminates among candidates on the basis of appearance or gender. Studies show that such biases do affect selection evaluations.[84]

The interview is at its best when used not to judge ability but to learn and understand the viewpoint and thinking of another person. This approach stems from nondirective counseling and can be adapted to many interview situations.[85] It is least appropriate in the employment interview since the interests of the applicant and the interviewer conflict: the applicant wants to get an offer and the interviewer wants to screen. Transfer or promotion interviews are not as subject to this conflict because both parties can be interested in assigning individuals to jobs in which their abilities will be most effectively used. This common interest, when established, improves the reliability of the applicant's statements. Nondirective interviewing and its relevant skills are discussed in detail in Chapter 18.

PREMATURE EMPLOYMENT DECISIONS

Decisions regarding employment seem to be colored by the fact that people are solution-minded, hence liable to make premature decisions. Some of the researchers at McGill University show that decisions regarding hiring versus not hiring are made early and that subsequent data tend to be used only to test the initial decision.[86] This tendency operates regardless of the order in which relevant information is supplied. In these studies, three types of information were given to the decision maker: biographical data (application form), description of personal appearance, and the interview notes. Regardless of which material was supplied first, the decision made after a scrutiny of the initial information tended to correspond with the final decision in 73 percent of 177 cases. Further, an initial rating of rejection was more likely to be upheld than one of acceptance.

The interviewer's behavior also is different in cases of acceptance and rejection. Once interviewers have decided to reject an applicant, they talk less and are less friendly, and the applicant is made to feel uneasy. The applicant's subsequent reactions thus tend to reinforce the interviewer's initial judgment. A later study showed that negative information about the job candidate disclosed at the beginning of an interview had more impact than if it came out later.[87]

If all sources of information are to play a more important part in the selection process, employment decision makers must find ways to delay their decisions. When decisions are made too early, subsequent information tends to be pigeonholed to support the decision. This approach to information evaluation excludes the gray region between the extremes, which should be thoroughly explored before the final classification step is taken.

A decision is like a theory in that it provides a frame of reference for factual information. These meanings restrict the varied interpretations that the same data might have if different theories were operating. Once a decision is made, it functions to screen and evaluate information. J. S. Bruner has used the term *gating* to refer to this selective attention given to new information, which progresses until the final stage when further information is gated out.[88]

Earlier it was stated that greater recognition has been given to the fact that interpersonal processes tend to be interactive, to be two-way processes. A recent study of the selection process demonstrates this. N. Schmitt and B. W. Coyle reflected that during an interview, the interviewer, as a representative of his or her company, is making an impression on the job candidate, as well as the other way around.[89] Their study showed that the interviewer's interpersonal style and method of conducting the job interview affected applicants' later decisions about the company involved.

THE CONTRIBUTION OF INTERVIEW TO ASSESSMENT

Data, no matter how objectively they are obtained, do not organize themselves; only human beings bring meaning to facts. The interviewer, according to Fraser, is in a position to integrate objective facts about a person and make a personality assessment.[90] This interpretive aspect of human judgment can be either a fault or a virtue. It requires both skill and insight to make it a virtue; ability to withhold judgment until the objective data are assembled is difficult. This conclusion is supported by the longitudinal investigation in the Bell System Management Progress study.[91] Skilled interviewers (psychologists), having access to biographical data and covering topics related to work goals, attitudes on social issues, and hobbies, were able to contribute information to individual assessments that subsequently were found to be related to progress in management. Variables reflecting career motivation, dependency needs, work motivation, and interpersonal skills were found to be related to individual differences in salary increases.

THE NEED FOR OBSERVANT SUPERVISORS

Supervisors must not assume that the problem of selecting and placing employees is a job strictly for the personnel department. The relating of jobs and people gives the personnel department statistical trends and cross-sections of many people, but each individual possesses a unique combination of abilities. An observant supervisor deals with large samples of individual behaviors and can see each person as a whole. For this reason, the army sergeant is often better able than the psychiatrist to judge a soldier's ability to stand up under fire. A supervisor is in a position to observe and discover special talents and interests and to distinguish between deficiencies in aptitudes and poor attitudes. Changes in behavior are important, and the skilled supervisor is sensitive to them and able to understand their meaning. *The*

judgment of qualified persons should not be overruled by tests.

VALUE OF THE EMPLOYEE'S RECORD

Test data are used not only for employment purposes but also for transfers and promotions. To match abilities and job requirements, the data serve the same purposes as in hiring. An additional source of information is available when a job change is involved: the employee's record in the company. Invariably, this information is used and, when properly interpreted, can be of great value. As a matter of fact, it is more complete than test information because it includes the whole person's performance in a life setting, not just cross-sections of certain abilities measured under test conditions. The rating of a person's job performance incorporates not only patterns of abilities, but also motivation, an indication of attitudes, personal and interpersonal adjustments, and the impressions made on supervisors.

Since employee ratings are often used as the criterion of success, a test constructor is satisfied when a battery of tests is found that correlates with merit ratings. However, when job-success predictions (based on candidates' test results) differ from later performance (as measured by merit ratings), managers often feel that the merit ratings must be wrong, rather than the test results. When job changes involve different abilities, the test may be a source of information, but insofar as similar activities are involved the record is more reliable. Further, the record provides information about a particular person and permits specific predictions, whereas a test merely indicates the probabilities of success.

In promoting people through the management ranks, executives wish to have certain assurances when making decisions, because poor choices may have serious consequences. Frequently executives call in consultants to test and interview their management personnel and then ask for assessments and recommendations. Granted that reputable consultants have certain skills, nevertheless their opinions, at best, are based on limited knowledge gained over a short period of time. These opinions should not be used as a substitute for an employee's performance record. Nor should the consultants be shown the performance record as an aid in their appraisal, because this will bias their assessment. When outside consultants are used, their assessment of an individual and the individual's record should be treated as supplementary data gained from different situations. Conflicting appraisals should not be viewed as suggesting conflicting decisions, but rather as posing a problem that requires further exploration.

When outside consultants assess managers, serious emotional problems can be created that may color the interviewer's assessment. Are those who fear the assessment the least capable, the most sensitive, the most ambitious, the least informed of the limitations of assessment, or the least stable? As yet no one knows the answer. Regardless of the effect of calling in specialists, the skilled interviewer must reassure the interviewee. All parties gain when the assessment leads to job placement in which the amount of responsibility is commensurate with the employee's ability and interest in using it effectively. But regardless of the values to be gained from assessment, the initiation of such a program should be carefully thought through in order to avoid widespread anxieties.

Management assessment can be a valuable supplement to other biographical data if used in accordance with its unique contribution.

A good interviewer can learn about a person's ambitions, concerns, important needs, and set of values. These understandings can aid in interpreting the employee's record and test data, and they can assist the person interviewed to better self-understanding and more realistic self-assessment.

AN ALTERNATIVE TO INTERVIEWING: THE ASSESSMENT CENTER

Recently the assessment-center approach to selection has been developed as an alternative to interviewing applicants for managerial positions.[92] It was hoped that this approach would lessen bias and increase objectivity in selection. Typically, such an approach combines groups of candidates and teams of evaluators in a standardized series of activities, including interviews, tests, work observation, biodata, and observation of individual contributions. The method uses a combination of information sources and a number of independent raters to increase predictive success.

Although the approach helps to counteract the biases present when only one rater or one performance measure is used, there have been criticisms of its effectiveness.[93] One writer cautions that the process must be evaluated objectively and retained or rejected on its merits.[94] Most evaluators find it enjoyable (many assessment-center-selection programs take place in resort hotels or other noncompany sites), but this is not evidence of its effectiveness. Moreover, this evaluation should not be turned into a rite of passage, as in a tribal initiation ceremony — this serves no valid selection purpose. In sum, candidates selected via assessment-center methods must be evaluated and their performance compared to that of candidates selected by alternative methods. Unless the former selects a greater proportion of successful managers, its relatively high cost cannot be justified.

CAREERS: THE PLANNING AND MANAGEMENT OF HUMAN RESOURCES

Many companies have had fast-track programs for an elite group of young managers for many years. Under these systems, executives and personnel managers select, for greater opportunity and more intense review, a subgroup of new employees who are believed to have high potential. This system is subject to all the drawbacks and biases of the unvalidated test or interview. It may produce a self-fulfilling prophecy: the knowledge that an individual is a fast-tracker may favorably influence supervisors' ratings. And then what of the individual who is not tapped for membership in this group? Is he or she doomed to a mediocre career?

In this age of assertiveness, employees who wish to become more in control of their careers have reacted in positive ways. Popularized texts on such topics as time management and career strategy have sold well,[95] and companies have also begun to respond with more information and help in determining employees' career goals and capabilities.[96] Providing guidance in this area can be of value to companies as well as to their employees. Using individual abilities more efficiently and fully is one way the company can get maximum return on its investment in organization members. Many efforts in this direction have, unfortunately, been relatively unsophisticated or half-hearted approaches proclaimed by personnel departments, but neither validated by

scientific methods nor backed by line managers.[97]

This section presents data from studies of various aspects of career development and occupational choice. The extent to which human resource planning becomes a useful and appreciated corporate tool will depend on how seriously management takes its responsibility for finding ways that help employees fulfill their capacities and career goals.

OCCUPATIONAL CHOICE

One critical stage in a business career is the transition from school to the first job. Evidence indicates that the transition is not easy, especially for minority group members. Unemployment rates for young people are often more than twice those of older workers, and the rates for minority youth are especially high — up to 40 percent during the 1970s.[98]

Various theories have been offered to describe the mental process by which an individual selects his or her occupation. One writer has postulated that choice of an occupation and effort in that occupation are based on a preference for consistency between self-esteem level, job demands, and expectations of others.[99] The definition of *self-esteem* used in this approach is a combination of personality variables and situational factors.[100]

The job that the individual eventually gets, is an outcome influenced both by internal goals and personality and by external factors, such as the attitudes of others and the job market at that particular time. Whether we perceive the greater impetus in the final outcome to be the strivings of the individual or the judgments of society depends on our evaluation of the locus of control of events.[101]

ORGANIZATIONAL ENTRY

A number of studies have suggested that factors in a person's initial response to the job and the organization have long-term effects on satisfaction and productivity. One area of investigation has been the effect on job turnover of receiving "realistic" versus "idealistic" information about the organization. Results suggest that management's being truthful about the bad and the good aspects of the organization is associated with lower turnover than that which occurs when one-sided reports are given.[102] This result was seen in studies of nursing students and military cadets, as well as in those of job applicants.

Several explanations are possible. Those people who joined after hearing the bad news as well as the good may have been more committed, or they may have felt more responsible for succeeding since they could not claim ignorance of conditions. Or perhaps realistic knowledge led to a better coping with situations and to lower frustration (see Chapter 4). Results of one study designed to test these possible explanations favored the last alternative as the most probable.[103]

Another important aspect of a person's initial impression at a job is that of the challenge. A study comparing initial perception of job challenge and performance five to eight years later showed a significant positive relationship.[104] Similar results were found at other large American firms and several federal agencies. The data showed that such differences could not be accounted for by relationships between personality characteristics and initial job assignments.

CAREER STAGES

One finding from the behavioral sciences[105] that has received widespread publicity in recent years is that normal human development does not stop with physical maturity, but continues through common, predictable stages and crises throughout adult life.[106]

Research reveals that motivation and attitudes about jobs and careers change as the maturing worker's perspective changes. Because the business environment is a dynamic and changing one, efforts toward self-development are not only intrinsically satisfying to many organization members, but also necessary if the organization is to survive and prosper. Unfortunately, some workers see change not as an opportunity for growth and novelty, but as a threat to their past achievement and status. Such issues are of extreme concern in research and development areas in companies. Various approaches to self-development were found to succeed better at some organizational levels than others during a study of research and development employees in one firm.[107] The probability of participation for lower-level employees was greater for career-planning techniques; self-analysis and action planning appealed to more managers.

Changes in the laws regarding the mandatory retirement age have brought to public attention the problems and concerns of middle-aged and older workers. Research in this area is still sketchy, but if the low birthrate in the United States proves to be a long-term trend, the average age of an American worker will continue to increase. Sophisticated, alert personnel executives will therefore be seeking new ways to maximize the effectiveness of older workers.

The United States and the Western world have often been characterized as having a youth-worshipping culture. Such attitudes and the negative opinions derived from them may have influenced company policies in the past. Human beings are held to be superior to other life forms on earth because they

MATCHING THE WORKER TO THE JOB

possess the greatest powers for accumulating knowledge on how to live better.[108]

Those people who have lived longer have also had a greater opportunity to accumulate knowledge and judgment. Age does not always indicate wisdom, but neither does it necessarily indicate senility. Moreover, recent evidence suggests that those who have survived in good health beyond the age of fifty-five are more likely than younger workers to be well-adjusted and able to cope constructively with stress and frustration.[109]

NOTES

1. See the following studies for findings on both sides of this complex and controversial issue: Katzell, R. A., and Dyck, F. J. Differential validity revived. *J. Appl. Psychol.*, 1977, *62*, 137–145; Schmidt, F. L., Berner, J. G., and Hunter, J. E. Racial differences in validity of employment tests: Reality or illusion? *J. Appl. Psychol.*, 1973, *58*, 5–9.

2. Smith, L. Equal opportunity rules are getting tougher. *Fortune*, 1978, *97*(12), 152–154ff.

3. Ross, I. Retirement at seventy: A new trauma for management. *Fortune*, 1978 *97*(9), 106–110ff.

4. Vidal, D. Sex differences in math studies analyzed. *New York Times*, July 21, 1976.

5. Argyris, C. Problems and new directions for industrial psychology. In M. D. Dunnette (Ed.), *Handbook of industrial and organizational psychology.* Chicago: Rand-McNally, 1976, pp. 151–184.

6. Whyte, W. How to cheat on personality tests. Appendix to *The organization man.* Garden City, N.Y.: Doubleday, 1957.

7. Dunnette, M. D., and Borman, W. C. Personnel selection and classification systems. *Ann. Rev. Psychol.*, 1979, *30*, 477–525.

8. Darlington, R. B. A defense of "rational" personnel selection and two new methods. *J. Educ. Meas.*, 1976, *13*, 43–52.

9. Dunnette and Borman, op. cit., p. 493.

10. For detailed discussion, see Nunnally, J. C., *Psychometric theory.* New York: McGraw-Hill, 1967; Bock, R. D., and Wood, R. Test theory. *Ann. Rev. Psychol.*, 1971, *22*, 193–224.

11. Sparks, C. P. Validity of psychological tests. *Personnel Psychol.*, 1970, *23*, 39–46.

12. Fleishman, E. A. Psychomotor selection tests: Research and application in the United States Air Force. *Personnel Psychol.*, 1956, *9*, 449–468.

13. Bennett, G. K., and Cruikshank, R. M. *A summary of manual and mechanical ability tests.* New York: Psychological Corp., 1942.

14. Shartle, C. L. A selection test for electrical troublemen. *Personnel J.*, 1932, *11*, 177–183; Vernon, P. E., and Parry, J. B. *Personnel selection in the British forces.* London: University of London Press, 1949, p. 230; Stead, W. H., and Shartle, C. L. *Occupational counseling techniques.* New York: American Book, 1940, Chapter 6; Wolff, W. M., and North, A. J. Selection of municipal firemen. *J. Appl. Psychol.*, 1957, *35*, 25–29.

15. Creativity, intelligence don't necessarily correlate, admen told. Report on speech presented by D. W. McKinnon at Sixth Annual Creative Workshop held by *Advertising Age.*

16. Getzels, J. W., and Jackson, P. W. *Creativity and intelligence: Explorations with gifted children.* New York: Wiley, 1962.

17. Torrance, E. P. *Encouraging creative behavior: Experiments in classroom creativity.* Englewood Cliffs, N.J.: Prentice-Hall, 1965.

18. Wertheimer, M. *Productive thinking.* New York: Harper & Row, 1959.

19. Maier, N. R. F., Thurber, J. A., and Janzen, J. C. Studies in creativity: V. The selection process in recall and problem-solving situations. *Psychol. Reports*, 1968, *23*, 1003–1022.

20. Maier, N. R. F., Julius, M., and Thurber, J. A. Studies in creativity: Individual differences in the storing and utilization of information. *Amer. J. Psychol.*, 1967, *80*, 492–519.
21. Torrance, op. cit.; Christensen, P. R., Guilford, J. P., and Wilson, R. C. Relations of creative response to working time and instructions. *J. Exp. Psychol.*, 1957, *53*, 82–88.
22. Colgrove, M. A., Stimulative creative problem solving: Innovative set. *Psychol. Reports*, 1968, *22*, 1205–1211.
23. Guilford, J. P. Intelligence: 1965 model. *Amer. Psychol.*, 1966, *21*, 20–26; Kettner, N. W., Guilford, J. P., and Christensen, P. R. A factor analytic study across the domains of reasoning, creativity, and evaluation. *Psychol. Mono.*, 1959 (No. *279*); Hendricks, M., Guilford, J. P., and Hoepfner, R. Measuring creative social intelligence. Los Angeles: University of Southern Calif., 1969, Report #42.
24. Cropley, A. J. Divergent thinking and science specialities. *Nature*, 1967, *215*, 671–672.
25. Maier, N. R. F. *Problem solving and creativity: In individuals and groups*. Belmont, Calif.: Brooks/Cole, 1970, Parts 1–4.
26. Buel, W. D. The validity of behavioral rating scale items for the assessment of individual creativity. *J. Appl. Psychol.*, 1960, *44*, 407–412.
27. Mednick, S. A. The associative basis of the creative process. *Psychol. Rev.*, 1962, *69*, 220–232; Maltzman, I., Belloni, M., and Fishbein, M. Experimental studies of associative variables in originality. *Psychol. Mono.*, 1964, *78* (No. 3).
28. Fleishman, E. A., and Hempel, W. E., Jr. A factor analysis of dexterity tests. *Personnel Psychol.*, 1954, 7, 15–32.
29. Garfiel, E. The measurement of motor ability. *Arch. Psychol.*, 1923, *9*(62), 32.
30. Fleishman, E. A. The description and prediction of perceptual motor skill learning. In R. Glaser (Ed.), *Training research and education*. Pittsburgh: University of Pittsburgh Press, 1962.
31. Treat, K. Tests of garment machine operators. *Personnel J.*, 1929, *8*, 19–28.
32. Hayes, E. G. Selecting women for shop work. *Personnel J.*, 1932, *11*, 69–85.
33. *Guide to the use of the General Aptitude Test Battery*. Washington, D.C.: U.S. Govt. Printing Office, 1958; Fleishman, E. A. Psychomotor selection tests: Research and application in the United States Air Force. *Personnel Psychol.*, 1956, *9*, 449–468; *The use of multifactor tests in guidance*. Washington, D.C.: American Personnel and Guidance Assn., 1957; Hall, R. C. Occupational group contents in terms of the DAT. *Educ. Psychol. Measmt*, 1957, *17*, 556–567.
34. Stead, W. H., and Shartle, C. L. *Occupational counseling techniques*. New York: American Book, 1940.
35. Kuhn, H. S. Articles bearing on industrial eye problems. *Transac. Amer. Acad. Opthal. Otolar.*, 1946, *50*, 175–178; Tiffin, J., and Wirt, S. E. Near vs. distance visual acuity in relation to success on close industrial jobs. *Suppl. Transact. Amer. Acad. Opthal. Otolar.*, 1944, *48*, 9–16; Tiffin, J., and McCormick, E. J. *Industrial psychology* (4th ed.). Englewood Cliffs, N.J.: Prentice-Hall, 1958, pp. 145–156.
36. Licklider, J. C. R. Basic correlates of the auditory stimulus. In S. S. Stevens (Ed.), *Handbook of experimental psychology*. New York: Wiley, 1951, Chapter 24.
37. For detailed discussions of sensory functions, see the following: Brant, H. F. *The psychology of seeing*. New York: Philosophical Library, 1945; Luckiesh, M., and Moss, F. K. *The science of seeing*. Princeton, N.J.: Van Nostrand, 1937; Hirsh, I. J. *The measurement of hearing*. New York: McGraw-Hill, 1952; Stevens, S. S., and Davis, H. *Hearing: Its psychology and physiology*. New York: Wiley, 1938; Pfaffman, C. Taste and smell. In S. S. Stevens (Ed.), *Handbook of experimental psychology*. New York: Wiley, 1951, pp. 1143–1171; Jenkins, W. L. Somesthesis. Ibid., pp. 1172–1190; Wendt, G. R. Vestibular functions. Ibid., pp. 1191–1223; Geldlard, F. A. *The human senses*. New York: Wiley, 1953; Tufts College Institute for Applied Experimental Psychology. *Handbook of human*

engineering data for design engineers, 2nd ed. Medford, Mass.: Tufts College, 1952; Rosenblith, W. A. (Ed.). Sensory communication. New York: Wiley, 1961; Brindley, G. S. Physiology of the retina and the visual pathways. London: Edward Arnold Co., 1960.

38. Kraut, A. I. Prediction of managerial success by peer and training staff ratings. J. Appl. Psychol., 1965, 60, 14–19; Edwards, R. C. Personality traits and "success" in schooling and work. Educ. Psychol. Meas., 1977, 37, 125–138.

39. Wesman, A. G. Faking personality test scores in simulated employment situation. J. Appl. Psychol., 1952, 36, 223–229; Borislow, B. The Edwards Personal Preference Schedule (EPPS) and fallability. J. Appl. Psychol., 1958, 42, 22–27; Dicken, C. F. Simulated patterns on the Edwards Personal Preference Schedule. J. Appl. Psychol., 1959, 43, 372–378; Hedberg, R. More on forced-choice test fakability. J. Appl. Psychol., 1962, 46, 125–127.

40. The study was made by W. J. Giese and F. C. Christy and is reported in Tiffin and McCormick, op. cit., pp. 180–181.

41. Humm, D. G., and Wadsworth, G. W. The Humm-Wadsworth Temperament Scale (1940 revision). Los Angeles: D. G. Humm Personnel Service.

42. Hedberg, R. "Real-life" faking on the Edwards Personal Preference Schedule by sales applicants. J. Appl. Psychol., 1962, 46, 128–130.

43. Edwards, A. L. Manual for the Edwards Personal Preference Schedule, rev. ed. New York: Psychological Corp., 1959.

44. Albright, L. E., Glennon, J. R., and Smith, W. J. The use of psychological tests in industry. Cleveland, Ohio: Howard Allen, 1963, p. 126.

45. Published by University of Minnesota Press, 1943; New York: Psychological Corp., 1945.

46. Hathaway, S. R., and Meehl, P. E. An atlas for the clinical use of the MMPI. Minneapolis: University of Minnesota Press, 1951; Welsch, G. S., and Dahlstrom, W. G. Basic readings on the MMPI in psychology and medicine. Minneapolis: University of Minnesota Press, 1956; Drake, L. E., and Oetting, E. R. An MMPI codebook for counselors. Minneapolis: University of Minnesota Press, 1959.

47. For excellent critical reviews, see: Cronback, L. J. Essentials of psychological testing (3rd ed.). New York: Harper, 1970, pp. 464–499; and Super, D. E., and Crites, J. O. The expanding list of primary abilities. In Appraising vocational fitness. New York: Harper, 1962, pp. 514–586.

48. (a) The Guilford-Martin Inventory of Factors G A M I N; (b) The Guilford-Martin Personnel Inventory; (c) The Guilford-Martin Temperament Profile Chart; (d) Guilford's Inventory of Factors S T D C R. Beverly Hills, Calif.: Sheridan Supply Co., 1943; (e) Guilford-Zimmerman Temperament Survey. Beverly Hills, Calif.: Sheridan Supply Co., 1949; (f) The 16 P. F. Test. Urbana, Ill.: Institute for Personality and Ability Testing, 1950.

49. Cattell, R. B. Personality theory growing from multivariate quantitative research. In S. Koch (Ed.), Psychology: a study of a science. III. Formulations of the person and the social context. New York: McGraw-Hill, 1959, pp. 257–327; Guilford, J. P. Personality. New York: McGraw-Hill, 1959.

50. Shartle, C. L. A clinical approach to foremanship. Personnel J., 1934, 3, 135–139.

51. Meyer, H. H. Factors related to success in the human relations aspect of work-group leadership. Psychol. Monogr., 1951, 65, 1–29.

52. Van Zelst, R. H. Empathy test scores and union leaders. J. Appl. Psychol., 1952, 36, 293–295.

53. Harrell, T. W. The personality of high earning MBA's in big business. Personnel Psychol., 1969, 22, 457–463.

54. Gellerman, S. W. Seven deadly sins of executive placement. Mgmt. Rev., 1958, 47, 4–9; Taylor, E. K. The unsolved riddle of executive success. Personnel, 1960, 37, 8–17; Stark, S. Executive personality and psychological testing. University of Illinois Bull., 1958, 55, 15–32; Michael, W. B. Differential testing of high-level personnel. Educ. Psychol. Measmt., 1957, 17, 475–490.

55. Nevis, E. C., Wallen, R. W., and Stickel, E. G. The thematic evaluation of managerial potential.

Cleveland, Ohio: Personnel Research and Development Corp., 1959; Harrower, M. R., and Steiner, M. E. *Large-scale Rorschach techniques.* Springfield, Ill.: Charles C Thomas, 1945; Piotrowski, Z. A., et al. Rorschach signs in the selection of outstanding young male mechanical workers. *J. Psychol.,* 1944, *18,* 131–150.

56. Taylor, E. K., and Nevis, E. C. The use of projective techniques in management selection. *Personnel,* 1957, *33,* 463–474.

57. Hillery, J. M., and Fugita, S. S. Group size effects in employment testing. *Educ. Psychol. Meas.,* 1975, *35,* 745–750.

58. Dunnette and Borman, op. cit.

59. Allport, G. W. The use of personal documents in psychological research. *Soc. Sci. Research Council Bull.,* No. 49, 1942; Ferguson, L. W. The development of industrial psychology. In B. H. Gilmer (Ed.), *Industrial psychology.* New York: McGraw-Hill, 1961, pp. 18–37; Guilford, J. P., and Lacey, J. I. Printed classification tests. *AAF Aviation Psychol. Research Prog. Repts.* Washington, D.C.: Genl. Printg. Offc., No. 5, 1947.

60. Kirchner, W. K., and Dunnette, M. D. Applying the weighted application blank techniques to a variety of office jobs. *J. Appl. Psychol.,* 1957, *41,* 206–208; Scollay, R. W. Personal history data as a predictor of success. *Personnel Psychol.,* 1957, *10,* 23–26; Dunnette, M. D., Kirchner, W. K., Erickson, J., and Banas, P. Predicting turnover among female office workers. *Personnel Admin.,* 1960, *23,* 45–50; Smith, W. J., Albright, L. E., and Glennon, J. R. The prediction of research competence and creativity from personal history. *J. Appl. Psychol.,* 1961, *45,* 59–62; Walther, R. H. Self-description as a predictor of success or failure in foreign service clerical jobs. *J. Appl. Psychol.,* 1961, *45,* 16–21; Lockwood, H. C., and Parsons, S. O. Relationship of personal history information to the performance of production supervisors. *Eng. Industr. Psychol.,* 1960, *2,* 20–26.

61. Fleishman, E. A., and Berniger, J. Using the application blank to reduce office turnover. In E. A. Fleishman (Ed.), *Studies in personnel and industrial psychology.* Homewood, Ill.: Dorsey, 1961, pp. 30–36.

62. Harrell, T. The validity of biographical items for food company salesmen. *J. Appl. Psychol.,* 1960, *44,* 31–33; Kornhauser, A., and Schultz, R. S. Research in selection of salesmen. *J. Appl. Psychol.,* 1941, *25,* 1–5; Kurtz, A. Recent research in selection of life insurance salesmen. *J. Appl. Psychol.,* 1941, *25,* 11–17.

63. Appel, V., and Feinberg, M. R. Recruiting door-to-door salesmen by mail. *J. Appl. Psychol.,* 1969, *53,* 362–366.

64. Owens, W. A. Background data. In M. D. Dunnette (Ed.), *Handbook of industrial and organizational psychology.* Chicago: Rand-McNally, 1976, pp. 609–644.

65. Mosel, J. L., and Cozan, L. W. The accuracy of application blank work histories. *J. Appl. Psychol.,* 1952, *36,* 365–369.

66. See, for example, Beirsmer, R. J., and Ryman, D. H. Prediction of scuba training performance. *J. Appl. Psychol.,* 1974, *59,* 519–521; Cascio, W. F. Turnover, biographical data and fair employment practice. *J. Appl. Psychol.,* 1976, *61,* 576–580; Erwin, F. W., and Herring, J. W. *The feasibility of the use of autobiographical information as a predictor of early Army attrition.* U.S. Army Res. Instit., Tech. Rept. TR–77–A6, 1977; Hinrichs, J. R., Haanpera, S., and Sonkin, L. Validity of a biographical information blank across national boundaries. *Personnel Psychol.,* 1976, *29,* 417–421.

67. Schmidt, F. L., Grunthal, A. L., Hunter, J. E., Berne, J. G., and Seaton, F. W. Job samples versus paper-and-pencil trades and technical tests: Adverse impact and examinee attitudes. *Personnel Psychol.,* 1977, *30,* 187–197.

68. See, for example, Gordon, M. E., and Kleeman, L. S. The prediction of trainability using a work sample test and an aptitude test: A direct comparison. *Personnel Psychol.,* 1976, *29,* 243–253; Mount, M. K., Muchinsky, P. M., and Hansen, L. M. The predictive validity of a work sample: A

laboratory study. *Personnel Psychol.*, 1977, *30*, 637–645; Anastasi, A. *Psychological testing*, 3rd ed. New York: Macmillan, 1968.

69. Williams, F. J., and Harrell, T. W. Predicting success in business. *J. Appl. Psychol.*, 1964, *48*(3), 164–167.

70. *Affirmative action and equal employment: A guidebook for employers*, Vols. 1 and 2. Washington, D.C., Equal Employmt. Oppor. Comm., 1979.

71. Drake, L. R., Kaplan, H. R., and Stone, R. A. Organizational performance as a function of recruitment criteria and effectiveness. *Personnel J.*, 1973, *52*, 885–891.

72. Scott, W. D., Clothier, R. C., and Spriegel, W. R. *Personnel management*, 6th ed. New York: McGraw-Hill, 1961, Appendix A, p. 565. Wagner, R. The employment interview: A critical summary. *Personnel Psychol.*, 1949, *2*, 17–46; Mayfield, E. C. The selection interview — a re-evaluation of research. *Personnel Psychol.*, 1964, *17*, 236–260; Heneman, H. G., Schwab, D. P., Huett, D. L., and Ford, J. J. Interviewer validity as a function of interview structure, biographical data, and interviewee order. *J. Appl. Psychol.*, 1975, *60*, 748–753; Landy, F. J. The validity of the interview in police officer selection. *J. Appl. Psychol.*, 1976, *61*, 193–198.

73. Dunnette, M. D. Personnel management. *Ann. Rev. Psychol.*, 1962, *13*, 285–314.

74. Harrell, T. W. *Industrial psychology*, rev. ed. New York: Rinehart, 1958, pp. 82–87.

75. Gagné, R. M., and Fleishman, E. A. *Psychology and human performance*. New York: Holt, 1959, pp. 375–376; Fear, R. A., and Jordan, B. *Employee evaluation manual for interviewers*. New York: Psychological Corp., 1943; Fear, R. A. *The evaluation interview*. New York: McGraw-Hill, 1958; McMurry, R. N. Validating the patterned interview. *Personnel*, 1947, *23*, 263–272.

76. Asher, J. J. Reliability of a novel format for the selection interview. *Psychol. Repts.*, 1970, *26*, 451–456.

77. Fraser, J. M. *Employment interviewing*. London: Macdonald & Evans, 1966.

78. Schmitt, N. Social and situational determinants of interview decisions: Implication for employment. *Personnel Psychol.*, 1976, *29*, 79–101.

79. Maier, N. R. F., and Janzen, J. C. The reliability of reasons used in making judgments of honesty and dishonesty. *Perceptual and Motor Skills*, 1967, *25*, 141–151.

80. Maier, N. R. F., and Thurber, J. A. Accuracy of judgments of deception when interview is watched, heard and read. *Personnel Psychol.* 1968, *21*, 23–30.

81. Asher, J. J. How the applicants' appearance affects the reliability and validity of the interview. *Educ. Psychol. Meas.*, 1970, *30*, 687–695.

82. See Peters, L. H., and Terborg, J. R. The effects of temporal placement of unfavorable information and of attitude similarity on personnel selection decisions. *Organ. Behav. Human Perform.*, 1975, *13*, 279–293; Rand, T. M., and Wexley, K. N. A demonstration of the Byrne similarity hypothesis in simulated employment interviews. *Psychol. Rep.*, 1975, *36*, 535–544; Wexley, K. N., and Nemeroff, W. F. Effects of racial prejudice, race of applicant and biographical similarity on interviewer evaluations of job applicants. *J. Soc. Behav. Sci.*, 1974, *20*, 66–78; Frank, L. L., and Hackman, J. R. Effects of interviewer-interviewee similarity on interviewer objectivity in college admission interviews. *J. Appl. Psychol.*, 1975, *60*, 356–360.

83. Ghiselli, E. E., and Barthol, R. Role perceptions of successful and unsuccessful supervisors. *J. Appl. Psychol.*, 1956, *40*, 241–244.

84. Dipboye, R. L., Arvey, R. D., and Terpstra, D. E. Sex and physical attractiveness of raters and applicants as determinants of resume evaluation. *J. Appl. Psychol.*, 1977, *62*, 288–294; Heneman, H. G. Impact of test information and applicant sex on applicant evaluations in a selection simulation. *J. Appl. Psychol.*, 1977, *62*, 524–526; Wexley and Nemeroff, op. cit.

85. Rogers, C. R. *Counseling and psychotherapy*. Boston: Houghton Mifflin, 1942.

86. Webster, E. C. Decision making in the employment interview. Montreal: Industrial Relations

Research Centre, McGill University, 1964; Springbett, B. M. Factors affecting the final decision in the employment interview. *Canad. J. Psychol.*, 1958, *12*, 13–22; Anderson, C. W. The relation between speaking times and decision in the employment interview. *J. Appl. Psychol.*, 1960, *44*, 207–268.

87. Peters and Terborg, op. cit.
88. Bruner, J. S. On perceptual readiness. *Psychol. Rev.*, 1957, *64*, 123–152.
89. Schmitt, N., and Coyle, B. W. Applicant decision in the employment process. *J. Appl. Psychol.*, 1976, *61*, 184–192.
90. Fraser, op. cit.
91. Grant, D. L., and Bray, D. W. Contributions of the interview to assessment of management potential. *J. Appl. Psychol.*, 1969, *53*, 24–34.
92. See, for example, Byham, W. C., and Wettengel, C. Assessment centers for supervisors and managers: An introduction and overview. *Publ. Pers. Manage.*, 1974, *3*, 352–364.
93. Finkle, R. B. Managerial assessment centers. In M. D. Dunnette (Ed.), *Handbook of industrial and organizational psychology.* Chicago: Rand-McNally, 1976, pp. 861–888.
94. Dodd, W. E., and Kraut, A. I. Will management assessment centers ensure selection of the same old types? *Proc. of Ann. Conven. of Amer. Psychol. Assn.*, 1970, *5*, 569–570; Hinrichs, J. R. Comparison of "real-life" assessments of management potential with situational exercises, paper-and-pencil ability tests and personality inventories. *J. Appl. Psychol.*, 1969, *53*, 425–433.
95. Lakein, A. *How to get control of your time and your life.* New York: New American Library, 1973.
96. Hall, D. T. *Careers in organizations.* Santa Monica, Calif.: Goodyear, 1976.
97. Walker, J. W. Human resource planning: Managerial concerns and practices. *Bus. Horizons*, 1976, *19*, 55–59.
98. Super, D. E., and Hall, D. T. Career development: Exploration and planning. *Ann. Rev. Psychol.*, 1978, *29*, 333–372.
99. Korman, A. K. Hypothesis of work behavior revisited and an extension. *Acad. Manage. Rev.*, 1976, *1*, 50–63.
100. See Dipboye, R. L. A critical review of Korman's self-consistency theory of work motivation and occupational choice. *Organ. Behav. Human Perform.*, 1977, *18*, 108–126 for a review and critique of Korman's approach.
101. Rotter, J. B. Generalized expectancies for internal vs. external control of reinforcement. *Psychol. Monogr.*, 1966, *80*.
102. Weitz, J. Job expectancy and survival. *J. Appl. Psychol.*, 1956, *40*, 245–247.
103. Ilgen, D. R., and Seely, W. Realistic expectations as an aid in reducing voluntary resignations. *J. Appl. Psychol.*, 1974, *59*, 452–455.
104. Berlew, D. E., and Hall, D. T. The socialization of managers: Effects of expectations on performance. *Admin. Sci. Quart.*, 1966, *11*, 207–223; Peres, S. H. *Factors which influence careers in General Electric.* Crotonville, N.Y.: Genl. Elec. Manage. Devel. Empl. Relns. Service, 1966; Buchanan, B. Building organizational commitment: The socialization of managers in work organizations. *Admin. Sci. Quart.*, 1974, *19*, 533–546; Dunnette, M. D., Orvey, R. D., and Banas, P. A. Why do they leave? *Personnel*, May–June, 1973, 25–39.
105. Erickson, E. H. *Childhood and society*, 2nd ed. New York: Norton, 1963; Levenson, D. J., Darrow, C., Klein, E., Levenson, M., and McKee, B. The psychological development of men in early adulthood and the mid-life transition. In D. T. Ricks, A. Thomas, and M. Roff (Eds.), *Life-span research in psychopathology*, Vol. 3. Minneapolis: University of Minnesota Press, 1974; Super, D. E. *The psychology of careers.* New York: Harper & Row, 1957.
106. Sheehy, G. *Passages.* New York: Dutton, 1974.

107. Miller, J. A., Bass, B. M., and Mihal, W. L. *An experiment to test methods of increasing self-development activities among research and development personnel.* Publ. TR-43. Rochester, N.Y.: Management and Research Center, Univ. of Rochester, 1973.

108. Young, J. Z. Evolution toward what? *New York Rev. of Books,* February 7, 1980, 45–46.

109. Vaillant, G. E. Creative adaptation: A medical horizon. *Creative Living,* Spring, 1979, 11–15.

SUGGESTED READINGS

Hall, D. T. *Careers in organizations.* Santa Monica, Calif.: Goodyear, 1976.

Hall, F. S., and Hall, D. T. *The two-career couple.* Reading, Mass.: Addison-Wesley, 1979.

Rosen, B., and Jerdee, T. H. The nature of job-related stereotypes. *J. Appl. Psychol.,* 1976, 180–183.

Rosen, B., and Jerdee, T. H. Coping with affirmative action backlash. *Bus. Horizons,* August, 1979, 15–20.

Schein, E. *Career dynamics.* Reading, Mass.: Addison-Wesley, 1978.

Wanous, J. Realistic job previews for organizational recruitment. *Personnel,* 1975, 50–60.

LABORATORY EXERCISE
MATCHING PEOPLE AND JOBS

A. DEVELOPING A TEST FOR A SPECIFIC JOB

1. Divide class into teams of five or six.
2. Each team will develop a test to measure one specific ability for the job of directory assistance operator in a telephone company.

B. TEAM ASSIGNMENT

1. Assume that one-third of the employees hired will become directory assistance operators. You need a test that will aid in selecting the best third of those available.
2. Description of the directory assistance operator's duties is as follows: Customers contact directory assistance operators to obtain telephone numbers of persons not yet listed, whose listings have changed, or whose number is unknown to the customer. These operators look up the requested numbers and transmit them to the customers. A number must be found quickly so that the customer is not kept waiting. It is often necessary to look under various spellings of the same name as customers frequently give incorrect spellings.
3. The instructor should serve as a resource person and be ready to supply information but not solutions.

C. GENERAL PROCEDURE

1. Make a list of the abilities that seem relevant to success on the job.
2. Rate the importance of these abilities on a five-point scale.

D. SPECIFIC PROCEDURES

1. The instructor will assign procedures D.2a and D.2b to different teams.

2. Alternate procedures
   a. Select a high-rated ability and develop a test to measure it. Only the materials available in the room are to be used. Telephone directories may not be furnished. The test should permit quantitative scoring and may be an individual or a group test.
   b. Select a high-rated ability that is susceptible to a rating by means of an interview. Develop a patterned interview format as well as a method for scoring.

E. DEMONSTRATION OF INSTRUMENTS

1. Each team should be given a chance to demonstrate its test on one of the other groups.
2. The instructor should impose time limits in accordance with time available and class interest.

F. DEVELOPING A TEST BATTERY

1. The various tests when combined form a test battery. The instructor should lead a discussion on which tests would make up the best battery.
2. If time permits, telephone directories could be supplied and the ability of class members to obtain telephone numbers of persons named by the instructor could be written down. Using a time limit, success could be measured by the number of correct responses.
3. The above scores should be related to test results. Use as time permits.
4. The instructor should also conduct a discussion on what part of the job was not measured by the test with telephone directories.

MATCHING THE WORKER TO THE JOB

DESIGNING
THE JOB
FOR
GREATER
EFFICIENCY

∎

∎

THE TWO PRECEDING CHAPTERS dealt with the problem of analyzing jobs in terms of human abilities. By selecting individuals who possess the abilities most essential to a given job, productivity is increased without workers having to expend more energy than before. A person unadapted to a job uses much energy for unproductive purposes and receives none of the satisfactions associated with proficiency.

In this chapter, the problem of job design is approached from the other side. How can a job be altered so that it will better fit the nature of human abilities? People differ in the degree to which they possess abilities, but they also have a great deal in common. Certain kinds of activities are unnatural for the way people are constructed. Any change in a task that makes it better fit the human organism should increase the productivity and job satisfaction of all people. The problem discussed in this chapter is to fit jobs to people, rather than people to jobs.

This approach should produce an increase in production without increasing the human energy expended. In this way, the method differs from the speed-up, which tries to increase production by increasing the energy output. Although job fit and speed-up are not inherently related, they have, unfortunately, become associated in the minds of many workers because changes described by management as aimed at increasing efficiency have, in many cases, resulted in job speed-ups.

EARLY APPROACHES

The first systematic attempt to discover the principles for designing jobs to fit the abilities of individuals may be traced to the work of Frederick W. Taylor.[1] He believed that the application of his principles of manage-ment, which went beyond merely changing work patterns, would benefit management, workers, and society in general. However, the desire for immediate gains resulted in partial applications and misapplications of his principles. Resistance by workers and unions to speed-up methods produced frequent failure to achieve the benefits he visualized.

Taylor originally conceived of scientific management as the cooperative effort by management and workers to determine the one best way to do a job, to select workers capable of doing the job that way, and to provide incentive pay for those selected who would work in the prescribed manner. Management was to provide the proper tools and sufficient material to work effectively. Information was to be collected from the workers and also by means of careful experimentation.

Taylor described one of the earliest applications of his principles in the coal yards of the Bethlehem Steel Company as "developing the science of shoveling. You . . . give each workman each day a job to which he is well suited and provide him with just that implement which will enable him to do his biggest day's work."[2] He put to experimental test with "two or three first-class shovelers" the question of what the optimum shovel load would be to obtain maximum productivity without overworking the employee. After about four months' experimentation, one conclusion was that, regardless of material being shoveled, a twenty-one-pound load was optimal. The company accepted this figure, provided the necessary number of the eight to ten different types of shovels required for different types of coal, improved their planning and measurement of the work by adding more staff, and selected the best workers on the basis of performance. The result, including the cost of

MATCHING THE WORKER TO THE JOB

new equipment and additional staff, was a reduction in the cost of handling a ton of coal "from between seven and eight cents to between three and four cents . . . $78,000 a year." The men received increased wages of approximately 60 percent more than they had been earning.

Taylor's followers and imitators, however, chose to concentrate on only two aspects of this approach, the determination of the one best way to do a job and the use of incentive pay to ensure conformity to the prescribed method of working. Moreover, systematic experimentation to determine the best way of working was replaced by systematic observation, analysis, and intuition — intuition that was often creative, but frequently psychologically unsound.

Examples of this approach to job design abound in the work of Frank and Lillian Gilbreth, a husband-and-wife team, who together revolutionized the work of many occupations. Gilbreth had learned the trade of bricklaying, an occupation that had been passed from one generation to the next with little alteration. While serving as contractor on a building project, he analyzed the job and found that eighteen separate movements were made in laying each brick.[3] By organizing the work pattern, he was able to reduce the movements to five and increase a bricklayer's production from 120 to 350 bricks per hour.

The Gilbreths' principal contributions to the study of job design dealt with the elimination of wasted movement, retention of the shortest movements, and simplification of work patterns by assigning different functions to different people consistent with their abilities. *Motion-and-time study* as it is practiced today owes its start principally to the general approach and specific methods developed by the Gilbreths.

THE AIMS OF MOTION-AND-TIME STUDY

Some jobs require proficiency in a combination of activities, which is rarely found together in one person. The breaking down of complex mechanical jobs in a plant permits the use of more specialized abilities. In this way, a larger proportion of the potential work force is eligible to perform each of the simpler jobs adequately. This breakdown of jobs is one characteristic of modern production methods developed from motion-and-time analysis. (It should be noted here that the advantages gained from "deskilling" jobs frequently are offset by their unfavorable effects on the motivation of the workers themselves.)

Another function of motion-and-time study has been to determine the most efficient way to execute a given operation and to induce people to work that way. The way a person performs a task has a great effect on the final efficiency attained, and this final efficiency may be independent of actual manipulative ability.[4] Analysis of an inspection job revealed that most workers tended to put their attention on the wrong aspect of an operation.[5] In visually examining tin plates for defects, inspectors watched the plate they were handling, which was, of course, in motion. This misplaced attention interfered with proper inspection, because it was difficult to see defects while the plate was moving. Altering the operation so that the plate inspected was not in motion greatly improved the inspector's efficiency.

Motion-and-time analysts have also examined the arrangement of work places to eliminate wasted effort in finding tools and handling materials. By rearranging the work space and having a convenient place for every tool used, the job was often greatly simplified. Proper tool arrangement enables the worker to develop automatic habits, because the same movement is always made to obtain a particular tool. The mere need of a tool calls up the special movement; without thinking, the worker makes the proper reach.

A fourth area for potential improvement in productivity and efficiency is proper design of tools for each job. Following Taylor's illustration of the benefits gained from the proper shovels for coal handling, many ingenious improvements have been introduced to relieve the worker of unnecessary activities. Drills suspended from springs within easy reach, special wrenches and screwdrivers, and all kinds of gadgets and conveniences suggest themselves when the job is analyzed. In addition to special tools and ways for mechanizing them, knee and foot pedals have been introduced, for example, to operate vises and other mechanisms requiring strength but not fine control. Chutes and conveyor belts are used to replace carrying, transporting, and delivering movements.[6]

Other factors often contributing to excessive energy expenditure and inefficiency involve uncomfortable work places and inconvenient work positions. The untrained supervisor is inclined to confuse comfort with loafing. However, if jobs are designed to permit sitting, the energy saved can be used for productive purposes.[7] In addition, an unnecessary source of irritation for the worker is removed.[8] Similarly, methods analysts have improved productivity by placing work benches at heights appropriate for the amount of lifting required.[9] Recent anthropometric studies of workers' physical measurements have provided information for equipment designers to plan work spaces that will comfortably fit most of the people likely to fill the jobs.[10]

Finally, attention is also given to the design of offices and plants to reduce movement. Operations related to one another should be physically related.[11] Lighting, noise, ventilation, plans to avoid congestion during shift changes, and facilities for eating, rest pauses, and medical care are also properly considered.[12]

GENERAL PRINCIPLES OF MOTION ECONOMY

Reliance on the ingenuity of motion analysts in developing the principles of motion economy has resulted in a variety of such principles. Interestingly, the few principles on which most analysts agree are those that treat the person most like a biological and psychological being and least like a machine. Some examples of principles concerned with workers' movements are given in the following discussion.

The right and left halves of a person's body are mirror images of each other. This means that movements of the two hands or arms are most simple when they are symmetrical; a pair of such movements does not disturb balance, whereas movement of either one alone does. For example, a supply of bolts on the left and a supply of nuts on the right will make their assembly a symmetrical pattern.

The notion of symmetrical movements can be extended to include the use of both hands and feet. If jobs are expertly designed, feet or knees can perform duties that neither cause fatigue nor interfere with hand movements. In this way, use of the feet and knees becomes a pure gain, since they can do heavier work than the hands. In fact, it is easier to flex all muscles together than to extend one limb and flex others.

Given human body structure, a person sitting with arms bent at the elbows can reach

The automotive industry's efficiency and productivity has been fostered in many ways, including division of jobs and convenient placement and specialization of tools. (Top: Bill Grimes, Black Star; bottom: Courtesy of Ford Motor Company)

DESIGNING THE JOB FOR GREATER EFFICIENCY

an area composed of two overlapping semi-circles with a radius of twelve to fourteen inches (or twenty-four to twenty-six inches, if the whole arm is used) — see Figure 11.1. The spaces enclosed by the lines are the work areas available to a person without disturbing the seated posture. The overlapping areas constitute the work space available to both hands and consequently delimit the space in which the hands can work conveniently together, as required in assembly work.

Rhythm is important to patterning and combining movements into behavior sequences. If jobs can be arranged to set up a natural rhythm, they are easier. However, some groupings or sequences of movements are easier than others, so that merely combining the movements with the smallest elemental times may not produce the shortest cycle operation. For example, two stroke movements of two different fingers require more time when made by fingers of one hand than when made by fingers of two hands. Manufacturers of typewriters fail to use this fact fully. Considering the frequencies and sequences of letters in the words used in the English language, the present keyboard does not permit the maximum number of strokes that require the alternate use of the hands.[13]

The amount of energy and movement required of the various limbs should be distributed according to their inherent capacities. Leg muscles are strong and should be used to operate heavy loads. For most people, one arm is stronger and more skillful than the other; therefore, the strong limb should do the greater share of the job. This would mean that jobs or machines would differ for right- and left-handed persons. Further, fingers vary in dexterity and strength; demands made upon them should be adapted to their capacities.

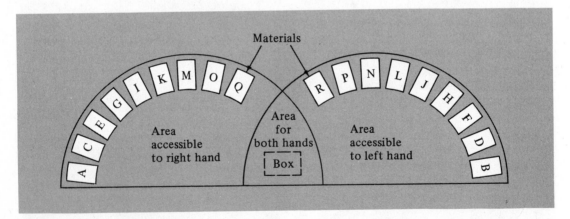

FIGURE 11.1 TYPICAL BENCH LAYOUT FOR ASSEMBLY WORK
A deck of eighteen cards can readily be assembled in the proper order by means of the arrangement shown above. The right and left hands simultaneously reach for cards in corresponding positions (Pairs *AB, CD, EF,* etc.) and slide them across the table into the box placed in a depression in the two-handed area.

SOURCE: Modified from J. Munro Fraser, *Psychology: General, industrial, social.* Sir Isaac Pitman and Sons, Ltd., London, 1951, p. 185.

MATCHING THE WORKER TO THE JOB

Another factor in efficient motion design is the replacement of straight-line movements with circular ones. A circular movement of the hand between two points is made more easily than a back-and-forth movement between the points, particularly if this movement must be made at high speed (see Figure 11.2). Starting and stopping movements waste energy. Well-executed acts of skill never involve jerky movements. Even the rapid up-and-down bow movements required in playing the violin are executed by circular arm and wrist movements.

Sometimes it is difficult or impossible to employ the principles of motion to the degree desired. In such cases, alternate ways to improve methods should be considered. For

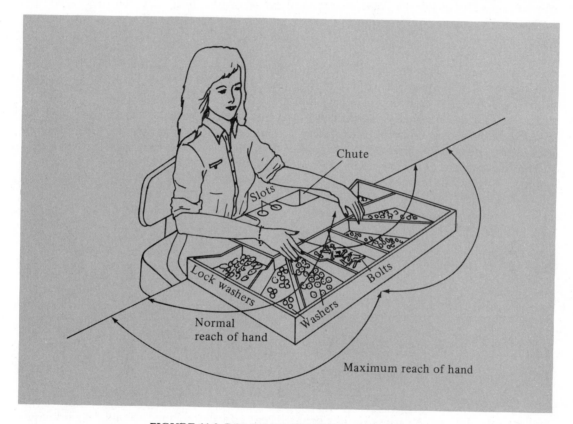

FIGURE 11.2 BOLT AND WASHER ASSEMBLY

Two assemblies are performed at the same time. Washers are moved across the table into recessed slots, and bolts are placed through washers. Lock washers (placed in the slot first) hold the other washers in place; the two complete assemblies are then lifted from their slots and dropped into chutes (shown to the right and left of the slots). The arms then continue their motion to the outside bins containing lock washers, and the next pair of assemblies is begun.

SOURCE: Redrawn from *Motion and Time Study: Design and Measurement of Work,* 7th ed., by R. M. Barnes. Copyright © 1980 by John Wiley & Sons, Inc. Reprinted by permission of John Wiley & Sons, Inc.

example, when jerky or zigzag movements cannot be replaced by curved movements, it is sometimes desirable to slow down an operation in order to escape the tiring effects of inertia. In other instances, conveyors and chutes can replace straight-line movements for moving an object from one point to another.

Picking up and handling objects requires a certain amount of precision, and jobs should be so designed that these requirements are simplified or reduced. Large movements are more primitive, and the progress of human maturation and development is one of achieving greater differentiation of muscle control, until highly detailed and specific movements can be made.[14] If fine and detailed movements represent a higher stage of development than gross movements, it follows that they are the more complex. Therefore, reducing the number of required fine movements produces some of the greatest savings in work methods. Smooth table surfaces can be used to eliminate grasping and handling, which are fine movements. Recesses cut into work space permit the assembling of sequences without handling.

TRENDS IN MOTION-AND-TIME STUDY

Two trends are apparent in this field. The first is the development of synthetic times for elemental movements. By timing the same element in a large variety of jobs or in controlled laboratory situations, a standard time is established for that element, which may then be applied to the development of time standards for new jobs in which it appears. In using predetermined elemental times, the analyst describes a new job in terms of its basic elements, then assigns the appropriate times to each. The sum of the assigned times, as in the older forms of time study, becomes the standard time for the operation. This and other systems of predetermined times make the same questionable assumption: a total job is the sum of its elemental movements. The proponents of this method claim, however, that the systems are more precise, therefore less liable to error, because they define smaller elements in specified contexts of job requirements.

A second trend is an attempt to overcome the resistance frequently expressed by workers to the application of time-and-motion study to their jobs. The basic assumption in this approach, usually called *work simplification,* is that if workers participate in improving their working methods and in setting standards, they will accept the changes more readily.[15] One procedure in work simplification is to have time-study experts train workers and supervisors in the principles and methods of motion economy and then to encourage them to apply the methods to improve their jobs.

The motivational advantage of having workers make decisions about the way they do their work is clearly consistent with the assumptions of group decision for gaining acceptance, outlined in Chapter 8. This fact may account for the fairly widespread adoption of work-simplification procedures in American business and for its many reported successes. It is not clear whether the successes are due to application of the principles of motion economy or to the motivation and ingenuity that workers apply when given a chance to decide how they should do their work. In any case, the involvement of workers in improving their work methods seems desirable.

LIMITATIONS OF MOTION-AND-TIME STUDY

Despite the apparent success of motion-and-time methods in industrial situations, critics are numerous. The criticisms take many forms, including doubt about the precision of the measurements themselves, questions about the validity of the assumptions underlying them, and citation of instances in which application of motion-and-time methods created new organizational problems, often of greater magnitude than those it was employed to solve.

CRITICISMS OF THE METHODOLOGY

Once a job motion has been established, the time required by the average worker has to be known so that proper pay rates are set. Determination of time standards relies on measurements made, often to the hundredths of a second. Even among successive ratings of experienced raters, however, discrepancies of the order of 15 percent have been found from one rating to the next. Even worse, these raters disagreed with one another's simultaneous ratings of the same workers by an average of 20 percent.[16] The magnitude of these discrepancies under highly controlled conditions are about the same as those reported by W. Gomberg in comparisons of the results of company-appointed and union-appointed time-study personnel.[17]

An additional source of error is introduced into time-study measurements by the fact that people work at different rates of speed. To compensate for such differences in setting a standard for "normal" production, the analyst applies a *leveling* or rating factor to the times recorded.[18] The leveling factor reflects the analyst's judgment that the worker timed was working "15 percent faster than normal" or "20 percent slower than normal," and so on. By applying the leveling factor to the observations — reducing the time taken by slow workers or increasing the time of fast workers — the analyst produces a normal time, that is, the time that it should take a qualified, thoroughly experienced operator working at "a pace that is neither fast nor slow" to complete a work cycle.[19]

Careful research has confirmed the intuition that the subjective leveling factor is an added source of error in time-study measurements. E. Ghiselli and C. Brown reported a study in which time measurements before leveling revealed that "the most rapid worker was 67 percent faster than the slowest worker."[20] Even after the leveling factor was applied, however, the standard time set on the fastest worker was 53 percent higher than that set on the time of the slowest worker. If the leveling factor were completely accurate, the two standard times should have been identical. K. A. Lifson, in another study, found that experienced time-study analysts rating the same group of workers (1) varied by as much as 30 percent on the average; (2) set different rates for the same workers; and (3) overrated slow workers and underrated faster ones.[21] The last finding explains why workers usually want standards for incentive pay set on the slowest worker.

Although the amount of error in time measurements uncovered by these studies is not large in absolute terms, it assumes considerable importance from the way in which time standards are applied. Often wage rates for different jobs are established on the basis of time studies. If the workers' perceptions of the relative difficulty of two jobs differ from the time-study results, much resentment and resistance to the introduction of standards can be expected.

CRITICISMS OF MOTION-AND-TIME-STUDY ASSUMPTIONS

The assumption that behavior can be analyzed by breaking it down into basic elements is known as the *atomistic* approach to psychology and has been challenged strongly by the *Gestalt* (configurational) approach, which contends that the whole act cannot be understood by an analysis of its parts. The function of any behavioral element is influenced by its relationship to other elements in the total behavioral pattern.

A series of laboratory studies by K. U. Smith using the Universal Motion Analyzer has shown that elemental times vary according to their position in a sequence.[22] The time it takes workers' hands to move from one point to another will be different if they first push a button than if they first turn a knob. Although the refined categories of synthetic time systems recognize this fact in part, they do not take into account the total pattern of behavior into which the elements are formed by the worker. A carefully controlled series of experiments by two German investigators showed that workers' actual performance on certain jobs deviated sharply from standards set on the basis of predetermined elemental times.[23] Their studies confirm the Gestalt position that analysis of jobs by fragmentation cannot lead to correct reconstruction of the total performance pattern any more than the study of all the pieces of a building can reveal how to construct the building.

Other studies have provided experimental evidence that casts doubt on certain additional motion-and-time assumptions about workers' behavior. One experiment demonstrated that hand travel time is approximately the same over a considerable range.[24] It appears that the hand accelerates more rapidly in moving a long distance than in moving a short one. However, the amount of travel time over a fixed distance varies considerably, depending on the type of manipulation that precedes or follows the movement.[25] The context within which the behavior occurs influences the amount of time that it takes.

In another study, complexity was shown to have little effect on the workers' performance.[26] Where complex tasks can be organized into manageable patterns, complexity is no barrier to good performance.

LOSS OF MOTIVATION AND JOB INTEREST

Another factor often overlooked by motion analysis is the type of motivation produced in the worker when jobs are fractionated in the name of efficiency. Several writers have contended that when jobs are oversimplified, workers become bored and feel alienated from their work.[27] Boredom can be costly, with increased accidents, wasted materials, poor quality work, absenteeism, and turnover. (The effects of boredom will be discussed further in Chapter 15.)

ONE BEST WAY OPEN TO QUESTION

A final important criticism of motion-and-time study concerns its assumption that there is one best way of doing a job. This assumption ignores individual differences. Because people differ in their aptitudes, it is reasonable to assume that they may work better using efficient but different methods. We need only look at sports champions to realize that each reached the top by adopting a style of play that fits his or her particular abilities. In an industrial study, it was found that the fastest workers in a sheet metal factory did the job differently from the average workers. The average workers could not be taught the method used by the superior workers because they did not have the necessary minimum aptitudes.

Training unskilled workers to use a single method in their work has the advantage of bringing everyone to a moderate level of performance. But insisting that superior workers use the same method deprives a company of the high productivity of the outstandingly able workers whose rare pattern of abilities may be better suited to a different method. The simpler the job, the more likely there is to be a one best way to do it, which fits the similarities among people. The more complex the job, the more individual differences in patterns of abilities will permit several successful work methods. In some instances, the best method may be one suited only to a limited number of persons. In any case, the concept of the best method must be considered in terms of "best for whom?"

PROBLEMS ARISING FROM TIME-STUDY APPLICATIONS

Any change or improvement in work arrangements may be resisted by employees not only because it is new, but also because it frequently threatens their security. The mere fact that management favors a new method arouses distrust and fear, and the intensity of these emotions is related to the degree to which workers distrust management. Distrust and resistance are increased whenever management tries to impose changes without gaining the workers' acceptance.[28] The need for skills in conducting discussions of problems involving changes in the work situation will become apparent in the exercise at the end of this chapter.

The application of time standards in busi-

ness has been criticized for ignoring their effects on the relations among work groups. W. F. Whyte documented numerous instances in which payments to workers based on time-study standards disrupted relations between work groups and created considerable labor-management strife.[29] E. Jaques made the point that workers have a fairly clear idea about what constitutes a fair pay rate for different jobs.[30] If wage rates assigned to such jobs on the basis of time standards conflict with accepted rates, antagonism and resistance can be expected. Workers evaluate the adequacy of their wages in comparison to the pay received by other workers with similar qualifications.[31] If the rates set by time standards run counter to the social system of the factory, they can produce more long-term problems than they are worth.

Although motion-and-time study has proved beneficial in increasing job performance and in establishing performance standards, it obviously cannot be applied uncritically. Establishing acceptable wage rates for different jobs seems to be the most controversial issue.

RECENT APPROACHES TO JOB DESIGN

A BIOPSYCHOLOGICAL APPROACH

What has been needed for years and neglected both by psychologists and engineers is a coherent theory of skilled performance based on human biological and psychological considerations. In simplified form, Smith contended that workers organize their motions in terms of the space that they see around them.[32] This space is organized geometrically, with respect to the vertical and horizontal axes of the body, corresponding, respectively, to the line of postural erectness and to the right-left symmetry of the body.

The basic and most primitive movements are *postural,* keeping the body erect in response to variations in gravitational stimulation. These are the first types of movements an infant learns. *Travel* motions (movements of body members) are organized, on the other hand, "mainly according to the bilateral symmetry of the body, with right and left members working together or in opposition." These movements must be integrated within the postural base. For example, when a tool or object is placed beyond a worker's normal reach, energy is wasted in restoring the body to an erect position since the job cannot be performed while off balance. Less obvious, however, is the conclusion that arm movements are probably better controlled in the horizontal plane than in the vertical; therefore, tools and materials should be placed around the perimeter of the normal working area, rather than suspended above it.

Manipulative motions (fine manipulation of the hands and the feet or the receptor systems of the head) form the third class of identified movements. These actions are learned, not as a series of discrete and unrelated events, but as an integrated pattern of perceptual-motor actions occurring within specific space-time relationships.

All the principles of motion economy stated earlier are consistent with Smith's principles as outlined here. Many "principles" still listed in motion-and-time-study books, as well as the basic assumptions criticized earlier, are consistent neither with the theory nor with experimental evidence. The most important contribution Smith's theory makes to job design is to provide a framework consistent with psychological evidence.

THE CHANGING NATURE OF WORK

With the development of complex equipment and engineering technology and the increased use of computers, machines are taking over much work formerly performed by human beings and are changing the kind of work allocated to employees.[33] One area of job design is the allotment of functions according to the superiority of either person or machine. Table 11.1 shows some ways in which the human being excels and some in which the machine excels.

The superiority of computers for handling data has encouraged researchers in this field to investigate mathematical models for decision making and solving problems, such as choosing a stock portfolio. A method called *bootstrapping* involves the replacement of decision makers with algebraic models of their judgmental processes. These models have been shown to work successfully in repetitive decision-making situations.[34] However, human beings are needed to supervise machines and to decide what goes into the computer. They also are the sources of many errors that computers are accused of making.

The extent of computer usage introduced does not totally depend on the development of superior machines, since human beings must make the decision regarding allocation. The need for jobs, foreign competition, and social attitudes all influence the extent to which automated machinery and computers are used. Even when access to computers is available to employees, some perceive computers as threatening and refuse to take advantage of them.

ENGINEERING PSYCHOLOGY

When designing equipment, engineers speak of systems having *inputs* and *outputs.* Materials are inputs when they enter the plant,

TABLE 11.1 COMPARISON OF FUNCTIONS OF HUMAN BEINGS AND MACHINES

ADVANTAGES OF HUMAN BEINGS OVER MACHINES	ADVANTAGES OF MACHINES OVER HUMAN BEINGS
1. Able to handle unexpected events, whereas machines cannot adapt to unanticipated contingencies	1. Information that can be stored is very large, whereas human capacity is relatively limited in the information it can handle in a unit of time.
2. Can organize bits of information into meaningful wholes (perception), whereas machines cannot perceive	2. Little or no decrement in function over long periods of time, whereas persons are subject to muscular fatigue, lapses in attention, and sensory decrement
3. Can accomplish similar results by alternative means, whereas machine may fail because of injury to part of it	3. Are excellent and rapid at arithmetical computation, whereas persons are relatively slow and subject to errors
4. Can change approaches, whereas a programmed machine is relatively inflexible	

SOURCE: Based on A. Chapanis, On the allocation of functions between man and machines. *Occup. Psychol.*, 1965, *39*, 1–11.

and the product is the output. Some systems are *open loops* in that they have no controls. For example, a broken window sets off a burglar alarm that continues to ring even after the police arrive. The purpose of controls is to introduce some kind of regulation, such as thermostatically controlled temperatures in a home. When the temperature falls below a certain point, the furnace will be activated. The heat generated by the furnace will in turn cause the furnace to shut off when it reaches the prescribed temperature. In this case, we speak of a *closed loop* system because the product produced sends a message (feedback) to the thermostat.

In fully automated plants, a person is needed only when something goes wrong, but in many work systems, a human being is needed to interpret the feedback messages and to make adjustments to meet changing needs. A familiar example of a system involving human judgment and machinery is

a truck and driver as illustrated in Figure 11.3. The driver has many *inputs* that are displayed by dials, sounds, the visual picture of the highway, sensations from the steering wheel, and so on. The driver responds to these messages by moving levers or pedals. The things done to operate the machine are the driver's *outputs*. Perceptions of movements, the response of the machine, and the message from the visual displays are the feedback that influences subsequent outputs. Transportation is the output of this system; wages, training, gasoline, company officers, and so on, represent inputs. The human being is the part of this system that cannot readily be replaced, even though there are instruments that measure some phenomena (for example, speed) more accurately than sense organs can.

Human responsibilities become greater as the sophistication of machines increases, because the whole system fails when the con-

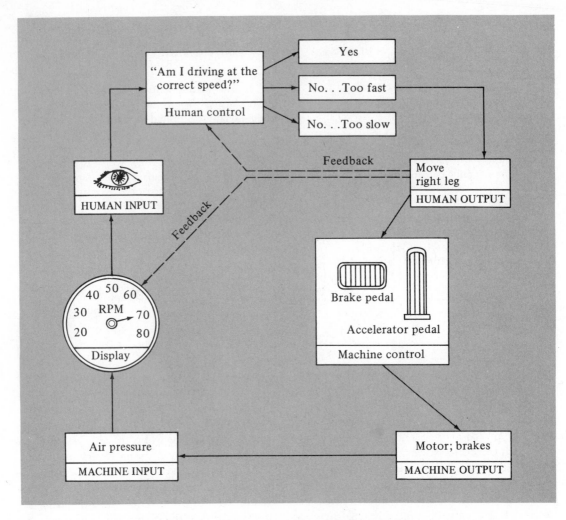

FIGURE 11.3 A PERSON-MACHINE SYSTEM

SOURCE: Redrawn from Laurence Siegel, *Industrial Psychology,* rev. ed. Homewood, Ill.: Richard D. Irwin, 1969, p. 316. © 1969 by Richard D. Irwin, Inc.

troller is inadequate. The research problems for the engineer involve developing improved ways of supplying information (for inputs to the operator) and designing controls that can be most accurately used. The task of the engineering psychologist is to test human ability (1) to process information when supplied in different forms, and (2) to operate controls of different design.[35] Also important is the environment in which the person must operate. By combining the skills of the engineer and the psychologist, these specialists can successfully integrate systems combining workers and machines.

MATCHING THE WORKER TO THE JOB

Visual and sound-producing cues are most common for displays of data, but the choice of the input *channel* depends not only on human sensory development but also on the work environment. Sound-producing cues would have disadvantages in a noisy environment, but would be better than visual displays if the operator has to move about the room, unable at times to see such data. Under certain circumstances, the olfactory channel (sense of smell) may be the best cue. Improvements in messages or displays are sought according to the need for precision, speed of response, need for vigilance, and so on.

P. M. Fitts and his coworkers made a continuous study of the relationships of the display of information and the design and arrangement of controls to pilot performance in military aircraft. Errors made by pilots in operating controls and in reading instruments were collected. They were then grouped into categories based on a psychological analysis of the causes of the errors. For example, 50 percent of the operating errors involved confusion of one control with another (for example, confusing flap and wheel controls), producing an unexpected and undesired change in the airplane's performance. Much of this confusion centered around the lack of uniform arrangements or operating characteristics of the controls, difficulty in distinguishing among different controls because of their identical shapes or close placement, and application of habitual sequences of control operation at inappropriate times. Recommended solutions to the first two types of problems focused on changes in control design, establishing standard places for controls and making them easily distinguishable.[36]

Analysis of errors made in many business situations would reveal numerous instances where job design is incompatible with the way in which workers are accustomed to act. Such analyses could lead to a redesign of parts of the equipment to make them compatible with well-learned work habits. Control devices, for example, are too often designed to operate in a direction opposite to the normal way. Many of us have experienced the problem of not knowing which way to turn off the hot water in a hotel, sometimes with scalding effects.

To make appropriate responses to inputs, the response alternatives should be readily distinguishable. This problem is acute when there is a large array of controls and quick responses are required. In a study of aircraft controls, tactual discrimination was found to be essential.[37] Various knob shapes were developed, eleven of them readily identifiable by touch. The shapes included spheres, cylinders, triangles, arcs, and cones.

Analysis of job errors could also be useful in pointing out specific training needs. The effectiveness of skill training can be enhanced substantially by concentrating on those aspects of the job that research has demonstrated to be especially difficult to learn.[38]

The advent of automation in industry has created many jobs that require workers constantly to monitor banks of instruments, watch for occasional deviations in dial readings, and react appropriately and quickly to remedy the situation indicated. Modern oil refineries, petrochemical plants, and nuclear power plants now operate automatically, with self-correcting feedback devices designed to handle slight deviations in subparts of the process.[39] The workers who staff these plants can do little, if anything, to improve productivity when the equipment is operating normally. The efficiency of automated production systems is measured by the least amount of *down-time,* that is, unproductive time.[40] When something goes

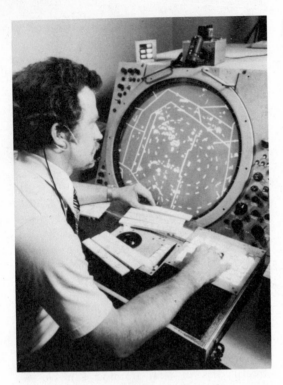

An air traffic controller's job demands constant monitoring of the radar screen and immediate response to emergency situations. (Fred Ward, Black Star)

wrong, however, they must make the necessary adjustments as quickly as possible, or damage to the entire production system may occur, as happened at the nuclear facility at Three-Mile Island, Pennsylvania, in 1979.

As events necessitating human intervention occur infrequently and at irregular intervals in an automated system, the question arises: how long can a person maintain adequate attention with no loss in speed and accuracy of response? This problem of vigilance[41] has been investigated extensively in connection with maintaining effective performance of radar operators. Experiments have shown that the speed and accuracy of responding to infrequent signals diminish

rapidly, as early as the first half-hour of viewing under difficult conditions. Alternating operators, improving the distinguishability of the signal, and providing operators with information about their own performance reduced the impairment in performance. However, anticipation of a telephone message about the job and addition of more signals served to reduce effective performance.[42] An interesting sidelight was the discovery of an optimum effective temperature range — that is, temperature-humidity combination — for performance, below *and* above which errors showed a marked increase.

The assumption that operators can maintain a consistently high level of performance over an entire eight-hour working day is open to serious question. Experimental study of the optimal conditions for work, such as rotation among different jobs, could yield important dividends in operating efficiency and worker satisfaction.

COMPUTER OPERATIONS

A variety of principles derived from experimental research has been applied to the design of jobs, as is illustrated in the description of the installation of the control console of a large computer. The designer had the task of identifying "an order of importance and a frequency of use (of the various dials and controls) . . . and the ease or difficulty for the operator in searching for, acquiring, and transmitting back information to the machine" and then applying "rigorously the relevant advice and knowledge available" from relevant research.[43]

The following illustrate the wide range of applications made and the research on which they were based.

1. Instruments and their related controls were grouped and color-matched according

to similarity. This system increased the faculty of identifying controls and enhanced the accuracy of activating the correct ones.

2. In one part of the console, four lights, usually unlit, glowed amber and were announced by the sounding of a chime to signal that attention was needed within the next five minutes. Use of chime as a general alarm to notify the operator to look for a light signaling trouble was based on research.[44] Experiments showed that operators' speed and accuracy in reacting to peripheral danger signals (like the amber lights) improved when a master tone (a chime) was introduced to announce the error, even though the peripheral signals were easily seen.

3. The engineer decided that vertical control panels would be least expensive to produce. Within these limitations, the findings of anthropometric studies of the sitting height, and vertical and horizontal reach (of the population likely to operate the console) were used to design a main central section forty-two inches wide with side limbs positioned fifteen degrees beyond a right angle from it and a desk height in front of it twenty-eight inches from the floor.[45]

This example of the cooperation of a human-factors specialist with the engineers responsible for equipment design illustrates the advantages that can accrue to business when the workers' characteristics as well as the engineering requirements are considered *before* the equipment is built. This type of cooperative effort at the design stage avoids many personnel problems that arise after machines are installed and can then be remedied only at considerable expense. In designing automated plants, F. C. Mann and L. R. Hoffman have pointed to the necessity of considering the total system (including the types of jobs and the grouping of personnel) in order to provide the optimal person-machine relationships for efficiency and worker satisfaction.[46]

HUMAN DECISIONS

The task of the operators in a machine system is to translate data supplied (input) into a form that is usable by the machine (output). This means that operators must evaluate inputs and make decisions or choices. These decisions include: "Did I or did I not receive a signal?" and "Which response is called for?" Factors that influence the time for such decisions include: the complexity, amount, and clarity of the input; the number of alternate responses; the degree of risk involved; probability distributions; and fatigue. Much research is involved in determining the optimum conditions that prevail for a given system.[47] At the present state of knowledge it has become apparent that more effective choices are made if the operator has a thorough and explicit knowledge of the task. This explains the great amount of training and knowledge required of astronauts, for example. Interestingly, fatigue appears to increase decision time, but not to affect reaction time once the decision is made.

DESIGNING JOBS FOR GROUPS

An airport control tower is an example of an interdependent work system. As an aircraft approaches for a landing, a control tower operator directs the activities of pilots, observing progress on radar. In a large airport, many aircraft continually arrive and depart, and at least two tower operators share the responsibility for their direction. The close cooperation required among the operators has been carefully studied in a series of experiments in which the tower operations were simulated in a laboratory setting.[48] The major conclusion from a number of studies comparing individual to two-person performance is that the teams are more effective than individuals, but that their efficiency per person is less. Team performance requires coordination between the members, which diverts each from the principal task of controlling the aircraft.[49] Thus, the job of each includes the ability to cooperate with the other member. This consideration accounts for the fact that the effectiveness of a team may not be the equivalent of the combination of their individual abilities.

A faulty approach to training for such jobs may be traced to thinking of them only in individual terms. Teaching workers how to do a job before putting them on the team often produces poorer team performance than when the team learns to work together as a unit. Work patterns learned individually frequently interfere with a person's ability to work in the group. Training of a team should be done on a unit basis, so all members know what they are to do and what they can expect from one another.

JOB ANALYSIS FOR IMPROVED SELECTION

The problems related to using tests, particularly intelligence tests, and other general and indirect measures of potential ability on a given job have led to increased interest in developing more sophisticated *direct* measures of success potential. Some industrial psychologists have analyzed jobs in terms of their particular components, not on the micro level of the time-and-motion-study engineers, but at the level of basic skills and abilities required for satisfactory performance. This approach has been used in some form for many years. However, according to one expert in this field, the ideal *behavioral taxonomy* (as these lists of job skills are called) has yet to be developed.[50] This scientist feels

that research in selection methods should develop a short, easily understood behavior-description inventory that can be administered to people in varied jobs and used to classify the jobs and to determine the aptitudes, skills, and so on, needed for each.

One promising recent development in this area is the technique of asking workers who perform a given job to participate in the efforts to describe its crucial elements. This approach, used successfully in determining job requirements for nurses,[51] fire fighters,[52] sales personnel, accountants, and research and development scientists,[53] has been termed by one researcher as *behavior observation scaling*. It is based on the comments of employees recalling critical incidents in their performance of their jobs. Attempts are made in collecting this data to avoid descriptions, attitudes, or personality traits, and to concentrate on behavior.[54]

Job analysis for purposes of selection has varied uses. In addition to providing a basis for a sound hiring system, it can be employed to maintain information files on special skills or talents of employees. Some efforts in this direction have been made in business. Records are kept, for example, on individuals with a facility for speaking foreign languages. Electronic data processing has made storage and retrieval of large quantities of data relatively simple and inexpensive. In the future, a complete and accurate analysis of all jobs in a firm could improve efforts to describe and differentiate jobs, relate personal abilities and job elements, and devise evaluation systems that consider job elements from the viewpoints of efficiency and performance, necessary qualifications, and potential for providing job satisfaction.

JOB DESIGN AND WORKER SATISFACTION

Research to date has generally led to the conclusion that the classical principles designed to reduce production time (make jobs as simple as possible; divide job units into the smallest possible units; put as much of the job under machine control as possible) are precisely those that (1) make the workers most dissatisfied with their jobs, (2) increase spoilage, (3) alienate workers from the company's goals, and (4) produce apathetic citizens.[55] Furthermore, when such simple jobs are placed together, the work groups thus formed appear to be the most militant and aggressive supporters of union-management conflict, often initiating wildcat strikes and other production-delaying tactics.[56] The costs of such labor strife are rarely attributed to the design of jobs, but may well offset the immediate advantage gained from oversimplification.

Faced with the fact that an adequate theory of job design is lacking, much can still be done to reduce boredom. Proposals will be made in Chapter 15. Proper consideration of all sides of the worker's position in the business environment can maintain a productive and satisfying society.

NOTES

1. Taylor, F. W. *Principles of scientific management.* New York: Harper, 1947.
2. Ibid., p. 57.
3. Gilbreth, F. B. *Motion study.* Princeton, N.J.: Van Nostrand, 1911, p. 88–89.
4. Seashore, R. H. Work methods: An often neglected factor underlying individual differences. *Psychol. Rev.,* 1939, *46,* 123–141.
5. Tiffin, J., and Rogers, H. B. The selection and training of inspectors. *Personnel,* 1941, *18,* 14–31.
6. Barnes, R. M. *Motion and time study,* 5th ed. New York: Wiley, 1963.
7. Gilbreth, F. B., and Gilbreth, L. M. *Fatigue study.* New York: Macmillan, 1919, pp. 104–108.
8. Koskela, A. Ergonomics applied to office work. *Ergonomics,* 1962, *5,* 263–264.
9. Bedale, E. M., and Vernon, H. M. *The effect of posture and rest in muscular work.* Industr. Fat. Res. Bd., 1924, Rep. No. 29.
10. Dempster, W. T., Gabel, W. C., and Felts, W. J. L. The anthropometry of the manual work space for the seated subject. *Amer. J. Physical Anthrop.,* 1959, *17,* 289–317; Hertzberg, H. T. E. Dynamic anthropometry of working positions. *Hum. Factors,* 1960, *2,* 147–155; Thomson, R. M., Covner, B. J., Jacobs, H. H., and Orlansky, J. *Arrangement of groups of men and machines.* Washington, D.C.: Office of Naval Research, Dec., 1958, ONR Rep. ARC–33.
11. Barnes, R. M. *Work methods manual,* 5th ed. New York: Wiley, 1963.
12. See Reed, R., Jr. *Plant layout: Factors, principles and techniques.* Homewood, Ill.: Richard D. Irwin, 1961.
13. Lahy, J. J. French psychologists improve typewriting. *Industr. Psychol.,* 1926, *1,* 333–337.
14. Coghill, G. E. *Anatomy and the problem of behavior.* London: Cambridge University Press, 1929; Pratt, K. C., Nelson, A. K., and Sun, K. H. The behavior of the new-born infant. *Ohio State Univ. Stud. Psychol.,* 1930 (10); Halverson, H. M. An experimental study of prehension in infants by means of systematic cinema records. *Genet. Psychol. Monogr.,* 1931, *10,* 107–286.
15. Lehrer, R. N. *Work simplification.* Englewood Cliffs, N.J.: Prentice-Hall, 1957; Mogensen, A. H. *Common sense applied to motion and time studies.* New York: McGraw-Hill, 1932.
16. Nadler, G. An analysis of the differences in the study from films of operations and the actual

operator. *Report of the 3rd Annual Motion and Time Study Work Session*, Purdue University, May, 1946; Mundel, M. E., and Margolin, L. *Report of the 4th Annual Motion and Time Study Work Session.* Purdue University, 1948.

17. Gomberg, W. *A trade union analysis of time study.* Chicago: Science Research Associates, 1948.

18. Barnes, R. M. *Motion and time study,* op. cit.

19. Niebel, B. W. *Motion and time study.* Homewood, Ill.: Richard D. Irwin, 1958, p. 265.

20. Ghiselli, E., and Brown, C. *Personnel and industrial psychology,* 2nd ed. New York: McGraw-Hill, 1955, p. 73.

21. Lifson, K. A. Errors in time-study judgments of industrial work pace. *Psychol. Monogr.,* 1953, *67,* No. 5.

22. Smaders, R., and Smith, K. U. Dimensional analysis of motion: VI. The component movements of assembly motions. *J. Appl. Psychol.,* 1953, *37,* 308–314.

23. Schmidtke, H., and Stier, F. An experimental evaluation of the validity of predetermined elemental time systems. *J. Industr. Engng.,* 1961, *12,* 182–204.

24. Chapanis, A., Garner, W., and Morgan, C. T. *Applied experimental psychology.* New York: Wiley, 1949.

25. Wehrkamp, R., and Smith, K. U. Dimensional analysis of motion: II. Travel-distance effects. *J. Appl. Psychol.,* 1952, *36,* 201–206.

26. Rubin, G., von Trebra, P., and Smith, K. U. Dimensional analysis of motion: III. Complexity of movement pattern. *J. Appl. Psychol.,* 1952, *36,* 272–276.

27. Blum, F. H. *Toward a democratic work process.* New York: Harper, 1953; Morse, N. C. *Satisfaction in the white collar job.* Ann Arbor, Mich.: Institute for Social Research, University of Michigan, 1953; Walker, C. R., and Guest, R. H. *The man on the assembly line.* Cambridge, Mass.: Harvard University Press, 1952.

28. Gotterer, M. G. Union reactions to unilateral changes in work measurement procedures. *Personnel Psychol.,* 1961, *14,* 433–450.

29. Whyte, W. F. *Money and motivation.* New York: Harper, 1955.

30. Jaques, E. *Equitable payment.* New York: Wiley, 1961.

31. Patchen, M. *The choice of wage comparisons.* Englewood Cliffs, N.J.: Prentice-Hall, 1961.

32. Smith, K. U., and Smith, W. M. *Perception and motion.* Philadelphia: Saunders, 1962.

33. Fitts, P. M. Engineering psychology and equipment design. In S. S. Stevens (Ed.), *Handbook of experimental psychology.* New York: Wiley, 1966.

34. Ashton, R. H. User prediction models in accounting: An alternative use. *Accntg. Rev.,* 1975, *50,* 710–722; Davis, R. M. A case study of graduate admissions: Applications of three principles of human decision making. *Amer. Psychol.,* 1971, *26,* 180–188.

35. DeGreene, K. B. (Ed.). *Systems psychology.* New York: McGraw-Hill, 1970; Fleishman, E. A. (Ed.). *Studies in personnel and industrial psychology.* Homewood, Ill.: Dorsey, 1967, Section 9; Chapanis, A. Engineering psychology. In M. D. Dunnette (Ed.), *Handbook of industrial and organizational psychology.* Chicago: Rand-McNally, 1976, pp. 697–744.

36. Fitts, P. M. and Jones, R. E. Analysis of factors contributing to 460 "pilot error" experiments in operating aircraft controls. In H. W. Sinaiko (Ed.), *Human factors in the design and use of control systems.* New York: Dover, 1961, pp. 332–358; Fitts, P. M., and Jones, R. E. Psychological aspects of instrument display. I. Analysis of 270 "pilot error" experiences in reading and interpreting aircraft instruments. Ibid., pp. 359–396.

37. Jenkins, W. O. Tactual discrimination of shapes for coding aircraft-type controls. In P. M. Fitts, *Psychological research on equipment design.* Washington, D.C.: Government Printing Office, 1947.

38. Parker J. F., Jr., and Fleishman, E. A. Use of analytical information concerning task requirements to increase the effectiveness of skill training. *J. Appl. Psychol.,* 1961, *45,* 295–302.

39. Mann, F. C., and Hoffman, L. R. *Automation and the worker*. New York: Holt, 1960.
40. Ibid.
41. For bibliography, see Davies, D. R., and Tune, G. S. *Human vigilance performance*. New York: American Elsevier, 1970.
42. Mackworth, N. H. Researches on the measurement of human performance. In H. W. Sinaiko (Ed.), op. cit., pp. 174–272; Mackworth, N. H., and Mackworth, J. P. Visual search for successive decisions. *Brit. J. Psychol.* 1958, *49*, 210–221.
43. Shackel, B. Ergonomics in the design of a large digital computer console. *Ergonomics*, 1962, *5*, 229–241.
44. Siegel, A. I., and Crain, K. Experimental investigations of cautionary signal presentations. *Ergonomics*, 1960, *3*, 339–356.
45. Floyd, W. F., and Roberts, D. F. Anatomical and physiological principles in chair and table design. *Ergonomics*, 1958, *2*, 1–16.
46. Mann and Hoffman, op. cit.
47. Schum, D. A. Behavior decision theory and man-machine systems. In K. B. DeGreene, op. cit.; Simon, H. A. *Models of man*. New York: Wiley, 1957; Miller, D. W., and Starr, M. K. *The structure of human decisions*. Englewood Cliffs, N.J.: Prentice-Hall, 1967; Hulbert, S. F., and Burg, A. Human factors in transportation systems. In K. B. DeGreene, op. cit.; Lee, W. *Decision theory and human behavior*. New York: Wiley, 1971.
48. Fitts, P. M., et al. Some concepts and methods for the conduct of system research in a laboratory setting. In G. Finch and F. Cameron (Eds.), *Symposium on air force human engineering, personnel and training research*. Washington, D.C.: National Academy of Science–National Research Council Publication 516, 1958.
49. Kinkade, R. G., and Kidd, J. S. *The effect of team size and intermember communication on decision-making performance*. Wright-Patterson Air Force Base, Ohio: WADC Technical Report 58–474, April, 1959.
50. Dunnette, M. D. Aptitudes, attitudes and skills. In M. D. Dunnette (Ed.), *Handbook of industrial and organizational psychology*. Chicago: Rand-McNally, 1976, pp. 473–520.
51. Smith, P. C., and Kendall, L. M. Retranslation of expectations: An approach to the construction of unambiguous anchors for rating scales. *J. Appl. Psychol.*, 1963, *47*, 149–155.
52. Heckman, R. W. *St. Paul firefighters test validation study*. Minneapolis: Personnel Decisions, 1973.
53. Dunnette, M. D., Groner, D. M., Holtzman, J. S., and Jackson, P. D. Job performance categories and rating scales for sales, technical and administrative jobs. Minneapolis: Personnel Decisions, 1972.
54. Flanagan, J. C. The critical incident technique. *Psychol. Bull.*, 1954, *51*, 327–358.
55. Walker and Guest, op. cit.; Argyris, C. The individual and organization: An empirical test. *Admin. Sci. Quart.*, 1959, *4*, 145–167.
56. Sayles, L. *Behavior of industrial work groups*. New York: Wiley, 1958; Singleton, J. W., and Druth, A. Interface: Man and machine: Two scientists look ahead. *Prospectives in Defense Mgmt.* June, 1969, 27–35.

SUGGESTED READINGS

Aldag, R. J., and Brief, A. P. *Task design and employee motivation*. Glenview, Ill.: Scott, Foresman, 1979.

Dunham, R. The measurement and dimensionality of job characteristics. *J. Appl. Psychol.*, 1976, *61*, 404–409.

Hackman, J. R., and Oldham, G. R. *Work redesign*. Reading, Mass.: Addison-Wesley, 1979.

Herzberg, F. *The managerial choice*. Homewood, Ill.: Dow Jones-Irwin, 1976.

LABORATORY EXERCISE
ROLE-PLAYING:
THE CASE OF THE CHANGE IN WORK PROCEDURES

(Students are asked not to read the case materials before participating in the laboratory exercise.)

A. PREPARATION FOR ROLE-PLAYING

The instructor will
1. Divide the class into groups of four persons each. Assign any extra persons to various groups as observers.
2. Read general instructions (E.1) aloud to all.
3. Assign roles. Each person is to read his or her instructions only.
4. Request role-players Jack, Kate, and Steve to wear name tags so that Gus, the supervisor, can call them by name.
5. Ask all Guses to stand up when they have finished reading their roles. Indicate that they may continue to refer as needed to the data supplied with their instructions.

B. THE ROLE-PLAYING PROCESS

1. When all the Guses are standing, the instructor will remind the Jacks, Kates, and Steves that they are waiting for Gus in his office. When he sits down and greets them, this will indicate that he has entered his office, and each should adopt his or her role.
2. At a signal, all Guses are seated. All groups role-play simultaneously.
3. Twenty-five minutes are required for the groups to reach a decision. If certain groups have trouble meeting this deadline, the instructor may ask the Guses to do the best they can in the next minute or two.
4. While groups are role-playing, the instructor will write a table on the chalkboard with the following column headings: *(1)*

group number, *(2)* solution, *(3)* problem employees, *(4)* expected production, *(5)* method used by supervisor, and *(6)* sharing of data.

C. COLLECTING RESULTS

1. Each group should report in turn while remaining seated as a group. The instructor will enter in column 1 the number of the group called on to report.
2. Each Gus reports the solution that he intends to follow. The solutions may be of three types: (a) continuation of old method (rotation through all positions); (b) adoption of new method with each person working his or her best position; (c) a compromise (new method in the morning, old in the afternoon); or (d) integrative solution containing features of old and new solutions (for example, each worker spends more time on best position; two workers exchange positions and third works on his or her best position; all three exchange but confine changes to work their two best positions). The instructor will enter type of solution in column 2 and add notes to indicate whether a trial period is involved, a rest pause is added, and so on.
3. Each Gus reports whether he had any special trouble with a particular employee. If so, the initial of the problem individual is entered in column 3.
4. Jack, Kate, and Steve report whether production will stay the same, go up, or go down as a result of the conference. The estimates of Jack, Kate, and Steve should be recorded as "0," "+," and "−" signs in column 4.
5. Group observers report on the way that Gus handled the group and how the

group responded. Enter a descriptive term in column 5 for Gus's method (for example, *tried to sell his plan, used group decision, blamed group, was arbitrary and somewhat abusive*). If no observers were present in a group, data should be supplied by the group itself. For leading questions about method, see instructions for observers (E.2).

D. DISCUSSION

1. Discuss the differences obtained and see if these can be related to Gus's attitude and the method.
2. List the kinds of resistance encountered. Classify them into fear, hostility, introduction of boredom, and so on.
3. Discuss the proper method for dealing with each of these kinds of resistance. (See Chapter 13 for analysis of resistance to change in this case.)

E. MATERIALS

1. General Instructions

You work in a plant that does a large number of subassembly jobs. Gus Thompson is supervisor of several groups, including the one with which we are concerned today. Jack, Kate, and Steve make up this particular group. The assembly operation is divided into three positions or jobs. Since the three jobs are rather simple and each of you is familiar with all of the operations, you find it desirable to exchange jobs or positions. You have worked together this way for a long time. Pay is based on a team piece rate and has been satisfactory to all of you. Presently each of you will be asked to be one of the following: Gus Thompson, Jack, Kate, or Steve. In some instances, an observer will be present in your group. Today, Gus, the supervisor, has asked Jack, Kate, and Steve to meet with him in his office. He said he wanted to talk about something.

2. Instructions for Observers

(May be omitted if desired)

Your job is to observe the method used by Gus in handling a problem with his group. Pay especial attention to the following:

a. Method of presenting problem. Does he criticize, suggest a remedy, request their help on a problem, or use some other approach?

b. Initial reaction of members. Do group members feel criticized, or do they try to help Gus?

c. Handling of discussion by Gus. Does he listen or argue? Does he try to persuade? Does he use threats? Or does he let the group decide?

d. Forms of resistance expressed by the group. Do members express fear, hostility, satisfaction with present method, and so on?

e. What does Gus do with the time-study data? (1) Lets group examine the table; (2) mentions some of the results; or (3) makes little or no reference to the data.

Best results are obtained if Gus uses the data to pose the problem of how they might be used to increase production.

3. Roles for Participants

Role for Gus Thompson, supervisor

You are the supervisor in a shop and supervise the work of about twenty people. Most of the jobs are piece-rate jobs, and some employees work in teams and are paid on a team piece-rate basis. In one of the teams, Jack, Kate, and Steve work together. Each one of them does one of the operations for an hour and then they exchange, so that all workers perform each of the operations at different times. The workers themselves decided to operate that way, and you have never given the plan any thought.

Lately, Jim Clark, the methods engineer, has been around and studied conditions in your shop. He timed Jack, Kate, and Steve on each of the operations and came up with the facts in the table on page 280.

Jim observed that with the workers rotating, the average time for all three operations would

	TIME PER OPERATION			
	POSITION 1	POSITION 2	POSITION 3	TOTAL
Jack	3 min.	4 min.	4½ min.	11½ min.
Kate	3½ min.	3½ min.	3 min.	10 min.
Steve	5 min.	3½ min.	4½ min.	13 min.
				34½ min.

be one-third of the total time, or 11½ minutes per complete unit. If, however, Jack worked in the No. 1 spot, Steve in the No. 2 spot, and Kate in the No. 3 spot, the time would be 9½ minutes, a reduction of over 17 percent. Such a reduction in time would amount to saving more than 80 minutes. If the time were used for productive effort, production would be increased more than 20 percent.

This made pretty good sense to you, so you have decided to take up the problem with the workers. You feel that they should go along with any change in operation that is made.

Role for Jack

You are one of three workers on an assembly operation. Kate and Steve are your teammates and you enjoy working with them. You get paid on a team basis, and you are making wages that are entirely satisfactory. Steve is not quite as fast as Kate and you, but when you feel that he is holding things up too much, each of you can help out.

The work is very monotonous. The saving thing about it is that every hour you all change positions. In this way, you get to do all three operations. You are best on the No. 1 position, so when you get in that spot you turn out some extra work and make the job easier for Steve who follows you in that position.

You have been on this job for two years, and you have never run out of work. Apparently your group can make pretty good pay without running yourselves out of a job. Lately, however, the company has had some of its experts hanging around. It looks like the company is trying to work out some speed-up methods. If they make

these jobs any more simple, you won't be able to stand the monotony. Gus Thompson, your supervisor, is a decent guy and has never criticized your team's work.

Role for Steve

You work with Jack and Kate on an assembly job and get paid on a team piece-rate. The three of you work very well together and make pretty good wages. Jack and Kate like to make a little more than you do, but you go along with them and work as hard as you can to keep the production up where they want it. They are your pals — they often help you out if you fall behind, so you feel it is only fair to try and go along with the pace they set.

The three of you exchange positions every hour. In this way, you get to work all positions. You like the No. 2 position the best because it is easiest. When you get in the No. 3 position, you can't keep up and then you feel Gus Thompson, the supervisor, watching you. Sometimes Kate and Jack slow down when you are on the No. 3 spot, and then the supervisor seems satisfied. Lately the methods man has been hanging around watching the job. You wonder what he is up to. Can't they leave people alone who are doing all right?

Role for Kate

You work with Jack and Steve on a job that requires three separate operations. Each of you works on each of the three operations by rotating positions once every hour. This makes the work more interesting, and you can always help out the others by running the job ahead in case one of you doesn't feel so good. It's all right to help out because you get paid on a team piece-

MATCHING THE WORKER TO THE JOB

rate basis. You could actually earn more if Steve were a faster worker, but he is a nice guy and you would rather have him in the group than someone else who might do a little bit more.

You find all three positions about equally desirable. They are all simple and purely routine. The monotony doesn't bother you much because you can talk, day-dream, and change your pace. By working slow for a while and then fast, you can sort of set your pace to music that you hum to yourself. Jack and Steve like the idea of changing jobs, and even though Steve is slow on some positions, the changing around has its good points. You feel you get to a stopping place every time you change positions, and this kind of takes the place of a rest pause.

Lately some kind of efficiency expert has been hanging around. He stands some distance away with a stop watch in his hand. The company could get more for its money if it put some of those guys to work. You say to yourself, "I'd like to see one of these guys try and tell me how to do this job. I'd sure give him an earful." If Gus Thompson, your supervisor, doesn't get him out of the shop pretty soon, you're going to tell him what you think of his dragging in company spies.

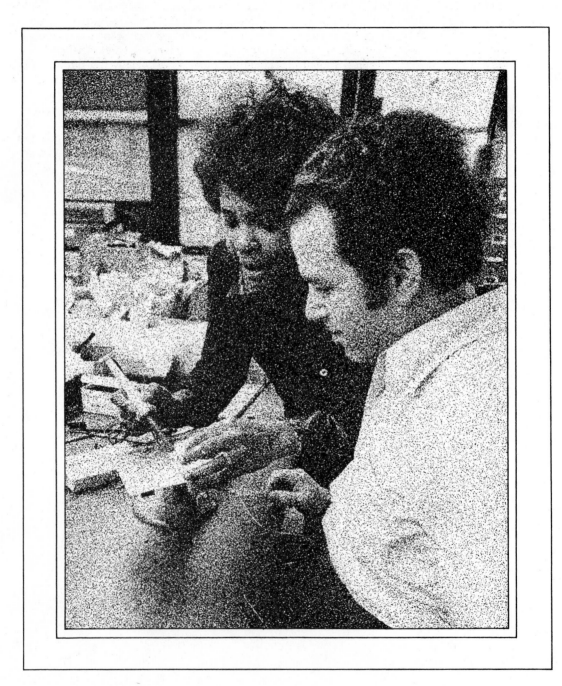

CHAPTER TWELVE

TRAINING
IN
ORGANIZATIONS

■

Aspects of Learning
Training Procedures
Evaluation of Training Methods
The Training of Trainers
Training the Hard-to-Employ
Professional Obsolescence and Continuing Education

■

BEFORE COMPLEX, AUTOMATED industrial machines were designed and human errors were not capable of causing great damage, experience alone was considered adequate to train for a job. Although training (apprenticeship) was accepted for the trades, companies had to be convinced that a training program for unskilled work paid for itself in improved performance (gains in production and decreases in breakage, absenteeism, and turnover).[1] With advances in technology, acceptance of training for operators as well as for management personnel became general. As a matter of fact, companies needed to be cautioned against extravagant claims that were often made by those who marketed programs. J. P. Campbell referred to the overemphasis of packaged programs as training "fads."[2]

A later review of training practices indicates that the patterns are still much the same.[3] Most trainers have little or no background in the behavioral sciences; programs are developed not on the basis of psychological principles but according to the latest wonder cure for a company's ills.

Also, in most companies, there is little follow-up on how effective their training programs are. Any evaluation done is usually too vague to lead to correction of specific problems or covers such minor points that it cannot produce significant improvements. Programs accumulate on an ad hoc basis in many cases because the company president went to a certain type of program and liked it, or because the trainer heard that a competitor's company developed a particular approach. Although program content has changed since the 1940s, the way programs are designed and implemented has not. This lack of progress is particularly regrettable because, although in some instances the goals of the company and those of the individual may clash, the training situation is one in which this conflict need not occur. Both personal and corporate development can result from well-planned and sophisticated corporate training programs.

Managers can influence programs by choosing training methods that are appropriate for the training objectives. The method that is best for one objective may be entirely inadequate for another. Sound-slides and movies have their applications; programmed learning has its uses; and participative approaches (including discussion methods, case studies, and role-playing) have theirs. But to contend that one method is superior to another, regardless of what is taught, is to miss the basic problem of training: teaching something specific. The objectives must determine the method, not the trainer's familiarity with it or admiration for it. The value of a program should be examined in terms of the relationship between the objective of the program and what is *learned* by the trainees. Too often a program is judged by its content (*what* is taught). This approach protects the trainer, since a class's failure to learn becomes the students' fault.

The degree to which trainees like a course or training program may also be misleading, since what persons get from a program may not always correspond with the training objective. However, interest and enthusiasm are assets to learning, and in order to do an efficient teaching job, the trainer must generate these feelings.

A well-designed and implemented training program must contain certain elements. First, training needs should be determined rationally and systematically. Next, those who require training (whether orientation, skill building, or refresher courses) should be selected. At this point, given knowledge of the needs and the individuals involved, appropriate training methods and topics should be developed. Finally, the program should include as an integral part of the original plan, provision for follow-up, evaluation, and reinforcement of training received.

Failure of a program to produce results might mean any of the following: (1) the training was a waste of time; (2) the method used was ineffective; (3) supervisors and trainers did not agree on how the job should be done; (4) the measuring procedure was ineffective; or (5) the training was discontinued before measurable gains were made.

Finding training methods appropriate to the training objective is of concern to line supervisors as well as to teachers and training supervisors. Regardless of how much training is done in a company before an employee reports to a particular supervisor, this supervisor must still do some training. Giving assignments, inspecting work, and upgrading performance should be thought of as training. Furthermore, the line supervisors should agree with the training content so that they reinforce rather than inhibit the desired behavior. Involving management personnel in setting training needs and goals is an essential way to obtain their acceptance of the program.[4]

ASPECTS OF LEARNING

SKILLED LABOR VERSUS JOB SKILL

Industrial jobs are commonly divided into skilled and unskilled work. When used in this sense, the term *skilled* refers to jobs requiring trade knowledge; *unskilled* refers to jobs requiring no special training. White-collar jobs are generally analogous to skilled positions in industry. The trades require both the learning of certain physical tasks and the acquisition of information or knowl-

edge. Carpenters, masons, electricians, and toolmakers thus possess knowledge as well as the ability to perform certain activities. These two aspects of learning are independent of each other. A person could possess trade knowledge to such a degree as to be able to tell others all the steps in constructing a building, yet be unable to saw a board at right angles. Another person might possess all the necessary separate skills, but be unable to construct the building. Knowing how a job should be done and being able to carry out the necessary operations are different learnings. In many blue-collar jobs, these two aspects of work are possessed by the same individual, but in some operations only physical effort is required of the worker; this is called *unskilled labor.*

Training activities in large companies include not only the learning of skilled trades but also supervisory training and executive development. Each of these activities involves a variety of kinds of learning, and since the best method of teaching depends on the kind of learning involved, it is important to study the various aspects of learning in general.

ASSOCIATIVE LEARNING

The formation of associations takes place in all types of learning, and it is through their formation that behavior is modified by experience. We experience objects with our sense organs, and we experience responding to the stimulation that they produce. When any of these experiences becomes linked with any other so that one of them arouses or recalls another, associative learning has taken place.

The essential condition for an association between two experiences is that the experiences must occur simultaneously or in close succession. Seeing a woman with a dog causes me to associate the two, so that on later occasions the dog reminds me of the woman. Food placed in a dog's mouth causes it to salivate but this relationship between the taste of food and salivation is inborn in the dog and is an unlearned response. However, if I ring a bell and then put food in the dog's mouth, I build up an association in the dog between the bell and food experiences. On later occasions, the sound of the bell alone causes the dog to salivate because of the association that links the bell and food experiences. This change in the dog's behavior is acquired through experience and represents simple associative learning, in contrast to trial-and-error learning, which always involves some selection in activity. The term *conditioned response* also is used to designate associative learning, particularly if a response or movement, rather than an idea, is aroused by a sensation.

Through a repetition of the same combination of experiences, associations accumulate and become more stable and permanent. Although some individuals form associations more quickly than others, all continue to profit by further repetition. There is, therefore, no final or complete stage of learning. Even if performance is no longer improved by repetition, the benefits of practice show up in less rapid forgetting.

Although all forms of learning involve formation of associations, only a few are limited to this aspect of learning. Job activities that depend most heavily on pure associative learning are those that require memorization. Examples of routine learning are spelling, recalling telephone numbers, and memorizing postal regulations.

SELECTIVE LEARNING (OPERANT CONDITIONING)

In selective learning a person must not only connect experiences, but must find out which things to connect.[5] Through trial-and-error, persons learn what actions on their part lead to what kind of results. The problem is to learn to make responses that lead to the desired results.

Practical situations demand two types of selection: *sensory* and *motor*. In *sensory* selection, the problem for the learner is to discover the conditions under which to express certain responses. For example, you may know that you should stop your car whenever a red light flashes, and that a constant green light means that you may continue. What should you do when new conditions arise, such as a constant red light, a blue light flashing, an alternating red and green light, and so on?

If you were rewarded for stopping when any kind of flashing light appeared and punished for stopping for a steady light, you would learn to select the essential condition that flashing lights require you to stop. This kind of learning requires more than the fact that two events occur close together in time. It also requires that pleasant or unpleasant consequences be connected with the response.

While a father is giving his child a bath, the child stands up in the tub, slips, and falls. What has the child learned? She may connect this unhappy experience with her father, the water, the bathroom, or standing in the tub. All factors were present at the time of the fall, but which one is selected in the association process determines what the child will avoid in the future. What do employees connect with disciplinary action, with accidents, with strict inspection, and the like? Most situations permit various possible connections, and good training should not leave this connection to chance.

Problems requiring *motor*, or movement, selection are the more typical kinds of trial-

and-error learning situations. They are characterized by the fact that they require the learner to discover what responses to make to a situation.[6] A cat locked in a box must discover that pulling a string will open a door, children must learn to balance food on a spoon in order to get it safely into their mouths, an employee must learn how to do a job to get praised or what not to do to escape reprimand. In this type of learning, a good many responses may be made to a general situation, and in order to learn what to do, the individual must unwittingly make the correct or desired response in the situation.

For learning to take place, the desired response must be within the individual's capabilities and must be connected or associated with the consequence. If the consequence is pleasant, the person is motivated to repeat the behavior; if the consequence is unpleasant, there is reason to avoid the action. To influence or control this learning in people, we often give rewards or punishments in conjunction with certain behaviors, hoping that the desired association will be made. Certain mistakes are frequently made with this method: (1) the individual leaves the situation without ever making the desired response; (2) the situation itself is rewarding, stimulating the individual to prolong the period before the desired response is made; or (3) reinforcement occurs so long after the desired response that no connection is made between responses and reward.

Responses that are seldom made are necessarily the ones that are most difficult to master. Dogs have a hard time learning to push levers upward to get food, but readily learn to push them down. The reverse is true for pigs. Motion-and-time study simplifies learning when the responses required come naturally or are more easily thought of by the person. In associative learning, this difficulty is not present because the desired response is under the trainer's control. The scientist can cause a person to connect a sound with a light by exposing the person to both, one after the other and can cause a dog to salivate in response to a bell by initiating the response, at will, by placing food in the animal's mouth.

SENSORY DISCRIMINATION

Many learning situations demand that a person respond in a certain way to one signal (stimulus) and in another way to a different signal (see Chapter 11). Whether to express a response or to withhold it raises a similar problem. When the stimulus signals are very different, the problem of training is primarily a matter of building up the proper associations. However, when two objects are very much alike, a different kind of difficulty is introduced.

The ability of the sense organs to make distinctions limits what an individual can learn. A child with poor vision may be unable to learn to read because of an inability to differentiate between letters; a color-blind man may make mistakes in matching fabrics; and a competent employee may make a mistake because of incorrectly hearing an assignment. Training methods not only should create situations that make optimum use of the sense organs (through such devices as lighting, glasses when needed, and contrast), but should train people to use the sense organ most useful for discrimination. A defect in a surface might be felt more easily than seen; a good piece of equipment might be selected more accurately by how it sounds when tapped than by how it looks; and a sound mounting for a motor might be detected with the sense of touch (vibration) more readily than with the sense of hearing.

ACQUISITION OF SKILL

Acquiring an act of skill requires not only a particular combination of movements in a specified sequence but also a given intensity of movement. In juggling balls, for instance, the balls must be tossed in a certain sequence, *and* they must be tossed at the proper height and in the proper direction. Of all the movements the juggler is capable of making, only certain ones should be made, and these must be performed with a given intensity. As learning progresses, the selected movements become more specific and closely knit, and interfering movements are dropped. The degree of skill is indicated by the stability of the pattern and the extent to which unessential and disturbing movements have been eliminated. Because such learning requires the discovery and selection of proper movements, it is a form of so-called trial-and-error learning. One aspect of learning is trying out movements, making mistakes, and trying some more.

The acquisition of skill differs from other forms of trial-and-error learning in that it largely depends on the muscle sense, as well as other senses.* This means that the response is an end product for most forms of learning, but for acts of skill, the muscular response serves also as a stimulus for further activity and in this capacity, it becomes a *means* to an end. When muscular activity serves as a guide to further behavior, the quantitative aspect of movement becomes highly important. In all learning, some kind of response is eventually made, but how it is accomplished is not always important.

All of us have experienced muscle sense when walking down a flight of stairs in the dark. Our reliance on the muscular sense becomes very apparent when an error in the pattern of movements is made. We have the "feeling" of having reached the floor and step forward. If the floor is a step farther down, the final movement is all too clearly inadequate for the situation.

UNDERSTANDING AND INSIGHT

At one extreme, a person may learn parrot-fashion and make correct responses without experiencing any deeper relationships; at the other extreme, he or she may learn something with complete insight and understanding. Appreciating the point of a joke involves more than knowing the meaning of each word. To understand something is to see a rich pattern of relationships in a situation or a passage, and these relationships give the situation a complex organization and structure. Intelligence enriches understanding and insights, and a person may be superior in these aspects of intelligence without being superior in others, such as ability to memorize.

Problems that permit understanding and insight are more readily solved than those that must be solved entirely by trial and error.[7] It has been shown that learning material that permits organization and understanding not only results in much better retention, but what is learned can also be applied and used in other situations.[8] Training methods that encourage insight and organization, therefore, will increase retention, improve judgments, and permit a more widespread application of knowledge.

---

* Small sense organs, located in the muscles, tendons, and joints, give a person the "feedback" by which posture and movement are sensed. This sense, known as *kinesthesis*, is essential to posture, walking, talking, and all other skilled activities.

MATCHING THE WORKER TO THE JOB

CHANGING ATTITUDES

Ordinarily the subject of developing or changing attitudes is not included under the topic of learning. Nevertheless, attitudes constitute an important segment of acquired behavior. One reason for giving them a separate (see Chapter 5) or unique treatment is their failure to be changed by traditional training methods. Attitudes contain a heavy loading of emotion, either pleasant or unpleasant; consequently they are associated with visceral responses, involving heart and circulatory changes, glandular secretions (especially from the adrenal glands), and inhibition of digestive processes. The fact that internal organ responses, not directly under voluntary control, are involved explains in part why attitudes cannot be changed by choice. Their close association with frustration also makes them a special case of acquired behavior. Since attitude problems are associated with many learning situations, it is important to recognize them as such and to deal with them appropriately.

TRAINING PROCEDURES

RULES FOR THE FORMATION OF ASSOCIATIONS

Since all learning requires associations, rules describing conditions that favor this process are of general value. However, associative connections are more important to some job

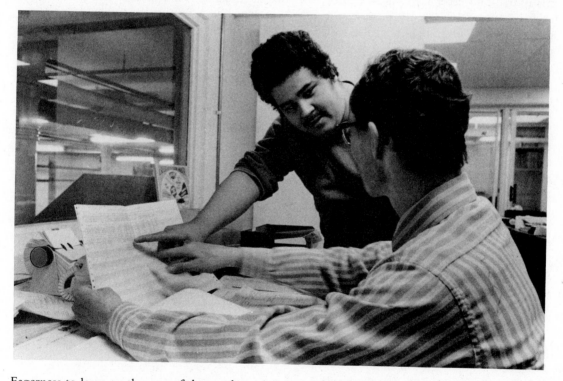

Eagerness to learn on the part of the employee is important in training, as is repetition of the various steps in a job process. (Donald Dietz)

situations than to others, and the value of specific associative bonds may differ.

1. *Frequency of repetition influences the number or strength of associations.*

This rule is most fundamental for memorization tasks. Its effect on pure memorization and understanding are different in that repetitions make simple associations stronger or more stable while they merely increase the opportunities to gain understanding. Once a relationship is understood, further repetitions are boring rather than helpful.

Trial-and-error learning profits from repetition in two ways: repetitions increase opportunities for selection, and they permit the stabilization of the essential associations. For many trial-and-error learning situations, the selective aspect of the problem is the big difficulty, and once it is achieved, further repetitions add little. Acts of skill profit greatly from repetitions because a whole chain or sequence of movements must be tied together. Learning the correct response in a sequence of choices, such as the route from one city to another, profits from repetition for a similar reason. Doubling the number of required associations approximately doubles the number of repetitions necessary to reach a given level of proficiency. However, the time requirement is four times as great because each complete repetition takes twice as long.

Repetition is perhaps the most commonly employed device of learning. We see it applied, almost ruthlessly, in advertising, propaganda, and training films. Although the principle is basic to memorization, there is more to learning and to inducing the buying of a product than the formation of associations.

2. *Attention and intention are important mental sets for learning.*

Although some learning may occur without conscious effort, it is an asset to learning if the experiences to be associated are dominant in consciousness and if there is an intent to learn. Intent increases attention, and attention in turn determines the experiences that will be most vivid to the learner. Conversely, it is extremely difficult to teach those who are brought unwillingly to the training situation. Learning gains result from anything that increases intention, such as motivating the person to learn, and from any procedures that make the relevant events or objects stand out in the learner's consciousness. Common methods for making experiences stand out are increases in size, intensity, duration, and distinctness of the stimulation. Introducing movement and sudden changes in intensity and size also increases the attention-getting properties of stimulus objects. These techniques are frequently used in advertising.

3. *Distributed or spaced repetitions are superior to massed or accumulated repetitions for most standard learning conditions.*

Numerous experiments have demonstrated that a given number of repetitions spaced over a period of days results in more learning than the same number of repetitions massed in a short period of time. The optimum interval between repetitions varies somewhat, but generally, intervals as long as a day or more are optimum.[9] This principle of making learning more economical by spreading the effort over a period of time holds for memorizing material, learning routes (mazes), and acquiring skills (for example, typing and archery), but it does not apply to conceptual learning. The extent of the advantage is greater for difficult (long) tasks than for easy ones. Under extreme conditions, massed trials produce inattention and boredom, resulting in a waste of time. No simple formula describes the way massed and spaced distribution of effort works because differences in motivation, interest, and even age influence the outcome. Massed practice is actually better when some of the activity serves the purpose of a warm-up period, and when long intervals produce too much forgetting between trials.[10]

The application of the principle of spaced learning to training may seem a simple one, but frequently certain practical conditions do not permit the trainer to set up ideal conditions. A new employee is not willing to spread the training time over a period of months by working an hour or so at a time. Practical solutions of the following types may be feasible: alternate job training with some useful but simple job activity; alternate training on very different aspects of the job, or high school students being employed on a part-time basis and the part-time employment being used for training.

The last method is used extensively in some banks and not only supplies trained employees for work after graduation, but permits both employees and supervisors to get acquainted before permanent employment is arranged. A telephone company has trained some operators on a half-time basis and others on a full-time basis. Both groups showed similar progress, and as a result it was found unnecessary to make any changes in the overall duration of the training period when half-time training was introduced.

4. *Whole learning generally is favored over part learning.*
Learning a complete meaningful unit is better than breaking the material into parts and learning them separately. A chapter studied as a whole gives a reader a better sense of organization and allows the formation of more meaningful interrelationships than the same amount of time devoted to studying it in small sections.

A complex task is first learned as a general impression of the whole, comparable to ex-periencing a large painting as a mass of bright color. As repetitions are permitted, more detail is noticed. In the painting, the viewer sees objects not noticed at first. Gradually, as repetitions continue, the minutest details acquire meaning. Figures in the painting formerly perceived as background may now add variety and subtleties.

Training programs should make use of the principle of repeating wholes by going over the entire program from the viewpoint of the overall relationships and then, on subsequent coverages, by working into more specific relationships. A supervisor should not expect perfection of any part of a beginner's work. Rather, many parts should mature together toward perfection as the finer details are mastered.

5. *Recitation or active repetitions are superior to passive reading or listening to another read.*
Reciting demands attention and concentration, locates weaknesses or gaps in learning, uses the process of recall, and demands the making of the very responses that will be required when the learning is utilized later on. These advantages apply to memorizing and to selective learning. A person learns a route through a city much better as the driver than as a passenger.

6. *Short-term memory shows rapid decrement.*
If given a number, a person forgets it unless it is repeated over and over, or unless it is given some meaning. If repetitions of the number are prevented, the recall of the number fades rapidly during an eighteen-second period. This phenomenon is called short-term memory and represents recall of experience before it has been stored in the brain.

7. *Grouping aids memory.*
Some meaningless numbers (telephone) or letters can be remembered better when grouped. An eleven-digit telephone number would require a considerable number of rep-

etitions to be memorized as a sequence. However, if given the meaning that the first digit is the long distance dialing number, the next three are the area code, the next three are the local exchange and the last four are the individual's number, the memory task is simplified even for short-term memory. Grouping is a method for imposing organization and meaning into material to be learned.

AIDS TO SELECTIVE LEARNING

To produce or control selective learning, the trainer must have some way of encouraging or discouraging responses. This is a problem in motivation. Reward and punishment are common ways for motivating behavior. Reward need not be in the form of a material object; praise and even describing a response as correct are effective. Punishments also need not produce physical pain to teach an individual what to avoid, since reprimand and the word *wrong* are effective. Selection can be accomplished by (1) excluding undesirable behavior (negative selection), (2) including only desirable behavior (positive selection), or (3) a combination of both.

The following principles facilitate the selection aspects of learning.

1. *The use of positive selection methods is recommended to trainers.*
A comparison of the merits of rewards and punishments as selectors involves a vast amount of conflicting and varied experimental data. Nevertheless, certain distinctions and general statements supporting use of positive selection methods can be made.

   a. Although training and discipline sometimes are difficult to distinguish, it is important to differentiate between such problems as teaching new employees their jobs and teaching employees to get to work on time.
   b. Most comparisons of the effects of reward and punishment involve two behavior possibilities, thus making avoidance of one synonymous with choosing the other.
   c. Most jobs that require selective learning are more concerned with what to do than with what not to do, and for this reason positive selection is the more economical.

2. *Knowledge of results is essential to selection.*
A training session in target practice led to no improvement because the trainees were not given their scores until the end of the period. They could not select the proper responses because it was impossible for them to know what they did correctly when they did it. Feedback of results should be immediate while the experience of the action made is still clear. The trainee must learn to discriminate between acts that lead to different results in order to control them. Failure to supply effective feedback will oblige the learner to use cues that are available and may be misleading. However, the feedback should be suited to the particular stage of learning. Supplying more information than the trainee can handle will only be confusing.[11]

Feedback also influences the motivational state of the trainee. Knowledge of results in the form of scores produces the experiences of success and failure, which can influence the amount of effort expended. The motivational effects on performance should be distinguished from the way the learned content influences performance.[12] Motivation can influence what is learned only insofar as it controls attention and intention. Variations in performance due to effort expended are motivational and will be discussed in Chapter 13.

3. *Cause-and-effect relationships should be made clear and meaningful.*

Learning to operate the controls of a machine is easier if we know something of the internal mechanisms.

4. *Individual instruction is needed to determine whether each learner is reacting to the proper aspect of the situation (sensory selection) and whether the learner is having difficulty in making the desired response.*

The trainer, in dealing with each person, individually, can evaluate progress and correct difficulty. To do this requires two-way communication and interpersonal relations skill, as well as insightful observation skills, on the part of the trainer.

CAUTIONS REGARDING DIFFERENTIATION PROBLEMS

It is important to recognize the part played by individual differences in sensory capacities. Before spending time training an employee, the trainer should be satisfied that the individual can make the sensory distinctions required. The first step in training inspectors might be to determine whether the trainees can differentiate satisfactory and unsatisfactory items. A common error in training is for the trainer to talk too much and fail to observe what the trainees are reacting to.

Training methods should conform to the sensory capacity involved. All learning requires a reaction to some sort of sensory stimulation. If vision is involved, then visual aids are appropriate. Thus, we can teach social relationships, the internal workings of a blast furnace, or the way to read a dial with the aid of movies, chalkboards, and models. However, sound movies, records, and auditory demonstrations are necessary to teach pronunciation, proper tone of voice to use on the phone, the meaning of sound signals, and the like. Because most people can read and hear words, much training utilizes visual and auditory methods. If a person has both read a passage and heard it spoken, double associations are formed and items from it can be recalled by two different routes, visual and auditory.

AIDING THE ACQUISITION OF SKILL

The basic dependence of acts of skill on the internal muscle sense causes unique difficulties in teaching skills. The associations required are those between sensations of movement and their execution. This means that the trainer cannot manipulate or control a necessary component of the training (the kinesthetic sense). One person can teach another that pushing a switch turns off a motor by demonstrating the relationship between the two events. Both events are under the trainer's control. However, we cannot teach another to juggle balls by demonstration because we cannot give the other person the sensations from the muscles involved. Teaching skills by imitation is greatly overrated.[13]

To teach motor skills effectively, somewhat different training methods are needed from those required in the acquisition of knowledge. The principles stated below are derived from the fact that skill is a form of trial-and-error learning in which the muscle or kinesthetic sense plays a unique role.

1. *Doing, not observing, is basic to forming the associations needed in the development of skill.*

The trainer must arrange for trainees to execute the skilled act, at the outset, as best they can. Time for demonstrations should be kept at a bare minimum. When danger and damage to equipment are possible, safe methods (training devices) for practicing the desired acts off-the-job should be used.

2. *The most useful function of the trainer is to aid trainees in the selection of movements.*

The trainer must be able to recognize correct movements by the way they *look* in order to inform the learner whether or not the skill is improving.

3. *Guiding the movements of another (as guiding a child's bicycle during the first ride) has some value in communicating the general idea during the early stages.*
It should be remembered, however, that guidance alters the sensations of movement because part of the muscle load is carried by the trainer.

4. *Directing attention to the feel of correct movements makes the reliance on this sense more conscious.*
It has been shown that, even in learning to relax, people profit from training in which they learn to recognize a state of relaxation from the feel.[14]

5. *Controlling perception has been found to be a helpful device in some training situations, and its possibilities should be investigated further.*
How should an information operator in the telephone company perceive and visualize a name in order to recognize it most quickly in the directory? Should a painter view a paintbrush as an extension of the hand or as a tool in order to produce the best stroke? Should a singer view the vibrato as a fast trill, as a single act, or as something else? These are questions coaches and trainers might ask when attempting to assist others in developing skills.

Experimentally, supervisors have done a better job of conducting a discussion when they viewed or thought of the participants as peers than when they viewed them as employees.[15] Seeing people as equals makes leaders more tolerant and permissive.

6. *The speed at which the movements in an act of skill are executed during training should match, as nearly as possible, the pace desired for the finished performance.*

Since the nature of the sensations from the muscles depends not only on the particular muscles involved but also on their rate of contraction and relaxation, the sensation of the correct pattern of movement can be achieved only if the action is properly paced. To hurry an act of skill or to slow it down results in inaccuracies and accidents. Judgment must be used in applying this principle to various training situations. Slow motions may be needed at times to permit a trainee to discover some of the finer details.

7. *Recognizing and dealing with tenseness is important to the trainer of skills.*
A perfect act of skill uses only the muscles essential to the act. All other muscles should be relaxed or used only to the extent that posture maintenance is required. A nervous or worried person tends unnecessarily to tense muscles not involved in a job activity. These partially contracted muscles send sensations to the brain and not only disturb the execution of the act of skill but also tire the worker.

Trainers should be understanding and considerate of feelings if they wish to reduce undesirable muscle tensions in learners who, because they are in a strange situation, are frequently in an anxious state. Expecting reasonable improvement rather than perfection should be the trainer's objective.

8. *To keep up interest in learning a task, proper incentives for improvement are important.*
Evidence from a number of investigations indicates that motivation increases not only the *willingness* to do more but also the *ability* to do more. Greater attention further improves the selection process and thereby increases the skill.

9. *In many instances of learning, a person reaches a stage in which apparent progress ceases.* Periods of this sort are known as *plateaus* in learning. Sometimes a plateau seems to be

inherent in the nature of the task, sometimes the method of learning is a factor, and sometimes the plateau appears to be due to reduced effort.[16] Whatever the cause, it is important that the trainee does not become discouraged by the seeming lack of improvement. The worker can be told that the plateau is temporary, that with a little more application it will soon pass. The mere knowledge that the phenomenon is characteristic of learning and not a unique characteristic often is all that is necessary to prevent an attitude of giving up.

10. *Attention to what the trainee does is important in the early stages of learning.*
After an act of skill is well learned, it is performed with little or no conscious attention to its various phases. During the early stages, however, there are so many things to watch that it is often confusing. The instructor can be of great aid in assisting the learner to apply efforts in the right place. Always the correct movements should be emphasized. To draw attention to wrong movements is harmful, in that it deprives the correct movements of necessary attention and may discourage the learner.

When movements have to be made in rapid succession, attention should be placed on the rhythm. A smooth act of skill is no more a mere aggregation of muscular movements than a triangle is a cluster of points.

Attention to the end result of the action pattern also tends to guide the execution of a pattern. We throw a baseball or drive a tennis ball where we look. Always, the attention must be well ahead of the movements, otherwise each separate unit becomes connected with the attention rather than with the preceding movement. In order to gain rapid and smooth performance, the pattern cannot be split into separate parts without necessitating separate acts of attention.

Thus, a unit of skill cannot be divided into parts that can be learned separately. Breaking up of a task into parts is feasible only when the parts are actually separate units of performance. Posture in golf, for instance, can be separated from the drive, whereas juggling a ball with one hand cannot be separated out of a pattern that uses both hands. In dividing jobs for production purposes, it is important that effective movement units be retained. Ordinarily, we think of a manufacturer's product in terms of the number of physical parts from which it is assembled. From the point of view of skill, we should think of the product as the assembly of units or patterns of skill.

BETTER LEARNING THROUGH UNDERSTANDING

Learning with understanding is superior to rote learning because retention is greater and the learning transfers to new situations. For example, a student who understands how to find the area of a parallelogram can use this understanding to find the area of many other geometrical figures. Some methods of teaching stimulate insights, whereas others encourage rote learning.[17]

1. *Training materials should be organized around principles.*
Sequences of illustrations, breakdowns of subject matter, comparisons of data, and visual aids should be presented to point up the basic principles.

2. *Discussion and free exchange of opinion should be encouraged.*
Discussion helps stimulate insightful experiences because extra time is spent examining various relationships. It takes more time to explore, analyze, and test ideas than to present them.

Discussion also requires the trainees to

take an active role, and the extra energy called up for this purpose serves as an aid to understanding. Understanding is always an active rather than a passive process, since the person must impose organization on the sensations supplied to the senses. The leader plays an action-provoking role by asking stimulating and exploratory questions.

3. *Periodically checking on the growth of trainees is essential because understanding declines rapidly when a person falls behind others.*

Trainers can profit from conducting discussions because they are made aware of the degree of comprehension and understanding achieved by their group members. When in possession of this knowledge, they can adapt statements and questions to the level of development the groups have attained.

4. *Requesting trainees to use their own words to summarize or restate a problem, restate another's viewpoint, and the like, aids learning because these assignments demand understanding.*

Only when there is understanding, hence communication, can the same idea be accurately expressed in different words by several people. Requesting group members to judge the accuracy of an interpretative statement made by one of them extends this procedure into a discussion process.

CHANGING ATTITUDES

Chapters 4 and 5 dealt with frustrations and attitudes, respectively, and such skills as listening, permissiveness, and acceptance were discussed. These skills, and the methods of responding to feelings by reflecting them, to be discussed in Chapter 18, may be regarded as effective ways for dealing with the feelings, attitudes, and frustrations of individuals. In Chapter 8, a method for achieving acceptance and agreement in groups was discussed. To complete the picture for dealing with attitudes as a training problem, only a brief statement of methods is needed.

1. *Permissive discussion methods, designed to encourage full expression of feelings and viewpoints, influence attitudes constructively because group members learn what the others think and feel.*

Individuals tend to adopt the attitudes of their group, and permissive discussions make the prevailing attitudes known. This influence of a group's attitude on individual attitudes is called *social pressure.*

2. *When frustrations are present, procedures designed to release hostile expression should be used.*

Attitudes that dominate during frustration are nonconstructive and often destructive and can change only if the state of frustration is reduced.

3. *As previously suggested, the method known as role-playing is especially suitable to attitude training.*

Role-playing permits the trainer to place trainees in a great variety of situations, so that they can better appreciate how situations influence the attitudes and actions of others. A first-line supervisor can be given the role of company president, employee with least seniority, worker with most seniority, or typist. In these different roles, the supervisor will experience some of the attitudes, feelings, and problems engendered by the situation. Such experiences make for greater understanding and tolerance.

4. *Pleasant experiences create favorable attitudes, whereas unpleasant experiences create unfavorable attitudes.*

Anything in a training situation that produces positive experiences tends to train attitudes in the direction of generosity. Good relations with supervisors cause attitudes toward a company to become more generous, thus resulting in more favorable opinions.[18]

EVALUATION OF TRAINING METHODS

THE LECTURE METHOD

Among various training methods,* lecturing is economical because it permits one trainer to cover a considerable amount of information with a number of persons. Many people learn more from hearing lectures than from reading, although for others the sight of a word facilitates learning better than the sound. Good lectures aid understanding and selective learning, but no lecture is efficient in helping people make simple associations unless it is conducted as a drill session. Lectures are of little value in changing attitudes, developing job skills, or training in human relations skills. However, lectures have more effect on attitudes than the written word.[19]

A. K. Korman has pointed out several potential problem areas with the lecture method. Some people who are uncomfortable with the traditional classroom approach may not be receptive; there is no direct tie between lecture topics and the job except at a very general level; individual differences in level of knowledge cannot be accommodated; and for those with poor preparation for dealing with abstract concepts, lectures can be difficult and threatening.[20]

The aspects of a training program that lend themselves to lectures are those involving principles and presentation of background information. Some companies have their officials talk to new employees to present the company history and its policies.

*Although research has not been carried to the point of permitting an exacting evaluation of certain training procedures, it seems desirable to give the reader some general idea of their relative merits. The following evaluations are the authors' opinions and should be considered as such.

Such talks give employees an impression of the company and of the officials. Some feeling for the history is communicated, and some idea of policy is gained, but if examinations are given, the speakers could be greatly disappointed by what was learned. One important factor in the success or failure of this method is the skill of the speaker.[21] The value of the method is also increased if a question-and-answer period is provided.[22]

SOUND MOTION PICTURES

The original cost of a sound movie is high, but since it can be used with many audiences, it is a relatively inexpensive investment for large companies. Many companies make their own films and also purchase films made by other companies. As a result, a randomly selected film library is likely to teach philosophies or values that are inconsistent with one another. By careful selection, however, a set of films consistent with a particular company's point of view may be assembled, but it will not be a complete resource for training.

A film's greatest value is in visual learning. A movie can show what actions lead to what ends, how something works, and how different functions relate to one another. In this way, too, the overall picture of a company operation can be taught even more effectively than by an actual trip through the plant. The sound film can be better than a lecture and demonstration combined.

A movie cannot teach any job skills, and its value for teaching interpersonal skills is grossly exaggerated. Human relations *principles* can be presented in movies as in lectures, though the drama and emotional appeals contained testify more to the films' superiority as an entertainment medium than as a teaching device. A movie might fail to train, yet serve to convince management that the company needs a training program. Unfortunately, management might settle for purchasing the film and using it to do the training job!

In recent years, cassette tapes and video materials have been used to train individuals because they permit an objective view of the worker's performance that can be seen and evaluated immediately. This method has advantages: instead of a trainer criticizing employees' skills or performance, they themselves can immediately see the areas where they are doing well and those where they need more help. Obviously, this technique works only in situations where the observable behavior is crucial. In many interpersonal situations, people may be unaware of

the immediate effects on others of their choice of words or their facial expressions. With the use of video materials, trainees can observe these effects more clearly because they are no longer concentrating on what *they* are saying, but on the responses their words produce *from others*.

DEMONSTRATIONS, VISUAL AIDS, AND SOUND FILM STRIPS

Direct demonstrations, visual aids for felt boards, and sound film strips are less expensive ways of accomplishing much of the effect of a movie. Like the movie, their main value is in aiding visual learning and associating sounds with visual descriptions. Demonstrations and visual aids permit some-

Visual aids in training lectures emphasize important points to trainees. (Courtesy American Telephone and Telegraph Company)

MATCHING THE WORKER TO THE JOB

what greater flexibility, as they can be adapted to the interests and level of the audience. However, this may also be a disadvantage in that trainers are given a certain amount of leeway. If their judgment and understanding are of lesser quality than those of the producer of the training material, they can use this leeway to reduce the value of the material.

One of the values of using so-called canned training material is that the prearrangement of materials prevents trainers from introducing their own pet notions. Although this approach eliminates some of the benefits of more personal approaches to training, it is preferable to poor training.

ON-THE-JOB TRAINING AND SIMULATION

Insofar as motor skills are required, the training facilities should be a duplication of the job situation. Supervised training on the job is ideal when the job requirements can accommodate low initial performance. If a certain level of proficiency is needed before work in the actual situation is to begin, off-the-job training, in which the actual jobs are set up for the use of trainees (vestibule schools), is often used. In other cases, facsimiles of the jobs are set up with hazards removed and opportunities for drill increased. In these improved situations, trainees can learn to climb utility poles without going high enough to injure themselves in case of failure; they can operate telephone equipment, with coaches serving as customers, and not disrupt service; sales personnel can be questioned by trainers acting as clients to see if they have mastered their knowledge of the product; and pilots can get practice in instrument flying and in handling emergencies by being enclosed in a simulated cockpit.

A unique feature of on-the-job training

and its equivalent in the vestibule school is that it is training through doing. Another feature is that instruction is primarily individual. Even when several persons are trained simultaneously, each receives opportunities to practice, and each should receive individual help on any particular difficulty or weakness.

JOB ROTATION AND RELATED MANAGEMENT TRAINING METHODS

A frequently used training method in industry is known as job rotation. The objective is to broaden an employee's exposure as well as experience. College recruits are often rotated among jobs, departments, and company locations before they are given a more permanent assignment. The rotation method also is used to broaden the experience of managers who are being groomed for executive positions.

The methods used for this purpose include fast-track plans for high-potential young managers, assistant-to entry jobs that give the incumbent immediate visibility and status in the firm, and mentorship, wherein an older, established successful executive guides a promising young management candidate through the company maze. In addition to these special programs for high-potential candidates, many large firms have management-training programs for all entering management-level employees. These programs serve the multiple purpose of acquainting the new employee with the people and tasks of the corporation, introducing the candidate to persons who may be interested in accepting the candidate for his or her first permanent job in the firm, and revealing to the new employee both promising and problem-ridden functional areas — to be sought out or avoided in future positions.

The difficulty with such methods is that

their usefulness and efficiency are highly variable from one firm to another. When upper-level executives take an active interest in newcomers, these methods can be very effective. Where the training benefits are considered secondary to getting work out, such programs are expensive failures. The initial response of individuals to companies is significant to their later performance and satisfaction (see Chapter 10).

THE CASE METHOD

The case method was developed at the Harvard School of Business and is one of the first deviations from the standard teaching method in that the teacher or trainer is not the source of knowledge.[23] Instead, learning occurs through participation in discussions and problem analysis. The idea of using case discussion evolved from legal training methods where cases are used as a basis for debate. The objective of finding the correct solution (which an authority supplies in traditional teaching) is replaced by the objectives of using facts effectively and of developing a convincing rationale for a position or decision.

Executive training programs frequently use the case method. A complex situation typical of a real-life problem is presented to a small group. The case becomes the theme for discussing "What to do?" "How could the problem have been prevented?" and "What are some of the policy issues involved?" The case method gives trainees practice in problem solving, and utilizes the benefits of discussion. It does not increase interpersonal skills materially, but many cases stimulate inquiry into effective leadership styles. One important insight gained from case discussion is discovering that *there is no one correct answer or solution* and that the best solution is often a matter of opinion or personal preference.

Another benefit of the case method is that it forces the trainee to make a decision, to take responsibility. Most forms of training, especially at the college level, involve the accumulation of knowledge or expertise. The case method requires risk-taking, in that it forces the individual to choose between alternatives in a crucial situation. In order to do so, priorities must be set and values established. In this aspect, the case method is far more representative of the manager's job situation than are theoretically oriented discussions or lectures.

THE INCIDENT PROCESS

Instead of presenting a group of trainees with a rather detailed account of a situation as required by the case method, the procedure in the incident process is to describe an event that requires action.[24] For example, a good employee wants special treatment. What should the supervisor do? Before coming to a decision, the group members are allowed to ask the trainer some questions. Since the incident usually is a real one, the trainer can answer pertinent questions.

Will the trainees seek out and obtain relevant information? This method offers training in getting vital facts and becomes a game in detective work. It is not skill training in ways to obtain information from a person, because the leader is ready and willing to answer any question; rather the skill requirement is in asking relevant questions. The next stage of the discussion requires the participants to make the decision and supply a rationale for it. They may make individual reports, which become the subject for discussion in the third stage. Finally, the leader tells what actually happened and why. This report may reveal background facts and considerations the participants failed to elicit during the first period. The values of this part of the process are similar to those in case discussion.

The potential major disadvantage of both incident process and case method is that they are highly dependent for success on the trainer's skill. The breadth and depth of insight that is achieved from a particular case or incident can vary widely, depending on how well the trainer leads the discussion, bringing out differing opinions, subtle but important facts, and underlying principles.

DISCUSSION METHODS

Insofar as participation is a motivating force, the use of discussion introduces motivation and involvement. It stimulates understanding, influences attitudes, and can give practice in problem solving. Because considerable time is consumed by a limited subject matter, the coverage is thorough, but there is a sacrifice of systematic organization and of wide content coverage.

The opportunity to take part in discussion enhances the probability of getting trainees involved and provides a built-in mechanism for clarification of issues through feedback. The group situation also supplies a powerful tool for positive or negative reinforcement of ideas through group pressure. This and other factors indicate the need for a well-trained discussion leader if time use is to be efficient.

If lectures or other methods of presentation are used to cover information for which there is general acceptance and discussion methods are used to deal with content for which acceptance is limited, both coverage and acceptance can be effectively and economically accomplished. The use of discussion methods for participative problem solving will be reviewed in Chapter 22.

PROGRAMMED INSTRUCTION

S. L. Pressey invented a method of teaching by exposing a statement with a blank in the frame of a machine.[25] The learner would fill in the blank and then see the correct answer by turning a crank. Students were required to continue a lesson until they mastered all the items. It would be similar to students taking a sentence-completion-type examination in which they could compare their response with the correct one. The so-called *teaching machine* is an apparatus that exposes the programmed sequence to be learned in one frame and the correct answers in another. This approach fitted B. F. Skinner's learning theory regarding repetition and immediate reward (reinforcement), and his support of this type of teaching gave it considerable status and many applications.[26] In more complicated programs the type of wrong answer exposes remedial material that the person can study.[27]

Programmed training permits the worker to learn individually so that differences in the rate of learning neither hold up fast learners nor stigmatize slow ones. School subjects in which the correct answer is not a matter of dispute lend themselves to programming. Another advantage of this method is that it requires the active response of the learner. At lectures and movies, audience members can tune out speakers at will and thus may miss crucial points. Programmed training requires that the learner maintain a high attention level throughout the lesson.

The expected superiority of the method for industry[28] was not initially supported by studies in which it was compared with the lecture-discussion method for teaching statistics and insurance fundamentals. It is evident that training for dealing with job problems is not the same as mere memorization of answers.[29] Programs have become much more sophisticated in recent years, and current programs provide much more challenge and stimulation.

However, problems still exist. For example, a large department store saved training costs by using programmed material to teach clerks to operate sophisticated cash registers. Successful performance required that a series of steps, including pressing the proper numerical and operation keys (for example, subtotal, sales tax), be taken in exactly the proper sequence. After several hours of practice alone in an isolated training room, most newly hired workers could perform the functions reasonably accurately. But when these new employees were sent to their first assignment, trainers observed a marked decline in efficiency, and there was high initial job turnover. In the real job situation, the new workers had to contend with impatient customers, labels that did not match the program's instructions, new products that had not been explained, and so on. The requirement of 100 percent accuracy in using the cash register was attainable under the ideal conditions of the training situation, but could not be maintained under the more stressful conditions of the work situation.

Another unexpected result with programmed training occurred in its use by a state drivers' licensing agency. Those people coming in to take the test were presented with slides of traffic situations and asked, "What should you do in these circumstances?" Four alternative responses were provided. This test seemed far superior to traditional paper-and-pencil tests, and it might have been, were it not for the program's response to wrong answers. The examination was taken in a room where several individuals were tested simultaneously. When an incorrect response was given, a loud buzzer sounded throughout the room.

The embarrassing effect, according to participants' reports, so upset them that it led them to make impulsive and incorrect later responses (resulting in more buzzing and stress). In this case, the concept of immediate feedback apparently was misapplied. Although knowledge of mistakes is important to learning, the negative factors involved in the choice of feedback method seemed to outweigh its benefits.

In both cases described, changes in method could have corrected the problems encountered. The difficulties lay not in the technique but in its misapplication by designers unfamiliar with psychological principles.

BUSINESS GAMES

Like war games, business games simulate a complex realistic situation in which groups compete with one another, and decisions made by one group have an effect on the others.[30] For example, two or more teams may represent competing business organizations in which decisions have to be made regarding production schedules for some months in advance. Decisions involving cost of storing, excess production versus inability to meet demands, cost of changing schedules, frequent adjustments versus long-range plans, possible gains versus losses from risks, and many other realistic considerations are introduced. The decisions are then processed — often by computers — and facts relating to market changes are used to feed back the consequences of each group's decision. The groups then are confronted with the next step in the decision process.

Business games invite much emotional involvement. The learning gained perhaps is the development of a better appreciation of the range of factors that must be considered in making effective decisions, of dangers involved both in risk-taking and conservative-ness, and of the value of cooperative discussions. Business or economic principles as such are not taught; the emphasis is on gaining managerial sophistication.

More recently, business games have been designed to serve more specialized purposes. For example, one such game has been developed to simulate situations involving organizational behavior, design, change, and development.[31] No computers are used, but the game is combined with a series of related readings that presumably help participants make more sophisticated choices.

The main benefit of business games is that the process is dynamic (as is the business environment) — situations change, factors that were crucial become peripheral, and new problems spring up from areas previously ignored or unknown. This approach prepares future managers for the immense complexity of the business environment and its active, ever changing nature. Some disadvantages of this training method are that alternatives may be artificially constricted by program design limitations, that trainees may substitute winning for learning as their main goal, and that participants may concentrate on the specific situation without generalizing the experience to other situations. Finally, because the process takes a lot of time, usually spread out over several weeks, and may use computer time, it is significantly more expensive than alternative training methods.

THE IN-BASKET

The in-basket method involves the characteristic matters or decisions that executives find on their desks.[32] How will they dispose of them? Trainees are confronted with a rush situation, limited information, and a list of action-demanding items that an executive might find in the in-basket. Disposing of matters by delegating decisions, replying by mail, setting up meetings, and delaying action are possibilities. The fact that action must be taken places the emphasis of this type of training on the doing process, which involves primarily mental skills rather than interpersonal skills.

This technique reveals the kinds of decisions executives must make under pressure and could serve a useful purpose in the selection of personnel, which, incidentally, was its original purpose. The training value resides largely in the subsequent discussion; members report their decisions to small groups that evaluate each report.

During in-basket training, the need for delegation, the failure to consider all alternatives, the importance of taking a look at the larger picture, and the detrimental effects of hasty decisions become apparent. A variety of self-insights are reported by trainees. All persons have an opportunity to learn what they may have overlooked in their own decisions.

ROLE-PLAYING

The role-playing method requires trainees to project themselves into a simulated interpersonal situation and play the parts of the persons and situations assigned to them. Role-playing can be limited to practice in the skills of interpersonal relations and of discussion leading. If this is done, attitudes are constructively influenced, the skills needed for effectively dealing with people are upgraded, and sensitivity for the feelings of others is increased. If role-playing cases are built around issues and organizational problems, the benefits of the case method are combined with the benefits of role-playing.[33]

To make the most of the time required for role-playing procedures, principles of behavior and of skill should first be learned by other methods. With a knowledge of principles as a background, good and poor practices become more than opinions for discussion.

Role-playing has been shown to be effective in improving two important components of sensitivity: observation and empathy.[34] Sensitivity is heightened by placing supervisory and management personnel in roles in which they experience attitudes and problems of people in situations different from their own.

Role-playing can also be used to develop self-insight and therapy. In such cases, the interaction processes and the feelings of the participants are more carefully analyzed and a greater degree of skill is required of the trainer.[35] When used to solve the participants' personal adjustment problems, it becomes therapeutic and is known as *psychodrama*.[36]

Role-playing in all its forms differs from the above-mentioned participation methods because it carries the training into the action phase. It is one thing to decide that a subordinate should be told "in a nice way" how to improve, and quite another thing to execute this decision. Deciding to delegate responsibility is still a long way from the act of delegating. Even making a decision and communicating it to others require very different skills. Interpersonal skills, emotional control, and sensitivity to feelings are central to role-playing, and when role-playing is followed by discussion, benefits can be derived from all these areas.

In recent years, a special use of role-playing has been employed for teaching managers interpersonal skills. The method was apparently originated by Melvin Sorcher at General Electric. It involves learning basic psychological skills and then practicing them through role-playing as described above. A third step, called *modeling*,[37] is added between these two processes. Trainees observe

a person skilled in interpersonal relations demonstrating an effective, successful way of dealing with a situation — then they role-play the same situation themselves.

Observation of an individual dealing with an interpersonal problem successfully may be helpful, but it has potential for misapplication in unskilled hands. The wholesale adoption of another's interpersonal style would be artificial and inadvisable, since it would probably be perceived by others as insincere. If the modeling phase is emphasized as *one possible* successful way of dealing with a problem and factors making it successful are stressed rather than specific words or actions, the approach could be improved.

In one test of modeling, an impartial panel evaluated managers on interpersonal skills; later, some received role-play modeling training, others did not. Before training, roughly one-fourth of each group was rated above average and one-fourth below average in this skill. All managers were rated again after the training sessions, but the panel was not aware which managers had received the training. Of the trained group, two-thirds were now rated above average, and all but a few were rated at least average. In the control group, evaluation percentages remained the same.

Although role-playing has been used successfully with management-level employees and some workers for a number of years, recent evidence suggests that special factors may be at work in situations involving disadvantaged groups. If the situation is not introduced properly or if attitudes are initially hostile, the method may not be successful.[38] Some trainees may feel that the situation is childish or artificial and may "ham it up" instead of approaching the problem seriously. As with many other methods, a skilled trainer is necessary to achieve maximum benefits.

T-GROUP TRAINING

The basic objective of the T-group (the *T* stands for "training") is to improve group interaction and communication by having participants develop an understanding of the impact that they make on others.[39] People know how others affect them, but they often have little knowledge of how others see them or how they affect others. A basic assumption of the method is that we cannot understand others until we understand ourselves. This is a common assumption among psychologists, but it is based on clinical rather than experimental data.

One approach is to organize small groups and have them meet for two or three hours daily for a period of two or more weeks. (Some concentrated programs are scheduled for a long weekend, eight or ten hours each day.) The trainer's function is to pass responsibility for discussion subject matter to the members. Before long, the members' conversation turns to themselves, and the leader finds ways to encourage the expression of feelings and opinions about personal reactions to one another. The discussion soon becomes frank, and these reactions become the main subject. Members often find themselves talking about some of their innermost feelings with the others, who show a surprising interest. Gradually people develop trust and expose their usually hidden sides; they find that bonds between them become stronger.

The inherent need of persons to be understood, the effects of authority on their freedom of expression, and the freedom of exploring what another meant by something become topics of discussion. The trainer might comment on unobserved expressions of feelings by making a statement such as "I wonder if John is as sure of what he said as he wants us to believe," or the trainer might say, "It seems that Judy has been very quiet this afternoon. Have some of you noticed that?"

Persons within some organizations who must communicate and work with one another are being sent to resort settings for T-group training. Some participants are hurt by the frankness, other strongly endorse the experience. Much depends on the skill of the trainer; various trainers are not in agreement as to the extent to which the leader should either actively facilitate the insights or do nothing and thereby frustrate the group into taking action.

T-group training and some role-playing methods have similar objectives — to facilitate interpersonal and group interaction. The former stresses freeing the individual from the shell of inhibition to improve communication with others; the latter stresses development of an understanding of others in order to penetrate their shells and make them feel free to communicate. T-group training tends to train participants; role playing, the leader. Perhaps the methods supplement each other; perhaps they are different attempts to do the same thing.

Much controversy centers on T-groups largely because they became as much a fad as a training method.[40] The fact that no obvious skills are required of the trainer permits persons who have once participated to feel competent to conduct training sessions. It is one training procedure where a little knowledge can be harmful rather than merely ineffective.

As data has accumulated on the T-group method, reservations in its use have developed in the minds of many organizational trainers. For example, B. M. Bass has collected evidence that the newly developed skills and attitudes may not result in increased organizational effectiveness.[41] W. G. Bennis has suggested that there may indeed be conflicts between T-group-engendered values and organizational values.[42] Some organizational members, writes C. Argyris, who are most in need of greater interpersonal skills, may dislike this approach a priori and refuse to participate.[43] Even if the method has beneficial effects in the long run, many companies have decided that its benefits do not outweigh the certain monetary and possible emotional costs.[44]

THE TRAINING OF TRAINERS

The potential benefits inherent in proper teaching are demonstrated by an experiment conducted under actual plant conditions.[45] Approximately eight hours of special training were given to the people who taught the operation of a stitching machine. The training emphasized (1) techniques of establishing favorable social interrelations, (2) methods for increasing motivation, and (3) procedures by which the trainer could guide and lead rather than push the workers. The training did not attempt to modify the former method of teaching the technical aspects of the work. The basis of the instruction, therefore, may be regarded as one which influenced the work environment by changing the attitudes of the trainer toward the job of teaching and toward trainees. The discussion method was used entirely.

Figure 12.1 shows the results of the trainer's effectiveness in teaching the stitching operations. The two solid lines show the progress of two new operators over a twelve-day period before the trainer received special training. After four hours of this training, two other operators were taught. The progress made by these operators is shown by the two broken lines in the graph's center. Finally, two operators were taught after the trainer received the full special training of eight hours. The progress made by these operators is shown by the two top lines. These results show that the workers' rates of improvement were directly related to the amount of instruction that their trainer had received. Despite the fact that individual differences in learning are marked, the benefits of the special training were so great that they predominated over variations in aptitude.

In this experiment, the training of trainers was confined to certain aspects of teaching workers. If striking improvements can be shown by limited instruction in interpersonal-relations skills, learning progress must be greatly influenced by the motivation and attitudes instilled by the trainer.

The modeling methods described earlier were used to train supervisors in coaching skills (for example, giving directions, discussing and reviewing performance), as well as in other interpersonal-relations situations. Results indicated that production was higher for employees working under trained (versus untrained) managers, whether the employees were supervisors or culturally disadvantaged workers.[46]

TRAINING THE HARD-TO-EMPLOY

In the United States today, there are two groups of unemployed people. The first is comprised of people temporarily between jobs. Of those unemployed in 1976, for example, 37 percent were out of work less than five weeks; only 15.2 percent were unemployed more than six months.[47] Data for 1976 also indicate that only half of the 7.5 million unemployed had left their jobs in-

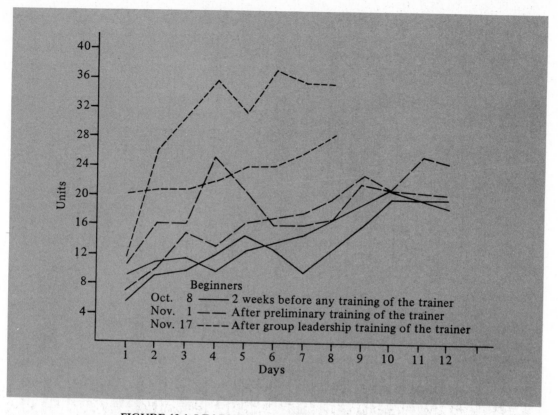

FIGURE 12.1 LEARNING CURVES OF SIX BEGINNERS

These employees were trained by the same instructor who received special training in the handling of employees. The curves show that the rate of learning increased as the instructor received more special training.

SOURCE: Courtesy of A. Bavelas

voluntarily — the rest either quit or were just entering (or re-entering) the job market.

The other group of unemployed consists of individuals variously described as the hard-core unemployed, the hard-to-employ, or the culturally disadvantaged.[48] Typically, members of this group have a history of chronic unemployment, parents with few or no job skills, and poor physical health (many need glasses and/or dental work). Few in this group have money to pay for private trans-

portation, most are school dropouts, many are members of minority groups.* When they have jobs, employer complaints about

*The official U.S. government definition of *hard-core unemployed* requires that a person must be a member of a poor family; be unemployed, underemployed, or hindered from seeking work; and be either (1) a school dropout, (2) a minority group member, (3) under twenty-two years old, (4) over forty-four years old, (5) handicapped, or (6) subject to special obstacles to employment.

such workers are numerous and serious: they are often late or absent; they resign without notice; they steal company property; and they are insubordinate.

Articles have described the problems of this group as America's most critical employment issue.[49] Compounding the problem of having few skills and little education to offer prospective employers are the negative attitudes toward business and the work environment. In recent years, special efforts have been made to train people with these problems. One study found that training in specific job skills was positively related to retention of hard-to-employ workers, and that efforts at attitudinal training were associated with higher levels of turnover.[50] Job-skills training seemed to enhance the worker's confidence that he or she would find a job and perform it satisfactorily, while the attitudinal training was perhaps perceived as attempts at manipulation. These findings are similar to those cited in Chapter 10 in which employees preferred direct measures of potential for job success.[51]

Personal counseling (discussed in Chapter 18) was found in another study to be positively related to retention. This relationship was particularly evident when the training took place over a relatively long period of time and employees could not immediately see the rewards of their efforts.[52]

In another study, on-the-job training of minority women influenced their probability of staying with the organization (an insurance firm) for at least two years.[53] Within a framework of consideration versus initiating structure, supervisors of the forty-one women hired were compared and analyzed in terms of percentage of workers retained. The findings suggest that consideration was positively related to retention, whereas initiating structure was negatively related. The

favorable attitudes of higher-level management also were found to be important in retaining higher proportions of these workers.

A major obstacle to both hiring and training the hard-core unemployed is that many are functionally illiterate, that is, they cannot read or make mathematical computations at the eighth-grade level. Not all functionally illiterate people fall into the category of the chronically unemployed, but many do. Their illiteracy affects not only their job potential but their daily lives. Of the approximately twenty-three million functionally illiterate Americans in 1979, it has been estimated that about one in four cannot calculate the correct change when given a cash register receipt and the denomination of currency used to pay for the purchase.[54]

Many of these people have failed in the public school system and will not consider remedial education using traditional training methods. Recent developments in computer-assisted training have been useful in reaching them. Computer programs developed by Control Data, for example, have been designed to make the "tutor" (who is given a name, such as *Speedy*) seem to be an encouraging, supportive friend who (unlike human trainers) never gives up, gets angry, or goes over the material too fast. In one experimental use of programs for the functionally illiterate, 90 percent of those participating said that they liked the class all or most of the time.[55] If performance results are equally good, it will provide a needed breakthrough in an area of continuing concern to both business and the American public.

PROFESSIONAL OBSOLESCENCE AND CONTINUING EDUCATION

A decline in productivity and/or creativity in mid- or late-career stages may be due either to a lack of technical updating or to changes in motivational factors. Study of engineers and scientists experiencing obsolescence has been extensive. One team of experts in this area has suggested that when technical obsolescence is widespread in an organization, it indicates that the organization — not its individual members — is outdated.[56] Such common practices as lack of recognition for technical contributions, product life rather than career orientation, and inadequate personnel planning are organizational precursors of technical obsolescence.

Other researchers have tried to tie level of obsolescence to personal characteristics. One study cites evidence that three characteristics — high intellectual ability, high self-motivation, and personal flexibility — are related to low mid-career obsolescence.[57]

H. G. Kaufman also has suggestions for creating organizational conditions that will minimize the development of technical and professional obsolescence.[58] These suggestions include having a challenging initial job, periodic job changes, positive work climate and good communications, a well-run performance evaluation and feedback program, and the opportunity to participate in management decisions. Personnel policies also can help: if the company selects for long-term needs, uses up-to-date assessment and testing methods, and offers career counseling, the chance of employees becoming professionally obsolete is lessened. Continuing career counseling is an aspect of training and development only recently recognized. E. H. Schein suggests that "creative individualism" is important in keeping organizations and members from using outdated methods and concepts, and that this mental set is fostered by tailoring specialized training and development programs to different career stages.[59]

Business is indirectly encouraging employees to counteract obsolescence in several ways. Frequently companies underwrite educational costs of part-time college courses taken by personnel. Many supervisors and managers are getting graduate business degrees in programs specifically oriented to their needs and interests. Others are participating in executive-development programs, lasting from four to thirteen weeks, in which concentrated efforts are made to convey up-to-date organizational concepts and managerial tools. All these efforts must be encouraged if business organizations are to be successful. Reliance on the "good old ways" of handling problems risks the development of an increasing gap between conception and reality. Training and retraining are key factors in dealing effectively with complex problems.

NOTES

1. Greenley, R. J. Job training. *Nat. Assn. Manuf. Labor Relat. Bull.*, 1941, *35,* 5–8; Lawshe, C. H., Jr. Eight ways to check the value of a training program. *Factory Mgmt. and Maint.*, 1945, *103,* 117–120. Lindahl, L. G. Movement analysis as an industrial training method. *J. Appl. Psychol.*, 1945, *29,* 420–436; Kelly, R. W., and Ware, H. F. An experiment in group dynamics. *Adv. Mgmt.*, 1947,

12, 116–119; Chaney, F. B., and Teel, K. S. Improving inspector performance through training and visual aids. *J. Appl. Psychol.*, 1967, *51*, 311–315.

2. Campbell, J. P. Personnel training and development, *Annual Review of Psychology*, 1971, *22*, 565–602.

3. Hinrichs, J. R. Personnel training. In M. D. Dunnette (Ed.), *Handbook of industrial and organizational psychology*. Chicago: Rand-McNally, 1976, pp. 829–860.

4. Zerfoss, L. F., and Maier, N. R. F. Improving staff procedure in training. *J. Indust. Train.*, 1952, *6*, 5–16.

5. Noble, C. E. Outline of human selective learning. In E. A. Bilodeau and I. M. Bilodeau (Eds.), *Principles of skill acquisition*. New York: Academic Press, 1969.

6. Thorndike, E. L. *Animal intelligence*. New York: Macmillan, 1911; Adams, D. K. Studies of adaptive behavior in cats. *Comp. Psychol. Monogr.*, 1929, *6*; Guthrie, E. R. *The psychology of learning*. New York: Harper, 1952; Guthrie, E. R., and Horton, G. P. *Cats in a puzzle box*. New York: Rinehart, 1946.

7. Köhler, W. *Gestalt psychology*. New York: Liveright, 1929; Wertheimer, M. *Productive thinking*. New York: Harper, 1945.

8. Katona, G. *Organizing and memorizing: Studies in the psychology of learning and teaching*. New York: Columbia University Press, 1940.

9. Woodworth, R. S. *Experimental psychology*. New York: Holt, 1938, Chapter 9.

10. Howland, C. I. Human learning and retention. In S. S. Stevens (Ed.), *Handbook of experimental psychology*. New York: Wiley, 1951, pp. 613–689.

11. Ammons, R. B. Effects of knowledge of performance: A survey and tentative theoretical formulation. *J. Gen. Psychol.*, 1956, *54*, 279–299.

12. Locke, E. A. Effects of knowledge of results, feedback in relation to standards, and goals on reaction-time performance. *Amer. J. Psychol.*, 1968, *81*, 566–574; Fleishman, E. A. Individual differences and motor learning. In R. M. Gagne (Ed.), *Learning and individual differences*. Columbus, Ohio: Merrill, 1967; Porter, L. W., and Lawler, E. E. *Managerial attitudes and performance*. Homewood, Ill.: Dorsey, 1968.

13. For a report of experiments on the acquisition of skills required for control of sensitive equipment, see Smith, K. U., and Sussman, H. Cybernetic theory and analysis of motor learning and memory. In E. A. Bilodeau and I. M. Bilodeau (Eds.), *Principles of skill acquisition*. New York: Academic Press, 1969.

14. Jacobson, E. *Progressive relaxation*. Chicago: University of Chicago Press, 1939.

15. Solem, A. R. The influence of the discussion leader's attitude on the outcome of group decision conferences. Doctoral dissertation, University of Michigan, 1953.

16. Book, W. F. *Learning to typewrite*. New York: Gregg, 1925, Chapter 15; Batson, W. H. Acquisition of skill. *Psychol. Monogr.*, 1916, *21*, 1–92.

17. Wertheimer, M. *Productive thinking*. New York: Harper, 1945; Katona, op. cit.

18. Maier, N. R. F., and Solem, A. R. Audience role playing: A new method in human relations training. *Hum. Relat.*, 1951, *4*, 287–294.

19. Wilke, W. H. An experimental comparison of the speech, the radio and the printed page as propaganda devices. *Arch. Psychol.*, 1934, No. 169.

20. Korman, A. K. *Industrial and organizational psychology*. Englewood Cliffs, N.J: Prentice-Hall, 1971.

21. Patten, T. D. *Manpower planning and the development of human resources*. New York: Wiley, 1971.

22. Meyer, H. E. A $900 lesson in podium power. *Fortune*, 1977, *96*(2), 196–198ff; Ehninger, D., Monroe, A. H., and Gronbeck, B. E. *Principles and types of speech communication*, 8th ed. Glenview, Ill.: Scott, Foresman, 1978.

23. Glover, J. D., and Hower, R. M. *The administrator: Cases on human relations in business,* 4th ed. Homewood, Ill.: Richard D. Irwin, 1963; McNair, M. P. *The case method at the Harvard Business School.* New York: McGraw-Hill, 1954.

24. Pigors, P. J., and Meyers, C. A. *Personnel administration: A point of view and a method.* New York: McGraw-Hill, 1961; Pigors, P. J., and Pigors, F. *Case method in human relations: The incident process.* New York: McGraw-Hill, 1961; Champion, J. M., and Bridges, F. J. *Critical incidents in management.* Homewood, Ill.: Richard D. Irwin, 1963.

25. Pressey, S. L. A simple apparatus which gives tests and scores — and teaches. *School & Society,* 1926, *13,* 373–376.

26. Skinner, B. F., The science of learning and the art of teaching. *Harvard Educ. Rev.,* 1954, *24,* 86–97; Skinner, B. F. *The technology of teaching.* New York: Appleton-Century-Crofts, 1968.

27. Hughes, J. L. (Ed.). *Programmed learning: A critical evaluation.* Chicago: Educational Methods, Inc.; Milton, O., and West L. J. *Programmed instruction: What it is and how it works.* New York: Harcourt, Brace & World, 1961.

28. Goldberg, M. H., and Dawson, R. I. Comparisons of programmed and conventional instruction methods. *J. Appl. Psychol.,* 1964, *48,* 110–114; Hedberg, R., Steffan, H., and Baxter, B. Insurance fundamentals — a programmed text versus a conventional text. *Personnel Psychol.,* 1965, *18,* 165–171; Nash, A. N., Muczyk, J. P., and Vettori, F. L. The relative practical effectiveness of programmed instruction. *Personnel Psychol.,* 1971, *24,* 379–418.

29. Seltzer, R. A. Computer-assisted instruction: What it can and cannot do. *Amer. Psychol.,* 1971, *26,* 373–377.

30. Kibbee, J. M., Craft, C. J., and Manus, B. *Management games: A new technique for executive development.* New York: Reinhold, 1961; Greene, J. R., and Sisson, R. L. *Dynamic management decision games.* New York: Wiley, 1959; Andlinger, G. R. Business games — play one. *Harvard Bus. Rev.,* 1958, *38* (March-April), 115–125; Rawdon, R. *Learning management skills from simulation gaming.* Ann Arbor, Mich.: Bureau of Industrial Relations, University of Michigan, 1960; and Cohen, K. S., et al. *The Carnegie Tech management game.* Homewood, Ill.: Richard D. Irwin, 1963.

31. Miles, R. E., and Randolph, W. A. *The organization game: A simulation in organizational behavior, design, change and development.* Santa Monica, Calif.: Goodyear, 1979.

32. Hemphill, J. K. (Ed.). Proceedings of the Conference on the Executive Study. *The in-basket technique.* Princeton, N.J.: Educational Testing Service, 1961.

33. Maier, N. R. F., Solem, A. R., and Maier, A. A. *Supervisory and executive development: A manual for role playing.* New York: Wiley, 1959.

34. Smith, H. C. *Sensitivity to people.* New York: McGraw-Hill, 1966.

35. Bradford, L. P., and Lippitt, R. Role-playing in supervisor training. *Personnel,* 1946, *22,* 358–369; Corsini, R. J., Shaw, M. E., and Blake, R. R. *Role-playing in business and industry.* New York: Free Press, 1961; Culbertson, F. M. Modification of an emotionally held attitude through role playing. *J. Abnorm. Soc. Psychol.,* 1957, *54,* 230–233.

36. Moreno, J. L. *Who shall survive?* Beacon, N.Y.: Beacon House, 1953.

37. Imitating models: A new management tool. *Bus. Week,* May 8, 1978, 119–120.

38. Elbing, A. O., Jr. The influence of prior attitudes on role playing results. *Personnel Psychol.,* 1967, *20,* 309–321.

39. Tannenbaum, R., Wechsler, I. R., and Massarik, E. *Leadership and organization: A behavioral science approach.* New York: McGraw Hill, 1961; Bradford, L. P., Gibb. J. R., and Benne, K. D. (Eds.). *T-group theory and laboratory method.* New York: Wiley, 1964; Gordon, T. *Group centered leadership.* Boston: Houghton Mifflin, 1955.

40. House, R. J. T-group education and leadership effectiveness: A review of the empirical literature

and a critical evaluation. *Personnel Psychol.*, 1967, *20*, 1–32; Campbell, J. P., and Dunnette, M.D., Effectiveness of T-group experiences in managerial training and development. *Psychol. Bull.*, 1968, *70*, 73–104.

41. Bass, B. M. The anarchist movement and the T-group. *J. Appl. Behav. Sci.*, 1967, *3*, 211–226.
42. Bennis, W. G. *Organizational development: Its nature, origins and prospects.* Reading, Mass.: Addison-Wesley, 1969.
43. Argyris, C. Problems and new directions for industrial psychology. In M. D. Dunnette (Ed.), *Handbook of industrial and organizational psychology.* Chicago: Rand McNally, 1976.
44. Wagner, A. B. The use of process analysis in business decision games. *J. Appl. Behav. Sci.*, 1965, *1*, 387–408.
45. This experiment was conducted by Alex Bavelas at MIT.
46. Burnaska, R. F. The effects of behavior modeling training upon managers' behaviors and employees' perceptions. *Personnel Psychol.*, 1976, *29*, 329–335. See also Hall, D. T., and Hall, F. S. What's new in career management. *Organ. Dyn.*, 1976, *5*, 17–33.
47. Guzzardi, W., Jr. How to deal with the "new unemployment." *Fortune*, 1976, *94*(4), 132–135ff.
48. See Piore, M. J. On-the-job training in the dual labor market: Public and private responsibilities in on-the-job training of disadvantaged workers. In A. R. Weber, F. H. Cassell, and W. L. Ginsburg (Eds.), *Public-private manpower policies.* Madison, Wisc.: Indus. Relations Research Assoc., 1969, pp. 101–132.
49. Super, D. E., and Hall, D. T. Career development: Exploration and planning. *Ann. Rev. Psychol.*, 1978, *29*, 333–372.
50. Goodman, P., and Salipante, P. Organizational rewards and retention of the hard-core unemployed. *J. Appl. Psychol.*, 1976, *61*, 12–21.
51. Schmidt, F. L., Grunthal, A. L., Hunter, J. E., Berner, J. G., and Seaton, F. W. Job samples vs. paper-and-pencil trades and technical tests: Adverse impact and examinee attitudes. *Personnel Psychol.*, 1977, *30*, 187–197.
52. Salipante, P., and Goodman, P. Training, counseling and retention of the hard-core unemployed. *J. Appl. Psychol.*, 1976, *61*, 1–11.
53. Beatty, R. W. Supervisory behavior related to job success of hard-core unemployed over a two-year period. *J. Appl. Psychol.*, 1974, *59*, 38–42.
54. Raloff, J. You're never too old. *Sci. News*, 1979, *114*(23), 394–396.
55. Raloff, ibid.
56. Thompson, P. H., and Dalton, G. W. Are R & D organizations obsolete? *Harvard Bus. Rev.*, 1976, *54*, 105–116.
57. Shearer, R. L., and Steger, J. A. Manpower obsolescence: A new definition and empirical investigation of personal variables. *Acad. Manage. J.*, 1975, *18*, 263–275.
58. Kaufman, H. G. *Obsolescence and professional career development.* New York: AMACOM, 1974.
59. Schein, E. H. Organizational socialization and the process of management. *Ind. Manage. Rev.*, 1968, *9*, 1–16; Schein, E. H. The individual, the organization, and the career: A conceptual scheme. *J. Appl. Behav. Sci.*, 1971, 7, 401–426. See also Hall, D. T. A theoretical model of career sub-identity development in organizational settings. *Org. Behav. Human Perform.*, 1971, *6*, 50–76; Holland, J. L. *Making vocational choices.* Englewood Cliffs, N.J.: Prenctice-Hall, 1973.

MATCHING THE WORKER TO THE JOB

SUGGESTED READINGS

Bowen, H. R. *Investment in learning*. San Francisco: Jossey-Bass, 1977.

Burnaska, R. F. The effects of behavior modelling training upon managers' behaviors and employees' perceptions. *Pers. Psychol.*, 1976, 329–335.

Ehninger, D., Monroe, A. H., and Gronbeck, B. E. *Principles and types of speech communication*, 8th ed. Glenview, Ill.: Scott, Foresman, 1978.

Goodman, P., and Salipante, P. Organizational rewards and retention of the hard-core unemployed. *J. Appl. Psychol.*, 1976, *61*, 12–21.

Kaufman, H. G. *Obsolescence and professional career development*. New York: AMACOM, 1974.

Mealiea, L. W. T. A. approach to employee development. *Supervis. Mgt.*, August, 1977, 11–19.

LABORATORY EXERCISE

ROLE-PLAYING:
BESSIE JOHNSON AND THE CHIEF EXECUTIVE OFFICER

A. GENERAL PREPARATIONS

1. Background information (D.1 and D.2) should be read aloud to the class by individuals selected by the instructor.
2. Then the class will divide into units of two. (If necessary, an extra person can serve as observer for one unit.) One person in each unit will read the role for Larry Joyce (E.1), and the other will read the role for Bob Walton (E.2).

B. THE ROLE-PLAYING PROCESS

1. When the role-players have had time to read their parts, they should put aside their roles.
2. The role-play will begin by Bob Walton greeting Larry Joyce and explaining the situation.
3. The role-playing should proceed for about twenty to thirty minutes.
4. When the role-playing has been terminated, the instructor should write down the solutions — if any — to the problem described.
5. The instructor should try to determine whether any units felt that a satisfactory decision could not be reached without Bessie Johnson's participation.
6. If there is time after class discussion, one individual may take the role of Bessie Johnson (as she is described in D.2) and role-play with a Larry Joyce and/or a Bob Walton to see what feelings will be expressed and whether a satisfactory problem solution can be found.

C. DISCUSSION QUESTIONS

1. What kinds of ideas for further training, if any, came up?
2. To what extent can further training be useful to Bessie?

3. How interested is Bessie likely to be in training to change her appearance and style? On what basis are your predictions made?
4. To what extent are companies justified in persuading employees to go along with a certain company image — through dress codes, social pressure, and so on?
5. What have been the benefits to Bessie and the company of her training thus far? What have been the limiting factors in that training?
6. Can training solve Bessie's problem?
7. Does Ashley Rush have a problem? Could training help him? Is he likely to get it?

D. MATERIALS FOR THE CASE

1. Background Information

Ashley Rush (A.R.) is Chairman of Parker Industries (PI), a manufacturer of specialty chemicals. When the board of Parker ousted the previous chairman three years ago, PI had $117 million in annual sales. Today it has more than $750 million in annual sales and continues to grow rapidly. Over the past thirty-six months, the stock's price has risen 75 percent. Skillful acquisition deals and wily bargaining on sales of low-profit divisions are how the industry analysts explain PI's phenomenal success. Company insiders give all the credit to A.R., the chief executive officer (CEO), and his golden touch.

Mel Lambertson is PI's vice president for public relations. He and Rush are returning to PI headquarters in A.R.'s limousine.

A.R.: Well, how was the trip, Mel? Worth your time?
Mel: I'd say so. I made a number of good contacts, talked to a lot of people.
A.R.: Get any commitments?
Mel: Well, nothing in writing, but . . .

A.R.: Right. Well, my trip wasn't too boring either. Went to a board meeting at Tuck. Talked to Parker Hudson. I think he'll be helpful to us on the Harper business. He said he would talk to Judd before we present it to Morgan Stanley — you know, sort of warm him up on the idea. Yes, that was all right.

Mel: While you were in the area, did you get a chance to visit the lab we acquired with Caplan-Mason? Nobody seems to know anything about it — just how it will fit into PI, and all.

A.R.: Yes. I just dropped in unexpectedly, and I'm glad I did. Talked to Bob Walton, the V.P. of research, who heads up the lab. Seemed reasonably intelligent, but we'll have to have Dr. Pyle read the reports. Must change one thing, for sure, though.

Mel: Yes? What's that?

A.R.: Well, you — of all people — are aware of how hard we've been working to develop the Parker Industries' image — you know — "Good grooming, better effort, best results?"

Mel: Sure. Betty tells me I mumble that slogan in my sleep.

A.R.: Well, the receptionist at the C-M lab has to be the living antithesis of that slogan.

Mel: No kidding, what's she like?

A.R.: Well, she's fat and sloppy, and when I saw her, she was wearing a purple dress with huge red flowers on it and about a quart of cheap perfume.

Mel: Good grief. Wherever do they find these people? Did you talk to Walton about her?

A.R.: Didn't get a chance. She really raps the image, all right. She could probably work in the mail room where nobody would see her, but not there in the reception area. What must customers think?

Mel: Well, it's a lab — maybe they don't get any customers out there.

A.R.: Use your head, Mel. Those audio-pulsars are a high-tech item — a lot of individual customer service by the scientists. They have all kinds of customers there. I mean, I don't even want people off the street to see her and think, "That's my image of Parker Industries." She probably wears hair-rollers to work on days when she has a big date.

Mel: Well, are you going to get her out of there?

A.R.: Right. I'm going to make a note to have Sheri get Buckman — C-M's president — tomorrow. This is ridiculous.

Mel: Right.

2. Larry Joyce's Speech

(The following is an excerpt of a speech by Larry R. Joyce, senior training specialist, Caplan-Mason Laboratories, to the American Association of Personnel and Training Managers' nineteenth annual convention.)

Motivating the Underprivileged Employee

. . . replied the farmer's daughter. So, you see, "underprivileged" depends on your point of view. [*Laughter*]

Now, I'd like to describe for you, as an illustration of the technique I've outlined above, an example from an individual with whom I have worked. Let's call her Becky Jackson. She is the oldest daughter of a man who was crippled in a steel mill accident. The father gets a little money from Workman's Comp, but in addition to Becky, the Jacksons' household includes two younger daughters, plus the son of one of the younger girls, all of whom are dependents.

I met Becky when she was sixteen years old and came to work at our firm as part of a school co-op program. She began working half days, sorting mail. When she finished high school, she began working for Caplan-Mason full time in the duplicating department.

In Becky's neighborhood in the central part of Elain, Ohio, a city where most people are employed at the steel mills, the majority are not employed full time. Of those who are, most are working in low-skill or heavy labor work. Now that their children are older, Becky's mother works part time as a domestic. But Elain is mostly a working-class town — there isn't much call for maids or housekeepers. Housekeeping in central Elain, by the way, is pretty difficult. If you've ever lived in a steel town or even driven through one, you'll recall that fine red dust that falls twenty-four hours a day and turns everything to a sort of pinkish-orange.

Most of Becky's girlfriends are either being supported by a man or living on Aid to Dependent Children money. But Becky had other ideas for herself: she wanted to get herself and her family out of the red-dust central city, get out of the duplicating department, do something with a little pizzazz, a little glamour.

I learned this little by little from Becky. She is a very cheerful, outgoing person, but she, like most of us, kept her dreams and ambitions to herself. Eventually, though, using the methods I've outlined to you, we built up a rapport. I explained to her about the company's tuition reimbursement program. She began to show a little interest, although she "hated school and that phony jazz," as she put it.

When she turned in her application for reimbursement for her first term at the local junior college, I was a little shocked. She had taken two courses: Introduction to Sociology and Black History. I sent the forms in to headquarters, and they returned them, saying that the courses were not related to her job. I was very much afraid that Becky would be knocked out at the start: not only could she not afford the tuition, but this rejection of her first tentative try at self-development would probably turn her off the whole idea. Well, fortunately, I found people at headquarters who were able to understand the problems of developing underprivileged employees. She got reimbursement for those courses and from then on got approval before taking course work.

I tried to interest Becky in learning typing and other secretarial skills, but she decided that was not her bent, and I had to agree with her. She is great working with people — very warm, very friendly and down-to-earth — but she doesn't have great manual dexterity or detail orientation, according to her aptitude test scores.

She was determined to get out of the duplicating department, though. To her, I guess, that department represented the kind of menial, low-status work that poor people had been limited to for many years. She looked around and decided that the perfect job for her was to be the lab's receptionist. Actually, the duties were well within her capabilities — she is friendly, remembers names and faces well, and can do the sorting and other clerical tasks assigned to fill in between visitors.

The receptionist at that time was a woman in her sixties, a very conservative, if not prejudiced, person. Her retirement date was about eighteen months after Becky's decision to aim for the receptionist's job. When she heard about Becky's ambition, she used all her influence — and after twenty-two years with the lab, she had some — to prevent Becky from replacing her. She succeeded in getting the job for her niece — a very nice young woman who soon found that she was pregnant and quit work six months later.

Again, Becky tried for the job. By this time, she had taken several general business courses and had acquired more poise and confidence. Unfortunately, the job was given to another woman, despite my own recommendation. This other woman also wanted the glamour spot, and she had more company seniority. So she got the job. But she couldn't *do* the job. She talked on the phone to her friends and left sales personnel and customers sitting idly by. She was absent frequently and generally lacked motivation. Everyone breathed a sigh of relief when she left to take a job with another company.

This time Becky got her job, and she is doing very well. Oh, she has a way to go yet — her hair style and dress are the ultimate in chic among her friends, but they don't fit the "dress for success" image. We're still working with her, and I have every confidence in her ability to be successful in this job. And she deserves it — she's come a long, long way from the relief-check mental attitudes of downtown Elain. Thank you, ladies and gentlemen.

E. ROLES FOR PARTICIPANTS

1. Role for Larry Joyce

You are Larry Joyce, thirty-five-year-old senior training specialist at Caplan-Mason Laboratories. Your background includes a lot of knowledge and experience with various training methods. You are particularly challenged when required to adapt teaching methods to an unusual case (as with Bessie Johnson, whom you called Becky Jackson in your speech). You were asked by Bob Walton, the head of Caplan-Mason to stop by and see him about an employee, but you don't know what the problem is or who the employee might be.

2. Role for Bob Walton

You are the forty-eight-year-old head of Caplan-Mason Laboratories and vice president of research for Parker Industries. Recently, you received a call from your boss (Dick Buckman) saying that Ashley Rush had noticed Bessie Johnson, the receptionist, and strongly disapproved of her appearance and style. You vaguely remember that Larry Joyce, the training specialist at C-M, thought highly of her. You got the definite impression that Rush wanted her moved to some job where she wouldn't deal with the public. But maybe some kind of training might help, so she could keep her job. You are not too sure if there is any such training or whether Rush would buy it, but you thought you'd get Larry's opinion. Perhaps he can help solve the problem.

PART

MOTIVATING
WORKERS
FOR
OPTIMUM
PERFORMANCE

FOUR

*Wants and needs are universal driving forces of human beings —
whether rich or poor, male or female, management or labor. This section
discusses how to use our knowledge of motivation to create situations in
which the wants and needs of all organization members are understood,
often shared, and made mutually harmonious.*

*Chapter 13 ("Job Motivation") presents some ways in which motiva-
tional principles (described in Chapter 3) can be applied to understanding
the basic wants of employees: methods of pay, levels of aspiration, task
novelty or stability, and so on. The remaining chapters in the section deal
with specialized areas of application: rating performance, boredom and fatigue, accidents and job turnover, and counseling. The common factor in
each situation is that by understanding the motivations and desires of employees, situations often regarded as insoluble problems can become opportunities to increase cooperation, interest, and productivity of employees.*

*Managers generally dislike performance reviews (as do employees) be-
cause they see them as negative motivational experiences — a judge/criminal
confrontation. Chapter 14 ("Evaluating Job Performance") presents a way
of viewing performance evaluation that releases constructive impulses from
both manager and subordinate toward the goal of improved performance.*

*Chapter 15 ("Job Fatigue: Physical and Psychological") describes the
physical and mental aspects of job boredom and fatigue. The discussion
shows that, to a great extent, such factors are affected by individual perceptions of the job (hence, individual motivation), rather than by the task itself.*

*Accidents, as Chapter 16 ("Accidents in the Workplace") points out, are
usually not entirely accidental, a matter of random chance. Although the
concept of accident proneness as formulated in the early twentieth century
was probably an oversimplification, the chapter indicates that motivational
factors (as well as frustration) influence individual accident rates.*

*Chapter 17 ("Analyzing Job Turnover") deals with job turnover — the
motivations that cause people to leave their jobs. Turnover is a costly problem for industry. The chapter differentiates between circumstances in which
turnover is preventable and those in which it is a constructive solution.*

*The section ends with Chapter 18 ("Counseling Skills for Managers")
and discusses a recommended method for communicating with, and understanding employees having many types of motivational problems. The
method is derived from clinical techniques, but detailed explanations are
given for adapting it for use by managers.*

*Overall, Part Four tries to create a new framework for viewing some
common problems of the work situation. Without training in interpersonal
skills and psychological principles, we tend to see people with motivational
problems as troublemakers — people who have little potential for improving
task performance and who, in fact, drag down the efforts of others. These
chapters present both insights to help managers view their employees as
people with soluble problems and data about skills needed to help managers
and employees find satisfactory solutions.*

CHAPTER THIRTEEN

JOB MOTIVATION

■

The Needs That Money Satisfies
Methods of Pay and the Values Created
Which Pay Method Is "Fairest"?
Extrinsic Versus Intrinsic Motivation
Achievement Theory Revisited   The Level of Aspiration
Nonmonetary Factors Affecting Performance
Social Factors in Motivation   Increasing Job Interest
What Employees Want in Their Jobs
Job Attitudes: Satisfaction, Involvement, and Commitment
Resistance to Change

■

M ONEY, IN ITSELF, has no incentive value. As our economic structure has made money a medium of exchange, however, it can be used to obtain the real incentives. Money is sought after in our society because of what it represents. In an experiment, chimpanzees were trained to work for poker chips, which they found they could exchange for food (the real incentive for their work). The chimpanzees even begged from one another to obtain the poker chips, and learned the difference between the high- and low-value chips.[1] In human beings, the exchange value of money has become so ingrained that people sometimes appear to be seeking money for its own sake rather than for what it represents.

THE NEEDS THAT MONEY SATISFIES

Before we can understand human beings' interest in money, we must appreciate the fact that although people in different income brackets receive the same kind of currency in their pay checks, they are not working for the same things and so are motivated differently. The order in which different amounts of income satisfy needs is roughly as follows:

1. Basic necessities of life (food, shelter, clothes, and the like)
2. Necessities for health and education
3. Luxuries (mostly acquired needs)
4. Social position
5. Power

The person who accumulates millions seeks power, and this need is real. People in lower income brackets wonder why the wealthy person seeks more wealth than is necessary for bodily needs and comforts. They do not understand the motivation to increase wealth because they have not tasted the power and influence possible with

money. Many people have said that they will stop working for money when they have obtained a certain amount. Such people fail to realize that they will develop other needs in the meantime and that these new needs will make them continue to strive.

That money represents the satisfaction of different kinds of needs becomes apparent if we speculate a moment on what people would do if they could not obtain social position and power by means of money. In such a case, these needs might most readily be satisfied by service to society. The success of a person then would become a matter of social, rather than financial, status. Instead of competing with one another for money chips, people would compete for other socially recognized indicators of merit. In the Bennington College community, where liberal leanings became associated with prestige, women developed nonconservative values, the most capable leaders showing a greater degree of liberalism than the less capable ones.[2] Prestige is not inevitably associated with wealth; rather, our culture has given money a prestige value.

METHODS OF PAY AND THE VALUES CREATED

Wages may be distributed by numerous possible methods, each having its unique effect on motivation and values. Since no single or pure method is universally accepted, in actual practice the effects are mixtures. A discussion of each method, however, will reveal its influence on behavior and help clarify why reactions to wage procedures are so varied.

PAY IN TERMS OF PRODUCTION
Payment in terms of the amount produced is intended to motivate workers to exert and

MOTIVATING WORKERS FOR OPTIMUM PERFORMANCE

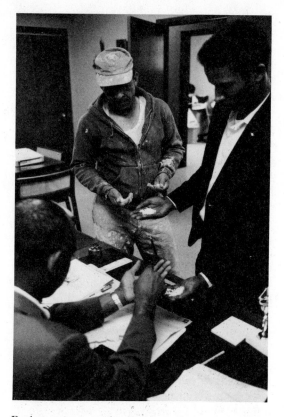

Basing wages on the number of items produced serves to give workers incentive to produce more, but quality of the product also is important. (Burk Uzzle, Magnum Photos, Inc.)

improve themselves to produce more goods. This method emphasizes individual differences, making superior ability a virtue. Efficiency and the production of goods become outstanding values, whereas culture and leisure come to be regarded as wasteful. Job security tends to be a matter of individual responsibility, and the standard of living varies among individuals doing the same kind of work. As strength and alertness decline with age, productivity also declines. Respect for old age is not encouraged by this pay method; the white-haired employee in the shop or office is not treated with consideration by the younger generation.

Although piece-rate methods use wages as an incentive to greater production, they do not necessarily motivate people to maximum effort.[3] If morale is bad, superior workers fear the reactions of average workers, who do not like the unfavorable comparison. Guarantees that the company will not change rates or discharge part of the labor force if production rises accompany the effective use of piece rates. When properly introduced, pay in terms of production is not opposed by labor.[4]

Experimental tests have shown that production increases with the introduction of incentive wage plans. In one study conducted during the 1930s, a change from an hourly to a bonus rate resulted in an immediate production increase of 46 percent and some additional advances during the next fifteen weeks.[5] The introduction of a piece-rate system resulted in another immediate increase of 30 percent. The two changes combined resulted in a production rate more than 100 percent above the initial figure. In general, employees regarded the piece rate as the fairest method of pay; there was less lost time and fewer instances of "troublesome" conduct when it was in use. But associated with piece rate were signs of greater stress: disagreements among workers, more fault finding with materials, and criticism of working conditions that interfered with productive activity. In one study, opposition to a group incentive came primarily from persons who did not understand the plan.[6] Large work groups also were more opposed than small ones.

However, incentive pay cannot be evaluated in isolation because the effect of a monetary incentive depends on the way other basic needs are satisfied, the economic situation of the worker, and the type of work.[7]

Incentive pay perhaps has its greatest value in monotonous work and is least valuable in machine-paced jobs. The emphasis on production in this pay method would perhaps create some problems in service jobs because it might motivate poor service and strain public relations. The difficulty of measuring and improving productivity in service and other white-collar jobs has been a continuing problem for business; the relatively low productivity of such jobs has been cited as an impediment to growth in the real (adjusted for inflation) gross national product.

Perhaps the greatest obstacle to incentive methods of pay is the employee's fear of the consequences of increased production. A survey showed that 40 percent of the manual workers believed a worker should turn out the average amount of work but not more. Of these, 41 percent were of the opinion that management would raise standards or cut rates if production increased, and 23 percent feared that they would be unpopular with the other workers if they did more than the average amount of work.[8]

HOURLY PAY

The method of paying wages by the hour or day fails to recognize the fact that individuals differ in ability. One person can put in time as well as another, so all people become "equal." As a consequence, the superior individual is not encouraged to exert beyond the point of a comfortable pace. Social pressure and the possibility of discharge might motivate substandard performers, but these factors then become negative incentives. The daily-wage method fails to use pay as an incentive to production but uses it only to get persons to report for work and put in their time.

To obtain any individual exertion, other incentives must be used; in actual practice, these are invariably present in one form or another. The policy of making promotions in terms of merit, for example, uses the principle of pay in terms of merit or productivity. However, this practice can lead to poor placement, since the job on the next level may require different abilities. Promotion can only be an effective reward if the new job uses the individual's strengths and makes no great demands on weaknesses. If promotion is an indiscriminate reward for good performance on the present job, employees tend to become stranded on jobs they are least able to perform.

Bonus methods combine day wages with piece work. Bonuses distributed at the end of the year are too remote to be highly effective, for the effectiveness of an incentive varies inversely with its remoteness. Thus, the use of short-range merit bonuses suggested by T. W. Costello and S. S. Zalkind might be expected to influence employee behavior more than an annual plan.[9]

The method of payment by the hour does not penalize old age. Neither differences in age nor differences in experience and ability influence pay; for this reason, older workers, as well as those who are less experienced or of inferior ability, favor it over piece rates. In many ways, it promotes a kind of equality, but in an artificial form.

Perhaps the strongest factor in making this method of pay acceptable is that it cannot be abused by management. Favoritism, discriminatory rates, and competition between workers to obtain personal increases are difficult to practice when the job determines the rate. Fear of abuses by management is the negative motivation that influences a choice in favor of hourly wages. On the positive side, there is security in knowing what the wages will be, regardless of inefficient supply lines or daily fluctuations in ability to produce. The fact that superior producers must make up for the wages paid the below-average producers might be argued both ways. Persons of superior ability always have to carry more than their share of the social burden, regardless of the specific economic arrangement followed. The question is, "What is the fairest way to do this so as to recognize merit and not degrade persons with less ability?"

THE SENIORITY METHOD OF PAY

Payment of wages in terms of length of service offers security in old age and makes a person's declining years pleasant and comfortable. Individual differences in ability are not recognized, as all people have the same ability to age. Like hourly wage procedures, this method of pay does not induce people to exert themselves unless other motivating factors are added.

This method of pay encourages young people of superior ability to seek employment in other organizations in which ability to produce is the basis for pay level. The less qualified people would remain in occupations where seniority pay methods were used, since they need only wait to get promoted.

It is sometimes argued that a person's worth to a company increases with experience and therefore the seniority method approaches pay in terms of merit or production. Although an employee in a nonmanagerial or nonprofessional job improves with experience, this improvement extends over a relatively short period and as already pointed out (Chapter 9), individual differences in aptitude usually more than offset differences created by training. However, some seniority increases would be justified on this basis.

To guard against the undesirable effects of seniority privileges, some companies follow the civil service procedure and give periodic increases within a job classification, but require a person to pass tests or qualifying examinations to become eligible for a higher job classification. This practice limits the progress that can be made purely on the basis of seniority and actually combines merit with seniority pay practices.

WHICH PAY METHOD IS "FAIREST"?

The motivational effects, as well as the desirable and undesirable ethical values of each of the four basic methods of pay, are summarized in Table 13.1. Regardless of how management might feel about each method, claims for each will be made at one time or another by some group of workers. Good producers feel unjustly treated if less competent workers receive as much or more pay than they do. Employees resent it if they are not paid when their machines break down and they cannot produce. Line crews for a utility play cards in a truck or at the garage during a storm and still feel that it is fair to receive full pay. They feel that because they put in their time the company should pay them for it. Demands for portal-to-portal pay reflect the feeling that the company purchases employees' time, and as long as they are on company property, they should be compensated.

Employees also talk about giving a company the "best years of their lives," and because of this, they expect to be compensated at rates in excess of others, regardless of productivity. The alleged fairness of seniority rights is an honest and understandable feeling and must be respected.

Cost-of-living increases and wages adjusted to a cost-of-living index are ways in which economic need has been recognized. The role of wage and salary increases in fueling the flame of inflation is a complex and

TABLE 13.1 EFFECT OF METHODS OF REMUNERATION

PURE PAY METHODS	BEHAVIOR MOTIVATED	ETHICAL VALUE	MAJOR OBJECTION	GROUP FAVORED
Production	Increased production	Recognizes individual differences	Creates insecurity	Capable employees
Time	Reporting for work	Prevents favoritism by equalizing wage rates	Merit not recognized	Insecure and below-average-ability employees
Seniority	Long service in a given company	Represents a form of advancement all can expect and control; security in old age	Discriminates against new employees	Employees with long service

controversial issue. But as long as the prices for basic items, such as food, housing, and fuel, rise the fastest, people earning low wages will be hardest hit and will continue to press for pay increases.

The last column of Table 13.1 shows the group that tends to be favored by each method. People on low-paying jobs desire and make demands for decent standards of living despite their lack of productivity. Superior producers have higher levels of aspiration and make demands for extra pay for their superior services, and old employees feel justified in being rewarded for their accumulated wisdom. We recognize and appreciate the justice in each of these demands because all these values have arisen in our society.

Since values that exist in society cannot be ignored by organizations, it follows that the best method of remuneration will depend on the ethical standards a given society wishes to perpetuate. Industry can influence these values by its method of remuneration, but it cannot arbitrarily decide on one method entirely to suit its own purpose and interests.

The psychological analysis of different pure methods of pay does not yield a solution to the problem of the best criterion of remuneration, not only because of varying notions of fairness and the differences in the incentive value of money, but also because pay is seen as a livelihood and represents income rather than compensation. In modern society, it is not uncommon for employees to feel that they own a job when they have one and are entitled to jobs if they do not. Furthermore, a decent standard of living, regardless of productivity, is accepted as a right. It is not surprising, therefore, that a review of the literature on compensation as a method of motivation in industry failed to support any particular plan or theory.[10]

Financial incentives may influence the level at which a person intends to perform, but the intention determines the performance.[11] Thus, setting a goal is an intention, and method of pay might influence it. But the resulting performance would tend to match the goal set.

Two methods of pay were experimentally compared: group piece rate and hourly. Under the piece-rate method the supervisor was

MOTIVATING WORKERS FOR OPTIMUM PERFORMANCE

more likely to get a preferred solution adopted, and the production intentions were higher than when the pay rate was hourly. However, when an innovative solution was developed by group discussion, the production-intention was highest and the frequency with which these solutions were developed was unrelated to the method of pay. Discussion influences intention, but the method of pay can serve a persuasion function. Nevertheless, problem solving fosters higher levels of intent to produce.[12]

The wage plan that may be effective for an office may be inadequate for a plant employing unskilled and temporary workers. Similarly, changes in social legislation, economic security, and labor organizations alter the needs of employees, and wage plans must be changed accordingly. Because of these varying considerations, wage plans must be evaluated in terms of motivating conditions as they exist. A knowledge of motivation, therefore, is a prerequisite for the evaluation of such plans.

The most successful plans in profit sharing have involved employee participation, which seems to be essential to obtaining a plan that is perceived as fair.[13] Both the Scanlon and Nunn-Bush plans owe some of their success to the relationship established between management and workers.[14]

Fringe benefits play an important part in labor-management negotiations. When employees find some company offering a desired benefit that their company does not give, they are inclined to register dissatisfaction. To deal with this criticism, one personnel director has suggested what might be called the "green stamp" plan. The company would offer a number of credit points and a basic package from which employees could select additional benefits to the extent of their credit points. Thus, employees with different needs and responsibilities could se-lect the benefits most suitable to their tastes and personal situations.

EXTRINSIC VERSUS INTRINSIC MOTIVATION

In recent years, business has increased the proportion of earnings paid to workers as wages and salaries and at the same time has increased the number of fringe benefits. Retirement plans, life and health insurance, coffee breaks, and paid vacations have been added to wages as rewards for workers. Each of these incentives is intended to influence satisfaction with working for a particular company rather than to increase the satisfaction of the work itself. As a matter of fact, individuals are motivated to get through their work so they can reach the desired incentives. To enjoy them, the employees must be away from work. *Behavior that is motivated by what it leads to is influenced by extrinsic incentives.*[15]

In contrast, leisure activity achieves none of the extrinsic incentives associated with work. Rather, we must often pay fees to participate and perhaps give up some wages. These represent negative incentives. Thus, with regard to the obvious extrinsic incentives, there is strong motivation to work rather than to engage solely in recreational activities. This motivational pattern is shown in the top half of Figure 13.1.

As this analysis of work and leisure activities does not explain why people prefer the latter, certain incentives must have been overlooked. To explain the motivation for recreation, it seems best to regard it as having a purpose or a goal in itself. Play is often defined as activity engaged in for the functional pleasure it affords. It has no ulterior motive.[16]

An activity that is satisfying in itself has

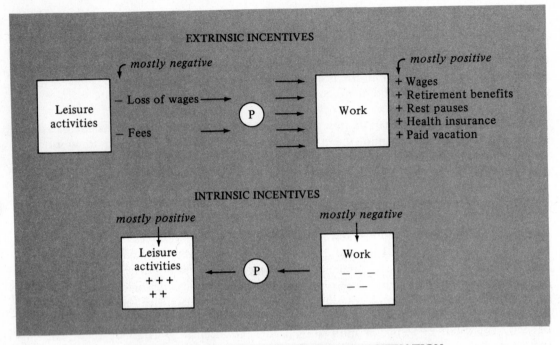

FIGURE 13.1 INTRINSIC AND EXTRINSIC MOTIVATION
Work and leisure activities generate different kinds of motivation. Extrinsic motivation is produced by giving people rewards (reinforcements) for doing something. The top part of the figure shows the positive incentives (plus signs) that follow work. Persons must perform the work to reach the incentives. Leisure has no such rewards and instead offers negative incentives (shown as minus signs) that must be experienced to reach the activity. Thus, extrinsic incentives clearly favor the work activity (as shown by arrows) over play. To offset this imbalance, we must consider the intrinsic motivational variables derived from the activity. What makes leisure activities more interesting than work? The lower half of the figure shows that some work activity contains negative incentives. Finding ways to remove negative incentives and ways to introduce positive incentives, as found in leisure activities, would be the best way to increase work satisfaction.

intrinsic motivation. A comparison of recreation and work activity indicates that work has more negative than positive intrinsic incentives, whereas recreation has more positive than negative incentives. The lower half of Figure 13.1 illustrates how the intrinsic motivational forces push the person away from work and in the direction of leisure activities.

In order for work to compete with recreation for people's time, most of the incentives used up to now in industry have been extrinsic. It would seem that more attention should be given to developing intrinsic motivation on the job. What can be done to remove some negative signs in the work situation and to introduce some plus signs? Making work situations more like recreational situations becomes a question that can lead to the generation of new forms of motivation.

Certainly we cannot claim that the hours for recreation are more favorable. Early hours for fishing and late hours for playing cards are not frowned upon, but would be sources of complaint in work situations. Similarly, energy expenditure does not explain the preference for play over work, because a person often expends more energy in sports than a company would dare expect on the job. Rules and regulations are present in both work and recreational situations, yet in one they are often taken as regimentation and in the other, they are regarded as essential.

Some factors favoring recreation seem to be more freedom in the choice of activity, freedom from criticism, less organizational structure, choice of companions, fewer status factors, less superior-subordinate conflict, and more opportunity to be oneself. It is also true that some people would rather work than play. This is indicated by the fact that wealthy persons, who are not in need of the extrinsic factors associated with work, may devote long hours to it. Usually their jobs are a challenge and contain the above-mentioned favorable factors. People who have jobs they enjoy and that, at the same time, offer them the extrinsic factors are indeed fortunate.

In recent years, a finding described by E. L. Deci has aroused both interest and controversy.[17] Basically, it suggests that the act of providing pay and/or other extrinsic rewards *in itself* reduces the intrinsic motivation of an activity. For example, Deci found that if a person is induced to do a task with low reward (low extrinsic motivation), the person will alter initial evaluation of its intrinsic properties to a more favorable light.[18] Moreover, in another study, it was found that the introduction of extrinsic rewards affected the perceived locus of causality (see Chapter 3) and feelings of competence and self-determination.[19] These findings are controversial, in part because they appear to conflict with principles of operant conditioning, which predicts that activities invariably become more attractive as reward for participation increases. Although this research has not been convincing to all, the principle (the nonadditivity of incentives) has found some support, according to one reviewer of the relevant literature.[20]

In the search for ways to increase the intrinsic motivation of work, opening opportunities for creativity (abundant in leisure activities like painting and carpentry) seems promising. One means — finding creative solutions to group problems — was discussed in Chapter 8. Encouraging employees to find creative answers (within the constraints of the area of freedom) in their individual tasks can be a part of every manager's job. Some studies suggest how this might be accomplished.[21] The growth of creativity, it appears, requires a situation in which both challenge and experience of success are possible. It also requires a trust in management, that is, that nonobvious solutions will be genuinely considered and objectively evaluated. In some jobs, such as those of research and development scientists, generating a climate where creativity can flourish is essential to success. In some firms, recognition of the special needs and motivations of engineering and other technical employees has led to the design of a unique reward system that recognizes employees' creativity and innovations.[22]

ACHIEVEMENT THEORY REVISITED

Although studies using the traditional need-for-achievement model (see Chapter 3) are still being carried out,[23] other researchers have questioned some of the traditional definitions of achievement.[24] One critique is based on the fact that jobs no longer fit the characteristics assumed in the McClelland studies, for example, a clearly defined task where some clear feedback on accomplishment is available. Further, McClelland's own studies show that values concerning the proper means to achievement and even the nature of success vary widely from one culture to another. Findings like this suggest caution in applying one culture's data about achievement to other cultures.

Some would-be modifiers of achievement theory contend that a more dynamic conception of human action is needed.[25] Deci's work has influenced this thought — that an activity can be overmotivated and therefore

can yield a decline in performance. Recent work in this area by J. W. Atkinson and others presents motivation for an immediate task in the context of the individuals' past decisions, present situation, and perception of future events and opportunities.[26]

Another somewhat controversial topic related to achievement theory deals specifically with the motivation of women, particularly those in jobs traditionally held by men. The original study by M. S. Horner, published in 1968, suggested that some women had a fear of success. In other words, these women felt that success in traditionally male-held positions (such as, in the United States, phy-

Women are being motivated to enter traditionally male jobs in greater numbers — here in a group of apprentice craft people at a training center. (Courtesy American Telephone and Telegraph Company)

MOTIVATING WORKERS FOR OPTIMUM PERFORMANCE

sicians or business executives) brought with it such high costs, in terms of a woman's social evaluation by others, that it was to be feared and perhaps avoided.[27] Replicative studies' conclusions have been mixed: some support, some fail to support the data. Some researchers attribute the failure to replicate data to possible "reactivity" on the part of study participants,[28] because values about the appropriateness of women in certain jobs have changed greatly in the years since the original study, perhaps affecting the studies' results.

THE LEVEL OF ASPIRATION

SUCCESS AND FAILURE AS REGULATORS

Success and failure are forms of reward and punishment because they satisfy or deny certain ego needs. What constitutes success or failure is a relative matter, and the psychological process that determines whether a particular action gives the satisfaction of success or the disappointment of failure is one's *level of aspiration.*[29]

Let us suppose a person is asked to roll marbles into a hole from a distance of twenty feet and to continue practice until able to make a score of nine successes in ten trials. In terms of actual achievement, the person may suffer continual failure and soon give up. However, this is not the way people operate. Regardless of the instructions given, each person adopts a criterion in terms of ability to achieve success. It might be getting one marble out of ten in the hole. If this leads to persistent failure, the level of aspiration might be lowered to one out of twenty marbles. If the performance results in repeated successes, the level of aspiration is raised. The difficulty of the situation, the ability of the individual, and the person's

attitude toward risk-taking largely regulate the level that a person's aspiration will reach. Success tends to raise the level and failure to lower it.

The level of aspiration functions as a regulator of success and failure and serves to protect the ego from frustration, while at the same time it keeps the goal ahead of actual achievement. Under conditions of normal and healthy functioning, a person never achieves the goal because the aspired-to goal moves ahead as it is approached. This permits the person to continue to exert effort. When the motive to achieve and the fear of failure are about equal, motivation is highest when the chances of succeeding are about equal to the chances of failing.[30] This amounts to competing with equals. So effective is the level of aspiration in serving as a realistic motivational objective that in one case it was possible to predict the success of hosiery work trainees by their level-of-aspiration scorings obtained during employment testing.[31]

Culturally imposed experiences of success and failure of males versus females and of whites versus blacks also seem to influence levels of aspiration. This has been measured by an activity similar to a pin-ball game.[32] The participants were asked to estimate on the basis of twenty previous trials the scores they would make on five successive trials. Comparison of black and white ninth-grade students (low socioeconomic level) showed that the black male estimates were based largely on chance with large shifts in estimates, whereas the white males were influenced more by previously made scores and their estimates were more stable and realistic. Females of both races were more cautious and less aspiring than males. The authors suggest that the black students are less inclined to believe that competence brings future reward and were reluctant to expect a direct relationship between good performance and high reward. Because females have learned that their ambitions are not as readily fulfilled as those of males, they tended to protect themselves from failure by setting their sights lower.

THE INFLUENCE OF SOCIAL PRESSURE ON LEVEL OF ASPIRATION

When persons are members of a group, their levels of aspiration are influenced by the performance of other members. Those below average in performance adopt levels of aspiration too high for their abilities; those above average adopt levels that are too low. To keep the level of aspiration of each individual commensurate with ability, therefore, only individuals of similar ability should compete with one another.

In the business situation, demands for production are usually calculated in terms of average performance. Low producers are under pressure, since their levels of aspiration tend to be raised by the superior work of the others. They become dissatisfied with their jobs and may quit, or they may rationalize their poor performance by blaming conditions outside themselves. They find fault with their equipment, their associates, or their supervisor. People with inferiority complexes are likely to have levels of aspiration too high for their ability.

In a job for which sixty units per hour was standard, turnover increased as the worker's performance approached sixty and reached a peak for the group that produced between fifty-five and fifty-nine units.[33] At sixty units, the turnover fell off sharply. The study design left little doubt that the turnover was caused by job dissatisfaction, and it is significant that the dissatisfaction was greatest for those just below standard. Apparently this group had set sixty as its goal

and, after exerting a great deal of effort, had failed. Those with definitely inferior ability were sufficiently far from standard so that the goal of sixty had ceased to raise their sights. It appears that a specific group objective influences the raising of aspiration level significantly only when it is close enough to an individual's potential ability to be a realistic possibility. In other words, a production goal must be perceived as realistic before it can exert a significant influence.

In contrast, workers with superior abilities tend to acquire levels of aspiration too low for their abilities. As a result, they experience success without exerting themselves. They tend to be self-satisfied and are content to take things easy while less capable ones exert themselves. Business suffers a great waste in potential production because it does not adequately use the abilities of superior workers. It is true that such individuals do highly satisfactory work, but in terms of potential ability, their accomplishment is low. Thus, business tends to push inferior individuals, some to the point of frustration, while neglecting to tap the latent talent of the superior ones.

Although the level of aspiration is influenced by previous personal successes and failures and by group standards, people with like personal and social experiences are by no means similar in their aspirations. Two influences accounting for these differences are possible. One appears to depend on personality variables. Persons showing greater anxiety about failure show larger variations in their levels of aspiration than those with lesser anxieties.[34] It appears that fear of failure causes persons to set their aspirations either defensively high or defensively low rather than realistically. Differences in affiliation needs also may cause variations in the influence of social pressure.

The other influence is more intellectual

and depends on judgment.[35] Although judgment is unfavorably influenced by emotional involvement and ego needs, the mere absence of such emotional factors does not assure realistic judgment. It is important to distinguish between poor judgments due to intellectual deficiencies and those due to emotional problems, because the method for dealing with the two causes necessarily differs. This need to diagnose is especially great in evaluating executives, because their decisions affect so many people.

Team membership also influences the goals set. Although groups and individuals set similar goals, groups seem somewhat less optimistic about reaching them (divided responsibility), and failure to reach the goal leads to lesser feelings of failure.[36]

RELATIONSHIP BETWEEN MOTIVATION AND PERFORMANCE

Figure 13.2 shows three possible relationships between performance and motivation. The solid line represents a relationship in which increased motivation leads to improved performance in equal increments. This possibility is unrealistic in that it fails to recognize the existence of a performance ceiling that is limited by ability. The dotted line represents a negatively accelerated relationship in which a performance ceiling is reached. This is a commonly accepted relationship. However, it has been shown (see page 329) that strong motivation may retard performance in some instances. Motivation produced by social facilitation has also been shown to impair learning, especially in the early stages.[37] Thus curves based on group performance on a variety of tasks might average out the negative and positive effects of increased motivation.

As discussed earlier, the findings on performance under conditions of high motivation reveal conflicting results. Increasing motivation sometimes is associated with an improvement in performance, sometimes with a decrease. The nature of a task used to measure performance is often crucial. High motivation would tend to increase the speed of running but might impair decision making. The curve represented by the broken line reflects reduction in performance with increased motivation and might accurately describe the influence of motivation in pressure situations.[38]

Attempts to oversimplify the relationship between motivation and performance also overlook individual differences in reaction to high motivation. Persons high in need achievement and those high in fear of failure differ in risk-taking situations.[39] Furthermore, pressures that motivate some people frustrate others, and when the frustration threshold is passed, behavior deteriorates rather than improves.

NONMONETARY FACTORS AFFECTING PERFORMANCE

Finding ways to incorporate more intrinsic motivation into the work situation requires innovation.[40] Nonfinancial incentives and methods for increasing job interest are forms of intrinsic motivation that lie in the direction of making work more like play. Additional gains can be accomplished if the recreation situation is used as a model for making practical adaptations suited to each particular work situation.

THE USE OF PRAISE

Praise is a form of ego satisfaction, and adults as well as children can readily be motivated with it. Too often, reprimand is the more natural procedure. Supervisors tend to

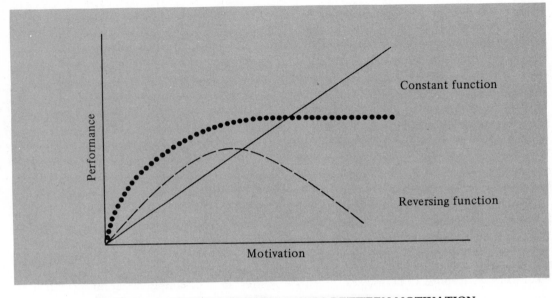

**FIGURE 13.2 POSSIBLE RELATIONSHIPS BETWEEN MOTIVATION
AND PERFORMANCE LEVELS**

SOURCE: From *Work and Motivation* by V. H. Vroom. New York: John Wiley & Sons, Inc., 1964.

expect good work, so they neglect to comment on such behavior but react to errors because they are frustrating.

A number of experimental studies have shown the effects of praise and reprimand on the quality and quantity of work of college students. These results are combined and averaged together in Table 13.2. Praise of their work was followed by improved work in 87.5 percent of the students and by poorer work in only 0.5 percent. Various expressions of disapproval of work caused from 11.9 to 66.3 percent of the students to do better, the number varying with the form of disapproval; poorer results occurred in from 10.7 to 65.1 percent of the cases. It is clear that praise for past efforts is distinctly superior to any form of disapproval.

Only one method of disapproval improves results more than it curtails them. This is private reprimand. All the other pro-

cedures listed in Table 13.2 cause the overall performance to decline. It is significant that the negative incentives fail to yield the intended results in proportion to the degree to which they damage the ego. Reprimand, ridicule, and sarcasm injure the ego and produce progressively poorer results. Public disapproval is more degrading to the individual than is privately expressed disapproval; thus, in the case of each of the three forms, the public form is more harmful in terms of work improvement than the private form is.

A comparison of work and recreational situations will reveal that praise and recognition for good performance are more common in the latter situations. In a game such as tennis, players often praise their opponents for good shots and console them for poor ones.

TABLE 13.2 COMPARISON OF POSITIVE AND NEGATIVE INCENTIVES

INCENTIVE	ORDER OF MERIT	PERCENTAGE SHOWING		
		BETTER RESULTS	SAME RESULTS	POORER RESULTS
Public praise	1	87.5	12.0	0.5
Private reprimand	2	66.3	23.0	10.7
Public reprimand	3	34.7	26.7	38.7
Private ridicule	4	32.5	33.0	34.5
Private sarcasm	5	27.9	27.5	44.7
Public ridicule	6	17.0	35.7	47.3
Public sarcasm	7	11.9	23.0	65.1

SOURCE: Modified from *Psychology for Business and Industry* by H. Moore. Copyright © 1939, McGraw-Hill. Used with the permission of McGraw-Hill Book Company.

EFFECTS OF PRAISE

To understand the variable effects of praise, it is essential to explore some of its functions and objectives. One is related to learning. Learning requires differentiation between correct and incorrect responses. Thus, rewards may serve merely to indicate correct responses, whereas punishment may indicate incorrect responses. Actually, any stimulus that is not highly distracting may act either as a punishment or a reward, depending on whether it accompanies responses that are designated as right or wrong.[41]

A second influence of praise is its effect on attitudes and morale. An athlete who is booed may suffer a loss of confidence, whereas cheers would build up confidence. Supportive behavior by teammates may act favorably on morale, whereas critical comments tend to isolate the individual. The source of praise may affect the recipient's attitude differently, but in either case, praise indicates acceptance of and liking for the person.

The third effect of praise is its influence on motivation. Praise often serves as a reward and makes the activity that leads to it attractive, whereas criticism can cause the individuals to avoid activity that leads to it. However, to serve in these capacities, the activity praised or criticized must be under the individual's control, that is, one must have a choice between alternative behaviors. Thus, the motivational effects can influence the attractiveness of activities that lead to praise, providing, of course, the person has ego needs that are satisfied by the praise. If the praise is perceived as recognition of work and effort, it is satisfying.

Finally, the effect of praise as an evaluation of the person or of a behavior must be included as an effect. As R. E. Farson has pointed out, praise may have a distinctly negative value in this context.[42] Inherent in the use of praise is the process of passing judgment. When one person passes judgment on another, the first can be seen as taking the role of a judge or superior person. Thus, if one person praises or criticizes another, a superior-subordinate relationship may be implied, and if the recipient does not accept this relationship, the comment may be resented.

Each of the four possible effects can occur, depending on the situation and the relationship between giver and recipient. *Praise seems to have its greatest value when given and received as recognition and is not perceived by either party as an attempt to control the behavior of the recipient.* When pay is perceived in this light, its influence on performance and satisfaction is greatest.[43]

KNOWLEDGE OF RESULTS

In Chapter 12 it was found that in order for individuals to show selective or discriminatory learning, they had to experience *what led to what.* Interests and motivation also seem to depend on a knowledge of what occurs as a consequence of behavior. A person would soon give up driving a golf ball if darkness prevented seeing where it went. In many situations, the learning and motivating aspects of the problem are so combined that their separate influences on improvement cannot be differentiated. Apparently both are aided by a knowledge of results, but frequently knowing how and to what extent such knowledge influenced each is desirable. Several experiments involving the acquisition of knowledge have shown that rates of improvement are at least 25 percent greater, and that interest is also greater, when persons are able to see what they are accomplishing.[44] It also has been shown that previously acquired skill is lost when reports of errors and progress are withheld.[45] Knowledge of results encourages both social and self-competition; failure to supply desired feedback may produce frustration.[46]

In one experiment, two groups of students were given a series of mental tasks requiring both accuracy and speed. One group was told to do its best; the other was told its results and urged to better them.[47] A total of 120 tests were made on the two groups. The final results showed that the group in which the individuals had knowledge of their scores did 16.5 percent better than the group that was urged to do its best.

Similar results were obtained in an experiment that required students repeatedly to lift a weight by flexing a finger and to continue until the finger was exhausted.[48] Eleven such tests were made at intervals of forty-eight hours. When the subjects knew the number of lifts their efforts had produced on previous occasions, they were able to make a greater number of lifts than when they had no knowledge of their previous scores. In 1980, the world's record for the one-mile run was set, and then beaten by a second runner within a few days. It may be surmised that knowledge of the new record motivated the second runner to beat it.

The extent to which improvement is a matter of knowledge of results and of self-competition cannot be determined. Certainly, keeping score is essential to competition, but whether knowledge of results introduces something additional has been questioned.[49]

Knowledge of results is essential to goal setting. In experiments using complex mental arithmetic tasks, it was found that supplying scores helped the person to set realistic goals.[50] Such knowledge, therefore, influences the *level of aspiration,* and the resulting benefits can be attributed to motivation.

Knowledge of results also influences team performance by facilitating communication and problem solving.[51] This is especially important when teammates must coordinate their activities. In one study, military defense problems were used with flight crews.[52] Two study teams that received feedback data and were given discussion opportunities improved an average of 42 percent, whereas two control teams improved only slightly more than 2 percent. The opportunity to analyze results served not only to improve teamwork but also to sustain motivation.

However, when group results are based on the summation of individual results, group feedback has little value. In an experiment in which individuals were grouped in teams, only slight improvement resulted from team-score feedback, but much greater improvement occurred when both team and individual scores were supplied.[53] Superior performers improved most from the information and showed a greater concern for personal success and failure than slow performers. When the task was changed so as to reduce the chances for success, the slow performers improved and showed more concern for group results. The fact that slow and fast performers respond differently to these conditions indicates that dependence on one another is important in attempts to upgrade team performance by motivational approaches.

COMPETITION

Individuals compete with one another not only for rewards but also for the mere satisfaction of winning. When prizes or monetary rewards are not at stake, the motivational factor must be based on some form of ego need. The person who wins may gain status, or social prestige, or experience need achievement, but we must also consider that the loser experiences failure and may lose status. Thus, each competitive situation can create both satisfaction and deprivation. We may argue that both effects have motivational possibilities, but the fact that these opposed effects may interfere with cooperation must not be overlooked. Sometimes the forces at work in competitive situations conflict with those involved in building positive job attitudes.

The efficacy of competition has been questioned by several studies. Greater productivity was achieved by groups of students encouraged to work cooperatively on problem-solving tasks (both puzzles and a human relations problem) than was obtained by those encouraged to work competitively.[54] A study designed to clarify these results found that noncompetitive, as compared to competitive, conditions favored attentiveness and involvement for both groups and individuals. But in this case, working in groups (rather than individually) was significantly related to development of high-quality solutions under both competitive and noncompetitive conditions.[55]

If self-serving behavior can be assumed to set up competition in conference groups, as appeared to be true in the seventy-two decision-making conferences studied in a business setting, competitive groups did not complete as many items on their agenda as did more cooperative (less self-serving) groups.[56]

The competition in recreational situations is usually healthy and motivates without causing hard feelings. Competition is involved in many play situations and is one of the basic motivating factors. However, disgrace for losing is seldom present, and face savers are furnished. The loser is credited with putting up a good fight and is praised for being a good sport; a poor showing is explained by bad luck or an off-day. In many games, chance plays a great part in determining the winner, and people can lose without feeling inferior. The experience of winning also is distributed among the members of a group because luck has no favorites.

When winning is a matter of skill, interest declines as soon as the same person begins to win consistently. If motivation is desired in competition, an element of uncertainty is necessary. We need merely reflect on how a sports event loses interest when the game is seen in a delayed broadcast and the outcome is known. Games and sports introduce uncertainty by having players compete with equals, limiting competition to equally graded leagues, making a certain difference in score the objective of play, and setting up various kinds of handicaps. These methods tend to give everyone a more nearly equal chance and therefore distribute winning and losing more equitably.

The importance of success and failure in competition was illustrated in a study that involved eight groups of children solving arithmetic problems.[57] This task was selected because the children already had mastered the essential skills and because productivity (number of problems correctly solved) was easily measured. Two conditions were tested: each of two competing teams was declared the winner on a fictitious basis in an irregular sequence, and one of two competing teams was fictitiously always declared the winner by an increasing margin.

Figure 13.3 shows the results of two

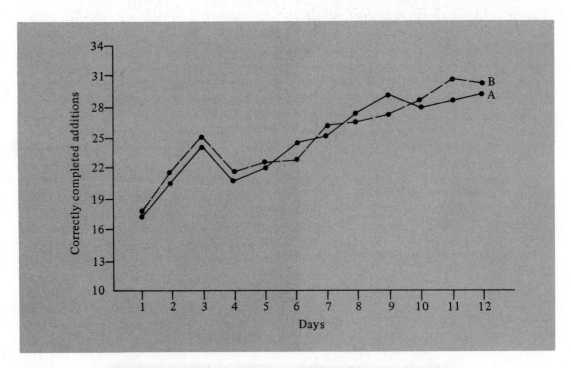

FIGURE 13.3 EFFECTS OF COMPETITION WHEN FICTITIOUS VICTORIES ARE RANDOMLY AWARDED TO BOTH TEAMS
The average number of problems correctly solved by the two teams of boys shows a rather progressive improvement over twelve successive daily tests. (Team A contained nineteen boys; Team B, eighteen boys.) The progress of two teams of girls showed similar trends.

Source: From Z. Bujas, N. Kopajtić, A. Ostojčić, B. Petz, and N. Smolić. An experimental contribution to the psychology of competition in public schools. *Acta Instituti Psychologici,* 1953, No. 18.

MOTIVATING WORKERS FOR OPTIMUM PERFORMANCE

groups of eighteen and nineteen boys, previously matched for ability, under the first condition. The trend over twelve daily tests shows a rather continuous improvement. The results for two groups of girls working under the same conditions show the same trend.

However, when one team was consistently declared victorious, the results were quite different, as shown in Figure 13.4. Here we find the victorious group (B) reaching a plateau and the losing group (A) show-

ing a decline from its best performance. The two groups begin with equal performance but separate after the fifth day. In this instance, repeated failure reduces motivation and repeated success fails to sustain motivation. Two groups of girls tested under the same conditions showed similar trends. When effort exerted by the losing group fails to show gains, motivation declines. It is possible that the fallacious feedback creates a distortion between effort expended and victory, and that this is an artifact influencing

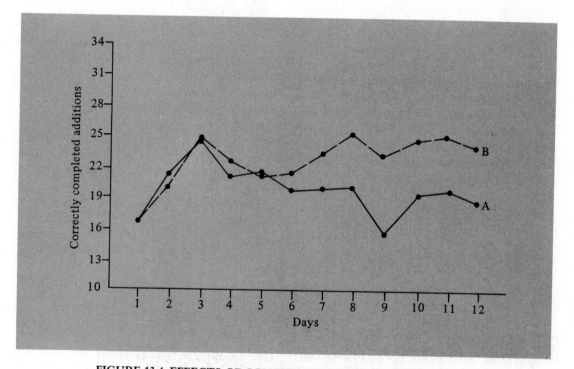

FIGURE 13.4 EFFECTS OF COMPETITION WHEN ONE TEAM WAS FICTITIOUSLY ALWAYS DECLARED THE WINNER BY AN INCREASING MARGIN

The average number of problems correctly solved by two teams of boys shows the winning team (B) leveling off, whereas the losing team (A) shows the effects of discouragement. (Team A contained twenty-two boys; Team B, twenty-one boys.)

SOURCE: From Z. Bujas, N. Kopajtić, A. Ostojčić, B. Petz, and N. Smolić. An experimental contribution to the psychology of competition in public schools. *Acta Instituti Psychologici*, 1953, No. 18.

the motivational condition. If this were an important factor, however, the motivational effects of the first condition (fictitious win/loss record) should have been less pronounced.

LIMITATIONS OF COMPETITION

A typical example of competition in business is that of giving prizes to first, second, and third place winners in sales campaigns. In order to distribute the opportunities for winning, breakdowns of territory are sometimes arranged. But winning is the rare and exceptional experience, hence such competition motivates only a few. Group competition has been used in connection with safety records. Frequently the motivation is so high that records are distorted, and *winning* instead of *safety* becomes the objective. In such safety drives, accidents often go unreported, and injured workers have been kept on the job so as not to have to report time-lost accidents.

Some supervisors have the authority and the desire to promote competition to increase production but claim the union would object, and this may be true. Such competition might be frowned on by workers because it would be regarded as a trick to exploit them. Further, it might shame slower workers, if not actually threaten their job security. Thus, the introduction of competition can make work more like play or more threatening, depending on how it is done.

If supervisors do not attempt to introduce competition directly but are concerned with job interest only, competitions arise spontaneously. These the supervisor can permit. Indeed, if no steps are taken to criticize poor work records, and instead attempts are made to spread out the experience of winning, these spontaneous competitions can help a supervisor make work seem more like rec-

reation. The use of group decision will help dictate how extensively this can be done. It is also important to recognize that there is little likelihood of suspicion if employees compete for records or scores that do not reflect production. These measurable items include attendance, punctuality, quality, safety, suggestions, housekeeping, and waste. At all times, it is important to be aware of the problem of fairness, and factors making for pressure and relaxed states should be examined. A certain amount of pressure is motivating and pleasant, but too much is frustrating.

Before setting up a competitive situation, managers should examine the possible motivational forces it will release. Since competition requires some kind of scoring method, motivation to obtain a high score is created. People will not only be motivated to perform better, but also to find other ways to improve the score. If amount of production is used as the criterion, workers may seek shortcuts that can reduce quality, increase accidents and waste, cover errors, or create problems for competitors; or it can lead to broken rules, falsified records, and poor service to customers. Thus, the score, rather than the production the score was designed to measure, becomes the goal. A fair criterion, one that cannot be faked, thus becomes a requirement in effective motivation through competition.

The goal should also be examined to determine whether it conflicts with other desirable objectives. Some goals are exclusive of one another, at least under certain conditions. For example, individual versus group results, helping a less able worker versus making a good personal record, competitive versus cooperative behavior, and personal pride versus consideration for others are pairs of objectives, both of which may be desirable, but attempts to increase one might reduce the other.

EXPERIENCE OF PROGRESS

Keeping score is an important part of any game. Without measured results or scores, there could be no effective competition, and knowledge of results would be limited. Scoring is also essential to creating the experience of progress.

It is sometimes stated that job performance on white-collar or service jobs cannot be objectively measured. However, job analysis reveals a variety of possibilities. The telephone industry has done a great deal in developing indices for measuring results on service jobs. For example, the effectiveness of a repair crew is measured in several dimensions, each determined monthly: (1) production — the number of visits per worker per day; (2) quality — percentage of repairs that required two or more visits within a month; and (3) service — percentage of times a customer called twice before the employee arrived. Other work groups have comparable indices for scoring quantity, quality, and service. These measures are in addition to records of tardiness, absenteeism, accidents, and a job-attitude index based on a questionnaire.

Indices of this kind, when used to measure rather than to criticize, are a source of interest to employees. All groups wish to know whether they are making progress, and employees watch the monthly or weekly charts of performance. New employees can readily be made to feel that their efforts are rewarded because they can see their improvement, but older employees do not have as much opportunity to experience progress. In groups that have already learned their jobs, nonthreatening scoring methods can be used to make work more enjoyable. When employees participate in designing fair methods of scoring, they can experience moving from one aspect of the job to another and experience progress by solving one problem after another.

One limitation here is that the more effectively a job is mastered, the more difficult it becomes to progress. Extra effort does little to reduce accidents, improve quality, or increase production if these are already near optimum. If effort spent is to be rewarding, improvement must show up clearly in the results. This fact suggests that progress charts should have units of improvement spaced farther and farther apart as improvement occurs. Figure 13.5 illustrates this method of charting so as to magnify progress. It is clear that Curve A communicates the fact of improvement more effectively than Curve B. This way of depicting progress is not deception if an improvement of from 96.0 to 96.5 is as difficult to achieve as an improvement of from 81 to 86. Progress is experienced by wage increases. Even when the income tax absorbs most of it, executives (as well as other highly paid persons) are sensitive to small increases in pay. Obviously it is not what the money will buy, but rather its meaning as a measure of success that has motivational value.

EXPECTANCY AND MOTIVATION

The belief that our effort will result in effective performance is a motivational factor that influences performance. It influences motivation even more than the belief that effective performance will lead to certain rewards.[58] It is also apparent that expectations of reward are more likely to influence persons in high positions than in low. It is not surprising, therefore, that employee job motivation increases at progressive levels of

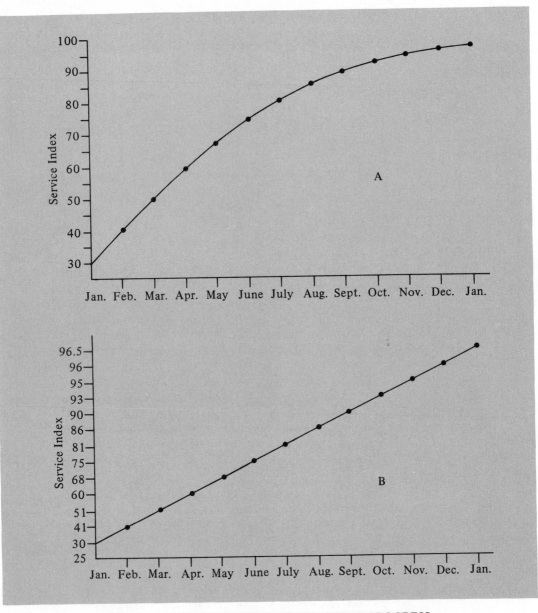

FIGURE 13.5 TWO METHODS FOR SHOWING PROGRESS

Curve *A* is the usual manner of showing progress in that the vertical axis shows equal steps. For skills that approach a ceiling, there is little experience of progress once a certain proficiency is reached. Curve *B* is plotted against a vertical axis on which the magnitude of the steps decreases as difficulty in improvement increases. This method permits the curve to continue to climb upward.

MOTIVATING WORKERS FOR OPTIMUM PERFORMANCE

management. Of course, we must not overlook the selective factor — positive motivation is an important trait in a person's promotability.

EXPERIENCE OF TASK COMPLETION

An important source of job satisfaction is sensing achievement. One basic factor in achievement is the experience of task completion. Activities that have definite completion points create involvement, and motivational forces to complete the task are set up. Regardless of whether the task is pleasant or unpleasant, the completion of the task becomes a goal, and the closer a person gets to the goal the stronger the force. One asset of many play activities is that games have completion points. Methods for increasing the experience of task completion in various types of work situations are discussed in Chapter 15.

SOCIAL FACTORS IN MOTIVATION

In sports we can observe what is called *social facilitation*. The enthusiasm of the performers influences the spectators, and the spirit of the spectators inspires the performers. It is recognized also that the enthusiasm of certain members of a team may spread to others, so that the total motivation of a group is more than the sum of the individual motivations. Group membership therefore becomes a source of motivation, and it may operate to increase the group's productive effort or it may operate to motivate the group to restrict its production.[59] Interdependence of team members and pride in group performance are constructive factors in group performance.[60]

Whether the superior performance of an individual is an asset or a threat to other workers depends on how the performance affects them. In recreational situations, superior performers are more likely to be regarded as assets, whereas in work situations, they are often seen as "rate-busters." The team situation seems to give the superior worker the opportunity to be helpful to associates, whereas when working as an individual, superior performance may appear as a threat to the less able — particularly when the supervisor uses the high producer as an example.

PARTICIPATION

A person who feels a member of a group must experience some form of participation. There can be varying degrees and several forms of participation, but it is generally accepted that participation in any form creates interest, and interest is an aspect of motivation. Employee committees and union representatives are sometimes asked to participate in management planning. The results invariably are in the direction of greater acceptance.[61] Of course, participation in decision making is the most complete form participation can take.

One theory dealing with task motivation and incentives focuses on the role of goal setting as central.[62] Locke argues that, in fact, orientation to work toward a goal is *the* primary motivating force of work behavior and level of effort. Goals can be both individual- and group-oriented. Workers may develop goals for themselves that are independent of both supervisor's and peers' goals. In business organizations, however, a great many task-related goals are mainly products of the group's norms and aims, as well as the dictates of higher management.

Independent of the above theoretical work, another writer publicized a more empirically based approach to the motivation of workers.[63] The method involved the joint designation of specific objectives or goals for employees (with their supervisors' guidance). Subsequent rewards in the organization were then supposed to be distributed in accordance with the worker's achievement of, or failure to achieve, these goals. As is true in so many cases, widespread attempts at implementation pointed out problems with the approach (as interpreted by managers). Objectives were sometimes generated by the supervisor, then forced on unwilling employees. In some jobs (for example, research scientist), specific goals and timetables for achievement were difficult to determine.

Although no perfect method of setting and accomplishing task goals has been achieved, the topic is still of much interest to researchers. It is still unclear, for example, whether participation in goal setting affects performance. Findings on the positive effects on job satisfaction seem more consistent,[64] although there is no universal agreement on this relationship either.[65]

Another approach has been to try to determine whether personality traits are significant in differentiating between organizational members who respond favorably to participation in goal setting and those who do not.[66] Thus far, results with this approach have shown few significant results.

Whether the ambiguities and conflicts in study results are effects of methodology or genuine differences from one task situation to another is not clear. According to one surveyor of the literature, most studies find no difference in performance between assigned and participative goal setting,[67] yet this seems to conflict not only with the large body of group problem-solving literature but also with many field reports of negative reactions to management-by-objectives

when the objectives are set unilaterally by management.

Conflicts and questions about various studies or approaches often indicate the magnitude of interest in an area of research, rather than the inadequacies of previous studies. Attempts are being made to understand the psychological processes underlying goal setting better — the roles of commitment and acceptance of goals, for example (which may clear up questions about the participation-performance relationship). D. F. Hall and L. W. Foster suggest that past success or failure directly affects goal-setting behavior (which would support some results of the need-for-achievement studies).[68] Thus, participation in goal setting leads to effort that increases performance and results in greater success; this success increases self-esteem and results in higher goals.

Another path for future research would be an analysis of ways in which external factors (pay, group pressure for conformity, economic conditions) affect goal-setting processes. Some researchers have reminded us that such factors may very well influence motivation in ways other than their effects on goal setting.[69]

Worker participation in management goal-setting decisions has been a way of life in many European countries, from West Germany to Yugoslavia, for many years. Whether this is to their overall benefit or not is still a matter of debate. As was suggested in Chapter 1, however, the desire on the part of American workers to participate in such decisions seems to have increased greatly in recent years.[70] Participation is seen by many not as a privilege, but as a right. Self-determination of our lives and taking responsibility for our own decisions have been topics of much discussion in the 1970s. It remains to be seen to what extent this means either

MOTIVATING WORKERS FOR OPTIMUM PERFORMANCE

self-expression at the expense of task-group goals[71] or the seeking of greater participation *as a group* in management decisions.

That some American companies are responding to these developing attitudes is exemplified at Texas Instruments, where employees throughout the hierarchy take part in planning and control aspects of their jobs. According to one employee, a former company president at Texas Instruments vetoed carpets for executives' floors on the grounds they might inhibit plant workers with dirty shoes from coming into management offices.[72]

If the pressure for employee participation in goal setting continues to be strong, we may anticipate a parallel continuation of research in the area. We may also see increased interest in one means of participation that has been shown to be effective in increasing satisfaction and performance when used properly — the group-decision method.

GROUP DECISION

The effectiveness of group decision as a method for increasing group effort has already been discussed in detail in Chapter 8. It is perhaps the most effective motivational procedure developed in social psychology. Although the forces that operate in group decision have not been isolated, it is probable that those listed below are important in making it an effective group procedure.

1. *Participation is carried to the point of action.*
Not only can members participate in a discussion, but they participate in determining what action should be taken. This effect makes a form of intrinsic motivation.

2. *Countermotivations are removed.*
Decisions sometimes are ineffective because there is a failure to accept them without reservations. When a group makes a decision, there is more complete acceptance.

3. *An acceptable and specific goal is set.*
It has been found that specific goals (for example, ninety units) are more effective than general ones (for example, improvement).[73] Goals set by outsiders may be as specific, but they are not as acceptable as specific group decisions. Specific and acceptable goals permit the clearest experience of progress.

4. *Social pressure is constructively used.*
All people are sensitive to the opinions of others, but sometimes these judgments hurt them. The child who is ridiculed by classmates for wearing shabby clothes is injured by social pressure, but the child who carries out the responsibilities of a class officer to gain the good will of classmates is positively motivated. Group discussion crystallizes the group judgment, and members feel positively motivated, not only to contribute but also to help others less able to do their share.

5. *The freedom and the right to participate give members recognition and ego satisfaction.*
This recognition in turn stimulates a sense of responsibility. There is nothing that develops the dignity of the individual and aids in emotional maturity as much as freedom and responsibility. Restriction is a form of regimentation and stimulates dependent behavior.

INCREASING JOB INTEREST

FITTING PEOPLE TO JOBS

Recreational situations give people an opportunity to choose the game or sport in which they wish to participate. If all persons were required to participate in the same games, there is little doubt that leisure interest in general would suffer. Work situations do not permit freedom of choice. An employee's selection of a position is often determined by (1) the jobs available at the time a choice is made, (2) the location of the job, (3) the wage or salary rates of various jobs, and (4) previous educational opportunities. These factors often conflict with a person's interests and aptitudes. Anything a company can do to place employees with their interests and aptitudes should improve job performance since both ability and motivation will be used to a greater degree.

MAKING JOBS IMPORTANT

Work is interesting and motivation is high when people see their duties as important. Motivation to do a good job declines when people do not understand the reasons for their jobs or feel they make no contribution to the total effort.[74] Job training should encourage an understanding of each job and should show how its activities relate to the success of the company. Company tours, films, and company meetings can furnish employees opportunities to see how their jobs relate to overall company operations. Supervisors should be aware of the need to respect the dignity of each individual.

During emergencies it is common for motivation to be extremely high. Utility executives are in full agreement that line crews can be depended on during storms and after disasters. Certainly, an important factor in their unique motivation is the feeling of importance and of being needed that is afforded the employees by a crisis.

WHAT EMPLOYEES WANT IN THEIR JOBS

NEEDS OF HOURLY WORKERS

The importance of nonfinancial factors in work is borne out by investigations of the wants of employees. In one study, 325 women factory workers in England were asked to arrange ten possible incentives in order of their importance.[75] High pay was found to be only sixth in importance. More important items were steady work and factors dealing with working conditions. In a similar study of 100 department store employees and 150 workers in other areas, it was found that the item of good pay was sixth and seventh, respectively, for the two groups in a list of twelve factors.[76] Opportunities to advance, to use their own ideas, and to learn, as well as steady work, were rated higher than good pay by these groups. Nonselling employees of a merchandising organization ranked good pay twenty-first in a list of twenty-eight items.[77] Factors having to do with fair and considerate treatment characterized the items thought to be more important.

In a comparison of union and nonunion workers, the amount of pay tied with working conditions for fourth place in a list of fourteen items among union employees and was in second place for nonunion employees.[78] The two groups differed to a marked degree on three items only. Union employees regarded fair adjustment of grievances and safety as highly important and put them in first and third places, respectively; nonunion employees put these items in the seventh and ninth positions. Chance for promotion was given third place by the nonunion employees and sixth place by the unionized workers.

Many items vary in importance, depending on the conditions under which the employees are working. The desirability of a good boss is more apparent when the employee does not have one. If promotions are made without regard to ability, this factor becomes the basis of a grievance.

A recent survey of workers' self-ranking

of their needs compared with estimates of their needs by union leaders and supervisors revealed some interesting discrepancies.[79] The average rank given each of the fourteen items is shown in Table 13.3. Security needs tended to rank high in all groups and were accurately judged by union leaders and managers. The greatest discrepancy in both the union leaders' and supervisors' judgments of the worker needs had to do with social needs (Item 5, "getting along with coworkers," and Item 6, "getting along with supervisors"). Factory workers ranked these items 4 and 5 respectively, whereas union leaders judged them to be 11.5 and 13, respectively, and supervisors judged them to be 11 and 12.5, respectively. Self-reported rankings of union representatives gave Item 5 a ranking of 2.5 and Item 6 a ranking of 13.

NEEDS OF MANAGERS

What people want from a job may reveal sources of positive satisfaction or avoidance of dissatisfaction. This was demonstrated in a study in which engineers and accountants in management were interviewed about past company experiences that had led to major satisfactions or dissatisfactions.[80] Each of 228 participants described at least one of each type of experience. It was found that this select group mentioned experiences of (1) achievement (41 percent); (2) recognition (33 percent); (3) work itself (26 percent); (4) responsibility (23 percent) and (5) advancement (20 percent) more often than salary (15 percent). This ordering places five satisfiers ahead of salary and indicates the importance of nonfinancial incentives. Even when salary is mentioned as a satisfier, it is in connection with recognition. Job security falls at the end of the list of sixteen items, apparently indicating that steady work is taken for granted at this level of management. There were eight sources of dissatisfaction that exceeded

the 10 percent frequency. Recognition, joy in the work itself, advancement, and salary appeared frequently in both columns, indicating that they remembered satisfaction when received and dissatisfaction when denied.

When the sources of satisfaction and dissatisfaction were added together, the order of the first eight items was recognition, achievement, work itself, company policy, salary, advancement, responsibility, and technical supervision. Interpersonal relations, another source was divided into three areas: subordinates, superiors, and peers. Relations with superiors was the largest source of dissatisfaction in the interpersonal-relations category. When this source was added to technical supervision, it became a major factor in dissatisfaction (35 percent).

JOB ATTITUDES: SATISFACTION, INVOLVEMENT, AND COMMITMENT

JOB SATISFACTION

The fact that *job satisfaction* has been a difficult concept to define and measure has not kept scientists and managers from trying to do so for the last fifty years. Job satisfaction is seen, for various reasons, as being extremely important. For some people, it is important for its own sake: workers should not be forced to do work that they hate or cannot take pride in. For others, satisfaction is a key to productivity, although efforts to demonstrate such a link conclusively have proved relatively unsuccessful.

Over time, knowledge has been accumulated about the factors that affect job attitudes, that is, the individual's favorable or unfavorable evaluations of total work environment — psychological and social, as well as physical. Clearly some work situations

TABLE 13.3 SELF-PERCEIVED NEEDS COMPARED TO JUDGMENTS OF MANAGERS AND UNION LEADERS

JOB FACTORS	FACTORY EMPLOYEES' SELF-RANKING	MANAGEMENT'S RANKING OF EMPLOYEES	UNION LEADERS' RANKING OF EMPLOYEES	MANAGEMENT'S SELF-RANKING	UNION LEADERS' SELF-RANKING
1. Steady work	1	2	1	1	2.5
2. High wages	3	1	2	2	10
3. Pensions, etc.	2	3	3	6	6
4. Not working too hard	8	14	8.5	14	14
5. Getting along with coworkers	4	11	11.5	7	2.5
6. Getting along with supervisors	5	12.5	13	10	13
7. Chance to do quality work	7	12.5	14	4	4
8. Chance to do interesting work	10.5	6	11.5	3	1
9. Chance for promotion	12	7.5	8.5	5	7
10. Good working conditions	10.5	9	6.5	9	8.5
11. Paid vacations	10.5	10	6.5	12	12
12. Good unions	13	7.5	10	13	5
13. Good working hours	6	4	4	11	11
14. Chance for raise	14	5	5	8	8.5
Number	65	16	6	16	6

SOURCE: From U. M. Gluskinos and B. J. Kestelman, Management and labor leaders' perception of worker needs as compared with self-reported needs. *Personnel Psychol.*, 1971, 24, 239–246.

MOTIVATING WORKERS FOR OPTIMUM PERFORMANCE

are more conducive to job satisfaction than others. Such factors as company attitudes toward employees and toward society in general, the type of supervisor, the cleanliness of the bathrooms, the lighting, ventilation, and attractiveness of the workplace — all give the site an atmosphere that influences the attitudes of employees.

Investigations show that employee work attitudes vary greatly from one company to another. In one study, data were obtained from 49,962 rank-and-file employees in 141 different groups from all sections of the country.[81] The average attitude score for the different companies showed significant variations and indicated that the employees could influence the score to an important degree. Such factors as type of work performed and wage level were relatively insignificant, whereas the type of boss and various forms of job satisfaction were very important. The importance of an immediate supervisor to the employees' job attitudes was apparent from the fact that departmental variation within a company was more marked than the differences between companies. Even when pay and hours of work were matched, wide departmental variation was apparent, and analysis revealed that the conduct of the immediate supervisors was the important factor. The importance of type of work and wages becomes evident, however, when other factors are equated. When jobs are classified according to ego involvement, job satisfaction is related to the type of work.[82]

Job satisfaction was shown to be important by demonstrating that a morale index was definitely higher among employees who were satisfied than among those who were dissatisfied on the following specific items:

1. A fair hearing and square deal on grievances

2. The prospects of a satisfactory future
3. The company's knowledge of the employee's qualifications and progress
4. Recognition of and credit for constructive suggestions offered
5. Friendly and helpful criticism of work or correction of errors
6. Pay increases when deserved
7. Recognition and praise for unusually good work
8. Selection of best-qualified employees for promotion when vacancies arise
9. Amount of work required not unreasonable
10. Pay at least as high as the going rate for the same type of work elsewhere
11. Freedom to seek help when difficult problems arise in work
12. Freedom from unjust reprimand
13. Satisfactory daily working hours
14. The company's vacation policy

The importance of these items in their influence on job attitudes is in the order listed. Many of the psychological satisfactions tend to be higher in the list than the purely material ones. However, the relative importance of various factors changes with the times. During periods when inflation rates are high, pay becomes a more important factor. Interest in pay also depends on the job: high-skill jobs make pay and working conditions less important than do low-skill jobs.[83]

Studies of job satisfaction (variously defined and measured) continue to pour out.[84] The first major study of job satisfaction that included intrinsic as well as extrinsic factors appears to be that by R. Hoppock in 1935.[85]

Since that time, scientists have labored to enumerate the psychological processes and the external (situational) factors involved. It has been suggested that a reasonable psychological definition of the concept of job satisfaction should take into account the *dynamic* (changing over time) nature of a person's self-concept, needs, values, and expectations.[86] A number of theorists feel that the key determinant of job satisfaction level is the perceived gap or match between the employee's job situation and important personal values.[87] Obviously, given that both individual and job environment are changing over time, satisfaction also increases and decreases over time, and one-time measures of satisfaction (such as questionnaires) cannot be expected to represent this fully.

RECENT FINDINGS IN JOB SATISFACTION RESEARCH

One study from the mid-1970s found that a high proportion (about three-fourths) of workers questioned expressed satisfaction with their jobs.[88] However, researchers doing *longitudinal studies* (over relatively long periods of time) cite evidence of a continuing decrease in satisfaction among American workers from the mid-1960s to the mid-1970s.[89] Whether this is due to rising expectations (mentioned earlier), deteriorating conditions, or other factors cannot be determined precisely.

A number of studies have sought to relate job satisfaction with some other specific job factors. For example, in the study by E. F. Adams et al., although positive correlations were found between satisfaction level and hierarchical level, differences were found between functional areas at a given level in the organization.[90] In another study, increased tension was found to be associated with lowered satisfaction, and perceived influence was found to be positively associated with satisfaction.[91] A study (described earlier) by Van Zelst demonstrated specifically that popularity within the group plays an important role in job satisfaction.[92] Group inter-

personal relations are clearly part of the job environment, yet it is important to consider their roles only along with others more frequently mentioned, such as pay, job properties (challenge, opportunity for creativity), supervision, and company policy.[93]

Studies, such as that by R. L. Hull and A. Kolstad in the 1940s,[94] have often shown pay to be listed relatively far down in a self-ranked list of job-satisfaction factors. It was noted, however, that at certain times, such as recessions or periods of high inflation, pay becomes a more significant factor in satisfaction. One study from the mid-1970s found that pay was related both to absolute level of pay and to perceived relative fairness, that is, to the degree that it met the individual's expectations.[95]

Money also played a role in still another study of satisfaction, but in a different way. P. H. Mirvis and E. E. Lawler attempted to quantify the costs of such factors as absenteeism, turnover, and low performance, which are held by many to be associated with low job satisfaction.[96] Another study that tried to evaluate whether low job satisfaction and absenteeism were positively related could not clearly establish such a relationship among the thirty studies reviewed.[97] Although this does not mean that no such relationship exists, the findings suggest that if there is, the relationship is more complex than first predicted and that there are probably other important but unknown variables influencing it.

Scientists have begun to turn from influences on job satisfaction intensively studied in the past (for example, pay, physical conditions, hierarchical level) to other, less obvious sources of influence. For example, J. P. Wilson et al. looked at the influence of organizational design and social structure on different types of workers.[98] Their results

MOTIVATING WORKERS FOR OPTIMUM PERFORMANCE

suggest that the hierarchical structure is associated with higher satisfaction for individuals who value security highly, whereas those who emphasize self-esteem are more satisfied in a relatively egalitarian social structure.

JOB COMMITMENT AND JOB INVOLVEMENT

Some researchers have begun using the terms *job commitment* and *job involvement* in place of *job satisfaction* for concepts that seem very similar. One reviewer has suggested that the latter term is broader in meaning;[99] however, all three seem to be positively related to the concept of *enriched jobs* (that is, positions where the incumbent has an increased role in planning and designing the task as well as in carrying it out); the three concepts' relationship to productivity, however, has not been clearly established. *Commitment* seems to be related to abstractions like *loyalty to* and *identification with* the company;[100] *causal factors* (personal characteristics, job characteristics, and job experiences) seem similar to those factors theorized for job satisfaction.

Unfortunately, the new terms do not seem to have solved the problems associated with the use of the older concept, job satisfaction. We still seem to be unable to find a universally acceptable description of the theoretical construct, and a clear link between that construct and the all-important issue of productivity.

Although relationships between job satisfaction and productivity are frequently obtained, they are not different measures of the same thing, and they are not invariably related.[101] A survey of railroad workers revealed that high- and low-producing sections did not differ in the degree to which they were satisfied with the work situation, the company, job status, and wages.[102] Productivity and job satisfaction both depend on many factors, and it is not surprising that they are related only under some conditions.

A review of studies of the relationship between job satisfaction and productivity also show mixed results, ranging from high positive relationships ($r = +.86$) to low negative relationships ($r = -.31$).[103] It is evident that the sources of satisfaction are only in part related to those inducing high productivity. Since satisfaction can come from the job, one's boss, company policy, work companions, and the challenge of the work, these mixed relationships are not surprising.

In some cases, high productivity is seen in association with low job satisfaction. This happens when people see their wants as incompatible with their realistic alternatives. If we ask people what accessories they want on a car, how important is comfort, and how much power they like in a motor, we may still not know much about the car they will actually purchase.

An industrial study showed that the most disliked feature of a job in Plant X was that it was machine paced.[104] However, 90 percent of the workers on this job came from another plant and from jobs that were not machine paced. Workers may stay on jobs in which they are unhappy in order to have high pay and security. Peoples' job choices frequently do not reflect the things that they want but rather the things that they fear. Fear of unemployment, therefore, may be revealed by the choice of a steady job. However, removal of the fear may not create positive motivation or satisfaction; rather, such a remedy is a method for avoiding trouble. In searching for factors that make for positive job satisfactions, we must go beyond the point of eliminating negative conditions.

A British study revealed that two-thirds of the employees on a bonus system of payment were dissatisfied because of the strain created, yet they failed to report their nervousness to the medical department because they feared they might be removed from a bonus job.[105] Such employees were in conflict because they disliked the pressure but felt the need for the extra money.

Although occasionally a study presents evidence of a relationship between job satisfaction and productivity,[106] many scientists would agree with T. R. Mitchell that a basic, generalizable relationship has not been shown.[107] The search for ways to increase productivity has grown more urgent as productivity increases have fallen off in the United States in recent years. Annual increases during the 1970s, for example, were one-half to one-third of an average of increases over the previous twenty years.[108] One economist has cited this phenomenon as the basic sickness of the American economy.[109] Failure by psychologists to provide managers with simple, reliable means of motivating employees to produce at high levels has left them relying on *demographics* (statistics about groups of people) for improvement.

Economists hope that the relatively slow growth of the labor force and the greater experience of women and youths hired in the 1970s will be forces that will help increase overall productivity. But reliance on these factors alone is inadvisable. Part of the problem is that managers are asking psychologists to produce ready-made, easy solutions to complex problems. Managers who want to increase productivity will find that the most direct and soundest route is that of trying to understand their workers in all their complexity and uniqueness.

One former blue-collar worker, now a sociologist, has written that workers tend to resist management attempts to increase production because of their experience: their reward for cooperating has been further demands for even greater output.[110] Moreover, managers lose their concern about people, he says, because of an excessive preoccupation with the product. Instead of viewing employees as their only route to success, some managers see them as obstacles to their own goal achievement.

RESISTANCE TO CHANGE

COUNTERMOTIVATION

Many misunderstandings arise because employees object to changes, such as the introduction of new machines and methods, adoption of higher standards growing out of improvements, and new policies. Often the changes are such that employees will benefit from them, yet they hesitate to accept them. Unions, for example, have frequently opposed work simplification programs and improved work methods, and it has therefore been claimed that they oppose efficiency. The forces operating in resistance to change may be regarded as countermotivations because they exert an influence in the direction opposite the intended or more obvious motivation. To overcome resistance to change, the forces acting upon individuals must be analyzed and dealt with according to their nature.

ANALYSIS OF THE CASE OF CHANGE-OF-WORK PROCEDURE

Let us examine the case described in the laboratory exercise at the end of Chapter 11 and study the kind of forces at work in resisting the change. The three workers on the subassembly jobs exchanged work positions every so often; this was their way of working. In Figure 13.6 this rotation method is called the *old method*. The time-study engineer, however, made an analysis of the work and found not only that each had a best position, but that no two had the same best position. It was therefore recommended to the supervisor that each work continuously on the position for which the worker had the fastest time. This method of work is called the *new method*. The problem as seen by the supervisor is to get the workers to move from the old to the new. The crew (shown as a circle) is on the side of the old method, and since they work on a piece-rate basis, they stand to gain by making the change to the new method. The arrow pointing to the plus sign indicates a force operating in the direction of change.

However, the workers object to making the change, not because of a disinterest in money, but because they anticipate boredom by the new method, fear rate cuts or layoffs,

and feel hostile toward the time-study engineer. These three factors are pictured as arrows pointing away from the new method and represent three forces opposed to change. Whether or not they change depends on how these forces combine and what changes may be introduced in them as a result of discussion.

Since the supervisor favors the *new* method and the group favors the *old,* a conflict between them is created by trying to get them to adopt the new method. The more this solution is pushed, the more the group tends to resist.

Two aspects of the resistance should be differentiated: emotional (fear and hostility) and situational (repetitious work). If the discussion remains at the emotional level, problem solving is hindered. The alternatives are limited to winning or losing. The leader needs to use skills to dissipate fears and hostility if the situation is to improve. But if the

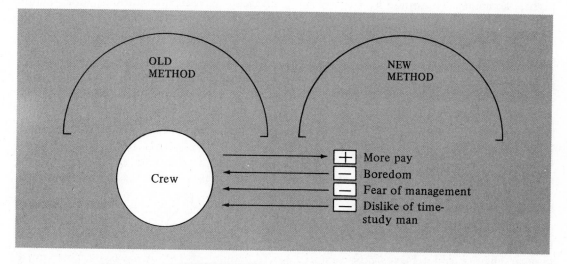

FIGURE 13.6 INTERACTING FORCES IN A PROPOSED CHANGE
The forces (arrows) are those set in motion when a supervisor suggests a change in work methods. The direction of the forces (to right or left) is determined by the positive (plus signs) and negative (minus signs) motivational conditions aroused or removed; they act upon the crew (circle), determining whether or not they will move from left to right.

discussion centers on the work situation and ways of reducing boredom, new possibilities emerge. These include: (1) two workers rotating while leaving the slowest worker on his or her best position; (2) all rotating between their two best positions; (3) rotating as before, but spending more time on their best positions; and (4) combinations of these. Such solutions are called *integrative* because they incorporate the facts about the causes of boredom (which the workers emphasize) as well as the facts obtained from the time study (which the supervisor emphasizes). A compromise solution would be a point between *old* and *new,* such as working the old method in the mornings and the new method in the afternoons.

Integrative solutions are of high quality because they deal with more of the facts, whereas the old solution ignores the facts of individual differences and the new ignores the repetitious nature of the work. Integrative solutions have been shown to have the highest acceptance (measured by faith in the solution).[111] Acceptance (Chapter 8) is a measure of the way that persons feel about a solution and hence influences their motivation to implement it. The greater acceptance is due in this case, in part, to the removal of distrust, since members of the group need not fear a solution that they helped develop, and in part to the dissipation of hostility toward the time-study engineer because they have used the data to achieve their own solution. Thus, the emotionally based negative motivational forces cease to be countermotivations. Although an integrative solution may not be the solution that the leader had in mind, it can be one that has high acceptance and achieves high quality. The emergence of an integrative solution from conflict is shown in Figure 13.7.

Persons trained in group decision are more likely to be successful supervisors in achieving high quality and high acceptance because they are less inclined to persuade or argue and more inclined to be considerate and entertain ideas contributed by the group.[112] Thus the group-decision approach as well as leadership skill is very important in motivating persons to adopt new ways.

UNION DEMANDS VERSUS EMPLOYEE WANTS

Why do workers strike for higher wages, fringe benefits, and shorter hours when these are often not rated as the items of greatest importance? The answer, in part, seems to be that if work is going to be unpleasant, employees will demand extra financial incentives to offset the undesirable conditions and shorter hours to escape the unpleasantness for as long a time as possible.

One important factor in determining the nature of a union's demands is strategy. If a union demanded better supervision, more pleasant working conditions, and better working companions, it would be difficult to prove whether the company had lived up to the contract. Hours and wages are measurable and are independent of opinion. When they are factors in contract negotiations, there is less misunderstanding of what is demanded and what is received. Pensions, paid holidays, rest pauses, and an annual wage are also objective and make good bargaining issues. Although union demands may reflect dissatisfactions, the nature of the demand may not reveal their source or nature. Sometimes employees cannot state specifically why they dislike a job, but they are sure of the degree to which they dislike it.

A study of 665 men and 639 women hourly workers showed that two-thirds of the men and half of the women did not want their children to do the same kind of

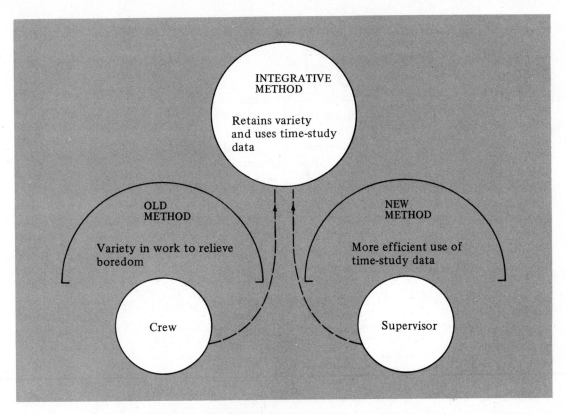

FIGURE 13.7 THE EMERGENCE OF NEW ALTERNATIVES
Conflicts may be resolved by the generating of alternatives that integrate facts favoring each of two conflicting alternatives. Feelings tend to polarize people in conflict and make resolutions difficult.

work.[113] Instead of material benefits, the study of their hopes and attitudes revealed needs for status and security, as well as such intangibles as self-respect and importance. It is clear that the intangible needs would be complex bargaining issues, and they would be difficult to express as demands; nevertheless, they might be major determiners of job satisfaction and, perhaps, productivity.

LIMITATIONS OF STATUS

The need for status and the need of workers to feel important create some interesting problems. Who is to generate the need satis-fiers, and will there be enough to go around? How can we increase the status of all work-ers when status implies the ranking of peo-ple? Granted, material conditions can be im-proved and the dignity of people increased, but is it realistic to assume that a genuinely egalitarian society is possible and that such a society would satisfy needs for status?

A WORD OF CAUTION

Questionnaires, studies of wants, or even good interviews cannot uncover what pro-duces the greatest satisfaction. Dislikes can be located more readily than satisfactions, but removal or correction of irritations is not the study of satisfaction. Happiness is a relative matter, and we can compare satisfactions only in the light of previous personal experience. The limiting factor is the unknown.

How happy would certain conditions, not ever experienced by a person, make that person? Most employees *could* not have recommended or requested group-decision methods in management. This way of leading groups first had to be invented before it could be experienced to any appreciable degree. Similarly, methods of interviewing, listening skills, improved work procedures, good lighting, fair employment tests, and so on, have been developed experimentally, and their value has then been tested in terms of the results produced. It is by this experimental method that new products are discovered, and through this method that major advances are made. When the experimental method is used to test *grounded theory* (theory generated from observations in businesses), we have the best of both worlds.

NOTES

1. Wolfe, J. B. Effectiveness of token-rewards for chimpanzees. *Comp. Psychol. Monogr.,* 1936, *12,* 1–77.
2. Newcomb, T. M. *Personality and social change.* New York: Dryden, 1943, p. 149. See also A. H. Maslow, *Motivation and personality.* New York: Harper, 1954.
3. Adams, J. S., and Rosenbaum, W. The relationship of worker productivity to cognitive dissonance about wage inequities. *J. Appl. Psychol.,* 1962, *46,* 161–164.
4. Davis, N. M. Some psychological conflicts caused by group bonus methods of payment. *Brit. J. Indust. Med.,* 1953, *10,* 18–26.
5. Wyatt, S. Incentives in repetitive work: A practical experiment in a factory. Indust. Health Res. Bd. Rep. No. 69, London, 1934.
6. Campbell, H. Group incentive payment schemes: the effect of lack of understanding and of group size. *Occup. Psychol.,* 1952, *26,* 15–21.
7. Mace, C. A. Incentives: Some experimental studies. London: Indus. Health Res. Bd. Rep. No. 72, 1935; Skinner, B. F. *Science and human behavior.* New York: Macmillan, 1953, Chapter 25.
8. What the factory worker really thinks about productivity, nationalization of industry and labor in politics. *Factory Mgmt. and Maint.,* 1946, *104,* 81–88.
9. Costello, T. W., and Zalkind, S. S. Merit raise or merit bonus: A psychological approach. *Personnel Admin.,* 1962, *25*(6), 10–17.
10. Opsahl, R. L., and Dunnette, M. D. The role of financial compensation in industrial motivation. *Psychol. Bull.,* 1966, *66,* 94–118.
11. Locke, E. A., Bryan, J. F., and Kendall, L. M. Goals and intentions as mediators of the effects of monetary incentives on behavior. *J. Appl. Psychol.,* 1968, *52,* 104–121.
12. Maier, N. R. F., and Hoffman, L. R. Financial incentives and group decision in motivating change. *J. Soc. Psychol.,* 1964, *64,* 369–378.
13. How to earn "well pay." *Business Week,* June 12, 1978, 143–145.
14. Lesier, F. G. (Ed.). *The Scanlon plan.* New York: Wiley, 1958; Nunn, H. L. *Partners in production.* Englewood Cliffs, N.J.: Prentice-Hall, 1961.

15. Andrisani, P. J., and Miljus, R. C. Individual differences in preferences for intrinsic versus extrinsic aspects of work. *J. Vocat. Behav.*, 1977, *11*, 14–30; Broedling, L. A. The uses of the intrinsic-extrinsic distinction in explaining motivation and organizational behavior. *Acad. Manage. Rev.*, 1977, *2*, 267–274.

16. See review by E. Klinger, Development of imaginative behavior: Implications of play for a theory of fantasy. *Psychol. Bull.*, 1969, *72*, 277–298.

17. Deci, E. L. The effects of contingent and noncontingent rewards and controls on intrinsic motivation. *Organ. Behav. Human Perform.*, 1972, *8*, 217–229; Deci, E. L. Notes on the theory and metatheory of intrinsic motivation. *Organ. Behav. Human Perform.*, 1976, *15*, 130–145; Deci, E. L., Benware, C., and Landy, D. The attribution of motivation as a function of output and rewards. *J. Person.*, 1974, *42*, 652–667.

18. Deci, E. L. *Intrinsic motivation.* New York: Plenum, 1975.

19. Deci, E. L., Cascio, W. F., and Krusell, J. Cognitive evaluation theory and some comments on the Calder and Staw critique. *J. Pers. Soc. Psychol.*, 1975, *31*, 81–85.

20. Notz, W. W. Work motivation and the negative effects of extrinsic rewards: A review with implications for theory and practice. *Amer. Psychol.*, 1975, *30*, 884–892.

21. Csikszentmihalyi, M. *Beyond boredom and anxiety.* San Francisco: Jossey-Bass, 1975.

22. More incentives for engineers. *Business Week*, July 10, 1975, 36F–36H.

23. See, for example, Rhode, J. G., Sorenson, J. E., and Lawler, E. E., III. An analysis of personal characteristics related to professional staff turnover in public accounting firms. *Decis. Sci.*, 1976, *7*, 771–800; Greenberg, J. The Protestant work ethic and reactions to negative performance evaluations on a laboratory task. *J. Appl. Psychol.*, 1977, *62*, 682–690; Hall, J. To achieve or not: The manager's choice. *Calif. Manage. Rev.*, 1976, Summer, 5–18.

24. For example, Machr, M. L. Culture and achievement motivation. *Amer. Psychol.*, 1974, *29*, 887–896.

25. Machr, ibid.

26. Atkinson, J. W., and Raynor, J. D. *Motivation and achievement.* Washington, D.C.: Winston, 1975; de Charms, R., and Muir, M. S. Motivation: Social approaches. *Ann. Rev. Psychol.*, 1978, *29*, 91–113.

27. Horner, M. S. *Sex differences in achievement motivation and performance in competitive and noncompetitive situations.* Doctoral thesis. Ann Arbor: University of Michigan, 1968.

28. Hoffman, L. W. Fear of success in males and females: 1965–1972. *J. Consult. Clin. Psychol.*, 1974, *42*, 353–358; Feather, N. T., and Raphaelson, A. C. Fear of success in Australian and American student groups: Motive or sex-role stereotype. *J. Pers.*, 1974, *41*, 190–201; Feather, N. T., and Simon, J. G. Fear of success and causal attributions for outcome. *J. Pers.*, 1973, *41*, 525–542.

29. Hoppe, F. Erfolg und Misserfolg. *Psychol. Forsch.*, 1930, *14*, 1–62. See also Lewin, K. *Dynamic theory of personality.* New York: McGraw-Hill, 1935, pp. 250–254; Starbuck, W. H. Level of aspiration. *Psychol. Rev.*, 1963, *70*, 51–60.

30. Atkinson, J. W. Motivational determinants of risk-taking behavior. *Psychol. Rev.*, 1957, *64*, 359–372.

31. Heller, F. A. Measuring motivation in industry. *Occup. Psychol.*, London, 1952, *26*, 86–95.

32. Strickland, B. R. Aspiration responses among Negro and white adolescents. *J. Person. Soc. Psychol.*, 1971, *19*, 315–320.

33. Coch, L., and French, J. R. P., Jr. Overcoming resistance to change. *Hum. Relat.*, 1948, *1*, 512–532.

34. Atkinson, J. W. (Ed.). *Motives in fantasy, action, and society.* Princeton, N.J.: Van Nostrand, 1958.

35. Frank, J. D. Individual differences in certain aspects of the level of aspiration. *Amer. J. Psychol.*, 1935, *47*, 119–128; Some psychological determinants of the level of aspiration. Ibid., 285–293;

Influence of level of aspiration in one task on level of aspiration in another. *J. Exp. Psychol.*, 1935, *18*, 159–175.

36. Zander, A., and Medow, H. Individual and group levels of aspiration. *Hum. Relat.*, 1963, *16*, 89–105.

37. Zajonc, R. B. Social facilitation. *Science*, 1965, *149*, 269–274.

38. Vroom, V. H. *Work and motivation.* New York: Wiley, 1964.

39. Atkinson, J. W. Motivational determinants of risk-taking behavior. *Psychol. Rev.*, 1957, *64*, 359–372.

40. Herzberg, F. One more time: How do you motivate employees? *Harvard Bus. Rev.*, 1968, *46*, 53–62.

41. Bernard, J., and Gilbert, R. W. The specificity of the effect of shock for error in maze learning with human subjects. *J. Exper. Psychol.*, 1941, *28*, 178–186.

42. Farson, R. E. *Praise reconsidered: Some questions about the functions of praise.* Rep. #16. La Jolla, Calif.: Western Behavioral Science Inst., 1962; Farson, R. E. Praise reappraised. *Harvard Bus. Rev.*, 1963, *41*, 61–66.

43. Opsahl and Dunnette, op. cit.; Vroom, V. H. *Work and motivation.* New York: Wiley, 1964.

44. Ammons, R. B. Effects of knowledge of performance: A survey and tentative formulation. *J. Gen. Psychol.*, 1956, *54*, 279–299; Bilodeau, E. A., and Bilodeau, I. McD. Variations of temporal intervals among critical events in five studies of knowledge of results. *J. Exp. Psychol.*, 1958, *55*, 603–612; Macpherson, S. J., Dees, V., and Grindley, G. C. The effect of knowledge of results on learning and performance. *Quart. J. Exp. Psychol.*, 1948, *1*, 68–78; Rao, K. V., and Russell, R. W. Effects of stress on goal-setting behavior. *J. Abnorm. Soc. Psychol.*, 1960, *61*, 380–388.

45. Bilodeau, E. A., Bilodeau, I. McD., and Schumsky, D. A. Some effects of introducing and withdrawing knowledge of results early and late in practice. *J. Exp. Psychol.*, 1959, *58*, 142–144.

46. Annett, J., and Kay, H. Knowledge of results and skilled performance. *Occup. Psychol.*, 1957, *31*, 69–79.

47. Book, W. F., and Norvelle, L. An experimental study of learning incentives. *Ped. Sem.*, 1922, *29*, 305–362.

48. Arps, G. F. Work with knowledge of results versus work without knowledge of results. *Psychol. Monogr.*, 1920, *28*, 1–41.

49. Chapanis, A. Knowledge of performance as an incentive in repetitive, monotonous tasks. *J. Appl. Psychol.*, 1964, *48*, 263–271.

50. Locke, E. A., and Bryan, J. F. Goal-setting as a determinant of the effect of knowledge of score on performance. *Amer. J. Psychol.*, 1968, *81*, 398–406.

51. Smith, E. E., and Knight, S. S. Effects of feedback on insight and problem solving efficiency in training groups. *J. Appl. Psychol.*, 1959, *43*, 209–211.

52. Alexander, L. T., Kepner, C. H., and Tregoe, B. B. The effectiveness of knowledge of results in a military system-training program. *J. Appl. Psychol.*, 1962, *46*, 202–211.

53. Zajonc, R. B. The effects of feedback and probability of group success in individual and group performance. *Hum. Relat.*, 1962, *15*, 149–161.

54. Deutsch, M. An experimental study of the effects of cooperation and competition upon group processes. *Hum. Relat.*, 1949, *2*, 199–232.

55. Goldman, M., and Hammond, L. K. Competition and non-competition and its relation to individual and group productivity. *Sociometry*, 1961, *24*, 46–60.

56. Marquis, D. G., Guetzkow, H., and Heyns, R. W. A social psychological study of the decision making conference. In H. Guetzkow (Ed.), *Groups, leadership, and men.* Pittsburgh: Carnegie Press, 1951, pp. 55–67.

57. Bujas, Z., Kopajtić, N., Ostojčić, A., Petz, B., and Smolić, N. An experimental contribution to the psychology of competition in public schools. *Acta Instituti Psychologici*, 1953, *18*, 1–14.
58. Arvey, R. D., and Dunnette, M. D. *Task performance as a function of perceived effort-performance and performance-reward contingencies.* Minneapolis, Minn.: Technical Report, Center for the Study of Organizational Performance and Human Effectiveness. University of Minnesota, 1970; See also Campbell, J. P., Dunnette, M. D., Lawler, E. E., III, and Weick, K. E., Jr. *Managerial behavior, performance, and effectiveness.* New York: McGraw-Hill, 1970; Porter, L. W., and Lawler, E. E., III. *Managerial attitudes and performance.* Homewood, Ill.: Irwin, 1968; Vroom, op. cit.
59. Schachter, S., Ellertson, N., McBridge, O., and Gregory, D. An experimental study of cohesiveness and productivity. *Hum. Relat.*, 1951, *4*, 229–238; Darley, J. G., Gross, N., and Martin, W. C. Studies of group behavior: Factors associated with the productivity of groups. *J. Appl. Psychol.*, 1952, *36*, 396–403. .
60. Berkowitz, L., and Levy, B. I. Pride in group performance and group-task motivation. *J. Abnorm. Soc. Psychol.*, 1956, *53*, 300–306.
61. Jaques, E. *The changing culture of a factory.* New York: Dryden, 1952; Nunn, op. cit.
62. Locke, E. A. Toward a theory of task motivation and incentives. *Org. Behav. Human Perform.*, 1968, *3*, 157–189.
63. Odiorne, G. *Management by objectives.* New York: Pitman, 1965.
64. See, for example, Ivancevich, J. M. Effects of goal setting on performance and job satisfaction. *J. Appl. Psychol.*, 1976, *61*, 605–612; Latham, G. P., and Baldes, J. J. The practical significance of Locke's theory of goal setting. *J. Appl. Psychol.*, 1975, *60*, 122–124; Greller, M. M. Subordinate participation and reactions to the appraisal interview. *J. Appl. Psychol.*, 1975, *60*, 544–549; Steers, R. M. Factors affecting job attitudes in a goal-setting environment. *Acad. Manage. J.*, 1976, *19*, 6–16.
65. White, S., Mitchell, T. R., and Bell, C. H. Goal setting, evaluation apprehension, and social cues as determinants of job performance and job satisfaction in a simulated organization. *J. Appl. Psychol.*, 1977, *62*, 665–673.
66. See, for example, Abdel-Halim, A. A., and Rowland, K. M. Some personality determinants of the effects of participation: A further investigation. *Personnel Psychol.*, 1976, *29*, 41–45; Arvey, R. D., Dewhirst, H. D., and Boling, J. C. Relationships between goal clarity, participation in goal setting and personality characteristics on job satisfaction in a scientific organization. *J. Appl. Psychol.*, 1976, *61*, 103–105; Latham, G. P., and Yukl, G. A. Effects of assigned and participative goal setting on performance and job satisfaction. *J. Appl. Psychol.*, 1976, *61*, 166–171; Latham, G. P., Mitchell, T. R., and Dossett, D. L. The importance of participative goal setting and anticipated rewards on goal difficulty and job performance. *J. Appl. Psychol.* (in press).
67. Mitchell, T. R. Organizational behavior. *Ann. Rev. Psychol.*, 1979, *30*, 243–281. See also Ivancevich, J. M. Different goal setting treatments and their effects on performance and job satisfaction. *Acad. Manage. J.*, 1977, *20*, 406–419, the results of which support Mitchell's position.
68. Hall, D. F., and Foster, L. W. A psychological success cycle and goal setting: Goals, performance and attitudes. *Acad. Manage. J.*, 1977, *20*, 282–290.
69. See, for example, Terborg, J. The motivational components of goal setting. *J. Appl. Psychol.*, 1976, *61*, 613–621.
70. See Yankelovitch, D. Turbulence in the working world: Angry workers, happy grads. *Psychol. Today*, 1974, *8*, 80–89.
71. Mills, T. M. *The sociology of small groups.* Englewood Cliffs, N.J.: Prentice-Hall, 1967, Chapter 7.
72. Ways, M. The American kind of worker participation. *Fortune*, 1976, *94*(4), 168–171ff.

73. See Chapter 8; also French, J. R. P., Jr. Field experiments: Changing group productivity. In J. G. Miller (Ed.), *Experiments in social process.* New York: McGraw-Hill, 1950, pp. 81–96.

74. Wickert, F. R. Turnover and employee's feelings of ego-involvement in the day-to-day operation of a company. *Personnel Psychol.,* 1951, *4,* 1–14.

75. Wyatt, S. Langdon, J. N., and Stock, F. G. L. Fatigue and boredom in repetitive work. Indust. Health Res. Bd., 1937, Rep. No. 77, pp. 43–46.

76. Chant, S. N. F. Measuring the factors that make a job interesting. *Personnel J.,* 1932, *11,* 1–4.

77. Houser, J. D. *What people want from business.* New York: McGraw-Hill, 1938, p. 29.

78. Hersey, R. B. Psychology of workers. *Personnel J.,* 1936, *14,* 291–296.

79. Gluskinos, U. M., and Kestelman, B. J. Management and labor leaders' perception of worker needs as compared with self-reported needs. *Personnel Psychol.,* 1971, *24,* 239–246.

80. Herzberg, F., Mausner, B., and Snyderman, B. B. *The motivation to work,* 3rd ed. New York: Wiley, 1959. See also Danielson, L. E. *Characteristics of engineers and scientists.* Ann Arbor, Mich.: Bureau of Industrial Relations, University of Michigan, 1960.

81. Hull, R. L., and Kolstad, A. Morale on the job. In G. Watson (Ed.), *Civilian morale.* Boston: Houghton Mifflin, 1942, pp. 349–364.

82. Gurin, G., Veroff, J., and Feld, S. *Americans view mental health.* New York: Basic Books, 1960.

83. Fairchild, M. Skill and specialization. *Personnel J.,* 1930, *9,* 28–71, 128–175; Adams, E. F., Laker, D. R., and Hulin, C. L. An investigation of the influence of job level and functional specialty on job attitudes and perception. *J. Appl. Psychol.,* 1977, *62,* 335–343.

84. For three overviews of this literature, see James, L. R., and Jones, A. P. Organizational structure: A review of structural dimensions and their conceptual relationships with individual attitudes and behavior. *Organ. Behav. Human Perform.,* 1976, *19,* 74–113; Berger, C. J., and Cummings, L. L. Organizational structure, attitudes and behaviors. In B. Staw (Ed.), *Research in organizational behavior,* Vol. 1. Greenwich, Conn.: JAI Press, 1978; Locke, E. A. The nature and causes of job satisfaction. In M. D. Dunnette (Ed.), *Handbook of industrial and organizational psychology.* Chicago: Rand McNally, 1976, 1297–1350.

85. Hoppock, R. *Job satisfaction.* New York: Harper, 1935.

86. Korman, A. K., Greenhaus, J. H., and Badin, I. J. Personnel attitudes and motivation. *Ann. Rev. Psychol.,* 1977, *28,* 173–196.

87. Katzell, R. A. Personal values, job satisfaction, and job behavior. In H. Borow (Ed.), *Man in a world at work.* Boston: Houghton Mifflin, 1964; Locke, E. A. What is job satisfaction? *Organ. Behav. Human Perform.,* 1969, *4,* 309–336; Likert, R. *New patterns of management.* New York: McGraw-Hill, 1961; Pelz, D. C., and Andrews, F. M. *Scientists in organizations.* New York: Wiley, 1966.

88. Kahn, R. L. On the meaning of work. *J. Occup. Med.,* 1974, *16,* 716–719.

89. Smith, F. J., Roberts, K. H., and Hulin, C. L. Ten-year job satisfaction in a stable organization. *Acad. Manage. J.,* 1976, *19,* 462–468; Smith, F. J., Scott, K. D., and Hulin, C. L. Trends in job-related attitudes of managerial and professional employees. *Acad. Manage. J.,* 1977, *20,* 454–460.

90. Adams, E. F., Laker, D. R. and Hulin, C. L., op. cit.

91. O'Connell, M. J., and Cummings, L. L. The moderating effects of environment and structure on the satisfaction-tension-influence network. *Organ. Behav. Human Perform.,* 1976, *17,* 351–366.

92. Van Zelst, R. H. Worker popularity and job satisfaction. *Personnel Psychol.,* 1951, *4,* 405–412.

93. Katz, R., and Van Maanen, J. V. The loci of work satisfaction, job interaction and policy. *Human Relat.,* 1977, *30,* 469–486.

94. Hull, R. L., and Kolstad, A., op. cit.

95. Dyer, L., and Theriault, R. The determinants of pay satisfaction. *J. Appl. Psychol.*, 1976, *61*, 596–604.
96. Mirvis, P. H., and Lawler, E. E., III. Measuring the financial impact of employee attitudes. *J. Appl. Psychol.*, 1977, *62*, 1–8.
97. Nicholson, N., Brown, C. A., and Chadwick-Jones, J. K. Absence from work and job satisfaction. *J. Appl. Psychol.*, 1976, *61*, 728–737.
98. Wilson, J. P., Aronoff, J., and Messe, L. A. Social structure, member motivation, and group productivity. *J. Pers. Soc. Psychol.*, 1975, *32*, 1094–1098.
99. Mitchell, T. R., op. cit.
100. Salancik, G. R. Commitment and the control of organizational behavior and belief. In B. M. Staw and G. R. Salancik (Eds.), *New directions in organizational behavior.* Chicago: St. Clair, 1976, pp. 1–54; Steers, R. M. Factors affecting job attitudes in a goal-setting environment. *Acad. Manage. J.*, 1976, *16*, 6–16.
101. Kahn, R. L., and Morse, N. C. The relationship of productivity to morale. *J. Soc. Issues*, 1951, *7*, 8–17; Wechsler, I. R., Kahane, M., and Tannenbaum, R. Job satisfaction, productivity and morale: A case study. *Occup. Psychol.*, London, 1952, *26*, 1–14.
102. Katz, D., et al. *Productivity, supervision and morale among railroad workers.* Ann Arbor, Mich.: Institute for Social Research, University of Michigan, 1951.
103. Vroom, V. *Work and motivation.* New York: Wiley, 1964.
104. Walker, C. R., and Guest, R. H. *The man on the assembly line.* Cambridge, Mass.: Harvard University Press, 1952.
105. Davis, N. M., op. cit.
106. See, for example, Organ, D. W. A reappraisal and reinterpretation of the satisfaction causes performance hypothesis. *Acad. Manage. Rev.*, 1977, *2*, 46–53.
107. Mitchell, T. R., op. cit.
108. Bowen, W. Better prospects for our ailing productivity. *Fortune,* 1979, *100*(11), 68–70ff.
109. Burton Malkiel, chairman, Department of Economics, Princeton University.
110. Shrank, R. *Ten thousand working days.* Cambridge, Mass.: MIT Press, 1978.
111. Maier, N. R. F., and Hoffman, L. R. Acceptance and quality of solutions as related to leader's attitude toward disagreement in group problem solving. *J. Appl. Behavioral Sci.*, 1965, *1*, 373–386.
112. Maier, N. R. F. An experimental test of the effect of training on discussion leadership. *Hum. Relat.*, 1953, *6*, 161–173; Maier, N. R. F., and Sashkin, M. Specific leadership behaviors that promote problem solving. *Personnel Psychol.*, 1971, *24*, 35–44.
113. Davis, N. M. The hopes of industrial workers for their children. *Occup. Psychol.*, London, 1953, *27*, 11–22.

SUGGESTED READINGS

Gray, J. L. The myths of the myths about behavior mod in organizations: A reply to Locke's criticisms of behavior modification. *Acad. Mgt. R.,* 1977, 121–129 (and Locke's response, 131–136).

Kidron, A. Work values and organizational commitment. *Acad. Mgt. J.,* June, 1978, 239–247.

Lawler, E. E. Reward systems. In J. R. Hackman and J. L. Suttle (Eds.), *Improving life at work.* Santa Monica, Calif.: Goodyear, 1977.

Locke, E. A. The myths of behavior mod in organizations. *Acad. Mgt. R.,* October, 1977, 543–553.

Luthans, F., and Kreitner, R. *Organizational behavior modification.* Glenview, Ill.: Scott, Foresman, 1975.

Patten, T. *Pay: Employee compensation and incentive plans.* New York: Free Press, 1977.

Schrank, R. *Ten thousand working days.* Cambridge, Mass.: MIT Press, 1978.

Terkel, S. *Working.* New York: Pantheon, 1974.

LABORATORY EXERCISE

DISCUSSION METHOD:
THE RISK TECHNIQUE

A. PREPARING FOR DISCUSSION*

1. Divide the class into discussion committees of five or six persons, each of which is to select a discussion leader. (In a small class, divide into smaller committees so that three or four committees may be obtained.)
2. The discussion problem is as follows: "What are the risks that a supervisor would take by practicing group-decision methods on the job with employees?"
3. Each risk should be briefly worded in very specific terms.
4. Each committee should divide its discussion into two phases:
   a. The listing of specific risks.
   b. The selection of the five most important risks.
5. The instructor will indicate when time is up for each phase.

B. COMMITTEE REPORTS

The instructor will receive the committee report and will
1. Call on each leader for a report.
2. Write a summarized statement of the risks on the chalkboard.

* This exercise is from N. R. F. Maier, *Principles of Human Relations*. New York: Wiley, 1952. Used with permission of Mrs. Ayesha Maier.

3. Check with the committee to see if the summary is accurate.
4. Summarize committee reports briefly.

C. COMMITTEE DISCUSSION — SECOND ASSIGNMENT

1. The instructor will ask each committee to discuss how their risks can be circumvented or reduced.
2. Allow about twenty minutes for evaluating each risk.

D. GENERAL DISCUSSION

1. Each committee report should be handled as follows:
   a. The committee will state its conclusions on how their risks can be circumvented or reduced.
   b. The class as a whole should then discuss the pros and cons of the issues raised.
   c. When various aspects and opinions have been voiced, the instructor will summarize the degree of agreement or disagreement.
2. Take a poll to determine the number of persons whose opinion of the group decision method has
   a. Gone up.
   b. Gone down.
   c. Remained unchanged.

CHAPTER FOURTEEN

EVALUATING
JOB
PERFORMANCE

■

■

THE RECOGNITION of differences in individuals' abilities (see Chapter 9) has suggested the desirability of evaluating the amount of work that they do on a job. Such measurements would not only bring to light the existing differences in ability, but would serve other purposes as well. Measurements would make it possible to differentiate between superior and inferior workers and thus permit analysis of their respective abilities. By measuring the characteristics of workers differing in productive capacity, it would be possible to determine whether specific abilities are present to a different degree in efficient and inefficient workers. These abilities might have to do with personality, intelligence, muscular coordination, sensory capacity, or body structure. A knowledge of the desirable characteristics would be very helpful in selection and placement of workers.

Efforts to design measuring devices have been going on since at least the sixteenth century, when Saint Ignatius of Loyola used a system of merit rating to evaluate the performance of Jesuit fathers. In the United States, General Motors has had a form of evaluation for some employees since 1918.

In measuring proficiency in work, we must distinguish between *merit* and *production*. Merit is a far more general aspect of proficiency than production; it includes productivity on the job as well as the other characteristics that make a person a valuable employee. We must also distinguish between production on jobs in which the number of units produced accurately represents how much a person has accomplished and production on jobs in which the accomplishment is complex and may not even involve direct contact with specific units of production. This chapter describes methods for measuring these different aspects of work and shows how each is used in evaluating performance.

MEASUREMENT OF WORK ON PRODUCTION JOBS

A production job is characterized by the fact that quantity is the only variable that must be considered when we wish to measure productivity. Counting the number of items produced is all that is required. Sometimes the parts produced can be delivered and recorded; in other cases, various types of counting devices are available or can be designed. Designing effective counters for various operations is an engineer's problem (see Chapter 11).

In actual practice, items produced vary in quality, so that evaluating a person's output by mere numbers is not fair. If a standard can be set up that sets the minimal quality level required, then this quality variable can be dealt with. Inspection methods that require that minimum standards be met take care of such qualitative features and permit measurement in terms of quantity, provided proper adjustments are made for defective production.

Whenever quality can be reduced to quantity by giving partial credit for repairable defects, individual production can be designated by a single score. Careful study of various kinds of work will suggest possible means for translating qualitative into quantitative features. To the extent that this can be done, evaluation of work output can be put purely on a production basis.

When people work in groups or teams, production must be measured by the team score. In such cases, employees should be matched on ability, and team spirit should be encouraged. The employees should have a voice in selecting teammates, and the company should cooperate in changing the make-up of the group to increase productivity, since one slow or uncooperative individual can destroy the efficiency of the whole team.

EVALUATION OF WORK ON NONPRODUCTION JOBS

A nonproduction job is one in which the work's quality plays a predominant part; this means that a complex pattern of quantities is involved in each unit of production. When a person's productiveness depends on a variety of considerations, it is impossible to use simple quantitative procedures. The work of a fire fighter, a police officer, a supervisor, or a teacher are examples of jobs that do not easily lend themselves to simple quantitative measurement. In such cases, it has been necessary to resort to human judgments to secure a measure of success on a job. Human judgments are subject to error, but if the source of the error is known, the judgments can become more trustworthy. But when we use indirect methods, we are actually measuring more than production; we are really measuring a person's merit or value to the company. Although productive ability is a very important aspect of merit, it must be recognized that merit is a more inclusive concept. A convenient expression for this relationship may be shown by the following formula:

Merit = Production $\pm$ Indirect contributions

Rating is a technique used to evaluate members of a group by comparing them with one another or with some standard. Thus, a supervisor might be asked to give each employee a letter grade of A, B, C, D, or E, according to the degree of proficiency and value on the job. This procedure seems little more than the usual method of passing an opinion on an employee, yet it is a distinct step forward. As the introduction of a grading system requires the raters to take some care in observing people's work, it encourages them to make comparisons. As soon as they make such comparisons, the raters are less inclined to use themselves as a model and are more likely to use the average person in the group as a standard. As pointed out in Chapter 9, an individual's ability has true meaning only when it is expressed in terms of its relationship to the abilities of other people.

PROBLEMS OF MERIT RATING

Many rating scales are designed so that one form can evaluate workers in a variety of jobs. A company may have three basic forms, one for the hourly paid, one for salaried, and another for management. The factors measured might be in such general terms as quality of work, quantity of work, dependability, attitude, and safety. An example of a simple rating form is shown in Figure 14.1.

A supervisor's rating form might include such job dimensions as leadership, planning, job knowledge, ability to train, emotional stability, productivity of unit, administration of safety, and communication skills. Most scales require the rater to assign a numerical value or a letter grade to each dimension to indicate judgments ranging from very superior to poor or unsatisfactory. Rating forms in actual practice differ considerably. The number of factors rated varies from as few as five to as many as twenty,

Name _____   Dept. _____   Date _____

Div. _____   When
assigned _____
Job grade _____

	Consistently superior	Sometimes superior	Consistently satisfactory	Usually acceptable	Consistently unsatisfactory
QUALITY OF WORK Accuracy, economy, neatness, etc.	☐	☐	☐	☐	☐

	Consistently above standard	Often above standard	Meets standard	Sometimes below standard	Consistently below standard
QUANTITY OF WORK	☐	☐	☐	☐	☐

	High in all respects	High in some respects	Satisfactory	Sometimes undependable	Consistently undependable
DEPENDABILITY Punctuality, judgment, follows instructions	☐	☐	☐	☐	☐

	Inspires others to work as team	Quick to volunteer or help others	Cooperative as general rule	Works well with some & not others	Works poorly with others
ATTITUDE Toward company, other employees, supervisor	☐	☐	☐	☐	☐

	Leads in promoting safety	Goes out of way to be safe	Respects rules	Sometimes violates safety	Disregards safety
SAFETY Respect for rules, influence on others	☐	☐	☐	☐	☐

COMMENTS:

INSTRUCTIONS:
1. Rate all employees on one factor before going to next factor.
2. Consider only performance on present job.
3. Place check mark in square that best describes employee.

FIGURE 14.1 MERIT RATING FORM

MOTIVATING WORKERS FOR OPTIMUM PERFORMANCE

and the number of grade steps range from three to eleven.

It will readily be conceded that problems, inconsistencies, and errors creep into measures based on subjective judgments. A knowledge of some of these deficiencies has helped to introduce certain refinements.[1]

THE HALO EFFECT

A common source of error in rating is the *halo effect*.[2] If raters have a generally favorable emotional response to a person, they tend to rate this person generously, whereas if they have an unfavorable impression, they tend to be overly critical. Evidence for the halo effect comes from two sources: different raters disagree on their estimates of individuals when confronted with the same information; and the ratings given a particular individual on a series of unrelated traits or characteristics show a striking correlation. First impressions, personal likes and dislikes, a tendency to generalize strengths or weaknesses of one behavior trait to other traits, and judgments influenced by the age or length of service of the employee[3] are the bases for the halo effect. It is not uncommon for a rater to assign approximately the same value to all traits.

The effects of this type of error can be reduced by having several observers rate the same workers. Various raters are likely to have different prejudices, and when they rate the same group of people independently, the various bases of the halo error tend to cancel one another. Obviously, this method can be practiced only when several raters are in a position to know the employees and their work well enough to pass judgment. *Raters who have slight contact with the work of a group only introduce an additional source of error.*

When it is not possible to have several supervisors rate the same individuals, it may be desirable to have workers rate one another. If they pass honest judgments, this procedure may be effective. Honest judgments, however, depend on the cooperation of the employees, and this exists only in plants that have fostered interpersonal trust in the past.

An effective method for reducing the tendency to give an individual the same rating on a number of traits is to require the rater to mark all employees on one trait before rating any on the next. In rating all employees successively on the same characteristic, the rater has to focus attention on a particular function, and the various individuals are compared within this one dimension. Tests with this method show that ratings given to an individual become more diversified.[4] This improved procedure thus achieves a result similar to that accomplished by increasing a rater's skill. To facilitate use of this procedure, the rating forms should have the names of employees listed under each factor, thus supplying a page for each factor rather than a page for each employee.

Because the nonproduction job requires consideration of several types of contributions that an employee may make, the process of rating should include measures of the various dimensions of the job. For example, a saleswoman may be judged not only in terms of her sales volume and the cost of her errors, for which objective measures may be available, but also for her effect on customers and her knowledge of the product. Certain aspects of her performance, indirectly associated with her production, should also be considered in merit rating. These considerations might include: her helpfulness to and congeniality with other sales personnel because of the effect such traits have on their work performance; her dependability in being punctual, because this may be important in planning for adequate job coverage; her relations with her supervisors, because this trait influences their assignments and peace of mind; and her care of the stock, because this activity aids other sales personnel and simplifies inventory.

In many types of work, these indirect aspects of production become so important that overall merit rather than quantitative productivity as such becomes the essential measure. As a matter of fact, they are so pertinent to the employee's value that they often overshadow the importance of production. Employees are more likely to be discharged for being troublemakers than for being incompetent.

Rating procedures are often used for employees who work on production jobs. Such characteristics as getting along with other workers, having a spirit of cooperation, and being dependable have become so essential that the method of merit rating rather than productivity rating is applied to both production and nonproduction jobs. These indirect factors also influence judgments of promotability and estimates of management ability. Although certain characteristics may be important in maintaining good interpersonal relationships, it is essential not to lose sight of the fact that productivity is the real goal, and that the indirect merit traits should influence this goal to some extent but should not become a substitute goal.

DIFFERENCES IN STANDARDS

Another source of error lies in the fact that all raters do not use the same standards. Some tend to rate all individuals relatively high, whereas some are inclined to be perfectionists and give few or no high ratings. Because of such differences, an *A* rating, for instance, does not always have the same meaning. One study found that 16 percent of the variance in rating accuracy was attributable to differences in such rater attributes as intelligence, personal adjustment, and de-

tail orientation.[5] Further evidence of rater bias was revealed in a study by W. C. Hamner et al., in which it was discovered that college students tended to give high ratings to same-sex workers.[6]

Attempts to correct this difference in standards have led to the use of order-of-merit ratings. In this method, the rater is asked to list the employees in rank order from best to poorest. This is somewhat difficult and time-consuming, particularly when large groups are involved. Also, it does not take into account the possibility that the quality of the individuals may show considerable differences in the various departments. The person in the middle position of a department may be superior to one in the highest position in another. As long as departments differ in the quality of the people they employ, it is difficult to know whether persons are rated high because of their own superiority or because of the inferiority of their associates.

Because the order-of-merit method is relatively time-consuming and also introduces other difficulties, it is not widely used. However, since the training of raters and the defining of standards help to bring the judgments of different raters closer together, the advantages of the order-of-merit method can be achieved, at least in part, in other ways.

THE IMPORTANCE
OF DEFINING DUTIES

A third difficulty arises because factors, such as leadership, dependability, safety, and even productivity, do not have the same meaning to all raters. To reduce this error, the functions must be defined in terms of on-the-job behaviors, and illustrations should be supplied. The meanings of the various ratings should also be illustrated. In the progression from simple to complex jobs, the problem of defining essential factors becomes more

MOTIVATING WORKERS FOR OPTIMUM PERFORMANCE

difficult. Job analysis (see Chapter 11) is a great aid in isolating essential behaviors to observe.

Definitions should avoid descriptions of persons and objectively define specific activities. Phrases like "gets work done on time," "follows safe practices," "notices things to do without being told" describe behavior. However, this practice causes a tendency to include a larger number of characteristics on the rating form, which leads to certain disadvantages.

THE NUMBER OF STEPS IN THE RATING SCALE

A rating scale should have no more steps than raters can reliably differentiate, yet should have enough to make the needed number of distinctions. Ordinarily we might suppose that the fewer the steps, the easier the job of rating and the greater the accuracy. However, one study revealed that optimum accuracy was reached with a nine-point scale.[7] This optimum number of steps may be expected to vary with the skill of the raters and with the complexity of the function rated, but nine may safely be considered as the largest number that should be used.

Another study revealed that raters are less willing to use a form requiring a two-point distinction than one requiring four distinctions.[8] People want to make qualifying evaluations, and when the number of steps is small, the number of borderline cases is large. Borderline cases make decisions difficult.

Most scales in use fall within the limits described and have four, five, or six steps. There is some question about whether an odd or an even number of steps is preferable. When an even number of steps is used, the procedure advocated is first to divide a group into the best and the poorest halves. Next, each of these is again divided, yielding four

groups. If six distinctions are desired, the two extreme groups are again split.

The character of the normal distribution curve suggests an odd number of steps. Most people's scores will fall in the center of the curve, and they are the ones who are much alike in ability. A classification for them is needed to avoid making many borderline distinctions. A scale with an even number of steps requires that the middle group be separated, obliging the rater to make distinctions between the many people who are the most alike.

THE NUMBER OF FACTORS RATED

The number of factors rated will naturally depend on the job's complexity. But the overall evaluation obtained from a few factors usually differs little from that obtained if many are used. One study showed that ratings on three characteristics (job performance, quality of work, and health) yielded the same results as ratings on twelve factors;[9] another study obtained equivalent results after fourteen seemingly independent items were analyzed and found to be reducible to six.[10]

Considerations other than the accuracy of ratings, however, must sometimes be taken into account. If employees and supervisors feel that ratings on a few items do not properly describe an employee, it may be desirable to use more items in order to achieve the confidence of both raters and those rated.

RATING AVERAGE PERFORMERS FIRST

In most practical rating situations, from eight to fifteen employees are involved. As both superior and inferior abilities are rare, such individuals are not likely to be properly represented in all groups. For example, the best producer in one group might be inferior to the best producer in another group. If we followed the common-sense rating procedure of using the extreme performers as points of orientation or as the ones to rate first, these two individuals would receive similar ratings.

The most dependable point of orientation is the group of near-average persons. Such persons are much alike and are sufficiently numerous, so that a few will be present in any group. These are the individuals on whom standards are based, and they should be thought of as satisfactory employees. Approximately half of a small group of people are similar with respect to any particular factor under consideration. Thus, in a group of ten employees, there should be four, five, or six persons who are most difficult to distinguish from one another with respect to each of the characteristics rated, be it productivity, dependability, or safety. These individuals should be rated as satisfactory (a rating of 3 on a five-point scale) on the factor under consideration. Once the middle ratings are assigned, the tasks of assigning ratings of one or two steps above and one or two steps below the typical persons are relatively easy.

THE WEIGHTING OF FUNCTIONS

Once employees have been rated on the way in which they perform various functions, the problem of combining the several ratings of a given individual into one score still remains. If a five-point scale has been used to evaluate functions A, B, C, and D, with values 5 through 1 indicating the best to the poorest performances, we could obtain a composite score by merely adding the numerical ratings. All functions would be treated as equal in importance, and no differential weightings would be involved. A rating form with four items would then produce a range in possible scores between 20 and 4.

Functions A and B, however, might be more important than functions C and D. In such a case, the ratings on functions A and B could be multiplied by some constant value, such as two. This would weight the first two functions, making the possible scoring range in our example 6 to 30. Another possibility would be to require minimum scores on certain functions. Thus, a worker who rates less than average in a certain important category might automatically be given an unsatisfactory rating in this function, or be considered for termination because of failure in the performance of an essential duty.

GROUP DECISION APPLIED TO MERIT RATING

In one company, supervisors tended to give high ratings to employees on high-skill jobs and low ratings to employees on low-skill jobs. This meant that supervisors were judging employees in part by the jobs they held, whereas the purpose of rating was to determine the proficiency with which they performed, whatever their jobs.

An experiment was designed to evaluate procedures for correcting this problem.[11] Twenty-nine supervisors were randomly divided into three groups. One group of nine was used as a control and given no training; a second group of nine was involved in a group decision as to what to do about the problem; and a third group of eleven was given a lecture on how to improve their rating skills. Measures of rating performance (indicating extent to which rating was influenced by job grade) were obtained before as well as after these attempts to improve the ratings were made.

The results showed that only the group-

MOTIVATING WORKERS FOR OPTIMUM PERFORMANCE

decision group improved significantly. There was no improvement in the control group, and the improvement in the lecture group was not statistically significant.

REFINEMENTS OF MERIT RATING

THE FORCED-CHOICE METHOD

Because merit rating plans reflect inaccuracies, persistent attempts have been made to improve the method of using human judgments to evaluate employees. One of these is the *forced-choice* procedure.[12] By this method, sets of four phrases or adjectives pertaining to the job are presented on a form. The rater is asked to indicate which of each set of four is most characteristic of the person rated and which is least characteristic. Examples of sets used for army officers are shown in Figure 14.2. In each set of four items, two are favorable and two are unfavorable. However, the rater does not know that only one of the favorable items is associated with success and only one of the unfavorable items with failure. The scoring takes into account only the checking of favorable and unfavorable items associated with good and poor performance. For example, a checkmark gives a plus value only when a crucial positive factor is checked as most characteristic and when a crucial poor factor is checked as least characteristic. Checking the alternative items that only appear favorable or unfavorable has no effect on the score, yet permits the rater to express likes and dislikes.

Among the variations of the forced-choice procedure are approaches that present blocks of two, three, four, or five statements, all either favorable or unfavorable, which discriminate among employees to differing degrees. The form using four favorable statements from which the rater is asked to choose the two most descriptive of the ratee was found most effective by J. R. Berkshire and R. W. Highland.[13] In addition to yielding high validities and acceptable reliability, this form appeared to be the most resistant to rater bias and was one of the two forms best liked by the raters.

The forced-choice method has proved its value over standard rating methods because it produces more objective evaluations, yields a more nearly normal distribution, and can be machine-scored, and also because the ratings can be related to valid indices of good and poor performance. To use this method, however, these prerequisites are needed: (1) a separate group of descriptive items for each job; (2) trained personnel available to develop the rating form; (3) objective agreement on the criteria of success and failure; and (4) willingness on the part of supervisors to pass judgment on employees even when they cannot tell whether they give one person a more favorable rating than another.

Forms may also be more acceptable if the rater is allowed to rate the degree to which an item selected from alternatives applies to the person rated. At least this was found to be the case when the form was used for self-rating.[14] Apparently the act of choosing an item that has little relevance to a person, even if it has more relevance than its alternative, makes the raters feel they are making judgments that are untrue. It appears that further improvements and simplifications are needed if the forced-choice method is to replace the less sophisticated rating method in business. Attempts to conceal from raters whether they are giving favorable or unfavorable ratings may reduce bias but at the

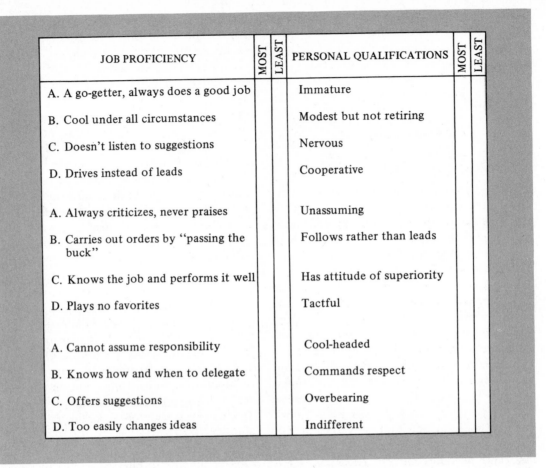

JOB PROFICIENCY	MOST	LEAST	PERSONAL QUALIFICATIONS	MOST	LEAST
A. A go-getter, always does a good job			Immature		
B. Cool under all circumstances			Modest but not retiring		
C. Doesn't listen to suggestions			Nervous		
D. Drives instead of leads			Cooperative		
A. Always criticizes, never praises			Unassuming		
B. Carries out orders by "passing the buck"			Follows rather than leads		
C. Knows the job and performs it well			Has attitude of superiority		
D. Plays no favorites			Tactful		
A. Cannot assume responsibility			Cool-headed		
B. Knows how and when to delegate			Commands respect		
C. Offers suggestions			Overbearing		
D. Too easily changes ideas			Indifferent		

FIGURE 14.2 SETS OF ITEMS IN FORCED-CHOICE RATING
The rater is asked to evaluate a subordinate by checking in each set of four items: (a) the one most characteristic, and (b) the one least characteristic. In each set of four items, one is related to success and another to failure, but the rater does not know the diagnostic items.

expense of cooperation. Yet this cooperation is essential to successful merit rating.

CHECK LISTS

To make employee evaluation as specific as possible, lists of positive and negative behaviors on a job have been developed, and supervisors are asked to check the descriptions that apply to a particular employee. This check-list procedure[15] has been refined

so that the items form a scale: each item has a value, depending on its importance.[16] Scale values are derived from preliminary research in which the pooled judgments of persons familiar with the job are used. Such persons are asked to arrange the potential items in various categories based on importance. Examples of items and their scale values for sale personnel are shown in Table 14.1. Only items on which the judges agree are used.

MOTIVATING WORKERS FOR OPTIMUM PERFORMANCE

TABLE 14.1 SCALED ITEMS APPEARING ON RATING FORM FOR SALES PERSONNEL

ITEM	SCALE VALUE
———— Is somewhat in a rut on some sales talks	32
———— Tends to keep comfortably ahead of the work schedule	56
———— Is a good steady worker	46
———— Is weak on planning	29
———— Is making exceptional progress	69

In rating a person, raters are asked to place a plus (+) sign, a minus (−) sign, or a question mark (?) in front of each item, depending, respectively, on whether they feel that the item applies, does not apply, or there is doubt. The actual rating is the average of the scale values of all items checked with a plus sign. Since the scale values do not appear on the form, the raters do not know how highly they have rated a given person. This method, like the forced-choice method, has definite merits in that it objectifies the rating procedure.

FIELD REVIEW

The field review is an approach to evaluating employee proficiency in which a member of the personnel department cooperates with the supervisor in developing employee ratings. The personnel specialist interviews the supervisor at the place of work, posing questions about an employee's performance like "What are his strengths?" or "Should she be promoted?" The personnel specialist later studies the notes and writes a tentative summary to be checked with the supervisor, who is invited to make additions or corrections. The supervisor is responsible for the final rating that is then prepared, but is aided by a trained person in its preparation and is freed of considerable detail work.

The field technique requires very competent personnel analysts plus management support. But the field review is advantageous in that supervisors frequently prefer to give oral ratings rather than the more usual written evaluations. Then, too, as the ratings are prepared by experts, they tend to be more readily comparable and more easily reviewed.[17]

CRITICAL-INCIDENT TECHNIQUE

The critical-incident technique developed by J. C. Flanagan is less a rating method than a procedure for collecting relevant data about employee performance.[18] Once a large number of incidents are recorded for each job under consideration, they can be analyzed to determine which incidents are critically associated with superior performance and which are associated with employee unsuitability, thus providing a basis for a scientifically constructed rating scale. This system provides standards for raters' judgments, accumulates observations of behavior upon which various raters can agree (rather than dealing with vague generalities or trait names that can be variously defined), and frequently helps decrease the influence of personal bias.

In one study, sixteen critical job requirements were developed for hourly employees of a Delco-Remy plant.[19] Through use of forms drawn up for the purpose, the time required for supervisors to record their observations usually took less than five minutes per day. In another study, managers were asked to report instances of behaviors associated with good versus poor sales personnel.[20] Out of 135 reported instances, 96 were obtained that could be used to relate to job successes. Of these, 61 were related to effective performance and 35 to noneffective performance. On the basis of these critical incidents, an evaluation form was developed. The form included such statements as "follows up quickly on requests from customers"; managers indicated the degree to which it described a particular salesperson by checking a five-point scale ranging from *strongly agree* to *strongly disagree*.

The job of chain store managers has been effectively analyzed by similar methods to appraise managerial effectiveness.[21] A major advantage of the method is that the behavior record of an employee is more complete and does not depend on recall, which may be incomplete and/or subjective. The record of the critical incidents also can serve as a basis for employee counseling because specifics rather than vague evaluative judgments are involved. Widespread use of the method is hindered by the costs involved since critical incidents even for similar jobs (selling different products) would have to be developed.

A refinement of this method, called BARS (behaviorally anchored rating scale), has been developed.[22] Rating errors have not been eliminated, however, and it is suspected that the problem may be that some raters are deviating from the required procedures.

SOME PERSISTENT PROBLEMS

CONFLICTING INTERESTS

A perceived need for the type of information that performance evaluation produces has resulted in its widespread use.[23] Despite the apparent need and the research that has been done to refine rating, few companies take advantage of the knowledge. One study showed that 32 percent of the companies surveyed offered no training at all, and few gave what might be regarded as adequate training to supervisors in making evaluations.[24]

Confidence in the rating results is also lacking. One study showed that 52 percent of the employees felt the ratings should not be considered in making promotions, and an additional 42 percent felt that the rating should count only 25 percent toward the decision.[25] Managers, too, resist filling out the forms and dislike the task of playing God.[26]

Attempts to make the ratings more objective have not solved the problem of acceptance, nor have attempts to reduce human error made rating procedures more acceptable to the supervisors who must use them. Furthermore, little progress has been made in evaluating critical employee behaviors.[27] This involves the problem of finding an agreed-upon criterion for successful performance.

COMMUNICATING THE PERFORMANCE EVALUATION

When performance must be discussed with the employee, the supervisor soon discovers that the employee accepts praise but reacts defensively to criticism. Thus, in striving to let employees know where they stand, the interview makes them feel that they are rejected or that the evaluation has been unfair.[28] To avoid trouble in an interview, supervisors tend to be overly generous — with the result that the evaluation has less value as a measure of performance and therefore is a poor basis for promotion or pay increases.

In many companies, the practice of discussing performance with the employee is followed throughout the various levels in the organization. When this is done, the objective is to improve employees' performance by getting them to correct weaknesses and letting them know their strengths. (Other techniques for developing employees will be discussed in Chapters 18 and 21.)

Behind the evaluation approach are two mistaken assumptions: that employees want to know where they stand, and that an employee will improve if told about weaknesses. Employees may say they want to know where they stand, but they do not like to be criticized, and they frequently show resentment when supervisors tell them where they stand. To help supervisors make their evaluations defensible, they are instructed to stick to facts or instances in these discussions. Supervisors have found that when they keep careful records so as to be able to do this, they are accused of spying. Some employees claim that small errors that occurred many years in the past are recorded or remembered and are the only reason for their being held back.

The second assumption implies not only that employees will correct their weaknesses when they know them, but also that they can correct them if they wish. However, because employees often challenge the supervisor's evaluation, they do not admit there is reason for changing. Some employees show their resentment of criticism by going to the opposite extreme in changing their behavior. One department head asked his assistant not to interrupt him with a problem when he was in conference. His assistant corrected this behavior: he never again entered his supervisor's office.

The problem of changing people through pointing out their weaknesses is complex. No one expects children to increase their intelligence if told that they are deficient, yet we often try to get employees to make more intelligent judgments by telling them to think things through. What if we suggest changes *only* when the new behavior is under a person's voluntary control. Immediately, differences of opinion arise as to what a person can control. Can a person be more aggressive, show more initiative, see jobs that need to be done, make decisions a bit faster, or speak more distinctly if merely told that it is required? We all know that in some instances these things can be accomplished easily, but in other instances a personality change seems to be involved. Indeed, if some people started suddenly to keep a neat desk, there might be reason for alarm.

MANAGEMENT AND EMPLOYEE VIEWPOINTS

When employees feel that they have been unfairly appraised or unjustly criticized, is this a solely defensive reaction, or is there a basis for honest disagreement? It is not uncommon for employees and managers to disagree on the question of what constitutes satisfactory job performance.

In a study of middle-management communication, both employee and manager were interviewed in detail regarding the employee's job.[29] Fifty-eight pairs of managers in five representative large organizations participated. Each job was examined from the viewpoint of the person who supervised it and that of the person who occupied it. Four areas were explored: (1) the actual duties required by the job; (2) the kinds of skills, knowledge, training, personality, and so on, essential to good performance; (3) the anticipated changes in the job in the near future; and (4) the kinds of obstacles or problems that the person met in performing the job. The interviews were analyzed and rated on a five-point scale to indicate the degrees of agreement, 0 indicating little or no agreement and 4 indicating high or full agreement. Special precaution was taken not to treat oversights, differences in ways of breaking down the job, and the number of details mentioned as disagreements. Despite the fact that the supervisor selected the employee job that was to be analyzed, the lack of agreement was striking. Table 14.2 shows the percentage of the fifty-eight pairs studied that fell into each rating category.

Agreement decreases in going from the first job area (duties) to the last (obstacles). Except for the area of job duties, the low-agreement categories (0 and 1) include more pairs than the high-agreement categories (3 and 4). Since a person's idea of job duties, job requirements, and obstacles faced would influence the rating of a job performance, we can see that a supervisor's evaluation of an employee's performance would have to differ from that of the employee. Thus it seems that the prevalent feeling that an evaluation made by a supervisor is unfair might have more than an emotional basis. Until

the two agree on the above job areas, there will inevitably be disagreement in rating performance. The use of job descriptions and previous experience of the supervisor on the employee's job does not remove the discrepancy.[30]

Clearly, the definition of job success is a complex question on many nonproduction jobs, yet proficiency has little meaning until this problem is settled. Finding an objective criterion of job success is essential to developing tests to select personnel, and it is also essential to training employees to perform more effectively. Yet should we assume that an answer can be found? Studies continue to show that organizational level affects rating.[31]

THE PERFORMANCE-EVALUATION INTERVIEW

CONFLICTING OBJECTIVES

The performance-evaluation interview has been selected for detailed treatment because

TABLE 14.2 COMPARATIVE AGREEMENT BETWEEN FIFTY-EIGHT MANAGER-EMPLOYEE PAIRS ON FOUR BASIC AREAS OF THE EMPLOYEE'S JOB

	0 ALMOST NO AGREEMENT ON TOPICS	1 AGREEMENT ON LESS THAN HALF THE TOPICS	2 AGREEMENT ON ABOUT HALF THE TOPICS	3 AGREEMENT ON MORE THAN HALF THE TOPICS	4 AGREEMENT ON ALL, OR ALMOST ALL, TOPICS	MEAN RATING
1. Job duties	3.4%	11.6%	39.1%	37.8%	8.1%	2.35
2. Job requirements (employee's qualifications)	7.0	29.3	40.9	20.5	2.3	1.82
3. Future changes in employee's job	35.4	14.3	18.3	16.3	15.7	1.62
4. Obstacles in the way of employee's performance	38.4	29.8	23.6	6.4	1.7	1.03

SOURCE: Adapted and reprinted by permission of the publisher from AMA Research Study No. 52, *Superior-subordinate communication in management*, p. 29. © 1961 by the American Management Association, Inc.

MOTIVATING WORKERS FOR OPTIMUM PERFORMANCE

The performance-evaluation interview is a critical interaction between supervisor and employee. (Elizabeth Hamlin)

A employee who has the opportunity to help determine the best method to do a job becomes motivated and interested in the work to be accomplished. (Peter Menzel, Stock, Boston)

it is widely used; many companies require all managers and supervisors to conduct such interviews annually.[32] Since the conduct of this interview can do harm as well as good, its undesirable features should be reduced as much as possible.

A supervisor must assist employees and evaluate their performance, and thus is both a helper and a judge. The first function is acceptable to employees and brings the supervisor in close touch with them; the second function builds a wall between them and causes employees to withhold information that will reflect unfavorably on themselves. As a helper, the supervisor needs to know the weaknesses of employees, but the role of judge stands in the way.

The major objectives of appraisal are wage or salary determination, job placement, and promotion. When the supervisor is required to tell employees about their strengths and weaknesses, these objectives are sacrificed to a considerable degree. The objectives of the performance-evaluation interview differ from those of the evaluation itself. The major purposes of the interview aspect of an evaluation program are to develop employee performance and to let employees know where they stand. (See Table 14.3) The first objective could be achieved through problem-solving interviews, but the latter requires communication of an evaluation. In the process of discussing an employee's eval-

TABLE 14.3 CAUSE-AND-EFFECT RELATIONSHIPS IN THREE TYPES OF PERFORMANCE-EVALUATION INTERVIEWS

METHOD	TELL AND SELL	TELL AND LISTEN	PROBLEM SOLVING
ROLE OF INTERVIEWER	JUDGE	JUDGE	HELPER
Objective	To communicate evaluation To persuade employee to improve	To communicate evaluation To release defensive feelings	To stimulate growth and development in employee performance
Assumptions	Employee desires to correct known weaknesses Any person who chooses can improve A supervisor is qualified to evaluate a subordinate	People will change if defensive feelings are removed	Growth can occur without correcting faults Discussing job problems leads to improved performance
Reactions	Defensive behavior suppressed Attempts to cover hostility	Defensive behavior expressed Employee feels accepted	Problem-solving behavior
Skills	Sales ability Patience	Listening and reflecting feelings Summarizing	Listening and reflecting feelings Reflecting ideas Using exploratory questions Summarizing
Attitude	People profit from criticism and appreciate help	One can respect the feelings of others if one understands them	Discussion develops new ideas and mutual interests
Motivation	Use of positive or negative incentives or both (Extrinsic in that motivation is added to the job itself)	Resistance to change reduced Positive incentive (Extrinsic and some intrinsic motivation)	Increased freedom Increased responsibility (Intrinsic motivation in that interest is inherent in the task)
Gains	Success most probable when employee respects interviewer	Develops favorable attitude toward supervisor, which increases probability of success	Almost assured of improvement in some respect

MOTIVATING WORKERS FOR OPTIMUM PERFORMANCE

TABLE 14.3 Continued

METHOD	TELL AND SELL	TELL AND LISTEN	PROBLEM SOLVING
ROLE OF INTERVIEWER	JUDGE	JUDGE	HELPER
Risks	Loss of loyalty Inhibition of independent judgment Face-saving problems created	Need for change may not be developed	Employee may lack ideas Change may be other than what supervisor had in mind
Values	Perpetuates existing practices and values	Permits interviewer to change own views in the light of employee's responses Some upward communication	Both learn since experience and views are pooled Change is facilitated

SOURCE: Reprinted from N. R. F. Maier, *The Appraisal Interview*. San Diego, Calif.: University Associates, 1976. Used with permission.

uation, he or she may be developed, but there is also the danger that the employee may lose job interest and work only to avoid criticism. Thus, conformity rather than initiative may be developed.

GUIDELINES FOR PERFORMANCE-EVALUATION INTERVIEWS

Several aspects of employee-supervisor relationships are relevant during the performance evaluation. The following guidelines are important for supervisors to bear in mind.

1. The supervisor's personal needs will influence the interview with any employee. For example, the treatment and appraisal of a highly satisfactory employee will differ depending on which of the following conditions holds. The employee is: (a) one of three persons fully qualified to fill a position opening up in the department; (b) the only person fully qualified to fill a position opening up; or (c) fully qualified to fill higher positions, but there are no prospects of any.

2. Employees are more likely to feel reprimanded than praised as a result of reports on their evaluations. Even if an employee has five strong points and only two weaknesses, more interview time will be spent on the weaknesses. This is because the favorable characteristics are not challenged. Praising a person first does not take the sting out of criticism that follows.

3. Criticism is most likely to be accepted when (a) it is constructive (that is, indicates what to do, rather than what is wrong); (b) employees feel that the supervisor is more competent in that area than they are; (c) the employee is still learning the job; and (d) supervisor and employee like each other.

4. If petty faults and unpleasant mannerisms are made part of an evaluation, they give the impression that the evaluation of

performance hinges on minor matters. Such problems should be handled on more appropriate occasions and should not await the annual performance evaluation.

5. There are many kinds of deficiencies. Some can be corrected easily; others require training; and in the case of still others, the process of correction may do more harm than good. Mannerisms may be forms of adjustment, bad habits, or neurotic manifestations. Deficiencies in job performance may be due to poor job aptitude, inadequate training, poor supervision, incomplete communication, or low motivation.

6. Effective job performance is often a matter of opinion. A supervisor and employee may have differing views on how best to carry out assignments, how to budget time, and which activities have priority or are the most important. In Table 14.2, research evidence was cited indicating that supervisors and their employees generally do not agree on the requirements or even on many of the duties of an employee's job. It is inevitable, therefore, that when a supervisor evaluates performance in terms of his or her frame of reference, the evaluation will appear unfair and unreasonable to an employee with a different frame of reference (see Chapter 5).

7. An employee is most highly motivated when free to participate in setting goals, determining priorities, planning, and deciding on the best way to accomplish objectives. There are usually several approaches to a job, and supervisors should not expect their ideas to be understood or accepted by all employees. These differences are good subjects for discussion and problem solving.

8. Performance can be viewed in the light of strengths and weaknesses. Usually a supervisor attempts to improve an employee's performance by correcting weaknesses. When weaknesses in performance are a mat-

ter of deficiencies in aptitude, they are difficult to improve. For this reason, performance can be upgraded by further improvements in strengths. Superior performance can be made even more superior, and this opportunity should not be overlooked.

9. Deficiencies in performance should be put in situational terms if they are to be discussed. When a person's behavior is criticized, he or she feels degraded and rejected, hence comes to his or her own defense.[33] When the *job* is examined, any deficiencies can be posed as problems to solve.

10. An employee's job performance can be improved in any of four ways: (a) change the employee; (b) change the duties or routines to capitalize on stronger abilities and interests; (c) transfer the employee to a more suitable job; and (d) change the group leader's manner of supervision. The performance-evaluation interview tends to concentrate on changing the employee, which is the most difficult way to accomplish improvement. The problem-solving interview permits improvement in performance by means of any of the four avenues.

Attempts to reduce the harmful effects of evaluation have led to a number of modifications of the procedure. One approach is based on an attempt to remove supervisory bias by a committee approach to the evaluation. In this method, each employee is rated by a committee in which a supervisor acts as group leader.[34] Another approach uses the interview to get employees to evaluate themselves.[35] Still another is to make the evaluation less subjective by relating it to objective job standards.[36] The extreme approach is to abandon the objective of letting the employees know where they stand and to concentrate on developing their performance through improved motivation and communication. In the process, employees get a good notion of how they stand without being told directly.[37]

JOB ANALYSIS AS AN AID TO MEASUREMENT OF PRODUCTIVITY

Because a knowledge of the job is an essential factor in measuring or evaluating performance as well as in selecting personnel, job analysis will be reviewed here with respect to its usefulness in evaluating performance.

A job description outlines the duties of a particular position, states the conditions of work, rate and method of pay, and factors relevant to training and promotion. The *job specification* is a description of the requirements an individual worker is expected to possess for a given job. Thus, the job description and specification supplement each other.[38]

All companies do not have job descriptions for the various positions, since occupancy of a position also teaches a worker what is expected. In larger organizations, a job analyst usually prepares job descriptions and specifications because the relationships between workers and management are likely to be more formalized. When job descriptions are desired, it is best to have experts work with both the worker and the supervisor to prepare descriptions acceptable to both.[39]

Job evaluation describes the process of grading jobs so that pay rates reflect the demands made on the employee. The value of a job increases as the amount of responsibility and the educational, intellectual, physical, and skill requirements increase, and as safety, working conditions, and health factors decrease. Thus, the same job with an added element of risk or less favorable working hours carries an increased value reflected in a pay differential, if job evaluation is used to set the rates.

Different procedures are used in evaluating the various jobs in a company, but most depend on some form of rating.[40] Once the key jobs have been rated and standardized with other companies, various jobs that may be specific within the company can be compared with the key positions. It should be emphasized that the job value refers to the job requirements and does *not* concern itself with the degree to which an individual meets these requirements. *Benchmark jobs* are used in company surveys to ensure equal pay for equivalent jobs within a community.

As in the case of job descriptions, a job analyst should seek the aid of supervisors and workers in arriving at acceptable job ratings. Both job descriptions and evaluations lean on a job analysis. The objective of *job analysis* is to determine the detailed requirements a worker should have for a particular job.

NEGATIVE ASPECTS OF JOB ANALYSIS

Job analysis tends to stereotype the job and may reduce the freedom of the employee to make decisions and to improve the work method. It assumes that the best work method is the same for all individuals. With the advent of participative approaches to management, job flexibility is increased. However, the extent to which such flexibility is an asset will vary with the job.[41] Since employees and supervisors do not fully agree on the job requirements, participative approaches should reduce differences and clarify the need for flexibility.

THE JOB PROFILE

Ratings can be improved if the job is analyzed to some degree and the ratings applied to different aspects of the job. This procedure can be carried much further if the analysis is in terms of the abilities required to do the job. A simple method for such an analysis is the use of the *job profile*. A card is prepared, listing all the skills that have a bearing on the job. Persons familiar with the job then rate the importance of each job skill.

In one study, six activities that seemed to revolve around the duties of supervisors were selected on the basis of hundreds of interviews with supervisors.[42] In chronological order, these were as follows:

1. Plans an activity
2. Decides to do or not do a certain thing
3. Organizes a group of persons to carry out the plans decided upon (delegates)
4. Communicates the program to the organization
5. Leads the organization toward the established goal
6. Analyzes the progress toward the goal

These six activities were then rated in their importance for various supervisory positions, thus yielding job profiles for supervisory positions at several levels in the organization.

Figure 14.3a shows the job profiles for the positions of section supervisor, general supervisor, and superintendent. The demands of the various supervisory behaviors increase in going from lower to higher positions.

Figure 14.3b shows how the merit ratings of John Doe, in his present position of section supervisor, can be made into a personal-qualifications profile. If we assume that Doe has the adequate job knowledge, his profile shows that he has five of the six other qualifications needed to become a general supervisor, but has not yet qualified as a superintendent.

By matching job and personal-qualifications profiles, we can combine merit ratings

and job-analysis results to improve job placement. It will also be apparent from the above illustration that this analysis of the supervisor's job presupposes a leader quite different from that described in Chapter 8. If job analysis were used exclusively as a means for specifying desired supervisory behavior, it would be difficult for new types of leaders to satisfy the qualifications and job specifications.

THE EMPIRICAL METHOD

The psychographic method analyzes a job in terms of human traits, but it does not escape direct dependence on human opinions, even though the opinions may be those of experts. To avoid this possible source of error, it is necessary to use more time-consuming procedures. One is the empirical method, which largely escapes the element of human opinion by comparing extremes.

Let us select for study a group of sixty people in a certain occupation. These individuals are then rated by supervisors (or individuals who have observed their work) on a five-point scale according to their proficiency. The score of each is the average of the supervisors' ratings. Thus far, the method uses the relatively crude rating procedure.

The next step is to divide the employees into three groups according to the scores attained. The one-third achieving the highest ratings are labeled superior workers; the third obtaining the lowest scores are labeled unsatisfactory workers; and the middle third, making intermediate scores, constitute the average workers. Conceding that errors in ratings have occurred, these divisions have placed some workers in the middle group who belonged in either the lowest or the highest groups, and placed some in the two extreme groups who should have fallen

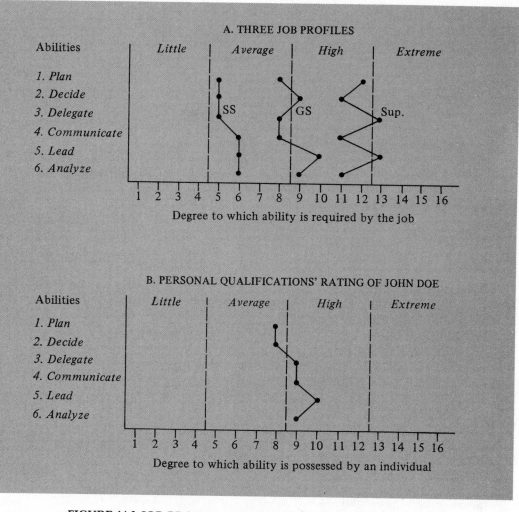

FIGURE 14.3 JOB PROFILE AND PERSONAL QUALIFICATION RATING

Figure 14.3A shows the profiles of section supervisor (Profile SS); general supervisor (Profile GS); and superintendent (Profile Sup.). These progressively higher positions require increasing amounts of the essential abilities. Figure 14.3B shows the qualifications of John Doe; these qualifications meet five of the job requirements of a general supervisor. By making profiles of jobs and personal qualifications, employees can readily be matched to jobs.

SOURCE: After H. F. Rothe, Matching men to job requirements. *Personnel Psychology,* 1951, 4.

in the middle group. The placing of unsatisfactory individuals in the superior group or of superior individuals in the unsatisfactory group would occur very seldom. If we now ignore the middle group and consider only the superior and unsatisfactory groups, we have two distinctly different samples of employees.

The third step is to study the characteristics of these two groups carefully. Any factor associated with success on the job should appear in different degrees in the two groups, and within each group, it should appear to a fairly uniform degree. By subjecting the groups to various measurements and tests, we may obtain many bases for comparison. The results frequently reveal that supervisors cannot always choose the important factors associated with success.

This empirical method permits us not only to locate the more important behaviors objectively, but also to determine their relative importance. The scores on the most important factors would show the most clear-cut differences in the two samples, and these could be given more thorough consideration. A knowledge of the important factors gives the rater a definite basis on which to judge, thereby increasing the accuracy of evaluative measurements.

Job analysis has importance beyond that of improving rating procedures. Once a job is analyzed in terms of the factors essential to success, tests can be devised to measure them. By using the results of these tests, people can be placed in jobs that best fit their particular abilities.

ROLE PRESCRIPTIONS

A person may be regarded as having a repertoire of behaviors so, as the situation warrants, he or she plays the roles of spouse, parent, employee, or supervisor. These roles are influenced by the expectations created by custom and past experience. Each of us behaves according to our role perception, but we are judged by the role perceptions of persons with whom we relate.

A person who performs a particular job has duties specified by the job description. However, performance is judged not only on how well these duties are carried out, but on how performance relates to what is expected. These expectations determine the role prescription, and this includes more than a description of the job.

Role prescriptions for the same type of work (sales, for instance) might be expected to vary between countries having cultural differences, but perceived roles can differ even within a company. Such expectations as giving help to associates, willingness to take suggestions, and being loyal to the company may be included even though unrelated to getting the job done. These expectations influence performance appraisal because such judgments are based on the relationship between what is expected and what actually occurs. A supervisor may be given an unfavorable rating for practicing group decision with employees if such behavior conflicts with the role prescription in the company. Role expectations are developed from past experience and can lead to conflict when organizational changes are introduced (see Chapter 21).

THE CRITERIA OF SUCCESSFUL JOB PERFORMANCE

The first question raised in any study of job success is: "What is good performance?" Is there a correct answer to this question or is it solely a matter of opinion? Since the supervisor evaluates employees and determines their merits, should the psychologist listen to the supervisor, or should the psychologist investigate the nature of success regardless of the supervisor's opinion? In middle-management positions, there is lack of agreement between managers and employees on various basic questions (see Table 14.2). When there is widespread disagreement, should we settle for an average? These and many other questions constitute what is called the *criterion problem*.

COLLEGE CRITERIA

Since most readers have had the experience of getting grades in school, we may profitably use the concept of successful college performance to illustrate the complexity of the criterion problem. It will be conceded that teachers do not always agree with one another on how grades should be given and that their students also disagree with teachers about grades received. To explore this, let us examine some goals of higher education:[43]

1. Necessary skills in writing, speaking, and listening
2. Self-reliance through ability to think clearly
3. Understanding of one's self and one's relationship to others
4. Growing convictions based on the search for truth
5. Understanding and appreciation of our cultural, social, scientific, and spiritual heritage
6. Intelligent approach to local, national, and world problems leading to responsible and responsive citizenship and leadership in life
7. Some practical understanding of another language
8. Professional competence based on high ethical standards in preparation not alone for the immediate job but for a lifetime of responsible leadership in professional activities
9. Healthful development of the body

Most readers undoubtedly will accept some if not all of these objectives, but it would be too much to hope that they would reach agreement on the relative importance of each. It is doubtful whether these goals have the same meaning to all educators, and it is probable that each of the nine items is made up of several more primary goals. This means that even the objectives are vague. Furthermore, it is likely that these several goals are not attainable by the same methods, so in striving for some goals, others would thereby be sacrificed.

Can success in college be scientifically measured under such indefinite conditions? Despite the lack of a satisfactory solution, school grades are given and used as the criteria for college success. Recently, critics have begun to call for reform in this area.[44] Evidence of the continuing trend of a generally broader conception of an individual's rights is the so-called truth-in-testing law that went into effect in the state of New York in 1980. Unfortunately, those who criticize current performance measures as unfair or arbitrary offer few, if any, realistic alternatives.

Similarly, business uses merit ratings as measures of success; even though they are subject to error, the crude measure is better than none at all. In the meantime, efforts to objectify the concept of success continue. The mere recognition of the fact that opinions of success are human judgments, made from particular points of view, represents progress. When value judgments are acknowledged as personally biased, tolerance increases and some conflicts can be resolved.

Since the objective of a business enterprise is to make money, it has been suggested that in this instance the criterion of success should be a measure of a person's worth, hence it should be reduced to a dimension of dollars and cents.[45] A single measure of success such as monetary worth would be the ideal type of criterion because this quantitative measure could then be correlated with scores on various kinds of psychological tests. Such a measure would be in operation if the salaries of baseball players reflected this worth. But the problems of equating batting averages with home runs, runs batted in, fielding records, and so on, suggests the number of difficulties involved.

Evidence shows that salary, when corrected for time on the job, is a better index of executive success than peer ratings and position in the hierarchy.[46] The index is further improved when it incorporates predicted salary increases. However, these combined measures remain at odds with peer ratings. At present, most researchers feel that the goal of a single measure is impractical and believe that the only accurate criterion must be multidimensional.[47]

PRACTICAL CONSIDERATIONS

The various criteria in common use include quantity of work, quality of work, learning time, experience, absenteeism, and safety. Each can be quantified and related to other measures, and little is gained by an attempt to reduce them to a single measure. As a matter of fact, the importance of each dimension varies from one job to another.

The desire to quantify can also lead to errors. A supervisor/rater would not be justified to regard one salesperson as superior to another because the sales volume of the first was greater than another's, since their territories might offer differing opportunities. Nor could it be assumed that one secretary was more proficient than another because one turned out more work, because the dictation given by one supervisor might be more difficult than that given by another. Differences in the same measures are often subject to what is called *contamination,* which means that the measures are influenced by variables other than the one measured.

Before any dimension of success is acceptable as a criterion, it must stand the test of *reliability*. This means that the measures should be relatively constant and not vary from one occasion to another. Thus, the measures of a group of workers made on two separate occasions should correlate highly with one another. Where production measures are used as the criterion, the correlations between two work samples often exceed 0.9. Low correlations indicate contamination and operation of chance factors.

THE CRITERIA FOR PROMOTABILITY

Merit rating forms frequently include a space for evaluating an employee's promotability.[48] This suggests that the evaluation of an employee's competence on the present job is related to competence on a higher-grade job. Chapter 9 pointed out that success on one job is related to success on another *only* when the two require similar abilities. This being so, promotability cannot be evaluated unless it is considered in relation to a specific job opening. Even if the duties on the higher-level new job are closely related to those on the old job (such as a promotion from supervisor of a small group to supervisor of a large group, or from first-line supervisor to second-line supervisor), the higher position is likely to make more demands on abilities common to both jobs. This means that unused capacities will have to be evaluated when the positions are similar, and unobserved abilities will have to be considered when the positions are different. Thus, the problem of promotion is similar to the problem of placement in that abilities and job requirements have to be matched.

MOTIVATING WORKERS FOR OPTIMUM PERFORMANCE

The difference is that in making a decision on a promotion, the supervisor has the employee's past record to turn to, which may be an advantage or a disadvantage, depending on how it is used.

Two major sources of error creep into making promotions. The first is the tendency to treat a promotion as a reward for above-average performance on the present job. If this practice were consistently followed, it would lead to staffing each job grade with average and below-average performers. This situation would occur because superior workers would be removed from the job as soon as an opening occurred and would continue to be promoted through the job grades until they became located in positions for which they lacked aptitude. Less capable workers would be kept in their jobs because they failed to demonstrate superior performance, and their discouragement would merely lower their performance further. Supervisors are inclined to be unhappy with this conclusion because they feel that promise of promotion is a way of motivating employees, and indeed it is. But must management mortgage future performance in order to motivate present performance?

The second source of error resides in the fact that we tend to favor promotion for persons we like. Promotion is regarded as desirable, and it is only human to want to be kind to those we like. Obviously this practice does not increase efficiency, and a company could not successfully compete if this practice prevailed. Family-owned businesses often fail when the management is kept in the family, and favored treatment dominates good judgment.

As a matter of fact, a supervisor may do a person a disfavor by promoting him or her. Many persons hold jobs in which they are unhappy because they cannot afford to give up a high job grade for a lower one in which they would be comfortable. Proper placement makes for greater true job satisfaction than the paycheck.

Promotability is not a characteristic of the person, but represents a relationship between ability and the requirements of the job under consideration: the degree of congruence between personality and a job profile. The most promotable person for a given job opening then would be the person whose personal qualifications best match the requirements of the job; and the degrees of matching of a group of candidates might be different from their relative merits on their present jobs. The only justification for devoting space on a rating form to the item of promotability is to indicate unused potential so that various persons might be considered for more demanding positions in the company. For the same reasons, a space for suggestions for lateral transfers might also be included in each employee's personnel file. If used consistently, such information can be useful to management in the process of long-term personnel and organizational planning.[49]

NOTES

1. Additional information regarding rating scales may be found in: Cronbach, L. J. *Essentials of psychological testing,* 3rd ed. New York: Harper, 1970; Ghiselli, E. E., and Brown, C. W. *Personnel and industrial psychology,* 2nd ed. New York: McGraw-Hill, 1955, Chapter 4; Strauss, G., and Sayles, L. R. *Personnel: The human problems of management.* Englewood Cliffs, N.J.: Prentice-Hall, 1960, pp. 527–540.

2. Thorndike, E. L. A constant error in psychological rating. *J. Appl. Psychol.*, 1920, *4*, 25–29.

3. Tiffin, J., and McCormick, E. J., *Industrial psychology*, 5th ed. Englewood Cliffs, N.J.: Prentice-Hall, 1965.

4. Stevens, S. M., and Wonderlic, E. F. An effective revision of the rating technique. *Personnel J.*, 1934, *13*, 125–134.

5. Borman, W. C. *Some raters are simply better than others at evaluating performance: Individual difference correlates of rating accuracy using behavioral scales.* Speech presented at the 1977 Ann. Conven. of Amer. Psychol. Assn., San Francisco.

6. Hamner, W. C., Kim, J. S., Baird, L., and Bigoness, W. J. Race and sex as determinants of ratings by potential employers in a simulated work-sampling task. *J. Appl. Psychol.*, 1974, *59*, 705–711.

7. Champney, H., and Marshall, H. Optimal refinement of the rating scale. *J. Appl. Psychol.*, 1939, *23*, 323–331.

8. Ghiselli, E. E. All or none versus graded response questionnaires. *J. Appl. Psychol.*, 1939, *23*, 405–413.

9. Ewart, E., Seashore, S. E., and Tiffin, J. A factor-analysis of an industrial merit rating scale. *J. Appl. Psychol.*, 1941, *25*, 481–486.

10. Bolanovich, D. J. Statistical analysis of an industrial rating chart. *J. Appl. Psychol.*, 1946, *30*, 23–31.

11. Levine, E., and Butler, J. Lecture vs. group decision in changing behavior. *J. Appl. Psychol.*, 1952, *36*, 29–33.

12. Sisson, E. D. Forced choice — the new Army rating. *Personnel Psychol.*, 1948, *1*, 365–381; Richardson, M. W. Forced choice performance reports. In M. J. Dovher and V. Marquis (Eds.), *Rating employee and supervisory performance.* New York: American Management Assn., 1950, pp. 35–46.

13. Berkshire, J. R., and Highland, R. W. Forced-choice performance rating: A methodological study. *Personnel Psychol.*, 1953, *6*, 355–378.

14. Waters, L. K., and Wherry, R. J., Jr. *Evaluation of two forced-choice formats.* Project MR005, 13–5001, Subtask 2, Rep. No. 10. Pensacola, Fla.: U.S. School of Aviation Medicine, 1961.

15. Probst, J. B. *Measuring and rating employee value.* New York: Ronald, 1947.

16. Richardson, M. W., and Kuder, G. F. Making a rating scale that measures. *Personnel J.*, 1933, *12*, 36–40.

17. Harrell, T. W. *Industrial psychology*, rev. ed. New York: Rinehart, 1958, p. 67.

18. Flanagan, J. C. The critical incidents technique. *Psychol. Bull.*, 1954, *51*, 327–358; Flanagan, J. C. A new approach to evaluating personnel. *Personnel*, 1949, *26*, 35–42.

19. Flanagan, J. C., and Burns, R. K. The employee performance record: A new appraisal and development tool. *Harvard Bus. Rev.*, 1955, *33*, 95–102.

20. Kirchner, W. K., and Dunnette, M. D. Using critical incidents to measure job proficiency factors. *Personnel*, 1957, *34*, 54–59.

21. Dunnette, M. D. Managerial effectiveness: Its definition and measurement. *Studies in Person. Psychol.*, 1970, *2*, 6–20.

22. Smith, P. C., and Kendall, L. M. Retranslation of expectations: an approach to the construction of unambiguous anchors for rating scales. *J. Appl. Psychol.*, 1963, *47*, 149–155; Schwab, D. P., Heneman, H. G., and DeCotiis, T. A. Behaviorally anchored rating scales: A review of the literature. *Personnel Psychol.*, 1975, *28*, 549–562.

23. National Industrial Conference Board. Personnel practices in factory and office. *Studies in personnel policy, no. 145.* New York: N. R. F. Maier, 1954.

24. Spicer, L. G. A survey of merit rating in industry. *Personnel*, 1951, *27*, 515–518.

25. Van Zelst, R. H., and Kerr, W. A. Workers' attitudes toward merit rating. *Personnel Psychol.*, 1953, *6*, 159–172.
26. MacGregor, D. M. An uneasy look at performance appraisal. *Harvard Bus. Rev.*, 1957, *35*, 89–94.
27. Kipnis, D. Some determinants of supervisory esteem. *Personnel Psychol.*, 1960, *13*, 377–391.
28. Kay, E., French, J. R. P., Jr., and Meyer, H. H. A study of threat and participation in an industrial performance appraisal program. *Mgmt. Developm. Employee Relat. Ser.* New York: General Electric, 1962; Meyer, H. H., Kay, E., and French, J. R. P., Jr. Split roles in performance appraisal. *Harvard Bus. Rev.*, 1964, *43*, 124–129; Maier, N. R. F. *The appraisal interview.* New York: Wiley, 1958.
29. Maier, N. R. F., Hoffman, L. R., Hooven, J. J., and Read, W. H. *Superior-subordinate communication in management.* Research Study 52. New York: American Management Assn., 1961.
30. Read, W. H. Upward communication in industrial hierarchies. *Hum. Relat.*, 1962, *15*, 3–15.
31. Heneman, H. G. Comparisons of self and superior ratings of managerial performance. *J. Appl. Psychol.*, 1974, *59*, 638–642; Klimoski, R. J., and London, M. Role of the rater in performance appraisal. *J. Appl. Psychol.*, 1974, *59*, 445–451.
32. Planty, E. G., and Efferson, C. A. Counseling executives after merit rating or evaluation. *Personnel*, 1951, *27*, 384–396; Rowland, V. K. *Evaluating and improving managerial performance.* New York: McGraw-Hill, 1970.
33. Meyer, H. H., Kay, E., and French, J. R. P., Jr. Split roles in performance appraisal, op.cit.
34. Rowland, V. K. *Improving managerial performance.* New York: Harper, 1958.
35. McGregor, D., op.cit.
36. Likert, R. *New patterns of management.* New York: McGraw-Hill, 1961.
37. Maier, N. R. F., *The appraisal interview.*
38. For occupational descriptions in general, see: Shartle, C. L. *Occupational information: Its development and application,* 3rd ed. Englewood Cliffs, N.J.: Prentice-Hall, 1959.
39. Scott, W. D., Clothier, R. C., and Spriegel, W. R. *Personnel management.* New York: McGraw-Hill, 1961, Chapters 9 and 10; Otis, J. L., and Leukart, R. H. *Job evaluation.* Englewood Cliffs, N.J.: Prentice-Hall, 1954; Prien, E. P., and Ronan, W. W. Job analysis: A review of research findings. *Personnel J.*, 1971, *24*, 371–396.
40. Patton, J. A., and Littlefield, C. A. *Job evaluation.* Homewood, Ill.: Richard D. Irwin, 1957; International Labour Office. *Job evaluation.* Geneva, Switzerland: La Tribune de Genève, 1960.
41. Filley, A. C., and House, R. J. *Managerial process and organizational behavior.* Glenview, Ill.: Scott, Foresman, 1969.
42. Rothe, H. F. Matching men to job requirements. *Personnel Psychol.*, 1951, *4*, 291–301. See also Fleishman, E. A. (Ed.). *Studies of personnel and industrial psychology.* Homewood, Ill.: Dorsey, 1967, pp. 5–13.
43. Dressel, P. L., et al. *Evaluation in higher education.* Boston: Houghton Mifflin, 1961.
44. Bayer, J. Nader, MPIRG question role of standardized tests. *Burnsville (Minnesota) Current,* January 30, 1980, 5a.
45. Brogden, H. E., and Taylor, E. K. The dollar criterion: applying the cost accounting concept to criterion construction. *Personnel Psychol.*, 1950, *3*, 133–154; Bass, B. M. Ultimate criteria of organizational worth. *Personnel Psychol.*, 1952, *5*, 157–174.
46. Hulin, C. L. The measurement of executive success. *J. Appl. Psychol.*, 1962, *46*, 303–306.
47. Dunnette, M. D. A note on the criterion. *J. Appl. Psychol.*, 1963, 47, 251–254; Fisk, D. W. Values, theory and the criterion problem. *Personnel Psychol.*, 1951, *4*, 93–98; Georgopoulos, B. S., and Mann, F. C. *The community general hospital.* New York: Macmillan, 1962, Chapter 5; Ghiselli, E. E. Dimensional problems of criteria. *J. Appl. Psychol.*, 1956, *40*, 1–4; Nagle, B. F. Criterion

development. *Personnel Psychol.*, 1953, *6*, 271–287; Ruch, C. H., Jr. A factorial study of sales criteria. *Personnel Psychol.*, 1953, *6*, 9–24.

48. Taylor, E. K., Parker, J. W., and Ford, G. L. Rating scale content. IV. Predictability of structured and unstructured scales. *Personnel Psychol.*, 1959, *12*, 247–266.

49. Meyer, H. E. The science of telling executives how they're doing. *Fortune*, 1974, *89*(1) 102–106ff.

SUGGESTED READINGS

Bigoness, W. Effect of applicant's sex, race, and performance on employer's performance ratings: Some additional findings. *J. Appl. Psychol.*, 1976, *61*, 80–84.

Cummings, L. L., and Schwab, D. P. *Performance in organizations: Determinants and appraisal.* Glenview, Ill.: Scott, Foresman, 1973.

Greller, M. M. The nature of subordinate participation in the appraisal interview. *Acad. Mgt. J.*, December, 1978, 646–658.

Lefton, R. E., et al. *Effective motivation through performance appraisal: Dimensional appraisal strategies.* New York: Wiley, 1977.

Maier, N. R. F. *The appraisal interview: Three basic approaches,* rev. ed. La Jolla, Calif.: University Associates, 1976.

LABORATORY EXERCISE

ROLE-PLAYING:
SENSITIVITY TO DECEPTION IN AN INTERVIEW

A. GENERAL PREPARATION*

1. The general instructions (D.1) should be read to everyone. The information regarding points received for each question should be placed on the chalkboard.
2. Two persons will be selected as role-players, one assigned the role of Professor Parker, the other, one of the two roles of Jensen, a student (in one of the roles, Jensen is honest; in the other, dishonest). Jensen's given name should be either Walter or Sheila.
3. Other class members will act as observers and be prepared to judge whether or not Jensen is honest.
4. Two chairs and a table should be arranged in front of the room to simulate an office.

B. THE ROLE-PLAYING PROCESS

1. When the role-players have had time to read their parts, they should put aside their role instructions.
2. Professor Parker should be in his office and shortly thereafter Jensen should be instructed to approach Parker and begin the role-play.
3. Role-playing should be continued until a decision is reached.
4. Leader should tabulate observers' opinions (a) on whether the decision was too lenient or too strict and (b) on whether Jensen was honest or dishonest. Parker's opinion also should be indicated, but Jensen should not reveal the role played.
5. Repeat with a different Parker and the other Jensen, assigning the alternate student role.

* From Maier, N. R. F. Sensitivity to attempts at deception in an interview situation. *Personnel Psychol.*, 1966, *19*, 55–56.

6. If the group interest is high and time permits, the process might be repeated with a third pair of role-players.

C. DISCUSSION

1. The identity of persons playing the honest and dishonest Jensens should be withheld for the time being.
2. The judgments of the observers for the different interviews should be compared.
3. Evidences of honest and dishonest actions on Jensen's part should be explored to determine whether agreement exists among observers.
4. A discussion about what Parker might have done to obtain more reliable evidence should be conducted.
5. The roles of the Jensens should be revealed at this point.
6. A list of the things learned from the case should be posted on the chalkboard.
7. Relevance to employment interviews should be explored.

D. MATERIALS

1. General Instructions

Walter (or Sheila) Jensen is a student in a college course taught by Professor Parker. The midterm consisted of five questions, each worth 20 points. Jensen received the following scores on the five questions:

- ☐ Question 1   15 points
- ☐ Question 2   14 points
- ☐ Question 3   13 points
- ☐ Question 4   12 points
- ☐ Question 5   9 points

- ☐ Total   63 points

The grade was a D, seven points below a C. He/she was particularly concerned with the small number of points received for Question 5. At the next class meeting, Jensen asked Professor Parker whether they could discuss a possible error in grading the test. Professor Parker took Jensen's blue book in order to be able to recheck the grading. It was then agreed that Jensen should come to Professor Parker's office the following day at 2 P.M.

At the agreed-upon time Jensen arrives and knocks on Professor Parker's door.

2. Role for Professor Parker

You asked your assistant to check Jensen's paper. After looking it over, she reported that she had been overly generous on the first two questions. However, on question 5, which had two parts, she had given nine points to Jensen's answer to the first part. She felt certain that the second part of the answer was not there when she had graded the paper originally, but had been added later.

After your assistant left, you looked over the exam and found that the answer to the first half of the question ended about three-fourths of the way down the right page of the blue book. Then in a less firm hand, but clearly present, there was the comment "see over." It seemed unlikely that the reader would have missed this comment, particularly since she knew the second part of the question had not been answered. The answer to the second part of the question as it now stands is very good and would have received ten points. It is the best section on the exam. This adds to your suspicion that it may have been added later. Jensen only needs seven points to raise his grade to a C.

It is not uncommon for students with D grades to try to get their grades raised. However, you do not like to see dishonesty practiced to achieve these ends.

It is about time for Jensen to arrive.

3. Role for Walter (or Sheila) Jensen (a)

You usually do not complain about your grades, but a D is going to look bad on your record. You feel that an error has been made in grading,

especially on question 5. There were two parts to this question. You finished the first part, leaving a little space at the bottom of the page in case you might wish to add something, and turned over the page to have a fresh space for the second part of the question. On examining your blue book, you feel quite sure that the grader may have forgotten to turn over the page. The last question was one that you knew most about, yet you received the poorest grade on it. This oversight on the part of Professor Parker seems the most plausible explanation. At least you would like to know what was wrong in your treatment of the question.

Before giving the blue book to Professor Parker, you added a note "see over" at the end of the page on which you had answered the first part of question 5. This will help the reader find the answer to the second half of the question and prevent the same oversight a second time.

4. Role for Walter (or Sheila) Jensen (b)

You usually do not complain about grades, but a D is going to look bad on your record. You feel that you can make a case for an error having been made in grading on question 5. There were two parts to this question. You had finished the first part, leaving a little space at the bottom of the page in case you might wish to add something. You forgot to answer the second part of the question. When you got the exam back, you found you could answer this part of question 5 without looking at your notes.

Since you need to improve your grade, you decided to answer the question, using the same ball point pen you had used during the exam. You feel quite sure that you can make a case that the grader had forgotten to turn over the page and did not see your answer to the second part of the question. You can claim that the last question was one that you knew most about, yet you received the poorest grade on it. Thus, you can suggest a possible explanation. At least you will tell him that you would like to know what was wrong in your treatment of the question.

Before giving the blue book to Professor Parker, you added a note "see over" at the end of the page on which you had answered the first part of question 5. You did this with pencil to show it had been added. This will help the reader find the answer to the second half of the question, and you can say you did this to prevent a second oversight.

CHAPTER FIFTEEN

JOB FATIGUE:
PHYSICAL
AND PSYCHOLOGICAL

■

The Nature of Fatigue   Ergograph Studies of Physical Fatigue
Applications of Ergograph Findings   Reactions to Sustained Work
Hourly Production as a Measure of Job Fatigue: The Production Curve
Muscular Tension   Value of Rest Pauses
The Effect of Length of Workday on Production
The Varieties of Psychological Fatigue
Fatigue, Motivation, and Energy Expenditure
Work Decrement in Mental Operations
Monotony and Its Relationship to Efficiency
The Psychological Effects of Repetition
Methods of Eliminating Boredom in Industry
The Psychological Effects of Incomplete Tasks
Adapting Laboratory Findings to the Job   Job Enrichment

■

A NY STUDY OF FATIGUE must control not only the actual physical activity, but also the indefinite environmental factors that influence a worker's outlook and attitude toward the work. It has now become very apparent that emotional stability and mental health cannot be divorced from fatigue; emotional conflicts and attitudes are so closely related to fatigue that it cannot be defined without involving the other factors.[1]

THE NATURE OF FATIGUE

For practical purposes, industrial fatigue may be defined as *a reduction in the ability to do work because of previous work.* As soon as we attempt to determine the nature of fatigue, differences in opinion arise, for it appears that the reduction in ability to do work is caused by a variety of changes, ranging from chemical to psychological. Previous activity of a particular part of the body alters its ability to continue to function, and some changes produced by this activity can be specifically localized.[2]

We may also approach the problem of fatigue by studying the "feelings" of fatigued persons. If physiological changes always correspond with psychological experiences, the two approaches might measure different aspects of the same thing. Unfortunately, the various evidences of fatigue do not always agree.

There is every reason to believe that an individual's attitude is an important factor in the ability to do work, but the presence of this attitude cannot be detected by any physiological measures. The complexity of the fatigue phenomenon was illustrated when an experimental group of twenty-four college students were confined in a lecture room all night without sleep and were kept active by reading, listening to music, dancing, and so on.[3] At 6 A.M. the students went on a six-mile quick walk, after which they were tested for two hours. A comparable control group of twenty-five students were given the same tests after a normal night's sleep.

With respect to subjective reports, 100 percent of the experimental group reported some fatigue (87.5 percent said that they were exhausted or very tired). Only 12 percent of the rested group rated their condition as very tired (none rated it exhausted) and 28 percent reported no fatigue or slight fatigue. But with respect to performance on twelve psychological tests requiring reasoning, spatial judgments, verbal tests, and locating printing errors, there were no significant differences between the groups.

There was some suggestion that under conditions of fatigue, other mechanisms and mental processes replace the initial ones, so that the individual changes methods for carrying out a function, and this substitution covers up the effects of fatigue. A similar phenomenon appears to occur in muscular effort when a person holds a certain load at a constant height. At first the person performs the task with the muscles best adapted to it, then includes other muscle groups. Finally, muscles not at all involved at the outset become activated, and the work is done with a larger number of muscle groups.

ERGOGRAPH STUDIES OF PHYSICAL FATIGUE

The work of Angelo Mosso, an Italian scientist, has become a classic on the subject of physical fatigue.[4] He developed an instrument, known as the *ergograph*, which made it possible to investigate the relationship between fatigue and physical effort in a relatively isolated part of the body. By studying the activity of a limited muscle group, he

MOTIVATING WORKERS FOR OPTIMUM PERFORMANCE

was able to induce fatigue in a short time. Thus, he could study the phenomenon without greatly complicating it with such psychological effects as monotony and boredom, which are likely to accompany longer periods of work. (Fatigue was measured by recording contractions of a finger muscle lifting a weight.)

The use of the ergograph has established several important relationships, each of which has definite applications to business. Nine specific principles of fatigue are briefly summarized in the following paragraphs.

1. If the contractions with a given load are spaced one every two seconds or thereabouts, there is a gradual decrease in the amplitude of the contractions until finally no further contractions can be made. With a six-kilogram load, this stage is reached in about one minute. Reducing the load will again permit contractions, but fatigue for this load is soon complete.

2. If the contractions for the same load are spaced at long enough intervals (ten seconds, for example), there is no apparent evidence of fatigue. A six-kilogram weight can be lifted almost indefinitely under these conditions.

3. If work is measured in terms of the total weight lifted through a given space, the amount of work the finger is capable of doing is greater for light than for heavy loads. Thus a three-kilogram load can be lifted definitely more than twice as often as a six-kilogram weight.

4. A given load lifted in a fast rhythm produces more fatigue per lift than the same load lifted at a slower rhythm.

5. The time for complete recovery (that is, until the optimum performance can be duplicated) increases rapidly as the period of work is increased.

6. The activity of other sets of muscles reduces the ability of the finger to do work. Strenuous exercise preceding the test with the ergograph causes the stage of complete inability to lift the weight to appear more quickly than normally.

7. The ability of the muscle to do work is decreased by loss of sleep, mental activity, hunger, and anemia of the muscles. As a matter of fact, any condition that depresses or interferes with the nutritive state increases the susceptibility to fatigue.

8. The ability of the muscle to do work is increased by muscle massage, injection of sugar into the blood stream, good health, and a well-nourished body.

9. The rate of fatigue differs greatly in different people, but the principles listed above apply alike to all.

APPLICATIONS OF ERGOGRAPH FINDINGS

ENERGY EXPENDITURE

The first five principles of fatigue support the general conclusion that, with a given amount of muscular energy, more work can be done when this energy is spent gradually than when it is spent rapidly. There is a tendency, however, for people to work fast when they have a lot of energy available. Just as long-distance runners have to learn to keep their speed down and adjust themselves to a pace that they have learned they can maintain, workers need to be taught to spend their energy efficiently.

Another problem in the economical expenditure of energy lies in the fact that it is unnatural for people to rest before they are fatigued to an uncomfortable degree. Since recovery time increases rapidly as fatigue progresses, it is advisable for a worker to rest before fatigue has progressed very far or to work at such a pace that rest periods are unnecessary.

Motion-and-time studies have used some of the ergograph principles by spacing or spreading the work. The Gilbreths were strong advocates of fatigue elimination, and much of their effectiveness was attributable to their recognition of the problem of fatigue.[5] In motion-and-time studies, fatigue was reduced by (1) lightening the load, (2) introducing rest periods, and (3) pacing the work. Since any one of these methods serves the same purpose, the procedure that is adopted depends on the nature of the work.

Much industrial work does not involve heavy loads, but instead requires rapid movements. In some cases the movements may be paced; in other cases rest periods should be given to distribute the work properly. Although the best procedure for setting the pace of a production line has not been determined, it probably should be fairly constant throughout the day, except during the first half-hour, when it should be slower to permit warming up. It is fairly common practice to have the line move most rapidly in the early part of the day and to slow it down as the end of the work period is approached. This procedure is definitely contrary to the principles of fatigue. It is based on the mistaken belief that workers should spend their energy when they have it available. In practice, it requires workers to spend most of their working time in a fatigued condition.

THE GENERAL CHARACTERISTIC OF FATIGUE

The sixth point of the ergograph results indicates that fatigue is general in nature. If activity of one set of muscles reduces the ability of others to do work, then recovery must proceed most effectively when the person is completely relaxed. Unfortunately, workers who have the most strenuous occupations too often have the least accessible facilities for relaxation.

HEALTH AND NOURISHMENT

The seventh and eighth points of the ergograph results deal with the healthful state of the body. They suggest that employees' living conditions outside the plant play an important part in their ability to work. Some of these conditions can be improved by adequate remuneration, others, by educational methods.

A German investigator believes that the worker's travel time from home to work is a significant factor in fatigue.[6] This means that business would have to consider locating its plants near residential areas or to stimulate housing projects near its present plant locations. Furthermore, the applicant's address would become a factor in employment. There already has been a sharp trend in the direction of decentralization of business in this country; the suggested changes would also conserve both human energy and gasoline (fossil fuel energy).

Because food intake reduces fatigue, it may be considered a practical substitute for, or addition to, rest. Company restaurants that sell good food at low prices encourage healthful eating habits and are sound investments.

INDIVIDUAL DIFFERENCES

The rate of fatigue and recovery may differ for persons of equal strength. In sports, the feeling of fatigue is influenced by the person's self-evaluation of his or her capacity.[7] This influence may be partly a matter of personality. Because of the varied individual differences in fatigue, the work pace that suits one person may not be appropriate for another.

When people work in teams and are dependent on one another, it is advisable to match their susceptibility to fatigue as well as their ability. People should be carefully selected for jobs requiring endurance.

LIMITATIONS OF
ERGOGRAPH FINDINGS

It is reasonable to question whether ergograph results are applicable to industry. Laboratory and plant or office atmospheres are very different; also, completely fatiguing a finger is not the same as fatiguing the whole body to a lesser degree. Although the situations differ, similarity may exist. Considering the beneficial change in attitude that would probably accompany some of the practices mentioned, the total effect on employees might exceed that found in the laboratory.

The ergograph principles should be verified in actual work situations with real job holders, not only because work on a job involves the whole body and takes up a good share of a person's working hours, but also because attitudes and motivation have such subtle effects on productivity. Employees like rest pauses, not just because they are tired, but because they want time for coffee, personal telephone calls, and sociability. Often they want coffee just after arriving for work or shortly before lunch. In such instances, the rest period substitutes for a meal. Using lunch periods for shopping and rest periods for lunch prevents the fatigue reduction these breaks were intended to provide.

Company restaurants, rest periods, attractive and comfortable rest rooms, protection against hard cement floors, and stools to permit working while seated have been adopted to reduce workers' complaints. Invariably, these changes have been found to pay dividends in increased production. In one instance, just the installation of stools for workers increased production 32 percent.[8]

The ergograph finding that the detrimental effects of fatigue increase progressively was given some support by a practical investigation.[9] Its author advocated placing lunchtime one-third of the way through the workday to reduce cumulative fatigue.

REACTIONS TO
SUSTAINED WORK

ACCIDENTS AND FATIGUE

The relationship between hours of work and accidents was striking in industry when the hours of work were long and the accident rate was high.[10] With shorter hours, rest pauses, less heavy work, and a reduced accident rate due to accident prevention methods, this relationship is less evident.

Individuals differ in the way they compensate for fatigue, so whether fatigue influences accidents depends on the method of compensation as well as on the situation. Sustained effort may cause some to slow down, others to become more cautious, and still others to take a rest. Common effects of fatigue are reduced coordination, inattention, and falling asleep. Whether these changes result in accidents depends on the activity in which the individual is engaged as well as on the individual's method of compensation. However, fatigue in one form or another is regarded as a physiological factor associated with accidents in aerospace studies.[11]

IMPAIRMENT IN
HIGH-GRADE PERFORMANCE

The concept that fatigue effects may be covered up by changes in the way a task is accomplished is further supported by studies

Plant and company cafeterias and lunchrooms provide places where employees can relax and socialize. (Burk Uzzle, Magnum Photos, Inc.)

of pilot errors in Cambridge, England.[12] These investigations indicated a disorganization of receptor-effector processes at work. This meant that timing and the integrative functions were most readily affected by fatigue conditions and that their effect was most evident in tasks requiring high-grade performance and sustained attention and concentration.[13]

Loss of sleep may not impair a person's performance if the activity sustains attention. But if the activity is not a demanding one, the person tends to fall asleep. Thus, motivation may upgrade a person's performance and cover the lack of sleep, thereby masking the fatigue effects on performance.[14]

HOURLY PRODUCTION AS A MEASURE OF JOB FATIGUE: THE PRODUCTION CURVE

When the amount of production is left largely to the individual and is not paced by the speed of the production line or of a machine, hourly production gradually falls off during both the morning and the afternoon work periods. Typical production curves for morning and afternoon are shown in Figure 15.1. The work on which these curves are based is classified as medium-heavy.[15] The progressive falling off of production in both curves is attributed to fatigue and is characteristic of production trends on work not largely influenced by monotony effects.

MOTIVATING WORKERS FOR OPTIMUM PERFORMANCE

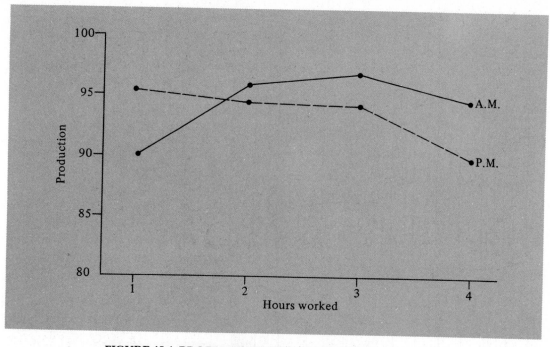

**FIGURE 15.1 PRODUCTION CURVES FOR MORNING AND
AFTERNOON WORK PERIODS**

The solid line indicates production during the four morning hours; the broken line indicates production during the four afternoon hours. The warming-up characteristics are absent in the afternoon period, but the fatigue effects are more apparent than in the morning period.

The morning curve shows a rise during the first hour, known as the *warming-up period*. The exact cause of the warming-up period is not known, but unquestionably this phenomenon depends on a variety of factors. True warming up is usually understood to entail certain physiological adjustments. Other factors, ranging from making the necessary tool arrangements to getting into a working attitude, also enter into the picture. It appears that the warming-up period is less than an hour and that in many instances, it is a matter of a few minutes. The psychological aspects associated with getting started probably are more delayed in actual practice than are the physiological adjustments.

Between the second and third hours, the combined production of a large group of workers usually reaches its peak. Thereafter, production gradually falls off. This continuing decrease reflects the presence of job fatigue.

The afternoon curve frequently shows no evidence of a warming-up period; if present at all, it is of shorter duration. Afternoon production ordinarily begins at a higher point than that which obtained at the end of the morning curve, showing the characteristic recovery that we would expect because of rest and lunch. Thereafter, the curve falls off more rapidly than in the morning, indicating incomplete recovery during the rest pause. The final hour usually shows the lowest production of the day.

Part of the low production at the end of a day may be due to a tendency to quit early or to begin putting away tools. As in the warming-up period, some extraneous activities are performed, and the decrease in production is unrelated to fatigue. The general downward hourly trend, however, reflects the condition of lowered production because of previous work and justifies the characterization of *job fatigue*.

Another feature of some production curves is the *end spurt*. It consists of a rise in production at the end of a work period and appears only in some instances. Evidence for the end spurt is most commonly found in work that does not require physical exertion. This temporary rise in production may be attributed to the motivation of approaching a goal, which in most cases is the end of the day.

The production curve thus reveals three characteristic features: the warming-up period, the end spurt, and the fatigue effects. Each is undoubtedly attributable to a complex set of factors, but all have basic causes which can be determined and which are worthy of investigation.

MUSCULAR TENSION

EYESTRAIN AND CONFLICT

S. H. Bartley designed an experiment in which he produced eyestrain in participants by using light flashes.[16] When the frequency of the light flashes was too fast for the pupillary muscles to follow and too slow to produce the effects of a continuous light, eyestrain quickly appeared. Bartley called this a *conflict situation*.

These results are in contrast to the findings of L. Carmichael and W. F. Dearborn who obtained no evidence of visual fatigue after six hours of continuous reading.[17] In the reading situation, eye movements were repeatedly made but no eye conflict was present. Instead, motivation and lighting were optimum. Apparently the interval between periodic eye movements is adequate for recovery. Combining both researches on experimentally produced eyestrain and on reading, it is apparent that conflict or excessive demands on eye-muscle activity must be carefully considered in evaluating fatigue-producing situations.

The reader may appreciate the fatiguing effects of a struggle between opposing sets of muscles by clenching a fist and holding it up rigidly. It is evident that holding the arm in a rigid position requires more effort of the muscles than if the forearm is moved back and forth. Muscles that pull against each other exert themselves a good deal, but accomplish little externally. The isometric system of muscle development is based on this finding. To what extent does this condition of contractions of opposed sets of muscles occur in nervous tension? The fact that the effects of eye movements involved in six hours of reading add up to much less than the effects of two minutes of looking at light flashes makes it clear that we must look beyond external movements to find the answer to fatigue problems. Doing nothing but holding a pose may be hard work.

A BUSINESS APPLICATION

Some emotional aspects of the eye-fatigue problem became apparent in a case where a new billing machine was introduced in an office. The machine was especially designed to cut down eye movements. On the previously used machine, the eye had to sweep from left to right to compare two sets of figures, but on the new one it was possible to maintain a fixed eye position for this comparison.

The first woman to operate the new machine complained of eyestrain after a few days, despite having been told that eyestrain would decrease with the new machine. Matters became more serious when five other workers, who soon were to receive identical billing machines, visited the manager and said that they would quit rather than use the new machines.

When the manager reported this problem to management, the response was that a lot of money had been invested in the new machines and that they would have to be used. It was up to the manager to "sell" the new machines to the workers. To meet this apparently insoluble problem, the following plan was evolved. The six employees who were to operate the new machines were asked if they would like to test various experimental methods of operating the new machines, the objective being to find a way to use them that was not tiring. They readily agreed to this proposal, and experimentation was begun as soon as the other five machines arrived.

The following three work patterns were tested, each one by two workers per day: (1) do a complete page (about ten minutes' work) and then rest for one minute; (2) rest for one minute after each half-page; (c) alternate rest and work periods of about one minute each. The finding showed that production remained the same for all three procedures, despite the large difference in the amount of rest. Furthermore, production was consistently, but not strikingly, higher on the new machines than it had been on the old ones. Since production was better on the new machines, the operators decided that they wanted to use them. They also argued that eye-rest pauses were needed to abolish eyestrain. They preferred the frequent short

units and settled on a routine of brief rests after each small unit of work. During the following year, no eyestrain was evident.

STRESS

Emotional problems create stress that is accompanied by inability to relax. Work performed with muscles that must pull against opposing muscles that are not completely relaxed creates a condition of conflict similar to eyestrain. This condition may account for the high incidence of fatigue in pressure situations.

VALUE OF REST PAUSES

EFFECT ON PRODUCTION

The introduction of rest pauses in work does not make possible a comparison between work with and without such pauses, because spontaneous rest pauses inevitably occur, whether or not they are recognized. The question of interest to business is whether or not externally introduced rest periods increase production.

The evidence clearly shows that increases of from 10 to 20 percent are common.[18] For instance, the introduction of a ten-minute rest pause in the morning work period for women engaged in labeling resulted in a 20 percent increase in production.[19] In another study, rest pauses of seven minutes, introduced in both morning and afternoon work periods, favorably changed the entire shape of the hourly production curves.[20] The best distribution of rest pauses has not been determined, but it may be expected to vary considerably with the type of work, length of the workday, length of the work week, individual differences, and the level of motivation.

The results of experiments with rest

pauses during moderate physical effort have demonstrated that about 18 percent of the workday for this type of effort should be devoted to resting in order to obtain optimum results. Brief rest periods given after short periods of work produce consistently better results than the same proportion of rest to work taken in longer periods. Using 18.2 percent rest for all test conditions, the greatest benefit of rest pauses has been obtained when rest has been distributed through the work period in one-minute stretches.[21] As the experimenter points out, however, frequent rest pauses interrupting the work can perhaps only be applied to jobs having no complex organization and involving no planning.

UNOFFICIAL REST PAUSES

Whether or not employees have rest pauses is not entirely under the control of management. Employees can pace their work so that short rest pauses are continuously taken, they can pause at intervals, they can go to the bathroom, and they can cause machine breakdowns.

Unofficial rest pauses actually reflect the employee's way of budgeting energy. When people work long days, they pace their work differently and work more slowly than when they work short days. H. M. Vernon studied the rest pauses taken by workers when they worked six- and eight-hour shifts.[22] For the six-hour shifts, the average rest per hour was 10.2 minutes and for the eight-hour shift it was 12.5 minutes. Thus, the percentage of rest per workday as 17.0 and 20.8, respectively, for the six- and eight-hour shifts. However, the workers did not take the rest pauses on the hour as may be suggested by these figures. It seems that each cycle of 16 or 17 minutes contained a rest and a work period.

SOME PRACTICAL PROBLEMS

It is generally agreed that a company's official rest pause should be introduced just before production would start to fall off. Because rest periods may be seen as interruptions and create unfavorable results, it may be desirable to permit the individual a certain degree of freedom in their arrangement. When a person is engaged in finishing a unit of work, an externally imposed pause may serve as an irritant because it disrupts the work pattern.

One of the difficulties encountered in studying the specific effects of rest periods on production is the fact that an improved attitude toward the company is frequently associated with their introduction. The effect of the better attitude tends to confuse the data, making it difficult to determine how much effect is attributable to rest gained and how much to the attitude factor.

THE EFFECT OF LENGTH OF WORKDAY ON PRODUCTION

During the depression of the 1930s, an attempt was made to distribute work among a large number of people by shortening the workday. During the war effort in the 1940s, on the other hand, an attempt was made to increase production by increasing the length of the workday. These procedures presuppose that production is a simple function of the number of hours worked. Considering the effect of fatigue on productivity, we may rightly question the validity of this supposition.

EXCESSIVELY LONG HOURS

What happens to productivity under conditions where people work long hours? In one case, a worker in a surgical-dressing plant refused to follow the workday maintained by the plant.[23] The hours were from 6:00 to 8:00 A.M., 8:30 to 12:30 P.M., 1:30 to 5:30, and 6:00 to 8:00 P.M.. Meals were eaten in the three free periods. The worker in question not only refused to work before breakfast, but also declined to return in the evening. When questioned, the worker claimed that it was possible to do more work by working only eight hours. Investigation revealed that this worker's output under an eight-hour per day schedule was 52,429 bobbins per month. This was the highest number produced by any worker on that job — 12 percent above the average and 6 percent above the next highest worker. Because it is unlikely that any one person could be that superior to the best workers in a group, the shorter workday appeared to be the most plausible explanation for the worker's productivity.

Another instance verified this finding. Under the pressure of World War II, England increased its work week from 56 hours to an average of 69.5 hours in the war industries.[24] The first effect of this increase was a 10 percent rise in production, but then production declined, and sickness, absenteeism, and accidents increased. By the end of two months, the average amount of time actually worked was only 51 hours weekly, compared with the average work week of 53 hours during the prewar period. Production was 12 percent below that previously attained. Six months later, the shorter week was restored with the result that production rose steadily to a higher point than ever before.

The English experience suggests that increased production does not necessarily result from large amounts of overtime work. Working extra hours results in some extra production, but the overall effects may be negative. Under the stress of great motivation, these trends may temporarily be altered, but eventually undesirable effects can be expected.[25]

OPTIMUM WORK WEEKS

During the depression years of the middle 1930s, the Waverly Press went on a six-hour day worked without a break.[26] The first effect of the change from eight to six hours was a 5 percent drop in production and a doubling of errors. As the employees became accustomed to the new work pattern, however, hourly production rose to 15 percent above the previous standard, and the errors were fewer than before the introduction of the six-hour day. Considering that errors were reduced, this means that production for a six-hour day was approximately the same as for an eight-hour day. A more efficient use of the six-hour day, such as interrupting it with a lunch period, might have made up for any slight difference that remained.

In a more detailed study, work weeks of thirty-six, forty, forty-four, and forty-eight hours were compared.[27] The hourly output for the forty-hour week was found to be the most efficient. The inefficiency of the shortest work week may have been due to loss in practice and improper work attitudes or to any of a number of other factors.

Apparently, the forty-eight-to-fifty-four-hour week is approximately the work pattern that yields the greatest *weekly output.* Only when the work period exceeds these hours is the decrease in hourly output sufficiently great to make the longer week less productive than the shorter week.

In deciding upon a most efficient work week, it is desirable to distinguish between its effect on hourly production and its effect on weekly production. From the standpoint of efficiency, measured in terms of production per hour, a work week of about forty hours seems to be the optimum under existing conditions. But if there is a shortage of labor and the purpose is to get the maximum amount of goods produced with the personnel available, then a work week in the vicinity of fifty hours is the optimum.

If there is an excess of labor and the goal is to spread the work, the reduction in either hours or days worked must be great enough to accomplish the objective, but this might require a reduction in weekly pay.

THE FOUR-DAY WEEK

If the length of the work week is held constant and the number of days worked is varied, a new work pattern emerges. There has been an interest in the forty-hour, four-day pattern. This would mean a return to the ten-hour day, which had been less productive than the eight-hour day for many types of work. Does the four-day week offset the fatigue of the long day? This, in part, depends on what the worker does with the time off. If used for long weekends, it reduces the Monday absenteeism that plagues business, but if workers still take an additional day off to achieve a four-day weekend, no reduction in absenteeism would occur.

Whatever the benefits or drawbacks of the four-day week, it has not become dominant. An alternative to the four-day week called *flex-time* has been introduced. As described in Chapter 1, this schedule requires some attendance at work five days per week during a five-hour core period. But outside this core period, workers have a great deal of latitude in selecting the additional working hours to reach the required weekly number (thirty-five to forty).

Although both attitudes and productivity figures were positive after a year of flex-time at one company studied, the researchers caution that responses to the use of such a program may be expected to vary because of the size and type of company involved, worker attitudes, and organizational values.[28]

Research is needed to test productivity under controlled conditions so that case studies, which may be selected to prove a bias, need not be used as evidence. Since fatigue principles may be violated, the productivity losses resulting may be overcome by improved attitudes and morale. Thus, tests over a period of time are needed to establish efficiency.

THE WORK SHIFT

Many companies operate three shifts in order to give twenty-four hours of service; others use two or three shifts to increase the productive capacity of the plant. As capital investment per employee increases, it becomes more necessary to operate several shifts, to reduce overhead.

A study of British industries revealed some problems and facts about the use of night shifts.[29] When the same individuals alternately work a day and a night shift, most of them are more productive on the day than on the night shift. (This finding corresponds to the general experience in the United States.) However, the absenteeism of a given individual is about the same for both day and night shifts.

Various problems are created by the shifts. Most employees prefer the day shift, the expressed reasons being better health and social life as well as higher output. The investigators found general agreement among the workers that the feeling of fatigue was greater for the night than for the day shift.

MOTIVATING WORKERS FOR OPTIMUM PERFORMANCE

Failure to get enough sleep at home when working on the night shift was claimed by 42 percent of the employees.

More difficult than the problem of rest, however, was that of adjusting to the change in mealtime when changing shifts. Sixty-two percent indicated this to be a problem, and 35 percent said the adjustment required more than four days. Most employees mentioned loss of appetite and digestive upsets in connection with shift changes.

Some of these problems affected productivity. The plants studied included some that changed shifts weekly, others every two weeks, and others monthly. Examination of production records of the two-week changes revealed that production was better on the second week than on the first week of the day shift. For the monthly changes, there was a slight but continued improvement for each successive week of the day shift. However, the night-shift schedules showed no such improvment. Because of the physiological adjustment problems that it creates, W. Bloom argues against shift rotation, particularly on a weekly basis.[30]

Shift rotation is an attempt to distribute the hardship or inconvenience to all employees. Although the changes introduce an additional problem of adjustment, rotation does permit all employees and their families to live a normal life part of the time. It is possible that some of the problems created by three shift operations can be solved by making the night shift more attractive. Differential pay is only part of this picture. Persons who live out of phase with other people also have problems with shopping, recreation, and social and community life. When a large number of persons work on a night shift, the possibilities of developing a more nearly normal pattern of life should be explored. Without shift changes, husbands and wives who work could more easily obtain jobs with similar hours. It now sometimes happens that husbands and wives work different shifts and are denied a home life, as well as a community life.

THE JOB OF THE EXECUTIVE

Although the trends of lightening physical work and shortening the work day apply to most employees, the executive's job has shown no such changes. Executives are working longer hours, lunch periods are usually used for meetings, dinner meetings or obligations are frequent, and on some occasions, breakfast meetings are held to increase scheduling opportunities for conferences.[31] Conducting conferences and holding interviews are stressful activities because they require constant alertness.

Frequently executives have little time for planning during the day, which means that this may be done during the hours intended for sleep. Since unfinished work or work in the planning stage is hard to forget, this continuous stress frequently becomes akin to worry.

The positions of executives are also less secure: they have no union steward to defend them, it is difficult for them to find other jobs at a comparable level on short notice, and good performance is difficult to measure, so that the necessity of making a good impression rather than doing a conscientious job becomes a distractor. Thus work pressure, long hours, and little opportunity to escape from job worries can become fatiguing.[32] But if the jobs are satisfying, the need for leisure is less because the work becomes more like play. The executives' perceptions of their jobs determine, in part, the fatigue effects of long hours.

Industrial physicians have expressed concern about executives' apparent reluctance to take time off from work.[33] Reasons that executives gave included the following: that work is a major source of satisfaction to them; that they experience feelings of insecurity about their jobs and power; or that they feel that asking for time off is showing weakness. In an effort to encourage executives to take periodic vacations, some firms have increased annual paid-vacation allowances, but are not permitting the time to accrue over more than one year.

Decision making, willingness to take risks, and generation of alternatives cannot be relegated to computers. With business consistently extending its trade to an international basis, functioning in a more restricted economic environment, and diversifying its products, executive responsibilities are increasing. The only long-term escape from pressure is through delegation. More and more, decision-making functions will have to be moved further down the hierarchy. Thus, reforms in the executive's job must be sought through improved organizational climates (see Chapter 20).

AUTOMATION AND DATA PROCESSING

With automation, the pace of the work is controlled by the machinery, and heavy work is largely eliminated. In many instances, the worker is present only to take action in the event that something goes wrong. In some modern chemical fabric plants, employees are so scarce that loneliness becomes a job-related problem.

Lack of sleep and fatigue affect attentiveness. Automation increases the cost of errors and the need for vigilance, and the difficulty of maintaining attention increases as improved mechanization reduces the probability of a failure.[34] Thus, an attendant must be ready to act when an incident occurs, but the required concentration is hard to maintain when action is required only a few times a day.

In air transport, a similar type of attention is needed. In these cases, emphasis is placed on decreasing fatigue by reducing distractors in the physical environment. However, these fatigue-reducing conditions also encourage sleep, particularly if the employee has had inadequate rest. Long east–west flights also cause fatigue and physiological upset because of the required rapid adjustment to time-zone changes.

Loss of developed skills, boredom, loneliness, and reduced job satisfaction are problems that can be created by automation, and these factors affect fatigue as well as motivation. The problem of boredom and the ways to reduce it are considered later in this chapter.

LEISURE AND RECREATION

As incomes rise and working hours decline, off-the-job activities play a more important part in a worker's system of values.[35] Leisure can be an opportunity for enjoying creative activities, acquiring skills and knowledge that promote the individual's job potential, strengthening family bonds, escaping the stresses of work, recuperating from fatigue, and preparing for retirement. The continuing popularity of correspondence courses, specialized adult training, and the like, suggests that many people are using these hours to acquire new skills required by positions to which they aspire. Resting or taking part in activities like jogging or running, designed to relieve job tensions or to regenerate energy so that employees may return to the job more zestfully, is another positive approach. During leisure hours, the do-it-yourself trend has fostered making articles that range from original fabrics to furniture, and rising costs have led many people to learn to make electrical or plumbing repairs at home.

Both the do-it-yourself trend and the popularity of back-packing and camping dramatize the findings of a study in which 76.8 percent of the 125 automobile workers questioned replied that they would spend more time with their families if their leisure were increased.[36] Here leisure functions as a family unifier for the person whose work and commuting requires being away from home most of the day. C. G. Wrenn proposed that occupation and leisure be considered not as a polarity but as a fusion.[37] This concept suggests that work not be restricted to employed activities and that unpaid work can fulfill a moral end (work considered to be a virtue by society) and be satisfying at the same time. Working outside of a person's occupation may have particular significance if the work done for pay is not personally satisfying and makes the person feel insignificant.

There is no guarantee, however, that leisure will be constructively used. Leisure time can also be used to develop interests or activities that conflict with job progress, break family ties, increase fatigue, or make for unhealthy distractions (for example, increased drinking). Freedom from work in a work-oriented society can be an emotionally disturbing experience. Statistics show that suicides occur more frequently on weekends, holidays, and vacations.[38] The constructive use of leisure is of concern to business and society as a whole, and it requires training.

In the past, leisure time was often a negative experience to people living in a culture that valued work as the primary justification for human existence.[39] But a basic change in attitude seems to be taking place. One effect of the new attitudes regarding the "proper" activities for women has been a parallel change in expectations (by many, at least) regarding "proper" activities for men. Today, the role of the father as parent is more emphasized than ever before,[40] and other nonwork sources of self-esteem are similarly encouraged. It is to be hoped that one long-term outgrowth of women's efforts to change their societal role will be to broaden cultural concepts for both men and women as to what consititutes acceptable and normal sources of individual self-actualization and development.

PREPARATION FOR RETIREMENT

Workers should learn to develop recreational interests and good physical fitness habits while they are still young so that these can replace work when they retire. The leisure time resulting from the changing work patterns of modern society can be used profitably to prepare for retirement, so individuals will not equate job loss with death or uselessness, as is frequently the case.[41] Membership in various groups — whether religious, political, cultural, volunteer, or activity-based — begun during the early years can both stabilize the individual's activities and make for a positive self-concept upon retirement. The long-term effects of changes in mandatory retirement laws can only be guessed at now. Whether economic factors or motivational ones will keep employees at work past the age of sixty-five is as yet unknown.

THE VARIETIES OF PSYCHOLOGICAL FATIGUE

Performance is more than a simple demonstration of ability and/or effort. J. P. Campbell and R. D. Pritchard have cited eight separate factors affecting performance.[42]

Employees should plan for their retirement not only in a monetary way, but also in usage of leisure time through various activities and hobbies. Here a retired executive (right) is acting as a volunteer senior consultant aiding minority businessmen as part of Raytheon Company's Minority Vendor Program. (Courtesy Raytheon Company)

Some of these are external factors, but others, relating to motivation, are determined by individual psychological responses. One type of response is psychological fatigue.

The term *psychological fatigue* designates the more elusive factors causing work decrement. It includes the falling-off in efficiency of work commonly referred to as *mental fatigue*, as well as the phenomena of *monotony* and *boredom*. The influence of attitudes and motivation on work decrement also should be considered under this category.

Insofar as true mental fatigue exists, it

may be a decrement in the functioning of nerve and brain centers. Monotony and boredom are influenced by the way a person views a task, causing the output to fluctuate rather than to fall off progressively. The manner in which a job is perceived is an individual matter, but certain kinds of tasks and work atmospheres are more likely to induce monotony and boredom. All these experiences are special forms of fatigue that are probably psychological rather than physiological.

Motivation is a factor in all forms of fatigue in the sense that the rate of fatigue for almost any type of task varies inversely with the intensity of the motivation. When motivation is low, fatigue effects appear early; when motivation is high, evidence of fatigue may not be apparent until considerable physical exhaustion is manifest.

Psychological fatigue is an important aspect of work unrest as well as of work decrement. Mental conflicts and frustrations are commonly associated with work, and therefore it is important to determine methods for reducing their incidence.

FATIGUE, MOTIVATION, AND ENERGY EXPENDITURE

A MOTIVATION THEORY OF FATIGUE

Work energy is not stored in a person in such a way that it can be drained off like opening a valve. Rather, it is more appropriate to think of this energy as inaccessible until motivation exists; even then, only a given amount becomes available for a specific kind of activity. As a result, the energy for a given task may be depleted without greatly reducing the total supply. It is as though the energy were rationed and a particular job must have a high priority in order to get a significant share of energy. For instance, after a day at the office, a person may be too tired to work overtime, but if someone suggests a bowling game, the needed energy is available. The person's basic supply of energy is not totally depleted by work, but the portion allocated to work-related tasks has been expended. If many allotments are made, the total supply is reduced. Rationing then becomes more strict; higher priorities are needed, or smaller allocations are made. Thus, the total supply of a person's energy is limited, but is seldom if ever depleted, because rationing prevents it. The depletion commonly experienced as boredom is the spending of an energy assignment. Motivation controls the distribution of energy; thus, it is the key process in the rationing procedure.

Figure 15.2 describes the relationships between the total supply of energy, the portion allocated to a given task, the effect of motivation on the task allocation, and the relationships between fatigue, motivation, and energy expenditure. In each of the six conditions the large circle represents the total energy of an individual. The smaller circles within the large circles represent allocations of energy for specific tasks; their size indicates amounts of energy allocated. These amounts vary directly with the degree of motivation that a particular task can arouse in an individual. Diagrams A and B represent energy allocations given differing degrees of motivation for the same task in two different people. Diagrams C and D represent conditions after work on the tasks has been completed; the shaded portions of the circles indicate that half the allocated energy of each has been spent. Spending half the allotted energy creates a relative degree of fatigue, and this fatigue is the same for both

people represented in diagrams C and D, even though the amount of energy spent for condition C is more than twice as great as for condition D. Diagram E illustrates the condition in which a person expresses fatigue for Task I. However, when Task II, an activity with high motivation, is presented, energy for it is made available from the total reserve. The fact that an incomplete circle of energy is shown for Task II indicates stricter rationing conditions created by the reduced energy supply. Diagram F describes a condition in which many activities have been performed, each having enough motivation to obtain new allocations. Several incomplete circles indicate stricter rationing. When the total supply has been reduced so that all tasks are curtailed, the condition of exhaustion is approached.

According to this view, high motivation makes more energy available, and low motivation releases a lesser amount of energy for a given task. It follows, then, that the problem of reducing fatigue can be approached either by making more energy available or by efficiently using the quota of energy that has been made available. Raising motivation reduces fatigue by increasing the allocated energy supply, whereas such factors as rest periods and slower work pace reduce fatigue by increasing the efficiency of the expenditure of energy, regardless of the amount allotted. Since these two types of influence on fatigue are altogether different, we can understand why the curve of fatigue does not always follow the same trend. People sometimes perform heroic deeds and show surprising degrees of endurance without apparently succumbing to fatigue. These exceptional feats appear superhuman only because we try to interpret them in the light of the more common and limited allotments of energy; actually, unusual amounts of energy were made available in such instances.

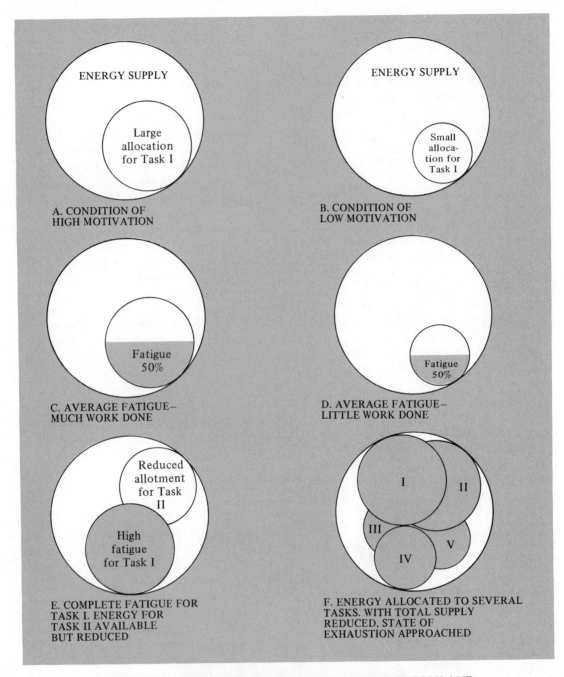

FIGURE 15.2 RELATIONSHIPS BETWEEN ENERGY SUPPLY AND
ENERGY AVAILABLE FOR A TASK

Although this theory awaits further experimental confirmation, it represents an attempt to account for certain qualitative relationships between fatigue and energy expenditure. It also permits a distinction between fatigue and exhaustion, which existing evidence seems to require.

EXPERIMENTAL FINDINGS

Some experimental support of the theory that energy is distributed according to the task motivation comes from an experiment using animals. Evidence from animal behavior in a problem of this kind is useful, since it shows that the phenomenon is a fundamental process (in that it affects more than one species). Also, the data are not distorted or confused by higher mental processes, which may affect perception and indirectly influence results.

In the experiment in question, rats were trained to run a certain distance along a path before they made a turn that led to food.[43] Animals were required to begin at the starting point, make a right turn, and run to the sixth turning point before making a left turn, at the end of which they found food. The positions of the starting unit and of the food units were changed from trial to trial, but the distance between them was always the same. Since identical paths led off the main route at one-foot intervals, the only way for the rats to locate the correct turn was by learning to run a certain distance; that is, to recognize when they had spent a certain amount of energy. With motivation held constant (twenty-four hours without food), the problem was learned with considerable accuracy.

Changes in motivation were then introduced. When motivation was increased by lengthening the period of food deprivation, the animals made the turn approximately one unit farther along the path; when the

motivation was decreased, the animals made the turn about one unit too soon. In other words, when the animals were highly motivated, they underestimated the energy they had expended; when they were poorly motivated, they overestimated it. If these errors in estimating energy expenditure can be produced by motivation, it appears that motivation influences the energy supply, and in this manner distorts the judgment of how much has been spent. In other words, spending half of a large amount of energy feels subjectively very much the same as spending half of a small allotment of energy.

This interpretation of motivation as a factor determining the supply of energy is consistent with the results of a number of other experiments that show a relationship between motivation and learning behavior, as well as with common experiences concerning the relationship between motivation and industrial work. So-called lazy people seem to have a deficiency in energy, yet we may be surprised at their endurance when sports are involved. Since their energy is available only for certain activities, it is a problem in motivation to make energy accessible for job activities.

WORK DECREMENT IN MENTAL OPERATIONS

FINDINGS ON MENTAL FATIGUE

Assuming that motivation can be kept fairly constant during a laboratory experiment, evidence shows that both speed and accuracy decrease as the work period continues.[44] Tasks such as mental multiplication of two- or three-place numbers, reciting the alphabet backward repeatedly, and memorizing words or syllables produce evidence of fatigue within an hour. Also, signs of warming-up and end spurts often appear.

As in the case of physical work, rest periods delay the onset of the work decrement. In general, frequent short rests seem more effective than a few long ones. The actual percentage of rest required for mental work is probably less than that for physical labor.

E. Bornemann emphasized the degree of involvement in a task as a factor in determining rest pauses.[45] He developed a method for measuring involvement and found that it is greater in office work (involvement ranges from 50 to 100 percent) than in manual work (involvement ranges from 30 to 60 percent). Although office work may not be fatiguing physically, the high degree of involvement introduces a new factor for consideration. The study recommends short breaks (five or ten minutes) because recovery is rapid for fatigue effects resulting from psychological involvement in a task. In a military study, it was found that ten-minute rest periods following each half-hour's duty facilitated detection of visual signals to a significant degree.[46] Here, too, a high degree of psychological involvement may be assumed since constant attentiveness is necessary for successful performance.

Inspectors looking for occasional rejects among batches of items on a conveyor belt, sonar specialists listening for the different echo, radar observers looking for targets on the screen, motorists checking the road for traffic signs — all are activities that involve receiving stimulus information, but for which few of the stimuli are signals for action. Such tasks require little muscular effort, and decrements in their function are attributable to mental fatigue.[47]

PHYSIOLOGICAL CHANGES IN MENTAL WORK

Muscular fatigue was never seriously questioned as a phenomenon because it was possible to demonstrate the physical presence of fatigue products when muscles were activated. If true mental fatigue exists, it is reasonable to assume that the fatigue products should be found in brain or nerve tissues. Highly refined methods of measuring heat, oxygen consumption, and carbon dioxide production have made it possible to demonstrate increased metabolism when nerve tissue functions. It has been established that there is a resting metabolism, an activity metabolism, and reduced levels of functioning with continued use.[48] The reduced functioning of the nerve with continued use demonstrates fatigue. By reducing the magnitude of nerve responses, nerve tissue is protected from exhaustion.

Evidence of physiological changes produced by mental operations and unrelated to emotional factors has been reported by A. Ford.[49] He used an electronic indicator developed to measure changes in the functioning of the heart. Subjects lying in relaxed positions on cots were required to do mental arithmetic problems for a period of twenty-seven minutes with alternating three-minute intervals of work and rest. To ensure against changes produced by accompanying muscular contractions, electrical responses measuring even twitches were recorded. Under these carefully controlled experiments, it was found that (1) the electrical output of the heart increased 6 percent; (2) as work continued most subjects showed a decreased output, which represented adaptation to the work load; and (3) most subjects showed faster heart rates during mental work than those during rest. However, this study does not indicate whether the results were directly related to the mental effort involved or were a by-product of the greater stress experienced during test versus rest periods.

MENTAL BLOCKING

Work that requires constant alertness and attention is subject to interferences known as *blocking*.[50] Most people have observed that, when adding a column of numbers, they reach momentary stages at which they find themselves repeating a sum several times before going on to the next one. Then, for a while, they find they can continue from one number to the next in smooth succession until another block occurs. The same effect may be observed if a person attempts to repeat a word over and over. The blocks are only a few seconds in duration, and several may occur per minute.

The phenomenon of mental blocking becomes objectively apparent when we measure the continuous results of mental work. If a person is asked to name a series of colors, give the opposites of a list of words, or add a series of sums, and if the responses are recorded on a revolving drum so that each response makes a mark, it is found that these marks are irregularly grouped. A few responses occur rapidly, then there is a delay, followed by another set of responses.

The blocks or lapses in performance are associated with the making of errors. Mistakes in arithmetic tend to occur at the points where the blocks occur. Long blocks not only produce errors, but materially delay the speed of work. In plants in which constant attentiveness to the work is necessary, these blocks may cause accidents.

There are wide differences among people in the length of their mental blocks, as well as in the frequency with which these occur. Individuals who tend to perform slowly in experimental tests also are likely to be the ones who have long or frequent blocks.

Blocking probably functions as an automatic method of resting; for this reason an activity requiring attention can go on with only brief interruptions. Continued work, however, produces an increase in the length and frequency of blocking incidents, and this phenomenon probably accounts for the decrement in mental work that gradually appears as the work period continues.

Repetitive work with its resultant monotony can cause working rates to vary and fall. (Eric Hartman, Magnum Photos, Inc.)

MONOTONY AND ITS RELATIONSHIP TO EFFICIENCY

The experience of monotony is often regarded as the curse of modern efficiency. It is claimed that repetitive work makes robots of people and that it destroys such human values as pride in one's craft and individuality. There is a general belief that boredom and dissatisfaction are common in our present methods of production. To what extent these conditions are assumed to exist by people who do not actually do the work, and to what extent a state of boredom really does influence production, are issues worthy of consideration.

SOME DEFINITIONS

Both the terms *monotony* and *boredom* have been used to describe the undesirable effects of repetitive work. These terms have somewhat different connotations and should be more specifically defined. One writer has pointed out that reading a book may be boring without being repetitious and that work that is repetitive but does not require attention might not be boring.[51] He suggests the term *tedium* for the undesirable effects of repetitious activity. This use of the term is very close to the way the term *monotony* is used by the British investigators who have done most of the work on this subject.[52] For the purposes of this book, the terms *tedium* and *monotony* are employed to describe the state of mind caused by repetitive work. They refer to the experience of sameness without implying emotional distaste. The term *boredom* will be used as a more inclusive term, taking in the person's unfavorable feeling for the task being performed.

Boredom has been defined as the result of a wide gap between a person's level of competence (relatively high) and task demands (low).[53] This state is contrasted with *anxiety*, which (the author of this research argues) occurs when the gap between competence and task demands is in the opposite direction (demands high, competence low).

It follows from the distinction between boredom and monotony that boredom will be affected more than monotony by the following factors: (1) the personality of the individual; (2) attitude and mood; and (3) the perception of the task performed. This means that individuals might not agree on the task that was most boring; individuals might show more boredom one day than another, and some people might become adjusted more readily to boring tasks than to monotonous ones.

In one study, ten persons were rotated between five repetitive jobs.[54] They spent one month on each task and were then asked to rate the jobs from zero to five according to the degree of boredom. The zero rating was for the job in which boredom was completely absent and the five for jobs in which it was always present. On one of the jobs there was agreement: all ten persons assigned it their highest or second highest boredom ratings. Agreement ended at this point, however. The average boredom ratings given for the five jobs varied from 4.2 to 1.7. Individual ratings ranged from 1.8 to 2.9. The authors of the study also pointed out that superior intelligence and an outgoing personality increase a person's susceptibility to boredom. A study made in the United States demonstrated a relationship between boredom and poor adjustment.[55] These relationships indicate that boredom is a complex experience, influenced by personality and intellectual factors as well as by the activity performed.

BUSINESS FINDINGS

Monotony and boredom become specific topics under the general heading of fatigue only when it can be shown that performance of work that produces them also results in a productivity decline not attributable to muscular fatigue.

The British studies, in general, agree in indicating that the mental state of monotony is associated with definite fluctuations in the rate of working and with a fall in production. Some of the findings of the British

MOTIVATING WORKERS FOR OPTIMUM PERFORMANCE

investigators have been questioned by investigators in this country.[56] In these studies, the close relationship between the experience of boredom and output was not reproduced and individual differences were found to be very marked. There is general agreement, however, that workers tend to slow down, talk, become restless, and show variable production when bored. The motivating effect of the end of the work period, causing an end spurt, was also found to be a characteristic of repetitive jobs.

Letting the mind wander seems to be one way of escaping monotony. If daydreaming does not interfere with the ability to do good work, it is probably a useful adjustment, but if constant alertness is imperative, it may cause errors and accidents. Obviously, the best adjustment to repetitive work will vary with the nature of the job.

That a good deal of the loss in production in repetitive work is due to the specific condition of boredom rather than to muscular fatigue is indicated by the facts that (1) afternoon monotony effects do not exceed those of the morning, as might be expected from accumulated fatigue, (2) the anticipation of the end of the work period tends to abolish signs of monotony, and (3) intelligent workers are more subject to monotony effects than are less intelligent ones. These facts indicate that a knowledge of the mental effects of repetitive work is highly important, since such information might suggest methods for eliminating this mental condition.

THE PSYCHOLOGICAL EFFECTS OF REPETITION

THE PROGRESSIVE STAGES OF SATIATION

Much has been learned about physical fatigue by performing experiments in which a few muscles were worked to the point of exhaustion. Experiments to seek a corresponding phenomenon for mental activity have been performed in the laboratory. By confining the activity to very simple operations and having them repeated indefinitely, marked changes in behavior were produced.[57] In these experiments, the term *satiation* was used. The process may be defined as the stages a person goes through in reaching mental exhaustion for a particular activity; emotional reactions characteristic of boredom may also appear.

College students in these satiation experiments were asked to draw vertical lines on a sheet of paper following a specified pattern. As subjects filled one sheet of paper after another, the paper supply was replenished. They were not allowed to stop and rest. Gradually the quality of work declined, until it was sometimes difficult to make out what had been done. Only the retention of a particular pattern seemed to connect the later products of work with the earlier ones. After about four hours, the average subject could not continue, that is, was satiated on this task. The stages of (1) variability, (2) reduction in quality, (3) difficulty in continuing to make the necessary movements, and (4) complete inability to go on with the work characterized the course of satiation.

To demonstrate that the satiation could not be attributed to the fatiguing of the musculature involved, the experimenter merely changed the instructions. Subjects who could not write any more were told to finish the page or to write their names on the sheets, and their ability to write was completely restored.

Another aspect of the experiment showed that variability in work delayed the onset of complete satiation. Individuals who were ingenious in finding variations in the execution of the task were able to continue longer.

When the experimenter introduced variations in the task, the stage of complete satiation was postponed. However, each change in instruction became less beneficial, so that eventually a whole type of activity was satiated.

The experiment was next tried on a group of unemployed men who were paid a small sum per hour to serve as subjects. These men worked a full eight-hour day, and their work continued to be as neat and accurate at the end of the day as it was at the outset. Unlike the college students, they found the work highly pleasant. One asked to have the job on a permanent basis.

The difference in performance of workers and college students was found to be due to the difference in the way the work appeared to them. To the unemployed workers, as each hour passed, they had moved along in the day and had earned more money. Analysis of the psychological experiences of the college students revealed that they tended to have the experience of marking time, going in circles, being on a treadmill; in other words, they experienced "getting nowhere." The paper supply did not diminish, they did not approach an end, and their activity achieved nothing; yet they felt they had to continue because they had consented to serve in the experiment.

The effect of the perception of a task on motivation and performance can also be illustrated by the case of a problem employee who worked in an industrial research laboratory. The employee's job required the processing and testing of new types of experimental plastics in small sample batches. The employee was asked by a visitor, "What do you do?" He replied, "I make little pieces of plastic, then put them into machines until they break." The surprised visitor persisted. "But what do they *do* with your work?" He responded, "They throw it away."

Although the scientists who were developing the new materials would probably describe the testing process in a very different way, it was not surprising, given his perception of his job, to find that this employee had chronic problems of absenteeism, safety violations, and alcoholism.

The absence of the experience of a *goal* or an *end* toward which an individual moves seems to be the cause of satiation, a cause that depends completely on the way he or she views the task.[58] In the writing experiment, a particular view of the task was encouraged by the situation, but in on-the-job situations, much variation may be expected. The same task may appear quite unlike to people with varied backgrounds, attitudes, and intellects. A particular person may not view a task in the same way on two occasions, or may react differently to two tasks that another feels are very similar. What appear to be unimportant modifications in the arrangement of a task may actually change the whole outlook of a group of dissatisfied workers.

ATTITUDE TOWARD THE TASK

It might be supposed that unpleasant tasks would be satiated more quickly than pleasant tasks. This assumption was not borne out by experiments on satiation. On the contrary, pleasant and unpleasant tasks were satiated at the same rate, both more quickly than tasks that did not generate emotional reaction. This finding suggests that satiation is something more than mere dislike for a job. It is a condition of being disturbed because of the failure of an action to lead to anything, rather than because of the inherent nature of the task. It also appears that reducing emotional involvement in the task may reduce satiation. Perhaps daydreaming and background music are helpful in industry because they dominate the person emotionally and so make the task a secondary, hence more neutral, activity. The physiological condition of the person also was found to influence susceptibility to satiation.[59]

METHODS OF ELIMINATING BOREDOM IN INDUSTRY

The method of dealing with the problem of eliminating boredom will naturally vary for different types of work. In order to alter the way in which a job is experienced, it may be necessary to make changes in the work pattern.

JOB ROTATION AND JOB ENLARGEMENT

If variability in a task delays the onset of satiation, it may be said that a change in work is as good as a rest insofar as satiation is part of the general state of fatigue. For this reason, any changes in work that are instituted must give the person the *experience* of doing something different. What one person regards as different may be the same old grind to another. When high degrees of skill are not at a premium, it is probably expedient to permit employees to exchange jobs for days or parts of days. Variability on the same job should also be permitted. Different ways of doing the job, fluctuations in pace, and other variations that the worker may adopt serve the purpose if they are not extensive enough to interfere with skill or to increase muscular fatigue. Rotating between simple jobs or positions on an assembly line and combining several simple jobs introduce variety by enlarging the job.[60]

A few illustrations will suffice to show how this principle of variation may be applied. J. R. P. French reported improvement in job attitudes as a result of variation within a job.[61] He had women working on a sewing operation fill out *pacing cards*. The cards divided the shift into hourly work periods, and the workers were requested to indicate the hours of the day during which they wanted to work at slow, medium, and fast paces. They were encouraged to introduce variations in these paces and to try out a variety of plans. This planned variety in pacing had a beneficial effect on both attitude and productivity.

In a central office housing telephone equipment, it was found that two types of maintenance jobs were a constant source of difficulty. These were the jobs of the solderers and the dusters. The duty of the duster was to go over the equipment constantly to keep it clean; that of the solderer was to check the many wires and correct any loose or faulty contacts. Job attitudes were poor; the workers fought; turnover was high. The employees complained of being overworked. Assuming the jobs to be monotonous and recognizing that the training problem was a minor one, the workers were given the opportunity to change jobs. All accepted the opportunity. Half of them dusted and half soldered, but every two hours they exchanged jobs. The two supervisors of the twenty employees agreed that conditions had improved and continued to improve for the following year at least. Also interesting was the fact that the dusters now dusted as much on a half-time basis as they had previously full time. A similar though somewhat smaller improvement occurred with the solderers.

The use of job rotation to counteract boredom resulting from automation also should be considered. In training operators for new jobs in a fully automated plant, rotation among the jobs was instituted. This practice was continued beyond the training stage and was found to be an important factor in the increased job interest that the operators experienced in the modern power plant.[62] A comparison was made of the feelings toward rotation of operators not removed to the new power plant (and not having experienced job rotation) with operators moved to the new plant (and having experienced it). The response of the operators who had experienced rotation showed that 70 percent "liked rotation very much," whereas only 37 percent of the operators who lacked the experience anticipated that they would like it, and 17 percent indicated they would "dislike it a lot." Perhaps concern about the new learning required dampened the expectations of those who had not experienced rotation.

Both job rotation and job enlargement contribute to job interest and job satisfaction for many people because they increase job complexity. The power plant study demonstrated that the satisfaction from job rotation did not come from greater mobility or more contacts with fellow workers. The evidence indicates that job interest is a function of job duties. If job enlargement and job rotation can be incorporated in the work while remaining within practical limitations of training costs, it seems advisable to do so on jobs that require attention and cannot be reduced to simple habits.

RELATING THE JOB TO THE LARGER PICTURE

In general, the term *red tape* refers to activity that is experienced as boring and unnecessary. If employees do not understand what a detailed record is used for, they react to it as unnecessary. Teaching employees how their work fits into the total organizational task might change some perceptions of red tape.

Giving employees responsibility and opportunities for judgment is also effective in accomplishing this end. Too often, the supervisor tells a skilled worker exactly what to do on a repair job without saying why or giving the worker a chance to get involved in the task. Assignments can become opportunities for involving the workers in problem solving if the supervisor welcomes their ideas about how to do the job.

THE USE OF PACING METHODS AND AUTOMATIC WORK HABITS

Our analysis has shown that repetitive work creates mental satiation and perhaps boredom as well, not because the activity is repetitive, but because it creates the experience of not making progress. If the experience can be changed, but the activity left the same, the boredom will partly disappear. This point suggests that repetitive work should be made automatic whenever possible. A job that is second nature to a worker frees the mind. For instance, we do not get bored with walking because our thoughts can be on other things. However, if we perceive walking consciously as picking up the feet and putting them down again, this activity would seem very dull. Walking, however, permits contemplation, daydreaming, and conversation.

Since many jobs are as automatic as walking, conversation and daydreaming should be encouraged in these cases. Industrial research has shown that monotony disappears when daydreaming is prevalent.[63] A survey in Germany revealed that about 90 percent of the factory workers preferred repetitive, rhythmic tasks because these gave them a chance to think of other things while working.[64]

However, taking the mind from work may interfere with keeping up a work pace. It takes attention to keep going at a rapid speed. Industrial research has demonstrated that jobs repetitive in nature may benefit by external pacing methods. For example, production on a job involving the sorting of metal plates rose nearly 18 percent when a metronome was used to set the pace.[65]

THE EFFECTS OF BACKGROUND MUSIC

The use of background music in plants and offices has become fairly common.[66] English studies of the effects of musical programs on simple assembly operations showed production increases up to 6 percent when production on days with music was compared to that on days without music.[67] In an assembly plant in which music was customarily played, the effectivenss of fast, slow, and mixed programs was studied.[68] The scrappage rate was found to be less when either fast or slow music was consistently played than when there was no music or when fast and slow musical programs were alternated. Musical programs also were reported to have a beneficial effect on employee attitudes.

Subsequent studies tend to support the general finding that some production increases are obtained and that favorable effects upon employees' states of mind occur.[69] The increase in production varies considerably with the job and with the shift. Simple repetitive jobs that can be performed well while talking seem to benefit most by music. In one investigation, no production increase was obtained, but the job studied was a complex one, in that judgment, thought, and working cooperatively with another person were required.[70] However, employees thought their production was better with music. One overview of research findings indicates that music seems to encourage young, inexperienced workers to increase production on routine jobs. No significant effects were found for older skilled workers.[71]

Although music may be beneficial for a number of reasons, one of the most favorable effects is its influence on boredom. It takes the mind from the work as well as frees the brain of the obligation of initiating activity. Moreover, progress may be experienced by moving through a musical program, even if the job tends to give the experience of getting nowhere.

THE PSYCHOLOGICAL EFFECTS OF INCOMPLETE TASKS

Modern production methods are characterized by the division of the manufacturing of an industrial product into many units or subassemblies. Each worker makes or assembles only a part, so that few employees have the experience of turning out a complete object. Is it essential to job satisfaction that the task be completed?

It is a common occurrence for a person to put off starting a job near the end of the day. This behavior indicates a general tendency to avoid starting something that cannot be finished. Since this is the case, it is unjust to regard such activities at the end of the day as simply avoidance of effort.

THE NONCOMPLETION OF TASKS (THE ZEIGARNIK EFFECT)

To obtain an index of the effect of preventing the completion of a task, one experimenter measured the influence of work interruption on memory.[72] Subjects were asked to perform a group of twenty simple tasks, such as modeling animals or stringing beads. Half of the time, participants were allowed to finish the tasks, but during the other half, they were interrupted and completion was prevented. At the end of the experiment, the subjects were asked to list all the tasks that they had performed. The incompleted tasks were remembered twice as frequently as the completed ones. Retests given some time later showed the same difference. A finished task was easy to forget; an unfinished one lingered in the memory and even bothered participants. When permitted to finish the incompleted tasks later, participants were relieved and the memory difference disappeared. The psychological uneasiness and memory persistence caused by leaving a task unfinished has been named the *Zeigarnik effect*, after the woman who performed the original experiments.

Other aspects of the experiment made it clear that a certain energy system is built up when a task is being performed and that it is the strain of the unspent energy that influences the memory. A strong emotion tended to break up these strains, indicating that the energy system had its basis in emotional energy. Fatigue tends to reduce the energy available for a task, and when the experiments were performed under conditions of fatigue, there was less difference between the effects of completing and not completing tasks.

The experimental evidence demonstrates that the performance of a task sets up a psychological condition that demands its completion. The strength of this demand varies with the task, the stage of interruption, and the individual. More recent evidence indicates that tasks left uncompleted by one person may cause another to feel the need to complete them.[73] Unfinished tasks as such, depending on how they are experienced, seem to have a disturbing effect and must be carefully considered in investigations of job satisfaction.[74]

Tasks that have a definite point of completion are the most affected by interruption. For example, when modeling a clay dog, the task is not finished until the animal is complete. Interruption of such tasks invariably caused definite reactions. In contrast, the activity of stringing beads was often experienced as completed despite the interruption. A partly finished long string of beads may also be a completed smaller string.

The point at which a task is interrupted is a very important factor. Other things being equal, interruptions toward the end of the task create a stronger desire for completion than interruptions occurring toward the beginning. As the goal or end of the task is approached, the motivation to complete it rises and the tension created by interruption increases.

TASK COMPLETION AND MOTIVATION

The experiments on task interruption clearly demonstrate that the completion of a task represents a strong goal or incentive. Anything that is done to permit experiences of task completion would represent a kind of motivation and as such should be considered in connection with methods for increasing motivation on the job. Sometimes the very factors that induce efficiency unintentionally have introduced another form of inefficiency and job dissatisfaction through job segmentation. This is the basis for one criticism of the assembly-line method.

REDUCING INTERRUPTIONS AND INCREASING TASK COMPLETION

Two approaches to the application of the experimental findings are possible: (1) to do what is feasible to prevent interruptions, and (2) to create additional kinds of completion experiences. Each method suggests a variety of innovations. Preventing interruptions means not only elimination of unnecessary interruptions, but also reorganization of the situation so that the purpose of the interruption is viewed differently.

For example, a boy is playing in the yard, and his mother wants him to come in for lunch. For the good of the child and the convenience of the mother, his play must be interrupted. Frequently a child resists interruption and does not come when called. If force is used, an emotional scene rather than a pleasant lunch may result. Let us suppose, however, that the mother realizes that the child is pretending that he is trucking freight to Chicago. Under these circumstances, she could point out that she owns a restaurant on the road to Chicago and ask if the truck driver would like to stop for a meal. The child can now stop for lunch without his play being interrupted. Moreover, the mother makes capital of the situation in that the child now eats like a truck driver.

Interruptions can frequently be prevented by specifying stopping points. A girl can be told that she will have to come home after one more ride on the merry-go-round; children might agree to a five-inning baseball game and experience this point as the stopping place; poker players find it easier to quit at a reasonable hour if they set one additional hand as the completion point.

Another method of preventing interruption is to remind a person of an approaching appointment, thereby providing an opportunity to come to a stopping place. In this case, the burden of finding a good stopping point is left to the person interrupted. The reader will recall frequently looking over a task to see how much there is left to do and indeed may have already looked ahead in this chapter to see how many more pages remain. This will be particularly true when the reader has an engagement and must leave soon. If many pages remain, one may settle for reading to the end of a section.

There are two ways to create new or additional completion points: (1) grouping small units together, and (2) dividing a long job into sections. These two methods of increasing the experience of completion are shown in Figure 15.3. Method I applies to repetitive assembly and inspection jobs where progress cannot be experienced because each unit is too small to be perceived

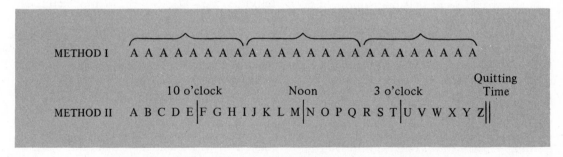

FIGURE 15.3 METHODS FOR INTRODUCING COMPLETION POINTS

Method I illustrates repetitive activity that has no terminal point. Inspecting ball bearings delivered on a belt and dropped into a chute would be an example. If the inspected bearings are dropped into boxes that fill up, each full box becomes a complete unit. Method II illustrates a long job that may not be finished for days, weeks, or months. Such a job lacks completion experiences, too, even though it is not repetitive. If the job is planned and objectives are set for each hour or two, workers experience reaching these points as the completion of a succession of units. These units are the natural rest pauses.

as the completion of something. Method II applies to construction jobs that have a specific completion point, but one that is too far in the future to permit experiences of progress and the frequent satisfaction of finishing something. The size of the unit of work that seems most effective in actual practice is a unit that requires one to one and a half hours to finish.[75]

ADAPTING LABORATORY FINDINGS TO THE JOB

AVOIDING JOB INTERRUPTION

If the tendency to complete a task is a source of motivation, it should be constructively used. It is most characteristic of persons who become engrossed in their work. Constant frustration by interruptions forces such people to cease becoming engrossed in what they are doing. In one study, it was found that the typical first-level supervisor was repeatedly interrupted and engaged in approximately four hundred to six hundred different episodes during the working day.[76] Thus, it would seem that one source of fatigue tension might well lie in the many interruptions that prevent task completion.

Little changes in the layout of a job may do much to eliminate the frustration produced by the intrusion of others. Since a person may not be aware that these interruptions are the causes of friction, they continue undetected by management. In the painting department of one plant in Detroit, there was constant friction between inspectors and workers. It was the practice of the inspectors to point out to the painters places that they had missed and to have them correct the oversights as they were discovered. After an analysis of the effect of noncompletion of tasks, the job was rearranged. A worker with a pail of paint was delegated to accompany the inspector and to fix up the places missed by the regular painters. This procedure eliminated the inspector's interruption of the workers. The result of this minor change in the inspection methods was to establish harmony in the whole department and to increase production.

It is common in industry for friction to arise between people working on different shifts. Part of this trouble is undoubtedly attributable to the fact that one worker must finish a unit begun by another.[77] This unit, the product of two people, is frequently below standard quality, and the worker who finishes it often blames the poor quality on the person who started the work.

INCREASING THE EXPERIENCE OF COMPLETION

Management should be vitally concerned with having its employees experience their tasks as complete units or wholes. These units may be a box of one hundred parts, the complete assembly of a unit of a radio, or the finishing of a set of orders. If pay is given in terms of these arbitrary units, these activities can achieve the same status as building a complete unit. Completion of a task is an experience that can be influenced by the way the job is set up. One or the other of the two basic methods for creating artificial units described in Figure 15.3 can be applied to practically any job.

Boredom in the plant department of the telephone industry is most pronounced in jobs concerned with maintenance of central office equipment. There is little challenge in diagnosing trouble, and the job is very confining since a person can work for hours within a space of a few feet. There is never a real experience of progress; when the job is finished, the worker must start the whole operation again. Outside workers, on the other hand, feel very little boredom even if they constantly do the same work over and over. They at least go from one location to another.

In one plant, method I of Figure 15.3 was applied by subdividing the frames on which the employees worked with chalk lines. The effect of the lines was to create blocks of work. Each square of work bounded by lines was given a tag with a red and a green side. When the red side was up, it meant that the work on the unit had not been done; the green showed that the job was finished. No tag meant that someone was working on that unit.

Each block required between one and two hours to complete. The worker made the choice of the unit on which to work. The selections made permitted progressive jumps from one end of the frame to the other, so that in a single day a worker not only worked in different parts of the room but progressed from one end to the other.

The benefits of this pattern of work were immediately apparent. No unit was ever left without a tag: once a person selected a block, it was worked on until it was finished. Every time workers completed a unit, they took a short break. Even lunch and quitting time revealed no untagged units. The employees liked the plan, and supervisors reported that complaints decreased and difficulty meeting work schedules was eliminated.

An application of method II for creating extra completion units was tried out with telephone installers. It is characteristic for these installers to do three, four, or five complete installations per day, but not three and a half or four and a half. In this case the installation job was divided into units A, B, and C, representing work inside the house, at the pole, and between house and pole, respectively. Work records were kept on the number of units completed, and the super-

visor talked in terms of these units rather than of installations. In the crew on which this method was tested, it was found that production records of ten, eleven, thirteen, fourteen, and sixteen units occurred about as frequently as production scores of nine, twelve, and fifteen units. The first set of scores represents incompleted installations, the second set represents completed ones. The fact that workers responded to these arbitrary units as readily as to natural ones suggest that artificial units can become realistic, as far as completion experiences are concerned. The relationship between performance and goals and the negative relationship between performance and boredom is borne out by laboratory research.[78]

JOB ENRICHMENT

Job enlargement may be regarded as a way of removing boredom from work, and job enrichment, as a way of adding interests or satisfiers to it. As discussed in Chapter 13, a job can be made more motivating by either removing the negative features or introducing positive ones. Increasing completion experiences therefore represents a form of job enrichment.

The concept of job enrichment has been very popular; many studies supporting its value have appeared in the literature.[79] But other studies have indicated that job enrichment is not perceived as desirable by all employees.[80]

A more sophisticated approach has been developed that takes account of differences in employees' viewpoint.[81] In this method, through an initial survey the potential of a job for enrichment, the current level of employee satisfaction, and the employee's desire for greater responsibility are measured. Differing responses can then be selected based on the individual worker's interests and aspirations. This technique recognizes that some instances of poor performance may be due to nonmotivational factors and that low motivation may be caused by non–work-related factors.

Participation in solving job problems and searching for ways to make work more interesting can facilitate job enrichment. Since certain job changes may increase challenge for some workers and frustrate others, it is important that job enrichment not be forced on workers by experts, yet experts may be needed to spark the ideas of workers. Problem-solving discussions with subordinates could generate ideas that would enrich jobs. The fact that such discussions are seldom held in organizations indicates the untapped potential for making work more interesting.

NOTES

1. Bartley, S. H. Conflict, frustration and fatigue, *Psychosom. Med.*, 1943, *5*, 160–163; Cattell, R. B., and Schierer, I. *The meaning and measurement of neuroticism and anxiety.* New York: Ronald, 1960, Chapters 9 and 10; French, G. W. The clinical significance of tiredness, *Canad. Med. Assn. J.*, 1960, *82*, 665–671; Schwab, R. S., and DeLorno, T. Psychiatric findings in fatigue. *Amer. J. Psychiat.*, 1953, *109*, 621–625.

2. Bartley, S. H., and Chute, E. *Fatigue and impairment in man.* New York: McGraw-Hill, 1947, Chapter 2; Karpovich, P. V. *Physiology of muscular activity.* Philadelphia: Saunders, 1959; Ryan, T. A. *Work and effort: The psychology of production.* New York: Ronald, 1947, Chapters 3, 4, and 5; Viteles, M. S. *Industrial Psychology.* New York: Norton, 1932, Chapter 21.

3. Bujas, Z., Petz, B., Krković, A., and Sorokin, B. Analysis of factors in intellectual performance under fatigue and without fatigue. *Acta Instituti Psychol.*, 1961, *23*, 11–22.

4. Mosso, A. *Fatigue.*, Trans. by M. Drummond and W. B. Drummond. New York: Putnam, 1904.

5. Gilbreth, F. B., and Gilbreth, L. M. *Fatigue study.* New York: Macmillan, 1919.

6. Gärtner, H. Ermüdungsüberwindung vom Standpunkt der Hygiene. *Mensch u. Arbeit*, 1952, *5*, 156–170.

7. Dimitrova, S. Dependence of voluntary effort upon the magnitude of the goal and the way it is set in sportsmen. *Internatl. J. Sport Psychol.*, 1970, *1*, 29–33.

8. Mezerik, A. G. The factory manager learns the facts of life. *Harper's Mag.*, 1943, *187*, 289–297.

9. Bornemann, E. Psychologische Wege zur Verminderung der Ermudung in Betrieb und Schule. *Mensch u. Arbeit*, 1952, *5*, 133–144.

10. Vernon, H. M. *Industrial fatigue and efficiency.* London: Routledge, 1921.

11. Directorate of Aerospace Safety. *Psychophysiological factors in major USA aircraft accidents.* Norton AFB, Calif.: USAF Study, 1962, 39–62.

12. Fraser, D. C. Recent experimental work in the study of fatigue. In E. A. Fleishman (Ed.), *Studies in personnel and industrial psychology.* New York: Dorsey, 1961, pp. 473–478.

13. Takahuwa, E. The function of concentration maintenance (T.A.F.) as an evaluation of fatigue. *Ergonomics*, 1962, *5*, 37–49.

14. Wilkinson, R. T. Effects of up to 60 hours sleep deprivation on different types of work. *Ergonomics*, 1964, *7*, 175–186.

15. Goldmark, J., et al. Studies in industrial physiology: Fatigue in relation to working capacity: I. Comparison of an eight-hour plant and a ten-hour plant. *Publ. Health Bull.*, 1920 (106).

16. Bartley, S. H. A factor in visual fatigue. *Psychosom. Med.*, 1942, *4*, 275–396; Bartley, S. H. Conflict, frustration, and fatigue, op. cit.

17. Carmichael, L., and Dearborn, W. F. *Reading and visual fatigue.* Boston: Houghton Mifflin, 1947.

18. For a detailed discussion, see Viteles, op. cit., pp. 470–482; Vernon, op. cit., pp. 98–115.

19. Vernon, H. M., and Bedford, T. *The influence of rest pauses on light industrial work.* Industr. Fat. Res. Bd., 1924, Rep. No. 25.

20. Farmer, E., and Bevington, S. M. An experiment in the introduction of rest pauses. *Nat. Inst. Industr. Psychol.,* 1922, *1,* 89–92.

21. Shepherd, G. Effects of rest pauses on production. *Personnel J.,* 1928, 7, 186–202.

22. Vernon, H. M. The influence of hours of work and of ventilation on output in tin plate manufacture. *Industr. Fat. Res. Bd.,* 1919, Rep. No. 1.

23. Muscio, B. *Lectures in industrial psychology.* London: Routledge, 1920

24. *The Nation,* April 11, 1952, p. 412.

25. Bartley and Chute, op. cit., Chapter 2: Vernon, H. M. The influence of hours of work and ventilation on output in tin plate manufacture, op.cit.

26. *Kalends.* Baltimore, Waverly Press, 1937, *3* 5–8.

27. Miles, G. H., and Angles, A. The influence of short time on speed of production. *J. Nat. Industr. Psychol.,* 1925, *2,* 300–302.

28. Golembiewski, K. T., Hilles, R., and Kagno, M. S. A longitudinal study of flex-time effects: Some consequences of an organizational development structural intervention. *J. Appl. Psychol.,* 1974, *10,* 503–532.

29. Wyatt, S., and Marriott, R. Night work and shift changes. *Brit. J. Industr. Med.,* 1953, *10,* 164–172.

30. Bloom, W. Shift work and the sleep-wakefulness cycle. *Personnel,* 1961, *38,* 24–31.

31. Wilensky, H. L. The uneven distribution of leisure: The impact of economic growth on "free time." In E. O. Smigel (Ed.), *Work and leisure.* New Haven, Conn.: College and University Press, 1963, pp. 107–145.

32. Schoonmaker, A. N. *Anxiety and the executive.* New York: American Management Association, 1969.

33. Meyer, H. E. The boss ought to take more time off. *Fortune,* 1974, *89*(6), 140–142ff.

34. Mast, T. M., and Heimstra, N. W. Effects of fatigue on vigilance performance. *J. Engr. Psychol.,* 1964, *3,* 73–79.

35. Faunce, W. A. Automation and leisure. In E. O. Smigel (Ed.), *Work and leisure.* New Haven, Conn.: College and University Press, 1963, pp. 85–106; Henle, P. Recent growth of paid leisure for U. S. workers. In W. Galenson and S. M. Lipset (Eds.), *Labor and trade unions.* New York: Wiley, 1960; Meany urges 35-hour work week. *Det. News,* November 12, 1963, 6d; U.S. labor: Affluence vs. influence. *Newsweek,* November 25, 1963, 85–88.

36. Faunce, ibid., pp. 92–95.

37. Wrenn, C. G. Human values and work in American life. In H. Borow (Ed.), *Man in a world at work.* Boston: Houghton-Mifflin, 1964.

38. Wrenn, ibid.

39. Huizinga, J. *Homo ludens: A study of the play element in culture.* Boston: Beacon Press, 1955; Berger, B. M. The sociology of leisure. *Indus. Rel.,* 1962, *1*(2); Weiss, R., and Reisman, D. Some issues in the future of leisure. *Soc Prob.,* 1961, *9,* 78–86; Kaplan, M. *Leisure in America: A social inquiry.* New York: Wiley, 1960; Kerr, W. *The decline of pleasure.* New York: Simon & Schuster, 1962.

40. Spock, B. "The family is changing." In *Baby and child care,* revised. New York: Pocket Books, 1977, pp. 37–38.

41. Harlan, W. H. The meaning of work and retirement for coal-miners. In E. A. Friedmann et al. (Eds.), *The meaning of work and retirement.* Chicago: University of Chicago Press, 1954, pp. 53–98.

42. Campbell, J. P., and Pritchard, R. D. Motivation theory in industrial and organizational psychology. In M. D. Dunnette (Ed.), *Handbook of industrial and organizational psychology*. Chicago: Rand-McNally, 1976.

43. Crutchfield, R. S. Psychological distance as a function of psychological need. *J. Comp. Psychol.*, 1939, *28, 447–469.*

44. A good summary of this work can be found in Bartley and Chute, op.cit.

45. Bornemann, op. cit.

46. Gergum, B. O., and Lehr, D. J. Vigilance performance as a function of interpolated rest. *J. Appl. Psychol.*, 1962, *46, 425–427.*

47. Mackworth, J. F. *Vigilance and habituation: A neuropsychological approach.* Baltimore, Md.: Penguin, 1970; Alluisi, E. A. Sustained performance. In E. A. Bilodeau and I. M. Bilodeau, *Principles of skill acquisition.* New York: Academic Press, 1969.

48. Brink, F., Jr. Excitation and conduction in the neuron. In S. S. Stevens (Ed.), *Handbook of experimental psychology.* New York: Wiley, 1951, pp. 50–93.

49. Ford, A. Bioelectric potentials and mental effort: I. Cardiac effects. *J. Comp. Physiol. Psychol.*, 1953, *46, 347–351.*

50. Bills, A. G. Blocking: A new principle in mental fatigue. *Amer. J. Psychol.*, 1931, *43,* 230–245; Bills, A. G. Fatigue, oscillation, and blocks, *J. Exp. Psychol.*, 1935, *18,* 562–573; Warren, N., and Clark, B. Blocking in mental and motor tasks during a 65 hour vigil. *Psychol. Bull.*, 1936, *33,* 814–815.

51. Baldamus, W. Incentives and work analysis. *University of Birmingham studies of economics and society,* Monogr. Al, 1951, 1–78.

52. Wyatt, S., Fraser, J. A., and Stock, F. G. L. *The effects of monotony in work.* Indust. Fat. Res. Bd., 1929, Rep. No. 56.

53. Csikszentmihalyi, M. *Beyond boredom and anxiety.* San Francisco: Jossey-Bass, 1975.

54. Wyatt, S., Langdon, J. N., and Stock, F. G. L. *Fatigue and boredom in repetitive work.* Indust. Health Res. Bd., 1937, Rep. No. 77.

55. Smith, P. C. The prediction of individual differences in susceptibility to industrial monotony. *Amer. Psychologist,* 1951, *6,* 361.

56. Rothe, H. F. Output rates among butter wrappers: II. Work curves and their stability. *J. Appl. Psychol.*, 1946, *30,* 199–211; Smith, P. C. The curve of output as a criterion of boredom. *J. Appl. Psychol.*, 1953, *37,* 69–74.

57. Karsten, A. Psychische Sättigung. *Psychol. Forsch.*, 1928, *10,* 142–154. These experiments are also described in Lewin, K. *A dynamic theory of personality.* New York: McGraw-Hill, 1935, pp. 254–257.

58. See Locke, E. A., Cartledge, N., and Kuerr, C. S. Studies of the relationship between satisfaction, goal-setting and performance. *Organ. Behav. Human Perform.*, 1970, *5,* 135–158, for a more complete discussion of the relationship between experience of progress, performance, and satisfaction.

59. Freund, A. Psychische Sättigung in Menstruum und Intermenstruum. *Psychol. Forsch.*, 1930, *13,* 198–217.

60. Schoderbek, P. P., and Reif, W. E. *Job enlargement: Key to improved performance.* Ann Arbor, Mich.: Bureau of Industrial Relations, University of Michigan, 1969.

61. French, J. R. P., Jr. Field experiments: Changing group productivity. In J. G. Miller (Ed.), *Experiments in social psychology.* New York: McGraw-Hill, 1950, Chapter 6.

62. Mann, F. C., and Hoffman, L. R. *Automation and the worker.* New York: Holt, 1960.

63. Wyatt, Fraser, and Stock, op. cit.

64. Arendt, H. *The human condition.* Chicago: University of Chicago Press, 1958.

65. Reinhardt, H. Rhythmus und Arbeitsleistung. *Indust. Psychotechn.*, 1926, *3,* 225–237.

66. Benson, B. E. *Music and sound systems in industry*. New York: McGraw-Hill, 1945.

67. Wyatt, Langdon, and Stock, op cit.

68. Humes, J. F. The effect of occupational music on scrappage in the manufacturing of radio tubes. *J. Appl. Psychol.*, 1941, *25*, 573–587.

69. Kerr, W. A. Effects of music on factory production. *Appl. Psychol. Monogr.*, 1945, *5*; Smith, H. C. Music in relation to employee attitudes, piece-work production and industrial accidents. *Appl. Psychol. Monogr.*, 1947, *14*.

70. McGehee, W., and Gardner, J. E. Music in a complex industrial job. *Personnel Psychol.*, 1949, *2*, 405–417; Newman, R. I., Jr., Hunt, D. L., and Rhodes, F. Effects of music on employee attitude and productivity in a skateboard factory. *J. Appl. Psychol.*, 1966, *50*, 493–496.

71. Uhrbock, R. S. Music on the job: Its influence on worker morale and production. *Personnel Psychol.*, 1961, *14*, 9–38.

72. Zeigarnik, B. Über das Behalten von erledigten und unerledigten Handlungen. *Psychol. Forsch.*, 1927, *9*, 1–85.

73. Henle, M., and Aull, G. Factors decisive for resumption of interrupted activities: The question reopened. *Psychol. Rev.*, 1953, *60*, 81–88; Horwitz, M. The recall of interrupted group tasks: An experimental study of individual motivation in relation to group goals. In D. Cartwright and A. Zander (Eds.), *Group dynamics*. Evanston, Ill.: Row, Peterson, 1953, Chapter 25.

74. Atkinson, J. W. The achievement motive and recall of interrupted and completed tasks. *J. Exp. Psychol.*, 1953, *46*, 381–390; Cartwright, D. The effect of interruption, completion and failure on the attractiveness of activities. *J. Exp. Psychol.*, 1942, *31*, 1–16; Marrow, A. J. Goal tensions and recall. *J. Gen. Psychol.*, 1938, *19*, 3–64.

75. Cox, D., and Sharp, K. M. D. Research on the unit of work. *Occup. Psychol.*, London, 1951, *25*, 90–108.

76. Walker, C. R., Guest, R. H., and Turner, A. N. *The foreman on the assembly line*. Cambridge, Mass.: Harvard University Press, 1956, pp. 123–124.

77. Roy, D. F. Work satisfaction and social reward in quota achievement: An analysis of piecework incentive. In W. Galenson and S. M. Lipset (Eds.), *Labor and trade unionism*. New York: Wiley, 1960, pp. 361–369.

78. Locke, E. A., and Bryan, J. F. Performance goals as determinants of level of performance and boredom. *J. Appl. Pschol.*, 1967, *51*, 120–130.

79. Herzberg, F. The wise old Turk. *Harv. Bus. Rev.*, 1974, *52*, 70–80; Horn, P. Worker involvement pays off. *Psychol. Today*, 1975, *9*, 89; Ford, R. N. *Motivation through the work itself*. New York: AMACOM, 1969.

80. Brief, A. P., and Alday, R. J. Employee reactions to job characteristics: A constructive replication. *J. Appl. Psychol.*, 1975, *60*, 182–186; Robey, D. Task design, work values and worker response: An experimental test. *Organ. Behav. Human Perform.*, 1974, *12*, 264–273; Suzansky, J. W. *The effects of individual characteristics as moderating variables of the relation between job design quality and job satisfaction*. Ph.D. dissertation, Stevens Inst. Technol., Hoboken, N.J. Wanous, J. P. Individual differences and reactions to job characteristics. *J. Appl. Psychol.*, 1974, *59*, 616–622.

81. Hackman, J. R., and Oldham, G. R. Development of the job diagnostic survey. *J. Appl. Psychol.*, 1975, *60*, 159–170; Hackman, J. R., Oldham, G. R., Janson, R., and Purdy, K. A new strategy for job enrichment. *Calif. Manage. Rev.*, 1975, *17*, 57–71.

SUGGESTED READINGS

Behling, O., Schriesheim, C., and Tolliver, J. Present theories and new directions in theories of work effort. *Journal Supplement Abstract Service*, Amer. Psychol. Corp., 1976.

Csikszentmihalyi, M. *Beyond boredom and anxiety.* San Francisco: Jossey-Bass, 1975.

Hackman, J. R., Oldham, G. R., Janson, R., and Purdy, K. A new strategy for job enrichment. *Cal. Mgt. R.,* 1975, 57–71.

Horn, P. Worker involvement pays off. *Psychol. Today,* 1975, 89.

Wrenn, C. G. Human values and work in American life. In H. Borow (Ed.), *Man in a world at work.* Boston: Houghton Mifflin, 1964.

LABORATORY EXERCISE

ROLE-PLAYING:
THE CASE OF THE PARASOL ASSEMBLY

(Students are asked not to read the case materials before participating in the laboratory exercise.)

A. PROCEDURE*

1. Eight persons are needed for this problem, one to play the part of the supervisor and the other seven to be subassembly workers.

2. If the room permits, arrange eight chairs in a circle, spaced to correspond to the positions of the workers shown in Figure 15.4. Chairs for observers should be arranged to form a circle or semicircle outside the ring of eight chairs. The desired pattern will simulate a theater-in-the-round.

3. The instructor will select seven students to play the roles of the workers and ask them to take their places in the circle.

4. Name tags should be placed on each person to indicate which of the workers he or she is portraying.

5. The instructor will select a person to play the role of Helen Benton, the supervisor who is to remain apart from the group of workers until the role-playing begins. The chalkboard should be used to show names of workers arranged in a circle.

*Case taken from Maier, N. R. F. The quality of group decisions as influenced by the discussion leader. *Hum. Relat.,* 1950, *3,* 155–174, with the permission of the Journal.

6. The observers are to analyze the effectiveness of Benton's leadership.

7. The instructor will read the general instructions (F.1) aloud to everyone. Permit a question period to clarify any points regarding work of this type. All persons should be encouraged to participate at this point.

8. Benton and the seven workers read their assigned roles (F.2, F.3).

B. THE ROLE-PLAYING-PROCESS

1. The role-players finish reading their instructions and put them aside.

2. The instructor checks to see whether the person playing Benton has any questions.

3. At a signal, Benton joins the group, who are seated in their work positions, and the case begins.

4. Approximately three-fourths of an hour is necessary to role-play this case.

5. If the instructor feels it is advisable to help the supervisor or to discuss some especially crucial aspect of the case, he or she should feel free to interrupt.

6. After an interruption, the role-playing continues, ignoring the interruption.

C. ANALYSIS OF THE QUALITY OF THE SOLUTION

1. Observers discuss the quality of the solution in terms of its objective excellence,

disregarding its acceptance by group members for the time being.

2. A high-quality solution should (1) give workers who wish and are able to do more a way to do it, and (2) acknowledge the existence of boredom and permit its reduction.

D. ANALYSIS OF GENERAL ACCEPTANCE

1. Determine which workers will cooperate with the new method, which are neutral, and which will cause trouble.
2. What could Benton have done to improve the acceptance? Discuss.

E. GENERAL DISCUSSION ON QUESTIONS

1. How should Benton have stated the problem to her group to stimulate problem-solving behavior?
2. How might Benton have made use of some of the differences of opinion in the group?
3. How could Benton have used the mention of such things as boredom, fear of breaking up the team, rotation, a bottleneck, and so on, to raise the level of thinking or to prevent the group's thinking from staying in a rut?

F. MATERIALS FOR THE CASE

1. General Instructions

Visualize a subassembly situation in which seven persons, working in a circle, assemble carburetors. The article enters the circle at one point, and workers add their pieces and push the unit to the next worker. When the unit leaves the circle, it is a completed carburetor. This work arrangement is diagrammed in Figure 15.4. It is called a *parasol assembly* because of the circular arrangement.

Suppose that there are four such parasol sub-assembly stations, each one with a supervisor. Suppose further that Station A assembles 85 units per day; Station B, 80 per day; Station C, 60 units per day; and Station D, 50 units. It is a fact that Station D previously assembled 60

units. The supervisor was dissatisfied with the production and reprimanded the group. Following the reprimand, production fell to 50 units per day. (Production scores should be posted on the board).

The assembly work is simple and requires a minimum of training for each step. The aptitude requirement is primarily good finger dexterity. The materials for each assembly position are located in bins which are kept supplied by material handlers. Thus, each worker has the essential material at his or her elbow. The job has been divided by motion-and-time experts to ensure that the positions are of equal difficulty. Pay is based on hourly rates.

The total plant production depends on receiving the required number of assembled units from these four stations. The production is now so low that the plant production as a whole has had to slow down. The desired quota is 300 parts per shift for the four stations combined.

We are concerned with Station C producing at the rate of 60 units. The work piles up at the position of Joe. The unit must pass through him (position 3) and he always has several piled up waiting for him. Supervisors on nonproduction jobs are not willing to accept Joe as a transfer. Joe is a man of sixty with thirty years of service in the company. Emphasis on improving production has brought his deficiencies to light.

2. Role for the Supervisor, Helen Benton

You are the new supervisor of Station C and have been instructed to get production up. The job has been analyzed by motion-and-time-study experts and the amount of work at each position is practically the same. The no. 3 position (Joe's position) is, however, slightly easier than the others in that one less motion is required. Undoubtedly, the previous supervisor put Joe there to reduce the bottleneck. You have received training in group-decision methods and are going to try to work out your problem by this method. You have therefore stopped the production line for a discussion. You understand that what you do is your problem. You cannot pass Joe to another supervisor. You find Joe a likeable per-

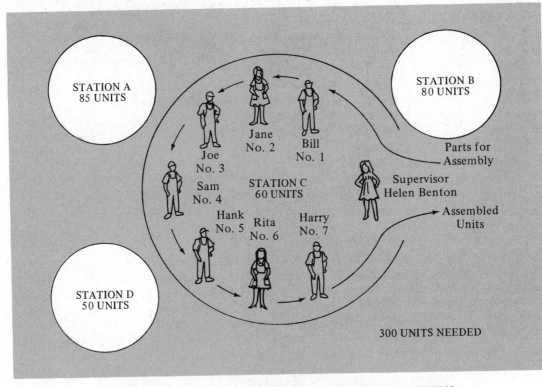

FIGURE 15.4 DIAGRAM OF FOUR SUBASSEMBLY STATIONS

The stations represent four groups of assemblers who work in teams and assemble carburetors. All groups do the same work and the combined output is 275 units, just 25 short of what is needed. The supervisor of station C wishes to raise her group's production. There is a bottleneck at the no. 3 position. Work piles up here, and the worker seems unable to keep up the pace. How can the problem be solved?

son, and it is your impression that Joe gets along well with the other workers in the unit.

3. Roles for Assembly Workers

Bill, No. 1
You find you can easily do more work but have to slow down because Joe gets behind. In order not to make him feel bad, you hold back. You don't want to get Joe into trouble.

Jane, No. 2
You and Bill work closely together, and you usually are waiting for your part from Bill. This waiting for the part is more prevalent in the latter part of the day than in the beginning. To keep busy, you often help out Joe who can't keep up. However, you are careful not to let the supervisor catch you helping Joe because she might let Joe go.

Joe, No. 3
You work hard but just aren't as fast as the others. You know you are holding things up, but no matter how you try, you get behind. The rest of the workers are fine people and have more energy than you do at your age.

Sam, No. 4
Joe has trouble keeping up and you sometimes grab Joe's part and finish it for him when the boss isn't looking. Joe is a bit old for the pace

MOTIVATING WORKERS FOR OPTIMUM PERFORMANCE

set, and he feels the strain, For you the job is easy, and you feel the whole job is slowed down too much because of Joe. "Why couldn't Joe be given less to do?" you ask yourself.

Hank, No. 5

You feel a bit uneasy on this job. There isn't enough to do, so you have to act busy. If only Joe could speed up a bit. Why don't they move him out of the group? Is the company so blind that they can't see where the production trouble is?

Rita, No. 6

You are able to keep up with the pace, but on the last assembly job you were pressed. Fortunately Joe is slower than you are, so he keeps the pressure off you. You are determined that Joe not be moved off the job. Somebody has to protect people from speed-up tactics.

Harry, No. 7

You get bored doing the same operations over and over. On some jobs, you get variety by working fast for a while, then slowly. On this job you can't work fast because the parts aren't fed to you fast enough. It gets you down to keep doing exactly the same thing over and over in slow motion. You are considering getting a job some place where they can keep a person busy. Maybe this new supervisor will get things going.

CHAPTER SIXTEEN

ACCIDENTS
IN
THE
WORKPLACE

■

Mechanical Safety Devices
Indirect Safety Measures   *Psychological Safety Devices*
Accident Proneness
Psychological Tests and Accident Frequency
Other Personal Factors Related to Accidents
The Clinical Approach to Accident Proneness
The Case-Study Approach   *Generating Positive Safety*
Attitudes
Application of Causation Model to Accident Prevention

■

PREVENTION OF ACCIDENTS may be approached from the viewpoint of the engineer or of the psychologist. The method of the engineer is to remove the hazard from the work by changing the operation of dangerous machinery, designing and installing safety devices, and inspecting the safety of the building and the machinery with a view to structural or functional changes. Simple improvements include enclosing moving parts, such as belts and gears; using different colors of paint to make stationary and moving parts more readily distinguishable; attaching guards so that the body cannot come in contact with rotating saws; designing safety goggles; and building floors or platforms to reduce chances of falling, slipping, or receiving electric shock. This approach has been a major factor in the reduction of industrial accidents in modern plants.

The psychological approach involves dealing with the human factors in accidents. Training employees to use safety methods and to become aware of hazards, developing attitudes of cooperation, reducing fatigue, and properly selecting people for their jobs are some of the psychological aspects of accident control. For safety devices to work properly, they must be used properly. Therefore psychological aspects of accident prevention cannot be separated from mechanical ones.

MECHANICAL SAFETY DEVICES

The designing of safety devices is largely an inventor's problem, and some operations must be greatly altered to permit safe procedures. Like the motion-and-time engineer, the safety engineer must have originality and mechanical ingenuity. However, certain general principles apply to most situations and serve as points of departure for further improvements. A common safety method is the use of guards that do not admit a part of the body, but do admit material to be brought next to the cutting edges of machinery. Another approach is the use of contact switches that break the electric circuit so that the hands must continue to press buttons as long as the machine is operating. Protective devices, such as special gloves, glasses to protect the eyes, and tools to hold the part to be cut or drilled are familiar safety aids.

The purpose of safety devices is to eliminate the danger points. Each one may be designed to remove a specific hazard; therefore, each safety mechanism may be in some way unique. But safety devices have some features in common and certain minimal specifications that must be met. The three most important psychological requirements of mechanical safety devices are examined here.

GOOD SAFETY DEVICES CANNOT BE DISENGAGED

A psychological problem arises when employees are required to use new safety devices, for many workers like to do the job in the old way, or worry that using safety devices is cowardly. They may feel that the new gadget slows production and that they are experienced enough to get along without it. Because of such reactions, workers must be educated to value safety methods.

Moreover, safety devices should be designed in such a way that they cannot be disengaged. The device that interrupts the electric current and prevents a machine from running when hands are not pressing down the safety button is intended to be of this

MOTIVATING WORKERS FOR OPTIMUM PERFORMANCE

Safety aids (top photo) like this auto welder's gloves and glasses, help protect against accidents. (Michael Hayman, Black Star) Bottom: Ample lighting in plants reduces the causes of accidents. (Courtesy of Clairol)

ACCIDENTS IN THE WORKPLACE

439

type. However, some operators circumvent this safety feature by jamming the button with a piece of wood to keep it depressed. The ingenuity of engineers in designing unbeatable safety devices seems to be a challenge to the ingenuity of workers with negative safety attitudes.

The best kind of safety device is one so arranged that the workers must use it in order to produce. When this arrangement is impossible, psychological motivation must be introduced. When workers are trained from the outset to operate a machine with a safety device, the problem of circumventing the device is less likely to arise.

GOOD SAFETY
DEVICES ARE FOOLPROOF

A second requirement for a safety device is that it be foolproof. A device that is only safe half the time may increase accidents because the worker may consider the machine safer than it really is and become less cautious.

Since people adjust to the perceived level of danger, existing points of hazard should be made more obvious. Safety devices that guard completely against one type of accident may leave other sources of danger untouched. Some safety devices may merely change the type of accident in a plant by protecting workers from one hazard and, at the same time, making them unaware of others. Hazards that remain should always be made clear to the workers while they are being trained. When hazards are clearly evident, the accidents that do occur tend to be without relation to the nature of the hazard.[1]

GOOD SAFETY
DEVICES DO NOT
INTERFERE WITH PRODUCTION

Safety devices that interfere with work are unsatisfactory because workers resist using them since they reduce productivity. It should be the goal of safety engineers to construct safety devices that do not handicap the work pattern. Actually, the work pattern can be improved by the motion analysis involved in planning such devices. With properly developed devices, production may be expected to increase because workers can apply themselves entirely to their work, instead of having to divide their energies between self-protection and work, a situation that rapidly induces fatigue.

INDIRECT SAFETY MEASURES

ELIMINATION OF FATIGUE

That fatigue is most conducive to accidents when it is extreme is indicated by the difference in the effect of long and short days on the accident rates of men and women. H. M. Vernon cites the case of a shell factory in England that changed from a twelve-hour day to a ten-hour day. This change did not materially alter the accident rate among men, but it reduced the accident rate among women by more than 60 percent.[2]

In the United States during the 1930s, the accident record was about 45 percent higher for women than for men. A good deal of this higher accident rate among women was attributed to accidents that occurred after the seventh hour of work.[3] It is probable that some of the fatigue in women was due to the fact that they have generally had more home responsibilities before and after work than men have. In some European countries, when home and work tasks were combined, work weeks for women averaged seventy hours and higher.[4] More recent studies have suggested that women represent a lower risk of accident repetition than do men.[5]

The relationship between fatigue and accidents is not limited to the purely physical aspects of fatigue that result in loss of skill, but includes such psychological factors as absent-mindedness and inattention arising from boredom. The weekly accident trend is often a mirror image of the production trend. Both the beginning and the end of the week show high accident frequencies.

GOOD LIGHTING

Accidents are about 25 percent greater under artificial lighting than under natural lighting, but these figures are influenced by seasonal variations. Day- and night-shift work also involve differences other than lighting. Driving accidents occur most frequently at dusk, and night driving is more hazardous than day driving.[6]

CONTROLLED ATMOSPHERIC CONDITIONS

Both temperature and humidity have been shown to be directly related to accident frequency.[7] In mining, minor accidents progressively increase as the temperature in different areas rises from 62 degrees to 85 degrees Fahrenheit. In mining sites having the highest temperature, the minor-accident frequency was over three times that of areas having the lowest temperature. Major accidents showed little relation to temperature, however.

For machine work, the optimum temperature for the English worker was found to be 67.5 degrees. An increase of 35 percent in accidents was obtained by a drop in temperature to 52 degrees or a rise to 75 degrees. It is probable that optimum temperatures vary with the way the worker dresses and

the temperature to which the worker is accustomed at home. Recently, the federal government established laws affecting thermostat settings in many businesses. The long-term effect of these regulations on accidents and performance is still unknown.

It is probable that conditions that are optimal for production will also favor a minimum of accidents. The problem of atmospheric conditions in relation to production will be considered in Chapter 19.

PSYCHOLOGICAL SAFETY DEVICES

SAFETY COMMITTEES

One method of ensuring employee participation is for each plant to have a safety committee, along with several subcommittees if the number of employees is large. Such committees should include both workers and a safety officer. Such a group, meeting regularly and reviewing reports, complaints, and suggestions from workers, helps to maintain safety consciousness.

A safety committee should serve in an educational capacity to prevent accidents and should watch for careless workers and potential hazards. Suggestions from workers have frequently led to constructive safety measures. With an active committee, social pressure will be exerted on the worker who declines to use safety measures and is generally careless.

New safety rules set as a result of the passage of the federal Occupational Health and Safety Act (OSHA) have changed the nature and scope of safety committees. To avoid possible citations, fines, or other penalties, companies must be able to *prove* they have sufficiently described safety hazards and trained workers in safe job methods.

SAFETY CAMPAIGNS AND POSTERS

The use of posters and slogans is often effective in raising support for safety. As in all advertising, the appeal should be simple, reasonable, and constructive. Emotional appeals may have temporary value, but if they arouse fear, they may do more harm than good.[8] A frightened worker is not a safe worker. Although a gruesome picture invariably attracts attention, it seldom creates a desirable effect.

Perhaps the most important requirement for an effective poster is that it contain a positive message. Advertising a remedy for cold feet has more appeal when the description is headlined "warm feet" than "cold feet." People whose feet are cold respond favorably to the goal of warm feet but are not attracted by a discussion of cold feet. A poster that says, "Don't have accidents," neither describes what you do want to have nor tells you *how* not to have the accidents. The following statements illustrate helpful information that could appear on posters placed in appropriate locations:

☐ Pedestrians Cross Here
☐ Smoking Permitted in the Next Aisle
☐ Wear Hard Hats Here
☐ Gasoline Fumes in This Area

Specific forms of behavior conducive to safety can be advertised in appropriate departments and serve a constructive purpose. The important thing is to approach safety in a positive, educational way rather than in a negative, moralistic way.

SAFETY HABITS

The discussion of training in Chapter 12 emphasized the desirability of stabilizing an efficient behavior pattern and building it into a strong habit. Training should include safety as one characteristic built into work habits. There are certain ways of holding a tool, specific body postures, and a few methods of applying pressure that are relatively safe, even if slippage or inaccuracies occur. On the other hand, certain movements that are unrelated to the job can expose the person to injury and should be eliminated. The proper methods of work must be known to trainers and taught to new employees.

Safety methods that are added to a job are more difficult to learn. The use of safety goggles is not part of the actual grinding operation; thus the operators must decide whether to use them each time they sharpen a tool. The probability of an unfavorable decision is increased (1) if the goggles are left behind and must be retrieved, (2) if the goggles are uncomfortable or (3) if they interfere with vision. To the extent that safe methods can be incorporated into the job as a habit and not tacked on as a precaution to be taken, the problem of job accidents will be reduced. Incorporation of safe behavior into the job is facilitated if the activity is pleasant or helpful, and is resisted if it is unpleasant.

Study of various industrial operations from the viewpoint of safety can lead to the building of habits that are highly dependable and natural. These habits may be thought of as *psychological safety devices*. Like the design of mechanical safety devices, the design of safety habits requires ingenuity.

When safe work habits have been made a part of the work pattern, it is unnecessary to warn employees to attend to the danger in their work. They can relax, assured that their habits will make their actions safe. The importance of stabilizing safe work habits is illustrated by the method used by many electricians to wire buildings. The current can be off or on during wiring, but the procedure is different under the two conditions. Given that in some cases the electrician must wire with the current on, the best approach is to teach only the "current on" procedure and always wire under those conditions. With a single procedure, a worker does not constantly have to be checking whether wires are "live" or not. Accidents caused by the workers' absent-minded handling of a live wire are largely prevented by this method. Eliminating absent-minded behavior is difficult; telling people not to be absent-minded is little more effective than telling them not to be the kind of human beings they are.

In many cases, the officially taught pattern of work may not be inherently superior to others, but safety demands that one method be used exclusively. If the five parts of a hypothetical job are always performed in the order A-B-C-D-E, accidents arising from several sources may be avoided. First, one worker can take over where another left off without the possibility of any misunderstanding as to what remains to be done; second, the worker can be interrupted after finishing part C and, upon returning, can pick up the job efficiently by noting that C has been done and D must be done next; and finally, there is a routine to follow without having to remember the five acts individually.

MOTIVATING SAFETY

Because some people openly disregard safety, some writers have been led to believe that accidents are sometimes a goal, that persons sometimes unconsciously wish to punish themselves in order to remove guilt feelings.[9] Other researchers have suggested that accident proneness may be related to some workers' impulsive wish to impress others with their "bravery."[10]

Another hypothesis is that workers have accidents to get time off the job. This assumption has been tested statistically.[11] Employees who had been with the company for four years were divided into two groups; those having no accidents (two hundred persons) and those having one or more accidents (eighty-nine persons). It was postulated that if persons had accidents to get time off, then those having accidents should absent themselves more from the job for other reasons also. Analysis of the data showed that the accident-free group averaged 15.0 noninjury absences and the accident group averaged 24.4 noninjury absences. This difference was not removed when job hazard was considered. One interpretation of the results may be that poor emotional adjustment is the cause of both types of absence. Accidents may occur because a person is preoccupied with other issues and behaviors, not because a person wishes to escape guilt or work.

Another aspect of accidents that makes tham appear as a positive choice is the presence of *countermotivation*. Two conflicting aspects of a job may both be emphasized: safety and production. Furthermore, the emphasis for each may come from different sources: the safety department promotes safety and the supervisor presses for higher production. Although the two goals are not always in conflict, close inspection will reveal instances in which they are. No job is so completely analyzed and controlled that hurrying and shortcuts are not possible. Hurrying introduces new hazards, and shortcuts often circumvent safety practices.

The influence of hurrying on accidents was clearly demonstrated in a survey of home injuries.[12] Table 16.1 shows that ordinary hurrying was responsible for more than one-third of the accidents that occurred in or around the home. Dispensing with activities designed to make work safe makes

TABLE 16.1 PERCENTAGE OF HOME INJURIES DUE TO VARIOUS BEHAVIORS

CAUSE	PERCENTAGE
Hurry	35
Not paying attention; absorbed, distracted	22
Excitement (except hurry or anger)	11
Doing wrong thing, but knew better	11
Doing wrong thing, but did not know better	7
Just wanted to do it; don't know why	8
Anger	4
Attention getting, "showing off"	2

SOURCE: Based on data from the University of Michigan School of Public Health, *Investigation and application of home injury survey data in development of preventative procedures*, 4th ed. 1953, p. 457.

a person appear to disregard safety, but strong motivation may cause people knowingly to take greater risks. Not wearing goggles saves the machinist the time and effort of getting them and putting them on; not wearing a hard hat when passing through certain structures makes it unnecessary for the worker to look after the hat; and not shutting off the motor to remove something from the machinery eliminates two acts. When a supervisor criticizes a person for doing less work than the others, motivation to cut corners is introduced.[13] The conflicting reinforcement between fast and safe performance is a frequent cause of accidents.

Safety measures may not only interfere with production, but also cause the worker some distress. This unpleasantness may stem from several sources, ranging from discomfort to attitudes. Safety belts, goggles, respirators, and other devices to be worn are often resisted because they are uncomfortable. Electrical workers, in one instance, avoided using hard hats because these caused them to be mistaken for lower-status construction workers. To conclude that employees are not interested in safety because they violate rules is to overlook important aspects of motivation.

ACCIDENT PRONENESS

SPECULATION CONCERNING THE DISTRIBUTION OF ACCIDENTS

Who has accidents and how do they happen? It may be assumed that accidents happen on a chance basis, that is, that everyone is equally subject to them and that having accidents is a matter of bad luck. It may be assumed that having an accident will make a person more careful, hence less subject to future accidents. It is also reasonable to assume that having an accident so upsets individuals that they will tend to have additional future accidents because of a loss in confidence or a heightened tension. Finally, the possibility exists that some individuals are prone to have accidents because of their biological and psychological makeup.

RESULTS OF INVESTIGATIONS

One of the earliest studies to test these hypotheses about accident proneness dealt with an analysis of the distribution of accidents among 648 employees in a shell factory.[14] The distribution of accidents obtained is shown in Table 16.2. This distribution does

TABLE 16.2 DISTRIBUTION OF ACCIDENTS

NUMBER OF ACCIDENTS	NUMBER OF WOMEN	
0	448	
1	132	622 workers had a total of 216 accidents, or 96 percent had 72 percent of the accidents.
2	42	
3	21	
4	3	26 workers had a total of 85 accidents, or 4 percent had 28 percent of the accidents.
5	2	

SOURCE: From M. Greenwood and H. M. Woods, *The incidence of industrial accidents with special reference to multiple accidents.* Industr. Fat. Res. Bd., 1919, Rep. No. 4.

not conform to chance expectancy. On the basis of chance, only 8 percent of the workers should have between three and five accidents. The finding that 96 percent of the workers had 72 percent of the accidents, while 4 percent of them had 28 percent of the accidents suggests that accidents are not random. The fact that a large number of workers had no accidents means that the period of observation was too brief to allow members of this group enough time to differentiate themselves.

Another approach, cited in the same investigation, involved comparison of the accident frequency of 198 workers during two successive periods. This analysis revealed that 136 of them had no accidents during the month of February, whereas 62 workers had one or more accidents (an average of 1.3 accidents) during the same period. From March to July, the 136 workers in the no-accident group had an average of .16 accidents per month, whereas the 62 workers in the accident group had an average of .35 accidents per month, or more than twice as many. This finding reveals that accidents not only fail to follow a chance pattern, but that they tend repeatedly to involve the same individuals.

That the accident rates of the workers during the second period did not exceed those during the first period indicates that there was no increase in the tendency to have accidents. This suggests that accidents are not associated with the same individuals because a previous accident has made them more susceptible. To explain the facts, there remains only the possibility that accidents are associated with certain people because they have behavior characteristics that make them susceptible to accidents.

The importance of the individual's characteristics in the incidence of accidents is also apparent when the relationship between two separate accident records of a group of individuals is measured. To indicate this relationship, accident scores of one observation period may be plotted against the scores of a second period. Correlation coefficients between two such periods commonly range from .37 to .72.

A comparison of accident scores of persons in two different work situations does not show as close a relationship as does a comparison of accident scores of those persons over two periods in the same situation. This suggests that certain individual characteristics predispose greater accident proneness in one situation than in another.

Studies suggesting that accidents were related to individual personality factors gave rise to the concept of *accident proneness,* and early investigators made it one of the important factors in the causes of accidents.

ACCIDENT LIABILITY

Accidents depend on the behavior of the person, on the degree of hazard in the situation, and on pure chance. For example, a person may be cut by plate glass while walking past a store window. Let us suppose that he just happened to be going by when someone else broke the window. This is the kind of injury that, from the standpoint of the person injured, may be described as due to chance — an accidental combination of circumstances. However, if store windows are broken frequently, in this case a person going down a street in the shopping district will be exposed to considerable danger. Although chance would still operate, the frequency of injuries would increase. The probability of chance combinations leading to injury is the measure for the degree of hazard. If a person is cut by flying glass because of slow reflexes, she has made a personal contribution to the accident. The differences in the degree to which various people contribute to accidents is the measure of proneness. The term *accident liability* includes all these factors and represents a more inclusive concept for evaluating accident data.[15]

Although a person's accident *record* also depends on all these factors, an individual's accident *liability* is not the same as an accident record. Liability refers to the expectation of a person having a given degree of likelihood of accident working under a constant degree of hazard and having an average amount of luck, whereas the record shows what actually happened. This is analogous to saying that a particular baseball team may be more likely to win than its opponent, but the actual score for a game may be different from this likelihood. Like a team's standing, probability of accidents is a statistical concept.

Because of this approach to accident analysis, it is apparent that the accident proneness of an individual should not be decided from limited evidence. To be accident prone, a worker must have more than a fair share of accidents, not because of exposure to more dangers, exposure for a greater percentage of the time, or a run of bad luck, but because of personal acts that contributed to the accidents. A driver's liability for car accidents may be high because he or she drives a lot, drives at excessive speeds, drives while drunk, has a car with poor brakes and faulty lights, has poor vision in one eye, is too small or large to operate the vehicle properly, drives for long periods without rest, is worried, has poor coordination, or takes drugs. Only those factors that are characteristic of the person and would not necessarily apply to another driver placed in the same situation can be classified as aspects of accident proneness. A person with high liability may be accident free for a considerable period because of good fortune or because others make special allowances.

ACCIDENT PRONENESS
RE-EXAMINED

If the term *accident proneness* is confined to the *permanent* characteristics of an individual that contribute to accidents, we must exclude inexperience, age, fatigue, and temporary worry or frustration from the concept. *It is doubtful that accident proneness so defined will reveal a single set of traits that accident repeaters have in common.* The traits that contribute to accidents probably differ from one situation to another, since there are a great variety of ways in which to have accidents.

More recent studies have tended to de-

MOTIVATING WORKERS FOR OPTIMUM PERFORMANCE

emphasize the concept of accident proneness as a major cause of accidents, although the debate as to its usefulness as a psychological concept continues.[16] A survey of 27,000 industrial and 8,000 nonindustrial accidents indicated that the accident repeater contributed only .5 percent of them, whereas 74 percent were due to relatively infrequent experiences of a large number of persons.[17] Is this decline in evidence for accident proneness due to changing causes of accidents because of modern safety development or to better statistical analyses? Probably both factors as well as others are involved.

The comparison of job groups shown in Table 16.3 reveals that accident frequency for utility workers is associated more with the job than with the individual. The average rates for the various job groups range from .12 to .65 per worker. Evidence of accident proneness was uncovered only after close scrutiny of individuals with multiple accidents, and only six clear-cut instances were found. This small number of accident-prone individuals suggests that accident proneness as a permanent trait may be relatively rare. We must also take into account the fact that the utility workers studied were a select and relatively stable group of employees, that is, accident-prone workers on the hazardous jobs may have been screened out.

Comparison of the accident rate of the same individuals while in the same jobs over two comparable periods of time is a more accurate test of accident proneness than accident frequencies alone, and this method reveals some evidence of accident proneness.[18] In a modern chemical company, the correlation of accident scores of individuals for odd and even one-year periods was found to be .349 (significant at the 5 percent level of confidence). The correlation for

TABLE 16.3 ACCIDENT FREQUENCY RATES FOR JOB GROUPS MATCHED IN TERMS OF HAZARD EXPOSURE

JOB GROUP	NUMBER OF EMPLOYEES	NUMBER OF ACCIDENTS	ACCIDENT FREQUENCY RATE
Lineman 1/C	160	72	.45
Lineman 2/C	112	35	.31
Lineman 3/C	34	22	.65*
Groundman	189	47	.25
Maintenance 1/C	43	9	.21
Maintenance 2/C	34	4	.12
Maintenance 3/C	28	5	.18
Meterman 1/C	36	7	.19
Meterman 2/C	79	11	.14
Meterman 3/C	22	8	.36
Total	737	220	.30

* Significant at .01 level of confidence.

SOURCE: From P. L. Crawford, Hazard exposure differentiation necessary for the identification of the accident-prone employee. *J. Appl. Psychol.*, 1960, 44, 192–194. Copyright 1960 by the American Psychological Association, and reproduced by permission.

scores of unsafe behaviors (recorded by supervisors trained to make these observations) for odd and even one-week periods was .875 However, the second measure is subject to rater bias.

Comparison of accident rates of the same persons over two periods are distorted because the worst offenders in the first period tend to be eliminated. However, data based on South African bus drivers, where this selective factor was minimal, show correlations of accident frequencies over two four-year periods as follows:[19]

Difficult traffic conditions	(N = 43)	.66
Easy traffic conditions	(N = 46)	.36

When discipline for accidents was introduced, some improvement was evidenced in individual records, and as high offenders were removed, improvements of 21 to 41 percent were recorded between 1952 and 1960.

W. Kerr believes that accident proneness must be supplemented by two additional concepts, both of which involve the work climate.[20] One is the *goals freedom-alertness* theory that treats the accident as defective behavior caused by restrictions on the individual's freedom of action. The work climate should be such as to upgrade pride and initiative. The other is the *adjustment-stress* theory, which deals with accidents caused by the individual's stresses. These are caused by internal environment (disease, emotional stability, and so on) or by the external environment (excessive temperatures, noise, pressure). Lack of freedom and stress in the work climate may cause individuals to be accident repeaters on certain jobs or under certain conditions. Insofar as the work climate causes individuals to do things that lead to accidents, accident proneness is not their basic cause, but insofar as the persons react differently to situational factors, human characteristics are involved. If individual differences in these traits systematically cause differences in the number of accidents, accident proneness is indicated.

PSYCHOLOGICAL TESTS AND ACCIDENT FREQUENCY

Differentiating between accidents caused by a person's tendency to generate potential accident situations and those caused by an inability to deal with the situation when in an accident is helpful. For example, the fast driver or the driver who neglects to check the car brakes may get into accident situations, but may show unusual skill in manipulating the car and thus avoid a collision. Skill and rapid perception help, but continually generating the conditions for such situations will result in an accident record. Another individual may conscientiously try to avoid accident situations, but when in one, may either lack sufficient skill to cope with it or panic and lose whatever skill he or she possessed. Such a person also acquires an accident record, because accident situations cannot always be avoided.

It is puzzling to find that some highly skilled individuals have more accidents than less skilled persons. Actually, such individuals do not have the same accident exposure. The skilled person may work on a narrower margin of safety and so be exposed to greater hazard. For example, young drivers may show greater skill than older drivers in handling a car, but at the same time have more accidents. Because of their superior skill, they may be overconfident, drive faster, and allow less distance for passing other cars. If something goes wrong, they have little leeway for avoiding an accident.

This situation suggests that accident

proneness may be a rather complex phenomenon and that the factors involved need not be the same for all accident-prone individuals. However, if accident proneness is to have any application to business, it is necessary to determine the factors that are associated with accident susceptibility and to develop tests for detecting their presence.

SENSORIMOTOR TESTS

Measures of muscular coordination are related to certain types of accident proneness. In one investigation, this group of abilities was measured by a dotting test, by speed in reacting to a signal, and by adjustment of muscular performance in accordance with changing signals.[21] When over six hundred employees were divided into two groups according to test scores, the poorer half of the test performers had 48 percent more accidents than the better half. The poorer quarter had 51 percent more accidents than the better three-quarters, indicating that elimination of 25 percent of the poor performers on such tests would significantly decrease accidents. The relationship between the test score and accident rate also existed when the data were analyzed according to the occupation of the employees. Other investigations have revealed similar relationships between motor coordination and accidents.[22]

The relationship between test scores and accidents also increases with length of time on the job.[23] Apparently, the causes of accidents become more uniform with experience, and the sensorimotor tests reveal this persisting personal factor in accident causation.

Of great practical importance is the fact that there is a definite relationship between accident-proneness tests and proficiency on the job. By selecting employees who do well — that is, score low — on accident-proneness tests, managers can reduce accidents and improve the caliber of the employees at the same time.

EMOTIONAL STABILITY AND PERSONALITY TESTS

Instruments that measure the degree of emotional reactions (in terms of chemical changes) and tests that measure tremor have been found effective in showing a relationship between certain aspects of emotionality and accident frequency.[24] Accidents by taxicab drivers were greatly reduced by the use of psychological tests, among which tests of emotional stability were found to be highly important.[25] Even closer relationships are found when an individual's responses are measured under disturbing and distracting conditions.[26] For example, taxicab drivers who made five or more errors on such tests averaged three accidents, whereas those who made fewer than five errors averaged only 1.3 accidents.

In the extensive research on South African bus drivers, applicants were screened for motor skills and then given projective personality tests. Despite their having adequate motor skills, poor risks could be detected from the personality tests. High-accident producers were immature, impulsive, hostile, and inclined toward aggression. Disciplinary and accident records showed correlations of .45 and .57 with the personality test scores and were significantly correlated with each other (.42). After refining the personality tests, prediction of accident risks became strikingly accurate. Of those passing the test, 80 percent were successful drivers, whereas only 14 percent of those failing the experimental test were successful on the job.

In another study a high-accident group was compared with a low-accident group matched for age, education, intelligence, sex, socioeconomic background, and exposure to hazard.[27] The responses of the high-accident group to a sentence-completion test indicated that they were significantly different from the matched group with regard to self-centeredness and the presence of a negative attitude toward employment. The matched group was higher on responses indicating optimism, trust, and concern for others. These findings were replicated in a study published twenty-one years after the one cited above.[28]

Moods also seem to be highly important. In one study it was found that half of four hundred minor accidents occurred while the employees were emotionally low, although this emotional condition existed only 20 percent of the time.[29] Production was 8 percent higher during the happy moods, showing that emotional conditions favorable to accident prevention are also favorable to production.[30]

INTELLIGENCE TESTS

The investigations that revealed that accidents were related both to sensorimotor coordination and emotionality showed no relationship between accidents and intelligence.[31] One study in a vocational school did demonstrate a relationship between intelligence and accidents, but in this case it is difficult to know to what extent the intelligent students acquired skill more rapidly and so avoided accidents, and to what extent they were permanently less accident prone.[32]

RATIO BETWEEN MUSCULAR AND PERCEPTUAL SPEED

In examining the characteristics of accident-prone and accident-safe individuals, the relationship between motor and perceptual speed was quite different in the two groups.[33] Individuals who were quicker at recognizing differences in visual patterns than they were in making purely muscular manipulations tended to be accident-safe. Individuals who were slower in recognizing visual patterns than they were in making muscular responses were inclined to be accident prone. Of the 42 percent who made scores of −10 or less, 82 percent had accidents. When this test was used in the selection of eighteen new employees, the accident index of the new group was 70 percent below the previous average, despite the fact that the plant had already achieved a low accident record by means of a safety program.

TESTS OF VISUAL SKILLS

Vision plays an important part in many occupations, and accidents often are associated with defective vision.[34] In a study made in a paper mill, the vision of 52 accident-free employees was compared with that of 52 workers who had one or more serious accidents.[35] It was found that 63 percent of the no-accident group passed the eye test, whereas only 33 percent of the accident group passed it.

Two groups of employees were distinguishable after a ten-year study of a fertilizer plant — an accident-free group and an accident-repeating group.[36] A visual-acuity test was administered to employees who were matched on age, education, experience, and pay. The accident-free workers scored significantly better both on monocular and binocular vision than the accident repeaters.

Setting up the visual requirements of a job and testing workers for them, rather than using an arbitrary test, is now required by law. This more specific approach also simulates the critical-incident method and may be expected to generate greater acceptance by job candidates. A specific method should be extended to other sense capacities because it is probable that hearing, touch, smell, and other sensory requirements are essential to safety in specialized occupations.

PHYSICAL EXAMINATIONS

Pre-employment physical examinations can serve as a protection against injury and resulting compensation claims. One company reduced its back-injury claims by 93 percent by introducing such examinations.[37] The cost of poor safety practices may not be immediately obvious, but eventually manifests itself. In one small plant, so many workers had histories of job-related back injuries (and therefore could not lift heavy objects) that, on occasion, work was stopped while a

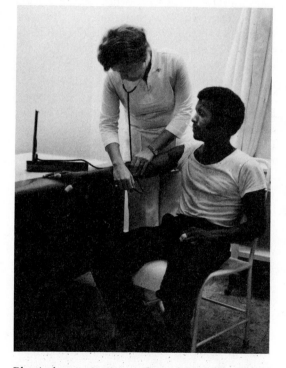

Physical examinations of employees can reveal information important in hiring decisions and job determination. (Frank Siteman, Stock, Boston)

search was made for someone who could do the required heavy work.

To the extent that it can be ascertained through physical or other examination, evidence of alcoholism should be considered a negative factor specifically because of accident risk, aside from other considerations. A matched set of known alcoholics and non-alcoholics was compared for accidents and absenteeism in a British plant by an observer working in the plant.[38] The results indicated that the alcoholics had 2.5 times as many days absent and 3.6 times as many accidents as the nonalcoholics had.

OTHER PERSONAL FACTORS RELATED TO ACCIDENTS

FRUSTRATION AND ACCIDENT PRONENESS

Since widely different tests were found to be related to accident records, it is apparent that accident proneness is not a specific trait, and the manner in which it reveals itself will vary with the job. Thus, jobs involving avoidance of risks might be related to personality traits, and those involving coordination might be related to the sensorimotor abilities. The study of South African bus drivers clearly revealed that the drivers with the best skills did not have lower accident rates.[39] Driving requires both skill and emotional stability, and since traffic situations are stressful, the latter ability becomes relatively more important in driving than in other occupations.

Insofar as accidents are related to such personality traits as hostility and emotional immaturity, we may question the use of personality tests as measures of accident proneness since these behaviors may be temporary conditions. Thus, the frustrated person shows aggression, regression, and fixations, all of which are in opposition to constructive and safe behavior. However, as pointed out by the studies of South African bus drivers, the hostile behavior is not always present, but in many it lies near the surface. Thus, we may describe individuals as differing in frustration thresholds, and the proneness aspect of the personality test would be the frustration threshold rather than the state of instability.

More complete and precise knowledge of the relationship between frustration and accidents may well lead to better means of preventing accidents. For example, it may be found that some behavioral manifestations of frustration may be more or less often associated with accidents than others. Knowledge of an individual's (1) characteristic means of dealing with frustration (for example, aggression versus regression) and (2) tolerance for frustration may be useful guides in making assignments or recommendations for transfer.

EXPERIENCE

R. H. Van Zelst plotted the monthly accident rates of 1,237 workers in a newly opened copper plant against their length of experience.[40] He found that the accident rate dropped from nearly 6 per 1,000 hours to around 3.5 during the first five months. After the initial drop, no further improvements occurred during the remainder of the five-year period studied. His investigation shows experience to be an important factor in accidents during the early stages only. A comparable group of employees who left the company before the end of the five-year period showed a similar learning trend, but leveled off at a higher rate (in the vicinity of 4 accidents per 1,000 hours). Part of the con-

tinued decline with experience over extended periods of time, shown in some studies, may be due to greater turnover rate of accident repeaters.

Experienced workers may offset potential accidents and accident-proneness. In one case at a small chemical plant, a well-liked and ambitious young worker frequently left plant equipment and materials in unsafe states. Only the older workers' willingness to cover for him and recheck his work prevented several serious plant accidents. Management suspected this situation, but was reluctant to dismiss the worker without actual proof of negligence. The problem was solved by the workers themselves. When the near-accidents continued after the young worker had been six months on the job, employees told him that they felt he was unsuited for the work and they would no longer "clean up after him." Soon after, he took another job.

The fact that experience and safety are related suggests the importance of proper training and guidance for new employees. If accidents are reduced by experience, many of them can be eliminated by training. Practice on hazardless duplicates of machinery, such as are used in achievement tests, would develop basic skills.

AGE

In a well-controlled study, Van Zelst compared a group of 639 young workers (mean age = 28.7) with approximately three years' experience, with 552 older workers (mean age = 41.1) having about the same amount of experience.[41] The plot of the monthly accident rate over an eighteen-month period showed that the older group's rate fluctuated in the vicinity of 3.4 per 1,000 hours as compared to 4.0 for the younger group. Not once during the period of the study did the younger group have as good a record as the older group. This study clearly indicates that the age factor in accidents is not entirely a function of experience. In the transportation industry, accidents were found to decline with age, but data were often contaminated with differing exposure times and experience. With exposure time matched, the older age group still tended to be safer.[42]

Several studies have related high accident rates to impulsive, risk-taking behavior.[43] A review of the relevant literature by J. B. Miner and J. F. Brewer led them to the conclusion that accident proneness is often a personality maladjustment.[44] This is *not* a permanent characteristic of the individual, but manifests itself during adolescence and early adulthood. The maladjustment is manifested in risky behavior, often accompanied by a hatred of management and a defiance of company rules, including those relating to safety.

These findings are particularly interesting in light of similar findings by sociologists studying crime patterns. A finding that has held up over many years is that, although a relatively large percentage of American adolescents (one-fourth to one-third or more) are involved in some kind of conflict with the law, the percentage drops off dramatically by the age of thirty.[45] For some, apparently, crime is a career, whereas for others it reflects merely a temporary attitude of rebellion, nonconformity, risk-taking, and defiance of "the establishment."

One specific study of the relationship between age and accidents found accidents to be most frequent in the ages ranging from seventeen to twenty-eight years, after which the rates declined steadily to reach a low point for the fifty-five to sixty-five-year-old workers.[46] These findings may also bear on the relatively high driving accident (and insurance) rates of younger drivers.

THE CLINICAL APPROACH TO ACCIDENT PRONENESS

M. Viteles has emphasized the importance of carefully studying accident-prone individuals, diagnosing their difficulties, and recommending specific remedies.[47] By means of this approach, the accident rate of forty-four accident-prone workers dropped nearly 50 percent within one year.

That this procedure is valuable is shown by its reduction of accidents. However, such an analysis of accidents is largely subjective. To conclude, for example, that an accident is attributable to a faulty attitude is an interpretation of the facts rather than a statement of them. The person who had the accident may actually lack the necessary coordination, a deficiency that may have caused the development of an inferiority attitude and defensiveness, whereupon the person's attitude is judged to be faulty.

A similar source of error is present in psychological analyses based on human judgments. When two people are engaged in an argument, we may ask how it started and be told that the cause was a disagreement over politics. Yet it may also be true that the two thoroughly dislike each other; the political issue may be incidental. Analyzing the causes of arguments will not necessarily clarify such hidden factors. Similarly, the analysis of accidents by this procedure has limited value and is not a substitute for methods that relate individual characteristics and accident proneness. This is probably why the testing method and the clinical method do not agree more closely on the nature of accident proneness. For the present, both approaches should be used. The testing method is particularly valuable in selecting employees, whereas the clinical approach is important in helping the accident repeater.

THE CASE-STUDY APPROACH

An accident may involve a complex series of events, and a change in any one of them may alter the outcome. Thus far we have discussed the characteristics of individuals and their relation to hazards. The varied factors can give us statistical relationships. What can be learned by careful analysis of specific accidents? The case-study approach has been successfully used by the Harvard Medical School.[48]

Their analysis — or case study — of a fatal automobile accident indicated that it was not the result of a single cause but the outcome of a complex chain of events, all of which contributed to the tragic occurence. Significant causative factors included tire failure caused by negligence on the part of a garage mechanic; inadequate skills on the part of the driver; inadequate highway safety equipment (no retaining barrier); and failure of drivers and passengers to use seat belts. (It is interesting to observe that the garage mechanic, who may be regarded as the initial cause of the accident, will never know he contributed to the deaths of several persons.)

GENERATING POSITIVE SAFETY ATTITUDES

THE SUPERVISOR'S DILEMMA

Disciplinary action often follows accidents or safety violations. Regardless of how supervisors feel about punishment, they may be required to administer penalties. What does a supervisor do when an employee is found breaking a company regulation for which disciplinary action is specified?

Many supervisors have described the dilemmas they face when a good worker commits a violation. They know that laying off a worker often creates hardships, destroys friendly relations, and causes negative job attitudes. Sometimes grievances are filed, and when this occurs, their decisions are frequently reversed. Supervisors also know that they can get into trouble if they ignore violations because this is seen as unfairness or playing favorites. Management must demand strict enforcement of company regulations. Aside from concern for workers' safety, failure to enforce safety regulations can make the company liable for penalty by OSHA officials. In the interests of stricter enforcement, campaigns and training programs may be instituted to make supervisors more safety conscious. Supervisors, frustrated by such experiences, resolve the dilemma by not seeing the violations.

THE INFLUENCE OF THE UNION STEWARD

When supervisors fail to invoke penalties, they give such excuses as: (1) the violation was in doubt; (2) the penalty is too strict; (3) the worker cannot afford the layoff; or (4) the employees will resent the disciplinary action.[49] In a simulated experiment, excuses of this sort were largely eliminated by creating a situation in which there was no doubt about the violation of a nonsmoking rule; the penalty was a three-day layoff; and the supervisor had already laid the worker off. What would be the supervisor's response when the union steward attempted to get the decision changed?

The results are shown in Table 16.4. Only 34.9 percent of the supervisors did not alter their decision (with another 13.4 percent unable to settle the matter in the allotted time). Both outcomes resulted in a good percentage of grievances. Supervisors who took a less rigid stand and did some problem solving retained the union steward's good will and

MOTIVATING WORKERS FOR OPTIMUM PERFORMANCE

TABLE 16.4 DECISIONS REGARDING PUNISHMENT FOR VIOLATIONS CHALLENGED BY THE UNION STEWARD

DECISION	FREQUENCY (PERCENTAGE)	RESULT IN GRIEVANCE (PERCENTAGE)
Full three-day layoff	34.9	45
Reduced layoff	4.6	
Warning	22.7	
Forgiven	7.5	
Consult higher management	8.7	2
Consult workers	3.5	
Other	4.6	
No decision	13.4	43

SOURCE: From N. R. F. Maier and L. E. Danielson, An evaluation of two approaches to discipline in industry. *J. Appl. Psychol.*, 1956, *40*, 319–329. Copyright 1956 by the American Psychological Association, and reproduced by permission.

even gained some assistance in promoting safety. In these instances, grievances were rare.

The legalistic stand of determining guilt and invoking punishment, even if accepted by the company philosophy, is not supported by supervisors in general. They are inclined to recognize the feelings of the workers and to think in terms of future safety and the effects on morale.

The training of supervisors should be in terms of positive motivation. Obviously workers do not want to have accidents, so attempts to make accidents less attractive by punishment misses the point. If people behave in unsafe ways, it is due to the presence of conflicting goals. Punishment is frequently seen as the price for getting caught and therefore often motivates employees to find ways to avoid detection or to reduce the pain of the penalty.

We should not conclude that all forms of punishment for safety violations can or should be abolished. Instead, the need is to find better ways to accomplish objectives by studying the motivational alternatives.

GROUP DECISION AND SAFETY

The supervisor will find many uses for employee participation and group decision in dealing with safety. The group-decision approach is advantageous for the following reasons: (1) there are mutual interests in safety goals; (2) the problems can readily be stated in situational terms; (3) the workers have much information to contribute (which they withhold when punishment is part of the picture); (4) social pressure will keep more individuals in line with the group decision; and (5) sources of danger not noticed by safety engineers may be uncovered.

Employee participation is effective in dealing with the safety of the group in which there are varied reactions: many who accept safety regulations; some who object to working with others who are unsafe, but who cannot expose them because of group loyalty; others who have violated regulations, but have not been caught; and violators who have been reprimanded. Varied experiences and viewpoints can lead to new approaches to safety as well as to better understanding.

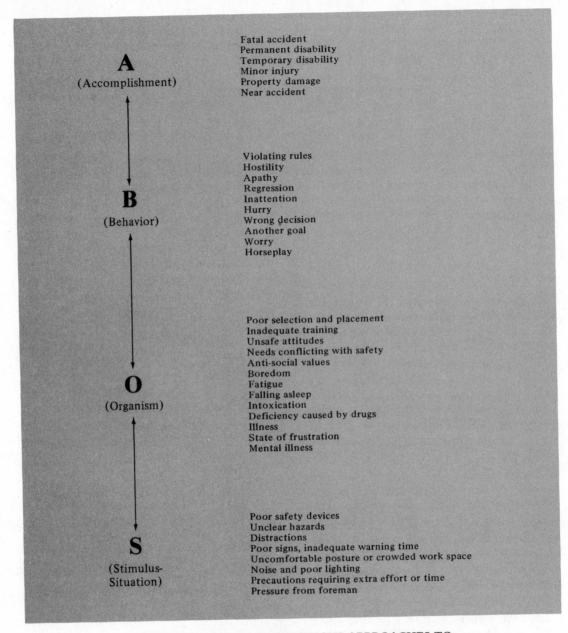

A
(Accomplishment)

Fatal accident
Permanent disability
Temporary disability
Minor injury
Property damage
Near accident

B
(Behavior)

Violating rules
Hostility
Apathy
Regression
Inattention
Hurry
Wrong decision
Another goal
Worry
Horseplay

O
(Organism)

Poor selection and placement
Inadequate training
Unsafe attitudes
Needs conflicting with safety
Anti-social values
Boredom
Fatigue
Falling asleep
Intoxication
Deficiency caused by drugs
Illness
State of frustration
Mental illness

S
(Stimulus-
Situation)

Poor safety devices
Unclear hazards
Distractions
Poor signs, inadequate warning time
Uncomfortable posture or crowded work space
Noise and poor lighting
Precautions requiring extra effort or time
Pressure from foreman

**FIGURE 16.1 SUMMARY OF VARIOUS APPROACHES TO
ACCIDENT PREVENTION**

There are many approaches to safety. These include the *S*, the *O*, the *B*, and *A*, and the relationships among them. Although causation is a function of the interaction of *S* and *O*, it is essential to analyze the whole causation model to explore completely the potentials for increasing safety. The items listed in each of the four divisions summarize the progress that has been made in isolating the types of factors involved.

MOTIVATING WORKERS FOR OPTIMUM PERFORMANCE

COUNSELING SKILLS

The modern supervisor must also deal with individual problems. Persons with emotional problems are temporarily accident prone, regardless of whether the source of the disturbance is on the job or outside. Frequently the supervisor is expected not only to be sensitive to a worker's emotional condition but also to acquire some elementary skills in dealing with such employees. In this capacity, the supervisor acts as a helper or counselor rather than as a critic or judge. A presentation of the counseling skills that can safely be used by supervisors at all levels of management will be found in Chapter 18. These skills are an extension of the interpersonal-relations skills discussed in Chapters 4 and 5.

APPLICATION OF CAUSATION MODEL TO ACCIDENT PREVENTION

The study of accidents involves a consideration of the four variables discussed in Chapter 2: the accomplishment, the behavior, the individual or organism, and the situation. Figure 16.1 shows how each is involved.

The accomplishment (A) is largely a matter of probability. Whether a fall results in an injury is largely beyond the control of the individual involved. But the situation in which the fall occurs can reduce the probability of injury. Thus the various accomplishments should be studied to determine whether they relate to the other factors in the causation sequence.

The behaviors (B) of the persons involved also need to be evaluated to determine those most likely to lead to the various accomplishments. Although the behavior is caused by the interaction of the situation (S) and the organism (O), it is important to isolate and classify the behavior that have the greatest probability of leading to accidents. Behaviors known to be associated with accidents are shown in the figure.

Advances made in the prevention of accidents fall into two types: changes in the organism and changes in the situations in which the individuals behave. The varied factors in the S and O that are associated with accidents are also shown in Figure 16.1. Methods for removing these sources have been found effective.

NOTES

1. Keenan, V., Kerr, W., and Sherman, W. Psychological climate and accidents in an automotive plant. *J. Appl. Psychol.,* 1951, *35,* 108–111.
2. Vernon, H. M. *Accidents and their prevention.* London: Cambridge University Press, 1936.
3. Mezerik, A. G. The factory manager learns the facts of life. *Harper's Mag.,* 1943, *187,* 289–297.
4. Jorgensen, S., and (Verser), G. G. Casselman. Woman power: A national and international survey of the working woman. Working paper No. 44. Ann Arbor: Bureau of Business Research, University of Michigan, 1971.
5. McIver, I. *Behavioral approaches to accident research.* New York: Association for Aid of Crippled Children, 1961
6. De Silva, H. R. *Why we have automobile accidents.* New York: Wiley, 1942, pp. 18–21.
7. Vernon, *op. cit.,* pp. 75–85; Viteles, M. S. *Industrial psychology.* New York: Norton, 1932, pp. 364–368.

8. Howland, C. I. Changes in attitude through communication. *J. Abnorm. Soc. Psychol.*, 1951, *46*, 424–437; Vernon, op. cit., pp. 259–264.
9. Fenichel, O. *The psychoanalytic theory of neurosis.* New York: Norton, 1945.
10. Miner, J. B., and Brewer, J. F. The management of ineffective performance. In M. D. Dunnette (Ed.), *Handbook of industrial and organizational psychology.* Chicago: Rand-McNally, 1976, pp. 995–1029.
11. Hill, J. M. M., and Trist, E. L. A consideration of industrial accidents as a means of withdrawal from the work situation. *Hum. Relat.*, 1953, *6*, 357–380.
12. University of Michigan School of Public Health, *Investigation and application of home injury survey data in development of preventive procedures,* 1953.
13. Altman, J. W. Behavior and accidents. *J. Safety Res.*, 1970, *2*, 109–122.
14. Greenwood, M., and Woods, H. M. *The incidence of industrial accidents with special reference to multiple accidents.* Industr. Fat. Res. Bd., 1919, Rep. No. 4.
15. Mintz, A., and Blum, M. L. A re-examination of the accident proneness concept. *J. Appl. Psychol.*, 1949, *33*, 195–211; Mintz, A. The inference of accident liability from the accident record. *J. Appl. Psychol.*, 1954, *38*, 41–46.
16. De Reamer, R. Accident proneness: Fact or fiction. *Supervisory Mgmt.*, 1956, *3*, 1–14; Kirchner, W. K. The fallacy of accident proneness. *Personnel*, 1961, *38* (6), 34–37.
17. Schulzinger, M. S. Accident proneness. *Industr. Med. and Surgery*, 1954, *23*, 151–152.
18. Whitlock, G. H., Clouse, R. J., and Spencer, W. F. Predicting accident proneness. *Personel Psychol.*, 1963, *16*, 35–44.
19. Shaw, L., and Sichel, H. *Accident proneness: Research in the occurrence, causation, and prevention of road accidents.* Oxford: Pergamon Press, 1971.
20. Kerr, W. Complementary theories of safety psychology. *J. Soc. Psychol.*, 1957, *45*, 3–9.
21. Farmer, E., and Chambers, E. G. *A psychological study of individual differences in accident rates.* Industr. Fat. Res. Bd., 1926, Rep. No. 38.
22. Vernon, op. cit., p. 40.
23. Farmer, E., and Chambers, E. G. *A study of personal qualities in accident-proneness and proficiency.* Industr. Fat. Res. Bd., 1929, Rep. No. 55.
24. Farmer and Chambers, ibid.
25. Snow, A. J. Tests for chauffeurs, *Industr, Psychol.*, 1926, *1*, 30–45.
26. Wechsler, D. Test for taxicab drivers. *J. Personnel Res.*, 1926, *5*, 24–30.
27. Hersey, R. B. Emotional factors in accidents. *Personnel J.*, 1936, *15*, 59–65.
28. Davids, A., and Mahoney, J. T. Personality dynamics and accident proneness in an industrial setting. *J. Appl Psychol.*, 1957, *41*, 303–306.
29. Hersey, R. B. Rates of production and emotional state. *Personnel J.*, 1932, *10*, 355–364.
30. Davids and Mahoney, op. cit.
31. Farmer and Chambers, op. cit.
32. Henig, M. S. Intelligence and safety. *J. Educ. Res.*, 1926, *16*, 81–87.
33. Drake, C. A. Accident-proneness: A hypothesis. *Character and Person.*, 1940, *8*, 335–341.
34. Stump, F. N. Spotting accident-prone workers by vision tests. *Factory Mgmt. and Maint.*, 1945, *103*, 109–112.
35. Wirt, S. E., and Leedke, H. H. Skillful eyes prevent accidents. *Annual News Letter*, Natl. Safety Council (Industr. Nursing Section), November, 1945, 10–12.
36. Menon, A. S. Role of visual skill in safe operational behavior. *Psychol. Annual*, 1970, *4*, 18–21.
37. Stewart, R. D. How to manage your injury problems. *Personnel J.*, 1970, *49*, 590–592.
38. "Observer" and Maxwell, M.A.A. A study of absenteeism, accidents, and sickness payments in problem drinkers in one industry. *Quart. J. of Studies on Alcoholism*, 1959, *20*, 302–312.

39. Shaw and Sichel, op. cit.
40. Van Zelst, R. H. The effect of age and experience upon accident rate. *J. Appl. Psychol.*, 1954, *38*, 313–317.
41. Van Zelst, ibid.
42. McFarland, R. A. *Human factors in air transportation.* New York: McGraw-Hill, 1953.
43. See, for example, Miner and Brewer, op. cit.; Kunce, J. T. Vocational interests and accident proneness. *J. Appl. Psychol.*, 1967, *51,* 223–225.
44. Miner and Brewer, op.cit.
45. Silberman, C. E. *Criminal violence, criminal justice.* New York: Random House, 1978.
46. Schulzinger, M. S. *The accident syndrome.* Springfield, Ill.: Thomas, 1956.
47. Viteles, op.cit.
48. Schwartz, R. L. The case for fast drivers. *Harper's Mag.,* 1963, *227,* 65–70.
49. Maier, N. R. F., and Danielson, L. E. An evaluation of two approaches to discipline in industry. *J. Appl. Psychol.,* 1956, *40,* 319–329.

SUGGESTED READINGS

Accident Facts, a review of recent information on accident factors, published periodically. Chicago: National Safety Council.

Shaw, L. and Sichel, H. *Accident proneness: Research in the occurrence, causation, and prevention of road accidents.* Oxford, Eng.: Pergamon Press, 1971.

LABORATORY EXERCISE
ROLE-PLAYING:
THE CASE OF THE SAFETY BELT

(Students are asked not to read the case materials before participating in the laboratory exercise.)

A. PREPARATION FOR ROLE-PLAYING

1. This case requires two persons to role-play and a third to act as an observer.
2. The class is to separate into units of three and distribute themselves by units as widely as possible in different parts of the room. (If the class is not divisible by three, one or two teams of two persons should be formed.)
3. Each group counts off: one, two, three.
4. The instructor will assign to the *ones,* the role of Jim Welch, the supervisor (E.1); to the *twos,* the role of Bill Smith (E.2); and to the *threes,* the task of the observer (E.3).
5. Each person should study his or her part only, and when finished, should lay it aside.

B. THE ROLE-PLAYING PROCESS

1. When persons with roles have finished studying their parts, the instructor will give the following directions:
   a. The Bill Smiths are to stand on a chair next to a wall and pretend to be working on top of a telephone pole.
   b. The Jim Welches are to move some distance away and await the instructor's signal to begin.
   c. The observers are to stay close enough to hear the conversation of their pair but are to be as unobtrusive as possible.
2. An opportunity should be given for any questions.

3. On signal, the Jim Welches approach the Bill Smiths and begin the action.
4. The observers are to inform the instructor when their role-players have finished.
5. When approximately two-thirds of the role-players have finished, the instructor should ask the others to settle their problems in the next two minutes.

C. COLLECTING RESULTS

1. On the chalkboard, the instructor will prepare column headings under which to record results for each group of role-players.
2. Each observer should report on the following:
   a. The solution reached
   b. The method used by the supervisor to influence the future behavior of the employee
   c. An estimation of each participant's satisfaction with the interview.
   d. The key things done or said by the supervisor that caused the interview to take a turn for the better or for the worse.
3. The supervisors should report on whether or not
   a. the employee has gone down in their estimation.
   b. they think the employee will be safer.
   c. they think the employee's work will suffer.
4. The employees should report on whether or not
   a. the supervisor has gone down in their estimation.
   b. they will work more safely in the future.
   c. their other work will suffer.

D. DISCUSSION QUESTIONS

1. What conclusions can be drawn from the results obtained?
2. Why was the worker not laid off by more of the supervisors?
3. Can a supervisor get into difficulty by warning rather than by laying off a worker?
4. What are the pros and cons of not discussing Smith's probable safety violation at all and holding a safety meeting with the whole crew instead?

E. MATERIALS FOR THE CASE

1. Role for Jim Welch, Supervisor

You are the supervisor of a repair crew of the telephone company. You have twelve workers who go on jobs. They usually work alone or in pairs. As supervisor, you spend your time visiting work locations, checking on progress, and giving such help, training, and instruction as may be needed. You are also responsible for the safety of your workers, and the company judges you partly on the safety record of your crew. At the present time, a company safety drive is on. The slogan is, "No job is so important that it cannot be done safely." The company has passed a ruling that anyone found violating a safety practice will be laid off for three weeks.

You have just driven up to the place where Bill Smith is working. You stop your car some distance away (you cannot drive directly to the work location) and see Bill working on top of the pole. As you stop the car, you have a distinct impression that Smith just snapped his safety belt. Apparently he was working without using his belt, and this is a safety practice violation.

Smith is an employee with twenty years of service. He has four children ranging in age from five to twelve. He is a good workman but is quite independent in his thinking. You wish to do what you can to correct this man and give him a better attitude toward safety. You have been a supervisor of this crew for two years and don't know too much about Bill's past record. You have ten years of service with the company.

2. Role for Bill Smith, Repairman

You are a member of Jim Welch's repair crew in a utility company. You have been in the company for twenty years, and for the past two years, Jim has been your supervisor. You feel you know the job and consider your technical knowledge perhaps somewhat greater than that of Welch, who has worked in the company for a total of ten years. You believe Jim has done a fair job as supervisor but feel that he supervises too closely.

You usually work alone on repair jobs except for several visits a week from your supervisor. You are now working on top of a pole and haven't bothered to snap your safety belt. You are a careful worker and use it when it is necessary, but you find it uncomfortable and in the way, and so frequently you don't bother to snap it. By winding your leg over the cross bar and hooking your foot against the pole, you can hold yourself firmly in place when working in a particular position. Actually, there are a lot of hazards in your work that the company hasn't bothered about. Work pressures, poor tires on your truck, an uncomfortable belt, and supervisors who are more interested in catching someone at a violation than in helping to do a job — all are factors that cause a person to have accidents, but the company ignores these things. The only time you ever had a scare was when a former supervisor made you work on a wet pole after a rain.

Welch has just driven up, so you hasten to snap your belt. There is an annual safety drive on, and the company has threatened to lay workers off for safety violations. You can't afford time off. You have four children, and living expenses use up all your earnings. You are quite sure Jim didn't see you snap your safety belt. He is walking toward your pole now.

3. Instructions for the Observer

You will witness an incident in which Jim Welch, the supervisor of a telephone repair crew, either catches a worker or thinks he has in a safety violation. Note how the supervisor opens the

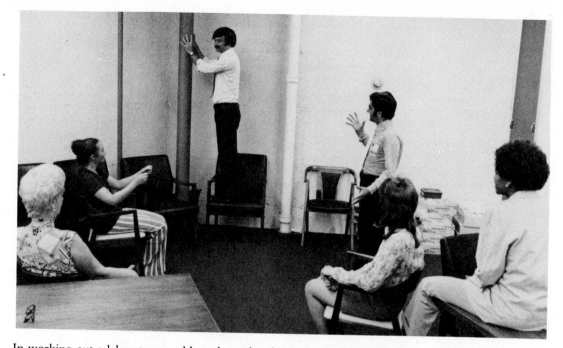

In working out a laboratory problem through role-playing, students can gain insight into supervisory programs by imagining themselves in a given situation. Only the simplest props are needed (the person standing on a chair represents a man working on a telephone pole; the other man is playing the foreman and the woman is the observer. (Frank Siteman, with cooperation of Stride-Rite Corporation)

conversation and observe whether he wants the worker to come down off the pole. Does he use an approach that makes the man feel at home, or does he put him on the defensive? Make notes of the things the supervisor says that are key factors in determining whether the interview becomes pleasant or unpleasant and whether the worker confides, exaggerates, or lies.

You will be asked to report on the method used by the supervisor to promote safety. He will be attempting to motivate the worker by means of fear if he punishes, threatens to punish, discusses accidents, and so on; he will be using positive motivation if he praises the worker for his record, requests his help in training others in safety, or tries to get him to participate in safety meetings. It is possible that the supervisor will try to get the worker to talk in

order to learn about his attitude, or the supervisor may do the talking and try to sell the man on the merits of safety. He may attempt to determine whether a safety violation occurred, or he may go so far as to avoid finding out the actual facts.

In reporting the solution, it is necessary to state whether the worker is disciplined, warned, forgiven, or whether the violation is overlooked or ignored. The solution may include some follow-ups, such as training others, group meetings, and new duties, and these should also be reported.

When the role-playing is finished, you will be asked how the participants feel toward each other. Do not ask the participants this, but form your own opinion. In this way you will learn how sensitive an observer you are.

CHAPTER SEVENTEEN

ANALYZING
JOB
TURNOVER

■

Job Turnover: Costs and Causes
Specific Factors Related to Labor Turnover
Discovering Employee Needs
Discharging Employees   The Exit Interview
New Ways to Deal with the Problem of Discharging Employees

■

S EPARATIONS OF EMPLOYER and employee come about for many reasons. Some are inevitable; others may be avoided. A knowledge of the basic factors in avoidable labor turnover may lead to a reduction in the rate of turnover and create a saving in hiring and training costs.

JOB TURNOVER: COSTS AND CAUSES

Savings through reduction of job turnover may be considerably more than they first appear. Replacing an employee who has been in service for many years may require hiring and training several persons before a relatively permanent employee is again found. In addition, new employees are more subject to accidents, cause more breakage, and make more errors than experienced workers, so that costs of replacing a worker may greatly exceed direct hiring costs. The average cost of hiring college graduates continues to be high as is the turnover rate for recruits during the first five years.[1]

Another important aspect of turnover is the fact that it reflects conditions in a plant.[2] A company perceived as having high turnover is often regarded unfavorably by employees and by society. We can, however, determine some of the faulty practices that lead to unnecessary job turnover, but to do this, we must understand its causes.

Unavoidable forms of turnover are constant factors and influence all forms of work, as well as all organizations. Death, permanent disability, retirement, and change of residence cause separations that fall into this category.

Turnover caused by layoffs and seasonal conditions may depend on factors beyond employers' control, but these can be influenced to some degree. By carefully planning work, it is possible to approach a uniform production schedule so that a permanent staff is employed throughout the year. In other cases, part-time employment may be arranged to handle extra work demands. Such individuals may be semipermanently employed during rush periods without disturbing the balance of the labor market. In handling lower levels of unexpected demands, overtime is frequently the best solution. Successful maintenance of a permanent staff promotes the formation of a work force with greater trust in management.

Discharges required because the employee is incompetent can be reduced by better selection methods and by shifting employees into work for which they may be better fitted. A low rate of discharge does not mean that employment methods are satisfactory, however. A company that lacks competition and does not measure individual productivity may have a low discharge rate because of its low production standards. Such a situation invites the entry of competition and eventual bankruptcy of the firm.

Resignations that occur because employees prefer to work elsewhere are the most revealing. To what extent was the job accurately described when the employee was hired? Often the employment interviewer is only concerned with determining whether the employee is satisfactory and forgets that the job and company must also be satisfactory to the employee. The job may even be misrepresented during the interview in order to induce a desirable candidate to take the job.[3] Sometimes job candidates do not meet the supervisor for whom they will work. This one-sided interviewing condition may account for a large proportion of employee departures during the first three months of employment.[4]

Quitting a job may also be an individual employee's method of retaliation — a form of aggression arising from frustration. The same conditions that cause this type of turnover also cause grievances.[5] When employees have little opportunity for re-employment elsewhere, they express their frustration by interfering with production (being wasteful of materials, sabotaging equipment, defying company rules).

Although job dissatisfaction of some sort is a major factor in resignations, there are other reasons for quitting. Emotionally maladjusted persons wander from job to job. Other workers may be working in a field for which they have little talent.

To determine the kind of individuals who voluntarily leave their employment, it is important to distinguish between the resignation of satisfactory and unsatisfactory employees. If those who quit are inferior in workmanship, the separation may be desirable; if the resignations are predominantly among the more satisfactory employees, then the condition is serious. In job turnover, a selective factor is operating that can either raise or lower the quality of the permanent working force.

SPECIFIC FACTORS RELATED TO LABOR TURNOVER

LENGTH OF SERVICE

An analysis of turnover in terms of length of service shows that, even when turnover is high, a large proportion of the employees are stable, whereas a minority move from one job to another.[6] This means that some positions must be filled repeatedly. Turnover is highest for persons who have been with a company less than a month and drops rapidly during the first year. In one company it was found that 80 percent of the employees leaving the job had served less than three months.

The relationship between turnover and length of service constitutes an argument for seniority rewards, depending on the cost and complexity of training. Data showing this relationship reveal also that there is a moving labor supply that is responsible for most of the expense of hiring and training. In some cases, when training costs are small and pay is low (for example, fast-food franchises), companies may tolerate, if not encourage, high turnover rates.

AGE

If part of the unstable labor supply is due to trial-and-error job seeking, we would expect young employees to show higher labor turnover than older employees. This point is supported by an analysis of labor turnover in relation to age.[7]

The importance of responsibility in preventing turnover is shown by the fact that labor turnover again increases among workers who are over thirty-five years of age and reaches another high point at about forty-five years. This new high point in turnover comes at an age when family responsibilities begin to decline because children have reached working age.

For workers over forty-five years of age, the average length of service increases rapidly. In the past, this fact has been due partly to the reluctance of companies to hire older workers. Whether the new laws in this area will change the pattern will be seen during the coming years.

MARITAL STATUS

Although the proportion of married people increases with age, a separate analysis of the data in terms of marital status shows that it is one of the factors that influence the age trend in turnover rate. Among common laborers, the average length of service for married men was found to be about three times as great as that for single men. It is probable that marriage makes for both stability and responsibility, factors that reduce turnover rate under normal conditions of employment.

RELATIONSHIP BETWEEN
TURNOVER AND
JOB COMPLEXITY

Since the relationship between intelligence and turnover varies for different jobs, we may expect job complexity to be an important factor in causing people of low versus high intelligence to show different degrees of dissatisfaction for the same job. This point has been clearly verified by a study made of clerical workers.[8] Tests of mental alertness were given to employees at the time of hiring. The jobs were classified into five categories (A, B, C, D, and E) according to their level of difficulty, A jobs being the least difficult, and E jobs the most difficult. In analyzing the data, the average-scoring individuals were eliminated so that comparisons between the two extreme groups could be made. The extreme groups were those with mental-alertness scores below 80 and those with mental-alertness scores above 100. The first part of Table 17.1 shows the results for individuals who scored above 100. In originally placing the individuals, the tendency was to assign a greater proportion of them to the more complex jobs. Even so, thirty months later, the proportion of these individuals in complex jobs had increased (because of the high turnover of low-scoring individuals), whereas the proportion of these individuals in simple jobs decreased (because of their own high turnover).

The second part of the table shows the results for individuals who scored below 80.

TABLE 17.1 RELATIONSHIP BETWEEN INTELLIGENCE AND JOB COMPLEXITY

GRADE OF WORK	PERCENTAGE SCORING 100 OR BETTER		
	ORIGINAL GROUP	30 MONTHS LATER	PERCENTAGE OF TURNOVER
A (most simple)	26	0	100
B	20	0	100
C	45	27	72
D	46	51	53
E (most difficult)	50	57	41
	PERCENTAGE SCORING UNDER 80		
A	50	57	37
B	53	50	62
C	53	36	50
D	30	23	58
E	13	7	66

SOURCE: From M. A. Bills, Relation of mental alertness test score to positions and permanency in company. *J. Appl. Psychol.*, 1923, 7, 154–156. Copyright 1923 by the American Psychological Association, and reproduced by permission.

MOTIVATING WORKERS FOR OPTIMUM PERFORMANCE

After thirty months, the complex jobs had a lower proportion of low-scoring individuals, whereas simple jobs showed no such loss.

The last column shows that turnover among individuals with high scores declined as job complexity increased, indicating that a basic cause in turnover among these individuals may have been dissatisfaction with work that was too easy for them. For individuals who scored below 80 in mental alertness, turnover tended to increase with job complexity, suggesting that these individuals were dissatisfied with work that was too difficult for them. Thus, individuals with above- or below-average intelligence were dissatisfied with their jobs for different reasons, and a determining factor in this difference in behavior was the complexity of the job. This study also demonstrates that turnover functions as a selective process by which the individuals who remain are more suited to their work.

TURNOVER AND JOB SATISFACTION

An organization's concern for promoting job satisfaction influences not only motivation but also turnover resulting from dissatisfaction with the job or the company. This voluntary turnover depends in part on the ease of finding another job that is perceived as more desirable (the pull), as well as on the degree of dissatisfaction with the present job situation (the push). By using a model to predict turnover (based on prior studies of job satisfaction), it was possible to do better than chance to predict turnover among scientists and engineers.[9] Measures of job satisfaction were made while the participants were employed, and comparisons were made between those who quit within five years and those who stayed. The same questionnaires also indicated that the best performers tended to give responses similar to the turnover groups.[10]

In a longitudinal study of voluntary turnover in a manufacturing firm, it was found that the rate fluctuated with the labor-management relationship. During periods of harmony the rate was low, and during periods of unrest it was high.[11] Thus, the attitude toward the company was related to turnover.

Five aspects of job satisfaction for clerical workers were explored: kind of work, pay, supervision, promotional opportunities, and coworkers.[12] On the basis of the results, the company made a number of changes, which included more intracompany transfers, altered wage policies, merit-raise procedures, and certain job changes. At the time of the survey, turnover was 30 percent. In one year, it fell to 18 percent, and a year later it was 12 percent. During the two-year period, significant improvements in job satisfaction were obtained in four of the five job-satisfaction indices.

Job analysis and interviews with job incumbents may be useful ways to determine relationships between job satisfaction and turnover. In one large tire-manufacturing firm operating several hundred retail outlets for its products, retail store managers lasted an average of six months before quitting. Since training for this job was intensive and costly, turnover at this level constituted a real problem.

Discussions with a number of the store managers leaving the position revealed a common cause of dissatisfaction. The complexity of administrative work involved in the job had led the company to consider only candidates with college degrees. But when business was brisk, managers were expected to help by changing tires and doing other garage work. This manual labor conflicted with the self-concepts and job expectations of the new managers, so they left to find positions more suitable. Eventually, the company found it less expensive to hire high school graduates who were less reluctant to "get their hands dirty," even though many had more difficulty with bookkeeping and other administrative duties than their predecessors had.

TURNOVER AND ABSENTEEISM

Lack of job satisfaction may be expected to influence absenteeism as well as turnover, but differing motivations are also present. Quitting a job implies the availability of an alternative, whereas absenteeism is largely an avoidance response. It has generally been found that both absenteeism and turnover are related to dissatisfaction with the job, but the overall relationship is usually significant for absenteeism only.[13] The attitude toward the firm and the monotony of the job seem to influence both absenteeism and turnover, but the relationships differed even when two similar manufacturing firms in the same geographical area were compared.[14] Broad generalizations regarding the relationship between absenteeism and turnover therefore cannot be justified.

DISCOVERING
EMPLOYEE NEEDS

VARIOUS PURPOSES
A JOB MAY SERVE

Although it is desirable to relate certain general factors, such as intelligence and wages, to turnover, the importance of a good job/worker fit should not be overlooked. A job may serve any one of a number of pur-

poses, depending on the individual. Four general classifications of these purposes are discussed briefly.

1. *Temporary arrangement during period of transition*
Students on vacation and people waiting for a better job provide examples of this kind of job interest. Although many of these temporary employees (and they may not say they are temporary when they seek regular jobs) may be exploring vocational possibilities while employed, most are chiefly motivated by pay.

2. *Trial-and-error exploration of jobs*
One way to learn about jobs and companies is to hold a variety of jobs. Younger workers make up most of this exploratory group of employees. Usually they are not dependent on the job for a livelihood but can fall back on their family for help, and as a consequence, their major interest is not wages. Some expect to try out several jobs before deciding; others become interested and remain with a company to become part of the group of stable employees.

3. *Security and permanent occupation*
Many men and women enter occupations as seriously as they enter marriage. They have given the matter a good deal of thought and have taken a job that they believe they can endure, if not enjoy. They are a stable group of employees who will tolerate a good deal of dissatisfaction before quitting. To the extent that they do not find positive incentives in the work itself, they may pursue outside activities for satisfactions lacking on the job.

4. *Intermediate positions*
College graduates and others with high levels of aspiration accept positions with the understanding that they must start at lower positions and work up. They have their sights on the higher positions and experience

progress as they move up the corporate ladder. For such employees, the job is a central part of their lives, and they depend on job success for happiness.[15]

Clearly, the purposes that a job may serve will influence turnover in different ways. To expect all employees to respond to the same incentives and working conditions is unrealistic. There are many conditions that reduce turnover, but they are not cumulative; any one may be adequate if applied to the right person.

TRANSIENT EMPLOYEES

Employees who take a job as a temporary condition will select jobs primarily for their pay rates, and there is little the company can do to prevent these employees from quitting. If this type of turnover is to be reduced, the place to do it is in the employment office. In one study, the expression of interest in going to college was associated with clerical workers who stayed on the job three months or less.[16] Skilled interviews and the previous employment record can do much to detect the transient worker.

The short-term employee need not, however, be an undesirable one. Frequently such employees offer a high degree of skill or training in a specialized field of knowledge. The problem of transients is created primarily because the company does not know which employees are temporary. Employment interviews must not make permanence a condition of employment if deception in this matter is to be avoided. Sometimes married women applying for jobs are asked about their husband's job and the likelihood that the husband will be transferred. Unless this question is also always asked of male job candidates, it constitutes unfair discrimination.

FITTING EMPLOYEES TO JOBS

If employees are told what to expect on the job and if supervisors and employment interviewers know the job requirements, much job-hopping can be eliminated. In an investigation in which a clerical-aptitude test and an interest questionnaire were given, prediction of turnover was greatly improved.[17] The inclusion of an interview in which biographical background factors and job interests were explored added further relevant data.

Failure to do the job successfully is readily recognized by employees, and some are likely to quit even before they give themselves a fair chance to learn. Such employees can easily be mistaken for transients. In one case, candidates for lens-inspection jobs were given tests to determine whether they had the adequate visual skills for the job.[18] It was found that of those having adequate skills, 43 percent had been on the job eight months or more; of those lacking adequate skills, only 4 percent had as much as eight months' service. As a matter of fact, most of the employees lacking visual skills left the company in less than four months.

Employees who failed to make the production standard also were found to quit their jobs more readily than successful ones.[19] Those making just below standard experienced failure more acutely and showed a higher rate of quitting than those making well below standard. The experience of failure, rather than failure as objectively measured, seemed to be the determining influence.

REDUCING EXPERIENCES OF FAILURE

Proper selection and placement are obvious answers to turnover caused by job failure, but it must also be recognized that incompetence is not the only cause of perceived failure. Below-average performance and fear of being a failure are common experiences in any new undertaking. Beginners cannot compete with experienced operators, and although the supervisor does not expect top performance from them and often makes adequate allowances, new employees usually are not aware of the degree of understanding extended to them.

One approach to dealing with experiences of failure among beginners is to have a job-training program. It is the general experience of the telephone industry that the use of training classes reduces the anxiety of new employees. This benefit occurs because (1) the standards for learners are obviously different from those of experienced workers and apply equally to all members of the class, and (2) a coach is constantly present to give the attention and encouragement a learner requires.

Some research in Sweden with telephone operators demonstrates the value of training supervisors to take responsibility in getting new employees adjusted to their jobs.[20] When the telephone supervisors took the initiative for following the progress and development of new employees and saw to it that they were kept informed of the reasons behind regulations, an improved relationship between employees and supervisors developed. Employees so treated saw their supervisors as helpers rather than as critics; consequently, they went to them with their problems, accepted service monitoring, increased their production, and accepted responsibility on the job more quickly than others. In one company, employees were given training away from the job before being placed in the actual situation. As a result of this preliminary training, termina-

tions during the first thirty days dropped to 6 percent compared to 13 percent who quit when "broken in on the floor."[21]

Poor job aptitude is only one source of a failure experience on a new job. Employees who are new to a unit, whether beginners or transfers from another group, must make a social adjustment and become accepted by their new associates. Since job satisfaction is influenced by the satisfaction of needs, acceptance by peers becomes vital. Having an experienced employee assigned to help new employees get acquainted during the first week or two can reduce some of the experience of social failure.

PROBLEMS OF STABLE EMPLOYEES

How many stable employees stay with their companies because they are really satisfied, and how many are afraid to make the break? Security may be an undesirable influence if it causes employees to remain on jobs that give them no satisfaction. Both employee and employer lose by such an arrangement. Since there is a large percentage of stable employees, it is important to find ways to motivate and interest them.[22]

Long-term employees should be studied from the viewpoint of their interests. Interests change over a period of years, and job transfers as well as opportunities to help employees develop along new lines should be explored. A study of the changes in interests after employees had been on the job a number of years revealed that many were showing an interest in other kinds of jobs.[23] This shift in interest is a first sign of dissatisfaction, which eventually leads to turnover among less timid employees. Most companies have a diversity of jobs and are able to satisfy a variety of employees' interests if they are aware of them.

MOTIVATING WORKERS FOR OPTIMUM PERFORMANCE

AMBITIOUS EMPLOYEES AND DELEGATION

Higher-level employees often view working for a company as the process of progressing from one job to a higher one. Such employees see employment rather than a specific job as the source of satisfaction.

These people are motivated to find ways of speeding up the progression schedule. This frequently leads to such behaviors as discrediting associates who are seen as competitors, trying to make good impressions on superiors, and joining the "right" clubs. Although competence and job performance should be the determining factors in promotions, often ambitious employees completely overlook these as the means for getting ahead. The fact that methods of questionable relevance and ethics continue to be practiced by persons who want to be promoted suggests that these methods may be successful and that managers can be deceived.[24]

Employees who successfully use Machiavellian techniques to obtain advancement, discourage conscientious accomplishment and job interest in others. To derive true job satisfaction, an employee must experience accomplishment within the job itself. This means that the objectives of the job, not what the job will do for the person, must become the central interest of the employee. Frequently, the promise of promotion is used as an inducement to employees, but this too detracts from an interest in the intrinsic nature of the present job.

Stimulating job interest not only requires that the known principles of motivation be more effectively applied but also demands that supervisors make it a practice to discuss with their employees what the latter hope to get from their jobs. Supervisors will better understand the behavior of employees if they know how the employees see their jobs. These job discussions should cover (1) ways for improving the job; (2) methods for making work more satisfying, (3) opportunities for growing on the job, (4) suggestions for overcoming difficulties of communication, and (5) better delegation of responsibility. Within certain limitations, each job can be modified to some extent to suit the needs of the persons holding it. There is no reason why a predecessor should determine the complete job description, but it is natural for this to occur because the supervisor is often the previous holder of the employee's job. People differ greatly in how much responsibility and pressure they can stand. Frequently, it is easier to change assignments somewhat (always with the participation of those involved) than to try to find the person who completely suits the job.

ENGINEERS AND SCIENTISTS

The number of engineers and scientists employed in business has shown a marked increase in recent years, and this trend is likely to continue. Many of these specialists eventually move into management positions where they have little opportunity for scientific achievement. Questionnaires designed to measure various interests show engineers to be positively oriented toward the concrete and thinking along scientific lines, and to be negatively oriented toward dealing with people and expressing ideas.

Engineers who have progressed to higher positions in management, however, have broader interests. A study of engineers who left a company within two years after employment shows that some had interest patterns similar to those of the engineers in higher management.[25] Thus, a portion of the engineers who leave a company may be the very ones who would derive satisfaction

Job turnover of employees with specialized training, like scientists and engineers, can be reduced if their different interests and expectations are recognized. (Courtesy of Monsanto)

if they had greater opportunities to perform management functions. If such people are needed, adequate procedures for selecting them are not enough; ways to retain them should be found.

Studies of engineers and scientists working in business have found them unique in the extent to which they derive satisfaction from solving problems, creating, and innovating.[26] They also resist regimentation, resent close supervision, and expect freedom of movement. If they are promoted to supervisory positions, they lose their former opportunity for individual scientific achieve-

ment and must find satisfaction in interpersonal accomplishments since they now must work *through* people. This means they must undergo a change in their expectations as they advance in an organization. They may find themselves in a conflict situation because, in most organizations, advancement lies along managerial lines. "Dual-ladder" systems for progress via management talent or scientific talent have faltered because management positions have more power than scientific positions, though salaries may be equal. Management-training programs, which develop executive skills in dealing

MOTIVATING WORKERS FOR OPTIMUM PERFORMANCE

with people, may solve the problem in part by whetting the engineer's and scientist's appetite for management problems and by opening doors for other forms of innovation.

In situations where outlets for creativity and access to power are denied, frustration can become a serious and expensive problem. Scientists in a marketing-dominated food-processing firm, for example, were found to be engaging in frustration-induced behaviors that were expensive in both career and organizational terms.[27]

Since persons with specialized training have different expectations and interests, they often are isolated and limited in their friendships. A study of college recruits entering a three-year program of training revealed that when peer groups of three or more had opportunities to interact by being placed in the same department, their turnover rate was significantly below that of dyads and isolates.[28] When three or more trainees were assigned to the same department, 90 percent of 70 such persons were still with the company three years later, compared to 45 percent out of 84 for dyads and 51 percent out of 126 for isolates. The effect of "opportunity for peer-group interaction" on turnover exceeded that of scholastic performance (although more trainees receiving low grades left the firm than those whose scores fell above the median).

DUAL-CAREER FAMILIES

Some couples choose companies and the geographic locations for their jobs on the basis of the career opportunities afforded both partners. The trend for married women to work is expected to continue, and therefore some basic social and organizational changes in policy are required. More and better child-care centers will be needed; paid maternity leaves may become standard company policy; and new ways of dealing with housework and family responsibilities will have to be found.

The problem of dealing with home responsibilities can be solved in a number of ways. Husbands can share responsibilities, which will require changing some attitudes. Shorter work days and work weeks may supply some relief, and this trend is encouraging. One solution would be more inexpensive and competent domestic help. A number of firms offering specialized services from cleaning to plant watering to selecting wardrobes for busy executives have sprung up in recent years. National chains of child-care centers have appeared and may well follow the mushrooming development pattern in the 1980s that fast-food franchises did in the 1970s.

Changing work patterns have led to changes in home life. Today's families are more likely to eat at restaurants frequently and live in condominiums (no lawn-mowing or other home maintenance required). All problems in this area have not been solved, but the current trends do suggest that Americans are learning to adjust to the social changes brought about by dual-career families.

DEALING WITH PERSONALIZED NEEDS

Although employees may be classified according to their view of a job, these classifications are for convenience only, and each employee must be viewed as having a unique set of needs and values. Satisfaction with our lot in life does not require that all needs be satisfied, but the satisfaction must approach individuals' expectations if they are to achieve positive work attitudes.

In order to learn about employee needs,

the supervisor must be a good listener and must be willing to discuss ways for dealing with individual situations and problems. Running an office with general rules and practices may prevent grievances, but it also excludes the proper consideration of important individual needs.

DISCHARGING EMPLOYEES

LIMITATIONS OF FIRING TO UPGRADE THE WORK FORCE

Although many employees can readily leave one company for another, it has become difficult for companies to discharge unsatisfactory employees. To support a case for discharge, it is often essential to have (1) a permanent merit-rating record of the employee (to rule out a charge of discrimination), (2) memoranda indicating attempts to correct the employee's faults, (3) a copy of a final warning, and (4) a letter of discharge stating the reason for the action. Although criticisms and warnings are frequently ineffective procedures for correcting a poor performer, they are prerequisites instituted to safeguard against arbitrary action. Many companies do not permit a discharge to be made by the immediate supervisor, but require that it be handled by a department head or the personnel director.

In actual practice today, discharges of employees paid at an hourly rate are rare and the reasons given are more likely to be factors (such as dishonesty, lack of cooperation, excessive absences) other than incompetence.[29] Because of these complications, the risk of law suits, and desire for improved interpersonal relations, discharge ceases to be a practical method for upgrading personnel. Thus, the initial selection of employees and other methods to improve the working staff grow in importance as methods for upgrading the quality of employees.

LATERAL TRANSFER AS ALTERNATIVE TO DISCHARGE

Supervisors usually still have the authority to transfer employees out of their units. Although this procedure involves the cooperation of other persons, it remains a method for dealing with employees who are unsatisfactory because of poor job placement. One supervisor is rarely willing to accept another's unsatisfactory employee, but mutual interest can be established as supervisors find ways to exchange their "misfits".

CAPITALIZING ON THE PROBATIONARY PERIOD

Another opportunity for screening employees lies in the effective use of a probationary period. Most companies have a six-month probationary period, and the opportunity to be selective during this time is ample. Regardless of the length of the probationary period, it should be used to evaluate the employee's potential competence. Supervisors often tend to be overly generous in their reviews of new employees because they are reluctant to give an evaluation that leads to discharge. Biases in the direction of generosity must be carefully explored, and the considered judgment of several persons should be used so that none feels like a villain.

Observation of performance on the job over a period of a few months can serve as a good indication of an employee's aptitude for learning the job and of social and personal adjustment. These are traits the person brings to the job, and inadequacies are difficult to correct. Some undesirable traits can be developed after the employee is hired or are acquired in the work climate. They cannot be detected beforehand and should be corrected by improving the work environment and the supervision. Deficiencies acquired after employment that are due to off-the-job problems, aging, and altered job demands are responsibilities that companies may be expected to assume, as they have assumed responsibility for hospitalization and retirement.

Some rare employees put on their best behavior during the probationary period and, once secure, revert to their true selves. The appearance of such behavior indicates that the employee is capable of both forms of behavior; thus, satisfactory behavior is possible. This being the case, the problem for management is one of finding the motivation that induces the satisfactory behavior. Problem solving as a method for resolving differences will be discussed in Chapter 20.

IS DISCHARGE CRUEL?

Discharge of an employee, even when considered judgment indicates it to be the best solution, is often postponed. Executives do not like to dismiss a long-term employee who is unable to do the job. It is important to face this reality rather than to continue to delay action and live in a state of indecision and frustration.[30] If the employee cannot perform the job and if the supervisor who has the responsibility of handling the discharge is unable to accept and execute this decision, other alternatives must be generated. Postponing a decision may appear generous but the employee may actually be as unhappy with the situation as the supervisor.

Assuming that lateral transfers are out of the question, what alternatives remain? We assume that a lesser job with reduced pay would be unacceptable and are concerned about the employee's reaction. Demotion without reduction in pay is sometimes used, but it creates problems with other employees doing the same work. Paying the employee at a lower rate and at the same time paying an additional benefit from a personnel or retirement fund set aside for the purpose might be more acceptable to department heads who must pass on exceptional pay rates.[31] Another alternative is liberal severance pay.[32]

Often an employee's inability to perform a job does not reflect a deficiency in the person but arises and becomes apparent because the job has increased in complexity. When an employee cannot grow as fast as the job, a problem is created by growth or technical advances in the company. To blame a person for not growing as fast as the company amounts to holding the employee responsible for changes in the company. It has become a fairly common practice (resulting from union pressure) to assure employees that improvements in production methods will not jeopardize their jobs. This guarantee is essential to gain cooperation. Employees whose jobs have grown too fast for them are entitled to similar assurance, and when the situation is viewed in this manner, they are not seen as incompetent. Rather, it is the company's problem to relocate them or be ready to compensate them for their loss.

THE EXIT INTERVIEW

When managers discharge employees, they seldom give the whole or even the true reason for doing so. The objective is to give a reason that sounds plausible, or one that they can defend. This objective is also true when an employee quits.

On the one hand, some employees may not wish to appear critical of a supervisor, so they fabricate a plausible reason for quitting, such as a better offer, when actually they have accepted an equivalent position in another company. Others may blame the job or the supervisor for their leaving, whereas the real dissatisfaction is an inability to cope with the job's responsibilities. On the other hand, we should not assume that because an employee wishes to leave the company he or she is dissatisfied. An attractive offer or a desire to live elsewhere may have motivated the decision.

Continued probing during the exit interview can become a source of irritation, but failure to explore feelings may be interpreted as disinterest. In addition to providing good public relations, the objective of the exit interview is to offer an opportunity to communicate and learn, to explore alternatives, and to solve any problems of mutual interest. Skills in listening without criticizing and sensitivity to feelings are needed. These contrast with the more common practice of trying to persuade others to change their minds or attempting to get them to understand the company's position.

A skilled interviewer can learn a great deal about the company and about employees from the exit interview. In some instances, employees will change their minds and decide to remain with the company. In other instances, job changes, supervisory adjustments, or corrections of misunderstanding may make it possible to retain a good employee.

Listening skills are also relevant when an unwanted employee is leaving. Retaining the employee may no longer be an objective, but the public relations objective can be the same. The exit interview can be of assistance by helping the employee to analyze the job difficulties and to seek a more suitable job. Giving advice is likely to be a waste of time, but being able to talk freely helps a person face reality.

NEW WAYS TO DEAL WITH THE PROBLEMS OF DISCHARGING EMPOYEES

Whether because of more humanistic values or more regulations, companies have turned to some indirect, not to say devious, methods for getting rid of unwanted employees.[33] One company, for instance, capitalized on a decision to move its headquarters as a means for persuading some unwanted employees to resign. Those who were not wanted and whose moving costs were not going to be paid were told only to consider carefully the effects of the move from the Midwest to New York City on their lives. So skillfully was the subtle message given that of the 125 wanted employees, all but 3 moved, and only 7 of the 400 unwanted employees had to be fired. One unethical practice used in some firms (according to industrial physicians) is to pressure company doctors to overstate unwanted employees' medical problems in order to make them eligible for early retirement or long-term disability programs offered by the firms.

A more common and acceptable practice when executives are fired is using a specialized consulting firm to carry out what is euphemistically described as *out-placement*.[34] (Firing is considered so pejorative a term that it is rarely heard in business. Nearly everyone at executive levels is offered the opportunity to resign.) Out-placement consultants do not tell the employee that he or she has been dismissed, but meet with the individual immediately after the boss (or other company representative) conveys the message. The first role of the consultant, then, is to give the individual an opportunity to ventilate hostilities or to express hurt feelings without alienating the former employer.

Most executives provided with out-placement services (which include help in finding a new job) have lost their jobs as a result of company reorganizations or personality conflicts, rather than incompetence. This may be one reason why the success rate of finding the executive a new job at an equal or better salary is so high: some consultants claim that 80 percent of their clients have found such positions within six months.*

*A number of years ago, N.R.F. Maier recommended that an unwanted but unfireable executive be paid his normal salary for a year or so to stay home and stop damaging the company further. His suggestion was greeted with a combination of ridicule and horror. Today, however, the widespread practice of paying an executive "head-hunter" to uncover a job for an unwanted executive, then pretend to discover the executive independently, and to woo the unsuspecting manager away to the new job is common knowledge. In comparison with these Byzantine shenanigans, Maier's suggestion seems both modest and refreshingly straightforward. — G.C.V.

NOTES

1. Odiorne, G. S. How to get the men you want. *Nation's Business,* 1964, *52* (1), 70–72, 74.
2. Scheer, W. E. Reduce turnover: Increase profits. *Personnel J.,* 1962, *41,* 559–561.
3. Weitz, J. Job expectancy and survival. *J. Appl. Psychol.,* 1956, *40,* 247–249; Ilgen, D. R., and Seely, W. Realistic expectations as an aid in reducing voluntary resignations. *J. Appl. Psychol.,* 1974, *59,* 452–455.
4. Kilwein, J. H. Turnover as a function of communication during employment procedure. *Personnel J.,* 1962, *41,* 458.
5. Fleishman, E. A., and Harris, E. F. Patterns of leadership behavior related to employee grievances and turnover, *Personnel Psychol.,* 1962, *15,* 43–56.
6. Scott, W. D., and Clothier, R. C. *Personnel Management.* New York: A. W. Shaw, 1923, pp. 469–472, Scott, W. D., Clothier, R. C., and Spriegel, W. R. *Personnel management,* 6th ed. New York: McGraw-Hill, 1961, p. 466.
7. Scott, W. D., Clothier, R. C., Mathewson, S. B., and Spriegel, W. R. *Personnel management,* 3rd ed. New York: McGraw-Hill, 1941, p. 504; Guzzardi, W. The uncertain passage from college to job. *Fortune,* 1976, *93* (11), 126–129ff.
8. Bills, M. A. Relation of mental alertness test score to positions and permanency in company. *J. Appl. Psychol.,* 1923, 7, 154–156.
9. Farris, G. F. A predictive study of turnover, *Personnel Psychol.,* 1971, *24,* 311–328.
10. Pelz, D. C., and Andrews, F. M. *Scientists in organizations.* New York: Wiley, 1966.
11. Knowles, M. C. A longitudinal study of labour turnover, *Personnel Pract. Bull.,* 1965, *21,* 6–17.
12. Hulin, C. L. Effects of changes in job satisfaction levels on employee turnover *J. Appl. Psychol.,* 1968, 52, 122–126.
13. Talacci, S. Organizational size, individual attitudes and behavior: an empirical study. Doctoral dissertation, University of Chicago, 1959.
14. Kilbridge, M. D. Turnover, absence, and transfer rate as indicators of employee dissatisfaction. *Indust. Labor Relat. Rev.,* 1961, *15,* 21–32.
15. Meyer, H. E. The boss ought to take more time off. *Fortune,* 1974, *89* (6), 140–142ff. See also, Leibling, B. A. Beyond work stereotypes. *MBA,* 1978, August–September, 13–25, for a breakdown of the motivations of M.B.A. graduates in business.

16. Kriedt, P. H., and Gadel, M.S. Prediction of turnover among clerical workers *J. Appl. Psychol.*, 1953, *37*, 338–340.

17. Kriedt and Gadel, ibid.

18. Kephart, N. C. Visual skills and labor turnover. *J. Appl. Psychol.*, 1948, *32*, 51–55.

19. Coch, L., and French, J. R. P., Jr. Overcoming resistance to change. *Hum. Relat.*, 1948, *1*, 512–532.

20. Westerlund, G. *Group leadership: A field experiment.* Stockholm: Nordisk Rotogravyer, 1952.

21. Lawshe, C. H. Jr. Eight ways to check the value of a training program. *Factory Mgt. and Maintenance*, 1945, *105*, 117–120.

22. (Verser), G. G. Casselman, and Taylor, M. *Motivating for increased productivity.* New York: AMACOM, 1974.

23. Herzberg, F., and Russell, D. The effects of experience and change of job interest on the Kuder Preference Record. *J. Appl. Psychol.*, 1953, *37*, 478–481.

24. Odiorne, G. S. Maverickism — a new business value? *Michigan Bus. Rev.*, 1960, *12*, 2, 15–19; Machiavellian tactics for B-school students. *Business Week,* October 13, 1975.

25. Boyd, J. B. Interests of engineers related to turnover, selection and management. *J. Appl. Psychol.*, 1961, *45*, 143–149.

26. Herzberg, F., Mausner, B., and Snyderman, B. B. *The motivation to work.* New York: Wiley, 1959; Danielson, L. E. *Characteristics of engineers and scientists.* Ann Arbor, Mich.: University of Michigan, Bureau of Industrial Relations, 1960; Dunnette, M.D. A note on the criterion. *J. Appl. Psychol.*, 1963, *47*, 251–254; Pelz and Andrews, op. cit.

27. Verser, G. C. *The effects of an imbalance of power on new product development in marketing-oriented firms.* Doctoral dissertation, Ann Arbor, Mich: Univ. Microfilms, 1978.

28. Evan, W. M. Peer group interaction and organizational socialization: a study of employee turnover, *Amer. Sociol. Rev.*, 1963, *28*, 436–448.

29. Scott, Clothier, and Spriegel, op. cit.

30. Randall, C. When to fire him. *Atlantic Mon.*, 1963, *211*(1), 58–60.

31. Maier, N. R. F. How to get rid of an unwanted employee. *Personnel Admin.*, 1965, *28*, 25–27.

32. Big steel strives to thin its ranks. *Business Week,* Aug. 25, 1962, *1721*, 106, 108.

33. Gooding, J. The art of firing an executive. *Fortune,* 1972, *86*(4), 88–91ff.

34. Meyer, H. E. The flourishing new business of recycling executives. *Fortune,* 1977, *95*(5), 328–330ff.

SUGGESTED READINGS

Horn, P. W., Katerberg, R., Jr., and Hulin, C. L. Comparative examination of three approaches to the prediction of turnover. *J. Appl. Psychol.*, June, 1979, 280–290.

Porter, L. W., and Steers, R. M. Organizational, work, and personal factors in employee turnover and absenteeism. *Psychol. Bull.*, 1973, 151–176.

Price, J. *The study of turnover.* Ames, Iowa: Iowa State University Press, 1977.

Telly, C. S., French, W. R., and Scott, W. G. The relationship of inequity to turnover among hourly workers. *Adm. Sci. Quart.*, June, 1971, 164–172.

LABORATORY EXERCISE
ROLE-PLAYING:
THE PERSONNEL INTERVIEW

(Students are asked not to read the case materials before participating in the laboratory exercise.)

A. GENERAL PREPARATION*

1. The instructor will select three persons to participate in this case.
2. One person will play the part of Loretta Welch, personnel director of the company. This person leaves the room to study the role (G.4). *CAUTION:* He or she is to read *only* this role.
3. The instructor will read aloud the setting of the case (G.1) to the class as a whole, including the two participants who will play the parts of Ken Hardy and Walt Henderson.
4. The person who is to be Walt Henderson takes a seat at a table placed in front of the room. Walt is working at a drafting board. A copy of the dialogue (G.2) should be placed on the table.
5. Ken Hardy is also supplied with a copy of the dialogue.

B. READING THE DIALOGUE

1. Ken Hardy approaches Walt Henderson from behind and begins reading the dialogue.
2. Proceed through the complete dialogue.
3. When the scene is completed, Ken Hardy resumes his place in the class.
4. Walt leaves the room to study the material titled "Additional Information for Walt Henderson" (G.3).

* Case adapted from N.R.F. Maier, Dramatized case material as a springboard for role playing. *Group Psychother.*, 1953, *6*, 30–42. Materials reproduced with permission of Beacon House Inc., publisher, and J. L. Moreno, editor.

C. PREPARING FOR ROLE-PLAYING

1. The instructor asks the person who was given the role of Loretta Welch to return and take a seat at the table.
2. The instructor places another chair at the table and informs the class that Loretta Welch is in her office and will shortly conduct an interview with an employee of the company who has asked to see her on an urgent matter.

D. ROLE-PLAYING THE SCENE BETWEEN LORETTA WELCH AND WALT HENDERSON

1. The instructor asks Henderson to return and indicates that Loretta Welch is in her office and can see him now.
2. Role-playing proceeds to a natural termination point.
3. Role-players might agree to have another interview later on, or an interview between Hardy and Welch; or the single interview might end the incident, with Henderson deciding either to quit or to forget his problem.

E. SUBSEQUENT ROLE-PLAYING SCENES

1. Interviews or problems growing out of the first interview should be role played by assuming the time set for them has arrived.
2. If Hardy becomes a participant in role-playing, he should be instructed to assume that he has not witnessed the first role-playing interview.

F. DISCUSSION QUESTIONS

1. Did the interview between Welch and Henderson influence his final decision? Discuss.

2. Did Welch learn anything relevant in the initial interview? Discuss in detail.
3. Did Henderson have another offer or was he bluffing? Did Welch learn the facts?
4. What did Henderson need as a concession to make him remain with the company? Was this unreasonable?
5. Should Welch consult Hardy about any commitments that she makes to Henderson? If she did consult Hardy, did she antagonize him by assuming more authority than she had? Discuss.
6. What are the face-saving problems?
7. If time permits, other class members may try out some of their ideas by taking any of the parts and role-playing a brief scene with the appropriate person.

G. MATERIALS FOR THE CASE

1. Setting of the Case

The work place is a drawing table in a large drafting room of the Wilson Construction Company. There are thirty draftsmen in the office and two supervisors. Walt Henderson, a draftsman, is working busily as his supervisor, Ken Hardy, comes by. It is 10 A.M. Tuesday morning.

2. Dialogue

Ken: How's the work going, Walt?

Walt: Fine. All caught up.

Ken: Even that set of specifications of Joe's that I gave you to check yesterday?

Walt: Yep. Took it home and worked on it there so I wouldn't be too rushed today.

Ken: Well, now, I don't want you to have to be taking work home, Walt. I didn't know you were going to do that or I'd have asked Fred to help Joe out on it instead.

Walt: Oh! That's O.K. I didn't mind doing it. I knew Joe was going to have a rough time getting it all done by noon today, anyway.

Ken: What are you working on now?

Walt: Some plans for that little boat I told you I was going to build.

Ken: I see. Think you should be doing that on company time, Walt?

Walt: Well, I don't know. I've done all my own work and put in three hours of my own time last night to help Joe out. And besides I don't have my own equipment at home to do this drafting. What's the harm in it?

Ken: It just looks bad to be doing something like that on company time. You know that.

Walt: Well, when I have all my work done and more, what does the company expect me to do — twiddle my thumbs?

Ken: Now let's not get hasty. We went through all this last year when you got both of us on the hot seat with Johnson over that garage of yours that you drew up here. Remember?

Walt: Sure, I remember. And I still don't think it's anybody's business what I work on here so long as my own work is done and I don't bother anybody else.

Ken: That's what you think. Now let's get this straight. Nobody's telling you what to do before or after office hours, but when you're here drawing pay you're supposed to be earning it. And I don't want another mess like the one we had on that garage of yours. Understand?

Walt: Yes, but I don't see why we have to set up such rigid rules. Just because Johnson doesn't know how much work I turn out is no reason why you should take your cue from him.

Ken: Look, Walt, I'm not taking my cue from him. I didn't like the idea of you doing your own work here either, but I decided to let it pass. Then when the chief caught you at it and you didn't have the good judgment to be a bit more careful — well, you've got the wrong attitude.

Walt: How can you say that? You know perfectly well I turn out more work than anyone else. Is it my fault if you can't keep me busy?

Ken: Walt, I know you're a top-notch draftsman, but a good employee is something more.

Walt: Yeh — a good employee is a yes-man.

Ken: Not at all. A good employee works well with others. He's got to follow rules so that he doesn't set a bad precedent. Suppose the others brought their own work down here?

Walt: Well, make them do their job first.

Ken: How can I if they say I let you work on your personal things?

Walt: But I do company work at home and more than make up the time.

Ken: Walt, am I supposed to let you choose when and where you do company work? What a mess that would make if I had to keep track of everyone's homework. Anyway, we've never asked you to do work at home. When we have more to do than you can handle during working hours we'll pay you overtime.

Walt: Ken, I'm not asking for overtime. All I want is to be treated as an honest person. I've never gypped the company out of anything and whenever the company is behind schedule I've worked like the devil to help out. Now I've got a personal problem and all I'm asking is to borrow some of the facilities. Is that unreasonable?

Ken: I can see your side, Walt, but we can't give favors to some and not to others. I've just got to make a rule, and remember you've forced me into it. There will be no more personal work done during company hours. I'll let you finish this job, but that will have to be the end. I am not going to have the others say I play favorites. Sorry, but that's it.

3. Additional Information for Walt Henderson

Walt was disturbed by this conversation. At noon he called his friend Bill Alden, who told him they had an opening in the drafting department in his company (Jones Bros., Inc.). Walt asked him to check up on details. That afternoon Bill's boss, Mr. Hansen, called Walt and told him he was very anxious to have Walt come to work for Jones Bros. He told Walt that he would take him on Bill's recommendation and the salary he quoted was five dollars a week more than Walt was getting. From his description, the work seemed about the same as Walt was now doing. When Walt expressed interest, Hansen asked him if he could start next week. That would be next Monday. Since Jones Bros. had another applicant for the job, he asked Walt if he could let him know right away. Walt asked if he could have until Wednesday morning so as to have time to talk it over with his wife. Hansen said that would be O.K. He suggested that Walt give

the Wilson Company a good excuse for quitting so suddenly because he wanted to stay on good terms with the Wilson Company.

After this talk, Walt thought a bit and decided it would be nice to work in Bill's office. They had often compared companies, and although Walt had sometimes thought of making a change he could find little difference between the companies. Since he had eight years with the Wilson Company, he had some seniority and retirement benefits. Now he had a reason for quitting. He knew his wife would go along with any decision. The important thing to do now was to go to the personnel office and let the company know about his decision. Walt therefore called Loretta Welch of the personnel department and asked to see her on an urgent matter. Welch asked him to come right down.

4. Role for Loretta Welch

You are head of the personnel department of the Wilson Construction Company. Your department does all the hiring, and must O.K. all recommendations for changes in pay rates. You have the authority to turn down recommended increases and to make changes in job classifications and are in a position to influence personnel policy. Your door is open to employees who want to discuss company matters or even their own personal problems. You or your staff interview all employees who leave the company.

Walt Henderson of the drafting department has just called you and wants to see you on "an urgent matter." You've asked him to come right down. Just to prepare yourself on factual matters, you have looked up his record. He works for Ken Hardy, a drafting department supervisor, whom you regard highly, and Ken has given him a very good rating. The record shows Walt Henderson to be a top-notch draftsman. He has eight years with the company, which is about average for the drafting room. Walt Henderson is married, and has a four-year-old daughter. As his hobbies he has listed fishing and sailing. The door opens and Walt Henderson walks in.

CHAPTER EIGHTEEN

COUNSELING SKILLS FOR MANAGERS

■

Counseling and Interpersonal Relations
Nondirective Skills   *Accomplishments of Counseling*
Common Counseling Situations
Some Practical Considerations in Counseling
Location of Counseling Services   *Interview Objectives*
Basic Interviewing Principles
The Interview as a Whole   *Improving Job Contacts*

■

EMPLOYEES COMMUNICATE with their supervisors in many ways and on many occasions. A perceptive supervisor realizes that sensitive issues, especially personal ones, are not easily talked about by most people. To help employees express their questions and concerns, the trained manager has learned to respond effectively to each communication situation. Three of the most important — counseling, interviewing, and informal job contacts — are discussed in this chapter. In addition to descriptions of these situations, methods are given for improving the manager's skills in dealing with each type.

COUNSELING AND INTERPERSONAL RELATIONS

PROBLEMS IN MISUNDERSTANDING

We have already considered many of the principles and skills essential to success in dealing with people. Chapter 5 discussed misunderstandings arising between employees and supervisors because of the differences in their attitudes; it emphasized the importance of discovering other persons' attitudes in order to communicate effectively. Methods of helping frustrated people release their feelings were emphasized in Chapter 4. There we saw that constructive and cooperative behavior could result only from removal of frustration-producing obstacles. But even with frustrating conditions corrected, effective motivation was not assured. To deal effectively with employees who have differing sources of motivation, it is necessary to understand their needs — particularly their acquired needs.[1] The importance of discovering needs and of finding

positive, rather than negative, incentives was described in Chapters 3 and 13.

Research into the effects of emotional disturbance on productivity suggests that these problems are associated with lowered output.[2]

Whether we are faced with attitude problems, frustrated employees, or motivation difficulties — and any of these will introduce communication problems — the remedy lies in the same direction: a supervisor who sees difficulties with people as problems to solve and who wants to understand the employee's situation. Employees in this case are sources of information, and the supervisor must become adept at drawing them out. In any conversation, the person who talks the most is the one who learns the least about the other person. The good supervisor therefore must become a good listener.

Although most dealings with people do not involve unpleasantness or misunderstandings, instances that do occur are so disturbing that management personnel have become interested in the basic counseling skills. Supervisors generally agree that about 10 percent of employees present problems. H. Meltzer reported that these problems include almost the whole array of behaviors found in the clinic.[3]

Many so-called problem employees are known to higher management, which means that the problem employee is discussed at several levels of management. The inclusion of higher management in discussions about employees involves the use of expensive time. One president of a large company spent over half an hour describing a problem that his company had with an elevator operator. To know all the details, he must have had to deal with the matter over a period of months.

Certain valuable by-products of counseling skills accrue to supervisors for time spent in counseling activities. Ordinarily, misunderstandings come to a supervisor's attention when they become acute. However, a supervisor who has counseling skills may use them to prevent problems or minor disturbances. Anything done to make good conditions better or to reduce the number of temporary dissatisfactions and disappointments represents a gain. When interviewing a cross section of over 100 male and female employees, Maier found that more than 85 percent felt that there were times when they would welcome an opportunity to speak their minds. But only a scattered few said they ever discussed personal problems with their supervisor, and an even smaller number felt free to speak critically of an office situation.

THE SELECTION OF SAFE SKILLS

Important skills for dealing with emotionally disturbed people have been developed in clinics and counseling centers. Many of these skills have been carried out of the original settings and used in business. The Ford Motor Company, for example, had a counseling program as early as 1914 to advise employees on nontask-related problems.[4] The most extensive application to industry of a clinically sound method was described in the classic Hawthorne study.[5] However, any clinical or therapeutic procedures used by nonprofessionals must be foolproof. Sometimes a little knowledge is dangerous, but sometimes a little knowledge is better than no knowledge.

Fortunately the researches of Carl Rogers[6] and his students[7] have supplied procedures which, if practiced by skilled persons, seem to be as good as any known alternatives, and if practiced with minimum skill, at least per-

mit supervisors to do no worse than they would have done before training. Research findings suggest that counseling by those without psychological training will be accepted by employees and can help improve poor performance.[8]

THE NATURE OF NONDIRECTIVE COUNSELING

The counseling approach that lends itself best to interpersonal relations in business is nondirective, or client-centered, counseling. It is called *nondirective* because the counselor does not direct the client with advice; it is *client-centered* because the client, not the counselor, determines what will be discussed; interest centers on the client's feelings rather than on a diagnosis. The method differs from the popular view of counseling in that no diagnosis is made, no solution to a problem is supplied, and no advice is given. Rather, the counselor stimulates clients to uncover their problems themselves and to decide their own courses of action. A person is more likely to act upon a solution worked out personally because it is more acceptable. Giving advice, asking questions, making a diagnosis, and supplying the solution characterize the directive approach. Volunteered advice is notoriously unproductive; even people who ask for it seldom are pleased or moved to act by what they hear.

In actual practice, many skills used by directive and nondirective counselors are similar, and a counselor can use techniques that are neither solely directive nor solely nondirective. Nevertheless, it is important to differentiate between the two approaches in order to see their applications to business. A counselor may encourage a client to talk about problems either to make a diagnosis or to stimulate the client's self-analysis. The nondirective approach avoids diagnosis and therefore the risk of a wrong diagnosis.[9]

NONDIRECTIVE SKILLS

ACTIVE LISTENING

Philosophers in the past have spoken of the wisdom of listening, but the development and refinement of listening as a clinical tool is relatively recent. Listening means more than refraining from speaking. Listeners must demonstrate their desire to understand through their behavior and through their acceptance of the person, as well as of the person's statement. If counselors indicate doubt, surprise, disagreement, or criticism, they are acting as judge or critic; if they express agreement, pity, or even sympathy, they are acting as supporter. Judging stimulates defensive behavior; offering support stimulates dependent behavior.

The active listener's behavior includes a posture indicative of attention, a friendly facial expression, patience, and acceptance of pauses. Certain vocal expressions may rightly be included under listening. These include such expressions as "Uh-huh," "I see," "I understand," and "Do you want to tell me about that?" Even if directly asked to express an opinion, a counselor can avoid entering into a discussion by saying, "Would you like to tell me how you feel about it?" or "I think it is best for you to tell me about it."

ACCEPTING FEELINGS

If a person expressing hostile feelings is told by a supervisor that he or she is reacting unjustly, the employee may feel judged and rejected and become defensive. If the supervisor gives advice before understanding the person's true problem, the advice may be inappropriate and unacceptable. Nevertheless, hostile and childish feelings may require more than permissive listening; in this case, they can be accepted and verbalizaed by the counseling supervisor without either agreeing or disagreeing with them. Examples of verbal acceptance of feelings are:

- You must have been very upset to have walked out of his office like that.
- I can see that your feelings were hurt badly by that incident.
- I can see you were badly upset by my criticism of the job you did.

Such statements indicate sensitivity to feelings and avoid evaluation of them. If expressed in time, they may prevent defensive behavior, or in many instances, confrontation. When the listener feels attacked, it is difficult to avoid retaliation; a verbal acceptance of the feeling can prevent the situation from deteriorating. H. G. Ginott gives many examples of how arguments between parents and children can be avoided by accepting feelings.[10]

Acceptance should not be confused with agreement or approval. Ginott points out "a physician does not reject a patient because he bleeds. Though unpleasant such behavior is tolerated; it is neither encouraged nor welcomed. It is merely accepted."[11]

REFLECTING FEELINGS

Although listening and accepting feelings are easy to describe, they are difficult to execute. Ordinarily, communication is a give-and-take interaction in which persons exchange views. Evaluation by agreeing or disagreeing characterizes such exchanges. Counselors using nondirective techniques are asked to inhibit these natural tendencies by listening and being sensitive to feelings and carefully avoiding an act of judgment. Counseling skills must replace advice with some *useful* kind of verbal response. The method of responding to feelings by restating or *reflecting* them effectively satisfies this requirement. Since substituting one response for another is easier than withholding a response, training in reflecting another person's feelings helps the counselor avoid making judgmental responses.

Reflecting feelings seems awkward at first but supplements the benefits of listening; and at the same time, it makes it necessary for the counselor to speak. However, in order to reflect feelings properly, a counselor must listen carefully and selectively. Selective listening means paying attention to certain things in a speech. In a debate or argument, one listens selectively to the opponent and pays strict attention to see if the speaker violates facts or expresses inconsistencies. An opponent attacks what is said, not what is meant. A counselor, however, pays atten-

tion to feelings, and factual material is allowed to fall into the background. Inconsistencies indicate to the counselor the need for clarification through further expression. Because of this rationale, the technique of reflecting feelings is also known as "empathically understanding the client."

The method of reflecting feelings is analogous to the counselor or interviewer serving as a *selective* mirror. The counselor mirrors or restates some parts of the conversation and allows other parts to pass (Figure 18.1). Facts, incidents, justifications, details of arguments and reasons, the chronology and geography of events are relatively unimportant, but how the person feels about any of these things *is* important. These feelings must be reflected so they can be seen in a different setting. Seeing oneself in a home movie or on videotape gives one an objective look at one's physical appearance,

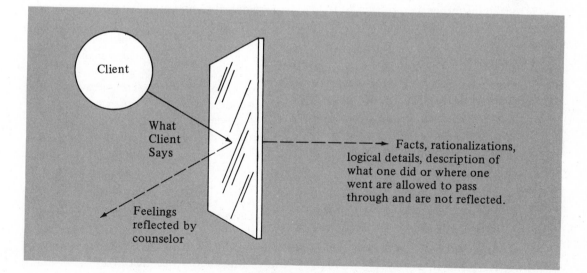

FIGURE 18.1 THE COUNSELOR SERVES AS A SELECTIVE MIRROR
A disturbed person may say many things (solid-line arrow) to a counselor. The counselor responds by allowing factual content to pass (broken-line arrow on right), but reacts to feelings by summarizing and restating them (broken-line arrow on left).

and what is seen sometimes comes as a surprise. The counselor helps people to be more objective about their feelings by restating them in different words.

An angry employee may say, "There is no reason why this promotion should not have been given to me. I've been with this company a long time, I've never taken advantage of sickness benefits, I work hard, and I certainly could use the extra money more than the person who got the job." An appropriate reflecting remark of a supervisor would be, "You feel that you were not treated fairly considering all you've done for the company." Any disputing or recounting of points in the argument given by the employee would violate the method of reflecting feelings since these are factual items or refer to things outside the person. Individuals who tell their life's story on a bus are not receiving nondirective counseling from listeners because events rather than feelings are being focused on. But if the listener responds to feelings rather than to events, such an encounter can become a counseling interview.

In learning to reflect feelings the following points should be observed:

1. Restate the other person's expressed feelings in your own words rather than mimicking or parroting the original words.

2. Preface reflected remarks, at first, with "You feel . . . ," "You think . . . ," "It seems to you that . . . ," "It sometimes appears to you that . . . ," and so on. Later in the interview, you can dispense with such prefatory phrases.

3. Formulate reflected remarks as statements, not as questions. Try to speak quietly and slowly, and with a neutral emotional tone.

4. Wait out pauses. Long pauses often enable a person to say things that are difficult to admit. Inexperienced interviewers often are embarrassed by pauses and make distracting remarks to fill them.

5. When many feelings are expressed, as in a long speech, only the last feeling area expressed should be reflected. (Confusion about many things is one feeling area, but feeling immature and hating one's mother are two feeling areas, and only the last should be reflected.)

6. Only feelings actually expressed should be reflected. It may be apparent that a person distrusts another, but distrust should not be reflected unless and until it is explicitly stated. A counselor who diagnoses or anticipates may injure the counseling relationship. Skilled counselors sometimes *lead*, in that they reflect feelings just a little ahead of those expressed, but unless this leading is accurately and skillfully done, it hinders the relationship and may frighten the client.

7. When a person makes contradictory statements ("I can't understand why Ralph did that," and "I know why Ralph acted that way"), the counselor should reflect each opinion when it is expressed and proceed as though no inconsistency were stated. Such changes in expression indicate progress and a clarification of feeling.

8. If a person cries during an interview, references to the act may be made in reflecting remarks, provided the person is not attempting to hide the tears.

9. Watch for mixed feelings involving a conflict between (1) what the person desires and feels is a duty; (2) what others think and what the person thinks; and (3) the person's values and those of society. These ambivalent feelings should be reflected.

10. Decisions, solutions, and constructive ideas may be reflected when they *predominate* over feelings of confusion, hostility, fear,

insecurity, rejection, and the like. The unskilled counselor is likely to overvalue the former and reflect them before a person is ready to act upon these possibilities. Searching behavior reveals many possible actions, and a counselor must not try to hasten the decision process.

11. In reflecting another person's state of mind, any indication of approval or disapproval should be avoided. It is important to refrain from questioning, probing, blaming, interpreting, giving advice, persuading, reassuring, and giving sympathy.

12. Diagnoses should be avoided. A diagnosis is a counselor's interpretation of why the disturbed person feels that way and leads to biased listening.

13. It is almost always safe to assume that what initially is presented as the problem is not the central one.

14. Avoid being solution-minded. Remember that the solution must come as a result of the person's own insight.

The method of reflecting feelings helps and supplements listening, and it introduces two additional values. First, it gives the counselor a way to pass the conversation back to the client when expected to give some kind of reaction or judgment. Even a direct question, such as "What would you do if you were in my place?" can be reflected by "You feel you would like me to tell you what to do." Second, the method stimulates further expression in the general feeling area reflected. Many of the everyday benefits of listening are never realized because the expression stops short of the important and more complete release of feeling.

Table 18.1 contains statements taken from case material, with four possible responses by a counselor or supervisor given in the right-hand column. The reader should attempt to select the best reflecting response before checking against the answers at the end.[12]

THE USE OF QUESTIONS

The unskilled counselor should avoid using questions as much as possible. Questions tend to direct the conversation and put disturbed individuals at a disadvantage, because usually either they do not know the answers or they do not feel free to give them.

Questions that are in the spirit of nondirective counseling may serve a convenient and helpful function, however. Questions such as "Would you like to tell me about it?" "Did that bother you a lot?" and "How did that make you feel?" stimulate further expression in a feeling area under examination. Such questions neither pry nor direct the course of the discussion. Care must be taken to avoid questions that can be answered by *yes* or *no*.[13]

When the counseling process has reached the stage of exploring various behavior possibilities, questions may be used to explore consequences. Such questions as "What do you think would happen if you did that?" "How would that affect the others?" and "Do you feel you could eventually adjust to that?" cause the person to evaluate not only actions but also the consequences of actions. However, none of the questions indicate approval or disapproval; they merely explore whether consequences of various actions have been considered.

ESSENTIAL ATTITUDES

The counselor's attitude toward a client will influence the skill with which these methods are practiced. The counselor who likes and respects other persons can do a better job of listening and reflecting feelings than one

(Continued on page 495)

TABLE 18.1 EXAMPLES OF GOOD AND POOR REFLECTED RESPONSES

REMARK	SELECT BEST RESPONSE TO REFLECT
1. The client has been on a new crew for three months. During a counseling interview, he said: "I don't know why it is, but I just don't feel as though I'm one of the gang. They are all nice enough fellows, but somehow they seem to have a closed circle and make me feel like an outsider. Maybe it's me; I don't know."	(a) Why don't you use the first chance you get to do the boys a favor? (b) It seems to you that the group doesn't accept you. (c) It seems that the others dislike you for some reason. (d) You don't think they will accept you if you give them some more time to learn that you are a nice fellow.
2. Client is a twenty-year-old woman. She states, "God, I hate my ma. She tries to run my life for me. I feel almost as strongly about my dad. He just sits back and lets her run everything, and never protests."	(a) You feel the father should be stronger than the mother. (b) You resent your mother for being too strong, and your father for being too weak. (c) You feel guilty because you can't accept the idea that you hate your parents. (d) Getting away from home for a while would relieve the immediate tension and give you a chance to work out this problem.
3. A clerical employee with ten years' experience told his supervisor: "I've been doing this job for years now and nobody had ever complained and now you send my work back and tell me to do it over. It isn't fair and it doesn't make sense. Maybe I do make mistakes now and then, but nobody is perfect and I don't know why I should get all the blame for what goes on around here."	(a) It isn't fair to ask you to correct your own mistakes. (b) Suppose you check your work before you bring it to me. (c) You think you are being blamed for not being perfect. (d) You feel that I am too strict.
4. The following statement was made by a woman during a counseling session: "There is nothing wrong with me. I only came to see you because my doctor insisted upon it."	(a) That may be true, but shall we wait and see? (b) You are resentful about coming here. (c) You really don't want to be here. (d) What do you think was her reason for sending you here?
5. During an interview with his supervisor, a member of a crew states: "I don't want to work with Jake any more. He's lazy and is always taking a superior attitude and complains about the rest of us not helping him as much as we should. He thinks he is too good for this kind of work and too good to work with the rest of us, and I'm sick of being around him."	(a) You feel that Jake ought to be disciplined in some way. (b) Jake doesn't want to cooperate, is that it? (c) Jake's attitude makes the work unpleasant. (d) You think Jake might fit in better somewhere else.

TABLE 18.1 Continued

REMARK	SELECT BEST RESPONSE TO REFLECT
6. A young woman whose work showed a sudden drop in quality was sent to the employment manager for an interview. One of the things she said on arriving was: "I don't know why I should be asked to talk to you about my work. I haven't complained, and I haven't time for this kind of chit-chat. So give me what help you have in mind and I'll be on my way."	(a) You came to see me because you were sent and not because you feel any need for help. (b) Don't you feel that with my experience in the company, I might be of some help? (c) You feel irritated for coming here because you don't think I can help you. (d) You mustn't jump to conlusions. Often people need help when they are unaware of this need.
7. Man — age fifty-nine: "I couldn't let my son help me now that I'm down and out. I've got that shred of pride left — because you see I remember when he was a kid and I didn't turn my hand to help him. I traipsed around the country — his mother died when the kid was born — and I let the relatives push him around and stuck him in foster homes — and now — it certainly was like a knife stuck in me when we met the other day and he said, 'We can make a go of it together, Dad — I've got a little money saved up.' No — No — I won't let him do it. I will clear out of here. It'll be hard — but — I haven't done one thing for him — or anyone else for that matter."	(a) What was your married life like? Had you and your wife planned for a child? (b) Have you thought what it will mean to your son if you don't let him do this thing which he wants to do for you? (c) I see what you mean. You feel that you don't deserve the help he wants to give because in the past you did nothing to earn it. And your statement that you never have done anything for anyone else makes it look as if it might be a real problem for you to accept responsibility for helping others, and to accept help from others. (d) Your behavior in the past makes you unworthy of the help your son wants to give you now, is that what you mean?
8. In the middle of a counseling interview with her boss, a fifty-eight-year-old woman said, "You don't want me here, you just want young women. I'm getting old, so I guess I should get out."	(a) It's not true that I favor the young women employees. (b) You believe I'd like to have you leave because of your age. (c) You feel you have reason to believe that I prefer young girls. (d) I can see that I must have done something to hurt your feelings.
9. A supervisor was discussing the work of a young man about a year out of high school. The supervisor was trying to determine why important details on procedure were often overlooked or clearly violated. Suddenly the young man shouted "You're the worst supervisor I've ever had. If a person shows initiative, you work him over. I refuse to follow silly rules."	(a) Why don't you check with me before you make a change in procedure? (b) You resent me for criticizing your work. (c) Perhaps it's my fault that I didn't train you on the correct procedures. (d) You feel I should have someone else go over your work.

(Continued on next page)

TABLE 18.1 Continued

REMARK	SELECT BEST RESPONSE TO REFLECT
10. In a counseling interview, a young woman talked at length about her husband's lack of consideration, going into considerable detail to justify why she should divorce him. After a pause, she remarked that she never had long-term relationships with anyone. "Other people seem to have old friends, but I get tired of them after I get to know them. Maybe I expect too much of people."	(a) You feel a divorce may be the solution to your problem. (b) You think perhaps you should reconsider your divorce. (c) After you get to know people, they cease to be interesting. (d) It seems now that expecting too much of friends may interfere with long-term relationships.
11. Man — age forty-one: "I've been married four times and each time I've thought, 'Boy, this is the real thing!' None of them has ever been like this girl. She's the most beautiful girl you ever saw — and dance! And she dresses like a million dollars. She's out of this world!"	(a) You're really enthusiastic about her. (b) How does she compare with your other wives? How did you feel about them before you married? (c) If she's anything like you seem to feel she is, she must be quite a catch. Maybe this time you'll stick. (d) Doesn't it strike you as odd that every time you've felt the same way?
12. Woman — age thirty-five: "I'm determined to get ahead. I'm not afraid of hard work. I am not afraid to take a few hard knocks — if I can see my goal out there in front. And I'm not averse to climbing over a few people — who get in my way — because this means a lot to me. I can't be satisfied with just a mediocre job. No, I want to be somebody."	(a) You feel that you just have to be out on top no matter what you may do to others. (b) You see yourself as a deeply ambitious person, is that it? (c) What do you suppose is behind this strong determination of yours to get ahead? (d) Strong ambition can be a real asset to any woman. Are you really sure, though, that you mean it when you say you're not adverse to climbing over those who get in your way? Couldn't that turn out to do you more harm than good?
13. Man — age twenty-nine: "I keep remembering how I walked out on Mary and the two kids. Five years ago — the law never caught up with me — I thought I was pretty smart — but now — God, but I was a heel. I don't see how I could do it. And I'm so ashamed I can't look people in the eye. Now I can't find her — not a trace. Her relatives won't tell me where she is. I don't blame them — but how could I have done it? Just because it was tough going. I	(a) There are a number of things you might do to try to find her. You could list her as a missing person and get police help. You could get a private detective agency to handle it for you. You might even be able to get a court order that would force the relatives to give her address. (b) When did you decide that you wanted her back? Tell me the circumstances. (c) The hopelessness there seems pretty clearly connected with feelings of guilt.

TABLE 18.1 Continued

REMARK	SELECT BEST RESPONSE TO REFLECT
tell you, I'll never have any self-respect. Never! And I — I don't know what to do — or how I can try to rectify my big mistake. I don't know — !"	(d) As you see it then, your past behavior is just plain unforgivable.
14. A secretary began to cry when asked whether or not she had finished typing a first draft of a speech the personnel director was preparing and said, "Everything I do is wrong. I just can't do anything to please you. I don't mind when you criticize me to my face, but when you start writing me up as if I were a case — a good joke — well, I just can't take it." (Assume that the speech included a humorous anecdote about a secretary.)	(a) There is no reference to you as a person in that speech. (b) You feel I criticize you too publicly. (c) I'll be glad to take that out, but aren't you being a bit sensitive? (d) You feel I'm making fun of you in that story.

Correct responses: 1 — b, 2 — b, 3 — c, 4 — c, 5 — c, 6 — a, 7 — d, 8 — b, 9 — b, 10 — d, 11 — a, 12 — a, 13 — d, 14 — d.

who dislikes or feels superior to a person. In nondirective counseling, certain attitudes, beliefs, and values are consistent with, and supportive of the methods. Fortunately, these same attitudes are consistent with the leadership skills discussed in Chapter 8. This means that training in counseling will improve problem-solving leadership abilities and vice versa.

The following values, beliefs, and attitudes toward people are consistent with the development of skill in nondirective counseling:

1. A belief that individuals are basically responsible for themselves and a willingness to let them keep that responsibility.

2. A belief that people are capable of solving their problems once interfering obstacles are removed and that most people basically want to do the right thing.

3. An appreciation of the fact that every solution to life's problems must conform with a person's values and beliefs, and that individuals know their own feelings and aspirations better than an outsider does.

4. The development of an acceptant attitude is crucial because a person will bring out hidden feelings only when confident of being understood and not judged. A permissive atmosphere is necessary if a person is to express absurd, unconventional, contradictory, or hateful feelings.

5. Two kinds of acceptance are involved: (a) acceptance of the disturbed person as a worthy individual whose problems merit attention and (b) acceptance of what is said as being important and of interest. Because disturbed individuals feel that they are "different," it is especially important that the counselor be able to show an attitude of acceptance. Thoughts and feelings expressed must also be accepted if they are to stimulate the expression of even more guarded and deep-seated feelings.

6. A profound respect for the importance

of feelings in learning to live a full life. In most situations, people are asked to justify or give reasons for their opinions. Innocent remarks such as "I don't like that person," "I don't feel comfortable there," or even "I don't like olives" are met with the question "Why?" and a person who cannot supply good reasons may be judged as biased or not too bright. Since feelings are so often misunderstood, they frequently are withheld. The counselor must respect the dignity of feelings, no matter how unreasonable they at first appear, in order to help another person express them.

Experience in listening and in reflecting feelings will assist in developing the attitudes and beliefs described above, and these states of mind in turn will assist in refining the skills. Training in listening, in reflecting feelings, and in essential attitudes should be carried on simultaneously and is perhaps best accomplished by role-playing procedures. P.F.C. Castle has shown that interpersonal-relations training of supervisors that produced a change in attitude resulted in an improvement in their behavior.[14]

ACCOMPLISHMENTS OF COUNSELING

ATTITUDES AND NEEDS ARE DISCOVERED

The importance of preventing misunderstandings as well as correcting them has been emphasized throughout this book. Supervisors can have more satisfactory dealings with employees if they know why one employee turned down a particular promotion; why another showed resentment when an unwanted job was not offered; what is behind the lack of cooperation between two otherwise good employees; why certain employees violate company rules; or why a change in work procedure is resisted by a certain individual. Our moral judgment of a person who takes advantage of another person changes when we discover that the person injured was perceived as an enemy.

Nondirective-counseling skills provide a way for recognizing and dealing with misunderstandings caused by differences in attitudes and needs even when the question of therapy is not raised. Not only does the nondirective interviewer better understand an employee but the employee gains better self-awareness. A person's own attitudes and needs may be vague and confusing until they are expressed. The mere telling of a complex experience clarifies it by showing hitherto unperceived defects, inconsistencies, and gaps in continuity.

Because the nondirective approach to people respects attitudes and needs as well as clarifies them, sincerity and skill in its use become important assets for many interview and face-to-face situations. Furthermore, the basic skills are essential to group leadership where accepting climates are prerequisites to eliciting innovative contributions.

FRUSTRATED CONDITION IS REDUCED

Any procedure that permits expression of hostile and regressive behavior without introducing unfavorable experiences reduces tensions and relieves frustration. The process of obtaining relief from emotional tension through the mere expression of feeling (such as talking out loud about a deeply felt problem) is known as *catharsis*. Supervisors who understand the process of frustration and who can furnish a climate in which employees can gain relief from frustration, will be able to deal with many types of emotional behavior problems. Some of the situations may be temporary,[15] and catharsis is all that

MOTIVATING WORKERS FOR OPTIMUM PERFORMANCE

is needed; others may continue so that the relief will not be permanent. However, even temporary relief may be sufficient to introduce some problem-solving behavior and create opportunities for readjustment.

Many frustrations go back to childhood experiences. Memories of unjust punishment or parental rejection may be vague and seemingly forgotten, but their emotional effects remain strong and can color adult reactions to marriage, reprimand, managers, or failure. If these pockets of feeling are located and the childish hostilities are expressed, marked changes in meanings may occur and behaviors can become more mature. A state of frustration common to a whole group may be released through feedback sessions. In this instance, the discussion leader uses permissive skills and the ability to reflect feelings in a way that will stimulate further expression in a group discussion.

TRUE PROBLEM IS LOCATED AND ACCEPTED

In a state of frustration, people are inclined to blame others, insist that there is nothing they can do, doubt the worthwhileness of life, and generally bemoan their misfortune. But regardless of how unfortunate persons may be, they must come face-to-face with the present. If they are to achieve an adjustment, each must ask "What can *I* do about it?" Suppose a young man, through no fault of his own, has lost an arm. Quite naturally he feels that his problem is the loss of an arm and that there is nothing to do about it. An artificial arm is a poor solution. As he sees it, his problem is insoluble. Before problem-solving behavior can occur, a person must be confronted with a soluble problem. Strictly speaking, the loss of an arm is an obstacle rather than a problem. Problem solving is the search for a way to circumvent, remove, or overcome an obstacle that

is blocking progress toward some goal. This goal must be a part of any description of a true problem. If our young man's goal is to live a happy life, then his problem becomes, "How can I get the most out of life with the limbs and abilities I have?"

Accepting reality — including personal deficiencies, injuries, and bad luck — is the first prerequisite to solving life's problems. As long as people blame others and hide weaknesses or faults, they have not located the difficulty in a way that permits them to solve the problem. Looking backward, thinking of what might have been, and wishing are important feelings; they must be expressed so that they do not stand in the way of discovering the soluble problem.

Only as persons obtain relief from frustration are they able to focus on their true problems. Until then, they are too preoccupied with feelings to be able to see a problem. If anyone points out how they should constructively view their situations, they are unable to accept the counsel and instead may feel more than ever that they are in an unsympathetic world. Until persons are ready to *accept* their problems, they are unable to see them, and from the good advice given to them, they merely learn that no one understands.

An individual who seeks consolation or pity is not accepting the true problem, but merely wants others to join in the misery. Because pity comforts but does not stimulate problem-solving behavior, it is as important for the counselor to avoid giving pity as it is to avoid criticizing.

PROBLEM SOLVING IS STIMULATED

Problem-solving behavior is characterized by exploratory or searching activity and a ready recognition of existing realities. Various approaches to goals must be examined and evaluated before the best decision is reached. Listening and reflecting ideas helps this process because it stimulates the flow of ideas. A person persists in an idea if it is challenged, but when the idea is accepted and reflected, he or she has to go beyond it. Furthermore, the restatement of an idea in other words enriches it, encourages new meanings, and stimulates examination of different approaches.

Once a difficulty is recognized as a problem, questions may serve a useful purpose. A counselor or a supervisor can increase the range of a person's or a group's thinking by asking good questions. A question can take a person out of a rut in thinking, cause exploration of various ideas, stimulate evaluation of good and bad features of various alternatives, and generate an interest in, or a search for, facts without imposing, evaluating, or suggesting.

RESPONSIBILITY IS DEVELOPED

People who have difficulty coping with life's problems often are dependent persons. They look to someone to get them out of one difficulty after another. Frequently, the background reveals parents who have always made all the decisions. Such individuals have been denied the opportunity to become emotionally mature; even if a counselor or friend gave them good advice and even if they took it, the basic problem — that of immaturity — would not have been solved. Nondirective counseling, from the outset, makes no pretense of solving clients' problems. Instead, they are told that they must decide and do what they think best. The role of the counselor is that of helping persons to help themselves.

Nothing creates a sense of responsibility as quickly as having responsibility. This principle is basic to group decision and basic

to the success of nondirective counseling. The counselor gives individuals responsibility for solving their own problems, even for returning for other visits. If a client asks, "Do you want me to come again?" the counselor may reply, "That is up to you. If you feel that you would like to come again, the time is yours." Clients who have been requested to visit a counselor and show resentment on their first visit usually return voluntarily.[16]

SOLUTIONS FIT PERSONAL VALUE SYSTEMS

When persons can be induced to solve their own problems, the solutions conform with their personal sets of value. Solutions supplied by other persons overlook individual differences in values. If persons act on decisions that are contrary to their value systems, they often develop guilt feelings, and these may become more serious than the original problem. Examples of decisions that may conflict with some systems of values and not with others are given below.

1. A pregnant woman who does not want a child has an abortion.
2. A boy participates in vandalism under peer social pressure.
3. A supervisor discharges a long-term employee who is incompetent.
4. An employee dishonestly collects sickness benefits knowing that other employees have done it.
5. Parents place their retarded child in a state institution.

Whether decisions of this type will create future problems cannot be judged from the facts alone. Only persons whose value systems do not conflict with the actions can avoid subsequent feelings of guilt.

THE COUNSELOR CAN SERVE AS AN EXPERT

Once persons have gotten rid of feelings that interfere with solving problems, they often are in a position to solve them. The counselor or supervisor often has useful knowledge to assist in the solution. The very information or relevant facts that may be avoided because they are threatening to a disturbed person become realities that must be faced in the problem-solving stage. The counselor should be willing to assist a client in obtaining information that can help in solving problems and making decisions.

In supplying information, the following precautions should be observed by a counselor.

1. Do not try to change a disturbed person's feelings by supplying information to prove the person wrong. Understanding is needed instead.

2. Do not supply information to sell your point of view. Remember that attitudes select facts.

3. Do not avoid giving facts when the person *really* wants them. People often desire knowledge and information to solve problems or even out of curiosity. The nondirective approach can irritate a problem solver. (Distinguish between requests for information that are based on the desire to know and those that are wishes for assurance.)

4. Do not supply overwhelming amounts of information. Get feedback on how information is received and whether it is welcome. The supplying of information should be a two-way process.

Counselors play dual roles: on one hand, they facilitate the client's expression of feeling (to deal with frustration); on the other, they aid in the problem-solving process (to develop constructive action). For example,

students who do not know what courses to take often are advised by a vocational counselor. The skilled counselor will explore whether the indecision is due to fears, conflicts, and pressures from home, or whether they need knowledge about professional alternatives. Information on courses are supplied only when the student is ready to explore alternative choices realistically.

COMMON COUNSELING SITUATIONS

Counseling-derived skills can be helpful in dealing with a myriad of situations — an anxious new employee, a frustrated boss, an angry customer. But in some instances they are essential. Some of the more common situations in which this is the case are presented here.

THE POSSIBILITY OF ALCOHOLISM

When an employee is frequently absent and/or unproductive, a number of causes are possible. The individual may have serious family problems, a physical disease, an alcohol-abuse problem. The final determination of alcoholism must be made by a qualified professional. At no time should a manager describe an individual as alcoholic without outside validation. On the other hand, job contacts in which the counseling techniques described above are used can give the manager some cues as to the kind of professional help or opinion (if any) that is needed.[18]

STRESS

The effects of stress on job performance have been discussed at length elsewhere in this text. One constructive outlet for stress, whether it derives from job or home conditions, is an employer or supervisor who is trained in active listening and other counseling-derived techniques. This type of listening need not be justified by humanitarian values alone. The physical and psychological effects of stress reduce productivity, and to the extent that the manager can reduce such effects, even temporarily, the opportunity for higher productivity is increased.

THE EFFECTS OF GROWING OLDER

Typically, in the past, the changes in physical and motivational responses that occur in every employee's life have been referred to by the somewhat negative term *aging*.[19] The ability of workers in their twenties to produce versus the ability of workers in their sixties exemplifies the usual approach.

Recently, however, the public has become aware through popularized reports that psychological development and maturation need not end when physical development does.[20] A number of predictable life crises temporarily affect individuals' lives, including their job lives. The "mid-life crisis" that commonly occurs when an individual reaches the age of thirty-eight to forty-three is an example. Adjusting to the thought of our mortality and to the idea that perhaps our career aspirations will not be met requires time and is painful. To the extent that counseling-derived skills can ease valued employees through such crises and can help them find new sources of motivation and self-esteem, they are valuable tools for the manager and supervisor.

NUMBER AND LENGTH OF INTERVIEWS

If counseling is to improve the emotional adjustment of a disturbed or confused person, a number of interviews may be required. Such interviews should have a time limit — for example, thirty to forty-five minutes. A prearranged time for terminating an interview makes it unnecessary for the interviewer to find an excuse for breaking off a long and sometimes unprofitable session. Then, too, the spacing of interviews allows a person time to consolidate gains and grow between visits.

The actual number of visits needed varies with the problem. Surprising improvements have occurred after one interview. However, for personal off-the-job problems involving personality difficulties, a skilled counselor regards ten to twenty visits as typical. Problems not stemming from a person's past require fewer visits because it is relatively easy to locate the disturbing factor or condition. An interviewer must not, however, assume that just because a problem points to a difficulty on a job, its true character has been located. Incidents that set off an emotional reaction must not be mistaken for causes.

Single interviews of the counseling type can and do solve some complex job problems, prevent others, and clarify still others. Some typical examples are briefly described to illustrate the opportunities for counseling that occur in business.

1. A phone-service employee appeared unusually stubborn when asked to cooperate by giving up his truck and accepting a ride to his work location with another driver. He

began by giving all kinds of excuses and defending his rights. Finally, he revealed that he was an epileptic — having very mild attacks or blackouts. He felt that as long as the company allowed him to drive, he was normal and just as good as anyone else.

His condition had eluded detection for twenty years because he had learned to cover up. He was able to anticipate an attack, and as soon as he felt one coming on, he would drive to the curb, put his head on the steering wheel, black out for a minute or less, rest a moment, and then drive on again. When someone was with him, he would explain that he was taking a quick nap to get over a sleepy spell. In the interview, he decided to visit the medical department. The doctor prescribed medication, which was a satisfactory remedy for his condition.

2. An employee had been repeatedly interviewed regarding a job change to office work. Over a period of twenty-five years, he had received training on three different jobs but was found unable to handle them. He now insisted that he be given another opportunity because of his health. His medical report did not substantiate his claims. The supervisor responded to certain references he made to off-the-job experiences, and before long he talked freely about them. His background revealed marital difficulties and adjustment problems going back to his childhood. Although these personal problems were not solved by the interview, it became apparent to the employee as well as to the supervisor that a job change would not help him. In this instance, counseling prevented further waste of interview time.

3. A young woman was in the process of leaving a company because she would not work the night shift as she had agreed to do. The personnel exit interview revealed that she could not work nights, because that would leave her husband at home with her

friend, whose husband worked nights. The two couples shared an apartment, and certain changes in the relationships between the couples had occurred since the time the woman had promised to work nights. The personnel office was able to arrange a different assignment for her.

4. A senior employee caused considerable trouble and talked about filing a grievance when he was bypassed in a promotion to a supervisory position. In an interview with his supervisor, he revealed that he did not want the job; rather, he objected to the man who got the promotion, imagining that the young man had told the supervisor some thing about the senior employee's poor hearing. Without refuting the charge, the supervisor helped the senior employee discover that his imagination had played tricks on him — also that he ought to get the hearing aid that his wife had been trying to induce him to buy for the past two years.

TIME AND PLACE

Time and place arrangements should take into account the employee's feelings. An interview should be of interest to both parties, and the employee should be given a choice of times available to the interviewer. The setting for the interview should be one in which the employee can feel at home. Elegant surroundings, being seated in an open area while the interviewer is protected by a desk, distractions, interruptions — any of these can make for a strained atmosphere. When suitable surroundings are not available at the plant, it is sometimes best to adjourn to the coffee shop. The president of one company wondered why she learned so much more from her division heads when she visited them in the field than when they came to her office. She failed to realize that executives' office furnishings often reflect their high position and introduced a barrier to communication. Most supervisors, however, are close enough to those who report to them so that their offices are familiar places. If not, steps should be taken to make them more familiar.

KEEPING CONFIDENCES

Confidences should be strictly kept. To use nondirective methods to gain information that will be used to the detriment of an employee will cost more in the long run than the immediate gain or saving warrants. Even so, the method will not usually cause employees to give a supervisor the incriminating evidence that they give to a professional or religious counselor. The fact that a supervisor is an authority figure is one of the limitations of counseling as practiced by supervisors. However, not all problems involve this limitation, and it is not necessary to confine counseling to nonsupervisors. Rather, counseling skills make people better supervisors.

If employees do say things to supervisors that they may later regret, the supervisors should show by their manners that they have not been upset. With experience in listening they will learn not to be angry when employees tell them frankly how they feel.

On some occasions, a counseling interview may disclose a problem that can be solved by making changes or by involving other people. The implementation should always be worked out in discussions with the employee to avoid any feeling that confidences have been betrayed, even when the change is to the employee's advantage.

LOCATION OF COUNSELING SERVICES

The management of a company might recognize the value of counseling and wish to make the services available to its employees. How should this be done? The company could hire professional counselors and make them a part of either the medical or the personnel department, or it could train its supervisors and thereby expand the scope of their responsibility. The arguments in favor of each alternative are shown in Table 18.2.

Inspection of the table reveals that each approach has distinct advantages. Perhaps the greatest disadvantage in the use of expert counselors is that the service is not readily used. Only a limited number of employees seek help when the service is available in medical and personnel departments. The experience of Western Electric and the Ohio Bell Telephone Company, who pioneered in

TABLE 18.2 LOCATION OF COUNSELING SERVICE

ADVANTAGES TO TRAINING SUPERVISORS	ADVANTAGES TO USING EXPERTS IN MEDICAL OR PERSONNEL DEPARTMENTS
1. More available to employees	1. More skillful service
2. More natural part of job relationship	2. More confidential
3. No stigma involved	3. Less conflict due to other duties
4. Job performance known to counselor	4. No bias due to knowledge of person's work history
5. No induction of program needed	5. No emotional involvement in the case
6. Skill acquired for counseling useful in other supervisory functions	

counseling programs, showed that it was rather difficult to get employees and supervisors to accept counselors. Supervisors felt threatened by the program because they felt employees could unjustly criticize them. The general experience was that acceptance of the counseling program required from one to two years.

The strongest arguments against training supervisors for counseling are problems arising from a lack of skill and time. However, a limited amount of skill will assist the supervisors in dealing with superficial disturbances, and it can do a great deal in helping them prevent problems. Furthermore, the basic counseling skills are prerequisites to interviewing and to handling many communication problems. Persons with serious mental illness, of course, require professional treatment.

Perhaps the ideal method is a combination of the two approaches. Training supervisors permits them to deal with some emotionally disturbed employees and at the same time gives them an understanding of the role an expert might play. If counselors and psychiatrists are available through the medical or the personnel department, they pose no threat to supervisors, but instead become sources to which difficult cases can be referred.[21] An understanding supervisor can do a great deal to motivate an employee to visit the counselor.

Today, the trend in management training is toward increasing the amount of time and emphasis devoted to listening and to rudimentary counseling skills. Most supervisors welcome this training and see it not as an increase in their work loads but as an aid in the performance of their jobs. There is also an increase in placement of psychologically trained persons in personnel departments, and a trained counselor in the department is not uncommon.

H. Meltzer describes opportunities for the skilled personnel manager to improve the mental health of employees.[22] These occur in various interviews conducted (orientation, evaluation, follow-up, and exit), in daily rounds, in attendance at monthly departmental meetings, in safety committee meetings, in contributions to supervisors' meetings, in dealing with supervisory training problems, and in counseling. Meltzer advocates a *projective* type of interviewing, in which the specific purpose of the interview is considered, and the opportunity to learn about the employee is created. Details of background, attitudes, feelings, history of frustration, and sources of pleasure and tension are useful in understanding reactions that appear to be more irrational than the situation warrants. Skilled personnel in key positions can accomplish much to make supervisory personnel aware of mental health problems and to create an appreciation for counseling skills.

INTERVIEW OBJECTIVES

Unlike the usual face-to-face talks between supervisors and employees, interviews are held off the job. Ordinarily arrangements for a time and a place are made, which makes them somewhat more formal than routine job contacts. Each interview has a purpose of its own, whether an employment interview, a performance-evaluation interview, an exit interview, or a change of assignment. A casual visit between employee and supervisor is not called an interview, because it lacks a formal purpose. Job interviews differ from counseling interviews in that they are not client-centered but have an objective of their own. This does not mean, however, that the two objectives cannot be combined. Each kind of interview can be concerned with how the employee feels about a job, a transfer, development, or reasons for leaving.

Interviews have been used as fact-gathering devices and as ways to learn about another's potentialities. Their value for accomplishing these objectives is extremely limited, and frequently more confusion than clarification is accomplished by them. When objective methods (application blanks, school grades, transcripts, and so on) for obtaining facts are available, they should be used in preference to an interview. Memories may play tricks, the motivation of the person interviewed may be to withhold information, and the interviewer may change questions and style, thereby making comparisons between interview results unreliable. With proper precautions, accuracy can be increased. In order to permit comparisons between responses of interviewers, the standardized interview has been developed.[23]

The interview can have a unique value and perform a real service to all management personnel (interviewers and interviewees alike) if it is used to discover the interviewee's attitude toward some particular thing. It is this aspect of the interview that is directly related to all interpersonal-relations problems and that makes use of nondirective-counseling skills. When interviews conducted by psychologists were used to assess management potential, they obtained useful judgments of career motivation, dependency needs, and interpersonal skills that were correlated with management's overall assessment of the individual (including the interview data).[24] Various judgments also were related to salary progress (period between assessment and the end of experiment).

BASIC INTERVIEWING PRINCIPLES

ESTABLISHING A MUTUAL INTEREST

People speak frankly and freely only when the interviewer is accepting and understanding. In such a situation, two people can cooperate to achieve a common objective — that of solving the interviewee's problem. This working relationship makes the interviewer a helper rather than judge.

But the fact that interviews have a purpose or objective of their own introduces some conflict. For example, in an employment interview, the employment manager's objective is to screen the applicants and hire the person best suited for the job, but the applicant's objective is to be hired. When people want to be judged favorably, they are motivated to distort facts, cover up faults, fail to mention troubles, and even lie about age. They hide true feelings and say they do not mind working nights if this may be a job condition.

Cooperative behavior occurs when there is a *mutual interest*. In the case of job placement, it is not difficult to find an interest that both parties share. Employees want jobs that will make use of their special aptitudes and training, and this is what a company may reasonably want. If this mutual or common interest is established (which it can be, providing the employee already has been hired), an employee will honestly express preferences and disclose true feelings and aspirations.

In any interview requiring cooperation, a mutual interest becomes the meeting ground for discussion. The Kinsey interviewers capitalized on a general curiosity and interest in science to obtain cooperation.[25] Some interviewers attempt to find a person's interests on matters not relevant to the interview. They talk about golf, fishing, or family to warm up to the task. Artificial warming up is of questionable value; not only may it be seen as a trick, but it may also keep the employee in an anxious state. The purpose of an interview should be established as soon as possible, and this purpose should be of interest to both parties. It is unwise to distort the truth in order to find a common interest. To tell employees that the company has their interests at heart is not likely to be believed, but to say that the company thinks that satisfied employees are good employees will make sense to them. Employees will feel freer to speak their minds about conditions if they can see why their opinions are of interest to the company.

Let us examine some interview problems in the light of the principle of mutual interest. In the case of a company making extensive studies of each accident in order to improve its safety record, if penalties for negligence are imposed, a mutual interest with employees who have been involved in accidents will be rare. The company behaves as if it wants to find someone to punish, and the employees know that they want to escape punishment. If, however, the company does not desire to punish but merely to discover the cause of an accident to guard against future accidents, a common interest can readily be established. It then becomes possible for an employee to reveal that she had been out late the night before and fell asleep on the job. Together interviewer and employee can discuss the problem of how to prevent such conditions in the future. Perhaps in hazardous work the workers should report when they have not had enough sleep and be given a different assignment on such days. Regardless of how management views the practicality of such an approach to accidents, cooperation will improve only if and

when an acceptable common interest is found.

In conducting interviews concerning transfers, promotions, and demotions, a supervisor can easily locate mutual interests, and in the process of listening and reflecting feelings can learn the nature of the problems the changes will create. Frequently, reasonable adjustments, compromises, and new ideas emerge if an employee's aspirations and development of abilities are part of the interview.

An exit interview contains an obvious common interest in that a company is able to learn from people who are leaving how the company can improve as a place to work, and employees leaving the company often appreciate an opportunity to talk on this subject. As a matter of fact, between 30 to 40 percent of employees resigning from one company changed their minds and decided to remain when properly interviewed.[26] This suggests the desirability of holding exit interviews before an employee has made other commitments. It would even be better to hold interviews when an employee has a complaint.

Interviews designed to inform employees at all levels in the organization of their evaluation or appraisal have a mutual interest if they are approached from the viewpoint of employee development. However, to accomplish growth and development, the best approach is not the "telling" kind of interview. Rather, the employees may be asked to evaluate themselves; this can be done with a high degree of insight (often approaching a counseling-type interview) if the interviewer has received training in the nondirective approach.

When the interviewer's objective is to let the employees know where they stand or to warn them of demotions unless radical changes in behavior are made, the supervisor is clearly functioning as a judge. With this relationship established, it is more difficult to find a common interest. As a result, communication is faulty, acceptance frequently is low, and in some instances, more problems are created than are solved.

THE USE OF QUESTIONS

Questions can direct or channel the topic of discussion. In client-centered counseling, the counselor does not wish to channel the discussion. But as each interview has a specific purpose, questions should control the topic of discussion. A question can direct the discussions and still be open-ended as far as the exploration of feelings is concerned. Examples of such questions are

1. "How do you feel about transferring to another district?"
2. "What are some of the problems you see in taking over this new work?"
3. "Do you see any disadvantage to this new method of operation?"
4. "What are the aspects of your job that you feel allow most opportunity for improvement?"

Open-ended questions specify the general topic, yet allow the interviewees a great deal of freedom. To the extent that the employee interviewed can select from a great range of possible reactions to a question, the interview is employee-centered and indicates an interest in employees and their feelings. If the intitial expressions of feelings are accepted and effectively reflected, such an interview approaches the counseling interview.

As confidence and trust grow during an interview, questions may move from the general to the specific. Examples of specific questions that will be honestly answered in a well-conducted interview are:

☐ Do you sometimes work without your safety belt? Under what conditions?
☐ How many days do you think you would be absent on account of sickness if the company didn't pay for sickness?
☐ Which employees do you feel are more qualified for supervisory positions than you are?
☐ How many times would you say that your immediate supervisor criticized you unfairly during the past year?

When mutual interests and a respect for differences in attitudes are present, a problem is frequently brought into focus. Suppose an employee feels that a transfer to another division may reduce chances for promotion because the change is into a job classification where opportunities for further progress are few. If interference with an employee's progress is not the manager's intent, the problem of how to prevent this condition is worth consideration. In this instance, questions such as "Do you see any disadvantages in this transfer?" or "How do the various divisions compare with respect to promotional opportunities?" would lead to more detailed analysis and perhaps an interest in fact finding. Stating that opportunities for progress are equally present on all jobs is not likely to be true nor convincing.

STIMULATING PROBLEM SOLVING WITH QUESTIONS

Good questions direct attention to other areas and broaden the scope of thinking. Routine solutions to problems tend to appear first and discourage further searching. Problem solving can be facilitated by such questions as "Are there some other approaches?" and "Can you think of some additional possibilities?" An interviewer can play a constructive role by encouraging the continuation of the problem-solving process.

Sometimes the ideas submitted by employees for approval are of questionable value, yet by rejecting them, the supervisor discourages future suggestions. Instead of rejecting the idea because it has a fault, the supervisor might question, "How could we do that without being accused of favoritism?" or "How would that machine work in a cold climate?" Such questions pose problems for which the employee may have answers, or they may point up the obstacles that have been overlooked. Either alternative leads to a constructive exchange rather than a rejection.

Many interviews can be upgraded by joint problem solving regarding the work situation or work relationship. Each party has information, and questions serve a useful purpose in stimulating exploratory behavior. However, the questions should not put a person on the defensive.

THE INTERVIEW AS A WHOLE

PROBLEM SOLVING
VERSUS TELL-AND-SELL
AND COUNSELING STYLES

Thus far, the interview has been treated in general terms with emphasis on listening and problem solving. The similarity between this *problem-solving* type of interview and the *group-decision* method is evident, and development of skills in either area will help in the other. The basic difference between the two approaches is that in the interview, the supervisor deals with a person rather than a group. The style of interview that corresponds to the autocratic style of leadership may be called the *tell-and-sell method*. In this

kind of interview, supervisors have the information and the solution, which they *tell* to the interviewee. In order to get the ideas accepted, the manager must convince the interviewee of their merits — this consitutes the *sell* aspect of the interview. Like the autocratic style of leadership, the tell-and-sell interview fits traditional ideas of how managers should interact with employees.

There is a place for the tell-and-sell style of interview. Sometimes it is the interviewer's objective to transmit information, and high acceptance of the objective is relatively unimportant. But when acceptance, employee development, upward communication, or the use of the interviewee's ideas and initiative are desired, the problem-solving approach is recommended. The counseling type of interview, discussed in the previous section, also has a counterpart in group processes. Feedback sessions in which employees air concerns and complaints require leaders who have nondirective counseling skills.

The interview styles also may be combined. For example, the *tell-and-listen* style of interview combines the telling aspect of the tell-and-sell method with the counseling type of interview. In practice, this method has objectives similar to those of consultative management, in which the manager encourages feedback and participation, but retains control of the decisions made. Thus, the tell-and-listen style stops short of gaining the major benefits of participation in that it limits influence to that of making suggestions. However, it permits release of expression and some upward communication when practiced sincerely.

The tell-and listen interview would be most useful in situations where the decision is beyond the interviewer's control. An employee who is discharged must be told, but this does not preclude the desirability of listening to the person. Likewise, a person who is incompetent must be told, but an interviewer can still listen to the individual's expression of feelings. Bad news of any kind requires telling, but the pain can sometimes be reduced by permitting feelings to be expressed.

INTERVIEW SITUATIONS

Space does not permit a discussion of all types of interview situations. Each has its own purposes and its pitfalls, but the various skills discussed and the relevance of attitudes applies to them all. In Table 18.3 the more common interview situations of interest to the manager are outlined, along with specific objectives to strive for, and pitfalls to guard against. This table is a convenient guide for the reader in the application of the various skills to specific interview situations.

EFFECT OF INTERVIEW STYLE

The problem-solving interview may be used in an appraisal program, although it may not completely conform to the viewpoint of the program. Nevertheless, it is a plan for improving performance by increasing job interest, developing an employee's problem-solving ability, and solving job problems. It has its greatest merit when used with superior employees or with employees who are reluctant to conform to bureaucratic procedures.

Employees and supervisors frequently do not have the same picture of the employee's job as we saw in Table 14.2. The problem-solving interview offers an opportunity to prevent problems arising from these communication failures and permits the employee to participate in solving problems that require a resolution of differences. The duties of a supervisor vary in priority, in the degree of freedom, and in the methods by which they can be performed. Delegation is a matter of degree. When do employees require approval of decisions? How much freedom and how much responsibility do they want? How much initiative is expected of them? These questions are seldom resolved. Furthermore, the answers do not depend on the job alone, but on the supervisor's viewpoint and the employee's ability.

Once these matters are clarified, problem-solving interviews can be used to solve current problems raised by either employee or supervisor. New goals, ideas, obstacles, plans, and preferences constantly arise and are good topics for discussion in the problem-solving interview. (The discussion of problem-solving in Chapter 8 and the case at the end of Chapter 20 should be reviewed in this connection.)

The tell-and-listen type of interview conforms with the spirit of most performance-evaluation programs and permits upward communication because the employee is encouraged to respond. It also reduces some of the possible frustrations the employee might experience because the supervisor is expected to permit the employee to express any unpleasant feelings generated by the evaluation and by the recommendations made. A degree of problem solving also can be incorporated into this interview plan.

The tell-and-sell approach is perhaps most representative of the styles used in evaluation interviews. It has the same major objectives as the tell-and-listen plan, but in place of an emphasis on listening to gain acceptance, the supervisor tries to persuade (sell) the employee to change. This approach can lead to arguments with subsequent face-saving problems; further, it tends to encourage conformity. These are two possible undesirable by-products that reduce the chances for true improvement. Although this plan is perhaps the most widely used, it is recommended

TABLE 18.3 SPECIFIC OBJECTIVES AND PITFALLS IN COMMON INTERVIEW SITUATIONS

TYPE OF INTERVIEW SITUATION	SPECIFIC OBJECTIVES TO STRIVE FOR	PITFALLS TO GUARD AGAINST
Employment	Screen applicant Discover work attitudes Discover interests	Applicant is motivated to make a favorable impression. "Factual" information has limited accuracy. Personal bias and premature judgment lead to poor decisions.
Lateral transfer	Make best use of employee's ability Capitalize on employee's strong interests Discover aspirations for advancement	Employee may feel forced to accept change. (Permit choice without penalty.) Interviewee may be reluctant to mention hardship and lack of interest in new job. Employee may be afraid of failing.
Promotions	Inform employee of new opportunity Discover aspirations Discover attitude toward added responsibility	Joy of good news often hides anxiety. Anxiety should be released and verbalized. Anxiety does not indicate incompetence.
Appraisal	Evaluate past job performance, not the person Improve future job performance Opportunity to use problem-solving approach	Criticism produces defensive behavior. Perception of job duties and requirements may differ for employee and superior. Degree of delegation should be clarified. Employee's job problems may not be known to supervisor.
Problem solving	Discover problems faced by employee Share problems involving employee's interests Encourage employee to be critical of old methods Stimulate employee to reveal ideas	Employees are reluctant to admit having problems. Employees are reluctant to disagree with supervisors.
Exit	Find real cause for leaving Determine whether decision should or can be reversed	Employees are inclined to give reasons that are convincing or acceptable to the supervisor rather than the real reason. If anger is expressed and accepted, employee may feel better.

that the other two plans be given more widespread application.

IMPROVING JOB CONTACTS

THE NATURE OF JOB CONTACTS

Job contacts, like counseling and interviewing situations, involve the supervisor and a single employee rather than a group of employees. However, job contacts are work related and take place in the normal operation of the job. It is through job contacts that personal motivations, job interests, and job satisfactions are likely to be uncovered. The psychological principles most appropriate for application to job contacts are found in the two chapters on motivation. A knowledge of widespread differences in abilities and needs among individuals is also valuable because it permits the supervisor to adapt expectations of performance to the person's capabilities and motivations. The chapter on attitudes is relevant in that communication failure and the need for sensitivity to differing viewpoints is essential to prevent misunderstandings. Finally, the chapter on frustration should help the supervisor locate persons with emotional problems and discover which aspects of the job cause resentment.

The chapters on groups and leadership emphasize the group as a whole and the need for avoiding favoritism. Despite the fact that supervisors are expected to be fair and impartial, they are also expected to treat each person as an individual. How is this to be done?

To take an extreme illustration, an amputee does not want to be helped to do everything, but would feel resentment if expected to compete in activities in which the handicap was a disadvantage.[27] Finding what special treatment is needed requires considerable insight. Individual differences between workers follow a similar pattern. The employee with a child expects certain privileges; the superior worker may expect extra considerations and recognitions; the low-aptitude individual is degraded if compared to others; the person who does not desire to advance resents being criticized for lacking ambition. Thus, people differ in many ways, and the supervisor who responds to these differences without showing favoritism will have warmer interpersonal relationships.

How can supervisors be expected to know all about their employees? There are many opportunities on the job for learning these things without taking up job time. Unofficial contacts occur when employees report for work, are met in the elevator, happen to be seen during the lunch hour, and so on. These meetings call for small talk, and during such conversations, a supervisor can learn of individual interests, family ties, important events in their lives (new baby, engagement, and the like). Later conversations can pick up from earlier fragments, and soon supervisors not only learn to know the employees as individuals, but find each more interesting in certain respects. Research indicates that in companies where informal contacts were mainly initiated by employees they had a less favorable view of their work place than did employees in firms where supervisor-initiated contacts predominated.[28] During job contacts, supervisors learn about each employee's job attitudes and interests. These added bits of information permit them to work with people as individuals, without showing the kind of consideration regarded as unfair by others. If questionable special treatment is requested, they can always resort to group-decision procedures to resolve conflicts.

Unofficial contacts with employees can provide a supervisor with opportunities to learn about their interests and personal lives. (Donald Dietz)

UNIQUE OPPORTUNITIES
IN VARIOUS JOB CONTACTS

Although most contacts have a job-related purpose, each can serve as a unique opportunity for improving interpersonal relations and for avoiding problems and misunderstandings. We have divided the job contacts into (1) unofficial or chance meetings; (2) those involved in giving job assignments; (3) inspecting, examining, or evaluating a job that has been done or is being done; (4) giving an individual employee some job training; and (5) introducing a new employee to other employees in the immediate situation. These five types of contacts have

the common feature of informality and should remain unstructured; developing good interpersonal relations is a common objective. Each also has a special purpose.

Higher-level managers, because of their rank in the hierarchy, have an especially difficult time overcoming barriers to communication with lower-level employees. Executives in several firms have found ingenious methods for handling the problem.[29] One delivers important memos in person; another rents tennis courts and meets managers through round-robin matches; one company president makes it a habit to eat in the company cafeteria twice a week, sitting in the first empty seat that he finds and conversing with whoever is present.

Table 18.4 shows how various types of contact can achieve objectives of an interpersonal nature. The last column deals with points to which the supervisor may wish to become especially sensitive. Review of this table reveals how the various principles discussed in the preceding parts of the book can be applied in the daily routines of a job. Counseling and interviewing skills also have a place because sensitivity becomes an important aid in interpreting the feedback in any communication, especially when rank differences exist.

OVERCOMING BARRIERS
TO COMMUNICATION CAUSED
BY DIFFERENCES IN RANK

Students and teachers may have observed how the relationship between teacher and class members chills after the first examination is returned. Performance-evaluation interviews also tend to strain relations between supervisors and employees. Job contacts can be used to reverse this trend and facilitate the supervisor's image as a helper rather than as a judge. Such gimmicks as the boss or teacher asking employees or students to call

TABLE 18.4 JOB CONTACTS AND THEIR UNIQUE OPPORTUNITIES

TYPE OF CONTACT	EXAMPLES	INTERPERSONAL-RELATIONS OBJECTIVES	CRITICAL POINTS TO OBSERVE
Unofficial	Morning greeting Meeting on elevator Coffee break	Treat as individual Increase job satisfaction	Changes in attitude Personal problems Needs and outside interests

Job assignment	Work on new project
	Special job
		Permit participation
		Generate ideas
			Feelings of unfair
			  treatment
			Possible
			  misunderstanding
			  (Have employee
			  summarize given
			  assignment)

Job inspection	Checking workmanship
	Analyzing results
	Measuring output
		Help employee to
		  improve
		Constructive
		  suggestions
		Generate ideas
		Give feeling of progress
		Be helper rather than
		  critic
			Defensive behavior
			Individual differences
			Communication failure
			  in assignment
			Face-saving responses

On-the-job training	Teaching a new job
	Teaching a new
	  employee
		Improve skill and
		  knowledge
		Create job interest
		Give feeling of progress
		Demonstrate your role
		  as helper
			Discouragement
			Individual differences
			Lack of interest
			Lack of aptitude

Inducting new employees	New employee in
	  company
	Transferred employee
	New employee in
	  special group
		Make employee feel
		  free to come to you
		  for help
		Make employee feel
		  welcome and
		  important
		Get employee to be
		  group member, not
		  member of subgroup
		Reduce high turnover
		  of new employees
			Induction process
			  requires a week or
			  more
			Need for companions
			  for lunch
			Discouragement
			How group members
			  react
			Insecurity

them by their first names or asking to be regarded as pals will not solve the problem. Parents cannot successfully be pseudo-friends of their children because children want and need a parental relationship. Similarly, employees and students need an official figure to be in charge of the activity.

Although holding a supervisory position and sometimes being inaccessible when needed may be seen as threatening, employee contacts can reduce the threatening perceptions of the boss and encourage the image of a coach, who is a source of information about the job and the company and also a person busy with many responsibilities. This new perception may require some changes in the behavior of managers, and the benefits may not be immediate because many employees have gained unfavorable perceptions from prior experiences.

New employees' relations with management are strained not only by the difference in rank, but also by having a stranger as a supervisor, and by having work associates who are strangers. Peers also pass judgment and determine the social status of a new member. The group-decision method helps the acquaintance process because it permits group interaction. Also, the supervisor is recommended to pay extra attention to new employees. In addition, more experienced employees can be asked to help get the new employees acquainted with others in the group. Thus, the introduction of employees — along with meeting them informally, assigning them work, evaluating their performance, and training them — provides managers on every level with the opportunity for employee contact and the bettering of their relations.

NOTES

1. Gavin, J. F. Employee perceptions of the work environment and mental health: A suggestive study. *J. Vocat. Behav.*, 1975, *6*, 217–234; Gavin, J. F., and Greenhaus, J. H. Organizational tenure, work environment perceptions and employee mental health. *J. Vocat. Behav.*, 1976, 7.
2. Steiner, M. E. The search for occupational personalities. *Personal*, 1953, *46*(6), 28–38.
3. Meltzer, H. Frustration, expectation and production in industry. *Amer. J. Orthopsychiat.*, 1945, *15* 329–343; Meltzer, H. Mental health realities in work situations. *Amer. J. Orthopsychiat.*, 1963, *33*, 562–565.
4. Bellows, R. *Psychology in business and industry.* Englewood Cliffs, N.J.: Prentice-Hall, 1961.
5. Roethlisberger, F. J., and Dickson, W. J. *Management and the worker.* Cambridge, Mass.: Harvard University Press, 1939; Roethlisberger, F. J. *Management and morale.* Cambridge, Mass.: Harvard University Press, 1941.
6. Rogers, C. R. *Counseling and psychotherapy.* Boston: Houghton Mifflin, 1942; *Client-centered therapy.* Boston: Houghton Mifflin, 1951.
7. Snyder, W. U. *Casebook of non-directive counseling.* Boston: Houghton Mifflin, 1947; Axline, Virginia M. *Play therapy.* Boston: Houghton Mifflin, 1947.
8. Berg, I. A. Employee counseling in well-rounded personnel program. *Publ. Personnel Rev.*, 1970, *31*(3), 185–189; Hunt, R. G., and Lichtman, C. M. Counseling of employees by work supervisors: Concepts, attitudes, and practices in a white-collar organization. *J. Counsel. Psychol.*, 1969, *16*, 1–6.
9. Hunt, W. A. Diagnosis and non-directive therapy. *J. Clin. Psychol*, 1948, *4*, 232–236; Patterson, C. H. Is psychotherapy dependent on diagnosis? *Amer. Psychologist*, 1948, *3*, 155–159; Rogers, C. R. Significant aspects of client-centered therapy. *Amer. Psychologist*, 1946, *1*, 415–422; Hart J. T., and Tomlinson, T. M. (Eds.). *New directions in client-centered therapy.* Boston: Houghton Mifflin,

1970; Rogers, C. R. A theory of therapy, personality, and interpersonal relationships as developed in the client-centered framework. In S. Koch (Ed.), *Psychology: A study of a science,* Vol. 3. New York: McGraw-Hill, 1959.

10. Ginott, H. G. *Between parent and child.* New York: Macmillan, 1965.

11. Ginott, H. G. *Between parent and teenager.* New York: Macmillan, 1969, p. 32.

12. Matarazzo, R. G., Phillips, J. S., Wiens, A. N., and Saslow, G. Learning the art of interviewing: A study of what beginning students do and their pattern of change. *Psychotherapy: Theory, Research, and Practice,* 1965, *2,* 49–60.

13. Erickson, C. E. *The counseling interview.* Englewood Cliffs, N.J.: Prentice-Hall, 1950.

14. Castle, P. F. C. The evaluation of human relations training for supervisors. *Occup. Psychol.,* London, 1952, *26,* 191–205.

15. Roethlisberger and Dickson, op. cit.; Maier, N. R. F. *Frustration.* New York: McGraw-Hill, 1949. Reissued Ann Arbor, Mich.: University of Michigan Press, 1961. Maier, N. R. F. Frustration theory: Restatement and extension. *Psychol. Rev.,* 1956, *63,* 370–388.

16. Rogers, C. R. *Counseling and psychotherapy,* op. cit.

17. Bordin, E. S. *Psychological counseling,* rev. ed. New York: Appleton. 1968: Fenlason, A. F., Ferguson, G. B., and Abrahamson, A. C. *Essentials in interviewing.* New York: Harper, 1962; Patterson, C. H. Counseling: Self-clarification and the helping relationship. In H. Borow, *Man in a world at work,* Boston: Houghton Mifflin, 1964; Barrett-Lennard, G. T. Dimensions of therapist response as causal factors in therapeutic change. *Psychol. Monogr.,* 1962, *76,* 562, 7; Moos, R. H., and Clemes, S. R. Multi-variate study of the patient-therapist system. *J. Consult. Psychol.,* 1967, *31,* 295–303.

18. Gibson, W. D. They're bringing problem drinkers out of the closet. *Chem. Week,* November 15, 1978, 85–86ff; Presnall, L. P. *Recent findings regarding alcoholism in industry.* New York: National Council on Alcoholism, 1967.

19. See U.S. Dept. of Labor, *Comparative job performance by age: Office workers.* Bull. 1273. Washington, D.C., Government Printing Office., 1960.

20. Sheehy, G. *Passages.* New York: Dutton, 1976.

21. Himler, L. E. Psychiatric treatment: brief psychotherapy procedures for the industrial physician. *Intern. Med. and Surgery,* 1956, *25*(51), 232–236; Occupational rehabilitation following mental illness. *Intern. Med. and Surgery,* 1960, *29*(10), 480–483; Psychiatry in industry. *Intern. Med. and Surgery,* 1962, *31*(10), 450–452. The application of psychiatry to industry. *Report of Committee on Psychiatry in Industry.* No. 20. Topeka, Kansas: Group for the Advancement of Psychiatry, 1951; Van der Veen, F. Basic elements in the process of psychotherapy: A research study. *J. Consult. Psychol.,* 1967, *31,* 295–303.

22. Meltzer, H. Mental health realities in work situations. *Amer. J. Orthopsychiat.,* 1963, *33,* 562–565.

23. Howland, C. I., and Wonderlic, E. F. Prediction of industrial success from a standardized interview. *J. Appl. Psychol.,* 1939, *23,* 537–546; McMurry, R. N. Validating the patterned interview. *Personnel,* 1947, *23,* 2–11.

24. Grant, D. L., and Bray, D. W. Contributions of the interview to assessment of management potential. *J. Appl. Psychol.,* 1969, *53,* 24–34.

25. Kinsey, A. C., Pomeroy, W. B., and Martin, C. E. *Sexual behavior in the human male.* Philadelphia; Saunders, 1948.

26. McMurry, R. N. *Handling personality adjustment in industry.* New York: Harper, 1944.

27. Dembo, T., Leviton, G. L., and Wright, B. A. Adjustment to misfortune — a problem of social-psychological rehabilitation. *Artificial Limbs,* 1956, *3,* 4–62.

28. Bagley, C. D., Hage, J., and Aiken, M. Communication and satisfaction in organizations. *Hum. Relat.*, 1975, *28*, 611–626.
29. Meyer, H. E. How the boss stays in touch with the troops. *Fortune, 91*(6), 153–155.

SUGGESTED READINGS

Bronfenbrenner, U. Nobody home: The erosion of the American family. *Psychol. Today*, 1977, 41–47.
Hunt, R. G. *Interpersonal strategies for system management: Applications of counseling and participation principles.* Monterey, Calif.: Brooks/Cole, 1974.
Roberts, K. A., and O'Reilly, C. H., III. Failures in upward communication in organizations: Three possible culprits. *Acad. Mgt. J.*, June, 1975, 205–215.
Vaillant, G. E. *Adaptation to life.* Boston: Little, Brown, 1977.

LABORATORY EXERCISE

SKILL PRACTICE:
THE DIANA TUCKER CASE

A. PREPARATION

1. The instructor will appoint one class member to read the part of Diana Tucker and another to read the part of Traver Norton. Assigning parts ahead of time will permit them to become familiar with the script (D.2).
2. Arrange two chairs at the sides of a table so that Diana and Traver face the class as well as each other.
3. The readers will bring a copy of the script with them (D.2). Other class members should not refer to the script before or during the exercise.

B. READING THE SCRIPT*

1. The instructor will read aloud the preliminary material (D.1, Situation).
2. Diana and Traver are asked to take their positions at the table.
3. Class members are instructed to listen to each of Diana's statements, think of an appropriate response, using the reflecting-feelings method described in this

*Used with permission of the interviewee.

chapter, and then write the response down.
4. Diana will then be asked to begin reading the script.
5. The instructor will ask several volunteers to read the response that they would give to Diana's words. Participation should be distributed around the class so that all members get a chance to respond.
6. After several suggestions have been made, the instructor will ask Traver to read the first response. At this point, participants can compare their responses to that of the interviewer, Traver Norton.
7. The script reading will continue in this manner; at the end of the reading, the instructor will read the follow-up information to let the class know the results of Diana's decisions.

C. DISCUSSION

1. Use class discussion to evaluate the counseling session. What would have happened if Traver had tried to advise, had directed the course of the interview by asking probing questions, or had made critical judgments about Diana's behavior

and feelings? What would the results have been if Traver had tried to diagnose Diana's problems?

2. Discuss any difficulty that class members might have experienced in reflecting feelings. Did they find that they had to listen more closely in order to reflect feelings than they ordinarily would? Discuss the merits of the reflecting-feelings method of counseling.

3. At what point did Traver anticipate Diana's feelings and find that she was reluctant to agree with his interpretation?

4. To some extent, the issues discussed were characteristic concerns of women in the 1970s. Other problems discussed were not exclusively those of women. Point out which themes seem dated and which are longstanding problems relating to achieving adulthood and responsibility, and are not exclusive to one historical period or gender.

5. Traver occasionally violated some principles of nondirective-counseling techniques. Point out some of these occurrences. What effect did these lapses seem to have on Diana's responses?

D. MATERIALS FOR THE CASE

1. Situation

The following material is an edited version of a transcript made in 1974 of a dialogue between Traver Norton and Diana Tucker in which Traver practiced the use of nondirective-counseling methods as part of a graduate business school course. Traver had some previous experience as a personnel manager and some training in undergraduate-level psychology, but was not a professional psychologist.

Diana Tucker, twenty-five years old, was a graduate student in primary education at the time of the interview. She was married to Andrew, a graduate student in business. Diana volunteered to help Traver with the course assignment, which was to tape record a session, using reflecting-feelings-counseling techniques. She

was not emotionally disturbed — the session was not intended to be therapeutic.

Diana begins the session with an opening remark, which she had prepared as a possible topic for their discussion.

2. Script

Diana: All this year, it seems I've gotten myself all caught up with (*pause*) . . . I guess I didn't expect psychologically to have to become aware of myself and the way I act and the way I relate to other people. As a result of courses in school, I'm becoming more aware of how much I've been *pushed under* by society as a woman, through your basic "Dick, Jane, and Sally" characters. You know, my mother saying, "You've been married four years — when are you going to have a kid?" — that kind of thing. Now, I'm much more aware that they're happening and trying to get myself up and out of that.
Traver: Um-hmm.

. . .

Diana: And I'm always surprised when people say, "Well, you've got a husband, you don't have to worry about how you look now." (*Laughs*) Things like that. (*Laughs*). Ah, like, "Andrew has a good job, why do you . . . you don't have to . . . or "Well you're going to be having kids anyway, so it's really sort of a waste that you're even going to graduate school." I guess it's never hit me that hard before now. Since I've been out of undergraduate school, I seem to be more aware of it. . . . A lot of times I'll go out and visit my sister in the suburbs, and she's pregnant with her second child and doesn't work. She spends time with her child, but she doesn't, you know, do a lot of activities, the way I would. She just sort of sits there and talks. And it's such a *relaxing* . . . so easy . . . just to fall into that, you know, suburban housewife . . .
Traver: It seems very appealing to you.
Diana: Yeah, it's very appealing. You have time to talk with people and get to know them. You'd have time to read if you want to read. You don't really have to give society anything . . .
Traver: So, the . . .
Diana: . . . so at the same time, I can go out

there and mix with her friends and say, "My gosh, why am I fighting all these things? Why am I trying to buck the system and be something that I really don't have to be? I'm probably going to have more headaches trying to break down barriers. Why go through it? I don't have to."

Traver: So there's some ambivalence . . .

Diana: Yeah, exactly — a lot of ambivalence. You know, I'm sure I'll go through with my education and work, because I just can't rationalize (*laughs*) just sitting home all day, just thinking. I just can't fathom that. I just know that my life will be very different from hers, and at the same time, hers looks really comfortable.

. . .

Diana: I think, too . . . I'm in graduate school and teaching and working, and I'll ask another woman — you know, if I'm in a cocktail party situation and I'll ask them what they do. They *know* that *you* are out in the world working, and I think defenses go up. I don't know what to say then . . . That's why I'd really like to work under somebody that's been through the gamut.

Traver: You feel like . . .

Diana: I want an example to look at to see how they handle these situations. I don't know that I'm handling them myself terribly well (*laughs*).

. . .

Traver: So you have this feeling of wanting to go to school, wanting to help others.

Diana: I think that my father gave each of us, his children, a role to play. Um, one sister's the big *thinker,* she's sort of way up here, and I'm the one who takes these high, lofty ideas and tries to really *do* stuff. But I don't know where it came from . . . maybe Andrew partly. Because he very much wants a wife that he can be proud of, in the sense that she's a real go-getter and respected in the community. He encourages me more than anyone else. And I always say, "Oh, why am I applying for jobs in all these school districts? It's ridiculous, let's take a loan out and forget the whole thing and we can start having kids next year." And he'll say, "Well, you can do it, but you know you'd be very unhappy next year if you did something like that." And . . . he's right, I would look at it as giving up.

Traver: And he provides . . .

Diana: Oh, he provides a lot, oh, yeah. I would never have had enough confidence to apply to the schools I applied to for graduate school.

. . .

Diana: Frequently, I'll just say to Andrew, "Why aren't you the typical husband and want a kid and have that whole *masculine ego* kind of thing that you want to prove that you can be a father?" He doesn't have any of that. Which is to my advantage in some ways. He will always say, "Well, it's your decision."

. . .

Diana: I don't think many women think about working versus staying home to care for children that much. They usually, they probably fall into it, by way of their husband . . .

Traver: They don't decide, they just fall . . .

Diana: . . . into whatever it would be. Either they have to work for economic reasons or their husbands don't want them to work, won't let them, or they have a child and they can't work — those are the choices. But I'm in a position of *extreme choice* (*laughs*). I was talking to someone the other day who was saying, "I don't envy you growing up now because you have complete choice to do anything you want to do." The money is more available, there are more scholarships and loans and the pill, and here you are . . . There are more efficient types of appliances, they whip up your dinner in two seconds. So you *are* living in a time of extreme choice and, ah . . .

Traver: And there can be such a thing as *too much* freedom.

Diana: Well, that's true. I think that's what's come out of all this. I've made a decision, but it's taken this year to do it.

Traver: So you feel as though you have resolved your ambivalence.

Diana: Yeah, ultimately. Even though I still break down and say, "Why do all this?"

Traver: It seemed to me as though you hesitated a minute before you said you'd made your mind up.

Diana: Yeah. The thing is, I kind of resent sometimes that it is so much up to me and . . . for most *men,* for most husbands, the decision is totally up to them.

Traver: Um-hmm.

Diana: But for most women, there's input from the husband as to . . . what he doesn't want his wife to . . . usually it's a negative thing.

Traver: Um-hmm.

Diana: I don't have any constraints at all (*laughs*).

Traver: And you resent . . .

Diana: I . . . you know, I think it would . . . if somebody told me what to do, I'd . . . but at the same time, I . . . maybe I'm too . . .

Traver: No, it's okay. What did you start to say?

Diana: At the same time, I want somebody to tell me. It's a lot easier if somebody tells you what to do.

Traver: Um-hmm.

Diana: And Andrew will *never* let me fall into that easy . . . sometimes I get angry, saying, "Well, why don't you just tell me?" It'd be so much easier if you had a husband that dictates the way you live. You can complain all you want, but it's *easier.*

Traver: And if something goes wrong . . .

Diana: You can just . . . yeah, exactly. You can just say, "See, Andrew, *you* . . ." But he won't, he won't do that for a second, ever. He says, "It's up to you. I'm not going to make your decisions." Some people, some women . . . would like to have the freedom . . . and I do. It's an ideal situation to be in. (*Pause*) But yet, there are just *those days* when you want somebody else to do the deciding. And in that respect, I guess that is what I'm talking about. When you're a victim of your upbringing — you're so *used* to having a lot more directives being thrown, I think, and there are people telling you how you should act and . . . and that kind of thing. And, now, really, you're completely free to do, go — I guess, do anything. And it's kind of *scary,* I think. I guess that may be part of all this.

Traver: That maybe you won't . . . take advantage of the opportunity or . . .

Diana: No, to be this . . . I've always been pretty independent, but (*pause*) the way I've tried to describe it is: throughout your life you're always preparing for the future, you go to school and you're preparing yourself, and you go to college and you're preparing yourself. You teach for a year and that's a learning experience, and graduate school. You're preparing yourself. And then, all of a sudden, the future's *there.* Okay? Now, that's it. Then you live from year to year. But everything you've been preparing for, you've sort of *put off,* you can keep putting off. "Well, it's not the real thing, I'm still preparing myself, I've still got another chance." All of a sudden, you've got to *decide,* you know. There you *are* (*laughs*). It's no more, "I'm gonna . . ." You're not preparing yourself any longer. This is it. You make it or break it. And, uh, it's sort of scary to be there (*laughs*).

Traver: Taking responsibility for your *self.*

Diana: Yeah. Exactly.

Traver: And how you turned out.

Diana: Yeah. This is it. You're a person now (*laughs*). You're not preparing yourself to be one any more. You know, you're always learning and all that kind of thing, but I think that by this time, your style of life has to . . . you know, your definite beliefs aren't being altered significantly.

Traver: So, sometimes you get so frustrated that you feel it would be better to decide anything rather than go on.

Diana: Yeah (*laughs*).

Traver: Why are you laughing?

Diana: Because, I don't know, I guess because that's probably true. I should do, like, a cost-benefit analysis (*both laugh*), you know, and list all the benefits under each alternative and the costs against me . . . I don't know. I guess I'm laughing because I've gone through this. I go over it in my mind a lot.

Traver: So it's something that really is a central concern for you.

Diana: Yeah, oh, yeah. Because I think it's determining my *life,* what I'm going to do, how I'm going to do, how I'm going to live, what I want to be — all that stuff. And I guess I just never . . . I've been living a lifestyle throughout . . . my growing up. I don't know why I feel that all of a sudden I'm *ending.* I *do* — I really feel like I'm coming to a . . . sort of the *end* of being able to take off in any direction.

Traver: Um-hmm. It's true, isn't it?

Diana: I do feel like it's very much an ending.

Traver: Writing the final chapter to the book.

Diana: (*Laughs*) Yeah. Well, I don't know. I don't know why I . . . I suppose it is.

Traver: So some of the reluctance to decide . . .

Diana: (*Pause, then very softly*) . . . is putting it off? (*Pause*) I don't know. (*Pause*)

Traver: How does that feel?

Diana: (*Pause*) Maybe it is. (*Pause*) The thing is, there are things, you know, that I *always* wanted to do. I always wanted to have a flashy car, and I always wanted to have a motorcycle, silly stuff, and I'm really . . . you know . . . saying, like, I'm never going to *do* it now. I . . . you know . . . I'm too old, almost. Probably the next kind of car I'm going to get is going to be a certain kind for a reason . . .

Traver: A station wagon . . .

Diana: Yeah.

Traver: . . . for all your children.

Diana: For all your children. Right. (*Pause) That* you're not going to do all the things you really want to do. (*Pause*) I don't know. How much longer do we have to go on with this thing?

Traver: You want to have it over with.

Diana: Yeah.

Traver: We can stop if you want.

Diana: Yeah, okay.

3. Follow-up Information

Diana Tucker left the university after she and her husband graduated. Shortly thereafter they had a child. She began to look for part-time employment and could find nothing suitable in the field of education. After about a year, she returned to school and eventually received a degree in accounting. She now works full time for one of the "big eight" accounting firms. She and Andrew have hired a housekeeper to take care of their son until he reaches school age.

PART

THE
ORGANIZATION
AND
THE
ENVIRONMENT

FIVE

Early writers on interpersonal relations generally were concerned with helping a manager generate stability in the work situation. Their focus was on matters inside the company, their goal was to develop an organization that would function like a well-oiled perpetual motion machine. Individual member components might change, but The Organization would go on forever.

Several factors shattered this vision of administrators and theorists. Thousands of companies failed during the Depression of the thirties; thousands of others prospered during and after World War II; and great international conglomerates were created in the fifties and sixties. People began to realize that factors outside the organization — government, national economic policies, wars, and alliances — could have tremendous effects on the success of individual firms. At the same time, organization members became aware of the effects businesses had on the environments in which they were located — both the physical environments in which employees worked and their psychological environments. Thus, more than ever before, people in organizations became aware of the levels of interdependence necessary to keep organizations going — interdependence between individuals, between departments in the company, and between the company and other organizations (customers, suppliers, government agencies and institutions).

This perspective resulted in the development of new tools and methods for understanding and dealing with new or recently perceived problems. The world is changing at a hectic pace, and often difficulties on the other side of the globe have a direct impact on American business. The approaches described in Part Three — from bringing in outside consultants to organizational problem solving — are designed to enable managers of the 1980s to grasp and deal with these broader and more complex problems.

Chapter 19 ("Physical and Socioeconomic Environments of Organizations") outlines the impact of the work situation's physical aspects on productivity and attitude and the effect of outside factors on the organization's goals and functions. Chapter 20 ("The Psychology of Organizations") parallels earlier discussions of individual psychology and group social psychology, covering problems relating to most or all organization members. Chapter 21 ("Organizational Development") deals with a multitude of approaches to correct long-term, broadly based ills that arise from organization-wide problems. Finally, the text concludes in Chapter 22 ("Problem Solving at the Organizational Level") with suggestions for expanding the techniques of problem solving, developed for use by middle managers and small groups, to deal with more general organizational problems.

CHAPTER NINETEEN

PHYSICAL
AND
SOCIOECONOMIC
ENVIRONMENTS
OF ORGANIZATIONS

■

The Physical Location of the Plant or Office
Illumination and Job Performance
Air Pollution and Work
The Effect of Noise on Work
Other Physical Environmental Factors
The Organization's Relationship to the Outside World:
The Socioeconomic Environment

■

IN EARLIER CHAPTERS, the necessity of understanding a frame of reference or context was shown to be essential to the correct interpretation and understanding of human behavior. Two concepts about the context of human beings — both within organizations and in other aspects of their lives — have been widely discussed in recent years. The first is the concept of *ecology*, that is, a network of interdependent organisms and physical phenomena making up the web of life in a given area. The second concept — *open-systems theory* — is derived from general-systems theory and describes an organization within the context of its social, political, and economic environment.[1]

Although Gestalt psychologists for many years have stressed the importance of understanding a phenomenon as it relates to its background environment, they have not generated the widespread interest in environmental issues that the ecology and open-systems-theory movements have. *Environment* as a term has become related to issues ranging from industrial safety to strip mining to political activism by organizational representatives.

In our discussion of environmental issues in this chapter, we differentiate three conceptions of the word *environment*. The first, the *psychological environment*, is often referred to as the *organizational climate* and represents individual perceptions of the values, attitudes, and expectations of those within a given organization. This topic has been studied by organizational psychologists for a number of years and will be discussed in Chapter 20.

The second meaning of *environment* refers to the *physical environment* of the organization — the conditions under which employees work and their effect on performance. Interest in this area has been spurred both by concern about pollution or other misuse of the environment and by the passage of the Occupational Health and Safety Act (OSHA), which has resulted in the setting of legal standards for permissible levels of noise, air pollution and so on, in plants and offices.

Finally, general-systems theory has led many researchers to view an organization as an open system existing in an interdependent state of interaction with many other organizations (such as suppliers, government agencies, and customers). These constitute *the social, economic, and political environment* outside the organization.

Space limitations prevent an exhaustive review of all topics in the areas of physical and socioeconomic environments. In this chapter, however, some important issues in these two areas will be discussed.

THE PHYSICAL LOCATION OF THE PLANT OR OFFICE

CITIES OR SUBURBS?

The decision of where to locate a plant or office building is influenced by (1) the size and skill of the available labor supply, (2) the sources of raw materials, and (3) the proximity of major markets. In the past, rivers and railroads were highly influential factors in locating plants and, with the advent of the energy crisis, are again becoming significant. Since these considerations are not the same as those used to choose a home, we may infer that ideal plant locations and desirable places to live are likely to differ. Although some people have abandoned civilization to return to a more basic lifestyle, most will have no choice but to live in the area where jobs are available, which means that they will live near cities.

Cities once were desirable places to live because they offered excitement, culture, and entertainment in theaters, museums, libraries, parks, and concert halls. The modern city offers these, but offers smog, congestion, noise, and crime as well. The flight to the suburbs was a temporary escape from the deteriorating city, but has generated more problems than it has solved. The romance of most cities has declined, and love songs about cities are old songs.

Many college graduates, when given a choice, no longer prefer large cities as work locations, and many married applicants find the large city even less attractive, despite wage differentials. For the first time, companies are encountering a significant percentage of managers who refuse a promotion that involves a transfer to a city that they view as objectionable.[2] The migration from rural areas to cities has largely halted, since the rural population has been reduced to the level needed to supervise highly mechanized farm operations.

The need to restore some desirable features of city life is universally acknowledged, and business has become involved in the effort. Sensible government action is also necessary to find ways to make the cities attractive and habitable. Moving plants to outlying districts did not solve the problem, but merely promoted suburban living while the cities deteriorated further. Freeways also proved to be a short-sighted solution, since they too created new problems by promoting individual transportation at the expense of mass transit and by increasing air and noise pollution. Only when society's values move from individual freedoms to group freedoms will we find a long-term answer to the cities' problems.

SIZE OF CITY AND JOB SATISFACTION

Studies comparing job satisfaction and the size of a city show a negative correlation.[3]

However, the poorer the slum conditions as contrasted with overall prosperity, the greater was satisfaction with the pay received. In other words, when workers compare their wages to the poor situations of neighbors in a slum setting, this comparison may make the amount seem higher than the same wages when received by workers in a comfortable middle-class environment.[4] The community variables were not related to satisfaction with supervision and coworkers. Apparently the financial factor is the most important job satisfier when community conditions are unfavorable.

Rural workers were most satisfied with highly involving jobs, whereas city workers found satisfaction in lesser skilled work and fewer social contacts. Intrinsic job satisfaction seemed to be much lower in city workers.[5] It appears that many urban workers are alienated from middle-class societal norms because of living conditions, high urban growth, and increasing living costs.[6] Since rural workers also have more roots in the community in which they work, the values important to them may be attributed to their identification with the community.

A study of the mental health of city and small town workers (matched for age and sex) compared employees in two plants having similar jobs and patterns of management.[7] Results indicated that interpersonal family relationships were more positive for small-town workers, whereas mature responsibility regarding success and achievement was more developed in large-city workers.

Political climate and the news media might also be regarded as factors influencing values existing in organizations. The UAW sit-down strike in the automobile industry (1936–1937) had the support of the news media,[8] whereas at about the same time, the strike in the shoe industry (Johnstown,

Pennsylvania) found the news media against the workers. The extent to which the outcomes, favorable to the workers in the first and unfavorable in the second, were due to the pressures exerted by the media is a matter of speculation, but their potential influence on business must be recognized. Public support plays an increasing part in shaping organizational behavior.

ILLUMINATION AND JOB PERFORMANCE

The lighting arrangements in a plant are the particular problem of the lighting engineer, but a number of psychological questions concern the plant manager. The adequacy of lighting cannot be judged merely by trying it out; careful tests of human performance must be made under different lighting conditions to determine optimal conditions.

For example, white surfaces reflect from 80 to 85 percent of the light falling upon them, and medium gray reflects from 20 to 40 percent. Such colors as light green and sky blue reflect approximately 40 percent of the light they receive; cardinal red, about 16 percent. The lighting of a plant or office can be greatly improved by the use of pale-colored paints. The Munsell system of colors provides an admirable guide in selecting attractive colors that also have desired high or low reflective characteristics.[9]

When considering proper lighting, we should take into account the distribution of light, the intensity of the light, and its wavelength (color). Although each of these aspects has its own specific advantages, they are somewhat interdependent. For instance, increase in intensity alone may be a disadvantage if glare effects are thereby increased.

Indirect lighting is the best method for producing uniform illumination. In this type, all the usable light is reflected light; high points of light, caused by light from the source striking the eye directly, are out of the visual field. With the source of light directly overhead, it cannot strike the workers' eyes unless they purposely look up at it. In direct lighting, the source is concentrated at small points; thus, shadows, glare, and high points of light are at a maximum.

The disadvantage of indirect lighting is its cost, since considerable light is lost through absorption. The benefits, however, seem to be more than worth the extra cost. In a three-hour reading test, little fatigue and practically no change in ability to sustain clear vision were found under conditions of indirect lighting, while direct lighting had significantly poorer results.[10]

ILLUMINATION INTENSITY

Visual acuity increases with light intensity and is about equal to daylight acuity as 100-foot-candle intensity is approached. However, this degree of acuity is seldom required, and it is apparent that the desired amount of lighting will vary with the amount of detail in the work. For instance, for very fine work, such as distinguishing black thread on black cloth, intensities of 400-foot-candles have been recommended.[11]

Table 19.1 shows the recommended intensities for five types of tasks. The given levels of light intensity roughly represent the steps in visual requirements into which industrial work might be classified. These requirements are conservative and are considerably lower than those recommended by illuminating engineers.[12]

Industrial surveys indicate that production continues to rise as illumination is raised from 6- to 20-foot-candles, and that at 20-foot-candles the rise in production follows a sharper upward trend than does the increase in the cost of lighting.[13]

THE ORGANIZATION AND THE ENVIRONMENT

TABLE 19.1 RECOMMENDED LIGHTING INTENSITIES

VISUAL CONDITION	LIGHT INTENSITY (FOOT-CANDLES)
Most severe work requirements	40 to 50
Tasks comparable to discriminating 6-point type*	30 to 40
Situations requiring reading of handwriting and the like	20 to 30
Reading newsprint and the like	15 to 20
Reading good-sized print (10-point) on good paper†	10 to 15

* This line is set in 6-point type.

† This line is set in 10-point type.

Source: From M. A. Tinker, Illumination standards for effective and easy seeing. *Psychol. Bull.*, 1947, *44*, 435–450. Copyright 1947 by the American Psychological Association, and reproduced by permission.

In general, industrial surveys show production increases ranging from 8 to 27 percent with increased illumination, the actual increase depending on the kind of work. That the type of work is a factor in the extent of the increase shows that the rises in production cannot be attributed entirely to an improved attitude, but that improved vision and reduced fatigue continue to increase production even when the lighting intensity greatly exceeds minimum requirements. Since the cost of these improvements in lighting is low relative to the net gain in productivity, an improvement in practically all types of work may be expected. Increased intensity must be accompanied by facilities for uniform distribution of light. Increases in intensity may be disturbing if the light is not properly distributed. High illumination with direct lighting may actually be very disturbing.[14]

VISUAL SIGNALS

When lights are used as signals, they are most effective when they contrast with the visual field. A flashing signal light against a background of steady light is highly effective, but if the background is flashing, it serves as a distractor regardless of the nature of the signal light.[15] Background lighting that serves as a distractor is called *visual noise*.

Neon signs, Christmas lights, and so on, which line many of our highways and streets offer examples of such noise, which may interfere with ability to locate traffic signals.

EFFECTS OF GOOD LIGHTING ON MORALE

Good lighting is cheerful and stimulating. Undoubtedly, some of the improvement in production that results from proper illumination is attributable to the favorable attitude created by pleasant surroundings. Although individuals differ in the amount of light that they find most desirable, 65 percent of the subjects of one study judged intensities between 10- and 30-foot-candles the most comfortable for reading.[16] With 15- or 20-foot-candles, the majority of individuals could work under a lighting intensity close to that which they found most comfortable; at the same time, they would have an illumination that has been found to be highly efficient and economical from the production point of view.

Invariably, people prefer light of daylight color. Since this light is also superior to all others in visual efficiency, ideal lighting would demand the use of correcting filters on filament lamps in order to obtain daylight color, as well as the discontinuation of colored fluorescent lights.

AIR POLLUTION AND WORK

VARIOUS ASPECTS
OF THE ATMOSPHERE

Several properties of the air may be expected to influence the work of individuals, since they breathe air and their bodies are immersed in it.[17] These include (1) the chemical composition of the air, (2) the addition of substances given off by people through exhalation and perspiration, (3) temperature, (4) barometric pressure, (5) movement of the air, and (6) humidity.

The *chemical composition* of the air is often a cause for concern when the nature of a job involves dealing with dangerous gases or toxic particles suspended in the air. Workers in secondary lead smelters, for example, are required to wear respirators to avoid breathing lead particles.[18]

The *temperature* of the air obviously influences body temperature. The body tends to maintain a constant temperature by reflex responses that lower or raise its temperature. In cool air, excessive heat is lost by convection and radiation; this heat must be resupplied relatively rapidly if the body is to maintain a constant temperature. In very warm air (warmer than the skin), on the other hand, the body absorbs heat from the surroundings; thus, it must be cooled by the evaporation of perspiration and exhalation of heat through breathing. Atmospheric temperature, therefore, is a factor that influences the way the body must function to maintain a constant internal temperature. Recent studies indicate that, under some conditions, temperature can affect behavior, causing people to become more agressive.[19]

Barometric pressure changes somewhat from day to day, but marked constant differences are present in low and high altitudes. When the pressure is low — that is,

at high altitudes — the air is thin, and a person must breathe more air to get the necessary oxygen supply. The effects of barometric pressure on psychological functions are particularly important in aviation and in mountainous regions, but under usual conditions, the barometric variations are not sufficiently great to influence activity.[20]

The *movement* of air prevents stagnant air from accumulating about the body or around machinery. Any undesirable property of such air (for example, its temperature or moisture content) is removed by its mixture with other air in the room. Circulation thus prevents formation of pockets of warm and moist air. In plants that do not have forced circulation, there may be great variation in the cooling properties of the air in various parts of the same room, although the temperature difference may be very small.

The *moisture* content of the air may function in two ways. The heat conductivity of the air increases with humidity, so that on a cool day, humid air rapidly carries heat from the body (convection), and the air feels cooler than the temperature reading would indicate. On the other hand, humid air interferes with evaporation. Since evaporation of perspiration serves a cooling function, this process is inhibited by high humidity. Warm humid air feels relatively warmer because it interferes with evaporation to a greater degree. At between 68 degrees and 70 degrees Fahrenheit (21 degrees Celsius) humidity is negligible in its influence on the bodily function of maintaining a constant temperature.[21]

EFFECTS OF
THE AIR BREATHED

Investigations made by the New York State Ventilation Commission clearly showed that

THE ORGANIZATION AND THE ENVIRONMENT

the air that is breathed does not cause the symptoms produced by "bad" air, such as headache, drowsiness, and lassitude.[22] A number of people confined in an airtight chamber for several hours showed the symptoms only when this so-called bad air surrounded their bodies. Persons in the room who breathed "fresh" air through tubes showed the symptoms, and persons outside the room who breathed "bad" air from the room failed to show the symptoms.

The air that is breathed is harmful only when the oxygen content is reduced to 14 percent and the carbon dioxide is increased to 2.4 percent. Oxygen content seldom falls below 19 percent and carbon dioxide content rarely exceeds .3 percent, even in poorly ventilated schools and plants, because enough air is exchanged through the walls and around windows to maintain fairly constant proportions. But recent efforts to seal buildings to prevent heat loss may have negative side effects.

Body odor may influence some individuals who are sensitive to odors, and the suggestion or belief that air is "bad" may affect others, but a knowledge of the facts will decrease these effects. For example, employees working in a building that had no windows but had an excellent ventilation system constantly complained about the air. Their complaints and symptoms disappeared when the modern ventilation system was shown and explained to them. This example indicates that suggestion is one important contributor to the ill effects caused by breathing "bad" air.

In the past, the effects of general air pollution and localized industrial wastes on workers have sometimes been accepted, or only minimum precautions have been taken. A common effect of such pollution is eye irritation. Smog-induced irritations result mainly in reduced endurance and increased eyestrain and fatigue, rather than in serious loss of visual acuity.[23]

Atmospheric conditions that may not affect visibility can affect the pulmonary functions, causing such diseases as emphysema.[24] This is more serious and harder to detect as it may not immediately result in decreased performance. In many cases, it is much easier to avoid the construction of plants having concentrated areas of chemicals, fumes, or dusts than to try to counteract them. Knowledge of tolerance levels of common pollutants and the ability to recognize overexposure symptoms are necessary to avoid industrial accidents and long-term illnesses.

When exposure is unavoidable, such precautionary measures as goggles or respirators must be used to protect against dangerous industrial pollutants. One problem, however, stems from the perceptions and attitudes of employees. Some workers refuse to wear safety equipment because to do so would violate their self-image. Others simply do not fully realize the dangers involved. (It may be that the psychological defense mechanism of denial is operating.) Good safety practice requires the training and positive motivation of employees with respect to safety procedures (see Chapter 16).

EFFECTS OF THE AIR SURROUNDING THE BODY

The New York State Ventilation Commission's findings showed that the symptoms caused by "bad" air disappeared when the interference of such air with the regulation of body temperature was removed. Cooling, drying, or moving the air with fans corrected the conditions in the airtight room. Statistical studies relating weather conditions to behavior show that barometric pressure has little effect, whereas temperature and humidity have considerable effect on behavior. The production of plant workers, the errors of bank clerks, and the work of college students show variations with weather conditions.[25]

Weather affects employee behavior in still another way. One study demonstrated that punctuality was dependent on the weather.[26] On fine days, employees were more likely to be late than on bad days, despite the fact that bad weather interfered somewhat with transportation. It appears that on fine days employees are reluctant to go indoors and linger to enjoy the outdoor attractions.

EFFECTS OF VENTILATION ON PHYSICAL WORK

The New York State Ventilation Commission's investigations also showed that physical work was definitely impaired by high temperature and stagnant air. In one experiment, men were required to lift a five-pound dumbbell two and a half feet and were motivated by a bonus. They were tested under temperatures of 68 degrees and 75 degrees Fahrenheit, with the air either fresh or stagnant. Production was at its highest level when the temperature was 68 degrees and the air was fresh. The production under the least favorable conditions (warm, stagnant air) was nearly 24 percent below production under the most favorable conditions (cool, fresh air).

The trend of results shows that physical work is definitely influenced by atmospheric conditions that interfere with the maintenance of a constant body temperature. Radical differences between indoor and outdoor temperatures may disturb body adjustment as well as make the choice of clothing more complicated.

Tolerable limits of exposure to heat are a function of prior acclimatization and required workload. Although moderate heat has little effect on performance, extreme heat exposure can result in impairment of rhythmic sense and interval estimation.[27] An individual's performance is affected by cold long before potentially fatal exposure has been suffered. The body adjusts to cold by constricting blood vessels next to the skin and reducing the flow of blood, thus limiting loss of heat to the air. Strength and duration of effort are compromised by reduced circulation in the limbs, and shivering obviously interferes with fine motor coordination.[28]

EFFECTS OF VENTILATION ON MENTAL WORK

The experiments of the New York State Ventilation Commission have demonstrated that mental work may be performed as effectively under humid (80 percent), hot (86 degrees Fahrenheit), and stagnant air conditions as under optimal conditions (circulating air at 68 degrees and 50 percent humidity). Although the subjects showed some tendency to take rest pauses more frequently under the most unfavorable conditions, the surprising fact is that mental work, even under these conditions, was affected little, if at all. A more recent experiment requiring students to perform multiplication problems under hot versus comfortable conditions (109 degrees, 40 percent humidity, and 77 degrees, 40 percent humidity) also revealed no differences.

However, some increase in errors was found in a vigilance task that required the subject to keep a pointer aligned with a moving target when the temperature was 100 degrees as compared to 60 degrees.[29] Because statistical studies have shown some influence of weather conditions (temperature and humidity) on mental work performed outside experimental situations, the possibilities (1) that weather may affect moods

THE ORGANIZATION AND THE ENVIRONMENT

and so influence all forms of human activity, and (2) that extreme and continually unfavorable conditions may influence mental performance, must be entertained.

THE EFFECT OF NOISE ON WORK

RESULTS OF LABORATORY INVESTIGATIONS

The effect of noise level on performance is the subject of many recent studies.[30] When loud noises are introduced in a laboratory situation, the first effect is a startle reaction that definitely interferes with work, particularly mental work. Soon the individual adjusts and eventually performs better during the noisy periods than during the quiet periods that precede and follow it. The improved performance is attributable to a form of adjustment and to the fact that, at first, greater effort is expended. The extra effort seems to be great enough, so the distraction is not only overcome but work is actually improved.[31] Even the muscles show increased tension during noise. With continued testing, these tensions diminish, indicating that the noise becomes less disturbing from day to day and that the person has less difficulty in adjusting to it.[32] Actually it is the change that disturbs. Once subjects have become accustomed to the experiment, going from noise to quiet is about as distracting as the reverse.[33]

Although the general laboratory findings show performance during noise to exceed that during quiet, the nature of the various effects of noise must be separated. Noise can serve as a distractor, but concentrations on the task may counteract this influence. Noise as a distractor depends on its ability to compete with the task for attention. Its disturbing effect therefore depends on the nature of the task as well as the nature of the noise. This effect involves the processes of perception and motivation. Noise that is an accompaniment to a task is less disturbing than a noise that is not essential to the task.[34] Workers are less disturbed by the noise of machines that they are operating than is a nonmachinist working in an adjoining room.

Certain skills also may be relevant because perceptual organization is necessarily selective, in that figure and ground must be separated. In this case, the task becomes the figure and the noise becomes the background. People differ in ability to separate relevant from irrelevant sounds, an aspect of hearing quite different from auditory acuity. The importance of this selection in auditory perception becomes apparent when a person uses a hearing aid. Background noises then are difficult to separate from voices. Apparently, the reduced ability to localize the various sounds makes it more difficult to separate figure from background.

EFFECTS OF NOISE ON JOB PERFORMANCE

A comparison of the productivity of four typists when working in a quiet office and when working in a noisy office showed no significant difference when errors, amount typed, and the number of discarded letters were considered.[35] Reports on the feelings of fatigue, taken from time to time, also showed no clear difference between the two working environments. However, later studies have shown a decrement in mental work resulting from noise exposure.[36]

In an intensive investigation of the effects of reducing noise, measurements of the production of eleven weavers were made when they were working with and without ear guards that reduced the noise of the machines about 10 percent (from 96 to 87 dec-

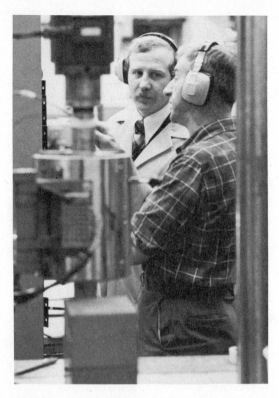

Sometimes working in a noisy environment is unavoidable; these men are wearing earphones (as required ·by the Environmental Protection Agency) that filter out most frequencies, but not the human voice. (Ann McQueen)

ibels).[37] Comparison of the productivity of the group when ear guards were in use and when they were not (alternate weeks) showed an improvement of only 1 percent in production with their use. However, the amount of production in weaving depends partly on the efficiency of the machinery and only partly on the skill of the worker. If the results are interpreted in terms of the reduction in time of the weaver's personal operations, then the improvement in efficiency amounted to 12 percent. Occupations that involve a greater proportion of personal per-

formance, therefore, may be expected to show a greater increase in efficiency with noise reduction.

The increase in production was considerably greater for weavers who reported that they were disturbed by the noise than for those who reported indifference, yet every weaver showed some improvement when using the ear guards. Interesting also is the fact that the benefits of the reduced noise were more marked in the morning than in the afternoon, and that the general effect was to produce a more regular rate of output. As may be expected, noise is more disturbing for mental than for manual work, with irregular, meaningful, and loud noises being the most distracting.[38]

In general, reports on the effects of noise in business show a variety of striking improvements with noise reduction.[39] For example, the work of assembling temperature regulators increased more than 37.0 percent, and errors fell to one-eighth of their former number when the work was moved from the proximity of a boiler shop to a quiet area. Office work increased 8.8 percent and typists' errors fell 24.0 percent with a noise reduction of 14.5 percent. The noise reduction also decreased turnover by 47.0 percent, and absenteeism by 37.5 percent.

A carefully controlled study compared work (threading cinefilm on perforation machines) in rooms with acoustic treatment with work in rooms not so treated.[40] Seven criterion measures were used; one showed a difference and was significant only at the 5 percent level. Rate of work, coordination, and other measures of performance seemed unaffected by ordinary noise levels, but there was some indication that noise increases the frequency of mental lapses.

The industrial studies generally agree that a reduction in noise is associated with some forms of improvement. When the noise level is decreased, production does not necessarily increase (except for a general attitude factor) but human error is less frequent.[41] One study suggested that task complexity influenced results.[42] Data indicate that people may have a reserve perceptual capacity that is usually unused. Should the perceptual demands of a task or of the situation increase, this reserve capacity may be drawn upon, maintaining task performance at a high level. This reserve may account for the results of studies showing that some background noise produces no decrement in task performance. By increasing task complexity and introducing a secondary task in this study, the reserve capacity was used, making it unavailable to draw upon when noise was introduced. Errors increased on the secondary task, although performance of the primary task was maintained.

EFFECTS ON HEALTH

Although the human body has great adaptability to its environment, this adjustment may be prevented when noise produces irritation. In an experiment using physiological measures of activity in the gastric and duodenal regions, it was found that the functional level was influenced by periods of intermittent noises.[43] Two conditions were tested. One group of subjects was able to prevent the noise, scheduled at thirty-second intervals, if they pressed a button during the five-second period before the onset of the noise. The other group had no control over the noise. The group that could control the noise showed increased physiological activity. The other group apparently adjusted, since they exhibited no increase in either gastric or duodenal activity.

These findings are in contrast with those of D. C. Glass and J. E. Singer, who suggest that people can adapt *on a short-term basis* to high-density noise.[44] But long-term exposure to noise pollution results in postnoise effects, such as decreased tolerance for frustration and impaired task performance. They found that when the noise was perceived as predictable or controllable, these negative aftereffects were less serious. Other studies of uncontrollable noise have confirmed its relationship to greater aggressiveness, less helping behavior, and a lower tolerance for frustration.[45] High noise levels have also been shown to be associated with elevated blood pressure.[46]

Some workers exposed to high noise levels (such as those directing planes taking off and landing) are now required to wear protective safety equipment, and standards for safe noise levels have been set. This requirement is necessary, in part, because the onset of deafness from chronic exposure to high noise levels is not immediately noticeable. In many cases, irreversible damage is done before the individual is aware of it. Partial deafness has become a common problem among former rock stars of the 1960s and 1970s.

EFFECT ON JOB ATTITUDES

Insofar as plant or office noise is of such character that it is generally unpleasant, its correction will lead to better job attitudes for the same reason that any consideration for the welfare of employees tends to produce a favorable reaction. Extreme quiet, however, also may be disturbing. In a quiet background, even the slightest noise may stand out and be more disturbing and disruptive than a constant background of noise.

The fact that noises are generally unpleasant may be a factor in social reactions and relations, even when they do not markedly influence individual performers.[47] Intermittent noises are certainly the most disturbing as far as emotional reactions are concerned, and noises that are meaningful (conversational) are the most distracting. In a highly motivated situation, these can be overcome by extra effort, but the necessity of overcoming them may create a source of irritation between individuals, particularly if an employee is the source of the noise.

VIBRATION

Helicopter pilots and air hammer operators are among the kinds of workers who cannot escape exposure to vibration. Vibration and sound are closely related, since vibrations reaching the body by air are acoustic. Mechanical oscillations between 20 and 20,000 frequencies per second (Hz) will be heard as sound, whereas airborne vibrations below 16 Hz will be perceived as vibration, not noise. Intense vibrations and noise produce stresses that are distracting and can produce an alarm reaction, anxiety, and irritation.[48] They can produce a temporary hearing loss and a decrease in fine motor coordination. If exposure to loud sound continues over long periods of time, the regaining of hearing acuity is delayed.

The eyeball has a critical resonance frequency that when approached, causes decreased visual acuity and impaired performance. At critical frequencies, vibration of the body produces greater perceptual impairment than vibration of the stimulus object does.[49]

Although prolonged exposure to intense vibration is detrimental, vibratory stimulation can be used to advantage. B. Gilmer lists fourteen situations in which vibration is useful. Among these are: (1) to alert or warn quickly; (2) where unusual stimulation is desirable; (3) as an aid to vigilance through warnings and redundance; and (4) where conditions handicap both the eye and ear.[50]

The air hammer operator is experiencing both vibration and noise. (Terence Le Goubin, Black Star)

J. F. Hahn demonstrates that although vibrotactile discrimination has advantages in certain situations, it is far less sensitive than visual discrimination.[51]

OTHER PHYSICAL ENVIRONMENTAL FACTORS

Most companies are sensitive to the need for attractive building designs and for creating comfortable lounges and making working conditions as attractive as the work permits.[52] Office space arrangements influence the manner in which employees form social

THE ORGANIZATION AND THE ENVIRONMENT

groups. Some offices are designed so that hundreds of desks occupy one section. Certain designers argue that such a situation offers more privacy than a room limited to four or six desks. A large open area offers one kind of privacy — that of not being an obvious member of a group. But such situations appear to be designed to prevent the formation of groups, which may be a factor in the alienation of employees in large offices.

Common sense seems to have persuaded some modern architects and managers to think that friendships detract from productivity. To take advantage of, rather than to destroy, natural groups, it is necessary to find ways to organize them around the job so that the friendship will lead to cooperation, good communication, and job interest. A unified group has little value to an organization unless it results in improved job satisfaction and productivity. Unity, however, can lead to increased participation and involvement in job activities.

General interest in the effects of perceived space on behavior and attitudes has developed into a specialized field called *proxemics*. The central concern in this field is the way that people use space as a means of regulating social interaction.[53] Basically, study in this area involves analysis of four phenomena: privacy, personal space, territoriality, and crowding.[54]

Psychological boundaries marking those persons who are in, or outside of, a group have received special study.[55] One important concept in human spatial behavior is that of perceived control. This was shown earlier in the chapter to be a factor in the effects of noise on performance and appears to be relevant to this aspect of behavior as well.[56]

Some research has combined the concepts of physical environment and social environment within the organization. These studies have suggested that physical settings have several psychological functions, such as feelings of security, social contact, and enjoyment. Before outsiders or managers intervene in organizations, they should make a thorough analysis of what the existing environment means to employees.[57] Choosing the correct means of effecting improvement, requires an accurate knowledge of the status quo.

THE ORGANIZATION'S RELATIONSHIP TO THE OUTSIDE WORLD: THE SOCIOECONOMIC ENVIRONMENT

The early theorists of classic management methods wrote as though individual organizations operated in separate vacuum packages, or closed systems.[58] They gave little or no consideration to an organization's relationships with representatives from the government, the local community, suppliers, or customers.

Then open-systems theory put an emphasis on exchange and interdependence, and provided a framework for a new way to understand organizations and their fit with other organizations and individuals.[59] Special areas of interest soon developed: (1) the definition and conception of organization-in-environment; (2) the concept of environmental change and uncertainty; and (3) the changing concept of corporate social responsibility. The trend overall is toward a greater sophistication in our current understanding of the organization as a dynamic system, whose survival and success depend on members' ability to recognize and deal with changing environmental needs and demands.

ORGANIZATION-IN-ENVIRONMENT

In the organization-in-environment concept,[60] environment is not an objective, constant artifact, but a conceptualization in the minds of organization members.[61] Different employees will have different ideas about which outside groups or individuals should be satisfied or appeased to ensure organizational success. For an executive, stockholders may be the most important group; for a product manager, customers will loom large; for the legal counsel, government agencies may seem the most crucial outside element.

Researchers in this area agree that organizations must deal somehow with all the relevant outside groups if they are to survive and prosper in the long run. They differ, however, in their approach to studying how organizations go about making the necessary adjustments. Some see the organization as a flexible system that persists by changing structure and form. Others perceive the organization over time as a succession of rigid structures that are developed, bloom, and die to be replaced by new, slightly modified versions.

In 1918, an inexperienced young manager named Alfred P. Sloan joined a new struggling organization, which manufactured automobiles.[62] By the time he retired, General Motors — as it was then known — had become the premier American manufacturing company and Sloan was a wealthy influential business executive. The question researchers would ask is: Was the company from which Alfred P. Sloan retired the same company he originally joined? What is the essence of an organization — its hierarchical charts and its standard procedures, its membership, its product lines? All of these change over time. Is there some insubstantial essence — an image, a reputation — that continues throughout its history, or is the company reborn with each new president, major policy change, and revised organizational design?

Recent theories about organizations have come a long way from those advanced by early writers on management methods. For example, J. C. Pock suggests that organizations can most usefully be thought of as hills in a sociological geography.[63] Following this concept, social groups and networks would be mounds and ridges, and economic systems could be thought of as islands or continents. The way a firm's members perceive their environmental niche is influenced by their oganizational set, according to some theories.[64] *Organizational set* refers to an a priori tendency by members to affirm certain aspects of the environment as more important than others. The degree to which this set is congruent with crucial factors in the environment is obviously related to the organization's ability to operate successfully. Differences in profitability (or other measures of success) within an industry thus can be conceived of in terms of the degree of fit between (1) organizational members' ideas about their company's environment and niche in that environment, and (2) the perceptions of that organization's responsibilities and role in the minds of influential outsiders (including customers, stockholders, and the general public).[65]

ENVIRONMENTAL UNCERTAINTY

In *Organization and Environment*, P. R. Lawrence and J. W. Lorsch showed that different industries succeeded in dealing with their respective environments by adopting different (most appropriate) strategies.[66] The best-fitting strategy for a given industry, it appeared, was one that was neither too elaborate nor too unsophisticated for the pace of *change* in that industry's environment.

The idea of relative turbulence or stability of environment has changed scientists' view of the *time dimension* as related to organizations, just as the open-system concepts have altered their view of the organization in space.[67] A *turbulent environment* is one characterized by relatively rapid change and relatively greater uncertainty in the prediction of future organizational needs and environmental demands. A *stable environment*, in contrast, is one in which environmental changes in needs and demands occur relatively slowly and/or less frequently and are reasonably predictable. The electronics industry is an example frequently used to illustrate a turbulent environment, and the container industry has been used as an example of a stable industry.[68]

Some factors in an organization that may be affected by the relative degree of turbulence in the environment include: (1) the number of levels in the organizational hierarchy; (2) the necessary degree of elaboration of interdepartmental liaison efforts; (3) the degree of elaboration of "boundary" positions and departments (that is, organization members who work mainly with individuals outside of the organization); and (4) the type and degree of long-term organizational planning and strategy. In general, if they are to be successful in the long run, companies operating in an environment where changes in competition, government regulation, or customer demands occur frequently must take a different approach to their business than companies operating in a stable environment.

Although early studies sought objective measures of turbulence or uncertainty, some scientists argue that this dimension also is to some extent a perception reflecting the attitudes or ideologies of organizational members.[69] An environment seen by one organization member as unpredictable, complex, and uncertain may be seen by another (who has different beliefs about the world, based on personal experience and early learning) as static and simple.

There may be a range of perceptions within successful companies about environmental complexity. However, a minimal level of awareness of crucial environmental factors should exist in order that the organization survive. Beyond that level, however, perceptions of greater complexity may be more or less appropriate and useful.

SOCIAL RESPONSIBILITY

Open-systems theory has confirmed the *permeability* of the boundaries between organizations and the outside world. Companies do not manufacture goods or provide services successfully without much informational exchange with relevant outside groups. Companies are and must be sensitive to changes in desires and demands of interested parties.[70]

In recent years, pressures and demands from outside groups have gone beyond the realm of product or service to attempts to influence company policies and practices. Should a company have a South African division or subsidiary, given that country's apartheid policies? Should stockholders or the general public have the right to demand changes in company hiring and promotion policies? How much and what kind of responsibility does a company have toward the community in which it operates?

Organizations sometimes must deal with opposing forces in the social environment, such as these two groups who are pro and con a nuclear energy plant. (Wide World Photos)

In 1980, a company that recycles metal from used auto batteries attempted to buy property to build a new plant in a small town in Pennsylvania. The conservation and reuse of metals and other nonrenewable resources have been strongly advocated by proenvironmental groups. The new plant would provide a number of jobs in a community that needed them. The management of the company was progressive and more than willing to conform to all government regulations — and, in fact, had a strong record of doing so in its other plants. Yet the town council was forced to turn down the company's proposal when angry citizens demanded that "such a plant" be banned from their community. To them, a smelter connoted dirt, pollution, and heavy industry. They were not willing to listen to a rational discussion of the subject.

One difficulty in trying to be a socially responsible company is that people do not agree on what constitutes social responsibility. For the battery-recycling plant's management, responsibility might be perceived as providing good jobs, reasonable pay, and safe working conditions. To citizens of that town, however, the mere existence of the

THE ORGANIZATION AND THE ENVIRONMENT

plant in their community constituted social irresponsibility.

A company cannot survive, whatever it produces or provides, if its policies and practices violate the norms and beliefs of the society in which it operates. For most organizations, recognizing and dealing with influences in the social environment are a part of the overall organizational task — a never-ending problem-solving process.

NOTES

1. Berrien, F. K. A general systems approach to organizations. In M. D. Dunnette (Ed.), *Handbook of industrial and organizational psychology*. Chicago: Rand McNally, 1976.
2. Bendian, R.K. Employee relocation: Motivations, concerns and expectations of the individual. Master's thesis. Minneapolis: Minn.: University of Minnesota, 1980.
3. Bass, B. M. *Organizational psychology*. Boston: Allyn & Bacon, 1965; Katzell, R. A., Barrett, R. S., and Parker, T. C. Job satisfaction, job performance, and situational characteristics. *J. Appl. Psychol.*, 1961, *45*, 65–72.
4. Hulin, C. L. Effects of community characteristics on measures of job satisfaction. *J. Appl. Psychol.*, 1966, *50*, 185–192.
5. Turner, A. N., and Lawrence, P. R. *Industrial jobs and the worker: An investigation of response to task attributes*. Boston: Harvard University Press, 1965.
6. Blood, M. R., and Hulin, C. L. Alienation, environmental characteristics, and worker response. *J. Appl. Psychol.*, 1967, *51*, 284–290.
7. Meltzer, H., and Ludwig, D. Community differences in positive mental health of younger workers. *J. Psychol.*, 1970, *75*, 217–223.
8. Personal communication with H. Meltzer.
9. The *Munsell Book of Color* contains charts and tables of aesthetic color combinations. Baltimore: Munsell Color Co., 1929.
10. Ferree, C. E., and Rand, G. Lighting in its relation to the eye. *Proc. Amer. Phil. Soc.*, 1918, *57*, 440–478.
11. Luckiesh, M., and Moss, F. K. *The science of seeing*. Princeton, N.J.: Van Nostrand, 1937, pp. 308 and 345.
12. Illuminating Engineering Society Committee. Report No. 1 Recommendations for quality and quantity of illumination. *Illuminating Engineering*, 1958, *53*, 422–432.
13. Luckiesh, M. *Light and work*. Princeton, N.J.: Van Nostrand, 1924, p. 267.
14. Ferree and Rand, op. cit.
15. Crawford, A. The perception of light signals: The effect of the number of irrelevant lights. *Ergonomics*, 1962, *5*, 417–428.
16. Ferree, C. E., and Rand, G. Good working conditions for eyes. *Personnel J.*, 1937, *15*, 333–340.
17. Ford, A. *A scientific approach to labor problems*. New York: McGraw-Hill, 1931, 134–144.
18. Moos, R. H. *The human context*. New York: Wiley, 1976; Waldbott, G. L. *Health effects of environmental pollutants*. St. Louis: Mosby, 1973.
19. Baron, R. A., and Bell, P. A. Aggression and heat: The influence of ambient temperature, negative affect and a cooling drink on physical aggression. *J. Pers. Soc. Psychol.*, 1976, *33*, 245–255; Griffiths, I. D. The thermal environment. In D. Canter and B. Stringer (Eds.), *Environmental interaction*. New York: International University Press, 1976, pp. 21–52; Rule, B. G., and Nesdale, A. R. Environmental stressors, emotional arousal, and aggression. In I. G. Sarason and C. D. Spielberger (Eds.), *Stress and anxiety*, Vol. 3. Washington, D.C.: Hemisphere, 1976, pp. 87–103.

20. Poffenberger, A. T. *Principles of applied psychology*. New York: Appleton, 1942, pp. 150–151.
21. Poffenberger, ibid., pp. 166–168.
22. *Ventilation: Report of the New York State Commission on Ventilation*. New York: Dutton, 1923.
23. Berkhout, J. Psychophysiological stress: Environmental factors leading to degraded performance. In K. DeGreene (Ed.), *Systems psychology*. New York: McGraw-Hill, 1970; Peterson, R. R. Air pollution and attendance in recreation behavior settings in the Los Angeles Basin. Presented at 83rd Ann. Conv., Amer. Psychol. Assn., Chicago, 1975.
24. Green, H. L., and Lane, W. R. *Particulate clouds, dusts, smokes, and mists*. London: Spon, Ltd., 1964.
25. Huntington, E. *Civilization and climate*. New Haven, Conn.: Yale University Press, 1924; Dexter, E. G. *Weather influences*. New York: Macmillan, 1904.
26. Mueser, R. E. The weather and other factors influencing employee punctuality. *J. Appl. Psychol.*, 1953, *37*, 329–337.
27. Hendler, E. *Unusual environments and human behavior*. New York: Free Press of Glencoe, 1963.
28. Fox, W. F. Human performance in the cold. *Human Factors*, 1967, *9*, 203–207.
29. Pepler, R. D. Warmth, glare and background of quiet speech: A comparison of their effects on performance. *Ergonomics*, 1960, *3*, 68–73.
30. Cohen, S., Glass, D. C., and Phillips, S. Environment and health. In S. Freeman, S. Levine, and L. G. Reede (Eds.), *Handbook of medical sociology*. Englewood Cliffs, N.J.: Prentice-Hall, 1977; and Glass, D. C., and Singer, J. E. *Urban stress*. New York: Academic, 1972.
31. Berrien, F. K. The effects of noise, *Psychol. Bull.*, 1946, *43*, 141–161; Ford, op. cit., pp. 154–155; Morgan, J. J. B. The overcoming of distraction and other resistances. *Arch. Psychol.*, 1916, *35*, 1–89.
32. Poffenberger, op. cit., pp. 133–317.
33. Ford, A. Attention-automatization: An investigation of the transitional nature of mind. *Amer. J. Psychol.*, 1929, *41*, 1–32.
34. Blum, M. L., and Naylor, J. C. *Industrial psychology: Its theoretical and social foundations*. New York: Harper & Row, 1968.
35. Kornhauser, A. W. The effects of noise on office output. *Indust. Psychol.*, 1927, *2*, 621–622.
36. Weinstein, N. D. Effect of noise on intellectual performance. *J. Appl. Psychol.*, 1974, *59*, 548–554.
37. Weston, H. C., and Adams, S. *The effects of noise on the performance of weavers*. Indust. Hlth. Res. Bd., 1932, Rep. No. 65.
38. Pollock, K. G., and Barlett, F. C. *Two studies in the psychological effects of noise, I. Psychological experiments on the effects of noise*. Indust. Hlth. Res. Bd., 1932, Rep. No. 65.
39. McCartney, J. L. Noise drives us crazy. Reprinted by the Natl. Noise Abatement Council, New York City, from the *Pa. Med. J.*, August, 1941.
40. Broadbent, D. E., and Little, E. A. J. Effects of noise reduction in a work situation. *Occup. Psychol.*, 1960, *34*, 133–140.
41. Broadbent, D. E., and Little, E. A. Effects of noise reduction in a work situation. *Occup. Psychol.*, 1960, *34*, 133–140.
42. Boggs, D. H., and Simon, J. R. Differential effect of noise on tasks of varying complexity. *J. Appl. Psychol.*, 1968. *52*, 148–153.
43. Davis, R. C., and Berry, F. Gastrointestinal reactions during a noise avoidance task. *Psychol. Rep.*, 1963, *12*, 135–137.
44. Glass, D. C., and Singer, J. E., op. cit.
45. Donnerstein, E., and Wilson, D. W. Effects of noise and perceived control on ongoing and subsequent aggressive behavior. *J. Pers. Soc. Psychol.*, 1976, *34*, 774–781; Sherrod, D. R., and Downs, R. Environmental determinants of altruism: The effects of stimulus overload and perceived control on helping. *J. Exp. Soc. Psychol.*, 1974, *10*, 468–479; Sherrod, D. R., Hage, J. M., Halpern,

P. L., and Moore, B. S. Effects of personal causation and perceived control on responses to an adversive environment: The more control, the better. *J. Exp. Soc. Psychol.*, 1977, *13*, 14–27.

46. Jonsson, A., and Hansson, L. Prolonged exposure to a stressful stimulus (noise) as a cause of raised blood pressure in man. *Lancet*, 1977, *1*, 86–87.

47. Pollock and Bartlett, op. cit.

48. Berkhout, op. cit.

49. Dennis, J. P. Some effects of vibration on visual performance. *J. Appl. Psychol.*, 1965, *49*, 245–252.

50. In Hawkes, G. R. (Ed.), *Symposium on cutaneous sensitivity*. Fort Knox, Ky.: U.S. Army Medical Research Laboratory Report 424, 1960.

51. Hahn, J. F. Unidimensional compensatory tracking with a vibrotactile display. *Perceptual and Motor Skills*, 1965, *21*, 699–702.

52. For a discussion of the architectural aspects of the organizational environment, see E. Pauley, Esthetics, architecture, and city and regional designs. In K. B. DeGreene, *Systems psychology*. New York: McGraw-Hill, 1970, Chapter 17.

53. Hall, E. T. *The hidden dimension*. New York: Doubleday, 1966.

54. Stokols, D. Environmental psychology. *Ann. Rev. Psychol.*, 1978, *29*, 253–295.

55. Knowles, E. S. Boundaries around group interaction: Effects of group size and member status on boundary permeability. *J. Pers. Soc. Psychol.*, 1973, *26*, 327–331.

56. Altman, I. *The environment and social behavior*. Monterey, Calif.: Brooks/Cole, 1975; Lefcourt, H. M. The function of the illusions of control and freedom. *Amer. Psychol.*, 1973, *28*, 417–425.

57. Alderfer, C. P. Organizational development. *Ann. Rev. Psychol.*, 1977, *28*, 197–223.

58. Thompson, J. D. *Organizations in action*. New York: McGraw-Hill, 1967.

59. See Berrien, F. K., op. cit.

60. This punctuation and the concept behind it are based on *Man-in-organization: Essays of F. J. Roethlisberger*. Cambridge, Mass.: Belknap Press, 1968.

61. Starbuck, W. H. Organizations and their environments. In M. D. Dunnette, op. cit., pp. 1069–1123.

62. Sloan, A. P. *My years with General Motors*. New York: Doubleday, 1963.

63. Pock, J. C. Definition and maintenance of organization boundaries: Working paper. Portland, Ore.: Reed College, 1972. See also Crozier, M. The relationship between micro- and macro-sociology. *Hum. Relat.*, 1972, *25*, 239–250.

64. Levine, S., and White, P. E. Exchange as a conceptual framework for the study of inter-organizational relationships. *Admin. Sci. Quart.*, 1961, *5*, 583–601; Hirsch, P. M. Processing fads and fashions: An organizational-set analysis of cultural industry systems. *Amer. J. Sociol.*, 1972, *77*, 639–659.

65. Levine, J. H. The sphere of influence. *Amer. Sociol. Rev.*, 1972, *37*, 14–27.

66. Lawrence, P. R., and Lorsch, J. W. *Organization and environment*. Boston: Harvard Business School, 1967.

67. See, for example, Emery, F. H., and Trist, E. L. *Towards a social ecology: Contextual appreciations of the future in the present*. London: Plenum, 1972.

68. Lawrence, P. R., and Lorsch, P. W., op. cit.

69. Stokols, op. cit. See also Clark, B. R. *The distinctive college*. Chicago: Aldine, 1970; Clark, B. R. The organizational sage in higher education. *Admin. Sci. Quart.*, 1972, *17*, 178–184; Dill, W. R. The impact of environment on organizational development. In J. Mailick and E. H. Van Ness (Eds.), *Concepts and issues in administrative behavior*. Englewood Cliffs, N.J.: Prentice-Hall, 1962, pp. 94–109.

70. Rhenman, E. *Organization theory for long-range planning*. New York: Wiley, 1973.

SUGGESTED READINGS

Alderfer, C. *Existence, relatedness and growth: Human needs in organizational settings.* New York: Free Press, 1972.

Davis, K., Frederick, W. C., and Blomstrom, R. L. *Business and society,* 4th ed. New York: McGraw-Hill, 1980.

Dulz, T. The concept of environmental uncertainty: Lawrence and Lorsch revisited. In W. Allen and P. Weissenberg (Eds.), *Proceedings, Eastern Acad. Mgt.* Hartford, Conn.: Eastern. Acad. Mgt., May, 1977, pp. 72–75.

Kimberly, J. R. Environmental constraints and organizational structure. *Adm. Sci. Quart.,* March, 1975, 1–8.

LABORATORY EXERCISE

ROLE-PLAYING:
THE PROMOTION INTERVIEW

(Students are asked not to read the case materials before participating in the laboratory exercise.)

A.. PREPARATION FOR ROLE-PLAYING

1. The instructor will select two players and give them their assignments at least a day ahead of time.
2. One person is to play the role of Trudy Pearce and should study carefully background information (E.1) and become thoroughly acquainted with special instructions for Trudy Pearce (E.2).
3. The other is to play the role of Jim Smith and should study carefully the background information (E.1) and become thoroughly acquainted with special instructions for Jim Smith (E.3).
4. The rest of the class should refrain from reading any of the materials in section E.

B.. ROLE-PLAYING PROCEDURE

1. The instructor will read the background information (E.1) aloud to the whole class and copy the schedule of jobs held by Smith on the chalkboard.
2. All persons not assigned a role are to act as observers.

3. The instructor will introduce Trudy Pearce to the class and seat her at a desk in front of the class, indicate that Pearce has an appointment with Jim Smith, and signal Smith to arrive for his appointment with Pearce.
4. The interview is then to be allowed to proceed to a solution or conclusion as in a real-life situation.

C. DISCUSSION ANALYSIS WITH OBSERVERS

Pearce and Smith may enter the discussion to evaluate the correctness of conclusions reached, but they should not divulge the nature of their special instructions.

1. Determine the degree to which Pearce established a mutual interest.
2. What use did Pearce make of various types of questions?
3. List feelings expressed by Smith.
4. Which feeling areas were thoroughly explored? Which not?
5. Obtain opinions on the degree to which Pearce understood Smith, and vice versa.
6. List cues that indicate there was a failure to communicate.

7. Did Pearce change as a result of the interview, or was she justified in maintaining her original estimation? List reasons.
8. How was Smith's attitude changed by the interview?

D. REPEAT ROLE-PLAYING OF INTERVIEW IF TIME PERMITS.

1. The class is to divide into groups of three.
2. The instructor will assign the role of Pearce to one member of each group, the role of Smith to a second member, and ask the third member to act as group leader and supervise the role-playing.
3. Role-playing should be terminated ten minutes before end of the class period.
4. Group leaders will hold discussion with role-players and evaluate the progress made.

E. MATERIALS FOR PROMOTION INTERVIEW

1. Background Information

The American Consolidated Chemical Company has chemical plants located in various sections of the country. The main plant is in Detroit. Important branches are at Houston, St. Louis, St. Paul, and Cleveland. All the products are manufactured in Detroit, but each ACCC branch specializes in making chemicals that either use raw material available in the locality or have a concentration of outlets in the area. Thus, the Cleveland plant manufactures products needed in the Cleveland area, and the Houston plant manufactures products that use petroleum derivatives.

Since the Detroit plant makes all the products, an experienced person can be moved from Detroit to any of the other plants. When a vacancy opens up in a particular department in Detroit, it is possible to fill the vacancy by choosing someone local or by bringing in an employee from a branch that produces the product corresponding to the one made by a particular department in Detroit. Thus, there has been a great deal of movement within the organization, and since the company has been expanding, opportunities for promotion have been good. Generally speaking, morale has been quite satisfactory.

Trudy Pearce is the assistant to the plant manager of the Detroit plant. One of her duties is to keep track of the college recruits and plan their development. The company hires several college recruits each year and from these selects the employees for promotion to and development in higher management positions. Pearce is about to have an interview with James Smith, a college graduate who was brought into the company ten years ago. The schedule below shows the positions that Smith has held during his ten years with the company.

2. Role Instructions for Trudy Pearce

Ever since Jim Smith graduated from college and joined the company as a college recruit ten years ago, you have kept an eye on him. During his first year in the company, you were impressed by his technical ability and even more

JAMES SMITH'S RECORD AT ACCC

Detroit	Dept. A	1 year	Regular employee
St. Paul	Depts. A, B, C	2 years	Regular employee
Detroit	Dept. A	1 year	Foreman
St. Louis	Depts. B, F	2 years	Foreman
Cleveland	Depts. D, E	1½ years	Foreman
Houston	Dept. G	1½ years	Foreman
Detroit	Dept. H	1 year	Foreman

by his leadership. After he'd had one year in Department A you sent him to St. Paul where they needed an employee with his training. He had made a good showing and worked in Departments A, B, and C. After two years, you brought him back to Detroit and made him a foreman in Department A. He did very well on this job, so you considered making some long-range plans for him. Here was a man you thought you could groom for an executive position. This meant giving him experience with all operations in all plants. To do this with the greatest ease, you decided to make him a foreman in each of the eight departments for a short period of time and to get him assignments in each of the branches.

During the past two years you have had some disturbing reports. Jim didn't impress Bill Jones, the department head at Houston, who reported that he had ideas but was always on the defensive. Since his return to Detroit, he has shown a lack of job interest, and the employees who work for him don't back him up the way they used to. You feel you have made quite a mistake in this man and that he has let you down after you've given him good build-ups with various department heads. Maybe the confidence you have shown in him and the praise you have given him during the several progress interviews have gone to his head. If so, he hasn't the stature it takes to make the top grade. Therefore, you have abandoned your plans of moving him up to superintendent at St. Paul (a two-step promotion) and think it may be best to send him to Houston where there is a job as general foreman in Department C. (Note that this is not the department in which Jones is the head.) This won't mean much of a promotion because you have moved his pay up as high as you could while he was a sort of roving foreman. However, you feel that he has earned some promotion even if he hasn't lived up to your expectations. This St. Paul position is still open, but unless you are convinced to the contrary, he doesn't seem up to it.

Of course, it's possible that Jim is having marital trouble. At a recent company party you found his wife to be quite dissatisfied and unhappy. Maybe she is giving Jim a rough time.

While you are waiting for Jim to arrive, you have his folder in front of you showing the positions he has held.

3. Role Instructions for Jim Smith

You have been with the American Consolidated Chemical Company for ten years now. You joined the company on graduating from college with a major in chemistry. At the time you joined the company you were interviewed by Trudy Pearce, and were told that a good employee could get ahead in the company. On the strength of the position, you married your college sweetheart and moved to Detroit. You preferred the Houston and St. Paul branches, but Pearce thought Detroit was the place to start. So you took your chance along with other college recruits. Because you were a good student in college and were active in college affairs, you had reason to believe you possessed leadership ability.

During your first few years, you thought you were getting some place. You got moved to Minnesota and felt Pearce was doing you a favor by sending you there. After the first year, you bought a home and got started on a family. During two years in Minnesota, you gained considerable experience in Departments A, B, and C. Then you were offered a foremanship in Detroit, and since this meant a promotion and you had a second child on the way, you decided to return to Detroit. When you came to Detroit, Pearce again saw you and told you how pleased she was with your progress.

Since this time, however, you have been given a royal run-around. They tell you they like your work, but all you get are a lot of lateral transfers. You have been foreman in practically every department and have been moved from one branch to another. Other people that came to the company, even after you joined, have been made general foremen. They stick in a given department and are working up while you

THE ORGANIZATION AND THE ENVIRONMENT

get moved from place to place. Although the company pays for your moves, both you and your wife want to settle down and have a permanent home for your children. Why can't people be honest with you? First they tell you what a good job you are doing, and then the next thing they do is get rid of you. Take, for example, Bill Jones, the department head at Houston. He acted as if you had done him a favor to go there, but you can tell he isn't sincere. Since you've gotten to know him, you can see through him. From little remarks he has dropped, you know he's been saying some nasty things about you to the home office. It's obvious that the Houston man is incompetent, and you feel he got rid of you because he considered you a threat to his job.

Your wife realizes that you are unhappy. She has told you she is willing to live on less just to get you out of the company. You know you could hold a superintendent's job, such as George Wilson got, who joined the company when you did, and he was just an average student in college. As a matter of fact, if the company were on the ball, they should realize that you have the ability to be a department head if George is superintendent material.

Pearce has asked you to come up and see her. You are a bit nervous about this interview because the news may not be good. You've felt her to be less friendly lately and have no desire to listen to any smooth manipulations. Last night you and your wife had a good talk about things, and she's willing that you should look around for another job. Certainly you've reached the end of your patience, and you're fed up with any more of her attempts to move you around just because someone is jealous of your ideas.

CHAPTER TWENTY

THE
PSYCHOLOGY
OF
ORGANIZATIONS

■

Theories of Human Behavior in Organizations
Systems-based Views of Human Behavior in Organizations
Organizational Climate
Organization Structure and Related Issues
Authority and Delegation in Hierarchical Organizations
Organizational Reporting and Control Systems
Cross-functional Relations

■

EVENTUALLY THE INTEREST in problems of the organization as a whole or in relations between groups and hierarchical levels in the organization generated studies in a new area called *organizational psychology*. This chapter considers some issues in this area, including theories of human behavior in organizations, organizational structure, cross-functional relations, and conflict management.

One of the benefits of this change in viewpoint from traditional industrial psychology to organizational psychology is the potential generalization of solutions from business organizations to other organizations. Government agencies, city departments, labor unions, hospitals, public schools, and colleges have psychological problems similar to those of business and industry, and the advances made in business are being examined to learn the extent to which the findings can be generalized. Public school principals are seeking to learn from business how to conduct appraisal interviews, how to deal with unions, and how to discipline. Business in turn is learning from the experiences of nonprofit organizations.[1]

THEORIES OF HUMAN BEHAVIOR IN ORGANIZATIONS

For many years, scientists have tried to isolate the key factors in determining human behavior in organizations. Some material in this area has already been discussed in Chapter 13. But several other approaches to understanding behavior in organizations have been generated by, and identified with specific organizational psychologists. Some of the better-known approaches will be summarized here, grouped into two broad categories. There are many different possible

basic approaches. The first consists of various scientists' analyses of how managers' styles and values affect their interactions with other employees, and thus significantly influence the values, policies, and practices at all levels of the organization. The second, more recent group includes the various approaches to understanding the organization as a group of subsystems and to understanding behavior as a product of varying pressures and demands from those within, and interacting with the subsystems.

ORGANIZATIONS AS DETERMINED BY HUMAN NATURE

The first approach in the scientific analyses of managers' styles and their effects focuses on the organization member as an individual. C. Argyris begins with individual motivations in order to study how these lead to group membership, either formal or informal.[2] However, organizations coerce workers to be dependent and subordinate, which often is a source of frustration. To facilitate effective interpersonal behavior within an organization, Argyris promotes T-group training, designed to develop self-insights in executives and to break down some of the communication barriers. Thus, *for him the basic problem in organizations is the need to develop warm interpersonal relationships and trust.* The influence of group membership on individual behavior is also emphasized by W. F. Whyte,[3] E. W. Bakke,[4] R. Dubin,[5] and R. R. Blake and J. S. Mouton[6] in their theories of organizational behavior.

ORGANIZATIONS AS DETERMINED BY LEADERSHIP STYLES

R. Likert developed a questionnaire that classifies management practices into four systems.[7] System I may be called the carrot-stick principle (in which rewards and punishment are used to control behavior). System II is more positive because emphasis is placed on rewards rather than on punishment. System III introduces considerable freedom and allows employees more initiative and increased responsibility. System IV involves the sharing of responsibility and authority throughout the organization, which assumes a degree of participation in group problem solving and decision making. Likert presents survey data to support the conclusion that, generally speaking, organizational effectiveness (cooperation, motivation, productivity) increases progressively from System I to System IV, but the various measures used are not completely confirmatory. Although managerial styles differ from one company to another, he found that the system used by top management tended to set the style for that organization.

Since questionnaire responses are influenced by the amount of consideration employees receive from their supervisors, a supervisor who is "people" oriented will appear to allow more freedom than one who is "production" oriented. The Likert systems tend to differ more in degree than in kind, and System IV falls short of the skillful practice of group problem solving. Even so, there appears to be a favorable trend from autocratic to more permissive and considerate climates in moving from System I to System IV.

Likert's system relies heavily on individual motivation achieved through the supervisor's supportive behavior, a paternalism that Likert attempts to integrate with group-decision concepts.[8] Like A. J. Marrow[9] and D. McGregor,[10] he makes a key issue of leadership styles.

The influence of K. Lewin (see Chapter 8), who described autocratic, democratic, and laissez-faire leadership styles, has been reflected in most organizational theories that emphasize leadership as the key factor. How these styles are adapted to the organizational hierarchy may differ with the organization because personalities, motivations, training, and conceptions of leadership are not the same. Also, because of differences among managers, we cannot describe an organization's leadership in specific terms. At best, we can describe the prevalent or average style, despite the fact that no one person might fit the average.

THEORIES X AND Y

Traditional organization concepts were primarily concerned with the problem of exercising centralized control over all operations. Finding the best ways to achieve this control thus became a vital concern. The importance of the human side was neglected, and theory was frowned on, because practical common sense was regarded as a virtue. McGregor countered this claim by pointing out that all managers follow a theory of human behavior.[11] McGregor called one common approach *Theory X* and showed that managers who follow it are assuming that (1) most people will avoid work if they can; (2) coercion and punishment must be used to get people to expend adequate energy to achieve organizational objectives; and (3) the average person prefers to be directed, wants to avoid responsibility, and needs security above all else. In contrast, he described a psychologically sound approach that he called *Theory Y,* which assumes that (1) it is as natural to expend mental and physical energy in work as in play; (2) people will exercise self-control to achieve goals that they accept; (3) people seek responsibility; (4) problem-solving ability is present in a large segment of the population; and (5) business does not use the full potential of its people.

Thus, Theory Y emphasized the need to practice psychological principles.

These two theories, however, were often based on averages. Most of the constraints in organizations were established because of the small percentage of people who seemed to be accurately described by Theory X. The major contribution of the discussion of Theories X and Y was that so-called common sense was actually the practice of an untested theory. Theories must be based on facts, not on assumptions or general attitudes, if they are to generate effective results.

One implication of McGregor's work is that managerial assumptions become self-fulfilling prophecies. Thus, if managers expect workers to cheat and set up the organizational system to prevent it, employees will often respond by withdrawing their trust, becoming resentful, and trying to "beat the system."

In the early 1980s, W. G. Ouchi, building on the widespread awareness of the Theory X/Theory Y research, wrote a popular book entitled *Theory Z: How American Business Can Meet the Japanese Challenge,* which described Japanese management styles for an audience of American managers.[12] Two other authors, R. T. Pascale and A. G. Athos also produced a book on the same topic, using a larger body of research data.[13] The inroads of Japanese-made products into markets that previously were held solely by American firms finally awakened American managers to the need for group consensus and the input of those at lower organizational levels — two main features of Theory Z.

These features and other aspects of Theory Z are similar to techniques described earlier in the discussion of group problem-solving skills (Chapter 8). Group problem solving was designed for American business personnel and, therefore, avoids the problems of adapting to the needs of American business and society a management system that is rooted in a culture with very different values. Too often, American managers want to solve all their interpersonal problems with one simple all-encompassing cure (as with T-groups in the 1960s and 1970s). Theory Z, with its emphasis on consensus and group problem solving, may well have some useful insights for American management, but it will not be the panacea that some managers continue to seek.

THE MANAGERIAL GRID

The managerial grid approach was originated by R. R. Blake and J. S. Mouton.[14] They proposed that if a manager's concern for productivity is plotted on a nine-point scale on the horizontal axis and concern for people on the vertical axis, each manager's style can be depicted as a point on a graph, or *managerial grid.* Each individual could then be given a "production, people" score, and the organization could be described in terms of the quadrant into which most managers fall. A tendency toward a "1, 1" system would indicate low concern for both people and production; a "1, 9" tendency would indicate low concern for production and high concern for people; and a "9, 1" system would indicate high concern for production and low concern for people. The ideal system would be one that approached "9, 9," that is, one that recognized the importance of both organizational members and the organizational task.

The suggestion that the managerial style of most managers in an organization will cluster in one quadrant of the managerial grid implies again that management style is not random in an organization, but is pushed in specific directions by internal and external pressures. These pressures may include; (1) the idiosyncrasies and values of the founder and/or current organization head; (2) the organizational task — which may require, for example, rapid adjustment to change (conducive to organizations with few hierarchical levels and low emphasis on status and power differences); and (3) demands of organizational members — for example, expectations of scientists that they will be relatively free from close supervision of their work.

INITIATION AND CONSIDERATION

The concepts of *consideration* and *initiating structure*,[15] (see also Chapter 7) make a qualitative distinction between consideration for people and activities related to getting the job done.[16] (Consideration should not be construed as permissiveness since it includes evaluation of performance.) These two dimensions of supervisory behavior have been measured by questionnaires. Consideration has been found to promote lower absenteeism, less turnover, and fewer grievances[17]; initiation in some cases led to increased productivity. Generally speaking, supervisors scoring high in the initiating dimension have been rated high by superiors and higher producing groups; leaders scoring high on consideration had more satisfied employees than those scoring low.[18] But again, the results cannot be freely generalized because size of group, the skill level of the manager, and the type of work performed influence the relationship. Some of the inconsistency in data has been clarified through studying the effects of consideration and initiating structure in a leader's behavior by distinguishing between jobs varying in interest and ambiguity.[19] When jobs are ambiguous, initiating structure is related to job satisfaction, whereas in routine jobs, the correlation is negative. As jobs increase in scope and autonomy, consideration becomes less important because job satisfaction comes from the work and is less dependent on consideration. It appears that both types of leader behavior have their place. The type of work is one factor to consider, but the needs of different individuals and the aspect of the work on which to use the behavior also must be considered.

Judgment and sensitivity about when to help and how much help to give and judgment in distinguishing between consideration and permissiveness are skill factors. These skills are difficult to measure with a questionnaire, yet they can be crucial determiners of the effect on organization members.

More recently, a serious question has been raised as to the *orthogonality*, or independence, of the two variables of consideration and initiating structure.[20] The suggestion is that a manager who initiates structure for employees *thereby affects their perception* of the manager's attitudes toward them as people.

SYSTEMS-BASED VIEWS OF HUMAN BEHAVIOR IN ORGANIZATIONS

The various approaches outlined in the previous section represent the conceptions of human motivation and behavior in organizations that are prevalent in many "progressive" companies today. Although many of these ideas have been questioned, these doubts have not yet resulted in their replacement by newer approaches. The ideas in this section represent more sophisticated approaches deriving from general systems theory.

THE ORGANIZATION AS AN ORGANISM

Haire draws an analogy between biological organisms and business organizations.[21] A single-celled organism performs all basic functions (feeding, locomotion, reproduction, and so on), but in larger organisms, specialized functions develop. The increased volume does not expose enough body surface to permit feeding through the membrane, so a circulatory system gradually evolves, and the complex organism develops a nervous system, a digestive system, a sensory system, and so on. The physiologist may study the functions of individual systems, but the *behavior* of the organism as a whole is the province of the psychologist.

Similarly, when a job grows and requires more than one person to do it, a helper is hired. Whyte has described how a diner run by one person flourishes.[22] The owner is cook, waiter, cashier, purchasing agent, and greeter. When the business grows, the functions become specialized, and waiters, a cook, and a cashier are hired. If the business expands into a chain of restaurants, managers are needed as well as financial and promotional help. Specialized functions that aid coordination, development, and support are described as *staff.* They increase with organizational size and are usually distinguished from *line functions,* which have to do with the company's product or the service that the company performs.

When does growth become self-destructive? An animal that is too large to be able to eat enough in one day to maintain itself cannot survive. Haire points out that a shelf bracket must be strongest where it receives the heaviest load, that is, where it is most likely to break.[23] If growth of organization can lead to self-destruction, then it becomes essential that a theory must locate the points of greatest weakness. Organization theories therefore may be expected to differ in terms of where organizational weakness is perceived.

Haire, using growth trends, has sought to find underlying laws for the growth process and the interdependence of size, shape, and function.[24] He has studied the growth patterns of four different companies and found sufficient similarities to encourage the belief that growth models can be developed.

ORGANIZATIONS AS DEPENDENT SUBSYSTEMS

D. Katz and R. L. Kahn see the organization as made up of groups of people, each group forming a subsystem, for example, the production, maintenance, and personnel functions.[25] Each subsystem develops group goals and values that frequently conflict with those of other subsystems. To view the subsystems as interrelated only so far as production is concerned is to overlook the potential conflict in values developed within the subsystem. Communication between subsystems is complicated by the invisible boundaries that separate them. Organizational psychology thus must be sensitive to groups and the dependence of individual behavior on group norms and loyalties.

Katz and Kahn think of the human aspect of organizations as role systems and see behavior as fulfilling roles. Thus, persons in a given position behave according to their perceptions of what their job requires. Persons behave differently as they assume different roles or as their positions change. When a union steward is promoted to a supervisor, behavioral changes occur in accordance with the new role.[26]

DECISION-MAKING MODELS

Another group of theories emphasizes the decision-making process as the essential factor in organizational effectiveness. They approach decision making with a logical analysis and attempt to develop mathematical models that might aid in the solving of problems.[27] For example, a formula might be developed for the amount of overtime that is justified, considering backlog of orders, production scheduled, availability of temporary transfers, and so on. When the need arises, the manager fills in the appropriate figures and solves the equation to reach a decision.

Many of the terms and metaphors used by Freud in his theories were borrowed from those used by physicists in theories being developed at the same time. Analogously, many scientists in recent years have borrowed some terms and conceptual frameworks from computer design and technology. Both human beings and organizations have been characterized as *information-processing systems* in these models.

Several of these approaches (for example, expectancy theory) have been outlined previously and will be mentioned only briefly. These approaches conceptualize individual decision making as being based on perceived alternative outcome probabilities and payoffs.[28] Other scientists have suggested that for certain managerial functions (repetitive decision-making situations), algebraic models of managers may make more effective judgments than managers themselves.[29]

These models have their limits, as do all models. It has been shown that nonrational factors influence perceptions of probabilities. For example, an event is judged more likely if its availability to recall is high (if it is easy to think of similar past events). But availability can be influenced by subjective factors, such as familiarity, recency, and emotional level.[30] Also, the natural starting points used by many individuals for judging past and future events have been shown to be less susceptible to fine-tuning through new data than a rational model of human behavior would suggest.[31] This approach places emphasis on the quality dimension of the decisions rather than the acceptance dimension.

It is not uncommon for a large group of workers to develop poor job attitudes because the manager will not, or is not allowed to, deviate from a decision reached by mathematics.

Other theorists have applied the information-processing model to the organizational system as a whole.[32] Complex organizational tasks are broken into component parts and solved by specialists. Examination of organizational tasks in these terms has led to increased study of the relationships between individuals representing different functional groups. Gestalt psychologists would urge caution in the use of models that require the breaking up of problems into parts, solving these subproblems, and then deriving an overall answer additively. Although success has been claimed for individuals using this method in some instances,[33] others have criticized it, suggesting that subdividing a problem may not make it any simpler psychologically.[34] Moreover, differentiated aspects of problems do not integrate themselves automatically into the overall solutions that maximize effectiveness for the organization as a whole.

An organization may be ineffective because its decisions do not use knowledge and logic sufficiently or because its decisions fail to gain the acceptance of the persons who must implement them. If the decision-making method depends on the *type* of problem, the use of models should be restricted to appropriate problems, and this requires human judgment. Not surprisingly, theories differ according to the problems selected as representative of those of the organization.

ORGANIZATIONAL CLIMATE

Chapter 7 pointed out that the style of leadership establishes a climate that influences the behavior of the group. Although each leader determines the group's climate, there are overall styles in the organization that create a general climate. Some organizations are described as punitive — control is largely maintained by rules and penalties administered through punishment. In contrast, some university administrations may be described as permissive because they allow students a high degree of freedom. Some organizations tend to be paternalistic, a style that is usually determined by the head (or founder) of the organization. Climates of this kind are largely influenced by the personality of the president. In the not-too-distant past, managers were untrained and operated the units on a common sense basis; of course, common sense was influenced by how supervisors had been managed when they were at lower levels. Thus, to some extent, the climate perpetuates itself but also changes along with the personal values of the person in control.

A further factor must also be considered: hiring and promotion practices involve the selection of individuals who satisfy the norms of the established leaders. In one organization, a person may be regarded as unfit for a promotion because of being too rigid and punitive, whereas in another, the same person might be passed by because of being too lax. Between companies, climates differ in friendliness, seriousness, graciousness, orderliness, criticalness, and so on.

Within a company's hierarchy, however, we often find that managers have traits in common. This homogeneity stems partly from the fact that people tend to prefer associates who are alike in personality and attitudes[35] and partly from the fact that they become more alike by working and socializing with one another. In this way, certain organizational value systems develop. Some

years ago, the hiring practices of the companies within the Bell System were such that it was frequently compared to a fraternity. But within any given organization a variety of managerial practices can exist.

Researchers have tried to relate organizational climate to other factors, such as the organization's internal structure.[36] For example, it has been suggested that in more decentralized companies, the greater responsibility/authority held at lower levels leads to a climate in which people are more willing to take risks, feel greater support for their individual efforts, and are more motivated to aim for high standards.[37] These feelings, in turn, lead to a greater sense of identification with the loyalty to the organization.

In attempting to make the concept of organizational climate more specific (since it can include a number of dimensions, such as organizational structure, behavioral events, and perceptions), J. P. Campbell, et al. has offered a definition of *organizational climate*. He defines the term as encompassing four major dimensions: (1) the individual's autonomy, or area of freedom; (2) the degree of structure that the organization imposes on any given job; (3) the way in which the reward system operates; and (4) the availability and nature of support from supervisors.[38]

ORGANIZATION STRUCTURE AND RELATED ISSUES

SIZE OF WORK GROUPS

As groups increase in size, the relative contribution of each member of the group becomes smaller. This inverse relationship reduces both self-centered behavior and the individual's sense of importance. The skill of the leader becomes a factor in such cases. As groups become larger, the demands on the leader become more numerous and complex.[39] Clique formation also increases with group size.[40]

The influence of group size on productivity has not been established. Too much congeniality as well as too little could interfere with production, so the skill of the leader becomes a determining variable. When group bonuses and group piece rates are incentives, effectiveness declines as group size increases from under ten to fifty.[41]

Although the nature of the task must be considered in determining the size of a work group, the general conclusion is that smaller groups perform better than larger groups because they interact more effectively and require less guidance from higher authority.[42] Most organizations are structured into hierarchies so that leaders seldom have more than fifteen employees in their groups. A supervisor who has as many as fifty workers usually has group leaders who may be considered as an intermediate level in management. Even when the intermediate level is not formally established, informal subgroups form.[43]

ORGANIZATIONAL SIZE

As organizations increase in size, the individual finds it more difficult to identify with them. School spirit has declined as universities have increased in enrollment, and blind loyalty has often been replaced by fault finding. If people are to have feelings of loyalty, they must have a sense of identification. In business, it has generally been found that the size of both the organization and the department influence absenteeism, tardiness, accidents, and strikes. Small plants (under 500 persons) have the best record.[44] A comparison of units in an airline, ranging from 172 to 3,205 employees, showed a decrease in absenteeism in the small units where identification with the organization was more evident.[45]

As there are many advantages in the growth and development of large organizations, the problem is to find ways to facilitate identification and involvement. Chapter 8 emphasized the potential uses of group decision making. Other methods involve the development of teams or smaller work groups. One task of organizational psychologists is to invent additional ways to develop

Managers can derive job satisfaction from both tall and flat organizational hierarchies, depending often on the organization's size. (Ann McQueen)

identity and a feeling of belonging not only in a person's work group, but also in the community.

ORGANIZATIONAL HIERARCHY

Organizational hierarchies vary in the number of levels of management (as many as eight or more); and for a given size, the hierarchy might be described as *tall* (having many levels) or *flat* (having few levels). Large organizations would require more levels than small, but control might be centralized (tall) or decentralized (flat). What are the relative merits of this structuring of control?

First, job satisfaction within a given organization is greater for persons occupying higher levels than for those in lower levels.[46] This is understandable considering the increased influence and challenge that higher positions allow. However, a selectivity factor operates in that job interest leads to promotion.

With regard to flat versus tall structures, complicating factors are organizational size and the type of work. Certain sizes and kinds of work lend themselves better to tall hierarchies, while others are suited by flat hierarchies. Companies may be subdivided either according to geographical dispersion or to functional specialization. A chain of stores lends itself readily to decentralization, so each store manager is in charge of all functions. The store manager's advancement would be one of moving from smaller stores to larger ones. In contrast, a utility is divided on a functional basis, so that sales, services, accounting, overhead lines, and maintenance are considered divisions. For a given type of industry, companies that have the average number of echelons are the most successful.[47] Since a number of factors influence the type of hierarchy established,[48] it is desirable to determine how the type of structuring, as such, affects organizational success.

A disadvantage to centralization is that executives become specialized and cannot readily be moved from one department to another. With decentralization, all unit managers have more freedom for independent action. But the freedom delegated to them might stop at their levels, unless they in turn share some decision-making functions within their divisions.

An early study using an attitude-survey approach reported that flat structures were associated with more positive job attitudes than tall structures.[49] Since then it has been found that the relationship is more complex. In a study in which large and small organizations were analyzed, job satisfaction in large and small organizations was related to structure in opposite ways.[50] Managers, whose job satisfaction had been measured by a questionnaire, were classified as belonging to tall, intermediate, and flat structures. In organizations of less than 5,000 employees, job satisfaction was greater for the flat structures, but for large organizations, the reverse was true. Failure to distinguish between organizational size may explain why the relationship with structure was not more apparent.[51]

The solution to organizational effectiveness does not lie in the direction of finding the one most effective organizational structure. How the structure already in existence functions may be more crucial. Are the failures due more to the people or to the structure of the organization? Companies that attempt to solve their problems by repeated structural reorganizations may create dysfunctions in behavior by upsetting communication channels. However, as pointed out in Chapter 19, failure to adopt an organizational structure that is appropriate for the degree of environmental turbulence in the

THE ORGANIZATION AND THE ENVIRONMENT

industry may result in the failure of the organization.

THE CLASSIC CONCEPT

The classic organization chart shows the hierarchy of levels of management as well as the lines of accountability. Figure 20.1 is a simplified example of such a chart. In this figure the plant manager would be in charge of a plant, and this manager and others in similar jobs might be accountable to the operating vice president, who would be accountable to the president. The president in turn would be accountable to the chairperson and the board of directors. Top management ordinarily would include persons involved with the overall operation of the company in such areas as policy-setting, finance, and public relations. Middle management begins at the level when functions become specific (manufacturing, marketing, quality control, and research and development) and may include many levels. In Figure 20.1, only three levels are indicated (the plant manager, department heads, and first-line supervisors), but in larger organizations, departments may have section heads, superintendents, and general supervisor levels between department heads and first-line supervisors. The first-line supervisor is the lowest level of management. This person supervises

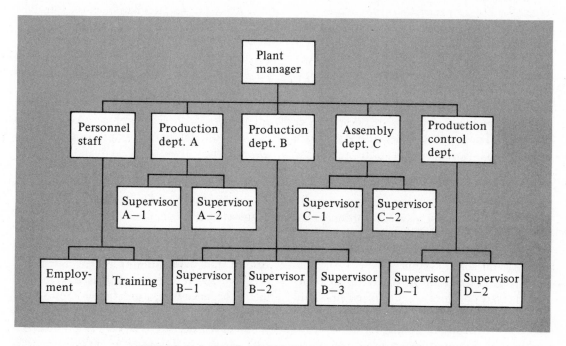

FIGURE 20.1 PART OF AN ORGANIZATION CHART
Three levels of management are indicated in the chart. The lines connecting the boxes show the supervisor-subordinate relationships.

nonmanagement people (hourly employees). Often the first-line supervisor is under pressure from both middle management and the union representing the workers (see also Chapter 7).

The chain-of-command concept implies that each person is accountable to an immediate supervisor and will receive assignments from that person only. This concept is intended to provide top management with effective control and coordination and to provide satisfaction to the employees, because they know what is expected of them and the criteria by which their performance will be judged. However, in actual practice, the chain of command does not always function in the manner in which its structure suggests. Some members have more influence than others, and many find it more expedient to take short cuts to avoid red tape.

Furthermore, pressures can come from varied sources to influence a person. A supervisor's boss may demand high production, the safety department may impose safety procedures that slow down production, and attitude surveys may supply higher management with evidence of poor worker attitudes. These varied expectations produce role conflict. Some organizations and some functions of an organization lend themselves more readily to the chain of command than others. In hospital settings, the nurse has a supervisor, but must also take orders from the doctors. Who is the real boss? Lack of clarity in supervisory roles makes for role conflict and role ambiguity.

In large organizations, the chain of command creates problems and is often slow and cumbersome. The president, if following the chain of command in getting a training program set up, would have to go through the vice president of personnel, who would go to the training department head, who would go to the training specialist to get a program prepared. The sources of misunderstanding in conveying this assignment would be great. Why not let the president discuss the problem with the specialist?

It is generally claimed that violations of the chain of command reduce employee satisfaction, as well as performance, and increase stress because they create role conflict and role ambiguity. Some research bears this out.[52] However, J. Woodward presents evidence that multiple-command relationships can be beneficial and satisfying.[53] In one organization, thirty supervisors received direction from five executives and twenty-eight reported that close association with five supervisors made them feel that they knew what was going on. The nature of the activity and the type of interpersonal relations involved appear to be crucial factors.

THE ROLE CONCEPT

In organizational psychology studies, a person in a given position is described as having a role.[54] Certain behaviors are expected of an individual in that position, and these constitute the person's role. The roles are not adequately defined; therefore, what is expected from the person who occupies a position is not always the same as what the occupier of the role *thinks* is expected.

How a role is perceived in a given organization is determined by several factors. One suggested list includes physical-technical systems (pressures imposed by the nature of the task itself), social-cultural systems (constraints and demands imposed by generally accepted social and ethical beliefs of people in the organization), and finally, individual opinions and attitudes of persons with whom the role-taker interacts.[55]

G. Graen suggests that earlier selection processes focused on matching the candidate with a fixed, or static, concept of the job.

More recent innovations, such as job enrichment, have demonstrated that a dynamic concept of a given role or position is more congruent with a changing organization in a changing environment.

Only when there is a great deal of distrust in an organization do disputes arise regarding whether an assignment falls within a job description. In labor-management disputes, this question may be raised, but in middle management, such disagreements are seldom aired.

Although violations of the chain-of-command principle may create role ambiguity and role conflict, these conditions can also arise from other sources, such as failures to communicate, different interpretations of the area of freedom, conflicts in goals or values, and personality clashes. The questionnaire method was used in one study to show that role conflict and ambiguity can be identified as separate factors.[56] Questions regarding how behavior is evaluated and the clarity of the job requirements were used to measure ambiguity. Questions relating to differences in values, the best way to do a job, reasonableness of assignments, the several roles involved, and incompatible requests were used to measure conflict. Both role conflict and ambiguity were negatively related to measures of need fulfillment and other job-satisfaction variables.

ROLE AMBIGUITY

According to R. L. Kahn et al., role ambiguity tends to increase with organizational size and complexity, rapid growth, frequent reorganizations, frequent changes in technology, and personnel changes accompanied by changes in management philosophies.[57] Individual differences exist in the ability to adapt to change. Nevertheless, the study showed that 35 percent of persons in a national sample was disturbed by not having a clear idea of responsibilities. Ambiguity was associated with increased tension, anxiety, fear, hostility, lowered job satisfaction, and loss of self-confidence. In many instances, lower production could be associated with these stresses.

Role ambiguity also is influenced by the supervisor. In general, studies show that the ability to give clear instructions and clear information is an important managerial skill.[58]

ROLE CONFLICT

Although the chain of command theoretically guards against a manager or supervisor having more than one boss, there still are other sources of role conflict. Kahn et al. cite several sources of conflict, including conflict tween supervisor's and subordinate's values or attitudes, gaps between role expectations and realistic ones, and conflict between expectations coming from different sources (for example, quantity and quality of output).[59] Whenever the person's job involves incompatible requirements, role conflict is a possible outcome. Surveys reporting the influence of role conflict are in general agreement that it "is associated with decreased satisfaction, coping behavior that would be dysfunctional for the organization, and experiences of stress and anxiety."[60]

BOUNDARY ROLES

The theory of organizations as open systems focused attention on those organization members who operate at the borderline, or *boundary,* of the organization.[61] Their functions involve the *acquisition* of raw materials and parts, capital, personnel, technology, information, and good will, as well as the *disposal* of goods, services, waste products, information, and so on. Job titles and departments on the boundary typically include marketing, sales, purchasing, recruiters, advertising, public relations specialists, and lobbyists.

As the turbulence of the environment grows, the need for, and dependence on such employees increases. These individuals have special problems. Persons with boundary roles are more distant, organizationally, psychologically, and often physically, from other organization members. Several factors—chiefly their constant interaction with outsiders—may cause role conflict for them. Periodic inspirational sales meetings and limited tours of foreign duty are examples of ways in which management tries to keep its boundary-role members loyal to the home organization.

BYPASSING

Bypassing is a term used when one intermediate level (or more) is skipped in communicating upward or downward in the chain of command. The dotted line *a* in Figure 20.2 shows an employee going to the boss's supervisor regarding some matter. Most supervisors would frown on this tactic, but suppose the employee wanted a transfer or questioned the boss's competence? Should the employee quit the company or should doors higher up be open? Some companies

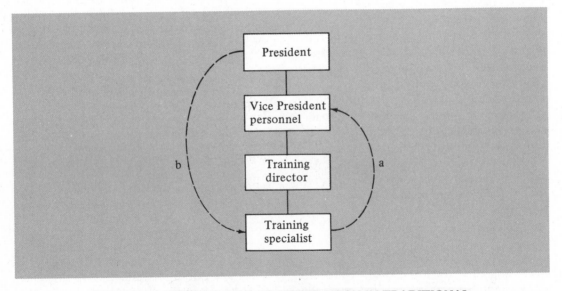

FIGURE 20.2 BYPASSING — FROWNED UPON IN TRADITIONAL MANAGEMENT THEORY

A training specialist had an idea that required extra money for the training department, which needed the approval of the vice president. The idea would be most likely to get approval if the training specialist could talk directly with the vice president (dotted line *a*). However, this would compel the specialist to bypass the immediate supervisor. Bypassing in the opposite direction (dotted line *b*) would occur if the president wanted to explore a problem in management training with the training specialist. It would be more fruitful to talk to the company expert in the field than with generalists, but this would involve bypassing two levels of supervision.

pride themselves on having an open-door policy because it permits upward communication.

In other instances, an employee wants clarification. For example, Barbara Kee's boss's supervisor has requested a report, which has been passed on to Barbara because she is an expert on the matter in question. If she asks questions of her boss, who in turn must talk to his boss, time is not efficiently used and many opportunities for misunderstanding are introduced. Certainly such a matter could be best handled if the person who was to do the job could talk it over with the person who requested it. How to do this without making Ms. Kee's boss feel bypassed is really the issue.

Bypassing also occurs when a higher level manager gives an assignment to a subordinate's subordinate (dotted line *b* in Figure 20.2) or to a specialist even lower in rank. In small businesses, this is a common problem because a top executive (often the owner) may change a production schedule when getting a big order is contingent on early delivery. In such instances, it is most efficient to deal directly with the person in charge of the production of the needed product. Shifting priorities and schedules may be good business in certain respects, but it may upset carefully made plans regarding work units that are dependent on one another. Such bypassing creates role conflict for the recipient and role ambiguity for the person bypassed.

Managers also bypass when they have lost trust in their immediate subordinate and detour because the person's subordinates are more competent. This practice creates new problems while avoiding others.

Instead of viewing bypassing as either desirable or undesirable, it seems best to pose situations that generate bypassing as problems to be solved. How can a manager get priority changes made when the need arises with a minimal disruption of ongoing plans? What should a manager do when an intermediate level of management complicates communication downward? When several levels of management and managers of different but concerned work groups are involved, group problem solving seems to be the way to resolve the various conflicts created. There is no simple rule; the chain-of-command relationship creates red tape and inefficiency, whereas ignoring formal relationships creates many forms of ambiguity and leads to loss of accountability. How to achieve the advantages and avoid the disadvantages of a practice generates a problem, and each problem needs to be solved separately because there is no general answer.

POWER AS A COMMUNICATION BARRIER

Supervisors tend to view their jobs in terms of their responsibilities. They must keep their subordinates busy, satisfied, and productive. Employees tend to view their supervisors' jobs as positions of power. These differences in perception are sources of misunderstanding, so differences in rank become communication barriers.

For example, an employee meeting a fellow employee in the washroom might say, "Having a nice smoke, Joe?" Joe might respond by offering a cigarette, saying, "Yup, have one." If the supervisor had entered and said the same thing in the same tone of voice, Joe's response might have been, "Yup, just finishing up, boss." If we take it a step higher and have the superintendent making the statement, Joe might have acted as if caught in the act and made a hasty exit. Thus, the meaning of the same words spoken in the same tone of voice with the same friendly intent changes, depending on the number of levels between persons.

The difference in level between hourly workers and company officials is so great that workers do not see officials as human beings, often referring to them as "the brass." The president of a company may, while on the golf course, merely express a wish that the weather were like that in California, and thereby give rise to a rumor that the plant is to be moved.

All environmental factors that suggest status (rugs, desks, secretaries in an outer office, special parking, and so on) strengthen the barriers imposed by rank, making upward communication a more serious problem. Subordinates keep bad news from management, cover up problems, avoid taking chances, protect one another, and in general, play it safe. Even though the supervisor does nothing to discourage free expression, the position alone is enough to inhibit it. The solution to this problem in an organization is not to abolish rank, but to make the barriers more permeable and eliminate needless status symbols. Communication proceeds much better when a discussion is held in the subordinate's office rather than in the manager's. Many top-management personnel follow this practice.

Awareness of the difference in perception is the first step in dealing with this communication barrier, because misunderstandings create defensive behavior which in turn increases the barrier. The development of discussion leadership skills is a second, but this requires management training.[62]

The influence of rank was demonstrated by a study that showed a correlation of .88 between an impartial observer's ratings of influence and rank in leaderless discussion groups.[63] When the discussion dealt with company matters, the correlation was higher than when it dealt with other topics.[64]

Employees also view their bosses in terms of the extent of their influence on higher management. Managers who are viewed as having high influence are more able to induce change in their subordinates than those who are seen as lacking in influence.[65] Whether perceived influence is desirable may be questioned. It may indicate that the supervisors are able to instill fear, and as such, they violate the leadership principles discussed in Chapter 8 and the motivational principles discussed in Chapter 13. Or it might indicate that they are willing and able to remedy conditions when employees complain. Power and influence represent two types of control and are the bases for different leadership styles. Persons concerned with change, such as staff specialists, often feel that they could accomplish more if they had more power to impose the change with the backing of higher management. Such changes lack the acceptance of the line organization, and communication barriers between staff and line (or different subsystems within the organization) become more firmly established.

AREA OF FREEDOM AND ORGANIZATIONAL LEVEL

Every management position has an area of freedom that determines the kinds of decisions the manager can make. Even though the manager and subordinate do not always agree on the exact boundaries, each manager's behavior is restricted by the job, company policy, legislation, and sometimes by union contracts. Within these boundaries, a manager can make the needed decisions or share the function with subordinates. Regardless of how much decision making is shared, the manager is still accountable for the results that the decision produces.

As we examine the area of freedom at different levels in the organization, the scope of the decisions' implications changes. Top management's area of freedom relates to such matters as financing, setting production goals, and establishing policies, all of which involve the company as a whole. Department heads are responsible for decisions that relate to their departments as a subsystem and involve the setting of department goals, integration of dependent functions, allocating departmental funds, implementing overall company policy, and so on. A superintendent's function would involve how to distribute overtime and how to keep company practices uniform. The supervisors' areas of freedom are less concerned with what to do and more with such decisions as how the job should be done and who should do it. They are also responsible for scheduling the work, maintaining discipline, and so on.

Thus, a top-management decision of an airline to purchase a new type of plane would take the problem out of the planning committee and put it into operations. The implementation of the decision would affect sales, ground service, flight crews, reservations, accounting, personnel, and flight scheduling departments in different ways, and each would have problems to solve. Within each department, the problem would go from middle management to the first-line level. How the problems change from higher to lower levels is partly a matter of delegation. At each level, certain functions are passed to the level below, and in this way, the successive boundaries for the areas of freedom are established.

DELEGATION

One vital key to an organization's effectiveness resides in the process of delegation. A manager gets things done through other people, but there is more to running an organization than getting the product or service out. Problems must be solved, plans must be made, and priorities must be appraised. These activities, as well as the production work, must be shared.

Perhaps the most important reason why the traditional concept of management is unrealistic is that accountability can become a threat and hence restrict freedom to solve problems. Executives may excuse their own mistakes, but how generous are they with the mistakes of others? In an effort to retain control at the top, organizations tend to be governed by rules and regulations that allow no ways to adapt to unusual or changing situations. For instance, employees who for personal reasons cannot get to work on time may be discharged even when they are willing to work after hours and this extra coverage would be beneficial to the company. Without delegation, there is little opportunity to deal with problems that are exceptions to the rules. The manager then merely serves to administer the regulations.

As organizations have become larger and technologically complex, more activities have been delegated, so that even the lowest-level supervisor has freedom to solve certain problems and make some decisions. The use of this freedom is part of their jobs, and whether they share this freedom with subordinates or make all decisions themselves is beside the point. How effectively they use this freedom is a matter of accountability.

In order to give each level of management opportunities to solve problems and to permit adaptation to changing conditions, it is in the interest of an organization to pass down as much decision making as possible. Thus, although individual supervisors cannot be permitted to set working hours because uniformity of hours may be essential, they should be able to make decisions about work assignments. In this matter, they may make the decision themselves or be influenced by their workers. Department heads may make decisions regarding space priorities in their sections, but they could delegate to their subordinates the responsibility of deciding how best to use the space.

In each case, the decision could be participative or unilateral, but the decision made indicates the area of freedom for the level below. As needs for problem-solving opportunities increase, the delegated areas of freedom might be expanded. But it also follows that the larger the area of freedom, the more able the manager must be in using it. The recent emphasis on management training indicates that the recognition of managers' skill requirement is increasing.

BOUNDARIES OF
THE AREA OF FREEDOM

Managers and their subordinates have quite different perceptions of the duties, responsibilities, and problems of the subordinate. There is more disagreement than agreement between them on these matters. The resolution to this discrepancy requires that a clear understanding between them be reached. This requires a discussion in which the perceptions of each are explored freely.

The effects of vague versus clear and large versus small areas of freedom were experimentally tested.[66] When the area of freedom is vague, subordinates behave as if they had less freedom than they actually have because they do not want to risk criticism. If the area of freedom is small, they are more inclined to do a poor job of problem solving because they think routinely. Merely telling managers how much freedom they have to carry out an assignment is not an effective way to delegate.

STAGES OF DELEGATION

As previously pointed out, the job description does not successfully determine or communicate the tasks that a manager should perform. With the same job description, two managers do not permit the same freedoms for their subordinates and two subordinates of the same supervisor do not perceive their freedoms in the same way. Subordinates differ in personality and ability, and see their assignments from different perspectives. Generally speaking, supervisors want their subordinates to be less dependent and to take more initiative, and subordinates, in general, feel they could do a better job if they had more freedom.

Both supervisor and subordinate favor the subordinates' having more freedom, yet subordinates do not take as much as is expected of them. The reason is largely fear. Employees assume that they can get into more trouble for what they *do* than for what they *fail to do*. Good decisions may not be noticed, but mistakes usually are. Such sources of inhibition, if real or imagined, can best be removed through clarification of delegation. Inconsistencies in a supervisors's behavior might be discovered as part of the problem.

Employees differ in experience, ability, and personality, and therefore they should not be given the same amount of freedom. Similarly, supervisors differ in that they are not equally ready to grant the same degree of freedom to others that their positions permit. Because of these differences, delegation should be tailored to fit the persons involved. In order to accomplish this, delegation should not be regarded as an all-or-nothing process, but one that involves stages; different degrees of delegation may be given for the different activities that a manager supervises.

Table 20.1 shows four stages of delegation. In Stage 1, the subordinates work without supervision. They are given the responsibility of performing their duties, but they have no authority to alter the job procedures

TABLE 20.1 STAGES OF DELEGATION

STAGE	AREA OF FREEDOM
1	Carrying out assignments, enforcing rules, giving assignments. No decision making other than who does what.
2	Stage 1 plus the expectation to make suggestions for improvement. Changes must be approved by supervisor.
3	Stage 2 plus participation in problem solving and decision making. Assume supervisor practices group decision.
4	Full delegation. Subordinates run things as they see fit. They are accountable for results but not how results are obtained.

or introduce changes. They have freedom to plan their work and make assignments. In Stage 2, the subordinates are expected to think and make suggestions to improve their operations, but they must obtain approval from higher management before making changes. Supervisors should be aware that vetoing too many suggestions will cause subordinates to revert to Stage 1. In Stage 3, a supervisor shares problem solving with individual employees, and with subordinates as groups when solutions involve the group as a whole. Training in group decision and group problem solving would tend to develop this type of delegation. Stage 4 represents full delegation. The managers run their units as if they were the owners. As owners, they are accountable and suffer if the operation is not successful. Like a head football coach who is not told by higher management how to run the team, having a poor season could cause termination of the job contract.

These four stages of delegation do not apply to all subordinates and to all duties in the same way. For example, the regional head responsible for installation of overhead lines in a telephone company might have decisions to make regarding (1) transferring crews, (2) permitting overtime, (3) setting production goals, (4) enforcing safety, and (5) making changes in work priorities. How much freedom should the department head give the regional heads since they differ in experience and ability?

Table 20.2 shows how the stages of delegation in each of these decision areas may be tailored to fit the employees involved. Sub-

TABLE 20.2 DELEGATION ACCORDING TO ABILITY AND DECISION AREAS

DECISION AREAS	CREWS	OVERTIME	PRODUCTION	SAFETY	PRIORITIES
Subordinate A	Stage 2	Stage 2	Stage 3	Stage 4	Stage 3
Subordinate B	Stage 4	Stage 3	Stage 4	Stage 2	Stage 3
Subordinate C	Stage 1	Stage 3	Stage 2	Stage 1	Stage 3
Subordinate D	Stage 1	Stage 1	Stage 2	Stage 1	Stage 3
Subordinate E	Stage 4	Stage 4	Stage 4	Stage 4	Stage 3

ordinates B and E are trusted and experienced, Subordinate D is new and developing. Stage 3 can be used for training; with respect to priorities, the group as a whole is consulted. As subordinates acquire more experience and as the supervisor develops more and more confidence in the judgments of certain individuals, the degree of delegation for various decision areas would change from year to year. These patterns of delegation should be reached through discussion, during which the needs of both supervisor and subordinate are frankly communicated. If one employee feels unfairly treated, the discussion in which priorities were set may not have been frank and open. Formal organization charts and job descriptions cannot be adapted to fit the personalities involved, and hence lead to reduced effectiveness, informal organizations, and job ambiguity.

MANAGEMENT BY OBJECTIVES

A procedure known as management by objectives (MBO) has been introduced, and a number of companies have been influenced by it (see also Chapter 13).[67] The basic concept is that managers of different levels in an organization should participate in reaching agreement on goals of mutual interest and define the major areas of responsibility in terms of the results expected of the subordinate. With specific measurable goals established, the contribution toward these goals can be assessed. Thus, a lower-level manager can be judged by results. Theoretically, this practice should lead to motivation to produce, and the manager would be appraised by results, not in terms of how they were produced.

In practice, several types of violations occur. Too frequently the higher-ranking manager dominates the goal setting and the subordinate submits, so the motivational value of goal setting by participation is lost. Then, too, the goals discussed often are not measurable, or they are too vague. A goal to outperform last year's record should specify in which ways and by how much. When asked to set goals, do lower-ranking managers assume that they must do better and hence set unrealistic goals, or do they play it safe and suggest low ones? Does the manager permit the subordinate to indicate in what way the subordinate expects certain kinds of help and does the manager explore these needs? Joint goal setting involves problem-solving skills on the part of the manager, and such interactions not only could lead to motivated performance but could go beyond mere goal setting by introducing improvements initiated from below.

Since management by objectives is more a philosophy than a training program, what can be expected when it is adopted by an organization? A study of the results in two companies revealed some positive gains.[68] There were some gains in satisfaction of higher-type needs (self-actualization) and in security needs when the program had good support of top management. Essential to improvement seemed to be the need for progress interviews with supervisors. Complaints also resulted.[69] These included excessive time spent in counseling and overemphasis on quantitative goals, the first of which is related to need satisfaction and the second of which reflects the need to escape measurement. Management by objectives seems to raise problems similar to those generated in performance-evaluation interviews. If problem solving occurs, performance can be improved by correcting the situation rather than the person, but when the supervisor stands in judgment and attempts to improve the person, defensiveness is likely to occur.

UPWARD COMMUNICATION

The fact that presidents of large organizations do not have the control that they are led to believe that they have is illustrated by the following incident. A company had a policy of giving its employees the day before Christmas off. Each year this "gift" was announced by the president. On one occasion, the vice president of personnel brought the official form to the president for his signature. The president noticed that the day to be announced as a holiday was December 23 and indicated that this was not company policy. The vice president pointed out that December 24 fell on a Saturday and since that was not a work day, he had assumed the day to be given as a gift would be December 23. The president said that since employees already had December 24 off, it would not be necessary to give it to them and refused to sign the proclamation. When December 23 arrived, no one except top management appeared for work. All others merely assumed they had the day off. No one ever told the president that his decision had been violated. Some time later, the president chided the vice president about his fears of a drop in morale. Communication depends on trust, and when fear is involved, bad news is suppressed. In this respect, subordinates show considerable cooperation.

An organization's hierarchy is designed to coordinate the functions of the various work groups. Middle management represents a link between top management and the first-level work groups. Facilitating communication through this hierarchy of middle management is one of the major problems in organizations. Traditionally, the direction of communication is downward. Yet it is well known that effective communication is a two-way street—both the receiver and the sender must be able to interact.[70] As a result of failure experienced while following the established channels, the lines of communication often are bypassed, unofficial channels (for example, the grapevine) are created, and even channels of communication outside the line organization arise. These represent detours developed because the official channels are inadequate. One company president has remarked that, as a middle manager coming up through the ranks, she had had better luck in finding out about organizational policy and personnel changes by calling her friends at a certain branch office than by calling headquarters directly.

Several types of communication channels exist outside the organizational chain of command. In recent years, opinion surveys have been found useful. Workers' opinions are surveyed, and the results are communicated directly to top management. Thus, the surveys represent one form of upward communication initiated by management.

Other channels are the suggestion box and the personnel department. The suggestion box gives the individual employee an opportunity to present an idea up the line without depending on a supervisor's approval. The personnel office can serve a communication function by interviewing disgruntled employees and persons who are quitting the company. The information gained can be shared with higher management.

The formation of a union by workers is an example of upward communication initiated by workers. The union serves as the voice of the workers, and its representatives deal directly with representatives of top management. In the absence of adequate upward communication via middle management, the union office becomes an influential communication channel. But in recent years rank-and-file failure to ratify tentative union agreements has become fairly commonplace, which indicates that union members may have difficulty communicating upward to union officials, as well as to management.

We have already seen how communication is facilitated in primary discussion groups. The discussion permits direct two-way communication. If first-line supervisors hold problem-solving discussions, they can become aware of the attitudes and ideas of their subordinates. What if the second-line supervisors also held discussions with the first-line supervisors who report to them. They would not only learn their opinions but also get some idea of the problems experienced by the first-line supervisors. In this way, each first-line supervisor would be a potential source of information. Similarly, the third level of management could have meetings with second-line supervisors, who would become sources of information not only for their own problems but also for the problems that had been communicated up to them.

If this type of process were practiced at each level, two-way communication inside the organizational structure, from bottom to top, would become a natural function. Even if some lower-level employees were not dependable or were reluctant to speak up, communication would not be blocked. Managers in the hierarchy would have as many sources of information as they had employees reporting to them. They need only the desire and the skill to use the available sources.

Figure 20.3 diagrammatically describes how the supervisor is both the leader (center of a circle) of a group of employees and a member of a group (point on circumference of another circle) reporting to a higher level. Thus, each member of management becomes a link between lower levels and a supervisor. In these two roles, each member

of management becomes a key figure in the communication channel inside the line organization.* The channel for one such chain is shown in Figure 20.3 as the vertical line starting with S_1 and reaching to top management.

The left part of the figure shows how improved communication can occur inside the organization if all levels of management hold problem-solving discussions. The small circle shows a ring of employees (e) who have opportunities to participate in solving problems when discussions are led by the first-line supervisor (S_1). The next circle shows how the first-line supervisors participate in solving problems with their supervisor (S_2). To complete the figure, these interlocking circles would have to be continued (to represent every hierarchical level) until the president was shown as the center of a group of vice presidents.

The right half of the figure shows the possible detours by which the workers communicate upward in the absence of an adequate channel inside the organizational structure. Because of inadequate upward communication, higher management must rely on surveys and the union to reveal worker attitudes and values. The need to improve the two-way communication inside the organizational structure increases as companies become larger and the gap between top and bottom widens because of an increase in intermediate levels. Upward communication within the organization can supply more constructive and accurate information for high-level decisions.

---

*Likert describes the supervisor who is a lower-level member of one group and also a supervisor to a group of employees as a *linking-pin,* serving a valuable coordinating function not only within the line, but between line and staff functions. Likert, R. *The human organization.* New York: McGraw-Hill, 1967.

THE ORGANIZATION AND THE ENVIRONMENT

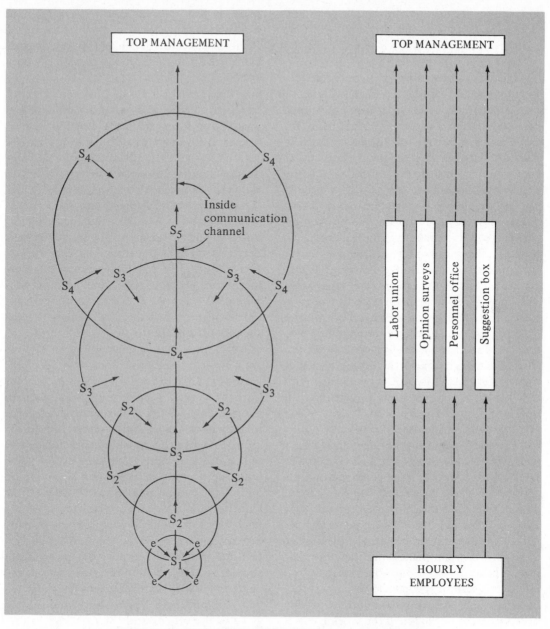

FIGURE 20.3 UPWARD COMMUNICATION CHANNELS

This simplified drawing is intended to show how each member of management is both the central figure for one circle and a peripheral figure on the next. This dual function of the supervisor can promote better communication in the organization, providing there actually is a two-way process, as in group discussion. The small arrows in each circle indicate communication from the several group members to the leader, while the solid vertical line shows a communication chain from bottom to top. Right diagram shows detours developed because of inadequate upward communication.

SOURCE: After N. R. F. Maier, *Principles of human relations*. New York: John Wiley & Sons, Inc. 1952. Used with permission of Ayesha Maier.

ORGANIZATIONAL REPORTING AND CONTROL SYSTEMS

Upward communication can be voluntary or involuntary. Budget reports, performance evaluation, production reports, and so on, are means that supervisors have for monitoring subordinates' productivity. Today, with the aid of data-processing equipment, much information about employee performance can be made available quickly for review by top management. In most companies, pay, promotion, and other rewards are tied to the results indicated in such reports. Therefore, they can be viewed as instruments for controlling both the organization and individual members' behavior.[71]

Using impersonal, quantified data as a basis for distributing rewards in the organization has been justified on the grounds that it is less susceptible to bias than feedback filtered through several layers of management. Yet resistance to cooperating with data gathering and analysis is common. If one purpose of this approach is to be more fair, why do people object to it?

One researcher has suggested several reasons.[72] First, the use of such systems interferes with the power balance in the organization—new and powerful "experts" arise, while others find their power, expertise, and alliances eroding. Second, the increased accuracy can be a threat as well as a blessing—after all, everyone makes mistakes, but few like to have them aired to top management. Finally, for some people, such impersonal measures of performance reduce intrinsic need satisfaction, the fun of the work itself.[73]

These concerns are exacerbated when a new measurement system deals with an area in which people feel inexperienced and vulnerable, or when it is imposed without their participation. People may prefer the company as it is or feel that rewards are too tightly tied to performance on the measures. Personality factors, such as low self-esteem, can make the measures especially worrisome.

When these conditions hold, control systems produce responses that are counterproductive for individuals and the organization. They may cause people to become rigidly bureaucratic and picky,[74] they may become uncooperative and unproductive, or they may produce a lot of invalid data. J. S. Berliner found, for example, that Soviet plant managers (who are rewarded for high volume) hoard supplies, purposely overorder, and buy on the black market—behaviors that help raise their own rewards but are inefficient for the economic system as a whole.[75]

Pressure to slant the data is higher when the individual reporting results sees the data as crucial to his or her standing in the organization. Other conditions that affect the accuracy of data include: (1) how clear it is, (2) how subjective it is, and (3) how much control the individual has over it. The information that goes on a person's performance evaluation is probably more difficult to influence than, say, an estimate of how many potential customers stopped at a trade booth run by that person. Most of the anxiety and duplicity involved in control systems arises from differences between management and employees about what should be measured and about how the information should be judged and used, and about the degree to which individual interests and rewards should be sacrificed when the greater good of the organization is at stake.

Unfortunately, as long as companies rely on extrinsic motivators (such as pay) to persuade people to work hard, there is little chance that the judges and the judged will agree on how control systems should operate. Ideally, control systems should be separated from rewards[76] and their information used to provide feedback in a participative system with moderately high but achievable standards. To institute such changes would be difficult, but if management were committed to this course, group problem-solving leadership skills could provide a reasonable way for developing a participative feedback system.

CROSS-FUNCTIONAL RELATIONS

INTERDEPENDENCE AND PEER NETWORKS

Viewing the organization as a set of interdependent subsystems points up the need to analyze the relationship of groups to one another and to the accomplishment of overall tasks. Researchers have hypothesized differences in the potential for conflict between groups, based on such characteristics as the type and frequency of their need for interaction.[77] In some companies, certain functions can operate with a minimal degree of interaction. But in other functions, such as that of product managers, day-to-day activities depend on the competence and cooperation of people in other functional groups.

Recently, R. M. Kanter indicated the importance of cross-functional relationships with peers, often called *peer networks*.[78] This importance was shown indirectly by the negative effect of lesser access to such networks on the power and performance of women managers and others. (Others would include those in staff or first-level supervisory positions.) Without a ready supply of highly desired information to trade, managers cannot "buy" the organizational resources and high-quality personnel that will ensure their future success.

DIFFERENTIATION AND INTEGRATION

Organizational efforts must be integrated in order to be effective. However, the problem of integration is more complex when task functions are highly differentiated. Specialization not only involves functional differences in work, but the persons who perform the functions differ in interests, attitudes, training, and job objectives. Thus, the problem of finding mutual interests between different units (so that cooperation is possible) increases with specialization. A manager who supervises several specialized activities must integrate these functions. This problem is quite different from that of a manager who has to integrate functions in different geographical areas. The specialized industries in general require greater effort to achieve the same level of integration as less differentiated industries.

Taking specialization of function into consideration because of the different environments, the variations in goal orientation, and the varying degrees of industry stability, P. R. Lawrence and J. W. Lorsch postulated the following: organizations having a relatively slow rate of technological change and low diversity in environment (for example, the container industries) should have less difficulty achieving integration than organizations having rapidly changing technologies and high diversity in job functions (for example, the plastics industries).[79] Their findings indicated that the most successful organizations were those that came closer to dealing with differentiation in a manner that was consistent with the type of industry and environment. Industries having a relatively slow rate of technological change were able to achieve integration between functions with little effort. The attitudes and goals of people in research and of those in production, for example, were similar enough that they could resolve conflicts involving their mutual areas through problem-solving conversations with one another. In the more differentiated industries, the outlook and job objectives of a research scientist and a production manager were so different that integration of function was achieved only with the help of a liaison person, *the integrator,* who understood both viewpoints and whose function was to help these specialists to communicate with one another.

When the problem of integration involves diverse functions, group problem solving could be highly beneficial. Both the specialists and the integrator would profit by training in group problem-solving skills.

Traditionally, a supervisor deals with only a few workers, and communication about the job is relatively simple. But in modern technical industries, an operator may have not only a supervisor, but a safety advisor, an engineering advisor, and a quality-control advisor as well. Obviously, the worker must deal with all these influences, and conflicts are inevitable. The same problems in communication also arise at higher levels. Thus, the importance of the integrative function is directly related to the amount of technological change and diversity in an industry.

H. J. Leavitt has worked extensively with communication problems in organizations, finding that control, satisfaction, cooperation, and competition often conflict.[80] Some suggested remedies are (1) decentralization to shorten communication channels and transfer more decision making to lower levels; (2) separation of staff functions from line to distribute responsibility of function; (3) use of committees to open up channels of communication; (4) increase in amount of horizontal communication to coordinate goals that might be in conflict; and (5) development of methods for sensing organizational conflicts to permit problem solving before they become acute. It seems that the need for these remedies would vary with the degree of differentiation and the amount of required integration. Some organizational structures and communication channels might serve one purpose, others a different purpose. All structures seem to suffer from a deficiency in upward communication.

Persons should not be restricted by structured channels that impede informal communication. Successful communication depends more on the skill of the people involved than on the formal structure of the organization.

CONFLICT MANAGEMENT

Conflict can be defined as a process that is started when one individual is frustrated by another. In some cases, the individual who is the source of frustration is perceived by the frustrated person as being the representative of a group, or the actions are perceived as representing the furtherance of group, rather than individual, goals.

Conflict, thus defined, inherently involves emotional factors. But people can differ in their opinions without conflict resulting. As L. R. Hoffman and N. R. F. Maier have shown,[81] when disagreement is handled skillfully, it can lead to more innovative solutions, rather than to emotional bickering or win-or-lose power plays.[82]

Many sources of conflict-provoking frustrations exist in the organization. One person gets promoted and the others who wanted the job are unhappy; limited budget funds mean that Peter is robbed to pay Paula; someone knowingly or unknowingly violates the rules or norms of another group or hurts another's feelings or embarrasses an individual in front of peers. Personality differences aside, different kinds of training, different organizational goals, and different control/reward systems generate the variances in perception that often lead to frustration and conflict.

A conflict is generated—rather than a group problem-solving session—because of the nature of a frustrated individual. The aggressiveness and childishness characterizing frustration block out more mature perceptions, such as recognizing the merit in another person's view or realizing that they have a mutual interest in finding a solution. Not seeing differences as problems to be solved, however, doesn't always lead to conflict. In the interests of getting on with the job, evidence of the underlying conflict may be suppressed.[83] The result may be a rigid system of set rules, which serve less and less well as demands outside and inside the organization change.

Conflict has been studied both as a process (A does this to B, B reacts, A responds and so on) and as a structural phenomenon. The latter stresses the long-standing pressures and constraints that frequently engender conflict.[84] The two models are complementary rather than competitive, for each illustrates different sources and kinds of conflict.

Obviously, the best way to deal with conflict is to avoid it through a problem-solving approach that focuses on the facts. This is not always possible, however, particularly when two or more groups are concerned. In some cases, conflict may be deliberately fomented for political rather than task-oriented, reasons. In this case, group members must begin by formulating the best means for moving the situation out of the emotional sphere and back onto a problem-solving track.

NOTES

1. Clark, B. R. *The distinctive college*. Chicago: Aldine, 1970; Clark, B. R. The organizational saga in higher education. *Admin. Sci. Quart.*, 1972, *17*, 178–184.
2. Argyris, C. *Interpersonal competence and organizational effectiveness*. Homewood, Ill.: Irwin-Dorsey, 1962.
3. Whyte, W. F. An interaction approach to the theory of organization. In M. Haire (Ed.), *Modern organization theory*. New York: Wiley, 1959.
4. Bakke, E. W. Concept of the social organization. In M. Haire, op cit.
5. Dubin, R. Stability of human organizations. In M. Haire, op. cit.
6. Blake, R. R., and Mouton, J. S. *Corporate excellence through grid organization development*. Houston, Tex.: Gulf, 1968.
7. Likert, R. *The human organization: Its management and value*. New York: McGraw-Hill, 1967; Bowers, D. G., and Seashore, S. E. Predicting organizational effectiveness with a four-factor theory of leadership. *Administration Sci. Quart.*, 1966, *11*, 238–263.
8. Likert, R. *New patterns of management*. New York: McGraw-Hill, 1967.
9. Marrow, A. J. *Making management human*. New York: McGraw-Hill, 1957.
10. McGregor, D. *Leadership and motivation*. Cambridge, Mass.: MIT Press, 1966.
11. McGregor, D., ibid.
12. Ouchi, W. G. *Theory Z: How American business can meet the Japanese challenge*. Reading, Mass.: Addison-Wesley, 1981.
13. Pascale, R. T. and Athos, A. G. *The art of Japanese management*. New York: Simon & Schuster, 1981.
14. Blake, R. R., and Mouton, J. S. *The managerial grid*. Houston, Tex.: Gulf, 1964.

15. Stogdill, R. M., and Coons, A. E. Leader behavior: Its description and measurement. *Res. Monogr. 88,* Columbus, Ohio: Ohio State Univ., Bureau of Bus. Research, 1957.

16. Lowen, A., Hrapchak, W. J., and Kavanagh, M. J. Consideration and initiating structure: An experimental investigation of leadership traits. *Admin. Sci. Quart.,* 1969, *14,* 238–253.

17. Fleishman, E. A., and Harris, E. F. Patterns of leadership behavior related to employee grievances and turnover. *Personnel Psychol.,* 1962, *15,* 43–56.

18. Filley, A. C., and House, R. J. *Managerial process and organizational behavior.* Glenview, Ill.: Scott, Foresman, 1969.

19. Fiedler, F. E. *A theory of leadership effectiveness.* New York: McGraw-Hill, 1967.

20. Argyris, C. Problems and new directions for industrial psychology. In M. D. Dunnette (Ed.), *Handbook of industrial and organizational psychology.* Chicago: Rand McNally, 1976.

21. Haire, M. Biological models and empirical histories of the growth of organizations. In M. Haire (Ed.), op. cit.

22. Whyte, W. F. *Human relations in the restaurant industry.* New York: McGraw-Hill, 1948.

23. Haire, op. cit.

24. Ibid.

25. Katz, D., and Kahn, R. L. *The social psychology of organizations.* New York: Wiley, 1966.

26. Lieberman, J. The effects of changes in roles on the attitudes of role occupants. *Hum. Relat.,* 1956, *9,* 385–402.

27. Cyert, R. M., and March, J. G. *Behavior theory of the firm.* Englewood Cliffs, N.J.: Prentice-Hall, 1963; Goldberg, W. (Ed.), *Behavioral approaches to modern management,* Vol. 1, *Information systems and decision making,* Vol. 2, *Applications of marketing, production, and finance.* Gothenberg, Sweden: Studies in Business Administration, 1970; Hedberg, B. *On man-computer interaction in organizational decision-making: A behavioral approach.* Gothenberg, Sweden: Studies in Business Administration, 1970; March, J. G., and Simon, H. *Organizations.* New York: Wiley, 1958; Marshak, J. Efficient and viable organizational forms. In M. Haire (Ed.), op. cit., pp. 307–320.

28. See Slovic, P., Fischoff, B., and Lichtenstein, S. Behavioral decision theory. *Ann. Rev. Psychol.,* 1977, *28,* 1–39; MacCrimmon, K. R. Managerial decision making. In J. W. McGuire (Ed.), *Contemporary management: Issues and viewpoint.* Englewood Cliffs, N.J.: Prentice-Hall, 1974, pp. 445–495; Barron, F. H. Behavioral decision theory: A topical bibliography for management scientists. *Interface,* 1974, *5,* 56–62; Kahneman, D., and Tversky, A. Subjective probability: A judgment of representativeness. *Cogn. Psychol.,* 1972, *3,* 430–454.

29. Ashton, R. H. User prediction models in accounting: An alternative use. *Account. Rev.,* 1975, *50,* 710–722; Dawes, R. M. A case study of graduate admissions: Application of three principles of human decision making. *Amer. Psychol.,* 1971, *26,* 180–188.

30. Tversky, A., and Kahneman, D. Availability: A heuristic for judging frequency and probability. *Cogn. Psychol.,* 1973, *5,* 207–232.

31. Slovic, P. From Shakespeare to Simon: Speculations—and some evidence—about man's ability to process information. *ORI Research Monogr.,* 1972, *12*(2).

32. March, J. G., and Simon, H. A., op. cit.

33. Armstrong, J. S., Denniston, W. B., and Gordon, M. M. The use of the decomposition principle in making judgments. *Organ Behav. Human Perform.,* 1975, *14,* 257–263; Gettys, C. F., Michel, C., Steiger, J. H., Kelly, C. W., and Peterson, C. R. Multiple-stage probabilistic information processing. *Organ Behav. Human Perform.,* 1973, *10,* 374–387.

34. Slovic, Fischhoff, and Lichtenstein, S., op. cit.

35. Newcomb, T. *The acquaintance process.* New York: Holt, Rinehart & Winston, 1961.

36. Payne, R., and Pugh, D. S. Organizational structure and climate. In M. D. Dunnette (Ed.), op.

cit.,pp. 1125–1173; Pugh, D. S., Hickson, D. J., Hinings, C. R., McDonald, K., Turner, C., and Lupton, T. A conceptual scheme for organizational analysis. *Admin. Sci. Quart.*, 1963, *8*, 289–315.

37. Litwin, G. H., and Stringer, R. A. *Motivation and organizational climate.* Cambridge, Mass.: Harvard University Press, 1968.

38. Campbell, J. P., Dunnette, M. D., Lawler, E. E., and Weick, K. E. *Managerial behavior, performance and effectiveness.* New York: McGraw-Hill, 1970. See also Tagiuri, R., and Litwin, G. H. *Organizational climate: Explorations of a concept.* Cambridge, Mass.: Harvard University Press, 1968.

39. Hemphill, L. Relations between the size of the group and the behavior of "superior" leaders. *J. Soc. Psychol.*, 1950, *32*, 11–22; Mass, H. S. Personal and group factors in leader's social perception. *J. Abnorm. Soc. Psychol.*, 1950, *45* 54–63.

40. Homans, G. C. *The human group.* New York: Harcourt, Brace, 1950.

41. Marriott, R. Size of working group and output. *Occup. Psychol.*, 1949, *23*, 47–57; Campbell, H. Group incentive payment schemes: The effect of lack of understanding and group size. *Occup. Psychol.*, 1952, *26*, 15–21.

42. McGrath, J. E. *A summary of small group research studies.* Arlington, Va.: Human Sciences Research, Inc., 1962.

43. Forehand, G. A., and Gilmer, B. Environmental variation in studies of organizational behavior. *Psychol. Bull.*, 1965, *62*, 361–382.

44. Cleland, S. *The influence of plant size on industrial relations.* Princeton, N.J.: Princeton University Press, 1955.

45. Baumgartel, H., and Sobel, R. Background and organizational factors in absenteeism *Personnel Psychol.*, 1959, *12*, 431–443.

46. Herzberg, F., Mausner, B., Peterson, R. O., and Campbell, D. F. *Job attitudes: Review of research and opinion.* Pittsburgh, Psychological Services of Pittsburgh, 1957.

47. Woodward, J. *Management and technology.* London: Her Majesty's Stationery Office, 1958; Bass, B. M. *Organizational psychology.* Boston: Allyn & Bacon, 1965.

48. Stieglitz, H. Optimizing span of control. *Mgt. Record,* 1962, *24*, 25–29. Lawrence, P. R., and Lorsch, J. W. *Organization and environment.* Homewood, Ill.: Irwin, 1969.

49. Worthy, J. Organization structures and employee morale. *Amer. Sociol. Rev.*, 1950, *15*, 169–179.

50. Porter, L. W., and Lawler, E. E. The effect of tall versus flat organization structures on managerial job satisfaction. *Personnel Psychol.*, 1964, *17*, 135–148.

51. Weiss, E. C. Relation of personnel statistics to organizational structure. *Personnel Psychol.*, 1957, *10*, 27–42.

52. Kaplan, N. The role of the research administrator. *Administrative Sci. Quart.*, 1959, *4*, 20–41; Blau, P. M., and Scott, W. R. *Formal organizations.* San Francisco: Chandler, 1962; La Port, T. R. Conditions of strain and accommodation in industrial research organizations. *Administrative Sci. Quart.*, 1965, *10*, 21–28.

53. Woodward, J. *Industrial organizations: Theory and practice.* London: Oxford University Press, 1965.

54. Ziller, R. C. Individuation and socialization: A theory of assimilation in large organizations. *Hum. Relat.*, 1964, *17*, 341–360; Ziller, R. C. Toward a theory of open and closed groups. *Psychol. Bull.*, 1965, *64*, 164–182.

55. Graen, G. Role-making processes within complex organizations. In M. D. Dunnette, op. cit., pp. 1201–1245.

56. Rizzo, J. R., House, R. J., and Lirtzman, S. I. Role conflict and ambiguity in complex organizations. *Administrative Sci. Quart.*, 1970, *15*, 150–163.

57. Kahn, R. L., Wolfe, D. M., Quinn, R. P., Snoek, J. P., and Rosenthal, R. A. *Organizational stress.* New York: Wiley, 1964.

58. Mandell, M. M. Supervisory characteristics and ratings: A summary of recent research. *Personnel,* 1956, *32,* 435–440.

59. Kahn et al., op. cit.

60. Woodward, op. cit.

61. Adams, J. S. The structure and dynamics of behavior in organizational boundary roles. In M. D. Dunnette, op. cit., pp. 1175–1199.

62. Bass, B. M., op. cit.

63. Bass, B. M., and Wurster, C. R. Effects of company rank on LGD performance of oil refinery supervisors. *J. Appl.Psychol.,* 1953, *37,* 100–104.

64. Bass, B. M., and Wurster, C. R. Effects of the nature of the problem on LGD performance. *J. Appl. Psychol.,* 1953, *37,* 96–99.

65. Pelz, D. C. Leadership within a hierarchical organization. *J. Soc. Issues,* 1951, 7, 49–55.

66. Epstein, S. *An experimental study of some of the effects of variations in the clarity and extent of a supervisor's area of freedom upon his supervisory behavior.* Doctoral dissertation, University of Michigan, 1956.

67. Drucker, P. *The practice of management.* New York: Harper & Row, 1954; Odiorne, G. *Management by objectives.* New York: Pitman, 1965.

68. Ivancevich, J. M., Donnelly, J. H., and Lyon, H. L. A study of the impact of management by objectives on perceived need satisfaction. *Personnel Psychol.,* 1970, *23,* 139–151.

69. Raia, A. P. A second look at management goals and controls. *Calif. Mgt. Rev.,* 1966, *8,* 49–58; Ivancevich, et al., op. cit.

70. Dubin, R. Stability in human organizations. In M. Haire (Ed.), *Modern organization theory.* New York: Wiley, 1959; Guetzkow, H., and Simon, H. A. The impact of certain communication nets upon organization in task-oriented groups. *Mgt. Sci.,* 1955, *1,* 233–250. Leavitt, H. J. Some effects of certain communication patterns on group performance. *J. Abnorm. Soc. Psychol.,* 1951, *46,* 38–50.

71. Woodward, J. (Ed.). *Industrial organization: Behavior and control.* London: Oxford University Press, 1970; Eilon, S. Problems in studying management control. *Intl. J. of Produc. Res.,* 1962, *1.*

72. Lawler, E. E. Control systems in organizations. In M. D. Dunnette, op. cit., pp. 1247–1291.

73. Hackman, J. R., and Lawler, E. E. Employee reactions to job characteristics. *J. Appl. Psychol. Monograph,* 1971.

74. Blau, P. M. *The dynamics of bureaucracy.* Chicago: University of Chicago Press, 1955.

75. Berliner, J. S. The situation of plant managers. In A. Inkeles and K. Geiger (Eds.), *Soviet society: A book of readings.* Boston: Houghton-Mifflin, 1961, pp. 361–381.

76. Lawler, E. E., op. cit.

77. March, J. G., and Simon, H. A., op. cit.

78. Kanter, R. M. *Men and women of the corporation.* New York: Basic Books, 1977.

79. Lawrence and Lorsch, op. cit.

80. Leavitt, H. J. *Managerial psychology.* Chicago: University of Chicago Press, 1964; Leavitt, H. J. Task ordering and organizational performance in the common target game. *Behav. Sci.,* 1960, *5,* 233–239.

81. Maier, N. R. F., and Hoffman, L. R. Acceptance and quality of solutions as related to the leader's attitude toward disagreement in group problem solving. *J. Appl. Behav. Sci.,* 1965, *1,* 373–386.

82. Deutsch, M. Toward an understanding of conflict. *Intl. J. of Group Tensions,* 1971, *1,* 42–54.

83. Van Doorn, J. A. A. Conflict in formal organizations. In A. de Reuch and J. Knight (Eds.), *Conflict in society.* Boston: Little, Brown, 1966, pp. 111–133.

84. Thomas, K. Conflict and conflict management. In M. D. Dunnette, op. cit., pp. 889–935.

SUGGESTED READINGS

Backhard, R., and Harris, R. T. *Organizational transitions: Managing complex change.* Reading, Mass.: Addison-Wesley, 1977.

Galbraith, J. R. *Organization design.* Reading, Mass.: Addison-Wesley, 1977.

Lawler, E. E., and Rhode, J. G. *Information and control in organizations.* Santa Monica, Calif.: Goodyear, 1976.

Melcher, A. J. *Structure and process of organizations: A systems approach.* Englewood Cliffs., N.J.: Prentice-Hall, 1976.

LABORATORY EXERCISE
ROLE-PLAYING:
PROBLEM SOLVING THE APPRAISAL INTERVIEW

A. PREPARATION FOR ROLE-PLAYING

1. The instructor will read general instructions (D.1) and write the organizational chart shown in Figure 20.4 on the chalkboard.
2. The class should then be divided into groups of three, one member being assigned the role of Stanley (D.2), the other the role of Burke (D.3) and the third the role of observer.
3. When the Burkes have finished reading their parts, they should stand and remain standing until further instructions are given.
4. When all of the Burkes are standing, the instructor should be sure that they know who their Stanleys are and that the observer is somewhat on the sidelines. The observer's presence is to be ignored by Stanley and Burke.

B. THE ROLE-PLAYING PROCESS

1. When the stage is set, the Burkes will be instructed to knock on Stanley's door (make-believe door) to present themselves for the scheduled interview.
2. Role-playing should proceed for about half an hour. Regardless of whether all have finished, they should have reached a point where comparisons of outcomes can be made.
3. When the interviews have been terminated, the instructor should ask each Stanley to assign two letter grades (A, B, C, D, or E) to Burke: one as an estimate

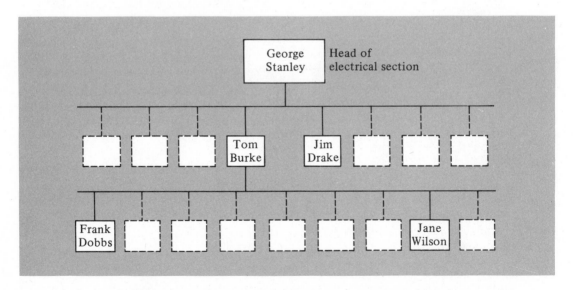

FIGURE 20.4 ORGANIZATIONAL CHART OF THE ELECTRICAL SECTION OF AMERICAN CONSTRUCTION COMPANY

The names of the persons that may be mentioned in this case are given, together with their positions in the organization. Only George Stanley and Tom Burke are involved in the role-playing.

THE ORGANIZATION AND THE ENVIRONMENT

of Burke before the interview; the other as a present estimate. These grades should be written down and not be visible to either the observer or Burke.

4. After Stanley has assigned the two grades, the observer and Burke should write individually on slips of paper the two grades that they think Stanley wrote. They should avoid being guided by what grades that they think should have been assigned. The appraisal judgments should be set aside for use in later discussions.

C. DISCUSSION

1. Each observer should report on any changes that will result from the interview. The instructor should check with the role-players to determine the accuracy of the observers' judgments. The instructor should briefly summarize points on the chalkboard.
2. After each observer has reported the changes expected, they should in turn report on Tom's job interest. These judgments also should be checked with Tom. The findings should be posted on the chalkboard.
3. The observers should report the before- and after-interview grades that they think Stanley assigned. Tom's opinion and Stanley's estimate should then be posted to test the observer's sensitivity as well as Tom's.
4. The observers should next be asked to go into a huddle with the Burke and Stanley whom they observed and point out opportunities that the two missed, where things went wrong, and why problem solving was not effectively used. The instructor should terminate these discussions after five minutes.
5. The instructor should summarize the discussion, evaluating the place of appraisal programs in organizations, the differences in job perception of supervisors and employees, and the potential use of problem solving in situations of this kind.

D. MATERIALS FOR THE CASE

1. General Instructions

George Stanley is the electrical section head in the engineering department of the American Construction Company. The work in the department includes design, drafting, cost estimates, keeping maps up to date, checking standards and building codes, field inspection, follow-up, and so on. Eight first-line supervisors report to George Stanley. The duties of the supervisors are partly technical and partly supervisory (see Figure 20.4).

Company policy requires that all section heads interview each of their supervisors once a year, the purposes being (1) to evaluate the supervisor's performance during the year, (2) to give recognition for jobs well done, and (3) to correct weaknesses. The company believes that employees should know how they stand, and that everything should be done to develop management personnel. The appraisal interviews were introduced to serve these purposes.

Tom Burke is one of the supervisors reporting to Stanley, and today we will witness an appraisal interview conducted by Stanley with Tom.

Tom Burke has a college degree in electrical engineering. In addition to his technical duties, which often take him to the field, he supervises the work of one junior designer, six draftsmen, and two clerks. He is highly paid, as are all the supervisors in this department because of the high requirements in technical knowledge. Burke has been with the company for twelve years and has been a supervisor for two years. He is married and has two children. He owns his home and is active in the civic affairs of the community in which he lives.

2. Role for George Stanley, Section Head

You have appraised all the supervisors who report to you and during the next two weeks will interview each of them. You hope to use these interviews constructively to develop each. Today you have arranged to interview Tom Burke, one of the eight first-line supervisors who report to you. Here is the information and his appraisal as given in your files.

Tom Burke: twelve years with company, two years as supervisor, college degree, married, two children. Evaluation: highly creative and original, and exceptionally competent technically. His unit is very productive, and during the two years that he has supervised the group, there has been a steady improvement. Within the past six months, you have given him extra work and he has had it done on schedule. As far as productivity and dependability are concerned, he is your top supervisor.

His cooperation with other supervisors in the section leaves much to be desired. Before you made him a supervisor, his originality and technical knowledge were available to your whole section. Gradually he has withdrawn and now acts more as a lone wolf. You've asked other supervisors to talk over certain problems with him, but they tell you that he offers no suggestions. He tells them he's busy or listens disinterestedly to their problems, kids them, or makes sarcastic remarks, depending on his mood. On one occasion he allowed Jim Drake, one of the supervisors in another unit, to make a mistake that he could have forestalled by letting him know the status of certain design changes, which he knew about and had seen. It is expected that supervisors will cooperate on matters involving design changes that affect them.

Furthermore, during the past six months, he has been unwilling to take two assignments. He said they were routine, that he preferred more interesting work, and he advised you to give the assignments to other supervisors. To prevent trouble, you followed his suggestion. However, you feel that you can't give him all the interesting work and that if he persists in this attitude, there will be trouble. You cannot play favorites and keep up morale in your unit.

Burke's failure to cooperate has you worried for another reason. Although his group is highly productive, there is more turnover among his draftsmen than in other groups. You have heard no complaints as yet, but you suspect that he may be treating his staff in an arbitrary manner.

Certainly if he talks up to you and to other supervisors, he's likely to be even more that way with his staff. Apparently the high productivity in his group is not due to high morale, but to his ability to use his people to do the things for which they are best suited. This method won't develop good draftsmen. You hope to discuss these matters with Burke in such a way as to recognize his good points and at the same time correct some of his weaknesses. Feel free to handle the interview in the manner that you think is best.

3. Role for Tom Burke, Supervisor

One junior designer, six draftsmen, and two clerks report to you. You feel that you get along fine with your group. You have always been pretty much of an idea man and apparently have the knack of passing on your enthusiasm to others in your group. There is a lot of "we" feeling in your unit because it is obvious that your group is the most productive.

You believe in developing your staff members and always give them strong recommendations. You feel you have gained the reputation of developing your employees because they frequently go out and get much better jobs. Since promotion is necessarily slow in a company such as yours, you feel that the best way to stimulate morale is to develop new people and demonstrate that a good worker can get somewhere. The two clerks in your unit are bright and efficient and there is a lot of good-natured kidding. Recently one of your clerks, Jane Wilson, turned down an outside offer that paid $125 a month more, for she preferred to stay in your group. You are going to get her a raise the first chance you have.

The other supervisors in Stanley's section do not have your enthusiasm. Some of them are dull and unimaginative. During your first year as supervisor, you used to help them a lot, but you soon found that they leaned on you and before long you were doing their work. There is a lot of pressure to get out production. You got your promotion by producing and you don't intend to let other supervisors interfere. Since you no longer help the other supervisors, your production has gone up, but a couple of them seem a bit sore at you. Frank, your junior designer, is better qualified than most of them and you'd like to see him made a supervisor. Since the company has some dead wood in it, Stanley ought to recognize this fact and assign such units the more routine jobs. Then they wouldn't need your help, and you could concentrate your efforts on jobs that suit your unit. At present, George Stanley passes out work pretty much as he gets it. Because you are efficient, you get more than your share of these jobs, and you see no reason why the extra work shouldn't be in the form of "plums." This would motivate units to turn out work. When you suggested to Stanley that he turn over some of the more routine jobs to other supervisors, he did it, but he was reluctant about it.

You did one thing recently that has bothered you. There was a design change in a set of plans and you should have told Jim Drake (a fellow supervisor) about it, but it slipped your mind. Drake was out when you had it on your mind, and then you got involved in a hot idea that Frank, your junior designer, had and forgot all about the matter with Drake. As a result, Drake had to make a lot of unnecessary changes, and he was quite sore about it. You told him you were sorry and offered to make the changes, but he turned down the offer.

Today you have an interview with George Stanley. It's about this management development plan in the company. It shouldn't take very long, but it's nice to have the boss tell you about the job you're turning out. Maybe there is a raise in it, maybe he'll tell you something about what to expect in the future.

4. Instructions for Observers

Read the roles of Stanley and Burke for background, to sensitize yourself to the problem. Do not participate in the interview or offer suggestions. Your task is to observe and evaluate. Do not discuss observations or conclusions with Burke or Stanley since you will report to the class as a whole.

Although the tell-and-sell method is usually followed by supervisors in situations of this type, we are concerned with whether Stanley tries to involve Tom Burke in problem solving. Pay especial attention to the following points.

1. Does Stanley praise or criticise? How are these evaluations received by Tom?

2. Does Stanley raise problems (a) to invite participation in solving them, or (b) to let Tom know about them?

3. Does Tom ask for certain things (for example, special treatment of any kind)? If so, does Stanley explore with him how to do it without creating new problems, or does he turn Tom down?

4. What skills does Stanley display that have been discussed in the course? List them as they occur.

5. At the end of the interview, indicate how you think Stanley or Burke might behave differently in the future.

6. Has Tom's job interest gone up, down, or stayed the same?

CHAPTER TWENTY-ONE

ORGANIZATIONAL DEVELOPMENT

■

Changing the Organization
Problems with O.D. Methods Used in the Past
New O.D. Techniques
Current Problems with Organizational Development
Action Research
Human Resource Development/Asset Management

■

CHANGING AN ORGANIZATION is a large undertaking. This book has described various approaches to increasing organizational effectiveness through the selection or training of management personnel. The illustrations of organizational changes described indicate the magnitude of the training problems when trying to change an organizational climate. Changes in organizational structure, new methods of production, the use of computers, and engineering-design changes represent changes in jobs and physical environment made to keep up with modern technology.

CHANGING THE ORGANIZATION

INTRODUCING CHANGE

Chapter 2 described how behavior (B) is a function of the situation or stimulus (S) and the nature of the person or organism (O). Changes required in B to increase an organization's accomplishment (A) therefore may involve either S or O or both. Some organizational changes are initiated by technical staffs or are recommended by outside consulting firms (experts in business and engineering technology); other changes may be initiated by the staff or by consulting firms whose members are trained in psychology or sociology. Regardless of the source of the change, the initiation is likely to come from persons other than those who have to change or to adapt themselves to the change.

Since change initiated from outside the group introduces a threat, it is often resisted. Each change situation has its own types of threat; therefore, the emotional condition should be diagnosed beforehand. Changes initiated through group problem solving, however, are usually welcomed. Involving people in change thus becomes an important part of the change method, but adapting it to each change situation raises problems in the application of group decision on an organizational basis. Changes required at one level (supervisor and workers) are relatively simple procedures, although getting a leader to try it out requires training (changing the O). In most instances the research on dealing with resistance to change has involved the use of outside leaders rather than actual supervisors.[1] However, the illustrations of group decision discussed earlier were initiated by line supervisors and their immediate subordinates. Because the negative results of resistance often become apparent only after the changes have been made (for example, a move to a new plant), they are discovered too late for correction. Thus, high-quality decisions fail because people are hostile or apathetic. Effective introduction of change in an organization is a complex problem, and the potential sources of fear must be anticipated in order to cope with them.

Changes initiated from the outside are obviously beneficial to those who initiate them, but what effect will they have on the recipients? It is to the interest of organizations to develop trust between organizational levels and between staff and line functions because higher management and staff personnel usually are the initiators of change. Job satisfaction increases in accordance with the degree of trust that subordinates feel their managers have in them and the degree to which there is participation in management decisions.[2]

Specialists in organizational development (O.D.) change organizations through either *structural* or *process interventions*. An example of structural intervention would be an organizational change in the reporting system that would give individual store managers greater responsibility and enable several levels of management to gain more control over their jobs. Such a structure could give managers more experience and at the same time reduce overly close supervision. Process interventions do not change the formal reporting system of the organization, but try instead to eliminate problems in interpersonal and/or intergroup relations, thus creating the conditions for permanent improvement. The long-term adjustment of organization members to the new style of interaction is called *refreezing* behavioral patterns and is the final step in the process of problem analysis, intervention, and change. Some aspects of the refreezing process include: (1) feedback of data about how members view their organization and themselves; (2) the presence of a change agent (see below) to act as a catalyst; (3) the frequent use of an off-site location to help people gain a new perspective on their jobs and attitudes; and (4) the creation and support by the change agent of behavioral norms for the change process, which help prevent psychological problems (anxiety, stress) and hostility or frustration.[3]

THE FUNCTION OF CHANGE AGENTS

Because changes involve emotions of fear and hostility, rational approaches are inadequate. The obstacles are the feelings of people, not engineering know-how. Since companies have had bad experiences with changes, it is not uncommon for them to utilize *change agents* to aid them. These are outsiders who work closely with the organization for a period of time.

The change agent has three advantages; being professionally trained, being an outsider, and being free of the organization's cultural biases. The change agent's function is to obtain information (through interviews, questionnaires, and observation) and to make a diagnosis of the organization's weaknesses and strengths.[4] The *diagnosis* points up obstacles and problems that need to be solved, the relative importance of acceptance, and how members of the organization can be involved in problem solving. Through problem solving with clients, certain actions or programs become apparent. A program of planned change is developed by making use of the outside agents' resources, knowledge, diagnostic skills, and group problem-solving leadership.

Interventions may range from the halting of a management meeting in order to analyze certain points in the discussion process to major changes.[5] Experts agree that successful permanent changes in an organization cannot be imposed from without. The change agent needs to work with and through *internal resource persons* who have developed the essential interpersonal skills and have an understanding of the importance of the acceptance dimension of decisions. C. Argyris uses the term *interpersonal competence* to indicate an essential ability in resource persons.[6] This competence is characterized by counseling and other interpersonal-relations skills and may be acquired through sensitivity training, role-playing, or training in counseling. If in a planned change program the change agent recommended special training for some executives, it would be called an *intervention*.

Most of the big changes are initiated at the level of top management, which then becomes the *point of entry*. Lesser changes (such as modifying safety or supervisory training programs, altering employment practices, and altering production-line procedures) may have points of entry at the level of superintendent, training or personnel departments, or the head of a particular plant. But these changes must have the support of top management if they are to succeed, and such support does not assure success. The general acceptance of a specific change depends on how individuals who have to live with the change feel about it. Change problems are difficult because both high quality and high acceptance are needed, which requires leadership skills. The employment of change agents is a method of obtaining the needed skills, but any skills developed inside the organization are important gains in management development. Chapter 22 is designed to help managers improve their skills so that they can make more complete use of group resources in solving problems that require both quality and acceptance.

MEASURING ORGANIZATIONAL CHANGE

One of the largest projects ever undertaken to change an organization through training was carried out in the Harwood Manufacturing Corporation after it merged with the Weldon Manufacturing Company to form the Harwood-Weldon Corporation.[7] Weldon had been a competitor of Harwood, about equal in size but with a different market because it produced a higher-quality product (pajamas). Harwood had been the site of many progressive experiments largely because Marrow, its president, was a social psychologist. The merger of this progressive company with one having an authoritarian style of management created the need to change the management style of the acquired organization. About one thousand people were involved in this change program.

The program included the use of change agents who introduced the following changes:

1. Redesigns of jobs, with workers in semi-autonomous groups

2. Employee training (new workers previously had been trained)
3. Retraining and coaching of poor performers
4. Sensitivity training for executives
5. Training seminars in interpersonal relations for supervisors and staff
6. Group problem-solving meetings at work-group levels
7. New production methods with a pay-rate increase
8. Employment selection tests (tests had not previously been used)
9. Discharge of chronic low performers

At the end of two years, productivity rose 30 percent, and survey data revealed changes in managerial behavior and employee satisfaction.

The research design permitted the identification of the causes of some improvements. Retraining and coaching contributed 11 percent; discharging poor workers, 5 percent; improved interpersonal relations, 5 percent; and group problem solving, 3 percent. Considering the extent of the changes made by group problem solving, the gain may seem small, however, when compared with what group problem-solving methods may accomplish (see Chapter 8).

Measuring changes in an organization is complicated by the fact that many managers and several levels of management are involved. Training in interpersonal skills or in group-decision methods does not necessarily cause all trainees to acquire such skills or to practice them. A two-week training program may change the managerial behavior of a few persons to a considerable degree, while not changing others at all. More training might change them, but there is no assurance that a given training approach will affect all participants, regardless of how extensive the program.

THE ORGANIZATION AND THE ENVIRONMENT

A change in one person in a crucial position, however, is sometimes sufficient to pay for a training program. The beneficial results attributed to some of the sensitivity programs are likely to be due to changes in certain key individuals. Often merely reducing the harm they do can lead to an overall improvement.

PROBLEMS WITH O.D. METHODS USED IN THE PAST

The National Training Laboratories at Bethel, Maine, developed *T-group methods,* also known as *sensitivity training.* These methods have influenced the thinking of many organizational psychologists who have tried to improve organizational effectiveness by training middle managers.[8] The underlying premise of this training (popular in the 1960s and early 1970s) is that attitudes and self-insights must be changed in order to achieve the type of leadership that makes for understanding, acceptance, and good communication.

T-group training lasts longer than other programs of management development. Reducing barriers of rank and holding frank discussions about interpersonal conflicts is done to help groups gradually develop trust and self-insights. The purpose of such sessions is to generate improvements in communication once the persons are back in their organizations, so that organizational effectiveness would increase. But convincing proof of such changes has been lacking, and many T-group programs have been dropped.[9]

Some shortcomings of T-group training are common to other intervention techniques used in the past (for example, "quick-and-dirty" questionnaire sampling). The difficulties are of two types. First, giving information without also giving the skills to use it may do more harm than good. People coming back from T-group training sometimes thought that they had become instant junior psychiatrists and often were inappropriately frank (or tactless) in ways that hurt long-standing relationships with other organization members.[10] Second, in some cases, merely wanting to change interpersonal style was insufficient because the organization's formal structure stifled or prevented it. Those who were willing to share problem-solving responsibilities with people in other functional groups, for example, had difficulties getting clearance to do so through the standard organizational channels.

NEW O.D. TECHNIQUES

SURVEY-QUESTIONNAIRE DESIGN

Problems in the past with questionnaire design have, in part, arisen from the fact that they were prepared in ways that emphasized psychometric (measurement of psychological factors) soundness or theoretical variables, rather than the accurate and complete identification of the organization's problems. Problems could arise because the data were taken over too brief a time, because little was known of the organization's history, or because insufficient qualitative data was collected to portray the organization in all its unique complexity.

One means of overcoming the inflexibility of standardized questionnaires designed on a theoretical basis was developed by H. Rosen and S. S. Komorita.[11] Their Ipsative Consequence Model has no predetermined structure of specific items. Instead, company employees (with the guidance of change agents) discuss the positive and negative consequences of possible changes and then evaluate them in terms of their perceived usefulness and chance of succeeding.

In a similar instance, O.D. consultants worked with a task force of employees to build, as a team, a questionnaire dealing with areas organization members considered to be important.[12] As part of the change process, consultants and clients also designed a system for feeding back information gathered on a periodic basis. In this particular case, no dramatic changes occurred in employee attitudes partly because organization members were free either to subscribe or not to subscribe to the program and feedback system. Those who chose to were more likely (the researchers found) to show beneficial changes.

TEAM DEVELOPMENT

Building positive group morale and identification with the task group and its goals has been a common aim of many change agents.[13] For example, W. L. French and R. W. Holliman proposed that management-by-objectives could be more successfully employed if assignments, goals, and so on, were worked out using group problem-solving techniques, rather than a series of one-on-one manager-employee discussions.[14] In addition to gaining the benefits of group problem solving described earlier (Chapter 8), it eliminated the time required for the manager to coordinate all the individual assignments and objectives.

Development of a team spirit in a task group builds morale and fosters group problem solving. (Courtesy of IBM)

THE ORGANIZATION AND THE ENVIRONMENT

FEEDBACK METHODS

Emphasis on the importance of giving feedback has increased greatly since the early days when surveys were sometimes made without reporting any results at all except to top management. Today, elaborate feedback systems have been developed that also stress the participation of organization members. In one such system, peers from different work groups met to discuss survey results with change agents and with one another.[15] Then they joined with representatives from other groups at various hierarchical levels to compare their different viewpoints. Intervention, in this instance, caused several structural changes to be instituted. Research suggests that methods like this increase both management's belief in the feedback's validity and its willingness to make the needed changes.

One generally recognized factor in successful feedback methods is the necessity for open discussion of results in task groups or other relevant groups. This discussion has been shown[16] to be significantly more satisfying than written reports and increases the perceived usefulness of the data.

JOB/FAMILY PROBLEMS

Greater awareness of the negative effects of job stress on both work and family life has led to various attempts to help workers and their families deal with it successfully. In one company, a two-day, off-site workshop was led by consultants to help husbands and wives cope more effectively with problems arrising from frequent, job-related trips.[17] Later, a comparison of problem-solving resources, coping ability, and carryover effects on organizational performance was made between workshop participants and nonparticipants. Participants generally scored higher in all three areas; moveover, they seemed to have developed (or released) more energy for dealing with other work-related issues.

A RECOMMENDED O.D. TECHNIQUE

People who fear change often do not understand the nature of their fears, which cannot be guarded against and so become anxieties. The first step in dealing with anxiety is to locate its source. Once the anxiety becomes resolved into specific fears, guarding against them becomes a soluble problem.

The *risk technique* is a group method for clarifying fears. The leader (or change agent) whose activity to this point has promoted change tends to build up anxieties. Managers in groups of fifteen or twenty-five are invited to discuss some of the dangers they see in the change program. This method has successfully been used in a management program designed to remove resistance to, and acceptance of group decision. The function of the leader is to post the risks on the chalkboard. Before each risk is posted, there should be sufficient discussion to make the danger specific.[18] Participants need not agree on the risk discussed, but they should try to understand it.

Typical examples of risks developed in discussion are shown in Table 21.1. Some of the risks represent misconceptions, some are imagined fears, some represent hostilities, others raise problems of how to adapt the learned principles to work situations. Participants differ in the number or nature of risks that they endorse, but the mere act of posting them reduces the anxiety (catharsis).

Once the risks are posted, methods for avoiding them become topics of mutual interest for problem solving. Such considerations as (1) the area of freedom, (2) the need to share data, (3) the realization that the participants in group decisions include only a

TABLE 21.1 RISKS POSTED FOR PRACTICE OF GROUP DECISION

1. Poor quality solutions would result.
2. Supervisor would lose status.
3. Not enough time for such discussions.
4. Groups would not be able to agree.
5. Management would lose control of the company.
6. Higher management would reverse decisions.
7. Employees would want raises because of their contributions to decisions.
8. Unofficial leaders (union steward) would take over.
9. Requires too much skill.
10. Poor morale because of conflicts resulting from discussion.
11. Discussions would be used to avoid doing work.
12. Decisions often would violate company policy.
13. Stockholders would object.
14. Decisions might violate union contracts.
15. Higher management would not permit me to use it.
16. Subordinates lack the essential information.

manager and immediate subordinates, (4) the importance of sharing information, and (5) the skill requirements of the leader then become relevant to an objective evaluation of their roles in the new situation.

The use of the risk technique lends itself to a variety of changes, especially those in which persuasion methods are inadequate. For instance, when a large airline was planning a merger with a smaller airline, employees of the smaller line were assured that the merger would not result in discrimination against them. They were even told that some might expect pay raises because the wage scale of the larger organization was higher. Entirely overlooked, however, was the fact that the merger would be a threat to the employees of the larger company. At their annual management-training program, held during the period when the merger was imminent, job attitudes were very poor, and there was more hostility than interest in the executive program. The trainer soon realized that the merger was of great emotional concern to all the participants. The merger was therefore made the discussion topic, and the negative features (risks) of the merger were posted. The first group of sixteen managers supplied twenty-three risks; the next group of fifteen supplied nineteen; and the third group of eighteen posted twenty-five. The exercise greatly reduced anxiety, and the cooperation in the training seminars was normal. Merely accepting and trying to understand the negative features of the merger reduced the anxiety.

When organizational changes arouse fears and hostility, the expression of these feelings in feedback sessions can have a great value in permitting the resumption of problem-solving behavior. The potential contributions of group problem solving to organizational development becomes a chapter in itself.

CURRENT PROBLEMS WITH ORGANIZATIONAL DEVELOPMENT

Making changes in the organization, whether structural or process-related, almost inevitably affects the power relationships of organization members. In the past, some change agents have ignored or overlooked this aspect of the consultant/client relationship often with negative results. More recently, researchers have suggested[19] that O.D. consultants must face these issues, and make every effort to see that the changes that they help generate do not foster conditions in which ability or creativity is stifled.[20]

Both consultants and managers must be aware of the long-term effects of the changes that they institute, and when necessary, make additional adjustments to eliminate unforeseen undesirable effects. Engaging organization members in skillfully guided group problem-solving sessions should be a significant factor in preventing counterproductive or dysfunctional changes.

ACTION RESEARCH

Many change agents have found that their experiences with various organizations have provided insights leading to the development of hypotheses and eventually theories of human behavior in organizations. Field-generated theory (see Chapter 1) is part of an approach to organizational behavior called *action research*. Unlike traditional research, the hypotheses tested are not derived from a priori general theories or creative invention, but are based on observation of ongoing processes and problems in companies. Although this approach to science is not likely to provide a general, all-encompassing theory of human behavior, it has great potential for generating concepts and approaches useful to managers in dealing with problems.

HUMAN RESOURCE DEVELOPMENT/ASSET MANAGEMENT

Many companies have found that they must take a more active role in selecting, training, and motivating employees if they are to compete successfully in the business world. For example, in the past, personnel selection involved "baiting the hook" with a strategically placed advertisement or a chat with a friend, followed by a patient wait until the right "fish" swam by.

Today, for several reasons, such a passive strategy is impossible, especially for companies in the forefront of their industries. Affirmative action, for instance, means going out and finding people who have the right potential but are often bypassed in traditional selection systems. In some cases, the "right fish" may not exist or may be in short supply. One manager in a high-technology company has stated frankly that because a certain job related to production control had relatively low status among engineering students, the company could not find enough trained people — of any degree of competence — for its growing needs. Therefore, they were hiring persons with some training and devising specialized long-term training programs to increase their competence.

A manufacturer of complex gear assemblies found that output of a relatively simple product was much higher in a small South Dakota plant than in other company plants. To take advantage of the pro-work attitudes in the South Dakota plant, it was decided to move some of the gear-manufacturing work to that area. Unfortunately, there was not one fully trained machinist in the town and not many elsewhere who were willing to move to South Dakota. As a result, the company undertook a program to use its own machinists, outside experts, and new recruits to develop the workers needed. Thus far, the company has found the program successful enough to continue to expand production at that plant.

Other personnel problems derive from the rapidly changing demands of the environment. *Manpower planning* used to be a term describing a fairly simple process: deciding how many people for what kinds of work a company should plan to hire over a given period. Today the process is vastly more complex. New problems and opportunities crop up at an ever-increasing pace; the greater diversity makes predictive accuracy more difficult. Also, the expectations and demands of current employees are changing. How many sixty-five-year-old employees in 1990, for example, will voluntarily retire and need to be replaced? Will continued inflation require longer careers? Will values change as the population ages so that the youth culture will no longer be a strong source of trends and values?

Companies that wish to maintain their leads in various industries are concerned about these and other aspects of human behavior in organizations. Competition long ago made managers aware that sophisticated asset management is a requirement for organizational prosperity. But for many, the realization that a company's *human* resources are assets that need to be studied, managed, and "well-invested" is a new one.

The tremendous growth of M.B.A. and managerial education programs in the United States in the past few years suggests that companies are aware that greater environmental/organizational complexity and interdependence requires more sophisticated managers. One lesson that these managers (and others) are learning is that acquiring a knowledge of the principles of dealing with people in an organizational setting is no longer optional. For the manager of the future, such knowledge is a prerequisite and a key to personal and organizational success.

NOTES

1. Coch, L., and French, J. R. P., Jr. Overcoming resistance to change. *Hum. Relat.*, 1948, *1*, 512–532.
2. Ritchie, J. B., and Miles, R. E. An analysis of quantity and quality of participation as mediating variables in the participative decision-making process. *Personnel Psychol.*, 1970, *23*, 347–359.
3. Beer, M. Technology of organizational development. In M. D. Dunnette (Ed.), *Handbook of industrial and organizational psychology*. Chicago: Rand McNally, 1976, pp. 937–993.
4. Lippitt, R., Watson, J., and Westley, B. *The dynamics of planned change*. New York: Harcourt, Brace, & World, 1958; Bennis, W. G., Benne, K. D., and Chin, R. (Eds.). *The planning of change*, 2nd ed. New York: Holt, Rinehart & Winston, 1969.
5. Schein, E. H. *Process consultation: Its role in organizational development*. Reading, Mass.: Addison-Wesley, 1969.
6. Argyris, C. *Interpersonal competence and organizational effectiveness*. Homewood, Ill.: Irwin-Dorsey, 1962.
7. Marrow, A. J., Bowers, D. G., and Seashore, S. E. *Management by participation*. New York: Harper & Row, 1967.
8. Bradford, L. P., Gibb, J. R., and Benne, K. D. (Eds.). *T-group theory and laboratory method*. New York: Wiley, 1964; Argyris, C. *Integrating the individual and the organization*. New York: Wiley, 1964; Bennis, W. G., and Schein, E. H. *Personal and organizational change through group methods*. New York: Wiley, 1965; Marrow, A. J., Bowers, D. G., and Seashore, S. E. op. cit.; McGregor, D. *The human side of enterprise*. New York: McGraw-Hill, 1960; Bass, B. M. The anarchist movement and the T-group: Some possible lessons for organizational development. *J. Appl. Behav. Sci.*, 1967, *3*, 211–227; Tannenbaum, R., Wechsler, I., and Massarik, F. *Leadership and organization*, New York: McGraw-Hill, 1961; Leavitt, H. J. *The social science of organizations*. Englewood Cliffs, N.J.: Prentice-Hall, 1963.

9. House, R. J. T-group education and leadership effectiveness: A review of the empirical literature and a critical evaluation. *Personnel Psychol.*, 1967, *20*, 1–52; Campbell, J. P., and Dunnette, M. D. Effectiveness of T-group experience in managerial training and development. *Psychol. Bull.*, 1968, *70*, 73–104.

10. Bass, B. M. The anarchist movement and the T-group. *J. Appl. Behav. Sci.*, 1967, *3*, 211–226; Wagner, A. B. The use of process analysis in business decision games. *J. Appl. Behav. Sci.*, 1965, *1*, 387–408; Bennis, W. G. *Organizational development: Its nature, origins and prospects.* Reading, Mass.: Addison-Wesley, 1969; Argyris, C. Management and organizational development: The path from Xa to Xb. New York: McGraw-Hill, 1971.

11. Rosen, H., and Komorita, S. S. A decision paradigm for action research: Problems of employing the physically handicapped. *J. Appl. Behav. Sci.*, 1969, *5*, 509–518.

12. Nadler, D. A., Mirvis, P. H., and Cammann, C. The ongoing feedback system: Experimenting with a new managerial tool. *Organ. Dyn.*, 1976, Spring, 63–80.

13. Fordyce, J. K., and Weil, R. *Managing with people.* Reading, Mass.: Addison-Wesley, 1971; French, W. L., and Bell, C. H. *Organizational development.* Englewood Cliffs, N.J.: Prentice-Hall, 1973.

14. French, W. L., and Holliman, R. W. Management by objectives: The team approach. *Calif Manage. Rev.*, 1975, *17*, 13–22.

15. Alderfer, C. P., and Holbrook, J. A new design for survey feedback. *Educ. Urban Soc.*, 1973, *5*, 437–464.

16. Klein, S., Kraut, A. I., and Wolfson, A. Employee reactions to attitude survey feedback: Study of the impact of structure and process. *Admin. Sci. Quart.*, 1971, *16*, 479–514.

17. Culbert, S. A., and Renshaw, J. R. Coping with the stresses of travel as an opportunity for improving the quality of work and family life. *Fam. Proc.*, 1972, *11*, 321–337.

18. Maier, N. R. F. *Principles of human relations.* New York: Wiley, 1952; Maier, N. R. F. *Problem-solving discussions and conferences: Leadership methods and skills.* New York: Wiley, 1963.

19. Pettigrew, A. M. Towards a political theory of organizational intervention. *Hum. Relat.*, 1975, *28*, 191–208; Vansena, L. S. Beyond organizational development. In P. T. Warr (Ed.), *Personal goals and work design.* New York: Wiley, 1975.

20. Singer, E. A., and Wooten, L. M. The triumph and failure of Albert Speer's administrative genius. *J. Appl. Behav. Sci.*, 1976, *12*, 79–103; Nord, W. R. The failure of current applied behavioral science. *J. Appl. Behav. Sci.*, 1974, *10*, 557–578.

SUGGESTED READINGS

Backhard, R., and Harris, R. T. *Organizational transitions: Managing complex change.* Reading, Mass.: Addison-Wesley, 1977.

French, W., and Bell, C. *Organizational development: Behavioral science interventions for organizational change,* 2nd ed. Englewood Cliffs, N.J.: Prentice-Hall, 1978.

Magusen, K. O. (Ed.). *Organization design, development and behavior: A situational view.* Glenview, Ill.: Scott, Foresman, 1977.

Weisbord, M. *Organizational diagnosis.* Reading, Mass.: Addison-Wesley, 1976.

LABORATORY EXERCISE

ROLE-PLAYING:
GOURMET COOKING, INC., AND THE COMPUTER

(Students are asked not to read the case materials before participating in the laboratory exercise.)

A. PREPARATION FOR ROLE-PLAYING

The teacher will:
1. Read the background information (E.1) to the class as a whole.
2. Divide the class into groups of six. Any remaining members should be asked to join one of the groups and serve as observers.
3. Assign roles to each group by handing out slips with these names: Dr. Lee Atkins, Jackie Belford, Craig O'Neill, Maria Bueno, Sara Krantz, and Grace Vincent. Ask each person to read his or her own role *only* (E.2). Instructions should not be consulted once role-playing has begun.
4. Pass out large sheets of blank paper (to be taped on wall or chalkboard) for use by each Dr. Atkins during group discussion.
5. Ask those playing Dr. Atkins to stand when they have completed reading their instructions.
6. When all those playing Dr. Atkins are standing, ask that each group member conspicuously display the slip of paper with the role name so that Dr. Atkins can identify each member by name.

B. THE ROLE-PLAYING PROCESS

1. The teacher will start the role-playing with a statement such as the following: "Dr. Atkins will lead a meeting of Ms. Vincent and the senior teaching staff in the GCI conference room; Dr. Atkins has not yet arrived. The purpose of the meeting is to discuss current problems related to the recent introduction of computerized methods at GCI. When Dr. Atkins sits down, this will mean that he or she has returned and the meeting will begin. What you eventually decide will be up to you as a group. Are you ready? Dr. Atkins, please sit down."
2. Role-playing proceeds for 20 to 30 minutes. Groups should be able to make some decisions during this interval.

C. COLLECTION OF RESULTS

1. Each change agent (Dr. Atkins) in turn reports the group decision(s). The instructor summarizes these briefly on the chalkboard by listing the group's decisions regarding computer usage at GCI in the future.
2. A tabulation should be made of the number of persons who (1) feel better about the situation after the discussion, (2) feel that they have had a fair hearing of their views; and (3) feel that their work situation vis-à-vis the computer will be more satisfactory in the future.

D. DISCUSSION OF RESULTS

1. Comparison of solutions may reveal differences in decisions regarding use of the computer (greater use, less use, no use, or the same amount of use) in the future. Discuss why the same facts yield different outcomes.
2. The quality of the solution can be measured by the efficiency and usefulness of the services and methods proposed for the future — whether computerized or not. Evaluate the probable efficiency of various solutions achieved.
3. The acceptance of solutions is indicated by a low number of dissatisfied participants. Evaluate solutions achieved on this dimension.

4. The usefulness of having an objective third party (change agent) can also be evaluated. To what extent was his or her approach helpful in achieving a satisfactory solution to GCI's problems?
5. List other kinds of organizational problems in which an objective outsider, skilled in organizational psychology, might make a significant contribution to problem solution.

MATERIALS FOR THE CASE

1. Background Information

Gourmet Cooking, Inc. (GCI), is an eight-year-old service organization; it provides a number of cooking programs in various cuisines to amateur and professional cooks. The company was started by Ms. Grace Vincent, the President and head of a staff of sixteen teachers, cooking aides, and administrators. The first lessons took place in her family room — now there is a new GCI School of Cuisine, furnished with everything from stainless steel sinks to Cuisinarts for each pupil.

Two months ago, Ms. Vincent hired a consultant, Nigel Martin, to update the company's mail-order advertising, class scheduling, accounting, and salary payment processes by using computerized methods. Initially the new programs did not run perfectly, and there were a few complaints from both customers and staff. Within a few weeks, most of these "bugs" were removed, however. The customers seem happier than ever with the new scheduling and billing methods. But the staff's complaints are increasing. To solve the problems associated with the staff's reaction to the new computerized methods, Ms. Vincent hired a second consultant, Dr. Lee Atkins, an organizational psychologist and change agent.

2. Role-Playing Instructions

Grace Vincent, President, GCI

Until a few months ago, you were very proud of GCI and looked forward to going to work each day. Now you are beginning to question whether it has been worth all the effort. When you first started giving gourmet cooking lessons, keeping track of fees and expenses was relatively easy, and your lack of business training did not create any difficulty. As the school has grown, however, you felt you were losing control of the financial side of things (although your familiarity with gourmet cooking enabled you to maintain control over the quality of teaching). Your accountant recommended using prepackaged computer programs for jobs like scheduling class times, paying bills, collecting student fees, advertising mailers, and so on. Since these areas had caused a lot of headaches in the past, you accepted the idea gladly and hired Nigel Martin to set things up.

Instead of being grateful for your efforts to achieve greater efficiency and control, some members of your teaching staff have done nothing but complain. They inflate small problems into giant dilemmas, refuse to provide input data, and sulk when you ask them to cooperate. You cannot get through to them or find out the basis for their complaints. Therefore, you have hired Dr. Atkins, an organizational psychologist, to meet with the group to find out why they object to the computer and what can and should be done.

Jackie Belford, Senior Instructor, "The Flavors of Provence"

You have worked with Gracie Vincent since the school started eight years ago. The two of you played bridge and cooked together for a number of years before that. When the classes got started, everything operated on a shoestring. Once, when the dish washer didn't show up, you and Gracie washed dishes for fifty-six students — veal parmesan — what a mess! But you laughed about it at the time. It wasn't really like work at all; it was more like being part of a team.

But the classes grew like Topsy. More students came and more teachers were hired. Soon you had to take your vacation at a set time, submit your lesson plans for approval — all kinds of rules and regulations. But you put up with it for friendship's sake and because you love the teaching.

But the computer is just too much. You never have felt comfortable with numbers. When those official-looking forms with all the little boxes and the paragraphs of instructions come to you, you really shiver. Sooner or later they will find out how dumb you are about this stuff. If things are going to be so mechanical and impersonal at Gracie's, maybe it would be better if a person like you just quit. Your husband, Harry, has been asking you why you stick with it when you don't need the money. Well, maybe this meeting will help to clear things up. It's worth one more try.

Craig O'Neill, Senior Instructor, "Scrutable Chinese Cooking"

When you came to GCI shortly after it opened, the teaching staff consisted of two sweet housewives, Gracie Vincent and Jackie Belford. Both of them were good cooks, but, frankly, the place needed a touch of class. Fortunately, your background and experience in international cuisine (including being a Master Chef at Edwin's, a Michelin three-star restaurant in Cincinnati) enabled you to provide the needed elegance. Your reputation attracted many new clients to GCI; Gracie always admitted this and treated you accordingly.

Now she has apparently forgotten your talents and past services and can think of nothing but this wonderful new computer. Well, can a computer make Canard à l'orange? Can a computer suffer? You hate all these new forms to fill out; all this ritualized red tape. Cooking is an art and you are an artist. If Gracie cannot see that, perhaps you will find someone who can.

On the other hand, working at GCI has many advantages over slaving at a hot stove all day. Maybe this professor can help you convey to Gracie your sense of discouragement about what has happened at GCI.

Maria Bueno, Instructor, "A Taste of Spain"

You came to GCI about two years ago because it had a reputation as a high-quality organization whose leadership paid well for good talent. Well, that part was true. You do get paid well, and the teachers are highly qualified. What you didn't know when you were hired was how unorganized the administrative side of things was. Your first pay check was two weeks late, and when it came, it was the wrong amount. The first semester you taught, one class had twenty-three people (three to each Cuisinart), and the other had a total of only four people. They told you that this was due to a scheduling mix-up on the part of Eunice, the bookkeeper and class scheduler. Well, it wasn't her fault, really. She was just overworked.

Then they brought in the computer whiz kid a few months ago. Things got worse for a while — typical computer bugs — but now they've got them mostly straightened out. Lately peoples' checks are on time and have all the proper deductions, classes are evenly divided, students have stopped complaining about mishandling of bills. If they can smooth out the rest of the bugs, maybe GCI could turn out to be a really good place to work. Dr. Atkins might be useful in helping you figure out how to make sure that the computer serves the staff members as a helpful tool, not an added complication.

Sara Krantz, Instructor, "France's Haute Cuisine"

You were recruited by Grace Vincent about one year ago because of your success at the New York Cookery International. NYCI is a sophisticated, up-to-date version of GCI — sort of what GCI would like to be in a few years.

One thing GCI has really needed, though, is help on the administrative side of things. At NYCI, pay-outs, scheduling, and all that routine stuff was computerized years ago. Since then, they've provided students with access, via computer, to thousands of recipes, cooking references, and other specialized services. When a student at NYCI wants to go into one area of the class more deeply, he or she can take (for a minimal extra fee) a programmed-learning course in the school's library. You've thought of other ways in which computers could be used in cooking schools and would like to see GCI get going. But for some reason, a few of the other teachers are not supportive of the recent changes. You can't understand this, but you hope that the meeting with Dr. Atkins will help clear things up. If they aren't going to get modernized, you're not sure that GCI is the right place for a future-oriented younger person like yourself.

Dr. Lee Atkins, Consultant

You have been called in because some of the senior teaching staff at GCI are having trouble adjusting to changes in the organizational system brought about by recently-introduced computerized methods for scheduling of classes, payment of salaries, and other administrative functions. They seem to be in conflict with Ms. Vincent and among themselves over the relative merits and costs of the recent changes.

To help them understand and deal with this situation, you intend to use the following method. First, you will write (on the large sheet of paper taped to wall or chalkboard that was provided for your group) two column headings, as follows: (1) Advantages of running GCI the old way — no computers; and (2) Advantages of running GCI the new way — with computer services. Then you will invite the group members to supply arguments for either position. Your responsibility is only to see that each argument is specific and is understood by everyone. Clarification, not agreement, is the objective at this point. As each argument is made, you will write it under the appropriate heading in abbreviated form. As emotional feelings are relieved, participants may be willing to contribute to both columns; even if they do not, they have the opportunity to see the situation from another's viewpoint.

Once all contributions have been made, you should summarize the situation: "It seems both points of view have some merits, so let's try to see if we can come up with a position that uses the merits of both." Ideas should then be solicited from group members for *specific* ways in which the benefits of both the old and new systems can be incorporated into future operations at GCI.

CHAPTER TWENTY-TWO

PROBLEM SOLVING
AT THE
ORGANIZATIONAL
LEVEL

■

Group Conditions Favoring Solution Quality
Group Conditions Detrimental to Solution Quality
Preconditions to Problem Solving and Decision Making
Processes Involved in Decision Making
Principles of Group Problem Solving
Principles for Evaluating Solutions
Improving Problem Solving in Organizations
Bargaining Versus Problem Solving
Problem-solving Discussion Procedures
Problem Solving: A Recapitulation
Conclusion

■

IN THIS CHAPTER, group problem solving will be discussed as a unique process. The problem-solving *process* should be distinguished from the *content,* or subject matter of the discussion. The same process might be used with problems having such diverse contents as finance, engineering, production, and sales. Usually participants are so involved with content that they are unaware of the process. The problem-solving process differs from such processes as arguing, persuading, bargaining, chatting, and exchanging ideas or information. It is a searching process involving idea generation.

If we diagrammed a problem-solving discussion, the conversation would zigzag among participants; the leader would talk less than participants once the process got under way. The leader's function would be to pose the problem, share any relevant information, restate ideas to facilitate understanding, and delay the evaluation process so that a solution would not be prematurely selected for the decision. The leader would be expected not to use any authority or power to promote favored ideas, but to be in charge of the process.

GROUP
CONDITIONS FAVORING
SOLUTION QUALITY

In Chapter 8, the leader was encouraged to share problems with employees to gain acceptance. In this chapter, training for the leader is being extended so that group problem solving can lead to higher-quality decisions as well. A group has certain assets as well as certain liabilities. If the liabilities can be avoided and the assets used to their fullest advantage, the group effort can be made creative.[1]

GREATER AMOUNT
OF KNOWLEDGE

A group has more knowledge and information than its most capable member. Since problem solving involves the processing of information, participants should feel free to share all information, rather than feel a need to defend preferred solutions and supply selected information. This willingness to share information depends on a problem-solving climate or attitude.

GREATER NUMBER
OF APPROACHES

Individuals get into ruts in their thinking and tend to persist in their initial approaches. Problem solving requires variety in thinking, and the group process generates more variety than the individual process. It also follows that the greater the differences in background of participants the greater the chances of innovation. In solving a technical problem, for example, a nontechnical member often contributes the most to innovation. A difficult problem requires a new approach; technical competence can be a handicap, to the extent that past thinking is repeated.

BETTER COMPREHENSION
AND ACCEPTANCE
OF THE SOLUTION

When a group of persons solves a problem or makes a decision, all participants understand the solution. They also are aware of the way it was reached and of the alternatives that were discarded. As a result, possible misunderstandings of the solution are avoided, the need to communicate the solution to others is eliminated, and persuasion is not required to gain acceptance of the solution.

GROUP CONDITIONS DETRIMENTAL TO SOLUTION QUALITY

SOCIAL PRESSURE

Social pressure is a major cause of conformity. The desire to be a good group member and to be accepted tends to inhibit disagreement and favors consensus. Majority opinions tend to be accepted regardless of whether their objective quality is logically and scientifically sound. In small groups, members strive to reach full agreement and feel the problem is solved when agreement is reached.In one study, unanimous agreement on the solution to an experimental problem was reached in over 75 percent of three-person groups, even though the groups disagreed with one another regarding the best decision.[2] Since the decisions differed greatly, all of them could not have been of high quality. Thus, social pressure favors acceptance of decisions at the expense of quality.

INDIVIDUAL DOMINATION

In most leaderless groups, a dominant individual emerges and captures more than an equal share of influence over the outcome. This is done through a greater degree of participation, persuasive ability, or stubborn persistence (fatiguing the opposition). None of these factors is related to problem-solving ability, so that the best problem solver in the group may not have the influence to upgrade the quality of the group's solution. L. R. Hoffman and Maier found that the mere act of appointing a leader causes that person to dominate a discussion.[3] Thus, regardless of problem-solving ability, an untrained leader tends to exert an undue influence on the outcome of a discussion.

PRECONDITIONS TO PROBLEM SOLVING AND DECISION MAKING

OPENMINDEDNESS

Participants frequently meet to discuss a problem, but often they have a solution in mind, and instead of solving a problem, they try to persuade one another. This prevents the group process of working together in search of a solution by replacing it with a conflict between members, all of whom may have committed themselves to solutions beforehand. If group problem solving is to occur, it is necessary that the members remain openminded. This condition is best achieved if the problem is not known beforehand.

AGREEMENT ON GOAL

An initial step in group problem solving is to determine whether there is agreement on the goal. Failure to reach agreement on solutions is often found to result from the fact that members have different objectives. If each participant favors a solution that gives a personal advantage, little cooperation is possible because members are in competition. One doesn't expect opponents in a card game to show their hands. Cooperation and trust are possible only when a goal of mutual interest is established. Finding this common goal therefore becomes a prerequisite to effective group problem solving.

SITUATIONAL VERSUS BEHAVIORAL PROBLEMS

Persons are more likely to cooperate in correcting or modifying situations than in changing themselves. When changes in themselves are suggested, they become defensive. It is essential that participants not be subjected to criticism if they are expected to cooperate in the problem-solving process. When the objective of participative problem solving is to improve work situations, it is most readily achieved. It is possible to restate all problems in situational terms, but this often is difficult. When we find fault or blame someone, we are concerned with a behavioral, rather than a situational, problem. Ability to restate the problem in situational terms is a skill.

PROCESSES INVOLVED IN DECISION MAKING

DIFFERENCES BETWEEN SOLUTIONS AND CHOICES

Two processes usually are involved in decision making: problem solving (PS) and choice behavior(C). The first is the discovery of solutions that constitute ways of getting around or removing obstacles; the second is the evaluation process that leads to the selection of a solution from among available alternatives. The model for decision making (D) therefore may be stated as follows:

$$D = PS + C$$

Objectively, a problem situation, as illustrated in Figure 22.1 is similar to a frustrating situation. Various obstacles stand between the person and the goal. The difference between frustrated and problem-solving behavior is that in the first case, the problem obstacle has become a source of irritation, whereas in the second, it is a challenge. To solve a problem, people must generate ideas or ways to remove or get around obstacles rather than fight or run away from them. Thus, problem solving is an *idea-getting process*.

Choices exist when we have two or more ways to get to a desired objective. In these instances, behavior is also blocked because it cannot proceed until one of the alternatives is selected. The selection among alternatives involves an appraisal of their relative merits. In Figure 22.2, alternative B usually would be selected because it is the shorter. Making a choice thus is an *idea-evaluation process*.

Some investigators use the term *decision making* interchangeably with *choice behavior*.[4] In their studies, the alternatives are supplied (for example, where to place bets in a gaming situation) and factors influencing the choice are investigated. Other investigators use the terms *problem solving* and *decision making* interchangeably, so that the solution reached is regarded as the decision. Studies of group decision, in general, follow this terminology, so that idea getting and idea evaluation are part of the discussion process. Since idea getting and idea evaluation are unique processes, depending on different conditions to facilitate them and subject to different sources of error, it seems desirable to treat them separately.

CAUSES OF LOW-QUALITY DECISIONS

Some decisions are of poor quality because a good alternative was not generated; others are poor because the best alternative generated was not selected. The *brainstorming* discussion method (see p. 609) generates many alternatives, but the selection process is inadequate, whereas in unsupervised discussions, the idea-generation process is terminated too soon.[5] Left to their own devices, untrained groups tend to (1) confuse facts, opinions, and diagnoses; (2) substitute opinions for facts; (3) fail to differentiate obsta-

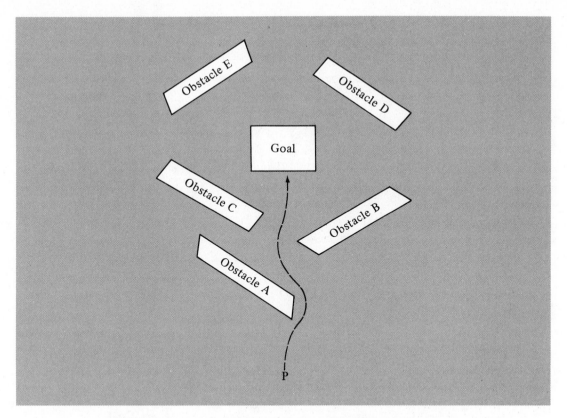

FIGURE 22.1 CHARACTERISTICS OF A PROBLEM SITUATION

Obstacles obstructing progress toward a goal present a problem. In this instance, the person (*P*) is prevented from reaching a goal and must find some way around the obstacles. The dotted line indicates a possible solution. Some obstacles are more readily circumvented than others. Thus, the search for surmountable obstacles and unusual ideas for getting around them are characteristics of good problem solvers.

cles and goals; and (4) pose solutions that bear no relationship to the diagnosis. Solutions are rationalized in that facts are invented to support them. Research shows that groups of college students do not engage in the problem-solving process merely by being placed in a problem situation, but that training or guidance is needed.[6] Training in systematic methods, the use of experimentally proven principles for encouraging idea generation, and idea evaluation can im-

prove a decision's quality as well as its acceptance.[7]

PRINCIPLES OF GROUP PROBLEM SOLVING

LOCATING SURMOUNTABLE OBSTACLES

Success in problem solving requires that effort be directed toward overcoming surmountable obsta-

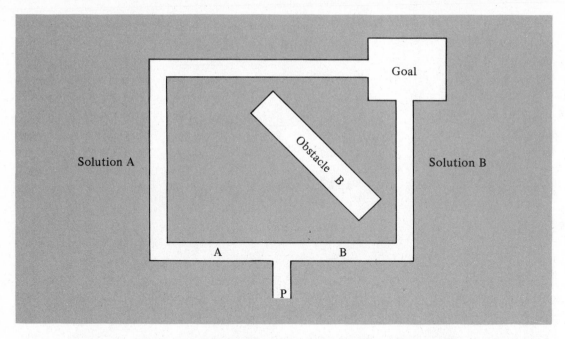

FIGURE 22.2 CHARACTERISTICS OF A CHOICE SITUATION
When there are two given ways of getting around an obstacle, a person's (P) behavior is blocked until one is chosen. Making a good choice between alternative ideas (shown as pathways A and B) requires idea evaluation.

cles. It is a common error to persist in overcoming obstacles or in trying to improve on ideas that lead to failure. There usually are a variety of ways to solve a problem. A disease might be conquered by immunizing people, sanitizing their environment, preventing germs from reaching people, preventing people from reaching the germs, or destroying the carriers of germs. Each approach has obstacles. Some approaches may have obstacles that can be overcome; others may have insurmountable obstacles. There is no way of predicting the most practical approach, but this should not prevent careful exploration of a variety of approaches. Success in solving problems requiring nonobvious solutions has been increased by instructing individuals to reconsider their original interpretation of the obstacle in-

volved and to avoid persisting in a given approach.[8]

The essential value of group thinking is that a greater number of possible approaches can be generated and fruitless persistence, which unfortunately is part of human nature, is offset by differences in viewpoint. The leader can do a great deal to reduce habitual ways of thinking by asking the group to think of unusual and different approaches. Difficult problems and creative solutions are most likely to require the uncommon and least obvious approaches.

A common source of insoluble problems is a tendency to blame others or to talk about what should have been done. Such discussion cannot lead to solutions, since the past cannot be changed. Discussions of how to correct an error or to prevent its recurrence

THE ORGANIZATION AND THE ENVIRONMENT

A group can generate many varied approaches to solving a given problem, and allowing a thorough examination of the problem is important to the problem-solving process. (David Tuttle)

focus on the present and the future, which can be altered. Another common failing is to recommend solutions that cannot be implemented. Discussions of what *someone else* (for example, the president) should do may be a solution for that someone else, but a good solution that is not implemented is no better than a poor solution that is not implemented. In such instances, the problem is how to influence that *someone* to adopt the favored solution.

Many problems posed by managers are insoluble because of the above two reasons: blaming and recommending solutions they cannot implement. If a group cannot locate surmountable obstacles, the problem is insoluble for them. Under such circumstances, the problem is one of accepting this reality and adjusting. Persistence in trying to solve insoluble problems leads only to frustration.

IMPORTANCE OF THE PROBLEM SOLVER'S LOCATION WITH REFERENCE TO THE GOAL

The starting point of a problem is richest in solution possibilities.[9] The solution to a problem may be envisaged as a route from the starting point to the goal as shown in Figure 22.3. The process of thinking about a solution is like proceeding along a path in a

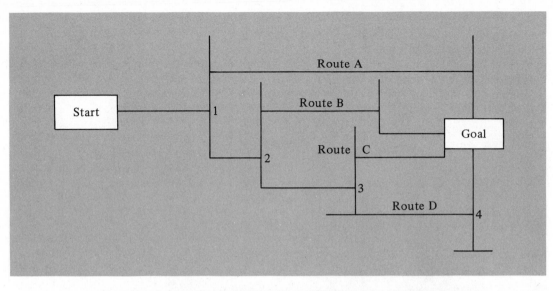

FIGURE 22.3 THE STARTING POINT IS RICHEST IN SOLUTION POSSIBILITIES

The first junction permits four alternatives; the second, three; the third, two; and the fourth, one. If routes *D, C,* and *B* are found to have insurmountable obstacles, but route *A* does not, it would be necessary to return to the first junction to solve the problem.

maze. Once persons start in a particular direction, they move away from other alternatives, and this reduces the number of possible directions to be pursued.

Each route may present obstacles. As discussion of a problem proceeds, successive obstacles may appear. A group may have successfully bypassed two obstacles along the way and then find difficulty with others faced at their advanced stage of progress toward the goal. Because of this partial success in moving forward, it is difficult for them to turn back and start all over again, yet a new start is the only way to increase the variety of solution possibilities. For example, a great deal of progress was made with propeller-driven planes; however, pilots were not able to fly above a certain height because of the lack of atmosphere. Increasing the power and design of the planes could raise the flying ceiling somewhat; neverthe-

less, the need for atmosphere limited the ceiling for propeller-driven craft. A plane with an entirely different type of engine — the jet — represented a fresh start in aviation.

In the usual problem situation, a group develops certain ideas about solutions. They move from the starting point in a particular direction toward the goal. A group that wishes to improve phone-answering services finds it difficult to think of approaches that do not limit personal calls. Hence, they think of different ways to curb such calls and lose sight of the original goal: improving phone-answering service. The tentative solutions reached become confused with the problem. This is why statements of problems frequently contain suggestions of solutions (in this case, how to get employees to refrain from making personal calls). Obviously such statements of problems describe more the nature of the solution than the original

THE ORGANIZATION AND THE ENVIRONMENT

goal and consequently prevent the search for other solution possibilities (for example, making personal calls during slack periods).

To appreciate the starting point of a problem better, the group should ask itself why it wishes or favors a certain solution. What purpose does this solution serve? Such a question may suggest the nature of the starting point of the problem. Spending time to explore the prime objective, therefore, represents a procedure for finding the starting point.

All solutions represent methods for reaching a goal, but frequently sight of the starting point is lost. Practical consideration requires that we reach a goal from the point at which we find ourselves. It may be unrealistic to get to an ideal goal from certain points. If a group could start from any point, more problems could be solved or more ideal goals could be reached, but this is not realistic problem solving.

EXPLORING THE PROBLEM AREAS

Problem-mindedness should be increased while solution-mindedness is delayed. The solution to a problem is a goal, and the motivational forces to reach it prevent a thorough exploration of the various factors in the problem.[10] Conflicting perceptions of the problem tend to remain unexplored and so appear as conflicting preferences for certain solutions. Thus, it is important that the perceptions of the problem be explored and facts bearing on the situation be discussed before members become committed to certain solutions. People often begin to suggest solutions before they fully understand a problem, or initially withhold essential information that they use later to reject solutions.

Experimental results show that the quality of a solution is upgraded if a discussion leader is instructed to explore the problem area with the group before beginning with the problem-solving discussion.[11] In observing the group problem-solving process, Maier has found premature concern with reaching a solution to be an almost universal fault for group members and especially leaders.

PERCEPTION OF THE PROBLEM AND CREATIVITY

Nonobvious statements of a problem stimulate creative thinking. Even when emotional involvement does not curtail creative thinking, the statement of the problem is important. Some statements offer little challenge and cause thinking to be routine. The question, "How do we take care of an increase in enrollment of 20 percent in this college?" merely suggests 20 percent more of what we are now doing. But the question, "How do we give a better education to 20 percent more students with a reduced budget?" requires original thinking.

A. R. Solem used the Parasol Assembly problem with 154 three-person groups who were asked to discuss the problem as a team of consultants.[12] The problem was posed to the groups in four different ways: how to (1) increase production of the assembly group; (2) capitalize on the fact that all other workers are faster than Joe; (3) reduce boredom of faster workers; and (4) permit each worker to adopt the pace he or she wishes.

The elegant solution to this problem is to have the group rotate positions periodically. This will permit the slower workers to move away from an accumulation of unfinished tasks, and faster workers to have extra work available to them. Each member thus contributes or takes from the accumulation according to ability, and production then is determined by the average ability rather than the lowest. This solution is elegant because it uses individual differences in ability, introduces variety to relieve boredom, allows for the substitution of another worker without disturbing the effectiveness of the procedure, and degrades no one for being slow. It assumes the work positions are simple and require no training, which is consistent with information supplied in the problem.

The frequencies with which the elegant rotation solution was recommended by the groups assigned the problem in the four ways were as follows: (1) 6 percent; (2) 8.6 percent; (3) 14.7 percent; and (4) 14.7 percent. The last two statements of the problem caused the groups to think more creatively than the first two. "Getting rid of Joe" was mentioned about equally often for the four conditions (ranging from 5.0 to 3.2 percent of the time).

The first two statements of the problem tend to make Joe the obstacle, which is rather obvious. They make the problem one of dealing with a bottleneck. The last two statements raise less obvious obstacles and channel thinking in new directions. The removal of these less obvious obstacles, however, does clear a path to the goal. The fact that groups under all conditions seldom suggest "getting rid of Joe" indicates that this rather obvious solution is seen by the consultants as one that the workers would not accept.

DISAGREEMENT AND CREATIVITY

Disagreement can lead either to hard feelings or to innovation, depending on the discussion leader. Persons who disagree often are troublesome to group members as well as to leaders. Disagreement indicates unwillingness to go along with others, yet cooperation is essential for achieving change and improvement. The person who is called a troublemaker in one group is hailed as a spark plug in another. Both conformity and deviant thinking have their place. Disagreeing for the sake of being different, as well as agreeing to obtain leader or group acceptance, hinders innovation. Conformity has merit in stabilizing relationships, but it is undesirable when it inhibits progress.[13]

Since life situations tend to foster conformity in organizations, it becomes necessary to promote, rather than to stifle, disagreement in group discussion.[14] Research studies have shown that heterogeneous groups are more innovative than homogeneous ones because differences lead to greater initial disagreement.[15] Groups in which disagreement with the leader is intense are more likely to develop innovative solutions than groups in which disagreement is mild. Table 22.1 shows that with strong opposition to the leaders' preferred solution, an innovative solution is developed in 45.8 percent of the groups as compared to 18.8 percent in groups with weak opposition. Innovative decisions depend on the generation of unusual alternatives, and when they are developed and adopted, the satisfaction of all participants is enhanced and acceptance is highest.

The leaders' attitudes toward persons who disagree are also important. Groups in which the leaders perceive disagreers as *problem employees* reach innovative solutions less often than groups in which leaders perceive disagreers *as idea generators*. Disagreers prevent the obvious alternatives from being adopted, and this blocking may create frustration, or it may lay the ground work for idea generation. When leaders try to persuade members to adopt their solution they may succeed or fail, but if opportunities to generate alternatives arise, something new can happen.

However, disagreement can also lead to argument (between nations, it leads to war), so groups must learn to use disagreement

TABLE 22.1 FREQUENCY OF THREE TYPES OF SOLUTIONS UNDER WEAK VERSUS STRONG OPPOSITION

TYPE OF GROUP	NO. OF GROUPS	SOLUTION		
		GROUP WINS (PERCENT)	LEADER WINS (PERCENT)	INNOVATIVE (PERCENT)
Weak opposition	48	14.6	66.7	18.8
Strong opposition	48	22.9	31.2	45.8

SOURCE: From L. R. Hoffman, E. Harburg, and N. R. F. Maier, Differences and disagreement as factors in creative group problem solving. *J. Abnorm. Soc. Psychol.*, 1962, *64*, 206–214. Copyright 1962 by the American Psychological Association, and reproduced by permission.

constructively.[16] The leader is in the best position to do this, but a trained leader *and* a trained group would be the optimum condition.

CONFLICT BETWEEN IDEA GETTING AND IDEA EVALUATION

The idea-getting process should be separated from the idea-evaluation process because the latter inhibits the former. When an idea is suggested, other group members tend to pass judgment on it. As a consequence, there is a reduced tendency to generate additional alternatives because the pros and cons of the first idea are being explored. Further, the person who generates ideas tends to be placed on the defensive and consequently hesitates to reveal ideas likely to be criticized. Since innovative and original ideas are unusual (hence the most questioned), evaluation stifles creativity.

The discussion method known as *brainstorming* imposes certain ground rules to prevent evaluation.[17] No one is permitted to criticize an idea, and the group is asked to suggest anything that occurs to them. Silly and humorous ideas are encouraged because they remove inhibitions and often suggest practical but innovative variations.

Problem-solving discussions can be made more productive if ideas are collected before they are evaluated.[18] The discussion of a particular idea should be limited to clarifying it. When clarified, it should be written out on a chalkboard or flip-chart for later evaluation. Persons who wish to criticize an idea should be asked to make an alternative suggestion. After a number of ideas have been collected, the process of evaluation can take place. This can lead to selection or interpretation of the ideas that seem to be the most practical.

Studies of problem-solving discussions reveal that ideas or solutions to a problem become accepted when they receive a certain amount of support.[19] Thus, solutions are often adopted before the less obvious alternatives are discovered. Because people are solution-minded, there is too much haste in adopting solutions.

PROBLEM SITUATIONS OBSCURE NEED FOR CHOICES

Problem situations should be turned into choice situations. Decision making involves both problem solving and choice behavior, but a situation in which the search for a solution is required (Fig. 22.1) tends to discourage further search once a workable solution is obtained. Task completion tends to be experienced (Zeigarnik effect) when the goal is reached, so the first solution suggested becomes the decision. To use the decision-making process, choice behavior should be included. In order to create a choice in a problem situation, two or more solutions need to be generated. Thus, the idea-getting process should be continued until the group is unable to generate additional solutions. When a dominant individual is part of the group, the second solution to the problem is two and a half times as likely to be innovative because the dominant individual has spent his or her influence on the first solution.[20] Innovative solutions are not necessarily of better quality, but if they are not generated, it is impossible to break away from the confines of the past.

CHOICE SITUATIONS OBSCURE NEED FOR PROBLEM SOLVING

Choice situations should be turned into problem situations. A choice situation like that described in Fig. 22.2 supplies alternatives, so there is a tendency to overlook the need to generate others. Often alternatives are supplied through learning and past problem solving, and when two or more are available, the perceived need to make a choice tends to dominate the activity. Thus, idea evaluation takes over. Whenever the need for making a change in a situation is suggested, two alternatives come to mind — the new versus the old — so that idea generation is often overlooked in change situations.

Every choice situation should be examined from the viewpoint of how to reach the goal in ways other than those already known. Just because there are two solutions to a problem does not preclude the possibility that others may exist.[21] In Figure 22.2, additional paths from p to the *goal* may be invented. Decisions can be improved by having good alternatives from which to choose, so the opportunities to generate ideas in choice situations should not be lost.

PRINCIPLES FOR EVALUATING SOLUTIONS

Once a number of proposed solutions have been generated, a group must select from among them. Two overall approaches are possible: eliminate the poorest ones or select the best. The first approach leads to defensive behavior. If member A finds fault with an idea suggested by member B, it is quite likely that B will attack A's solution when it is evaluated. It is not necessary to reject or devaluate any solutions; the group should merely select the best. Reaching agreement on the best solution, therefore, is the preferred method because it reduces face-saving efforts and saves time.

If the number of ideas generated is large, a straw vote to reduce the list is suggested. Each participant can be asked to vote for three solutions considered most workable. Between two and four alternatives usually stand out, and an equal number have little support. Solutions that have no chance of gaining group acceptance can be set aside so that evaluation may be confined to the solutions receiving substantial support. These should be evaluated in terms of the criteria discussed below.[22] A group might agree to score each solution on each of the criteria.

USE OF FACTS

A solution should deal with an obstacle that blocks progress toward a goal. If a solution to a production problem recommends the introduction of music and no facts indicate the existence of boredom, then the solution is not built on facts. Why then was it developed? Usually because music has been used

THE ORGANIZATION AND THE ENVIRONMENT

in other situations and produced favorable results. A common source of error in problem solving is overgeneralization. Generalization of solutions is successful only when the obstacles and facts in the two situations are basically identical. The tendency to ignore available facts is greatest when information is limited, but having limited information is no excuse for ignoring the facts that are available. In many situations, decisions have to be made on the basis of the available information, and high-quality solutions require that the solutions be congruent with the information. Good problem solvers require less information to solve problems effectively than the lesser skilled. The scientists who first accepted that the earth was round were influenced more by the facts and less by opinions popular at the time.

NEW PROBLEMS CREATED

Sometimes the solution to one problem creates a new problem. Solving a problem by giving privileges to one employee may create a new problem if several others request the same consideration. Similarly, the introduction of a more efficient work method might create a walk-out. If the new problem is readily soluble, progress results, but if it is more difficult to solve than the original one, the situation worsens. Each solution should be examined in terms of how its implementation might alter the situation by creating new problems.

CHANCES OF WORKING

A person often argues that one solution might work or that another solution might fail. When such issues are raised, the solutions should be rated in terms of the risks that would be taken and the odds involved. To expect every solution to produce results is often unrealistic, but to take long chances may be reckless. Risk taking may be desirable or undesirable depending on the relationship between potential return and chance of winning. Groups are more willing to take risks than individuals, but personality differences can affect willingness to take risks.[23]

COST OF IMPLEMENTING THE SOLUTION

Making choices always involves some value system. Beauty, speed, weight, size and cost determine choices depending on the dominant need. When several attributes have merit, choices become more complex. Business decisions often involve conflicts in value because the concept of a good solution may differ for sales, manufacturing, and research. In such instances, the relative values should be considered in determining the goal. When several solutions achieve the same goal equally well, secondary values may be considered.

RESPECTING PERSONAL PREFERENCES

Some solutions are disliked, but in order to reject them, participants are expected to give logical reasons. Other solutions are liked for emotional reasons, but participants try to defend them with facts. Solutions can be liked or disliked for emotional or unknown reasons, but when participants are required to justify their positions, unreal or untrue factors become part of the discussion.

For example, firing an incompetent manager might be a good solution to a problem, but may be rejected because the group does not like to hurt someone. Reasons given for rejecting this solution might be that they are not absolutely sure that the person is incompetent, that the replacement might be worse, or that the fault lies in not having developed the individual. Such rationalizations merely confuse the issue. If the group does not like the solution, the feeling should be accepted so that alternatives or ways to make the solution more acceptable might be entertained. Paying a termination bonus, offering training, or a transfer, and so on, might be practical alternatives.

Liking or disliking solutions should not have to be justified or explained. Such reasons should be respected and accepted as emanating from legitimate values. This does not mean that accepting feelings improves solution quality, but failure to respect them introduces interference and delays progress. When solutions are disliked, the evaluation should proceed to modifications or more attractive alternatives.

IMPROVING PROBLEM SOLVING IN ORGANIZATIONS

PROBLEM SOLVING BY INSIDERS AND OUTSIDERS

If problem solvers are given someone else's problem, they approach it as *outsiders* with no emotional investment in the solution other than having contributed to it. The major factor, therefore, becomes the quality of the solution recommended. Information tends to be freely shared, and in many instances, the same information is available to all participants. Examples of such problems are: finding the most efficient way to set up a job that other people will work at, building a bridge to carry a certain load in the cheapest way, and designing the safest possible car. Employees in staff and research units, as well as consultants, solve problems for others and therefore tend to approach the task as outsiders. Outsiders are prone to overlook the need to consider the acceptance that the solution must have by the persons who must implement the decision.

In contrast, when *insiders* solve problems, they deal with their own problems, and they must implement the solution. In such situations, (1) various alternatives represent gains for some and losses for others; (2) each participant may possess different areas of information, which are used to promote favored solutions and to reject others; (3) the information shared may be in conflict because it often is selective and exaggerated; and (4) there may be disagreement over the goals. The acceptance dimension thus becomes an important consideration, and quality may be overlooked. It has been shown that the quality of solutions to an experimental problem is higher when solved by outsiders than by insiders.[24]

HOW SOLUTIONS CREATE PROBLEMS

Often policy makers or experts have a problem because they have a solution in mind. Once a person accepts a solution, the problem of gaining the support of others is created. In this sense, solutions create problems, and if the needed support cannot be obtained, the implementation of the solution cannot be accomplished. Thus, many organizational objectives are sacrificed.

However, if a solution (for example, standardize company use of computers) has merit, it must be seen as accomplishing something (furnishing uniform data from various divisions). If the problem were posed in terms of how to achieve a certain goal without disturbing the goals of others (supply uniform data to the central office and at the same time permit each division to follow a system that suits its needs), the persons who are required to implement the solution could participate in searching for, and generating alternatives. The result might be the adoption of the solution that the leader

THE ORGANIZATION AND THE ENVIRONMENT

had in mind or one not previously entertained. The new solution may be either superior or inferior in quality to the leader's, but it will have greater acceptance. Whether the effectiveness of the greater support will offset any decrease in quality depends on how inferior the quality is and how important acceptance may be.

INDIVIDUAL VERSUS GROUP PROBLEM SOLVING

Group problem solving increases in importance as problems increase in complexity. No single individual can be expected to process all the ramifications of facts and ideas raised in many management decisions in a large company. Computers can handle part of the job, but they cannot make judgments or generate alternatives. An increasing number of managers, specialists, and technical experts work in teams, not because they want to, but because single individuals cannot do the job. This trend will continue, and it is imperative that the efficiency of group effort be increased before too many persons have gained negative attitudes from their experiences in working with untrained groups. The solution does not lie in returning to individual effort, but in improving group effort.

When an *individual* thinks, there is some organization built into the thoughts by the mere fact that the person is *one* organism. A *group of people* is made up of separate entities, and no central nervous system integrates or organizes their separate functions. If a group is to function effectively, some organization mechanism must be introduced, and this can quite naturally become the function of the group leader.

An analogy is found in the behavior of a starfish. The five rays respond to stimuli and can influence one another through physical contact. But for them to function in a unified response, each ray must send messages to the central nerve ring, which in turn collects the varied data and permits the integrative responses essential to effective locomotion, pursuit of prey, or feeding behavior. The central nervous system thus uses the messages it receives to integrate the data for the messages that it returns to the rays, rather than to serve as a source of data. If the central organization function is destroyed, the rays continue to respond, but as separate entities, responding and reacting independently.

The discussion leadership plays an important part in a group's performance. The controversy over whether persons working in groups are inferior or superior to the same number of persons working as individuals cannot be solved with a simple yes or no.[25] The answer depends on a group's leadership, on the nature of the problem, and on whether superiority is measured in terms of the quality of the decisions, the acceptance of the decision, or the number of ideas generated.

SKILL REQUIREMENTS OF THE LEADER

In Chapters 8 and 20, leadership skills were discussed in connection with group decisions and with successful interviews. In this chapter, the discussion leader is viewed as being in charge of the group *process*. It is the leader's responsibility to see that (1) idea getting and idea evaluation do not interfere with one another; (2) neither idea getting nor idea evaluation is overlooked when certain situations seem to require only one process; (3) participants do not become solution minded; (4) disagreement is used constructively; (5) the starting point is reconsidered from time to time; and (6) a variety of obstacles is located.

In addition, it is the leader's responsibility to indicate when idea evaluation is in order and to see that problem-solving principles are used. Serving as the integrator of the group process, the leader's role is to elicit ideas from the group, not to supply them. A leader's ideas are evaluated differently from those of other group members and tend to be either accepted or rejected. To prevent faulty evaluation, the leader should avoid expressing views unless the relationship in the group is such that these ideas receive the same treatment as those of others. The most common faults of discussion leaders are:

1. The tendency to take too much time in posing the problem, often restricting discussion by setting up ground rules. Clarification can come by way of members' questions. A short statement followed by a leader's willingness to wait out a pause is the surest way to get participation.

2. The tendency to suggest a solution by the way the problem is stated. A leader shows much more skill in stating a problem when at a loss about how to solve the problem. When the leader sincerely wants help, the group readily goes to the rescue. Often the leader poses a solution and thereby states the problem in terms of a choice: adopt or reject.

3. The tendency to respond to each participant's remark or question. True requests for information or clarification should be honored, but often members pose questions to draw out the leader's opinions. Many such requests can be turned back to the group. Getting members to respond to one another soon takes the leader out of the central position and allows group problem solving to proceed.

4. The tendency to withhold vital information, often for fear of hurting someone's feelings or for other considerate reasons. Facts are realities that cannot be avoided — only the way that they are used makes them

painful. An accident can be analyzed without blaming a person for an error.

Cognitive knowledge of these faults alters leader behavior insignificantly because the errors stem from habits based on traditional conceptualizations of a leader's functions. Each of the tendencies described can gradually be reduced through training with simulated problems. This was clearly evident in a study in which some leaders were given skill training in posing a problem and sharing data in a simulated problem situation.[26] They were trained to avoid suggesting solutions, to accept all ideas as possibilities, and to ask for other ideas. By keeping the searching process alive, avoiding persuasive situations, and not having a preference, the number of groups adopting innovative solutions rose to 68.0 percent as compared to 10.3 percent achieved under standard conditions. This was the highest innovative score ever achieved with this problem. Without the skill training and with only a knowledge of what to do, the other leaders were unable to execute the training principles and could be trapped by arguments.

It has been shown experimentally that two acts of the leader — how the problem is posed and the degree to which information is shared — significantly influence the quality of group solutions.[27] Leaders with some training performed these acts better than untrained leaders, but even with such training, the ratings were well below optimal.

Most training programs are in agreement regarding the values of participative management. Has this cognitive training influenced management skills in conducting problem-solving discussions? During the period 1952–1961, Maier used a role-play problem for training management personnel in problem-solving skills. A comparison of comparable groups during this period reveals no significant change in results over the period. High-quality solutions were no more likely to be achieved in 1961 than in 1952, but there is evidence to indicate an increase in permissive and persuasive methods.[28] Considerate treatment, however, is not an adequate substitute for discussion-leading skills, which greatly influence the quality of solutions to this problem.

The responsibilities described in this chapter, added to the interpersonal skills discussed earlier, give the leader's role a great deal of importance. In attempting to carry them out, the leader must be careful to avoid the accusation of being a manipulator. Since untrained participants do not distinguish between the *process* and *content* of discussions, this unusual role of the leader may be misunderstood. In order to capture the full value of the discussion process, it is best that participants as well as the leader become aware of the importance of the problem-solving *process* in determining the quality of decisions. By training groups in problem-solving skills, a problem-solving attitude is developed, so that the leadership function is greatly simplified by being shared.

BARGAINING VERSUS PROBLEM SOLVING

In bargaining situations, conflicting parties meet to iron out differences. A simple example is bargaining between a buyer and a seller. In such cases, a conflict in goals precludes cooperation. Instead, executing strategies, second-guessing the opposition's motives, and plotting to prevent one side's motives from being detected characterize the process.[29] Each tries to outwit the other and winning becomes an important incentive. The seller asks a price much higher than the going rate and the buyer's offer is far under it. Settlement is somewhere between the two initial solutions (prices), and each may perceive a victory. Persuasion and misrepresentation of intent characterize the bargaining process.

Studies of simulated bargaining situations indicate that potential mutual gains generate trust, whereas potential ability to inflict injury creates suspicion.[30] Threatening points of view introduce new factors, such as frustration and face saving. Pressures to reach agreement tend to evoke concessions but only when applied to both parties.[31] A bargainer who thinks the other is under pressure yields less, supporting the concept, "It pays to bargain from a position of strength."

Labor-management bargaining introduces additional factors. Not only do the participants meet to present different solutions, but they represent conflicting parties. Thus, even if discussion turned from bargaining to problem solving, the solution could not be adopted because the representatives would have to persuade the persons in authority. As the latter have not been present, they would not be influenced fully by the interaction between the bargainers.

Usually negotiation involves exchanging concessions — each party keeps some things and gives up others. Thus, the usual solution to the bargaining process is an alternative that represents a compromise between the two initial solutions. As long as the discussion is confined to the merits of two conflicting solutions, nothing new can enter the discussion. As failure to reach a solution becomes more costly (painful), making concessions becomes relatively less painful. It is analogous to the case of two parties fighting over an orange: each wants it, and to fight might involve damaging the orange. A compromise would be to cut the orange in half, each receiving half of what is wanted. However, if the opponents could have communicated and discovered that one wanted orange juice while the other wanted the peel (for candy), each could have had all that was wanted. This is characteristic of a solution as compared to a compromise.

The only problem solving that occurs in negotiation takes place during the period prior to the meeting. Each of the conflicting parties meets separately, and the bargaining representatives are made aware of guide lines and concession limits. Each side thus reaches a solution, and when the bargaining begins, one party poses its solution and the other party rejects it or counters with a different solution.

If the conflict between the parties is to be problem solved, it would be necessary for them to meet to discuss goals and see whether mutual interests could be located. Labor might demand an early retirement plan because the work is unpleasant. If unpleasantness of the work could be discussed, there might be ways other than escape from the job to solve the problem. Increasing job satisfaction might be more important than waiting for retirement and then facing boredom. However, the true factors are not revealed in bargaining, that is, the problem-solving stage is omitted because the parties reached solutions separately.

If mutual interests cannot be located, the solution does not lend itself to problem solving and becomes a matter of a choice between negotiating a settlement, a test of strength, or both. When solutions conflict, the problem-solving stage is passed over, and each side becomes committed to a different solution.

In conflicts between committed individuals, such as a union steward and a supervisor, confrontation can be avoided, and satisfaction for all parties can be achieved if each participant tries to understand the other's position.[32] This was demonstrated in an experiment using a simulated situation. The supervisor had laid off a worker for smoking in a restricted area, and the steward had promised to go to bat for the worker. Thus, both parties were committed to solutions and were in face-saving situations. If each persisted, future cooperation would be lost. If each gave in a little, compromises (for example, reduced layoff) could be achieved. Best results would be obtained if each understood the other's problem. Thus, the steward might assume responsibility for controlling smoking and tell other workers, that, in the future, regulations would be strictly enforced in exchange for rescinding this violation. Since the purpose of the rule was to control smoking, the supervisor would gain (assuming the union steward kept the promise), and the union steward would have carried out the promise to the worker.

A good resolution of a conflict, however, is not always acceptable to others who are involved. In a simulated study, a union steward was present to protect workers' interests in half the groups, and a time-study expert was present to aid a supervisor's cause in the other half.[33] The presence of the union steward resulted in less satisfactory solutions for the workers than the presence of the time-study expert, but workers having the union steward present felt that they had been helped, whereas workers having the time-study expert present did not. It appears that a union steward who was belligerent toward the supervisors made workers feel that someone was on their side, and hence they approved of the behavior, even though these efforts did them more harm than good. These findings support the conclusion that when people are frustrated and/or in a fighting mood, they might not accept a rational approach even if it were productive.

THE ORGANIZATION AND THE ENVIRONMENT

PROBLEM-SOLVING DISCUSSION PROCEDURES

THE TWO-COLUMN METHOD

When persons in conflict can and are willing to be brought together for group discussion, confrontation can often be prevented and the situation turned into a problem in which a mutual interest can be located. The two-column method of discussion is useful for accomplishing this aim.

When people are in conflict, discussion tends to polarize the positions so that the group with which one identifies has all the virtues and the opposition has all the faults. It seems improbable that a point of view having only faults should have any supporters, and yet each group in a conflict believes this.

A good procedure for reversing polarization is to designate two columns, one in which to post the merits of position A; the other, those of position B.[34] Participants are invited to supply arguments for either position. The discussion leader's duty is to see that each argument is specific and understood by everyone. Clarification, not agreement, is the objective. The point is then written in the appropriate column in abbreviated form.

As the columns increase in length, the same virtue might appear in both columns, and the points then neutralize each other. Soon emotionality is reduced, and some participants may begin contributing to both columns. This is a crucial development that could not have occurred earlier because it would have been a sign of disloyalty. Now, instead of there being a conflict between individuals, it is turned outward and becomes a conflict between the columns.

Once no further contributions can be made, the situation may be summarized as follows: "It seems both points of view have some merits, so let us try to see if we can come up with a position that recognizes the merits of both." This can become a problem of mutual interest and generate problem solving.

Situations that do not lend themselves to two alternatives may be handled by posting the positive and negative aspects of a single viewpoint in two columns. Having the strengths in one column and weaknesses in the other stimulates the group to search and discover ways to capture the strengths and avoid the weaknesses of an idea, thereby leading to its improvement.

The two-column method is similar to the risk technique described in Chapter 21. However, in addition to providing catharsis, the two-column method lays a foundation for locating mutual interests in conflict situations.

THE DEVELOPMENTAL DISCUSSION

The product of a discussion not only depends on the facts and the problem-solving skills of the people involved but also on the procedure followed. When groups are left to their own devices, some inefficiencies tend to arise.

1. Members bring up different aspects of the problem so the discussion is not synchronized.
2. Some aspects of the problem may not be explored.
3. The topics are not usually covered in a systematic or logical order.

Generally, there is too much initiation and too little listening. The *developmental discussion* was designed to synchronize and organize discussion so that participants can discuss the same aspects of the problem at the same time.[35] The procedure is to divide a problem into meaningful parts and discuss them in order. For example, a decision involving a promotion might be divided into the following five preliminary stages:

1. Listing the duties performed on the present job
2. Evaluating the person's performance by agreeing on a grade to assign to each duty
3. Listing the duties required on the new job
4. Assigning a grade to each (new duties raise questionable judgments)
5. Reaching agreement on the three duties that the new boss considers to be most important

In experiments in which some groups reached decisions following a *free* (no procedure specified) *discussion* and others a developmental discussion, striking differences in outcome occurred. In the case used in these experiments, Viola Burns was offered a promotion to a job different from her present one, but she was disturbed because she could not decide whether to accept it. Groups of three persons acting as consultants were given the same information and asked to decide which of three alternatives would be the best: (1) encourage her (because she is well qualified); (2) discourage her (assuming she would be unhappy and should wait

for a different opening); or (3) make no decision because the information is insufficient.

Table 22.2 presents the results. The first line shows the types of decisions reached when individuals were arbitrarily divided into groups (no discussion) and made the decision individually. *Encourage* decisions predominated and unanimous agreement appeared by chance in 23.0 percent of these groups. The free discussion resulted in a predominance of *Insufficient information* decisions. Disagreement over the other alternatives tended to cause a compromise on this intermediate decision (56.2 percent) with unanimous decisions reached in 76.5 percent of the groups. It will be seen that the *Encourage* decisions greatly outnumbered the *Discourage* decisions. The developmental discussion produced a predominance of *Discourage* decisions. Again, social pressure made for a high percentage of unanimous agreement (83.3 percent), but very few intermediate decisions occurred. Thus these groups were more decisive.

Two sources of error are inherent in this type of problem. The first is the influence of liking Viola (her description encourages this) — hardly a good criterion for promotion. The second is a desire to reward Viola for doing a good job by giving her a promotion,

TABLE 22.2 INFLUENCE OF FREE VERSUS DEVELOPMENTAL DISCUSSIONS

CONDITION	NUMBER	ENCOURAGE (PERCENT)	INSUFFICIENT INFORMATION (PERCENT)	DISCOURAGE (PERCENT)	UNANIMOUS GROUPS (PERCENT)
Individual	222	57.2	24.3	18.5[a,b]	23.0[d,e]
Free	153	35.9	56.2	7.8[a,c]	76.5[d]
Developmental	144	29.2	8.4	62.6[b,c]	83.3[e]

Note: Similarly superscripted figures are significantly different at the following levels: [a]$p < .01$, [b,c,d,e]$p < .001$.

SOURCE: From N. R. F. Maier. Prior commitment as a deterrent to group problem solving. *Personnel Psychol.*, 1973, *26*.

an unsound promotional procedure because superior ability on one job has little relation to ability on a different job. The developmental discussion tends to reduce these two sources of error, thus creating less indecision and the high-quality solution — *Discourage*. This solution is best for Viola and for the company.

This procedure can be used on all decisions involving promotion. In addition, many other problems lend themselves to logical breakdowns. Who gets the new equipment and which equipment should be discarded are separate problems arising whenever a new piece of equipment is introduced. Failure to separate these two parts of the problem leads to the assumption that the person with the worst equipment should get the new item. Budget problems may be broken down into categories, such as maintenance of present operations, essential new developments, ideal operating conditions, and so on. Thus, procedures as well as skills promote quality in decision making, but some skills are needed even in following procedures. If skills were unnecessary, the manager's job would be too simple to be challenging. It is the need for appropriate procedures, skills, and knowledge that make management a profession.

PROBLEM SOLVING: A RECAPITULATION

Attempts to improve organizations through development of communication channels, alteration of organizational structure, or consideration of organizational size tend to include the behavior of people. For example, supervising large groups requires more skilled managers than supervising small groups; supervising technical workers requires managerial styles different from those

supervising routine jobs; supervising researchers requires different leaders than supervising salesmen; and one employee prefers one kind of boss to another. Finding a solution to each type of situation poses new problems, because the solution that fits the average situation will be a poor fit for many others.

The solution to a problem should be designed to fit a specific situation. Attempts to generalize a good solution to other situations can fail unless the situations are essentially alike, and this cannot often be determined from the outside. Insofar as solutions need to be tailored to fit specific situations and the make-up of particular groups, there seems to be no alternative to the problem-solving approach.

However, the knowledge that problems can be solved as well as prevented by means of group discussion is not enough since group problem solving has liabilities as well as assets. There is no escape from the need for managers skilled in interpersonal relations and group interaction, and this need requires training of managers.

THE PROBLEM-SOLVING ATTITUDE

The problem-solving approach is characterized not only by the skills and principles already discussed but by an attitude — represented by a willingness to back away from an interest in a goal in order to explore the emotional investment in it.[36] It represents a desire to share information, to share the belief that persons with different personalities and training are not only interested in, but can contribute to, the search for ideas.

Withholding judgments of agreement and disagreement until full understanding of ideas is reached is essential to the problem-solving attitude. Value judgments are barriers to communication because they tend to cause ideas to be classified into already-known categories. New ideas, if classified into old categories, are stripped of any unique character they may have initially possessed. The problem-solving attitude is characterized by a search for differences in situations and ideas, and a reluctance to generalize solutions. Once a solution is decided upon, there is adequate time to find other situations that may profit from a similar one.

The problem-solving attitude also focuses on the present and the future. What has happened cannot be changed, but what can be done to prevent a recurrence or to correct damage already done represents a soluable problem.

Adapting to situations that cannot be corrected, rather than being distressed by them, is implied in the problem-solving attitude. Persons who have suffered a loss cannot adjust until they have accepted the loss and are ready to solve the problem of how to get the most out of life despite it. Often therapy is needed to help a patient change an attitude characterized by self-pity into a problem-solving state of mind. In a similar manner, groups must focus their thinking on things that can be done rather than concerning themselves with the past.

The problem-solving attitude requires the exclusion of fear so that participants can stimulate each other, rather than feel that they must screen their ideas in order to gain favorable evaluations. Trust seems to be an important ingredient, and trust requires the development of the attitude that more can be gained through cooperation than through selfishness. The development of this trust is a group change since a politically oriented person in a group can take advantage of naive trustfulness.

Groups that work together in problem-solving exercises and T-groups develop trust in a relatively short period of time. Trust is associated with the development of interpersonal respect. This type of respect is in contrast to the respect that stems from fear. Employees tend to regard supervisors who have high influence more highly than those with low influence.[37] High influence means, in these instances, power, and power represents the ability to instill fear.

In the past, individuals and groups have gained influence through their demonstrations of power. This has been a historical method for gaining influence and hence respect. The type of respect and influence gained without the use of power emerges from contributions in group problem solving and represents a basic change in the attitude from that found when members use manipulative methods to gain their own goals.

Groups should be trained to distinguish between attempts to influence one another and mutual problem solving. A knowledge of the difference helps to change behavior that is leading to conflict and polarization into behavior characterized by a discussion of goals, a recognition of differing perceptions of obstacles, and a search for alternatives. After a group has been trained, a reminder is usually all that is needed to cause the change.

EXTENDING USES OF PROBLEM SOLVING

Problem solving is likely to be attempted only when there is awareness of the problem, and it is most common when the content concerns things rather than people. Neglected areas of problem solving therefore are likely to be found in problems dealing with the management of people.[38] We have discussed in previous chapters the general problems of motivating individuals and groups, discipline, evaluating and developing employees, dealing with job stress and ambiguity, delegation, upward communication, how and when to bypass, the introduction of change, dealing with frustration, making jobs more interesting, and interpersonal relations. Problem solving each of these topics is aided by certain guiding principles, but exceptions need to be handled on an individual basis. Many of these problem situations arouse anger, and when this occurs, problem-solving behavior is inhibited.

If emotional involvement, common in dealings with people, is a deterrent to problem solving, it becomes desirable to work with situations in which things are going well, rather than after a breakdown occurs. That no obvious obstacles block the existing goal does not preclude the possibility of improvement (setting higher goals). Often future breakdowns can be avoided if they are anticipated and minor adjustments made. Preventive maintenance is possible with groups as well as with equipment.

Locating problems that are not acute requires sensitivity, but can be aided by a type of group discussion known as *posting problems*.[39] Instead of searching for solutions, the leader asks the group to describe obstacles that they encounter in the performance of the job. These problems should be briefly discussed and clarified before being written on the blackboard. No attempt should be made to solve them at the time of posting. Thus, attention is focused on problems rather than solutions. As people are experts in the things that they see as obstacles, participation is readily achieved if the items posted are accepted and not evaluated.

Groups that periodically work together can profit by becoming aware of each other's problems. Often the discussion becomes personal, but when a problem is located early, the emotional loading is less than if it surfaced later. The leader must be sensitive to face-saving situations and help members save face.

With a list of problems in hand, future discussion periods can be set aside for solving them. Some will disappear, the mere mentioning of them having improved communication and eliminated the problems. Others may be found to be reduced through the catharsis achieved in the discussion. For this reason, the problems should be examined from time to time and the opportunity to add new ones encouraged. Although the common complaint that time pressures do not permit such luxuries is voiced, we must consider the fact that preventive maintenance pays off when it applies to machinery, and machines are more easily repaired than people.

Group problem solving facilitates communication and can lead to the clarification of differences in goals. As much content of discussions associated with interpersonal conflict is based on misunderstandings, face-to-face discussions are needed to correct them. Once misunderstandings are removed, the true facts and motives can be explored. This predisposition to *problem solve* issues involving real or potential interpersonal conflict creates a climate that can pervade the whole management structure, so the organization can function as a unified organism. H. Levinson conceives of business as a problem-solving institution, and with proper use, group problem solving can approach an organizational philosophy.[40]

PROBLEM SOLVING: A SUMMARY

Participation in problem solving brings group members closer to agreement and tends to achieve acceptance of the solution as well as develop a sense of responsibility for its success. When this is the objective of

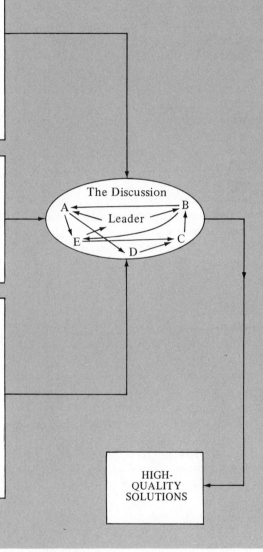

THE LEADER SHOULD:

1. State the problem in situational (not behavioral) terms as briefly as possible.
2. Share relevant information.
3. Obtain information from members.
4. Assume responsibility for the problem-solving process.
5. Avoid promoting a solution of his or her own.
6. Get the members to respond to one another.
7. Accept rather than evaluate contributions by clarifying and posting them.
8. Stimulate exploration of unusual obstacles.
9. Periodically summarize to indicate progress.

THE PROBLEM SHOULD:

1. Deal with a specific situation and not a general one.
2. Involve participants, and its solution should be of mutual interest to them.
3. Fall within the area of freedom of the leader for implementation.
4. Have a goal that is clear to all.

THE GROUP MEMBERS SHOULD:

1. Have mutual trust and willingness to share information.
2. Have minimal emotional involvement in a situation.
3. Delay solution preferences.
4. Prefer the problem-solving process to the persuasion process.
5. Perceive the leader as an integrator, rather than as an authority figure.
6. Perceive disagreement as a stimulant rather than as a threat.
7. Have developed a problem-solving attitude.

FIGURE 22.4 THREE SOURCES OF INPUT DETERMINE A SOLUTION'S QUALITY

a solution, the skill requirements are minimal. However, groups do not think systematically, and a variety of sources of error are present that tend to downgrade the objective quality of decisions.

When the success of decisions depends on the selection of solutions of high quality as well as high acceptance, three sources of input play a crucial part: the problem situation, the behavior of the leader, and the training and background of the employees.[41] The specific factors that promote high-quality solutions in each of these three sources are shown in Figure 22.4. The presence of all these factors is not essential to a high-quality outcome, but each contributes in its own way. When properly used, group thinking can be superior to the thinking of the best person in the group, but when improperly used, the group product tends to be that of the group's average thinking ability.

CONCLUSION

Consciousness of the scientific principles underlying organizational behavior provides a new framework, a new way of perceiving the world, and once learned, it cannot easily be dismissed. We may still become as frustrated and irrational as those untrained in this area, but we are more likely to recognize these feelings for what they are, to overcome them, and to find constructive solutions to problems.

The text contains descriptions of concepts and suggestions about behavior in many areas, from attitude formation to interviewing. But if any one concept is central to this volume, it is the idea of innovative problem solving. The manager who understands the principles involved in problem solving and who has achieved the necessary skills can turn disaster into hope and reconstruction, hostility into enthusiastic cooperation. More important, problem solving is an approach not only relevant to business but to personal lives: obstacles can be the genesis of despair and disillusionment, but they can also be seen as opportunities to exercise our individual creativity. In a world of automation, creative problem solving demonstrates that human potential for creative thought is as yet unchallenged by any computer.

NOTES

1. Crosby, A *Creativity and performance in industrial organizations*. New York: Barnes & Noble, 1968; Hyman, R., and Anderson, B. Problem solving. In D. Allison (Ed.), *Technical men, technical managers, and research productivity*. Cambridge, Mass.: MIT Press, 1969; Maier, N. R. F. Assets and liabilities in group problem solving: The need for an integrative function. *Psychol. Rev.*, 1967, 74, 239–249; Maier, N. R. F. *Problem-solving discussions and conferences: Leadership methods and skills*. New York: McGraw-Hill, 1963.
2. Maier, N. R. F. Prior commitment as a deterrent to group problem solving. *Personnel Psychol.*, 1973, 26.
3. Hoffman, L. R., and Maier, N. R. F. Valence in the adoption of solutions by problem-solving groups. *J. Person. Soc. Psychol.*, 1967, 6, 175–182.
4. Thrall, R. M., Coombs, C. H., and Davis, R. L. *Decision procedures*. New York: Wiley, 1954; Luce, R. D., and Raiffa, H. *Games and decisions*. New York: Wiley, 1957; Wallach, M. A., Kogan N., and Bem, D. J. Group influence on individual risk taking. *J. Abnorm. Soc. Psychol.*, 1962, 65, 75–86.
5. Clark, C. H. *Brainstorming*. Garden City, N.Y.: Doubleday, 1958; Dunnette, M. D., Campbell,

J., and Jaastad, K. The effect of group participation on brainstorming effectiveness for two industrial samples. *J. Appl. Psychol.,* 1963, *47,* 30–37; Maier, N. R. F., and Thurber, J. A. Limitations of procedures for improving group problem solving. *Psychol. Reports,* 1969, *25,* 639–656; Collins, B. E., and Guetzkow, H. *A social psychology of group processes in decision-making.* New York: Wiley, 1964.

6. Kepner, C. H., and Tregoe, B. B. *The rational manager: A systematic approach to problem solving and decision making.* New York: McGraw-Hill, 1965; Maier, Assets and liabilities in group problem solving, op. cit., Maier, N. R. F., and Thurber, J. A., op cit.: Thurber, J. A. *Measurement of process-product relationship in group problem solving.* Doctoral dissertation, University of Michigan, 1970; D'Zurilla, T. J., and Goldfried, M. R. Problem solving and behavior modification. *J. Abnorm. Psychol.,* 1971, *78,* 107–126.

7. Maier, N. R. F. *Problem solving and creativity: In individuals and groups.* Belmont, Calif.: Brooks/Cole, 1970; Maier, N. R. F. The integrative function in group problem solving. In L. R. Aronson, E. Tobach, D. S. Lehrman, and J. S. Rosenblatt, *Development and evolution of behavior: Essays in memory of T. C. Schneirla.* San Francisco: W. H. Freeman, 1970.

8. Colgrove, M. A. Stimulating creative problem solving: Innovative set. *Psychol. Reports,* 1968, *22,* 1205–1211; Maier, N. R. F. An aspect of human reasoning. *Brit. J. Psychol.,* 1933, *24,* 144–155; Raaheim, K., and Kaufmann, G. Level of activity and solving an unfamiliar task. *Psychol. Reports,* 1972, *30,* 271–274; Maier, N. R. F., and Casselman, G. G. Locating the difficulty in insight problems: Individual and sex differences. *Psychol. Reports,* 1970, *26,* 103–117.

9. Maier, N. R. F. *The appraisal interview: Objectives, methods, and skills.* New York: Wiley, 1958; Burke, R. J., Maier, N. R. F., and Hoffman, L. R. Function of hints in individual problem solving. *Amer. J. Psychol.* 1966, *79,* 389–399; Maier, N. R. F., and Burke, R. J. Influence of timing of hints on their effectiveness in problem solving. *Psychol. Reports,* 1967, *20,* 3–8; Maier, N. R. F., and Hoffman, L. R. Quality of first and second solutions in group problem solving. *J. Appl. Psychol.,* 1960, *44,* 278–283.

10. Kepner and Tregoe, op. cit.

11. Maier, N. R. F., and Solem, A. R. Improving solutions by turning choice situations into problems. *Personnel Psychol.,* 1962, *15,* 151–159.

12. Solem, A. R. *Some effects of discussion orientation on the development of insightful solutions.* Unpublished manuscript.

13. Maier, N. R. F., and Hayes, J. J. *Creative management.* New York: Wiley, 1962; Walker, E. L., and Heyns, R. W. *An anatomy for conformity.* Englewood Cliffs, N.J.: Prentice-Hall, 1962.

14. Hoffman, L. R. Group problem solving. In L. Berkowitz (Ed.), *Advances in experimental social psychology,* Vol. 2. New York: Academic Press, 1965, pp. 99–132.

15. Hoffman, L. R. Homogeneity of member personality and its effect on group problem solving. *J. Abnorm. Soc. Psychol.,* 1959, *58,* 27–32; Hoffman, L. R., and Maier, N. R. F. Quality and acceptance of problem solutions by members of homogeneous and heterogeneous groups. *J. Abnorm. Soc. Psychol.,* 1961, *62,* 401–407.

16. Collins and Guetzkow, op. cit.

17. Osborn, A. F. *Creative imagination: Principles and procedures of creative thinking.* New York: Scribner, 1953; Clark, C. H. *Brainstorming.* Garden City, N.Y.: Doubleday, 1958.

18. Brilhart, J. K., and Jochem, L. M. Effects of different patterns on outcomes of problem-solving discussions. *J. Appl. Psychol.,* 1964, *48,* 175–179.

19. Hoffman, L. R., and Maier, N. R. F. Valence in the adoption of solutions by problem-solving groups, op. cit.

20. Maier, N. R. F., and Hoffman, L. R. Quality of first and second solutions in group problem solving. *J. Appl. Psychol.,* 1960, *44,* 278–283; Maier, N. R. F., and Thurber, J. A. Innovative

THE ORGANIZATION AND THE ENVIRONMENT

problem solving by outsiders: A study of individuals and groups. *Personnel Psychol.*, 1969, *22*, 237–249.

21. Maier and Solem, op. cit.
22. Maier, N. R. F. *Problem-solving discussions and conferences.* New York: McGraw-Hill, 1963.
23. Coombs, C. H., and Pruitt, D. G. Components of risk in decision making: Probability and variance preferences. *J. Exper. Psychol.*, 1960, *60*, 265–277; Kass, N. Risk in decision making as a function of age, sex, and probability preferences. *Child Develop.*, 1964, *35*, 577–582; Wallach, M. A., and Kogan, N. The roles of information, discussion and concensus in group risk taking. *J. Exper. Soc. Psychol.*, 1965, *1*, 1–19; Wallach, M. A., Kogan, N., and Bem, D. J. Group influence on individual risk taking. *J. Abnorm. Soc. Psychol.*, 1962, *65*, 75–86.
24. Maier, N. R. F., and Thurber, J. A. Innovative problem solving by outsiders: A study of individuals and groups. *Personnel Psychol.*, 1969, *22*, 237–250.
25. Lorge, I., Fox, D., Davitz, J., and Brenner, M. A survey of studies contrasting the quality of group performance and individual performance. *Psychol. Bull.*, 1958, *55*, 337–372; Maier, N. R. F. Assets and liabilities in group problem solving. *Psychol. Rev.*, 1967, *74*, 239–249; Taylor, D. W., Berry, P. C., and Block, C. H. Does group participation when using brainstorming facilitate or inhibit creative thinking? *Administration Sci. Quart.*, 1958, *3*, 23–47.
26. Maier, N. R. F., and McRay, E. P. Increasing innovation in change situations through leadership skills. *Psychol. Reports*, 1972, *31*, 343–354.
27. Maier, N. R. F., and Sashkin, M. Specific leadership behaviors that promote problem solving. *Personnel Psychol.*, 1971, *24*, 35–44.
28. Maier, N. R. F. The integrative function in group problem-solving. In Aronson, et al., op. cit.
29. References to studies in bargaining may be found in Nemeth, C. Bargaining and reciprocity. *Psychol. Bull.*, 1970, *74*, 297–308; Siegel, S., and Fouraker, L. E. *Bargaining and group decision making.* New York: McGraw-Hill, 1960.
30. Deutsch, M., and Krauss, R. M. Studies of interpersonal bargaining. *J. Confl. Resol.*, 1962, *6*, 52–76; Deutsch, M. Trust and suspicion. *J. Confl. Resol.*, 1958, *2*, 265–279.
31. Komorita, S. S., and Barnes, M. Effects of pressures to reach agreement in bargaining. *J. Personal, Soc. Psychol.*, 1969, *13*, 245–252.
32. Maier, N. R. F., and Danielson, L. E. An evaluation of two approaches to discipline in industry. *J. Appl. Psychol.*, 1956, *40*, 319–323.
33. Maier, N. R. F., and Sashkin, M. The contributions of a union steward vs. a time-study man in introducing change: Role and sex effects. *Personnel Psychol.*, 1971, *24*, 268–278.
34. Maier, *Problem solving discussions and conferences,* op. cit.
35. Maier, N. R. F., and Maier, R. A. An experimental test of the effects of "developmental" vs. "free" discussion on the quality of group decisions. *J. Appl. Psychol.*, 1957, *41*, 320–323.
36. Maier, N. R. F. The problem solving attitude (Study 39). In N. R. F. Maier, *Problem solving and creativity: In individuals and groups.* Belmont, Calif.: Brooks/Cole, 1970.
37. Pelz, D. C. Leadership within a hierarchical organization, *J. Soc. Issues*, 1951, *7*, 49–55.
38. Maier, N. R. F. Extending the uses of problem solving (Study 40). In N. R. F. Maier, *Problem solving and creativity,* op. cit.
39. Maier, N. R. F. *Principles of human relations.* New York: Wiley, 1952, Maier, N. R. F. *Problem-solving discussions and conferences,* op. cit.
40. Levinson, H. *The exceptional executive: A psychological conception.* Cambridge, Mass.: Harvard University Press, 1968.
41. The relationship between leadership style and the characteristics of the situation are discussed in detail by Fiedler, who takes the position that different situations require different leadership styles. In Fiedler, F. E. *A theory of leadership effectiveness.* New York: McGraw-Hill, 1967; Sashkin, M.

Supervisory leadership in problem solving groups: Experimental tests of Fred Fiedler's "Theory of leadership effectiveness" in the laboratory using role play methods. Doctoral dissertation, University of Michigan, 1970.

SUGGESTED READINGS

The future role of business in society. New York: The Conference Board, 1977.

Carroll, A. B. (Ed.). *Managing corporate social responsibility.* Boston: Little, Brown, 1977.

Cavanagh, G. F. *American business values in transition.* Englewood Cliffs, N.J. Prentice-Hall, 1976.

Moffit, D. *America tomorrow.* Princeton, N.J.: Dow Jones Books, 1977.

Rowe, L. A., and Boise, W. B. (Eds). *Organizational and managerial innovation: A reader.* Santa Monica, Calif.: Goodyear, 1973.

AUTHOR/SOURCE INDEX

Clemes, S. R., 514n17
Clothier, R. C., 251n72, 391n39, 479nn6, 7, 480n29
Clouse, R. J., 458n18
Coch, L., 167n, 357n33, 480n19, 592n1
Cofer, G. N., 89n25
Coghill, G. E., 275n14
Cohen, K. S., 311n30
Cohen, N., 88n20
Cohen, S., 540n30
Colgrove, M. A., 248n22, 624n8
Collins, B., 116n9, 624nn5, 16
Connolly, T., 60n52
Cook, S. W., 116nn11, 12
Coombs, C. H., 622n4, 625n23
Coons, A. E., 155n12, 574n15
Cooper, J., 118n66
Corsini, R. J., 311n35
Costello, T. W., 356n9
Covner, B. J., 275n10
Cox, D., 431n75
Coyle, B. W., 242, 252n89
Cozan, L. W., 250n65
Craft, C. J., 311n30
Crain, K., 277n44
Crawford, A., 539n15
Crawford, P. L., 447n
Crites, J. O., 249n47
Cronbach, L. J., 56, 60n39, 249n47, 389n1
Cropley, A. J., 248n24
Crosby, A., 622n1
Crozier, M., 541n63
Cruikshank, R. M., 247n13
Crutchfield, R. S., 430n43
Csikszentmihalyi, M., 357n21, 430n53, 431
Culbert, S. A., 593n17
Culbertson, F. M., 311n35
Cummings, L. L., 18, 147, 156n17, 360nn84, 91, 392
Cyert, R. M., 574n27

Dahlstrom, W. G., 249n46
Dalton, G. W., 312n56
Danielson, L. E., 360n80, 455n, 459n49, 480n26, 625n32
Darley, J. G., 204n, 215n6, 359n59
Darley, J. M., 188n66
Darlington, R. B., 247n8
Darrow, C., 252n105
Davids, A., 458nn28, 30

Davies, D. R., 277n41
Davis, H., 248n37
Davis, K., 542
Davis, N. M., 356n4, 361nn105, 113
Davis, R. C., 6, 17n3, 540n43
Davis, R. L., 622n4
Davis, R. M., 276n34
Davitz, J., 625n25
Dawes, R. M., 574n29
Dawson, R. I., 311n28
Dearborn, W. F., 404, 429n17
DeCharms, R., 60n51, 357n26
Deci, E. L., 329, 330, 357nn17–19
DeCotiis, T. A., 390n22
Dees, V., 358n44
De Fleur, M., 117n31
DeGreene, K. B., 276n35, 277n47, 540n23, 541n52
DeLorno, T., 428n1
Dembo, T., 88n8, 514n27
Dempster, W. T., 275n10
Dennis, J. P., 541n49
Denniston, W. B., 574n33
De Reamer, R., 458n16
de Reuch, A., 576n83
De Silva, H. R., 456n6
Deutsch, K. W., 138n21
Deutsch, M., 116nn11, 12, 139n38, 358n54, 576n82, 625n30
Dewhirst, H. D., 359n66
Dexter, E. G., 540n25
Dicken, C. F., 249n39
Dickson, W. J., 89n27, 115nn1, 3, 118n54, 513n5, 514n15
Diener, E., 60n36
Dill, W. R., 541n69
Dimitrova, S., 428n7
Dinsmoor, J. A., 59n24
Dipboye, R. L., 251n84, 252n100
Directorate of Aerospace Safety, 428n11
DiVesta, F., 139n41
Dodd, W. E., 252n94
Dollard, J., 87n4
Donnelly, J. H., 576n68
Donnerstein, E., 540n45
Dossett, D. L., 359n66
Dovher, J. J., 390n12
Downey, H., 216
Downs, R., 540n45
Drake, C. A., 458n33
Drake, J. D., 118n51

Drake, L. E., 249n46
Drake, L. R., 251n71
Dressel, P. L., 391n43
Drucker, P., 576n67
Drummond, M. and W. B., 428n4
Druth, A., 277n56
Dubin, R., 18, 548, 573n5, 576n70
Dudek, D. H., 118n60, 188n17
Dulz, T., 542
Dunham, R., 277
Dunlap, J., 137n5
Dunnette, M. D., 17nn24, 31, 59n12, 60n34, 61n59, 118n49, 137n6, 215n9, 247nn5, 7, 9, 250nn58, 60, 64, 215n73, 252nn93, 104, 276n35, 277nn50, 53, 310n3, 311n40, 312n43, 356n10, 358n43, 359n58, 360n84, 390nn20, 21, 391n47, 430n42, 458n10, 459n44, 480n26, 539n1, 540n61, 574nn20, 36, 575nn38, 55, 576nn61, 72, 84, 592n3, 593n9, 622n5
Durand, D. E., 156n21
Durkin, H. E., 59n27
Dyck, F. J., 247n1
Dyer, L., 61n53, 360n95
Dyer, W. W., 59n13
D'Zurilla, T. J., 624n6

Eagly, A. H., 116n23, 117n32, 118n62
Edwards, A. L., 259n43
Edwards, C., 88n24
Edwards, J. D., 118n63
Edwards, R. C., 249n38
Efferson, C. A., 391n32
Eglash, A., 87n3
Ehninger, D., 310n22, 312
Eilon, S., 576n71
Eisenberg, P., 88n14
El-Assal, E., 117n31
Elbing, A. O., Jr., 311n38
Ellen, P., 87n3, 88n10
Ellertson, N., 359n59
Elms, A. C., 18n33
Emery, F. H., 541n67
Endler, N. W., 60n36
Epstein, S., 576n66
Erickson, C. E., 514n13
Erickson, E. H., 252n105
Erickson, J., 250n60

Erwin, F. W., 250n66
Evan, W. M., 480n28
Ewart, E., 390n9
Ewen, R. B., 215n2
Ex, J., 116n19

Fairchild, M., 360n83
Farmer, E., 429n20,
    458nn21, 23, 24, 31
Farris, G. F., 156n29, 479n9
Farson, R. E., 335, 358n42
Fatoullah, E., 118n65
Faunce, W. A., 429nn35, 36
Fayol, H., 6, 17n5, 144, 155n4
Fear, R. A., 251n75
Feather, N. T., 59nn5, 8, 357n28
Feinberg, M. R., 250n63
Feld, S., 360n82
Feldman, R. S., 87n3
Felts, W. J. L., 275n10
Fenichel, E., 458n9
Fenlason, A. F., 514n17
Ferguson, G. B., 514n17
Ferguson, L. W., 250n59
Ferree, C. E., 539nn10, 14, 16
Feshbach, S., 59n25, 87n5
Festinger, L., 106, 116n24,
    138nn26, 28
Fiedler, F. E., 148, 156n18,
    574n19, 625n41
Filley, A. C., 18, 391n41, 574n18
Finch, G., 277n48
Fine, S. A., 215nn8, 10
Finkle, R. B., 252n93
Fischhoff, B., 61n56, 574nn28, 34
Fishbein, M., 248n27
Fisher, B. A., 139
Fisk, D. W., 391n47
Fitts, P. M., 271, 276nn33, 36, 37,
    277n48
Flanagan, J. C., 277n54, 375,
    390nn18, 19
Fleishman, E. A., 35n4, 118n59,
    156nn13, 14, 247n12,
    248nn28, 30, 33, 250n61,
    251n75, 276nn35, 38, 310n12,
    391n42, 428n12, 479n5, 574n17
Floor, L. G., 157n43
Floyd, W. F., 277n45
Follett, M. P., 145, 155n9
Ford, A., 214n, 416, 430n49,
    539n17, 540n33
Ford, G. L., 392n48

Ford, J. J., 251n72
Ford, R. N., 431n78
Fordyce, J. K., 593n13
Forehand, G. A., 575n43
Foster, L. W., 344, 359n68
Fouraker, L. E., 625n29
Fox, D., 625n25
Fox, W. F., 540n28
Frank, J. D., 357n35
Frank, L. L., 251n82
Fraser, D. C., 428n12
Fraser, J. A., 430nn52, 63
Fraser, J. Munro, 241, 243, 251n77,
    252n90, 262n
Frederick, W. C., 542
Freeman, S., 540n30
Freeman, W. H., 87n1
French, E. G., 59n7, 138n22
French, G. W., 428n1
French, J. R. P., Jr., 113, 118n57,
    138n15, 167n, 357n33, 359n73,
    391nn28, 33, 421, 430n61,
    480n19, 592n1
French, W. L., 588, 593,
    593nn13, 14
French, W. R., 481
Freund, A., 430n59
Friedmann, E. A., 429n41
Fugita, S. S., 250n57

Gabel, W. C., 275n10
Gadel, M. S., 480nn16, 17
Gadlin, H., 18n33
Gagné, R. M., 12, 17nn23, 29,
    251n75, 310n12
Galbraith, J. R., 577
Galenson, W., 429n35, 431n77
Gardner, E., 89n25
Gardner, J. E., 431n70
Garfiel, E., 248n29
Garner, W., 276n24
Gärtner, H., 428n6
Gavin, J. F., 513n1
Geiger, K., 576n75
Geldlard, F. A., 248n37
Gellerman, S. W., 48, 59n20,
    249n54
Georgopoulos, B. S., 215n13,
    391n47
Gerard, H. B., 117n29
Gergum, B. O., 430n46
Gettys, C. F., 574n33
Getzels, J. W., 247n16

Ghiselli, E. E., 18n33, 216, 241,
    251n83, 265, 276n20, 389n1,
    390n8, 391n47
Gibb, J. R., 311n39, 592n8
Gibson, W. D., 514n18
Giese, W. J., 249n40
Gilbert, R. W., 358n41
Gilbreth, Frank B., 6, 17n2, 259,
    275nn3, 7, 400, 428n5
Gilbreth, Lillian, 259, 275n7, 400,
    428n5
Gilchrist, J. C., 138n23
Gilmer, B. H., 250n59, 534,
    575n43
Ginott, H. G., 89n29, 488,
    514nn10, 11
Ginsburg, W. L., 312n48
Gintner, G., 156n31
Glaser, B. G., 17n30
Glaser, N. M., 88n10
Glaser, R., 248n30
Glass, D. C., 533, 540nn30, 44
Glatzer, H. T., 59n27
Glennon, J. R., 249n44, 250n60
Glover, J. D., 310n23
Gluskinos, U. M., 348n, 360n79
Goffman, E., 149, 156n25
Gold, M., 138n8
Goldberg, H., 89
Goldberg, M. H., 311n28
Goldberg, W., 574n27
Goldfried, M. R., 624n6
Goldman, M., 139n40, 358n55
Goldmark, J., 428n15
Golembiewski, R. T., 17n18,
    429n28
Gombert, W., 265, 276n17
Gooding, J., 480n33
Goodman, P., 312nn50, 52, 313
Gordon, M. E., 250n68
Gordon, M. M., 574n33
Gordon, T., 311n39
Gordon, W. J. J., 17n20
Gotterer, M. G., 276n28
Graen, G., 58, 61n61, 558, 575n55
Grant, D. L., 116n11, 252n91,
    514n24
Green, H. L., 540n24
Greenberg, J., 88n23, 357n23
Greene, C. N., 188
Greene, J. E., Sr. and J. E., Jr.,
    116n13
Greene, J. R., 311n30

Greenhaus, J. H., 360n86, 513n1
Greenley, R. J., 309n1
Greenwald, A. G., 116n25, 117n25
Greenwood, M., 445n, 458n14
Gregory, D., 359n59
Greller, M. M., 359n64, 392
Griffiths, I. D., 539n19
Grindley, G. C., 358n44
Gronbeck, B. E., 310n22, 312
Groner, D. M., 277n53
Gross, N., 359n59
Grunthal, A. L., 250n67, 312n51
Gruvaeus, G., 116n4
Guest, R. H., 58n2, 276n27, 277n55, 361n104, 431n76
Guetzkow, H. S., 59n19, 358n56, 576n70, 624nn5, 16
Guilford, J. P., 228, 248nn21, 23, 249n49, 250n59
Gulick, L., 6, 17n4, 155n9
Gulo, M. J., 89n25
Gurin, G., 157n43, 360n82
Guthrie, E. R., 310n6
Guzzardi, W., Jr., 312n47, 479n7

Haanpera, S., 250n66
Hackman, J. R., 35, 60n37, 251n82, 278, 431n80, 432, 576n73
Hage, J., 515n28, 540n45
Hagstrom, W. O., 116n20
Hahn, J. F., 534, 541n51
Haire, M., 551, 552, 573nn3–5, 574nn21–27 passim, 576n70
Hall, D. F., 344, 359n68
Hall, D. T., 252nn96, 98, 104, 253, 312nn46, 49, 59
Hall, E. T., 541n53
Hall, F. S., 253, 312n46
Hall, J., 357n23
Hall, O. M., 116nn17, 22
Hall, R. C., 248n33
Halpern, P. L., 540n45
Halverson, H. M., 275n14
Hamilton, G. V., 88n10
Hamilton, J. A., 88n10
Hammond, K. R., 115n4, 116n4
Hammond, L. K., 358n55
Hamner, W. C., 35, 116n4, 370, 390n6
Hansen, L. M., 250n68
Hansson, L., 541n46
Hare, A. P., 138n31

Harlan, W. H., 429n41
Harlow, D. N., 155n8
Harrell, T. W., 236, 239, 249n53, 250n62, 251nn69, 74, 390n17
Harris, E. F., 35n4, 156nn13, 14, 479n5, 574n17
Harris, R. T., 577, 593
Harrower, M. R., 250n55
Hart, J. T., 513n9
Hartley, E. L., 155n5, 187n3
Hartshorne, H., 35n2
Haskins, J. B., 117n27
Hathaway, S. R., 249n46
Hawkes, G. R., 541n50
Hayakawa, S. I., 116n5
Hayes, E. G., 248n32
Hayes, John J., 117n48, 187n9, 624n13
Heckman, R. W., 277n52
Hedberg, R., 249nn39, 42, 311n28, 574n27
Heimstra, N. W., 429n34
Heller, F. A., 357n31
Hellriegel, D., 60n43
Hempel, W. E., Jr., 248n28
Hemphill, J. K., 215n9, 311n32
Hemphill, L., 575n39
Henderson, J. E., 118n66
Hendler, E., 540n27
Hendricks, M., 248n23
Heneman, H. G., 251nn72, 84, 390n22, 391n31
Henig, M. S., 458n32
Henle, M., 59n28, 431n73
Henle, P., 429n35
Herring, J. W., 250n66
Hersey, R. B., 360n78, 458nn27, 29
Hertzberg, H. T. E., 275n10
Herzberg, F., 47, 48, 52, 56, 59nn14, 29, 278, 358n40, 360n80, 431n78, 480nn23, 26, 575n46
Heyns, R. W., 187n13, 358n56, 624n13
Hickson, D. J., 575n36
Highland, R. W., 373, 390n13
Hill, J. M. M., 458n11
Hill, J. W., 155n8
Hill, T. S., 89n25
Hillery, J. M., 250n57
Hilles, R., 17n18, 429n28
Himler, L. E., 89n23, 415n21
Himmelfarb, S., 116n23

Hinings, C. R., 575n36
Hinrichs, J. R., 250n66, 252n94, 310n3
Hirsch, J. S., 59n27
Hirsch, P. M., 541n64
Hirsh, I. J., 248n37
Hoepfner, R., 248n23
Hoffman, L. R., 138nn25, 27, 187n6, 273, 277nn39, 40, 46, 356n12, 361n111, 391n29, 430n62, 572, 576n81, 601, 622n3, 624nn9, 14, 15, 19, 20
Hoffman, L. W., 357n28
Holbrook, J., 593n15
Holland, J. L., 312n59
Hollander, E. P., 157
Holliman, R. W., 588, 593n14
Holtzman, J. S., 277n53
Homans, G. C., 115n2, 575n40
Hooven, J. J., 391n29
Hoppe, F., 357n29
Hoppock, R., 349, 360n85
Horai, J., 118n65
Horn, P., 431n78, 432, 481
Horner, M. S., 330, 357n27
Horowitz, I. R., 89n24
Horton, G. P., 310n6
Horwitz, M., 431n73
House, R. J., 18, 148, 156n19, 215n11, 311n40, 391n41, 574n18, 575n56, 593n9
Houser, J. D., 360n77
Howe, H. F., 89n31
Hower, R. M., 310n23
Howland, C. I., 59n25, 310n10, 458n8, 514n23
Hrapchak, W. J., 547n16
Huett, D. L., 251n72
Hughes, J. L., 311n27
Huizinga, J., 429n39
Hulbert, S. F., 277n47
Hulett, J. E., Jr., 139n43
Hulin, C. L., 360nn83, 89, 90, 391n46, 479n12, 481, 539nn4, 6
Hull, C. L., 215n4
Hull, R. L., 350, 360nn81, 94
Humes, J. F., 431n68
Humm, D. G., 249n41
Humphrey, N. D., 88n21
Hunt, D. L., 431n70
Hunt, J. G., 156n20
Hunt, R. G., 513n8, 515
Hunt, W. A., 513n9

Opsahl, R. L., 356n10, 358n43
O'Reilly, C. H., III, 515
Organ, D. W., 361n106
Orlansky, J., 275n10
Orr, D. B., 215n9
Orvey, R. D., 252n104
Osborn, A. F., 624n17
Ostojčić, A., 338n, 339n, 358n57
Ostrom, T. M., 116n25
Otis, J. L., 391n39
Ouchi, W. G., 550, 573n12
Owens, W. A., 250n64

Parker, D., 61n54
Parker, J. F., Jr., 276n38
Parker, J. W., 392n48
Parker, T. C., 539n3
Parry, J. B., 247n14
Parsons, S. O., 250n60
Parsons, T., 138nn19, 20
Pascale, R. T., 550, 573n13
Patchen, M., 59n16, 276n31
Paterson, D. G., 204n, 215n6
Patrick, J. R., 88n10
Patten, T. D., 310n21
Patterson, C. H., 513n9, 514n17
Patton, J. A., 391n40
Pauley, E., 541n52
Payne, R., 574n36
Pelz, D. C., 138n30, 156n33,
    360n87, 479n10, 480n26,
    576n65, 625n37
Pennings, J. M., 188
Pepitone, A., 137n4
Pepler, R. D., 540n29
Peres, S. H., 252n104
Perkin, D. B., 118n51
Perrow, C., 145, 155n6, 156n15
Pervin, L. A., 215n7
Peters, L. H., 251n82, 252n87
Peterson, C. R., 574n33
Peterson, R. O., 575n46
Peterson, R. R., 540n23
Pettigrew, A. M., 593n19
Petz, B., 338n, 339n, 358n57,
    428n3
Pfaffman, C., 248n37
Pfeffer, J., 60n47, 119
Phares, E. J., 60n46
Phillips, J. D., 19n
Phillips, J. S., 514n12
Phillips, S., 540n30

Pigors, F., 311n24
Pigors, P. J. W., 218n, 311n24
Piore, M. J., 312n48
Piotrowski, Z. A., 250n55
Pirsig, R. M., 17n19
Planty, E. G., 391n32
Pock, J. C., 536, 541n63
Poffenberger, A. T.,
    540nn20, 21, 32
Pollock, K. G., 540n38, 541n47
Pomeroy, W. B., 514n25
Pondy, R. W., 119
Poor, R., 17n17
Porter, A., 89n33
Porter, D. T., 118n64
Porter, L. W., 35, 60n35, 61, 119,
    310n12, 359n58, 481, 575n50
Pratt, K. C., 275n14
Preiss, J. J., 117n47
Presnall, L. P., 88n18, 514n18
Pressey, S. L., 301, 311n25
Price, J., 481
Prien, E. P., 391n39
Pritchard, R. D., 60nn34, 40,
    61n60, 411, 429n42
Probst, J. B., 390n15
Pruitt, D. G., 625n23
Pryor, M. G., 119
Pugh, D. S., 155n4, 574–575n36
Purdy, K., 431n80, 432

Quinn, R. P., 89n32, 575n57

Raaheim, K., 624n8
Raia, A. P., 576n69
Raiffa, H., 622n4
Raloff, J., 312nn54, 55
Rand, G., 539nn10, 14, 16
Rand, T. M., 251n82
Randall, C., 480n30
Randolph, W. A., 311n31
Rao, K. V., 358n44
Raphaelson, A. C., 357n28
Rawdon, R., 311n30
Raynor, J. D., 357n26
Read, W. H., 391nn29, 30
Reed, R., Jr., 275n12
Reede, L. G., 540n30
Reif, W. E., 430n60
Reinhardt, H., 431n65
Reisman, D., 429n39

Reitz, H. J., 139
Renshaw, J. R., 593n17
Rhenman, E., 541n70
Rhine, R. J., 117n25
Rhode, J. G., 357n23, 577
Rhodes, F., 431n70
Ricciardi, F. M., 17n29
Richardson, M. W., 390nn12, 16
Ricks, D. T., 252n105
Ritchie, J. B., 592n2
Rizzo, J. R., 155n8, 575n56
Roberts, D. F., 277n45
Roberts, K. A., 515
Roberts, K. H., 360n89
Robey, D., 431n79
Robinson, H., 116n10
Roethlisberger, F. J., 89n27,
    115nn1, 3, 156n40, 513n5,
    514n15, 541n60
Roff, M., 252n105
Rogers, C. R., 89nn28, 32, 118n55,
    251n85, 487, 513nn6, 9,
    514nn9, 16
Rogers, H. B., 275n5
Rogers, M., 138n10
Rohrer, J., 117n45
Ronan, W. W., 391n39
Rosen, B., 253
Rosen, H., 587, 593n11
Rosenbaum, W., 356n3
Rosenberg, M. J., 116n21
Rosenblatt, J. S., 87n1, 624n7
Rosenblith, W. A., 249n37
Rosenthal, R. A., 89n32, 575n57
Rosenthal, S. P., 116n15, 16
Ross, I., 17n9, 247n3
Rothe, H. F., 385n, 391n42,
    430n56
Rotter, J. B., 56, 59n8, 60n44,
    252n101
Rowan, R., 145, 155n7
Rowe, L. A., 626
Rowland, K. M., 359n66
Rowland, V. K., 391nn32, 34
Roy, D. F., 431n77
Rubin, G., 276n26
Ruch, C. H., Jr., 392n47
Ruilmann, C. J., 89n25
Rule, B. G., 539n19
Russell, D., 480n23
Russell, R. W., 358n44
Ryan, T. A., 428n2
Ryman, D. H., 250n66

Steinman, D. O., 115n4
Stevens, S. M., 390n4
Stevens, S. S., 248nn36, 37,
  276n33, 310n10, 430n48
Stewart, R. D., 458n37
Stewart, T. R., 115n4
Stickel, E. G., 249n55
Stieglitz, H., 575n48
Stier, F., 276n23
Stock, F. G. L., 360n75,
  430nn52, 54, 63, 431n67
Stockbauer, J. W., 139n40
Stogdill, R. M., 155n12, 157,
  574n15
Stokols, D., 541nn54, 69
Stone, E. F., 60n35
Stone, R. A., 251n71
Stoner, J., 157
Stouffer, S. A., 139n44
Strauss, A. L., 17n30
Strauss, G., 389n1
Strickland, B. R., 357n32
Stringer, B., 539n19
Stringer, R. A., 575n37
Strump, F. N., 458n34
Suedfeld, P., 117n46
Summers, D. A., 116n4
Sun, K. H., 275n14
Super, D. E., 249n47,
  252nn98, 105, 312n49
Sussman, H., 310n13
Swanson, G. E., 88nn12, 19
Suzansky, J. W., 431n79

Tagiuri, R., 575n38
Takahuwa, E., 428n13
Talacci, S., 479n13
Tannenbaum, R., 311n39, 361n101,
  592n8
Tanofsky, R., 18n33
Taylor, D. W., 625n25
Taylor, E. K., 249n54, 250n56,
  391n45, 392n48
Taylor, Frederick W., 6, 17n1,
  258–259, 260, 275nn1, 2
Taylor, M., 480n22
Tedeschi, J. T., 155n8
Teel, K. S., 309n1
Telly, C. S., 481
Templeton, J., 155n2
Terai, T., 61
Terborg, J. R., 60n49, 116n7,
  251n82, 252n87, 359n69

Terpstra, D. E., 251n84
Theriault, R., 360n95
Thomas, A., 252n105
Thomas, K., 576n84
Thomas, R., 156n27
Thompson, J. D., 541n58
Thompson, P. H., 61n54, 312n56
Thomson, R. M., 275n10
Thorndike, E. L., 310n6, 390n2
Thrall, R. M., 622n4
Thurber, J. A., 247n19, 248n20,
  251n80, 624nn5, 6, 20, 625n24
Thurstone, L. L., 105, 116nn11, 14
Tiffin, Joseph, 202, 215n5, 216,
  248n35, 249n40, 275n5,
  390nn3, 9
Tinker, M. A., 527n
Tobach, E., 87n1, 624n7
Tolliver, J., 61n55, 431
Tomlinson, T. M., 513n9
Torrance, E. P., 228, 247n17,
  248n21
Tosi, H. L., 35
Treat, K., 248n31
Tregoe, B. B., 358n52, 624nn6, 10
Triandis, H. C., 117n30
Trier, H., 117n40
Trist, E. L., 458n11, 541n67
Tufts College Institute for Applied
  Experimental Psychology,
  248n37
Tune, G. S., 277n41
Turner, A. N., 413n76, 539n5
Turner, C., 575n36
Tversky, A., 574nn28, 30

Uhrbock, R. S., 431n71
Underwood, B. and B., 89n24
University of Michigan School of
  Public Health, 444n, 458n12
Urwick, L., 6, 17n4, 155n9

Vaillant, G. E., 86, 89nn34, 38,
  253n109, 515
Van der Veen, F., 514n21
Van Doorn, J. A., 576n83
Van Maanen, J. V., 360n93
Van Ness, E. H., 541n69
Vansena, L. S., 593n19
Van Zelst, R. H., 138nn12, 29,
  235, 249n52, 350, 360n92,
  391n25, 452, 459nn40, 41
Vernon, H. M., 275n9, 406,

428n10, 429nn18, 19, 22, 24, 440,
  456nn2, 7, 458nn8, 22
Vernon, J., 117n46
Vernon, P. E., 247n14
Veroff, J., 360n82
Verser, G. C., 88n16, 139n32,
  456n4, 479n, 480nn22, 27
Vettori, F. L., 311n28
Vidal, D., 247n4
Viteles, M. S., 17n16, 428n2,
  429n18, 453, 456n7, 459n47
von Trebra, P., 276n26
Vredenburgh, D., 188
Vroom, V. H., 59n18, 157,
  215n12, 334n, 357n38, 358n43,
  359n58, 361n103

Wadsworth, G. W., 249n41
Wagner, A. B., 312n44, 593n10
Wagner, R., 251n72
Waldbott, G. F., 539n18
Walker, C. R., 58n2, 138n13,
  276n27, 277n55, 361n104,
  431n75
Walker, E. L., 624n13
Walker, J. W., 252n97
Wallach, M. A., 622n4, 625n23
Wallen, R. W., 249n55
Walster, E., 61n58
Walther, R. H., 250n60
Wanous, J., 253, 431n79
Ware, H. F., 309n1
Warner, H., 116n4
Warr, P., 18n33, 593n19
Warren, N., 430n50
Warts, W., 117n28
Waters, L. K., 390n14
Watson, G., 59n26, 88n6, 137n3,
  139n42, 360n81
Watson, J., 592n4
Ways, M., 17n12, 88n13, 188n16,
  359n72
Weber, A. R., 312n48
Webster, E. C., 252n86
Wechsler, D., 458n26
Wechsler, I. R., 311n39, 361n101,
  592n8
Weed, S. E., 60n43, 156n24
Wehrkamp, R., 276n25
Weick, K. E., Jr., 118n49, 359n58,
  575n38
Weil, R., 593n13
Weiner, B., 60n45

SUBJECT INDEX

Ability(ies)
average, as basis for expectations, 198
defined, 210
as factor in performance, 196, 210–215
and motivation, 211–212, 294
relationship between, 207–210
sex and race differences in, 200–201
tests of, *see* Tests
variation in (shown on distribution curve), 197, 201–202
See also Job skill(s)
Absenteeism, 408
alcoholism and, 451
boredom and, 266
fatigue and, 407
in Hawthorne study, 95
job dissatisfaction and, 48, 470
leadership and, 147
organizational size and, 555
Acceptance of decision, *see* Decision making
Accidents
alcoholism and, 451
boredom and, 266, 441
case-study approach to, 454
experience and, 452
fatigue and, 401, 407, 440–441
frequency of, psychological tests and, 448–451
and frustration, 451–452
leadership and, 147
proneness to, 443, 444–454, 456
reduction/prevention of, 30, 31, 438–444, 453, 456

safety violations and, 444, 454–455
Accomplishment
as product of behavior, 24–26
in S-O-B-A sequence, *see* Stimulus
Accountability, *see* Responsibility
Achievement, 342
need for, 45–46, 52, 57, 329, 333
revisions of theory of, 329–331
Action research, 14, 591. *See also* Change
Activity, 68
as goal, 52–53, 57
Adaptive behavior, *see* Behavior
Advancement, *see* Promotion/advancement
Advertising, and behavior change, 114. *See also* Propaganda
Affiliation, *see* Group(s); Social needs
AF of L, personality tests of agents of, 235
Age
and ability to adjust and cope, 247
and accident rates, 452–453
and aging, counseling for, 500
discrimination on basis of, 223
and increase in average age of worker, 8, 246
and job turnover, 467
methods of payment and, 323, 324
and visual acuity, 230
Aggression, *see* Frustration
Air pollution, 528–531
Alcoholism

and accidents, 451
determination of, 499
American Telephone and Telegraph Company, 97
Anarchy, defined, 162
Anger, avoidance of, in dealing with frustration, 83
Anticipation, and behavior, 27, 42, 43
Applied psychology, *see* Psychology
Aptitude tests, *see* Tests
Area of freedom
boundaries of, 564
in group decision, 174–177, 179
and organizational level, 562–

Aspiration, level of, 331–333, 336. *See also* Failure; Success
Assessment center, 244–245. *See also* Interviews
Asset management, 591–592
Atmospheric conditions
and accident frequency, 441
effects of, 528–531
Attitude(s)
change in, 101, 105–115 *passim*, 289, 296, 297, 308
constructive, manager's acquisition of, 16
of counselor, 491, 495–496 (*see also* Counseling)
discovery of, in counseling, 496
of discussion leader, 180–181
dissatisfaction/satisfaction, *see* Satisfaction
effect of, on production, 94–97, 154

Attitude(s) (*continued*)
and facts, 99–101, 102–105, 108, 109, 111
fatigue/boredom and, 398, 420–423
fixation of, 75
frame of reference and, 97–98, 102–104, 108, 115, 382, 524
group affiliation and, 108–109
insight into, 95–96
job, 347, 349–352
  noise and, 533–534
meanings determined by, 99–101, 104–105
measurement of (and attitude scale), 105–106
nature and effects of, 97–105
and opinions, 98–99, 101–102, 108, 109
personality traits and, 233, 235
problem-solving, 619–620
punishment vs. reward and, 51 (*see also* Punishment)
"reconcile contradictions," 222
rest periods and, 406
results of studies of, 106–109
social, of supervisor/work leader, 235
social needs and, 44–45, 95–96
surveys of, 109–111
in testing, 237
See also Bias/prejudice; Feelings; Frustration; Morale; Motivation; Understanding; Values
Attraction/approach response, *see* Response(s)
Attribution theory, *see* Theory(ies)
Authority
experimental research on, 162, 164–167
location(s) of, 162, 168, 174
See also Leadership
Autocracy, 168
defined, 162
elimination of, 164–165
See also Leadership
Automation
and down-time, 271
and engineering psychology, 268–274
and fatigue/boredom, 410, 421

opposition to, 130, 268
See also Computerization
Availability principle (in frustration), 77–78
Average (on normal distribution curve), 197
Avoidance response, *see* Response(s)

Bargaining
contract, and frustration, 81
vs. problem solving, 615–616
wages as issue in, 354
BARS (behaviorally anchored rating scale), 376. *See also* Merit rating
Behavior
accomplishment as product of, 24–26
acquired, 29–30, 289
adaptive, 43, 68
  vs. unadaptive, 70–71, 73
analysis of, 22, 24–25
anticipation and, 27, 42, 43
changes/modifications in, 29–30, 107, 289
  and attitude change, 114–115
group decision making and, 182, 601–602
  punishment vs. reward and, 51
role changes and, 552
choice, *see* Decision making
cooperative, 95–97
extrovert vs. introvert, 78n
goal-oriented, 71, 79–81, 343, 566
group, *see* Group(s)
influences on/causes of, 22–26
  anticipation and, 27, 42, 43
basic, ignorance of, 27–28
different (of same behavior), 32–33, 33 (fig.)
excuses vs., 28
extrinsic/intrinsic incentives, 327
frustration, 68–72 (*see also* Frustration)
heredity, 29–30, 78
same (of different behavior), 33, 34 (fig.)
of interviewer for employment, 242
of leader, *see* Leadership

mutually supportive, *see* Cooperation
opinion determining, 98
in organizations, theories and systems-based views of, 548–553
perception and, 23–24
prediction of, 78
prevention/inhibition of, 24, 51
problem-solving, *see* Problem solving
purpose in, 25, 26–27
refreezing patterns of, 585
self-oriented, 55
small-group, research on, 126–132
in S-O-B-A sequence, *see* Stimulus
spatial, 535
stereotyped, 80 (*see also* Fixation)
understanding vs. evaluation of, 22, 24
variation of/variability in, 28–29, 68, 78 (*see also* Individual differences)
X and Y theories of, 549–550
See also Attitude(s); Expectations; Motivation; Performance/production; Response(s)
Behavioral taxonomy, 274. *See also* Ability(ies)
Behavior observation scaling, 274
Bell-shaped curve, *see* Normal distribution curve
Bell Telephone System, 554
  Management Progress Study, 243
  Ohio Company, 502
Benefits, salary, 327
Bennington College, 322
Bethlehem Steel Company, 258
Bias/prejudice
acknowledgment of, 387
in employment, 225
in "fast-track" programs, 245
in interviews, 240, 241–242
prejudice defined, 100
in testing/assessment (avoidance of), 237, 244
See also Attitude(s); Discrimination (racial, sexual)
Bimodal curves, *see* Normal distribution curve
Biodate approach (as testing alternative), 237–238

Biofeedback therapy, 87. *See also* Feedback

Blacks, *see* Minority groups

Blocking, mental, 417. *See also* Fatigue

Bootstrapping, 268

Boredom, 275, 412, 413
  and accidents, 266, 441
  defined, 418
  -efficiency relationship, 417–419, 427
  in learning process, 290
  methods of eliminating, 421–423
  See also Fatigue

Brainstorming, 602, 609. *See also* Discussion

Brainwashing, 115. *See also* Propaganda

Business games, *see* Training

Bypassing, 560–561, 566. *See also* Communication; Organization(s)

Cambridge, England, fatigue studies in, 402

Career planning and stages, 245–247

Case method, 300. *See also* Training

Catharsis, 83–85, 86
  defined, 83
  in problem-solving discussion, 617

Causation formula (S-O-B-A), *see* Stimulus

Change
  in attitude, *see* Attitude(s)
  in behavior, *see* Behavior
  functions of agents of, 14, 585–586, 589, 590, 591
  in motivation (with maturity), 246
  in nature of work, 268
  of needs and values, 350
  in organism, 30–31
  in organization, 584–592
  resistance to, 165, 352–354
  in stimulus/situation(s), 30, 31

Choice(s), *see* Decision making

"Classical management theory," *see* Management

Cognitive dissonance theory, 105–106. *See also* Theory(ies)

Communication

attitude surveys and, 109
difficulty in, 44, 105
discussion and, 113–114, 296
between groups, 136–137
listening and, 48, 95, 112–113, 476, 478, 488–496, 498, 500, 507–508
of needs, 48, 476
of performance evaluation, 376–377
persuasion, 113, 114, 170, 172
rank/power as barrier to, 511, 513, 548, 561–562
role-playing and, 112
upward, 562, 567–569, 570
value judgments as barriers to, 619–620
See also Bypassing; Interpersonal relations; Interviews; Understanding

Communism, 80, 115

Competition
  vs. cooperation, 135–136, 601
  intra- vs. intergroup, 11, 135–136
  limitations of, 340–341
  and motivation, 11, 337–341

Computerization, 272–273
  and bootstrapping, 268
  in evaluating hiring and promotional practices, 222
  See also Automation

Conditioning, operant, and conditioned response, *see* Learning

Conflict
  defined, 572
  in goals/motivation, 53–55, 340
  group, 132, 137
  within organization, management of, 572–573
  role, 559
  work group-management, 34–35, 130, 152–153
  See also Interpersonal relations

Conformity, 601, 608. *See also* Social pressure

Consideration, for people (vs. production), 146, 551

Consultants, in appraising employee, 244

Contamination (in measurement), 388. *See also* Evaluation

Contingency theory, *see* Theory(ies)

Contradictions, *see* Opinions

Control Data (firm), 227, 308

Cooperation
  vs. competition, 135–136, 601
  within group, 117, 133–134, 135–136, 137

Correlation coefficient(s), 208–209
  defined, 208
  of performance, business applications of, 209–210

Counseling
  acceptance of program of, 503
  accomplishments of, 496–499
  career, continuation of, 309
  common situations in, 499–500
  and counselor as expert, 499
  discontinuance of programs of, 96–97
  emotional, 456, 487
  frustration, 85–86
  of hard-to-employ, 308
  and interpersonal relations, 486–488
  nondirective (client-centered), 487–496, 498
  practical considerations in (number of interviews, time and place), 500–503
  questioning in, 491
  training for, 496, 503

Creativity
  convergent and divergent processes in, 228
  and "creative individualism," 309
  disagreement and, 608–609
  opportunity for, as incentive, 329
  in problem solving, 607–608
  tests of, 228–229

Criterion problem, 387. *See also* Evaluation

Critical-incident technique, 375–376. *See also* Merit rating

Cults, 80, 115. *See also* Propaganda

Curves, *see* Normal distribution curve

Cybernetics, 132–133

Deafness, 533, 534.*See also* Noise

Decision making
  and acceptance of decision, 168–
    174, 178, 179, 354
  in automated/machine system,
    273
  by chief executive officer, 151,
    410
  choice behavior in, 53–55, 56, 57–
    58
  distinguished from problem solv-
    ing, 602
  as problem solving, 609–610
  compromise in, 170
  delegation of, 410, 563–564
  failures in, 584
  group, see Group decision/
    problem solving
  interactive (within organization), 7
  organizational, models for, 552–
    553
  participation in, 55, 86, 169, 343,
    344–345
  premature, in employment, 242
  and quality of decision, 168–174,
    178, 602
  three locations of, 162
  training for, 302–303
  See also Problem solving
Delco-Remy Corporation, 375
Delegation
  of decision making, 410, 563–564
  stages of, 564–566
Democracy
  defined, 162
  fears of/ambivalence about, 165–
    166, 174
  majority-rule (voting type), 164
    (fig.), 168
  See also Group(s); Leadership
Demonstrations, see Visual aids
Difference, see Individual differ-
    ences
Direction (of management), 151.
    See also Leadership; Manage-
    ment
Director (of group), 149. See also
    Group(s); Leadership
Discrimination (racial, sexual),
    222–224, 241, 471
  in biodata approach, 237
  legal consequences of, 222, 223
  See also Attitude(s); Bias/prejudice

Discrimination (sensory)
  in learning situations, 287–288,
    293
  tactual, job design and, 271
Discussion
  group, 113–114, 296, 300–301,
    496, 601
  brainstorming in, 602, 609
  developmental, 617–619
  disagreement in, 608–609
  problem-solving procedures,
    617–619
  in learning process, 295–296, 301
  See also Communication;
    Group(s); Leadership
Disease, see Health
Dissatisfaction, see Satisfaction
Distribution curves, see Normal
    distribution curve

Ecology, concept of, 524
Edison, Thomas A., 11
Education, see Training
Edwards Personal Preference
    Schedule, 234. See also Tests
Ego needs, see Needs; Satisfaction;
    Success
Emotion, see Feelings
Empathy Test, 235. See also Tests
Employee(s)
  ambitious, 473 (see also Promo-
    tion/advancement)
  counseling of, see Counseling
  criticism of, 376–377, 381
  discharge of, 476–479
  evaluation of, see Evaluation
  fitted to jobs, 471
  as "human machines," 6
  job/family problems and, 589 (see
    also Stress)
  job wants and needs of, 8, 346–
    347, 354–355, 470–476, 496 (see
    also Needs)
  -management differences, 34–35,
    130, 377–378
  and manpower planning, 591–592
  orientation of, 44–45
  "problem" (disagreers), 608
  selection and placement of, 31,
    222–247, 274, 466, 476
  stable, problems of, 472

staff defined, 552
temporary/transient, 469, 470
turnover of, see Job turnover
See also Work
Employee's record, value of, 243–
    244
Encounter group therapy, see
    Group(s)
Engineers and scientists, and job
    turnover, 473–475
England
  studies of workers in, 346, 352,
    402, 408, 440, 441, 451
  wartime production in, 407
Environment
  organization in-, 536
  physical, 524–535
  psychological, 524
  social, factory as, 95, 96–97
  socioeconomic, 535–539
  uncertainty of (stability vs. turbu-
    lence), 536–537, 556, 560
Equal Employment Opportunity
    Commission (EEOC), 237,
    239–240
Equal employment opportunity
    legislation, 222
Equity theory, 57–58. See also The-
    ory(ies)
Ergograph, 398–400. See also Fa-
    tigue
Est therapy, 87
Evaluation
  contamination in, 388
  of frustration, 76–79
  of idea, vs. idea-getting process,
    609
  of problem solutions, 610–612
  for promotion, see
    Promotion/advancement
  vs. understanding of behavior, 22,
    24
  of work on production and non-
    production jobs, 366–367
  communication of (to employee),
    376–377
  criteria for, 386–389
  empirical method of, 384, 386
  by interview, 378–383
  job analysis as, 341, 371, 383–
    386
Executive, see Management

Expectancy theory, 57–58, 150. *See also* Theory(ies)
Expectations
  of behavior, leadership and, 149–150
  of performance, 198, 204
  of reward, as motivation, 341
Experience
  and accident rate, 452
  as basis for judging worker, 202–204
Experimental approach, 13
Extroversion, 78n. *See also* Behavior
Eyestrain, 404. *See also* Fatigue; Vision

Face-saving situations, *see* (Situation(s)
Facts
  attitudes and, *see* Attitude(s)
  use of, in problem solving, 610–611
Failure
  and aspiration level, 331–333
  competition and, 338–339
  experiences of, reduced, 471–472
  fear of, 45–46, 332, 333
  and frustration, 68 (*see also* Frustration)
Fairness
  as issue, 171–172, 186, 199
  of pay methods, 325–327
  in testing, 237
Fatigue
  and accidents, 401, 407, 440–441
  automation and, 410
  defined, 398
  ergograph studies and findings, 398–401
  eyestrain, 404
  mental, and work decrement, 415–419
  motivation and, 402, 412–415
  muscular tension and, 404–405
  and production, 401–408, 419
  psychological varieties of, 411–412
  repetition and, 419–422
  rest/recreation and, 401, 405–406, 410–411, 416
  See also Boredom

Fear
  and acceptance of decision, 170
  and behavior change, 51, 107
  of change, 584, 589–590
  of failure, 45–46, 332, 333
  frustration and, 74, 75
  and insecurity, 35, 44, 94, 267
  motivation through, 6, 215, 351
  power as cause of, 620
  in testing situation, 223
Feedback
  and biofeedback therapy, 87
  as catharsis, 84
  in engineering psychology, 269–271
  from group, 135, 137, 181, 337
  and improved morale, 31, 113
  in learning process, 292, 301, 302
  and motivation, 336–337
  and organizational change, 585, 589, 590
  sensory (kinesthesis), 288n
Feelings
  acceptance/reflection of, in counseling, 485–496
  and emotional adjustment/stability, testing of, 223–234, 449–450
  bias, 241
  conflict, and production, 31
  problems, 333, 456, 467
  problems, dealing with, 487
  resistance to change, 353
  stress in testing situation, 223
  See also Attitude(s); Counseling; Needs
Field approach, *see* Survey approach
Field review, 375. *See also* Merit rating
Films, film strips, *see* Visual aids
Fixation
  defined, 74
  frustration and, 72, 74–75, 77, 78, 80, 83
"Flex-time," *see* Working hours
Forced-choice method (of rating), 373–374.
  See also Merit rating
Ford Motor Company, 487
Four-day work week, *see* Working hours

Frame of reference, *see* Attitude(s)
Freud, Sigmund, 151, 553
Fringe benefits, 327. *See also* Wages/salary
Frustration
  and accident proneness, 451–452
  and aggression, 72–73, 76–83 *passim*
  attitudes developed through, 109, 151, 289
  and conflict, 572–573
  cost of, 76, 475
  dealing with/counseling for, 81–87, 296, 496–497, 499
  deprivation of needs and, 48
  evaluation of, 76–79
  expression of (catharsis), 83–85, 86
  and grievances, 467
  vs. motivation, 43, 48, 71–72, 76–79, 212, 215, 333, 548
  outlets for, 85
  punishment and, 51, 52, 74–75, 78, 83
  as reaction to problems, 68, 70–72
  -social movement relationship, 79–81
  and stress, 86–87
  symptoms of, 72–76, 77–86 *passim*

"Gating" of information, 242
General Electric Company, 304
General Motors Corporation, 184, 366, 536
Gestalt approach, *see* Psychology
Goal(s)
  absence of, 430
  activity as, 52–53, 57
  agreement on, in group problem solving, 601
  anticipated, 42, 43
  conflict in, 53–55, 340
  -needs relationship, 42, 49–50, 52, 133
  -oriented behavior, 71, 79–81, 343, 566
  -oriented groups, 79–81, 343
  -oriented motivational studies, 57
  participation in setting, 343–345
  real, 49
  realistic, knowledge of results and, 336

Goal(s) (*continued*)
substitute, 49–50
See also Satisfaction; Success
Graphs, *see* Normal distribution
curve; Scatter diagram, scattergram
Grievance(s)
analyzing, 31–32
defined, 31–32n
frustration and, 467
importance of adjustment of, 346
leadership and, 147
Gross national product, 324
Grounded theory, 14. *See also* The-
ory(ies)
Group(s)
affiliation with, 45–46, 108–109,
111, 113–114
attitudes/values within (in-
group/outgroup), 102, 130,
133–136, 137
behavior, models of, 132–133
characteristics of, 133–136, 613
cohesiveness of, 126, 133, 135,
137
competition (intra- vs.
intergroup), 11, 135–136
decisions by, *see* Group
decision/problem solving
discussion by, *see* Discussion
feedback from, 135, 137, 181, 337
field observation of, 131–132
frustration of, 79–80
goal-oriented, 79–81, 343
individual domination of, 601
interactions of (internal, external),
126
isolates, mutual pairs and stars in,
128, 148, 475
job design for, 273–274
-leader (director) relationships,
146, 148–151, 167–168
leadership of, 128, 149, 167–181,
601, 613
level of aspiration of, 333
-manager relations, 16, 34–35, 48,
130, 137, 152, 162, 164–167
models (mechanistic, organism,
conflict, cybernetic), 132–133
morale, 127, 136, 588
motivation, 343
as organism, 132
participation in, 343–345

productivity of, 366–367
relationships within, 16, 133, 136–
137
size, effects of, 134–135, 554–555
small, research on behavior of,
126–132
social status within, 96, 128, 130,
134
therapy (encounter or T-group),
87, 147, 620
training (T-group), 305–306, 548,
550, 587
Group decision/problem solving
accountability in, 174
adaptation of, to operating conditions, 174–179, 182, 264
area of freedom in, 174–177, 179
classification of problems in, 171–
174
concept of, 167–168
decision defined, 178
effectiveness of, 168–171, 345
group conditions detrimental to,
601
group conditions favoring, 600–
601
haste in, 607, 609
at higher management levels, 184–
186
vs. individual, 162, 613
industrial examples of, 181–184
locating surmountable obstacles
in, 603–605
in merit rating, 372–373
method clarified, 186
need for, in restricted production,
215
openmindedness in, 601
in organizational change, 591
at organizational level, 600–623
vs. participative management,
165–167
principles of, 603–612
processes involved in, 602–603
process vs. content in, 600, 615
risk in, 169
and safety, 455
selection of problems in, 178–179
summarized, 621–623
as supervisory method, 174, 354
time requirements for, 179
training for, 16, 179–181
why it works, 186–187, 345

Grouping (in memorization), 291–
292. *See also* Learning

Habit(s)
vs. fixation, 75
safety, 442–443
See also Training
Harper's Magazine, 213
Harvard Medical School, 454
Harvard School of Business, 300
Harwood-Weldon Corporation,
386
Hawthorne (Western Electric)
study, 6, 48, 83, 94–97, 112,
126, 487
Health
air pollution and, 529
noise and, 533
and nourishment (vs. fatigue), 400
and physical examinations, 451
stress-induced problems of, 76, 86
Hearst, Patricia, 115
Heredity
and behavior, 29–30, 78
and personality development, 233
Hierarchy, *see* Needs; Organiza-
tion(s)
Hours, *see* Working hours
Hugo, Victor, 33
Human resource development/asset
management, 591–592
Human resource planning (for career), 245–247

Idea-getting process, *see* Problem
solving
Ignatius of Loyola, St., 366
Illiteracy, 308. *See also* Training
Illumination, *see* Lighting
Incentives, *see* Motivation
Incident process, 300–301. *See also*
Training
Individual(s)
domination of group by, 601
vs. group, *see* Group(s)
manager relations with, 15–16
problem solving (vs. group problem solving), 613
Individual differences
in attitudes, 109
and "best" work method, 266–
267

consideration of, before changing organism, 31
and correlation of performances, 210
differences in experience and, 202–204
and fatigue, 400–401
in frustration, 78–79
as important variable, 201, 366
measurement of, 366–376
and methods of payment, 324, 325
nature of, 196–201
in needs, 48, 53
in perception, 148–150
Inflation, 8. *See also* Wages/salary
Information
    acquisition of, in management training, 16
    "gating" of, 242
    -job design relationship, 271
    -processing systems, humans and organizations as, 553
Initiating structure, 146, 551
Input/output
    defined, 268–269
    and input sources in problem solving, 622
Insecurity, *see* Fear
Intelligence
    and job complexity, 468–469
    tests, 206, 228, 450
Interpersonal relations
    counseling and, 486–488
    emphasis on, 6, 548
    group-management and within groups, *see* Group(s)
    and interpersonal competence, 585
    job contacts, 510–512
    leader-follower, 146, 148–151 (*see also* Leadership)
    management skill and, 15–16, 52
    managers' dissatisfaction with, 347
    and peer networks, 571
    praise/criticism as implication of, 335
    small-town vs. urban, 525
    training in, 496
    See also Communication; Counseling; Understanding
Interview
    assessment center as alternative to, 244–245

and basic interviewing principles, 504–506
and biodata approach, 348, 571
common situations of, 508
contribution of, to assessment, 242–243, 244
counseling, 501–510 (*see also* Counseling)
and discrimination/bias, 222, 237, 240, 241–242
EEOC requirements for, 239–240
in evaluating performance, 378–383
exit, 477–478, 505
and interviewing practices, 240–241, 505
misrepresentation of job in, 246, 466
objectives of, 503–504
problem-solving, vs. tell-and-sell, 507–508
progress, 566
Q by Q, 240–241
transfer or promotion, 242
Introversion, 78n. *See also* Behavior
Iowa Child Welfare Station, 73
Ipsative Consequence Model (as O.D. technique), 587
"Isolates," 128, 475

Japan
    cultural values in, 144
    heart disease in, 86
    management styles in, 550
Job analysis
    description, specification, evaluation, 383
    for improved selection, 274
    and job profile, 383–384
    as measure of performance, 341, 371, 383–386
    negative aspects of, 383
    and training, 12
Job attitudes, *see* Attitude(s); Satisfaction
Job complexity
    and job turnover, 468–469, 477
    and noise effects, 533
Job contacts
    five types of, 511
    improvement of, 510–512
    nature of, 510
    See also Interpersonal relations

Job design
    of automated plants, 269–273
    early approaches to, 258–259
    for groups, 273–274
    -information relationship, 271
    motion-and-time studies, 6, 259–268, 274, 287, 400
    recent approaches to, 267–275
    and worker satisfaction, 275
Job families, 210
Job fatigue, 404. *See also* Fatigue
Job interest/enrichment, 345–346, 422, 427–428, 473, 559. *See also* Motivation
Job rotation
    and enlargement, vs. boredom, 421–422
    in training, *see* Training
Job sampling, 238–239. *See also* Tests
Job skill(s)
    behavioral taxonomy as lists of, 274
    skill acquisition and, 288, 293–295
    skilled labor vs., 285
    See also Ability(ies)
Job training, *see* Training
Job turnover
    age and, 467
    ambition and, 473
    attitudinal training and, 308
    boredom and, 266
    costs and causes, 466–470
    and discharge of employee, 476–479
    engineers and scientists and, 473–475
    information about the organization and, 246, 466
    job complexity and, 468–469, 477
    job satisfaction/dissatisfaction and, 469–470, 472, 478
    leadership and, 147
    length of service and, 467
    level of aspiration and, 332
    marital status/dual careers and, 467–468, 475
    out-placement in, 478–479
    prediction of, 469, 471
    purposes (for employee) of job and, 470–471
    resignation and, 466–467, 478

Mechanical-relations tests, 227–228. *See also* Tests
Memorization, *see* Learning
Mental blocking, 417. *See also* Fatigue
Merit, distinguished from production, 368
Merit rating, 387
  group decision in, 372–373
  halo effect in, 369
  job analysis and, 383–384
  problems of, 367–373, 376–378, 388–389
  refinements in, 373–376
  See also Evaluation; Promotion/advancement
Minnesota Multiphasic Personality Inventory (MMPI), 234. *See also* Tests
Minority groups
  level of aspiration of, 331–332
  on-the-job training for, 308
  unemployment rates for, 245, 307
Modeling, *see* Role-playing
Money
  as measure of success, 341
  as satisfaction of needs, 52, 322
  See also Wages/salary
Monotony, 412, 418. *See also* Boredom
Morale
  defined, 136
  feedback and, 31, 113
  group, 127, 136, 588
  job satisfaction and, 349
  lighting and, 527
  national, defined, 136
  praise vs. criticism and, 335
  sociometry and, 130
  survey measurement of, 127
  See also Attitude(s)
Motion-and-time studies, 6, 259–268, 274, 287, 400
  and motion economy, 260–264, 268
  See also Job design
Motivation, 42–58, 548
  ability and, 211–212, 294
  changes in (with maturity), 246
  and choice behavior, *see* Decision making
  competition and, 11, 337–341
  to complete task, 424, 426–427

conflict in, 53–55, 340
and countermotivation, 345, 352, 354, 443
discussion and, 301
expectancy and, 341
experience of progress as, 341
experience of task completion as, 343
extrinsic vs. intrinsic, 327–331, 349
and fatigue, 402, 412–415
through fear, 6, 215, 351
feedback and, 292
frustration vs., *see* Frustration
goal-, 79 (*see also* Goal[s])
group, 343
importance of job and, 346
intensity of, 42
and job interest, 473
knowledge of results as, 336–337 (*see also* Feedback)
nonmonetary factors and, 333–343, 346
and overmotivation, 330
payment methods and, 322–327
positive, difficulty of, 51–52
power, 145, 322
praise as, 333–336
and production decrease, 213–214, 333
and production/performance, 210–212, 259, 343
-production relationship, 333
and professional obsolescence, 309
punishment vs. reward as, *see* Punishment
for safety, 438, 440, 443–444
situation/organism approaches to, 56–57
social factors and, 7, 211, 343, 345
success/failure and, 338–339
as testing factor, 223
"theories" of, 55–58
of women, 330–331
work-simplification procedures and, 375, 377
Motor coordination
  and accidents, 449
  and motion economy, 260–264
  tests of, *see* Tests
Movies, *see* Visual aids
Music, background, 423

National Training Laboratories (Bethel, Maine), 587
Nazi Germany, 80
Needs
  achievement, 45–46, 52, 57, 329, 333
  -achievement (*n*Ach) tests, 46
  acquired, 43–44, 49
  change in, 350
  dealing with, 48–49
  ego, 45, 331, 333, 335
  employee, *see* Employee(s)
  -goals relationship, 42, 49–50, 52, 133
  hierarchy of, 46–47
  of hourly workers, 346–347
  innate or natural, 43
  of managers, 347
  motivating, 42, 43–49, 57
  personality and, 45–46
  satisfaction of, *see* Satisfaction
  social, *see* Social needs
  See also Values
New York State Ventilation Commission, 528, 529, 530
Noise, effects of, 531–534
Normal distribution curve, 196–198, 211
  deviations from (bimodal and skewed), 205–207
  vs. restricted production curve, 212–215
  variations in, 201–202
Nunn Bush (profit-sharing) plan, 327

Obsolescence, professional and technical, 309
Occupational choice, 245
Occupational Safety and Health Act (OSHA), 441, 454
O'Connor Finger Dexterity Test Board, 200. *See also* Tests
O.D. (organizational development), *see* Organization(s)
Open-system theory, *see* Theory(ies)
Opinions
  vs. attitudes, 98–99, 108, 109
  change of, 114 (*see also* Propaganda)

Opinions (*continued*)
  contradictory, reconciled by atti-
    tudes, 101–102
  expressed, commitment to, 107
  improvement of (by changing
    facts), 111
Organism
  change in, 30–31
  group as, 132
  organization as, 551–552
  -stimulus interaction (S-O-B-A
    sequence), *see* Stimulus
Organization(s)
  change in, 584–592
    measurement of, 586–587
  conflict within, 572–573
  cross-functional relations in, 571–
    573
  as dependent subsystems, 552, 571
  development of (O.D.) 584, 587–
    591
  differentiation and integration of
    efforts of, 571–572
  hierarchy within, 555, 556–571
    and area of freedom, 562–563
    bypassing of, 560–561
    classic concept of, 557–558
    leadership, 162, 174–177
    role concept, ambiguity, and
      conflict of, 558–560
  human behavior in (theories and
    systems-based views of), 548–
    553
  improvement of problem solving
    in, 612–613 (*see also* Group de-
    cision/problem solving)
  information about (in interview)
    and job turnover, 246, 466
  leadership of, *see* Leadership;
    Management
  as organism, 551–552
  and organizational climate, 553–
    554
  and organizational psychology,
    548–573
  and organizational set, 536 (*see also*
    Environment)
  reporting and control systems of,
    570–571
  social responsibility of, 537–539
  structure and size of, 554–556
Organizational and Environment
  (Lawrence and Lorsch), 536

Orientation, importance of, 44–45
Orthogonality, 551
Out-placement, 478–479. *See also*
  Job turnover
Overtime, 466. *See also* Working
  hours

Parasol Assembly problem, 607
Peer networks, 571. *See also* Interpersonal relations
Perception, 104, 237
  and behavior, 23–24
  differences in, 148–150
  distortion of, in cognitive disso-
    nance theory, 106
  employee, of supervisor, 513, 551
  of problem, 607–608
  social, of discussion leader, 181
  in testing situation, 223
  visual, 232–223, 450
Performance/production
  ability as factor in, 196, 210–215
  attitude effect on, 94–97, 154
  "average," as basis for expecta-
    tions, 198
  consistency of, over entire day,
    272
  correlated, business applications
    of, 209–210
  criteria, 386–389
  early, as indication of potential
    skill, 204
  emotional conflict and, 31
  employee's record of, 243–244
  fatigue and, 408–409, 419 (*see also*
    Fatigue)
  improvement of, 382
  increased productivity sought
    (U.S.), 352
  intention and, 326–327
  job design and, 259–260
  job satisfaction and, 351–352
  job training and, 31
  lighting and, 526–527
  measurement of, 366–367 (*see also*
    Evaluation)
  merit distinguished from, 366
  motivation as factor in, 210–212
    (*see also* Motivation)
  noise effects on, 531–534
  nonmonetary factors affecting,
    333–343
  pacing methods and, 422–423

  payment in terms of, 322–324
  prediction of
    tests and, 225, 233, 239, 331
    weighted application blanks (in
      biodata approach) and, 238
  and productivity, importance of,
    144, 370
  and productivity-leadership rela-
    tionship, 146 (fig.), 150
  and productivity levels, range in,
    201
  restricted, curve of, 212–215
  sociometry and, 130
  speed of, leveling factor in, 265
  standards of, 168, 213–215
  supervision and, 30
  ventilation effects on, 530–531
Personality, 233
  disorder, vs. temporary frustra-
    tion, 86
  image of, in organization, 241
  and needs, 45–46
  tests, *see* Tests
Personnel specialist, 8
Persuasion, *see* Communication
Physical examinations, 451. *See also*
  Health
Pollution, *see* Air pollution; Noise
Popularity, and job satisfaction,
  134. *See also* Status
Power
  as communication barrier, 511,
    513, 548, 561–562
  fear caused by, 620
  as motivation, 145, 322
  need for, 46
Praise, use and effects of, 333–336.
  See also Motivation; Reward
Prejudice, *see* Bias/prejudice
Probationary period, 477–478
Problem(s)
  classification and chart of, in
    group decision making, 171–174
  of "saving face," *see* Situation(s)
  selection of, in group decision
    making, 178–179
Problem solving
  acceptance of reality in, 497, 620
  bargaining vs., 615–616
  behavior, 43, 68–72
    vs. frustration, 76–77, 81, 83, 84
    three types of, 229
  as choice behavior, 609–610

and creation of new problem, 611, 612–613
vs. creativity, 229
discussion procedures, 617–619
emotions and, 353
and evaluation of solutions, 610–612
extended uses of, 620–621
by group, *see* Group decision/problem solving
as idea-getting process, 602, 608
vs. idea evaluation, 609
individual vs. group, 613
by insiders and outsiders, 612
integrative solutions in, 354
and intent to produce, 327
as interview style, 507–508
and job enrichment, 428
organizational, improvement of, 612–615
personal values/preferences and, 498, 611–612
recapitulation of, 619–622
starting point in, 605–607
stimulation of, 497–498, 499, 506–507 (*see also* Counseling)
training in, 300, 614, 615
use of facts in, 610–611
See also Decision making
Production, productivity, *see* Performance/production
Profit-sharing plans, 327. *See also* Wages/salary
Programmed instruction, 301–302. *See also* Training
Promotion/advancement
criteria for, 388–389
"dual-ladder," 474
employee's record and, 243–244
government evaluation of, 222
interviews for, 242
job satisfaction vs., 473
as need satisfier, 52, 346
as reward for performance, 324
Propaganda, 80, 107, 114
Proxemics, 535
Psychiatric treatment, 86, 97
Psychodrama, 304. *See also* Role-playing
Psychological contract, 149
Psychology
applied, development of principles of, 10–12

applied, historical, current, and future role of, in industry, 6–10
atomistic approach to, 266
and biopsychological approach, 267–268
and employment tests, 223, 225, 235
engineering, 268–274
of fatigue, 411–412
Gestalt approach to, 13, 266, 524, 553
organizational, 548–573
and psychological effects of environment, 534–535
of safety, 438, 441–442
Public opinion polls, 108, 109. *See also* Survey approach
Punishment
dangers of, 51, 78, 83
and frustration, 51, 52, 74–75, 78, 83
as motivation, 6, 51–52
vs. prevention of behavior, 24, 51
vs. reward, 50–51, 55, 287, 292

Q by Q interviews, 240–241. *See also* Interviews
Questionnaires
in biodata approach, 238
in design of organizational development, 587–588
management job satisfaction measured by, 556
management practices classified by, 548–549
in personality testing, 233–234
role conflict and ambiguity measured by, 559
supervisory behavior measured by, 551
in surveys, 126–135 *passim,* 146, 147, 150
See also Survey approach; Tests

Rating, *see* Merit rating
Recognition, need for, 52
Recruiters, *see* Interviews
Red tape, perception of, 422. *See also* Boredom
Regression, frustration and, 72, 73–74, 77, 78, 80, 81, 83
Reinforcement (in learning), *see* Learning

Relationships
between abilities, 207–210
personal, *see* Interpersonal relations
Repetition
in learning, *see* Learning
psychological effects of (in work), 419–421 (*see also* Monotony)
Reprimand, 334. *See also* Punishment
Research, pure, value of, 10
Resignation (from job), *see* Job turnover
Resignation (state of mind), frustration and, 72, 75–76
Response(s)
attraction/approach, 50, 54
avoidance, 50, 51, 54, 55
Responsibility
and accountability, 174, 563
assumption of, by high-need achievers, 46
development of, 498
of leader, in group problem solving, 613–615 (*see also* Leadership)
as need satisfier, 52, 345
regression and, 74
social, of organization, 537–539
Rest and recreation, *see* Fatigue
Restricted production curves, 212–215. *See also* Normal distribution curve
Retirement
age of, 223
fears of, 44
preparation for, 411
Reward
expectations of, 341
praise as, 333–336
promotion as, 324
vs. punishment, 50–51, 55, 287, 292
See also Motivation
Rhythm
considered, in job design/training, 262, 295
tests of, 229
Risk technique, 589–590, 617. *See also* Fear
Role-playing, 14, 111–112
and attitude training, 296
within group, 127

Role-playing (*continued*)
  modeling and, 304, 306
  and role prescriptions (in job), 386
  as training method, 303–304, 614
Roles, organizational
  boundary, 559–560
  changes in, and behavior change, 552
  concept, ambiguity, and conflict of, 559
Rorschach Test, *see* Tests

Safety
  devices for, 438, 440, 441–442, 533
  employees' view of importance of, 346, 529
  habits of, 442–443
  indirect measures for, 440–441
  motivation for, 438, 440, 443–444
  psychological devices for, 438, 441–442
  and violation of safety regulations, 444, 454–455 (*see also* Accidents)
Salary, *see* Wages/salary
Satisfaction, 475
  activities and, 52–53
  job, 347–356, 472, 473, 584
    city size and, 525
    organization hierarchy and, 556
    popularity and, 134
    six sources of, 52
  and job dissatisfaction, 47–48, 127, 354
    and absenteeism, 48, 470
    job design and, 275
    major factor in, 347
    and turnover, 467–470, 472, 478
  management by objectives (MBO) and, 566
  money and, 52, 322
"Saving face," *see* Situation(s)
Scanlon (profit-sharing) plan, 327
Scapegoating, 72, 73, 82
Scatter diagram, scattergram, 208–210
Scorcher, Melvin, 304
Selection ratio, 225. *See also* Tests
Self
  perception of, 24
  and self-esteem, 47, 245
  and self-oriented behavior, 55

Seniority
  method of pay/rewards for, 325, 467
  union demand for rights of, 35
Sex roles, 411. *See also* Women
Shifts, *see* Work shifts
Situation(s)
  change in, 30, 31
  face-saving, 45, 50, 83, 337, 616
  manager control of, 14–15
  -person interaction, 23–24
  See also Stimulus
Skewed curve, *see* Normal distribution curve
Skills, *see* Ability(ies); Interpersonal relations; Job skill(s); Leadership
S-O-B-A formula, *see* Stimulus
Socialism, appeal of, 80–81
Social movements, -frustration relationship, 79–81. *See also* Group(s)
Social needs, 44–45
  and factory as social environment, 95, 96–97
  and social changes, 475
  and social facilitation, 343
  See also Status
Social pressure
  constructive use of, 345
  defined, 296
  in group problem solving, 601
  and honesty, 28
  and level of aspiration, 332–333
  and motivation, 7, 211, 343, 345
Sociogram (sociometry), 128. *See also* Survey approach
Staff, 552. *See also* Employee(s)
Standard of living, 44
  productivity essential to, 144
  relativity of, 81
  and wage demands, 326
Standards of performance, *see* Performance/production
Stanford University personality studies, 236
Status
  within group, 96, 128, 130, 134
  limitations of, 355
  as social need, 45
Stimulus
  and behavior variation, 28–29
  change in, 30, 31
  -organism interaction (S-O-B-A

sequence), 23–27, 25 (fig.), 30–31, 56, 456, 584
  response to, 273, 287, 288
  See also Situation(s)
Stress
  and accidents (adjustment-stress theory), 448
  counseling for, 499–500
  and fatigue, 405, 409 (*see also* Fatigue)
  frustration and, 86–87
  -induced health problems, 76, 86
  job/family problems and, 589
  in testing situation, 223
Strikes, 275
Success
  changing definitions of, 8
  competition and, 338–339
  and level of aspiration, 331–333
  salary/money as index of, 341, 388
Suggestibility, 74, 80
Suggestion box, 567
Supervisor(s)
  as applied scientist, 14–16
  and area of freedom (in group decision making), 174–177, 179
  attitudes of, and toward, 109, 110–111, 112–113
  and attitude surveys, 110
  and barriers to communication, 511, 513
  counseling by, *see* Counseling
  delegation by, *see* Delegation
  determination of needs by, 48 (*see also* Needs)
  as discussion leader, 177, 178
  duties of, 15
  employee- vs. job-centered, 145–146
  evaluation of performance by, 376, 379, 381–383
  as expert, 177–178
  in face-saving situation, 45
  and frustration, 81–82
  and grievances, 32
  and group decision as supervisory method, 174, 354
  and job discussion (with employee), 473
  as leader, 153–154, 165, 176
  observant, need for, 243
  perception of, 24

personality studies of, 235
regression in, 74
and safety violations, 454–455
training by and of, 285, 294, 472
(*see also* Training)
See also Leadership; Management
Survey approach, 12–14, 126–131
attitude surveys, 109–111
field observation, 12–13, 131–132
sociometry, 127–131, 133
See also Questionnaires
Survey Research Center (University of Michigan), 145
Sweden, supervisory training in, 472

Task completion, *see* Work
Teaching machines, 301. *See also* Training
Team development, 588. *See also* Group(s)
Temperature, *see* Atmospheric conditions
Tension, 58, 60. *See also* Frustration
Tests
of ability, 208, 210–211, 224–230
alternatives to, 237–239
aptitude, 31, 225–227, 230
battery of, 230, 236, 243
creative ability, 228–229
criterion for, 224, 236
criticisms of, 201, 211, 222, 223–224
culture-bound, 223, 237
dexterity, 229–230, 236
vs. employee's record, value of, 243–244
employment, 8, 222–237, 331
intelligence, 206, 228, 450
job-sampling vs., 238–239
mechanical-relations, 227–228
motor coordination, 229–230, 236–237, 238
*n*Ach (need-achievement), 46
norms for, 224
personality, 233–236, 449–450, 451–452
precision, 229
projective, 234–235
psychological, for accident-proneness, 448–451
reaction time, 229

reliability of, 224
results, as criteria of success, 387
results, vs. judgment of qualified person, 243
of rhythm, 229
Rorschach, 234, 236
sensorimotor, 449
of sensory abilities (vision, hearing, etc.), 230–233, 450–451, 471
Thematic Apperception, 234, 236
validity of, 225, 233, 236
See also Evaluation; Questionnaires
Texas Instruments Company, 345
T-group therapy, *see* Group(s)
T-group training, *see* Training
Thematic Apperception Test, 234, 236
Theory(ies)
achievement, revisions of, 329–331
attribution, 56–57, 114, 149
of behavior (X and Y), 549–550
cognitive dissonance, 106–107
contingency, 56, 57, 94, 148, 150
equity, 57–58
expectancy, 57–58, 150
grounded, 14, 356
leadership, 144–151
motivation, 55–58
open-systems, 524, 535, 536
Theory Z: How American Business Can Meet the Japanese Challenge (Ouchi), 550
Three-Mile Island accident, 272
Time
dimension, organizations and, 537
down-time, 271
-and-motion studies, 6, 259–268, 274, 287, 400
requirements for group decision, 179
See also Working hours
Time clocks, 28–29
Training, 284–309
attitude, 296, 308 (*see also* Attitude[s])
"business games" as, 14, 302–303
case method, 300
continuing (mid- or late-career), 309
for counseling, 496, 503

discussion methods, 301
distinguished from discipline, 292
effects of, on values, 46
evaluation of methods of, 297–306
"fads" in, 284, 305
of hard-to-employ, 306–308
in-basket method, 303
incident process used in, 300–301
in interpersonal relations, 496
job analysis and, 12
job rotation as, 299–300
leadership, 16, 147
management
and attitude/behavior change, 114
continuing, 309
for engineer/scientist, 474–475
fast-track plans in, 245, 299–300
growth of, 592
and "isolates," 128, 475
on-the-job/simulation, 299, 308
preliminary, 472
for problem solving, 300, 614, 615
procedures, 289–296
and production, 31
programmed, 301–302
role-playing method, 303–304, 614 (*see also* Role-playing)
specialized (engineering/scientific), and job turnover, 473–475
by supervisor, 285, 294
of supervisor, 472
team, 273–274
T-group/sensitivity, 305–306, 548, 550, 587
of trainers, 306
See also Learning
Transfer
vs. discharge, 476
employee's record and, 243–244
interviews for, 242
Truth-in-testing law (New York), 387
Turnover, *see* Job turnover
Typewriter design, 262. *See also* Job design

UAW strike (1936–1937), 525
Understanding
empathetic, 489 (*see also* Counseling)
vs. evaluation of behavior, 22, 24